COOK'S
WISDOM

COOK'S WISDOM

AUTHOR

Sarah Putman Clegg

ADDITIONAL TEXT BY

Mary Goodbody,
Carolyn Miller & Thy Tran

ILLUSTRATOR

Alice Harth

weldon**owen**

"Cooking is often
one disaster after another.
What you learn is the only thing
you can't fix is a soufflé."

—*Julia Child*

foreword

Nowadays fewer and fewer people have had a true understanding of cooking passed down to them. We once learned to cook by watching a parent or grandparent in the kitchen—seeing how they worked, discovering how they made adjustments to a recipe, and hearing their insights. Now, many people can only follow a recipe to the letter, unable to diverge from the stated steps and unable to compensate for gaps in the instructions or differing conditions in their own kitchens.

What if there was one compact book to which people could turn whenever they needed important everyday cooking information and needed it immediately? What if we could create the printed equivalent of having a knowledgeable companion standing by your side in the kitchen, one who could provide you with straightforward answers and commonsense advice at a glance?

This was the inspiration for *Cook's Wisdom*.

As the team of expert writers and editors went ahead with the project, they developed another goal for the book as well. They wanted to make it not just knowledgeable but also interesting and readable, a book you could pick up, dip into, and enjoy even when you weren't faced with a specific question or pressing problem. Consequently, they've done their best to make the entries intriguing and fun.

You're sure to find this book a welcome addition to your own kitchen library, one to which you'll happily turn again and again.

How to Use This Book

COOK'S WISDOM is an everyday cooking reference for real-life cooks. It is meant to be used alongside a cookbook, cooking article, or recipe. It provides background information, clarifies unfamiliar terms, explains the whys behind recipe instructions, and helps the cook identify and avoid potential problems and pitfalls.

In order to achieve these goals, the book presents its information in a carefully structured format with the following key features used consistently throughout:

ALPHABETICAL ORGANIZATION For ease of reference, entries are presented in alphabetical order, from "Abalone" to "Zucchini."

INGREDIENT ENTRIES Basic ingredients receive their own entries and include general guidelines on selection, storage, and preparation. Broader entries such as "Fish" and "Spice" provide detailed glossaries of ingredients included in that category.

COOKWARE AND EQUIPMENT ENTRIES Important kitchen appliances receive separate alphabetical entries. Broader entries under such headings as "Bakeware," "Baking Tools," "Cooking Tools," and "Cookware" contain detailed subentries on a wide variety of items.

COOKING METHOD ENTRIES Key cooking methods such as "Frying" and "Roasting" are covered by extensive explanations.

TECHNIQUES AND TERMS ENTRIES Detailed entries explain cooking techniques and terms, from "Adjusting the Seasoning" to "Zesting."

CHARTS Throughout the book, charts provide easy, at-a-glance references to information such as cooking times and methods for various grains or acceptable substitutions for common ingredients.

STEP-BY-STEP "HOW TO'S" Many entries contain basic methods for preparing ingredients or for performing specific cooking techniques, all explained step by step.

ILLUSTRATIONS More than 800 line drawings illustrate ingredients, types of equipment, and step-by-step instructions.

CROSS-REFERENCES The book is extensively cross-referenced to help you quickly find the information you need however you might first try to look it up. Cross-references at the end of many entries also direct you to similar or related terms, ingredients, equipment, or techniques.

everything from abalone to avocado

ABALONE With its sweet meat and beautiful shell lined with mother-of-pearl, this shellfish is native to the coasts of California and Alaska but is now rarely found fresh, and its harvesting is regulated. Most of us must settle for the canned version. If you come across live abalone in the fish market, snap it up, knowing you have a rare prize on your hands. Use it in recipes that call for squid, keeping in mind that, like squid, it overcooks easily and should be cooked for no longer than a minute or two.
Selecting Fresh abalone must be alive when you buy it. Check the meat inside the shell to make sure it moves when touched and that it looks plump and shiny. The shellfish should have a sweet smell, not an "off" odor. Canned and frozen abalone are available in Asian markets; frozen abalone is often pretenderized and can be very good.
Storing Live abalone should be kept refrigerated for no longer than 1 day. Canned abalone should be refrigerated after opening, covered with water, for not more than 4 days. Frozen will keep for 3 months.
Preparing Remove fresh abalone meat from its shell by running a knife under it to loosen it, and discard the innards, using only the large muscle. The meat of the abalone muscle is tough and must be tenderized by pounding to make it palatable. Use a meat mallet or rolling pin to pound and flatten the muscle to a thickness of ¼ inch or less. Score the meat, cutting a series of shallow slashes across its surface, to keep it from curling as it cooks.

ACHIOTE Another name for annatto seed. See SPICE.

ACID The word *acid* may not sound appetizing, but the sour substances it names play important roles in food and cooking.

Vinegar, lemon juice, and wine are examples of acids used in cooking for flavor and astringency, contributing a tart, sour, or bitter note to a dish.

Like salt, an acid can preserve food, as in the case of the vinegar used for pickling.

An acid can react with an alkaline, or base, substance to form a gas, a critical step in baking. Baking powder, a mixture of acid and alkaline substances, releases carbon dioxide gas when exposed to moisture or heat, causing a baked good to rise.

Lemons.

Acids break down proteins and are used to tenderize the surface of meats and fish. In the case of seviche, thin slices of fish or shellfish become firm and opaque when marinated in an acid, just as they would when cooked. On the other hand, acid added to vegetables and legumes will interfere with their cooking and softening.

Acids also act to prevent the discoloration of certain foods that occurs when they are cut and exposed to air. To slow the browning, lemon juice is commonly sprinkled or rubbed on the cut surfaces of fruits and vegetables.

See also BAKING POWDER & BAKING SODA; CREAM OF TARTAR; DISCOLORING; NONREACTIVE; VINEGAR.

ACIDULATED WATER See ACID; DISCOLORING.

ADJUSTING THE SEASONING
Many recipes instruct you to "adjust" or "correct" a given dish, usually near the end of the recipe. This means adding more salt, pepper, and any other appropriate herb or spice after tasting the cooked dish. Flavors meld and change as they cook, so it's important to gauge and adjust the seasoning to your liking just before serving. Take care to add seasonings in small amounts and to taste often when correcting. It is possible to add more but not to remove what you have already added. Also, do not taste a food until it has reached a stage at which you would consider it safe to eat. See also DONENESS; SEASONING; TASTING.

ADZUKI BEAN See BEAN, DRIED.

AGAR-AGAR See SEAWEED.

AIOLI (IY-o-lee) A pungent garlic-flavored mayonnaise that is highly popular in the south of France. The word derives from a combination of the Provençal words for garlic, *aïl,* and oil, *oli.*

Quick Bite

In Provence, aioli is traditionally served with poached salt cod and boiled green beans, carrots, beets, and eggs for a festive summertime meal called *le grand aïoli.*

ALCOHOL Wine, beer, and spirits are fermented or distilled beverages, usually created from fruits or grains, that contain a percentage of ethyl alcohol, which can be intoxicating. They are added to both savory and sweet recipes for flavor. These versatile beverages can also add welcome color to a dish, as in the case of a ruby red wine sauce for poached fruit, or they can be used for basting meat to give it rich color and flavor. Wine is an especially popular ingredient in sauces and braising liquids. Through reducing, the flavor of the wine may be intensified and its consistency thickened, delivering a pleasing, fruity taste and rich body to the finished dish.

Alcohol adds more than just flavor and color to food. When spirits or wine are cooked, the alcohol in them does not completely evaporate. Between 5 and 85 percent of the alcohol may remain, depending on the cooking time, temperature, and type of beverage.

See also LIQUEUR; REDUCING; SPIRITS; WINE.

AL DENTE (AL DEN-tay) This Italian phrase, which literally means "to the tooth," indicates that pasta has been cooked until it is tender but still chewy, offering some resistance to the bite. The same term is also sometimes used as an indication of doneness for certain sturdy vegetables, such as green beans, carrots, and asparagus, and for risotto.

Removing pasta for testing.

ALLSPICE See SPICE.

ALMOND See NUT.

ALUMINUM FOIL Found in virtually every American home, aluminum foil is one of the most versatile kitchen supplies. It is useful for lining broiling and roasting pans, for covering pans and baking dishes that lack lids, for cooking food in a pocket or pouch, and for wrapping cooked food to keep it hot. Use it to tent turkeys and chickens during the later stages of roasting to prevent overbrowning, and to shield the rims of pie crusts in the oven to keep them from scorching. Many home cooks line the bottom of the oven and the firebox of their grill with heavy-duty aluminum foil to deflect heat and ease cleanup.

When aluminum foil is used to line a pan, an oven, or a firebox, its shiny side should face outward. This deflects the heat most effectively, promoting even cooking.

ANCHOVY This tiny fish makes a big impression, attracting or repelling people in equal measure. Anchovies are indigenous to the Mediterranean and the Atlantic coastlines of Spain and Portugal and are used widely in the cuisines of those countries, as well as in Italy and southern France. They are an important ingredient in Caesar salad and in tapenade, a boldly flavored paste made from olives, capers, and anchovies. When added to a dish during cooking, the anchovy fillets will virtually dissolve, leaving only a surprisingly subtle, nonfishy dimension of flavor.

Selecting Anchovies are generally boned, cured, packed in oil, and sold in small cans. Rarely are they found fresh in the United States. Look for them in the canned fish section in 2-ounce jars or tins. Although jarred are generally more expensive, they offer better flavor and texture.

In Italy, anchovies are also commonly sold packed in salt, and many American chefs and cooks prefer those. In delicatessens, salted anchovies are typically sold by weight from a large opened can. They must be boned and rinsed before using.

Anchovy fillets.

Storing Once a can of oil-packed fillets is opened, transfer any leftover fillets and oil to a small glass or plastic container, cover, and refrigerate for up to 1 week. Add more olive oil if needed to keep the fillets covered. Salted anchovies should be kept in a tightly covered glass or other nonreactive container (salt is corrosive) or a zippered plastic bag in the refrigerator. They will keep for several weeks. Once the seal is broken on a tube of anchovy paste, the tube should be refrigerated. Capped securely, it will last for up to several months.

Preparing Lift oil-packed anchovies from their oil and drain on paper towels before using. Some cooks also rinse the oil-packed fillets under cold running water.

To prepare salted anchovies for use, rinse well under cold running water and scrape off their skins with a small, sharp knife. Split open along the backbone, cutting off the dorsal fins. Then pull out the spines and rinse the fillets well. Pat dry with paper towels, place in a glass or other nonreactive bowl, pour in enough olive oil to cover with a thin layer, cover tightly, and refrigerate. Use within 2 weeks.

ANISEED See SPICE.

ANNATTO SEED See SPICE.

APPLE It should be easy to eat an apple a day, considering they are perhaps the most common tree fruit in the world. There are some 7,000 known apple varieties in the world today. Of course, far fewer are available to the average shopper. The most common varieties sold in the United States are Red Delicious, Golden Delicious, Granny Smith, Gala, and McIntosh. Keep an eye open, too, for recently revived heirloom apples, old-fashioned varieties that fell out of favor with big commercial growers because of difficulties in large-scale growing, storing, and shipping. Many kinds with excellent flavor and texture can now be found in farmers' or specialty markets.

Selecting Look for unbroken skin with good color and no soft brown spots. Whenever possible, buy newly harvested local apples. Most apples are picked in autumn or winter; a few summer varieties (Maiden Blush, Transparent, Gravenstein) exist. The Australian crop helps to fill American fruit bins in the summer.

Although some apple lovers may insist that the sweeter apples, such as the Fuji and the Gala, are good for eating out of hand, while tarter, firmer ones, such as the Granny Smith, are better suited for cooking and baking, such tart and sweet distinctions are completely subjective. See the Apple Glossary at right for a few pointers.

Storing Because apples continue to ripen at room temperature, refrigerate them in the cold back part of the refrigerator for 1 week or longer. If you plan to eat them soon after purchase, they can be held at room temperature for a few days.

Preparing A small, sharp knife is all you need for peeling and slicing apples, although a vegetable peeler may be easier for

Apple Glossary

*E*ach apple variety has its own unique properties. Sample the range available in your local stores and farmers' markets to discover which ones you like. Following are some of the most popular varieties.

CORTLAND This red-skinned apple with snow-white flesh has a pleasing tartness and a firm texture. It is good for eating out of hand and for adding to fruit salads. Because it breaks down in cooking it is ideal for applesauce, although it is not as suitable for pies and the like.

EMPIRE Red- or green-skinned, this juicy apple with a tart-sweet flavor and creamy flesh is a cross between Red Delicious and McIntosh. It's good for applesauce and delicious eaten out of hand.

FUJI The Fuji, with its yellowish-green skin and juicy white flesh, has a sweet and slightly spicy flavor. This apple, developed in Japan in the 1960s, is particularly prized for eating out of hand.

GALA Native to New Zealand, the Gala is pleasantly sweet and crisp, with golden skin and a rosy overtone. It is best for eating raw, or for sautéing or slow baking.

GOLDEN DELICIOUS Sweet, juicy, and mild, this is probably the most widely available apple, good for eating raw, frying, and making pies. Its flesh does not darken as readily as that of other apples, and it holds its shape during baking.

continued

a

❧ Apple Glossary, continued ❧

GRANNY SMITH Originally from Australia, this bright green apple boasts white, firm, juicy flesh that is sweet and tart at the same time. It is good for eating, sautéing, and baking.

HONEYCRISP This large apple, with its streaks of red and green, has a juicy, crisp flesh and mellow flavor. Good for eating raw or for a wide variety of cooking methods.

IDA RED A good-looking red apple with a hint of green, this mildly tart fruit is prized for baking and cooking.

JONAGOLD This cross between the Jonathan and the Golden Delicious has red-streaked yellow skin and firm, sweet, juicy white flesh. Use it for eating or cooking.

JONATHAN Most Jonathans are used for baking and cooking, although the golden apples with red stripes and juicy yellow flesh are good eaten raw, too.

MCINTOSH This is a fall favorite, with its red skin and crisp, white, juicy flesh. Macs, as they are affectionately known, have flesh that softens when cooked, making good applesauce.

NORTHERN SPY Red-blushed with green undertones, this juicy, sweet apple makes wonderful pies and sauces and holds its shape when baked. It is good for eating raw, too.

PIPPIN The term *pippin* turns up in a number of apple names, but the best known of them is the Newtown pippin, usually simply called pippin. This all-purpose apple, with its pale green or yellow skin

and creamy flesh, has a bright, tart, full flavor and firm texture that make it a favorite in pies.

RED DELICIOUS A popular eating apple that looks just how we all imagine an apple should. Unfortunately, due to overlong storage or supermarkets' selling the Red Delicious out of its natural season, many specimens have a mushy and tasteless flesh. Shop for your Red Delicious at a farmers' market so that you can buy in season and taste

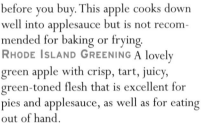

before you buy. This apple cooks down well into applesauce but is not recommended for baking or frying.

RHODE ISLAND GREENING A lovely green apple with crisp, tart, juicy, green-toned flesh that is excellent for pies and applesauce, as well as for eating out of hand.

ROME BEAUTY This large, red apple has sweet-tart, firm flesh and holds its shape when baked, which explains why it is among the most popular apples for filling with sweet or savory stuffings and baking whole.

WINESAP Sometimes called Stayman Winesap, this dark red apple has firm, crisp flesh and a sweet, winy flavor, characteristics that give it a loyal following among apple aficionados. It is not a good keeper, however, losing its crispness quickly. Its partisans recommend it for eating raw and for cooking.

YORK Mildly tart, this deep red apple with green stripes is a very good baking apple and makes fine applesauce.

the novice cook to use. Specially designed apple corers are available. Exposed apple flesh quickly discolors unless it is rubbed with lemon or other citrus juice. Since so many nutrients are in the skin of the apple, it is a good idea to leave it on when possible.

Quick Bite

Apples are grown widely, but those from colder northern climates are most prized. The Northeast and Pacific Northwest are the best-known apple-growing regions in the United States, with the largest crops coming from the states of Washington and New York.

See also CORING.

APRICOT Most apricots are canned, made into preserves, or dried, but once you experience a perfectly ripened fresh specimen, you will look forward to their brief season. Native to northern China, where they still grow wild, apricots are at their peak in July, but as they do not travel well, being easily bruised, they are not as widely available as peaches, nectarines, and other seasonal kin. They are small, too, less than half the size of a peach.

Selecting Look for fresh apricots with high golden color. When fully ripe, they will give slightly when gently pressed, similarly to a peach. Dark green unripe fruit will never ripen correctly. Light green unripe specimens may ripen satisfactorily.

Storing Eat ripe apricots as soon as possible. If you must store them, refrigerate them for up to 2 days. Those that are not fully ripe should be left at room temperature to ripen.

Preparing If a recipe requires peeled apricots, see BLANCHING.

See also DRIED FRUIT.

ARROWROOT See THICKENING.

ARTICHOKE Few vegetables look as forbidding as the artichoke. But for many cooks, this ungainly flower bud, harvested from a plant of the sizable thistle family, is a culinary treasure with a mild, nutty flavor to be savored. "Baby" artichokes are gaining in popularity and appearing on menus around the country, but most artichoke fanciers relish larger vegetables with more to them to enjoy. Baby artichokes are not immature artichokes, but simply small ones grown lower down on the plant. Whether large, medium, or small, all artichokes cultivated for commercial sale are Green Globe artichokes, which can be rounded or cone shaped.

Selecting The primary artichoke season is in early spring, followed by a second, smaller season in fall-winter. Buy artichokes that are heavy for their size. Look for tightly closed, olive green leaves and moist, healthy stems. A few purple streaks on the leaves are acceptable, but limp, brownish globes should be passed by. Some winter artichokes have black streaking, which indicates slight frost damage and is nothing to worry about. In fact, some artichoke lovers think these later vegetables are preferable to spring ones for their slightly nutty flavor. Baby artichokes should be olive green with tightly closed leaves.

If a recipe calls for artichoke hearts, use fresh ones or buy frozen or water-packed canned hearts, which are readily available in supermarkets. For cooked preparations, avoid small jars of marinated artichokes, as they add unwanted oil and flavorings to a recipe. They are, however, good in salads and as part of an antipasto spread.

Storing Sprinkle artichokes with a few drops of water and store in a perforated plastic bag in the coldest part of the refrigerator for up to 1 week. If cooking them on the day you buy them, leave them at cool room temperature. Once opened, marinated artichoke hearts will keep refrigerated for up to 2 weeks.

Quick Tip

Use only stainless-steel knives and cookware when preparing artichokes, since carbon steel, aluminum, and cast iron will discolor the vegetable within moments of cutting. No matter what you do, artichokes will darken somewhat, but fortunately this discoloration does not affect their flavor.

HOW TO *Trim an Artichoke*

1. Starting at the base, pull off and discard the tough outer leaves.

2. Cut the stem off flush with the bottom of the leaves and discard it.

3. Using a serrated knife, slice off the top 1 to 2 inches of the remaining leaves to remove the thorns, or use kitchen shears to trim off each thorny leaf top. If you are not cooking the artichoke immediately, sprinkle all the cut surfaces with lemon juice to minimize discoloring.

Removing the Choke Every large artichoke has an inedible fuzzy center, called a choke, that must be removed before eating. It is easiest to remove the choke after cooking since cooking softens the fibers, but some recipes direct you to remove the choke before cooking. Either way, there are several methods for removing the choke from an artichoke. You can halve the globes lengthwise and scrape the choke from either half with the edge of a spoon or with a small, sharp knife. You can also gently spread open the leaves from the top of a whole globe (this is easier after the top has been trimmed) and dig out the choke with a knife or spoon. This method is especially useful when making stuffed artichokes. After removing the choke this way, press the leaves back together to restore the artichoke's globe shape. If you want only the heart, you can remove all the leaves and then trim away the choke.

Artichoke hearts.

Or, you can serve a whole cooked artichoke with the choke intact and eat it as described in the section below entitled "Eating an Artichoke."

Baby artichokes can be as tiny as walnuts and do not have developed chokes, but you will still need to trim the stems, pull off the dark outer leaves, and cut away the spiny tops before cooking.

Artichokes are generally boiled or steamed, although they are also sometimes braised with other vegetables. They can be halved or quartered and roasted, as well. Baby artichokes are also delicious fried. If very young, they can be thinly sliced and eaten raw.

Quick Bite

Artichokes contain an acid called cynarin that causes most other foods or beverages you are consuming along with them to taste slightly sweet. This can make the crisp white wine with which you began your meal suddenly taste "off." To combat this effect, some cooks recommend serving Champagne or sparkling wine, rather than still wines, with artichokes.

Eating an Artichoke Eating an artichoke may sound like it takes a lot of effort, but the flavorful reward makes it well worth it. To eat large whole cooked artichokes, pull off the leaves one at a time, dip their thick, fleshy bases in melted butter, lemon juice, mayonnaise, vinaigrette, hollandaise sauce, or another dip, and then remove the sweet flesh from the bottom of each leaf by scraping it between your teeth. Discard the tough upper portion of the leaf. When you reach the last of the lighter-colored tender inner leaves, pull them out and discard them. If the fuzzy choke is not already removed, scrape it out with a spoon and eat the delicious heart.

See also BOILING; STEAMING.

ARUGULA Also known as rocket, this pleasantly peppery green has sword-shaped, deeply notched leaves usually no more than 2 or 3 inches long. Adding arugula to other milder salad greens results in a salad with a nicely sharp, spicy edge. It is much favored in Italy, where it is also used in pasta sauces and to top pizzas hot from the oven. Arugula can be added to soups and sauces, too.

Selecting Arugula is generally sold in small bunches, often with the root ends standing in a shallow tub of water to maintain freshness. Occasionally it is sold as prewashed loose leaves. Look for fresh-looking bunches of long, slender, young leaves. Do not worry if they droop slightly. Mature arugula can be too sharply flavored for all but the most hard-core aficionado.

Storing Wrap the stems in damp paper towels and slip the bunch into a loosely sealed plastic bag, or wrap it loosely in a kitchen towel. Store loose leaves in a plastic bag. Store in the refrigerator crisper and use within 2 days.

Preparing Trim thick stalk ends and rinse the leaves thoroughly under cool water. Shake dry or spin in a salad spinner. Toss with other clean, dry greens.

See also GREENS, SALAD.

ASIAN PEAR See PEAR, ASIAN.

ASPARAGUS Among the produce market's tastiest harbingers of spring, asparagus is most delicious in its true season—but very good fresh asparagus is available all year long. These tall, crisp-tender spears can be pencil-thin or as thick as a man's

a

thumb. Thin spears and thick each have their devoted followers. Steam or boil fresh spears vertically in an asparagus steamer or horizontally in a large frying pan (not a crowded saucepan) and serve hot, topped with melted butter and a squeeze of lemon juice, or cold, dressed with vinaigrette. Asparagus is heavenly when coated with olive oil and roasted in the oven or grilled. Slender spears are good sautéed in a bit of olive oil or butter and tossed with pasta; stockier spears are good additions to soups and stews. Canned and frozen are also available but are inferior to fresh.

Selecting Look for firm stalks and tight, dry, and often purple-tinged tips, avoiding those that are moist looking. The cut end should look freshly cut and not too dried out. If there is slight spreading at the top, the spears are still good. The length of the shoot should be all or mostly green. The white at the bottom should be discarded before cooking.

Most asparagus sold in the United States is green, but white asparagus, beloved in Europe, is becoming increasingly popular. It is the same vegetable, but given an exotic look and more delicate flavor by keeping the growing spears carefully covered with soil so only the tips emerge. This prevents sunlight from reaching the shoots and developing their chlorophyll. There is also a purple variety, which turns green when cooked and tends to be a little sweeter than regular asparagus.

Storing Cook asparagus as soon as possible after purchase. If you must store it, cut off an inch or so of the stalk at the base and set the bunch in a shallow pan of water for up to 4 days.

Preparing Bend the cut end of each spear until it breaks naturally. It will snap precisely where the fibrous, tough inedible portion begins.

Snapping off tough ends.

While the spears will be of unequal length, their flavor and texture will be uniformly glorious. If you favor a consistent length, trim snapped spears with a knife. If the spears have a thick or fibrous skin (check by taking a small bite), peel them to within about 1 inch of the tips.

Peeling asparagus.

Quick Bite

Canned white asparagus from Spain, particularly from Navarre, is full flavored and tender, ideal for serving with a vinaigrette made from Spanish olive oil and sherry vinegar. In some people's opinion, these tinned Iberian spears rival the best fresh asparagus.

AVOCADO Buttery and rich, this tropical tree fruit is mistakenly regarded as a vegetable. The primary ingredient in guacamole, it is also wonderful in salads or sandwiches, and is frequently served halved, pitted, and filled with shrimp salad, chicken salad, or a thick mustard vinaigrette. Avocados are at their best when served raw or only slightly heated, as their silky texture and mildly nutty flavor do not hold up in cooking. Although high in fat—they contain about 30 percent unsaturated fat—avocados also boast a good amount of protein for a fruit.

Selecting Avocados are available year-round, with a large winter harvest filling market bins in January and February and a large summer harvest from June through August. Two major varieties are commonly available: the dark green, dimple-skinned Hass (or Haas) and the smoother, paler green Fuerte. The former has a far richer flavor and texture. Look for dark, rough skin when buying Hass and smooth, un-blemished skin when buying Fuerte. Both varieties yield to gentle finger pressure when ripe. Avoid avocados that feel mushy or show signs of mold.

Storing Store ripe avocados at cool room temperature for up to 2 days, or in the re-frigerator for up to 1 week. Keep unripe avocados in a warm, dark place. After a few days, they should pass the pressure test. When this occurs, you may cut and use the Fuerte avocado, but let the Hass ripen a day longer; too often, avocados are served before they are fully ripe, denying the eater the fruit's full, rich flavor. To speed the ripening process, put the avocado in a paper bag with an apple, a banana, or a tomato. Ethylene gases emitted by the other fruit will hasten ripening.

To store a cut avocado, wrap it in plastic wrap, smoothing the wrap right onto the fruit's cut surface to seal out air and pre-vent discoloring.

Preparing Since the flesh of an avocado quickly turns brown when exposed to air, cut the fruit just before serving. Sprinkling the cut flesh with a little lemon or lime juice will help slow the discoloring.

HOW TO *Halve an Avocado*

1. Using a small, sharp knife, cut the avocado in half lengthwise, cutting carefully around the large, round pit at the center.
2. Rotate the halves in opposite directions to separate them.

3. Scoop out the pit with the tip of a spoon and discard. Or, holding the avocado with a pot holder or kitchen towel to protect your hand, carefully strike the pit with the heel of a large, sharp knife so that the blade lodges in it, and draw out the pit.

4. Ease a large spoon between the avocado flesh and the peel and gently scoop out the flesh, scraping as closely to the peel as possible. Alternatively, peel away the skin with the knife.

a

19

*everything from bacon
to buttermilk*

BACK BACON See CANADIAN BACON.

BACON A little bit of bacon goes a long way—although it's easy to eat more than just a little! Cut from the belly (called the side) of the hog below the spareribs, it is cured and usually smoked, which contributes to its irresistible flavor. Bacon is delicious with eggs, crumbled over salads, used to top baked dishes, and in sandwiches: the BLT—bacon, lettuce, and tomato—is an American classic. In the South, bacon fat is traditionally used to cook mustard, collard, and other sturdy greens.

Generally, bacon is about 50 percent fat, although leaner versions can be as low as 33 percent fat. As bacon cooks, its fat becomes liquid and separates from the meat, a process known as rendering. If fat rendered from frying bacon is not used for the recipe at hand, it can be poured off into a tightly covered container, stored in the refrigerator or freezer, and used for sautéing or frying other foods. If you don't wish to use it for cooking, pour the fat off into a coffee can or similar container, keep the can in a cool, dark place, and add to it until the can is full. Then discard the fat sensibly (never down the sink!).

Selecting Most people buy bacon already cut into slices and packaged in clear plastic in the meat section of the market. Look for rosy pink meat and ivory fat. Buy thin-sliced, regular-sliced, or thick-sliced bacon, depending on your preference. Look for thick-sliced apple wood–smoked bacon for especially good flavor. Butchers also usually sell slab bacon, which is often of better quality than presliced. The slab is covered with rind, which you can ask the butcher to remove. You can also ask the butcher to slice the bacon, or you can slice it at home as needed. Whole slab bacon stays fresher longer than presliced and is often less expensive as well.

Storing All bacon should be refrigerated in its original packaging or carefully wrapped in plastic until ready to cook. It keeps for up to 2 weeks and can be frozen for up to 2 months.

Preparing Most bacon is fried, although it can be roasted, too, with very good results. Cooking bacon in the microwave requires a rack to help it cook evenly. Drain bacon on paper towels before serving.

Bacon Savvy

- For perfect fried bacon, start with a dry pan. Heat the pan and bacon together over medium-low heat, tending it carefully and removing the slices when they are done to your liking—"soggy," crisp, or somewhere in between. If necessary, pour off the excess grease during cooking. Do not fall into the trap of cooking bacon over high heat. Cook it slowly.

- You do not have to separate bacon slices before cooking them—this often results in tearing. They easily separate once they begin to cook.

- To cook a large amount of bacon, place the strips in a roasting pan and roast in a 450°F oven until done to your liking. This can take 25 minutes. Separate the strips after 10 minutes and then turn

them every 5 to 10 minutes, carefully pouring off the grease as needed.
See also CANADIAN BACON; PANCETTA; PORK.

BAGEL A roll-sized traditional Jewish yeast bread, round with a hole in the center, like a doughnut. Plain, or water, bagels have white interiors and a somewhat chewier texture than yellow egg-enriched bagels. Onions, garlic, salt, poppy seeds, sesame seeds, or raisins and cinnamon are common flavorings.

Traditionally, bagels are briefly boiled before they are baked, which leaves them chewy and shiny. Their dense texture and round shape make them tricky to slice, which has given rise to a small kitchen gadget called a bagel slicer: the bagel is held vertically in the tool and then sliced with a guillotine-like action. A long, serrated bread knife can be used as well, but watch your fingers.

Bagels are sold in Jewish delicatessens and bakeries, many food markets, and in specialized bagel shops, where an assortment of cream cheeses, or schmears, both plain and flavored (lox, chives, vegetables, honey), also is typically available.

BAIN-MARIE (BAN mah-REE) See WATER BATH.

BAKER'S PEEL See BAKING TOOLS.

BAKEWARE See page 24.

BAKING Put simply, "baking" refers to the method of cooking food in the dry heat of an oven. The term is sometimes applied to the process of cooking uniform pieces of meat, poultry, or seafood with a small amount of fat or liquid (or a combination of foods mixed with a sauce) in an open pan or dish in the hot, dry air of an oven.

When these foods are cooked alone in the oven, however, the process is usually called roasting—harkening back to the days when meats were roasted over an open flame. More generally, "baking" refers to the process of making baked goods such as breads, cakes, pastries, and pies, which are then cooked in an oven.

For centuries, home cooks baked nearly every day. If they hadn't, there would have been no bread on the table or cakes and cookies to sweeten daily life. Today, many home cooks are nervous about baking, believing it is too complicated to tackle. Undeniably, baking requires more precision than most other home cooking, but with just a few ingredients and the right equipment, anyone can produce towering cakes, crisp cookies, bubbling fruit pies, and golden loaves of bread. And, as with everything, baking gets easier with practice.

Before You Begin First, read the recipe all the way to the end. (This is good advice regardless of what you are cooking.) Read it again and make a shopping list of any ingredients and equipment you do not have. Once you have all the necessary ingredients, measure them carefully or otherwise prepare them according to the ingredient list (chop, grate, sift) and put them in small bowls or other containers. Assemble all necessary equipment and utensils ahead, too, and prepare the pans for baking. This may mean greasing and flouring them or lining them with waxed paper or parchment paper, according to the recipe. Experienced bakers always "prep" this way, never as they go along, to avoid needless delays or oversights.

Preparing Ingredients For many cake and cookie recipes, eggs and butter should be brought to room temperature. This helps to form a smooth batter. Room-temperature egg whites foam more quickly than cold whites, but cold eggs are easier to separate, so if a recipe calls for egg whites or yolks only, separate the eggs right out of the refrigerator and then let them come to room temperature before beating.

For pie and tart doughs, cold ingredients should be kept cold, especially the butter or shortening. If the fat is allowed to melt before the crust reaches the oven, the pastry will not be as flaky.

Quick Tip

If you forget to allow enough time for eggs and butter to reach room temperature, submerge cold eggs in a bowl of warm tap water (not hot, or you'll "cook" the eggs) for about 15 minutes. Soften butter in the microwave on a low setting, checking it every 20 to 30 seconds to make sure it is not melting.

Measuring Ingredients When measuring ingredients for baking, remember that accuracy is the key. Until you are an experienced baker, save your experimentation for stir-fries and pasta sauces. If you don't follow a cake or cookie recipe precisely, there's a good chance it won't turn out. Bread making is a bit more forgiving. See MEASURING for more detail.

Check Your Oven Whether you are baking a loaf of bread, a cake, or a batch of cookies, an accurate oven is important. Use an oven thermometer—available at kitchen shops, hardware stores, and food markets—to determine the oven's accuracy. Seek out a mercury type over the less sturdy, less reliable spring-style thermometer. Hang it from the rack in the middle of the oven, and then turn on the oven. Check the temperature after at least 20 minutes have passed. If it is off by 25° or 50°F, adjust for it when baking. For example, if you set the oven for 350°F and the oven thermometer reads 375°F, reduce the knob setting to 325°F during baking

to compensate. Or, depending on the type of oven you have, call your local electric or gas company; most will send a technician to your house to calibrate the oven, thus eliminating the need to make an adjustment each time you bake. Nevertheless, it is a good idea to leave the thermometer in the oven all the time to track its accuracy.

See also BLIND BAKING; BREAD; CAKE; COOKIE; CUSTARD; FLOUR; MEASURING; MOUSSE; PAN SIZES; PARCHMENT PAPER; PIE & TART; QUICK BREAD; YEAST.

BAKING DISH See BAKEWARE.

BAKING POWDER & BAKING SODA These everyday pantry items give a lift to cakes and cookies, muffins and quick breads. Baking powder and soda are chemical leaveners, unlike yeast, which is a living microorganism. Baking powder and soda work by reacting with both liquids and heat to release carbon dioxide gas, which in turn leavens the batter, causing it to rise as it cooks.

Baking Powder Baking powder is a mixture of an acid and an alkaline, or base, that is activated when it is exposed to moisture or heat and releases carbon dioxide. Cornstarch is a typical element of baking powder, serving to absorb moisture, keeping the powder dry, and preventing a reaction until liquid is added.

The principle of leavening baked goods this way was first discovered in the late 18th century, when carbonate-rich wood ash was used to give quick breads a rise.

Quick Tip

If in doubt about the viability of baking powder, drop a generous pinch into a little warm water. If it fizzes or bubbles, it is still good. If it sinks to the bottom of the cup, discard it.

Nearly all baking powder sold today is "double acting," which means that it contains two acids that react at two different times. The acids are typically cream of tartar and either sodium aluminum sulfate or anhydrous monocalcium phosphate. The first dissolves more quickly than the second, reacting with the base and releasing some gas as soon as it is mixed with the liquid in a recipe. The second dissolves more slowly and reacts later, when the batter is exposed to the heat of the oven. This second reaction makes double-acting baking powder a reliable leavener.

In days gone by, only single-acting baking powder was available. This powder reacted when first mixed with liquid, which meant the batter had to be baked immediately. If not, the gases responsible for leavening might escape before the batter was cooked. Although many recipes still recommend that batters made with baking powder be baked promptly, time is not as crucial as it used to be. Even so, do not leave the batter sitting for more than about 20 minutes before baking.

Baking Soda Also known as bicarbonate of soda or sodium bicarbonate, baking soda is an alkaline, or base, that releases carbon dioxide gas only when it comes into contact with an acidic ingredient, such as sour cream, yogurt, buttermilk, or citrus juice.

When a recipe calls for baking soda alone, rather than baking soda and baking powder, an acidic ingredient must also be present in the batter. Because baking soda is single, rather than double, acting, wet and dry ingredients for batters should be mixed separately. Then, as soon as the two mixtures are combined, the batter must go directly into its pan and straight into a preheated oven. Baking soda is useful for other household tasks, too, from deodorizing refrigerators to loosening burned bits of food on pan bottoms.

Selecting Commercially sold baking powders and sodas are generally excellent. Check the sell-by dates, particularly on baking powder, which will eventually lose its effectiveness. Some brands of double-acting baking powder include aluminum compounds. If you have any concerns about ingesting aluminum, look for aluminum-free brands in supermarkets and natural-food stores. The best-known example is Rumford, which comes in a red canister and performs as effectively as those with aluminum compounds. Sodium-free baking powders are available as well. They are less powerful, however, and so the amounts called for in recipes should be doubled. Single-acting baking powder is nearly impossible to find these days.

Quick Bite

If only baking soda is used in a recipe with an acidic ingredient, it reacts with and neutralizes the acidic ingredient. To help retain some of that pleasant acidity, as in a recipe for buttermilk biscuits, both baking powder and baking soda are used. Baking powder has a built-in acid, which gives the batter a lift without neutralizing all of the acidic ingredient.

Storing Keep baking powder and baking soda in a cool, dry place, although this is more important for baking powder. Both will last for at least 4 months, or for 6 months at most. Discard them after this point if you don't want a batch of leaden biscuits or a pitifully flat cake.

BAKING SHEET See BAKEWARE.

BAKING STONE See BAKING TOOLS.

BAKING TOOLS See page 28.

BALSAMIC VINEGAR See VINEGAR.

Bakeware

Have you ever bitten into a seemingly perfect cookie only to discover an unpleasant charred bottom? Had the cookie been baked on a sturdy cookie sheet, it would have been burn free.

The taste and texture of baked goods are affected by the surface on which they're cooked. Inexpensive pans and cookie sheets will warp with use, causing poor heat conduction and unevenly baked cakes, cookies, and breads. The best baking pans cook evenly, brown nicely, and resist sticking or burning. If you hope to enjoy your own baked treats, you owe it to yourself to invest in quality bakeware.

Bakeware Materials Pans are available in several different materials, each with its own advantages and disadvantages. Note that darker-colored materials may require lower heat and shorter baking time than lighter ones.

ALUMINUM A superb conductor of heat, aluminum heats evenly, so baked goods brown evenly. Once removed from the oven, it cools quickly. Select anodized aluminum, which has been treated with an electrolytic process to make it harder, denser, and more resistant to corrosion. Insulated aluminum is also a good choice, since it heats more slowly than regular aluminum, avoiding burnt bottoms.

CAST IRON Durable cast iron absorbs and releases heat more slowly than other metals, turning out delicate muffins with fine, thin crusts and moist interiors.

GLASS AND CERAMIC These materials, used mainly for baking dishes and pie dishes or plates, encourage browning because the radiant heat is conducted and retained well by them. Foods bake more quickly in glass and ceramic bakeware, too, so you may need to reduce baking times and temperatures.

NONSTICK A nonstick coating ensures the easy release of baked goods and quick cleanup. Nonstick aluminum is a good heat conductor but is not always as sturdy as other materials, such as nonstick heavy-gauge steel. Look for a double-layer nonstick coating, and remember to use wooden or plastic utensils (such as a plastic spatula for removing cookies from a baking sheet) to avoid scratching the surface.

STEEL Heavy-gauge stainless steel is strong and easy to clean, a good choice for bakeware. Tinned steel is used in classic French baking; the shiny surface provided by the tin prevents overbrowning. Darkened steel pans, the choice of many professional bakers, are excellent absorbers and distributors of heat.

THE BASIC BAKER Following are the pans every home baker should have. While it is not necessary to buy every one of these pans at once, plan to stock your kitchen gradually with them over time. Note that

Quick Tip

Whatever the metal, a dark-colored pan absorbs heat more quickly than a light-colored one, and while this is desirable for some recipes, it can cause overbrowning of more delicate foods. Watch carefully and reduce oven temperature or shorten baking time.

the measurements given are taken on the inside of the pan.

BAKING DISH Used for everything from brownies to small roasts and lasagne, deep glass dishes (or metal pans) come in all shapes and sizes, but for the average home baker the most common are a 9-by-13-by-2-inch rectangular dish and an 8- or 9-inch square dish with 2-inch sides.

BAKING SHEET This rectangular metal pan with shallow, slightly sloping rims comes in several forms. The jelly-roll pan, so named because it is used to make sponge cakes that, after baking, are spread with a filling such as jelly and then rolled, is 10 by 15 inches with ½-inch rims. Half-sheet pans are 12 by 17 inches, half the size of large commercial baking sheets. Baking pans are handy for making rolls or croissants or may be used as roasting pans for small cuts of meat.

Quick Tip

A good baking sheet can play a strong supporting role for other bakeware. Placed beneath cake pans or under a soufflé dish, it will help retain more heat and conduct it into the cookware it accompanies, helping a cake or soufflé to rise higher than it otherwise would.

CAKE PAN Plan to buy at least two round cake pans in the sizes you are likely to use (check your recipes!): 1½ to 2 inches deep and 8 or 9 inches in diameter. American cake pans are not as deep as European ones. Choose good-quality, seamless, heavy metal pans. Square and rectangular pans also are often called for in some recipes— see Baking Dish, above, and Springform Pan, page 26.

COOKIE SHEET A flat metal pan, usually with a low rim on one or two ends, designed to allow for sliding cookies onto a cooling rack. Avoid very dark sheets, which will cause your baked goods to burn. Nonstick cookie sheets work well and are very easy to clean. Insulated cookie sheets, which have an interior air pocket between two layers of metal, guarantee that no cookie will ever have an overbrowned bottom. They do not, however, work well for thin, crisp cookies, which benefit from intense heat. You'll want two cookie sheets for big batches of cookies.

LOAF PAN Also called a bread pan, a standard loaf pan is 5 by 9 by 3 inches and may be metal or glass. A smaller pan, 4½ by 8½ by 2½ inches, is also useful. Metal loaf pans produce loaf cakes and quick breads with evenly browned crusts; glass dishes encourage fast browning, sometimes at the expense of the interior of the bread or cake. Can also be used for meat loaf.

MUFFIN PAN Standard muffin and cupcake pans have 6 or 12 cups, each capable of holding 6 to 7 tablespoons of batter. Muffin pans with jumbo cups or miniature, or gem, cups are also available. Muffin cups

continued

b

Bakeware, continued

can be lined with paper liners (although the crust is likely to come off with the paper) or greased before being filled. Special muffin pans include those with wide, flat cups for making thin, crisp muffins; and pans with cups in such whimsical or holiday-theme shapes as hearts, stars, teddy bears, dinosaurs, flowers, cars, or Christmas trees. Although aluminum and steel are common materials, cast-iron pans with nonstick surfaces are ideal for making muffins.

PIE PAN Buy metal pie pans or glass or ceramic pie plates in 9- and 10-inch sizes. Glass pie plates let you see how the bottom crust is browning, although they are sometimes overzealous heat conductors that lead to a brown crust and an undercooked middle. Look for a wide rim to hold up the fluted edge of the crust.

Quick Tip

If you like to bake pies containing especially juicy fruit, look in specialty cookware stores for a pie pan with a juice-saver rim—an extra-wide rim that includes a shallow trough to capture juices that bubble from the crust, thus preventing them from dribbling and burning on the oven floor.

SPRINGFORM PAN This deep, round cake pan with sides secured by a clamp is especially useful for cheesecakes and other solid

cakes. The sides expand when the clamp is released, making the cake easy to remove. A 9-inch diameter is the most commonly used size. Generally, springform pans should be used atop baking sheets to prevent batter from leaking onto the bottom of your oven.

Quick Tip

If a recipe suggests placing a springform pan in a water bath, wrap the outside of the springform in a layer of aluminum foil, shiny side in (unless the recipe instructs otherwise), to prevent water seepage. See also WATER BATH.

TART PAN A tart pan has shallow, usually fluted sides and perhaps a removable bottom. An 11-inch metal tart pan with a removable bottom and a 10- or 11-inch solid tart pan are the most useful choices.

THE WELL-STOCKED BAKER As you experiment with baking and discover your own personal favorites you may decide to buy a few special pans.

BRIOCHE MOLD Also called a brioche pan, this circular mold with deeply fluted sides is used to bake the classic butter-and-egg-enriched French bread loaf of the same name. Made of darkened steel, stainless or tinned steel, porcelain, or glass.

CHARLOTTE MOLD Named for a classic baked French dessert in which buttery ladyfingers enclose a Bavarian cream filling. Made of tinned or stainless steel, and with slightly slanting sides that ease unmolding, the round mold can range in size from 6 ounces to 2 quarts.

MADELEINE PAN Unless you plan to bake the small French sponge cakes known as madeleines, you won't need this pan. But if you want to make the buttery sweets that Proust made famous, you cannot manage without it. Also called madeleine molds, the pans have shallow shell-shaped depressions, each about 3 inches long and 2 inches wide. Most pans make 8 to 12 cookies at a time.

PIZZA PAN These pans are usually 12 to 17 inches in diameter, with a very low, angled rim (about $\frac{1}{2}$ inch high). Deep-dish pizza pans have $1\frac{1}{2}$-inch sides and may be rectangular (about 12 by 8 inches or slightly larger) or round. They often have removable bottoms and may be equipped with a pan gripper that clamps onto the side of the pan to hold it steady while you cut the pizza into slices or squares. Round pans are available with perforated bottoms to encourage a crisp crust. Some pizza pans are insulated, similar to insulated baking sheets, to prevent the crust from burning or becoming overbrown.

POPOVER PAN Similar to a muffin pan, but specially designed to accommodate airier popovers as they rise. Muffin pans will work for popovers, too, but they are not the best choice, as the cups are closer together (popovers need room to crown). Cookware stores also offer individual popover molds made of black steel, although custard cups or individual soufflé dishes may be used in their place. Avoid aluminum, which trans-mits the oven heat too quickly, overcooking the outside of the popover.

QUICHE DISH Similar to a tart pan, often made of steel with a removable bottom, with higher fluted sides to accommodate the deeper filling of a quiche. Quiche dishes made of ovenproof porcelain also double nicely as serving dishes.

SOUFFLÉ MOLD Designed with tall, straight sides so that the soufflé can rise straight and high, this dish is commonly circular, ranges in size from $\frac{1}{2}$ to 2 quarts, and is porcelain. It is handsome enough to carry to the table. Smaller, individual-portion soufflé molds are available in some shops as well.

TUBE PAN Any pan with a central tube, a feature that helps the center of a cake to rise and bake evenly, is called a tube pan, but several different styles exist. Angel food cake pans sometimes have removable bottoms and small "feet" (or a tall central tube) extending above the rim, which permit the inverted pan to stand clear of the counter during cooling so no moisture is trapped. Fluted tube pans, called Bundt pans, and fluted and flared kugelhopf (also called kugelhupf or gugelhopf) pans have fixed bottoms and no feet. Tube pans hold from $1\frac{1}{2}$ to 4 quarts of batter. For most uses, invest in one 10-inch tube pan.

Quick Tip

Tube pans can be used interchangeably with cake pans as long as they have the same capacity. But with more delicate recipes, such as for angel food cake, do not try to bake a tube pan recipe in a regular cake pan; the center of the cake may not cook properly.

See also PAN SIZES.

Baking Tools

Having the right tool for the job makes baking easier and more enjoyable. While you can roll out pastry dough with a wine bottle, or cut biscuits with an inverted water glass, these tasks go more smoothly with a rolling pin or a biscuit cutter.

If you buy good, sturdy tools, they will last for years and serve you well.

THE BASIC BAKER Every home baker should have the following tools. You don't need to buy every item listed here at once, but as time goes by, consider stocking your kitchen with most of them.

COOKIE AND BISCUIT CUTTERS Although some are made of plastic, the best cutters are made of metal, so that the cutting side holds its edge. Cookie cutters come in different shapes and sizes, from the basic round to holiday icons (jack-o'-lanterns, hearts, Christmas trees, Stars of David) and seasonal themes (leaves, flowers). Biscuit cutters are round and often fluted, and may come in nests of graduated sizes.

Quick Tip

A water glass will also work in a pinch for cutting cookies and biscuits. Thin crystal is best for slicing through dough.

COOLING RACK Because cakes, cookies, pies, and breads should be allowed to cool evenly, with air circulating on all sides, recipes call for cooling baked goods on wire racks. These come in squares, rectangles, or rounds and have small feet that raise them above the countertop. Most are made of chrome-plated metal, although some are made from stainless steel or nonstick aluminum. Buy sturdy racks that do not wobble on the counter. Have on hand two or three racks. You'll want enough to handle two cake layers or two sheets of cookies. Crisscrossing grids work well, leaving less of an indentation on your baked goods.

DOUGH SCRAPER Also called a bench scraper. This tool is used to lift dough (principally bread dough) as you work it, to scrape the remains of dough and flour from a board or countertop, and to divide pastry or bread dough into portions. Most dough scrapers have wooden or plastic handles and stainless-steel blades. Some have plastic blades, while others are constructed completely of stainless steel. All are rectangular, sometimes with rounded corners. Dough scrapers are also handy for scooping up and transferring chopped ingredients to a pan for sautéing, adding to a salad, or similar uses. Most such tasks executed by dough scrapers are relatively rugged work, so whatever type you decide on, look for a sturdy metal dough scraper that feels fairly hefty for its size. The little extra you might spend at the store will pay off in durability and efficiency at home.

FROSTING SPATULA Also called icing spatula or pastry spatula. This long, flat metal utensil with its slender, flexible, 6- to 12-inch-long blade resembles a round-tipped knife without a sharp edge. When the handle angles off the blade, the spatula is called an offset spatula. Both types will make frosting your cakes easier.

MEASURING SPOONS AND CUPS You will need a sturdy set of measuring spoons and two separate measures for dry and liquid ingredients. See MEASURING for more information.

MIXING BOWLS Stocking bowls in a range of materials, shapes, and sizes will help you tackle varied tasks more efficiently. For example, whipping egg whites and creaming butter call for deep bowls, while preparing and organizing ingredients for a cake call for a range of smaller bowls. See MIXING BOWL for more information.

MIXING SPOONS Wooden mixing spoons are favorites among cooks, although stainless-steel or sturdy plastic ones are also available. Wood does not conduct heat, so you won't burn your fingers, and wooden spoons are sturdy and inflexible, desirable qualities for most mixing tasks. They should be made of hardwoods such as beech or ash; softwoods can carry a resinous flavor. Segregate spoons used for baking from those used for savory preparations, as the latter may retain the taste of garlic and onions. Keep a mix of sizes for different tasks—small spoons for small quantities, large ones for mixing bowls of batter. See also SPOON.

PASTRY BLENDER Also known as a dough blender, this tool transforms fat and flour to a consistency suitable for pastry dough. It has a wooden or plastic handle anchoring a row of steel wires forming a U shape. The wires act as cutters, reducing pieces of butter or other fat to the size of small peas or the consistency of meal. See CUTTING IN for more detail.

Quick Tip

If a pastry blender is unavailable, you can use a fork, 2 table knives, or a food processor to cut in butter or shortening.

PASTRY BRUSH This important tool is used to brush water, egg washes, melted butter, or glazes on pastry. The brushes are made with natural or nylon bristles, with the latter usually no more than 1½ inches long and 1 to 2 inches wide. Goose-feather brushes are excellent for egg washes. Wash pastry brushes in hot, soapy water and keep them separate from brushes used for savory foods.

PREP BOWLS Baking is more relaxing when you precisely measure out, prepare, and line up all the ingredients before you start mixing. An assortment of small prep bowls helps you do just that. Look for glass or ceramic bowls, ranging from tiny vessels perfect for holding a single egg to larger sizes suitable for 2 cups of flour. Custard cups and ramekins also work.

continued

b

Baking Tools, continued

ROLLING PIN Rolling pins are available in different sizes and materials. For the most part, the type you choose is a matter of personal taste. Heavy, smooth wooden rolling pins are great for pie crusts and other types of dough. Some bakers prefer French-style pins without handles, either the straight dowel type or the kind with tapered ends, while others prefer pins with handles.

Professional models with good heft and ball bearings to keep the pin rolling smoothly are available. Marble or stainless-steel rolling pins are suggested for fine pastry work because they stay cool. Some rolling pins for pastry are even made with hollowed centers that can be packed with ice cubes, an elaboration that may go a bit too far. See also ROLLING OUT.

Quick Tip

If you're caught without a rolling pin, a clean wine bottle will work. Soak it in hot water, remove the label, dry it, and chill before using.

RUBBER SPATULA Also called a bowl scraper. This handy kitchen tool is used for getting every last bit of cake batter into pans, scraping down the sides of the mixing bowl when beating cookie dough, and scooping the last of the sour cream from its container. The best ones have blades made of silicone rubber, which won't melt or stick when used in a hot pan. Avoid plastic ones. The flexible blade is generally 2 inches wide by 3 inches long, although

smaller and larger ones are available. Some are slightly spoon shaped, which is great for stirring, folding, and scraping. Purchase a couple in different sizes for different tasks.
SIFTER Also known as a flour sifter or screen sifter. This is a metal or plastic canister fitted with two or three mesh screens and a handle that, when squeezed or turned, rotates an inside blade that forces

Quick Tip

If you don't have a sifter, a fine-mesh strainer with a handle is a good pinch hitter. Simply hold the strainer over a bowl and spoon in the flour or other ingredient. Then, gently tap the rim of the strainer with your hand to pass the contents through the mesh.

flour, lumpy cocoa powder or confectioners' sugar, or other dry ingredients through the screens to sift and aerate it. Sifters are sold in capacities ranging from 1 to 8 cups. A 2- or 3-cup capacity is most useful. See also SIFTING.
WHISK Wire whisks vary in length and diameter. The smallest are about 6 inches long, while the largest for the home baker are about 12 inches long. Three main types exist, each designed for a different task. Sauce whisks, which have somewhat elongated heads and relatively stiff wires, are used to mix ingredients thoroughly without adding excess air. Balloon whisks, which have rounded heads and more, thinner, lighter-gauge wires, are used to incorporate air into egg whites and cream. Flat whisks, sometimes called roux whisks, are used for whisking gravies and sauces. The flat shape allows you to get into the corners of a pan while also pressing out and smoothing lumps. As with rubber spatulas, you may need a couple of different sizes for different tasks. The best whisks have stainless-steel wires and sealed handles, so that no food can get into the handle. See also WHISKING.

THE WELL-STOCKED BAKER

Once you have the basic baking tools you need, you may want to add some specialty items that match your baking style.

BAKER'S PEEL Professional bread bakers use this wooden tool to slide loaves in and out of large ovens. Home cooks will find that a peel simplifies sliding a large loaf of bread dough or a fully loaded pizza onto a baking stone—and then retrieving it later.

BAKING STONE Also called a pizza stone, baking tile, or quarry tile. This is a flat rectangular, square, or round piece of unglazed stoneware used principally for baking breads and pizzas to produce crisp crusts. Appreciated for its efficient heat distribution, it is generally placed on the lowest rack or sometimes on the floor of the oven and preheated for at least 45 minutes or up to 1 hour before baking. The best ones are made of the same type of clay used to line kilns, as they are less apt to crack than ordinary clay baking stones. Wipe the cooled stones clean after use; do not use soap and water.

BREAD BOARD Any wooden board used mainly for kneading bread. Wood retains heat better than marble, tile, or granite, and yeast thrives in a warm environment, so home cooks whose kitchens have work surfaces in these materials often use a board for bread making.

CAKE ROUND Made of cardboard, this tool is used for both decorating and serving cakes. For easy frosting, a cake layer placed on a round can be balanced on the flat of your hand or on a decorating turntable. Each level on a tiered cake, such as a wedding cake, is supported by a cardboard round, which can be lifted off for serving. Buy cake rounds at cookware shops or bakeries or through catalogs, or cut rounds yourself from heavy, corrugated cardboard. See also FROSTING, ICING & GLAZE.

DECORATING COMB Also called a cake comb, an icing comb, or a comb scraper. These stainless-steel or plastic triangles with jagged teeth of varying size on each 3- to 4-inch edge are used to make decorative patterns in icings. Rectangular combs with a single serrated edge are also available.

DECORATING TURNTABLE Anyone who does a lot of cake decorating appreciates a turntable. Frosting and piping are much easier if you can turn the cake with a slight push and if it is raised above the work surface. An inexpensive "lazy Susan" works, but for the serious cake baker, a heavy metal turntable from a cookware shop or baking-supply house works best.

PASTRY BAG Also known as an icing bag, a decorating bag, a decorating tube, or a pastry tube. Pastry bags are made of plastic-lined canvas, plain canvas, polyester, nylon, or disposable plastic. Nylon and polyester are lightweight and easy to manipulate but can be slippery. The most useful bags are 8 to 12 inches long. Different pastry tips can be inserted into the narrow end of the conical bag, and frosting, whipped cream, or a similar mixture can be spooned into the wide end and piped out of the narrow end. If you plan to do much piping with a pastry bag, it is a good idea to have

continued

b

Baking Tools, continued

at least two bags, so that you can switch quickly back and forth between different colors of frosting without having to wash the bag. Pastry bags should be washed in warm, soapy water and turned inside out for drying. Be sure to keep bags used for savory preparations separate from those used for desserts. See also FROSTING, ICING & GLAZE; PIPING.

PASTRY BOARD Rolling out pastry calls for a smooth, hard, preferably cool surface. A pastry board may be made of hardwood or marble. Do not use it as a cutting board, or the surface will become rough (and marble will dull your knives). Marble boards stay cool, which is important for flaky pie dough. They can even be chilled in the refrigerator or on a cold back porch.

PASTRY CLOTH A piece of canvas cloth, measuring from 16 to 22 inches square, which facilitates rolling pastry by preventing it from sticking or sliding. Some are weighted or are fitted with clamps to hold them in place. Pastry cloths should be rubbed with flour before every use, and shaken and scraped clean afterward before storing. Wash them from time to time, since they may absorb fat and eventually become rancid. They are often sold accompanied by a rolling-pin sleeve made of the same fabric, which prevents the dough from sticking to the pin, a common problem for beginners. The sleeve must be rubbed with flour as well. See also PIE & TART; ROLLING OUT.

Quick Tip

In place of using a pastry cloth and sleeve, slip the dough between two sheets of waxed paper or parchment paper.

PASTRY CRIMPER Resembling large tweezers and sold in different patterns, pastry crimpers are used to seal together top and bottom crusts of pies and other filled pastries. The most common type is made of stainless steel and has serrated edges that can also be used to hull strawberries. See also CRIMPING; PIE & TART.

PASTRY WHEEL A tool used to cut out or trim rolled out pastry dough. Pastry wheels are circular straight or fluted blades attached to a handle that lets you roll them across the dough. They are useful for making strips or free-form shapes to top pies. Fluted pastry wheels are sometimes referred to as pastry jaggers for their jagged edges. Some manufacturers even produce double pastry wheels, with side-by-side blades that let you cut straight or fluted edges with a 180-degree turn of the handle.

PIE WEIGHTS Also known as pastry weights. These small aluminum or ceramic pellets are used to weight down pie dough when it is blind baked—that is, prebaked without a filling. A sheet of aluminum foil or parchment paper is fitted into the pastry-lined pan and then the weights are spread over the bottom to hold the pastry in place as it bakes. For more details, see BLIND BAKING.

Quick Tip

In a pinch, raw rice or dried beans work as pie weights. They should be discarded after a couple of bakings.

SCALE Choose a kitchen scale capable of weighing up to 10 pounds in no larger than $\frac{1}{4}$-ounce increments. The weighing bowl should be large enough to handle at least 2 cups of flour or an equivalent item. The best scales allow you to weigh ingredients in any bowl or container. Make sure that the scale weighs light items as accurately as it does heavy ones.

See also BREAD MACHINE; CROCKPOT; FOOD PROCESSOR; MIXER.

BAMBOO SHOOT A popular ingredient in the Asian pantry, bamboo shoots are ivory-colored, mild-flavored vegetables that provide refreshing, slightly crunchy texture. The shoots are harvested young and tender, when the bamboo plant, a grass related to edible grains such as wheat and oats, is green. Bamboo shoots are used in stir-fries and other typical Asian dishes.

Selecting Whole or sliced bamboo shoots canned in mild brine are more commonly available. Fresh ones are rarely encountered in markets outside Asia. Bamboo shoots also are found canned together with other vegetables such as water chestnuts and baby corn, usually labeled "stir-fry vegetables." Buy canned bamboo shoots in the ethnic-food aisle of the supermarket and in Asian markets.

Storing Once the can is opened, transfer the shoots to a plastic or glass container, cover with water, and refrigerate for up to 7 days. Changing the water once a day will keep them in good condition for up to another week.

Preparing Drain the canned shoots, slice them lengthwise if necessary, and use them in stir-fries or steamed dishes with beef, chicken, and/or vegetables.

BANANA Native to Asia, the banana is grown in most tropical regions of the world, with the largest and best crops coming from Latin America. The Cavendish is the familiar yellow variety found in most food stores, but other varieties are finding their way into markets with increasing frequency, particularly in areas where sizable Latin and Southeast Asian populations reside. These include lady's finger, apple, Canary, and Lakatan bananas. Most are small and plump, some are yellow, and others are rosy red. All taste, with varying degrees of sweetness, much like the Cavendish.

Cavendish banana.

Lady's finger bananas.

Bananas ripen well off the tree, so they are picked nearly mature but still green, making them less vulnerable to bruising. During ripening, they emit ethylene gas, which in turn prompts the other bananas in a bunch to ripen. Put green bananas in a

Quick Tip

If you notice your bananas are darkening quickly but you aren't ready to eat them, freeze them now to use later for banana bread.

loosely closed paper bag with other under-ripe fruits (tomatoes, avocados, peaches), and they will speed the ripening of their companions. As bananas mature, the flesh softens and sweetens, and the skin turns from light green to light yellow to bright yellow and finally to yellow speckled with

b

brown spots, at which point they are fully ripe, sweet, and tender.

Selecting For keeping around the house, buy bananas that are light green or light yellow with no, or very few, brown spots. Those with brown splotches are fully ripe and will quickly become overripe, unless you use them immediately. At this ripe stage, they don't travel well and may even bruise inside your shopping bag during the trip from market to home.

Quick Tip

Bananas can also be eaten as a frozen treat. Peel firm, ripe bananas and wrap them in plastic. They will keep for about 3 months. For an extra indulgence, dip the frozen bananas in melted chocolate.

Storing Bananas ripen nicely at normal room temperatures. If you choose less-ripe specimens, they will last for 5 to 7 days. If the fruit is ripe, refrigeration will not harm it, but the skin will turn black and the fruit may not last any longer than at room temperature. Peeled and wrapped in plastic, bananas freeze well for up to 3 months.

Preparing For slicing and mixing with other fruit, use firm, bright yellow bananas with only a few dark speckles. For banana bread and muffins, or for eating immediately out of hand, choose splotchier fruits, which will be softer and sweeter.

BAR See COOKIE.

BARBECUE SAUCE This tangy, thick sauce, an indispensable part of every pork or beef barbecue, varies from region to region—and from cook to cook. In many areas of the country, barbecue sauce is tomato based and slightly sweet and smoky. Other locales prefer a sharper-tasting vinegar- or mustard-based sauce. Trying

different barbecue sauces is half the fun of eating barbecue. Most barbecue and grilling books have recipes for a basic barbecue sauce, made with ketchup, vinegar, brown sugar, onions, chiles, and other seasonings, but this is only the beginning.

Storing After opening, barbecue sauce should be refrigerated. It generally will keep for several months.

Preparing Barbecue sauce is often brushed on meat and poultry during the last several minutes of cooking for added flavor. The sugar present in most sauces will burn if the sauce is applied before the last 15 minutes or so, which is why most barbecue sauces should not be used as marinades. The sauces may be heated and served alongside the meat.

BARBECUING Although many people use this term interchangeably with grilling, the two are not the same. Barbecuing is cooking meat outdoors in a closed chamber by indirect heat. A low temperature is maintained for a long time, using fragrant, smoky wood or high-grade charcoal. This slow method results in meat so tender that it literally falls off the bone. Pork is the most traditional meat for barbecue, although beef is often barbecued, too, particularly in Texas. Chicken, turkey, and lamb are not strangers to this outdoor method either.

Quick Bite

In the old South, barbecuing was done in pits, with the cooks tending the fire and the meat (commonly a whole hog) for hours. This often meant staying up all night, sipping drinks, spinning yarns, and turning the cooking process into a social event.

The sauce that is served with barbecue is determined by region. Barbecued pork in Tennessee and western North Carolina is paired with a tomato-based sauce. In eastern North Carolina, the pork is treated to a vinegar-and-red-pepper sauce, while in South Carolina, a mustard-seasoned sauce is typical. Traditional Texas beef brisket barbecue is served without sauce, and Kansas City beef barbecue is served with a sweet, thick tomato sauce.

Barbecued meat is cooked at temperatures maintained between 185° and 250°F. Most red meat is cooked until its internal temperature reaches 180° to 185°F, although some, such as brisket, needs to reach slightly higher temperatures. Chicken is cooked to an internal temperature of 170° to 180°F. Traditionally, the heat source is hardwood or high-grade charcoal, not electricity or gas. Before cooking, the meat is usually rubbed with a spice mixture, called a dry rub, or marinated.

Home cooks rarely barbecue meat in the traditional way. But those who do are known to turn the activity into a passionate hobby, which often includes building a cooker. Enthusiasts also experiment endlessly with different rubs, marinades, and barbecue sauces. Barbecue contests are held throughout the United States but primarily in the South and Midwest. They can be small, informal gatherings or large, high-stake events. Among the latter perhaps the best known are two annual contests, Tennessee's Memphis in May and the American Royal in Kansas City, Missouri.

See also GRILLING; MARINATING; RUB.

BARDING Laying thin sheets of pork fat, called *bardes* by the French, or bacon slices over meat or poultry is called "barding." They may be secured with kitchen string if necessary. This traditional technique keeps lean cuts of meat and the lean breast meat of poultry, notably game birds, from drying out during roasting. After cooking, the fat is removed and discarded.

Layering the fat.

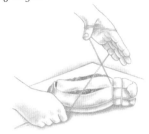

Securing with string.

BARLEY See GRAIN.

BASIL See HERB.

BASTING When a recipe calls for basting, it means to pour, spoon, or brush liquid over food, most often meat or poultry, to give it good flavor and color during roasting. Basting is not just for turkeys. Indeed, any large item, from a standing rib roast to a pork loin to a whole chicken, also benefits from it. While the food is roasting, pull out the oven rack and brush or spoon accumulated pan juices or another liquid over the meat. Some cooks use a bulb baster, also called a turkey baster, to pour liquid over the meat. A metal baster is a better choice than a plastic one, which might be warped or melted by the hot fat.

While basting is a time-honored technique for adding moisture to meat, it doesn't actually achieve this goal. Quite simply, meat cannot absorb moisture during cooking. In fact, meat always loses moisture when it cooks, and no amount of basting can moisten dried-out meat or poultry. Basting does help prevent the food from drying out too quickly, but the best way to prevent meat from drying out is to avoid overcooking it. Larger cuts generally have enough fat in their connective tissues and, in the case of turkeys, skin, to keep the food moist. Small, lean pieces of meat, such as chicken breasts and pork tenderloins, can benefit from barding to keep them juicy. For more detail, see BARDING.

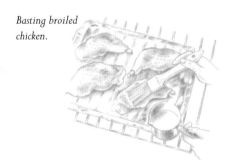

Basting broiled chicken.

Though it does not add moisture, basting does have its benefits. Basting liquids often are the accumulated pan juices, but they also can be melted butter, flavored or not, or various mixtures based on water, stock, wine, or beer. These all add flavor, and any that contain sugar or protein—in the form of butter, corn syrup, honey, preserves, stock or broth, wine, or beer—promote even browning. Too much sugar can cause scorching, however, so don't go overboard. Basting liquids also should include some fat, which is a flavor conductor.

BATTER Any smooth mixture that is thin enough to pour or spoon and that, when baked or fried, firms up to become a cake, bread, pancake, fritter, crisp coating, or similar item. Thinner batters are used to coat poultry, seafood, or vegetables, such as for batter-fried chicken or vegetable tempura. They rely

on properly heated deep oil to achieve the desired perfectly crisp, nongreasy results. So, too, do the slightly thicker batters that may be used to bind together diced or chopped ingredients cooked as fritters, from Indian *bhaji* to more familiar French- and American-style croquettes. Most batters consist of flour, eggs, and a liquid such as milk or beer. Many also contain sugar and butter. Batters differ from doughs primarily in consistency. The former are thinner and must be contained, while the latter are thick.

See also FRYING.

BAY LEAF See HERB.

BEAN CURD See SOY FOODS.

Bean, Dried

Beans, peas, and lentils (known collectively as legumes) are among the most healthful of foods. They are low in fat and high in protein, fiber, carbohydrates, vitamins, and minerals.

Beans are a practical, economical food with a long shelf life, keeping well for a year when stored airtight in a cool, dry cupboard. Some beans have been sown by farmers since the Stone Age and were a pantry staple in ancient Rome and Athens. Today, from Boston baked beans and split pea soup to hummus and black beans with rice, dried legumes star regularly at tables around the world.

Nevertheless, some people avoid cooking dried legumes because of the relatively lengthy preparation. Hard as small pebbles, dried beans require rehydrating to soften them. This is generally done by soaking them before cooking. Depending on your schedule, you can, however, select a long- or quick-soak method, or no soaking plus longer cooking. Lentils and certain other dried legumes, such as split peas, do not require soaking and cook quickly in comparison to beans.

Selecting Dried legumes are sold prewashed in plastic bags and in bulk in some supermarkets and in health-food stores. Choose clean-looking beans and lentils that show no signs of shriveling and buy them from stores with good turnover.

Storing Store dried legumes in a cool, dry cupboard in their packaging or in a tightly lidded canister or jar. They will keep for up to 1 year. The older the dried legumes, the longer they will take to cook and the more water they will absorb. Once dried beans are cooked, they must be refrigerated to prevent spoilage.

Cooked beans or lentils freeze beautifully. When cooled, put them in a tightly lidded freezer-safe container or spoon them into a zippered plastic freezer bag and freeze for up to 1 year.

Preparing Most dried beans are soaked before cooking. Lentils and peas do not require soaking. Before soaking beans or cooking legumes, regardless of method, rinse them in a colander under cold running water, scooping them between your fingers to make sure any debris washes away. Dried beans and legumes used to be packaged somewhat carelessly. Today, they are generally clean, although you should still check them. Some recipes instruct you to "sort" or "pick over" the beans before rinsing them, which simply means to discard any misshapen beans or foreign matter (small stones and the like).

Picking over beans.

There are three methods for preparing beans: the long-soak method, the quick-soak method, and the no-soak method.

continued

Bean, Dried, continued

HOW TO *Soak Beans*

Your choice of which of the three soaking methods explained below for dried beans will depend entirely on your schedule: how soon ahead of time you decide to prepare a bean dish; whether you have the beans in your pantry or have to go out and buy them; and how much time you have available to do the actual cooking of the beans.

LONG-SOAK METHOD

1. Put the beans in a large pot or bowl and add cold water to cover by 3 inches or more.

2. Soak at room temperature until visibly swelled and fully rehydrated, about 4 hours. Some recipes say to soak them overnight, but 4 hours is actually enough for any dried bean. If it suits your schedule, let the beans soak overnight or all day. Add additional water as necessary to keep them covered. Drain and proceed with the recipe.

QUICK-SOAK METHOD

1. Put the beans in a large pot and add cold water to cover by about 3 inches.
2. Bring the water to a rapid simmer over medium-high heat. Adjust the heat so the beans simmer vigorously for 2 minutes. Do not let the simmer turn into a full boil.
3. Remove the pot from the heat, cover, and let the beans cool in the liquid for at least 1 hour. Drain and proceed with the recipe.

NO-SOAK METHOD

Beans can be cooked without soaking. This is a satisfactory method, although soaking the beans will ensure even and thorough cooking. Omitting the step of soaking increases cooking times—but usually by no more than 30 to 40 minutes. To cook, drop the rinsed beans into boiling, lightly salted liquid and, when it returns to a boil, reduce the heat to very low, cover tightly, and cook until tender. Continue cooking as for soaked beans, adding more water as necessary to keep the beans covered. Test the beans for doneness every 10 to 15 minutes after the traditional cooking time is reached.

Quick Tip

Some cooks prefer cooking beans in a low (250°F) oven, rather than tending the pot simmering on top of the stove. Put the beans and cooking liquid in a covered casserole or Dutch oven and cook them for the same time as directed for stovetop cooking.

HOW TO *Cook Soaked Beans*

1. Put soaked and drained dried beans, or dried lentils or other legumes, in a pot and add cold water or stock to cover by several inches. Some recipes may say to add an onion, some garlic, herbs, or other flavorings at this point as well. Avoid acidic ingredients, such as tomatoes, which will toughen the beans and prevent them from softening.
2. Cooking beans with a bit of salt is not only acceptable, but preferable. Add about 1 teaspoon of salt to the cooking water for every 2 cups (about 1 pound) of dried beans. The old belief that salting will keep the beans from softening during cooking is based on the fact that an excessive amount of salt will interfere with their softening. A reasonable amount of salt will add good flavor and require only a slight adjustment at the end of cooking.
3. Bring to a boil over high heat, skim off the foam that rises to the top, and reduce the heat to low. Partially cover the pot and simmer the beans or lentils very gently. Slow cooking is essential; boiling the beans will cause their skins to split.

b

Cooking Times for Soaked Dried Beans

LEGUME	COOKING TIME*
Adzuki beans	30 to 40 minutes
Appaloosa beans	1 to 1½ hours
Black beans	30 to 60 minutes
Black-eyed peas (no soaking required)	35 to 45 minutes
Cannellini	1 to 1½ hours
Chickpeas	1½ to 2 hours
Cranberry beans	1 to 1½ hours
Fava beans	2½ to 3 hours
Flageolets	1 hour
Great Northern beans	1 to 1½ hours
Kidney beans	1 to 1½ hours
Lentils, green or brown or Puy (no soaking required)	30 to 45 minutes
Lentils, red or yellow (no soaking required)	8 to 10 minutes
Lima beans	1 to 1½ hours
Mung beans	45 to 60 minutes
Navy beans	1½ to 2 hours
Pink beans	1 hour
Pinto beans	1 to 1½ hours
Soybeans	2½ to 3 hours
Split peas (no soaking required)	35 to 60 minutes

Cooking times in this chart are based on 1 cup dried beans or lentils, measured before soaking, which yields about 2½ to 3 cups when cooked. (If you are using the no-soak method, remember to increase these cooking times by 30 to 40 minutes.)

4. Check the liquid level every 30 or 40 minutes, adding more as necessary to keep the beans fully covered at all times. This helps them cook more evenly.

5. Test for doneness by mashing a cooled bean against the roof of your mouth with your tongue or pressing it between your thumb and forefinger. The bean should be soft but not mushy, retaining some shape. Cook the beans longer if you prefer them softer.

Quick Tip

Partially covering the bean-cooking pot helps the beans cook evenly and keeps the liquid from evaporating too quickly before the beans are done. It's always a good idea to check the water level of the beans occasionally.

continued

Bean, Dried, continued

Dried Legume Varieties Many of the following dried legumes may be substituted for one another in recipes. As a rule of thumb, feel free to use any other legume of similar size, color, or shape, letting common sense and your own tastes be your guides. Some of the most versatile and interchangeable of beans are those of the haricot family, which includes the various types of white, kidney, and pinto beans.

ADZUKI BEAN Small, reddish brown, sweet-tasting bean popular in Japanese and Chinese cooking. Also used to make the sweet bean paste used in some Asian desserts.

APPALOOSA BEAN A light beige bean with black to brown spots. Related to kidney beans and used similarly.

BLACK BEAN Also called turtle, Mexican, or Spanish black bean. Small and shiny black. Used widely in Latin American cooking for pot beans, soups, and dips.

BLACK-EYED PEA Also called cowpea or black-eyed bean. Cream colored and kidney shaped, with a characteristic black dot with a yellow center and a mild flavor. Native to India and Iran and widely consumed in Africa, these legumes require less soaking than most dried beans and are the centerpiece of hoppin' John, a classic Southern rice dish.

BORLOTTI BEAN See Cranberry Bean, below.

BROAD BEAN See Fava Bean, below.

BUTTER BEAN See Lima Bean, below.

CANNELLINI These ivory-colored beans go into traditional Italian minestrone soup. Great Northern beans may be substituted.

CECI BEAN See Chickpea, below.

CHICKPEA Also known as garbanzo bean or ceci bean. Rich, nutty-flavored, large beige bean with a firm texture. These are the main ingredient in hummus, the famed Middle Eastern spread.

COWPEA See Black-Eyed Pea, above.

CRANBERRY BEAN Also called Roman bean or borlotti bean. Mild-flavored, mottled reddish bean that loses its color during soaking and cooking. They can be substituted for dried lima beans and for kidney beans.

FAVA BEAN Also called broad bean, English bean, or horse bean. Large, light brown bean with a slightly bitter flavor and grainy texture. See also BEAN, FRESH.

FLAGEOLET Small, flavorful, pale green or white beans traditionally served with lamb dishes in French cooking.

GARBANZO BEAN See Chickpea, above.

GREAT NORTHERN BEAN Also called white bean. Small, oval-shaped white beans. Can be used in place of other small white beans such as navy and white kidney. They share these beans' mild flavor and creamy texture. Often used in Boston baked beans.

KIDNEY BEAN Large, dark red, pinkish, or white kidney-shaped beans. Sturdy and versatile. Color determines their most common usage, although they are interchangeable if color is not a concern. Red kidney beans are used in many Southwestern dishes. Pink kidney beans are called red beans in Louisiana and go into red beans and rice. White kidney beans, sometimes mistaken for cannellini, are used in Italian dishes and can be substituted for navy or Great Northern beans. Red kidney beans can be substituted for cranberry beans.

LENTIL Small and flat, lentils may be green, brown, yellow, red, pink, or mottled. Mild flavored and quick to cook, they are extremely versatile. Ocher-colored lentils are widely used in Indian cooking, where they are called dal. Puy lentils are small, dark green French lentils with a pleasantly mild flavor. They make good salads and soups and blend well with meats.

LIMA BEAN Also called butter bean. Large, flat, white to pale green, sweet-tasting bean. Lima beans are also sold frozen and are sometimes available fresh. Can be substituted for kidney and cranberry beans.

MUNG BEAN Also called mung pea. Small, round, gray-green bean used primarily in Asian cooking. When mung beans are split, they are called yellow mung beans or *moong dal.*

NAVY BEAN Small white bean with a mild flavor. Versatile and sturdy, navy beans can be used in place of white kidney or Great Northern beans.

PINK BEAN A smooth, kidney-shaped, pale red bean that turns reddish brown when cooked. The sweet-tasting, meaty bean is similar to kidney and pinto beans but longer in shape.

PINTO BEAN A pale brown bean with darker, sometimes pinkish streaks, which disappear during cooking. Used extensively in Southwestern cooking, where their full, earthy flavor is appreciated. These may be substituted for kidney beans or pink beans.

RED BEAN See Kidney Bean, above.

ROMAN BEAN See Cranberry Bean, above.

SOYBEAN Ivory, green, brown, or black rounded beans with mild flavor and a firm texture. These require long cooking. Although dried soybeans are available, most people instead consume soy in other forms: tofu, tempeh, miso, soy milk, soy sauce, and other soy products. Soy is considered extremely healthful. See also SOY FOODS.

SPLIT PEA Small, pale green or yellow dried legumes. Split peas cook quickly and are used as side dishes or, in their best-known role, as the basis for split-pea soup.

WHITE BEAN Rather than being a specific bean, this is a group of beans that includes Great Northern beans, navy beans, kidney beans, and cannellini. See also Great Northern Bean, above.

b

Quick Tip

Look in specialty-food stores and mail-order catalogs for the many different varieties of long-lost heirloom beans currently being recultivated by enterprising growers. Seek out such beautiful, flavorful, and evocatively named types as the Black Valentine, Pebble, Eye of Goat, Swedish Brown, Gigante, Tongue of Fire, Bisbee Red, Wren's Egg, and Zuni Shalako.

A Word on the Unmentionable

If beans, which are high in fiber, are not cooked thoroughly, they are hard to digest. And even when cooked properly, beans cause gas in many people because of the complex sugars that, paired with the fiber, also contribute to flatulence. Eating beans regularly is a good way to acquaint your system with them and reduce the problem significantly. Vinegar and commercial anti-gas products such as Beano, which can be sprinkled on the beans just before eating, help—but they are not magic remedies.

Bean, Fresh

Long a garden staple, fresh beans fall into two categories: pod beans and shell beans. Pod beans, such as green beans, are consumed whole, outer pod and inner seeds. Only the inner seeds of shell beans can be eaten, and the pod is discarded.

Some of the more popular varieties of fresh shell beans are lima beans and fava beans.

Fresh beans are harvested when young and tender—in most cases, the younger, the better. When shell beans are grown to full maturity, their fully developed inner seeds can be dried to become dried legumes (see BEAN, DRIED). While some shell beans, most notably fava beans and cranberry beans, are available in their fresh state early in the harvest season, most shell beans are sold dried.

Selecting Fresh beans should be firm with good bright color.

Green, wax, and lima beans are sold frozen and canned. If you cannot find them fresh and have a choice, choose frozen beans over canned, which tend to have a tinny taste and soft, mushy texture. All the fresh shell beans described here are available dried and canned.

Quick Bite

With the exception of haricots verts, romanos, and Chinese long beans, pod beans are rarely labeled anything other than "green beans."

Storing Put fresh beans into a perforated plastic bag and refrigerate for up to 5 days. They are best, however, when eaten within 2 days of purchase, as their "snap" diminishes with time. Once shelled, fresh shell beans should be used within 2 days.

Preparing Trim off brown-tipped ends and remove any strings along the length of pod beans. Split open shell beans along their seams to remove the beans, easing them out with your thumb as necessary.

Shelling beans.

Fresh beans can be boiled, steamed, or added to soups and stews. Pod beans are often sautéed or stir-fried. Whatever recipe you choose, the important thing is not to overcook beans.

Fresh Bean Varieties

BORLOTTI BEAN See Cranberry Bean, below.

BROAD BEAN See Fava Bean, below.

BUTTER BEAN See Lima Bean, below.

CHINESE LONG BEAN Also called yard-long bean. Very long, rounded green pod bean used in Asian cooking and sold primarily in Asian markets, generally displayed bundled into loose skeins.

CRANBERRY BEAN Although usually eaten dried, the cranberry bean, a favorite of Italian American cooks, is available as a shell bean in some markets. The pod and inner seed should be the color of cream with a good representation of red speckles.

FAVA BEAN Also called broad bean, English bean, or horse bean. This shell bean is available fresh briefly in the spring in farmers' markets. Look for soft, pale green pods packed with pale green beans that resemble lima beans. They have a pleasingly bitter flavor.

Once removed from the pods, the beans should be peeled of their tough outer skin, which is slightly toxic, more so late in the season. To remove it, blanch the shelled beans for 1 minute in boiling water, let cool, then pinch the beans to remove the skin.

Skinning fava beans.

If the beans are young and fresh and no bigger than your thumbnail, skinning them may not be necessary, although some cooks find that even the skins of young beans impart too much bitterness. Fava beans are also sold dried.

FLAGEOLET Small, flavorful, pale green or white shell bean used in traditional French cooking. Flageolets are also sold canned and dried. The fresh beans can be difficult to find in the United States.

GREEN BEAN Also called snap bean, string bean, or runner bean. Green beans are eaten whole, pod and seeds, and taste mild and fresh with grassy overtones. The most familiar green bean is several inches long with a rounded pod. Buy evenly green ones that look as though they will snap decisively when broken. To prepare green beans, simply snap off the stem end and remove any strings along the length of the bean.

HARICOT VERT Also called French green bean or filet bean. Small, slender, dark green, young pod beans favored in France. Delicately flavored, they are more elegant, and commensurately expensive, than other green beans.

LIMA BEAN Also called a butter bean, the lima grows in wide, flat green inedible pods. Small beans are called baby limas. Look for green, velvety pods. The inner seed, the sweet-tasting edible portion, should be as green as possible. Avoid any with a white cast. Fresh lima beans may be difficult to find in some regional markets, while dried, canned, and especially frozen ones are commonly available.

ROMAN BEAN See Cranberry Bean, above.

ROMANO BEAN Also called Italian bean. A green pod bean, similar to green beans, but with slightly broader and more flattened pods and a somewhat more robust flavor and texture.

SNAP BEAN See Green Bean, above.

STRING BEAN See Green Bean, above.

WAX BEAN This is a green bean that is yellow rather than green. It has the same other characteristics as the green bean.

b

BEAN SPROUT See SPROUT.

BEATING Mixing vigorously until a single ingredient such as eggs or a mixture such as cake batter is smooth, well blended, and aerated. This is often accomplished with an electric mixer, although you can beat batters by hand with a spoon, whisk, manual egg beater, or fork. Eggs for scrambled eggs or French toast are commonly beaten by hand.

See also BATTER; DOUGH; EGG; FOLDING; MIXER; MIXING; WHIPPING; WHISKING.

BÉCHAMEL See SAUCE.

BEEF From the basic cheeseburger to the elegant standing rib roast, beef means eating well. Nothing satisfies a meat lover like a buttery beef tenderloin or a hearty beef stew, a sandwich piled high with corned beef or a juicy hamburger hot off the grill.
Beef Labeling Beef is graded by the United States Department of Agriculture (USDA) according to tenderness, flavor, and juiciness. All of these relate to the amount of white marbling, or intramuscular fat, the beef has. The best beef, with the most marbling and finest flavor, is graded "prime." Rarely is prime beef available anywhere but at premium butcher shops and steak houses. Most beef sold to consumers is "choice" or "select." It is generally leaner, although the leanness also depends on where on the animal the cut originated. Cuts from more active muscles, such as chuck and round, are naturally tougher and leaner than lightly used muscle sections, such as the rib and short loin. Though federal law mandates that all meat must be inspected, grading is voluntary. It is possible to find ungraded meat, but for assurance of quality, one should buy only prime, choice, or select grade beef.

In addition to the USDA grades, there is an increasing number of private labels or brands. For example, beef labeled "Certified Black Angus" is from the cattle of the same name, which is prized for its high-grade, top-quality beef. Although certified Angus beef may cost more than the meat of other breeds available at the market, it is preferred by many home cooks and restaurant chefs for its consistent quality.

Find a reliable butcher selling good meat at an independent shop or a supermarket, then develop a relationship with him or her. You will get good beef if you become a loyal and interested customer.

In recent years, with growing concerns for eating healthfully and light, beef was often dismissed as too high in saturated fat and cholesterol. Today, beef is bred to be more than 25 percent leaner than it was several decades ago, with less marbling and less outer fat in all grades. It is also generally sold in smaller cuts than it once was, with fewer roasts and more steaks, strips, and cubes, all of which are appropriate for lighter cooking methods such as grilling, broiling, and stir-frying. With these changes, cooks are starting to rediscover beef's healthful qualities, including its abundance of protein, iron, phosphorous, zinc, and B vitamins.
Selecting Look for bright red beef with light marbling (internal fat), fine texture, and nearly white outer fat but not much of it. The more marbling, the more tender and juicy the beef, and the best kind of marbling consists of many small deposits of intramuscular fat, rather than a few large globs. Vacuum-packed meat will appear purplish, but its color should brighten upon exposure to air. Be sure to press the meat (even through plastic) to make sure it feels firm. For ground beef, if you have a good butcher, ask him or her to grind it fresh for you. Otherwise, buy it already ground

✹ Beef Glossary ✹

Beef cuts.

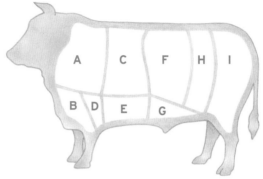

Cuts of meat are not labeled consistently from one region of the country to another—or even from one butcher shop to another. The following terms are based on the more universal primal cuts, large sections of beef that are then cut by the butcher into individual steaks and roasts. Understanding the nature of the primal cuts will help you decide what to buy for dinner and how to cook it. Never hesitate to ring the bell for the butcher at the supermarket and ask questions about a particular cut.

CHUCK (A) The muscular shoulder section, source of chuck steak, chuck roasts, and stewing beef, all tougher cuts best cooked by moist methods such as braising or stewing. Chuck roast makes the best pot roast. Ground chuck, a common type of ground beef, has a high proportion of fat, a robust flavor, and makes juicy hamburgers.

Chuck roast.

FORESHANK (B) Sold cubed or cut into bone-in slices, best suited for stewing, braising, or making stocks.

RIB (C) The meat nestled between the rib bones is flavorful, juicy, and tender. Rib cuts include flavorful rib-eye steaks for broiling or panfrying, short ribs for braising, and tender rib roasts and rib-eye roasts for oven roasting. A standing rib roast is a truly grand cut of beef, reserved for special occasions.

Standing rib roast.

BRISKET (D) Cut into flat or pointed half briskets, which are often cured and simmered as corned beef. Briskets may also be braised.

Brisket.

continued

b

Beef Glossary, continued

b
_

Quick Bite

When briskets are cured, they become corned beef. The "corn" in "corned beef" refers to corns, or grains, of salt used in the curing process.

PLATE (E) Source of short ribs and stew beef for braising and stewing, as well as ground beef. The inner muscle is sometimes sold as skirt steak, the traditional cut for fajitas. Good for braising, broiling, and grilling.

Short ribs.

Skirt steak.

SHORT LOIN (F) Source of the finest steaks, T-bone, porterhouse, club, top loin, tenderloin (also known as filet mignon), fillet, and strip. Tenderloin cuts, from the bottom of the section, are considered the finest cuts of beef. Tenderloin roasts are wonderful for roasting or broiling.

T-bone steak.

Fillet steaks.

FLANK (G) Source of lean flank steak, for braising, grilling, and stir-frying, and ground beef.

Flank steak.

SIRLOIN (H) Source of sirloin steaks for broiling or roasting, as well as ground beef. Ground sirloin falls between ground chuck and ground round in terms of fat content and has a rich beef flavor.

Sirloin steak.

ROUND (I) Source of round (or rump) roasts for braising, broiling, or grilling, as well as ground beef. Ground round is extremely lean but a little tough. Top round is the most tender part of this beef section.

Boneless rump roast.

from a reliable vendor. Look for even red color and nice white fat throughout the meat. Avoid dark, brownish meat and grayish fat. Also pass up any beef that looks excessively moist or that has two-tone coloration.

Storing Leave meat in its wrapper and store it in the coldest part of the refrigerator, which is usually at the back of the bottom shelf, or in a meat drawer. (A refrigerator thermometer will tell you for sure.) If any juices are seeping from the store packaging, wrap the package in a layer of plastic wrap. Do not unwrap meat until just before cooking because unnecessary exposure to air adds to deterioration. Beef can be held for about 4 days in the refrigerator; in a cold meat drawer (with temperatures hovering around 30°F), it will keep for up to 5 days. Ground beef will keep for 2 days but is best if cooked on the day it is purchased. It also freezes well.

To freeze steaks, chops, and roasts, trim any excess fat, wrap the meat in freezer-weight plastic or put it into a zippered plastic freezer bag, and freeze for up to 10 months. Ground beef freezes best if divided into small amounts—patties, meatballs, or small meat loaves. Discard any beef that develops an "off" smell.

Preparing Beef cooks more evenly and stays juicier if it is allowed to come to room temperature first, but the time it takes to come to room temperature varies depending on the cut. Leave it on the counter for up to 2 hours, if possible, before cooking. This may not help a large roast, which will likely still be cold in the center after only 2 hours, but it will take the chill off a tenderloin. To be safe, however, don't leave any cuts of beef out for more than 2 hours, and don't leave ground beef out for more than 30 minutes.

Before cooking, trim excess fat from the outside of beef cuts, leaving a thin coating

to protect the meat while it cooks. Cutting away all the fat contributes to dried-out meat. Meat that is not marinated should be trimmed just before cooking; meat that will be marinated should be trimmed before marinating.

Beef can be broiled, roasted, grilled, panfried, stewed, braised, and made into baked dishes and soups. As a general rule, the more tender cuts of beef—T-bone, sirloin, porterhouse, and strip steaks—benefit from quick, dry-heat methods of cooking, such as broiling, roasting, and grilling. The tougher, leaner cuts, including chuck, rump roast, and brisket, benefit from moist cooking, such as stewing, braising, and pot roasting. See the Beef Glossary at left for more details.

Beef that is roasted, grilled, or broiled (that is, cooked by a dry method) should be allowed to stand and "rest" for 5 to 25 minutes (depending on the size of the cut) before being carved. This gives the meat's juices, which rise to the surface during cooking, an opportunity to settle and redistribute themselves throughout the roast. The meat also firms up during the process and thus becomes easier to carve.

Doneness Temperatures for Beef

Rare	120° to 130°F*
Medium-rare	130° to 140°F*
Medium	140° to 150°F*
Medium-well	150° to 160°F
Well-done	160° to 165°F

Although these internal temperatures yield what many cooks feel are the optimum taste and texture, some are lower than those suggested by the U.S. Food Safety and Inspection Service guidelines; see Beef Safety, page 48, and DONENESS.

The best way to determine when beef is properly cooked is to gauge its internal temperature with an instant-read thermometer. When inserting the thermometer, make sure it does not touch bone, which can produce an inaccurate reading. Take the beef from the oven when the temperature reaches the lowest temperature in the range. The beef continues to cook from residual heat while standing.

Beef Safety In recent years there has been a good deal of media attention given to the need to cook meat properly in order to kill any potentially harmful bacteria. To make sense of these warnings, it is essential to understand the differences between whole cuts of beef, such as steaks and roasts, and ground beef. It is possible for the outside surface of beef cuts to become contaminated with bacteria during processing. These surface bacteria are rendered harmless by cooking, even if the interior is left rare or medium-rare. A problem arises, however, with ground beef, since during the grinding process any contamination on the surface can be mixed throughout the meat.

Ground beef should be cooked thoroughly, to 160°F in the center, to be perfectly safe. Steaks, roasts, and other whole cuts may safely be eaten rare if the surface of the beef has been cooked to 160°F, for example, if the surface is well seared, which would kill any bacteria.

Hands, utensils, and work surfaces that come into contact with raw beef must be washed in hot, soapy water to prevent bacteria spreading throughout the kitchen or to other foods.

See also CARVING; FOOD SAFETY; STOCK; individual cooking methods.

BEET Grandma might be surprised by the fuss being made over this hardy root vegetable. Beets were unglamorous kitchen staples for generations, but now they are showing up on every fashionable menu.

Also called beetroots, many boast a deep, rich red color combined with a sweet, earthy flavor and tender texture, making them a great favorite with chefs and home cooks alike.

Although beets will always be associated with their lovely deep red color, today it is not unusual to find pink, golden, white, and even striped beets in the market. These festive-looking vegetables have more or less the same flavor and texture as their red cousins, but provide unexpected color to dishes where the red beet is more commonly found.

Beets are served warm as a side dish, cold in salads, pickled, or made into the famous beet soup, borscht. Young, fresh-looking, bright green beet greens from small or medium-sized beets are delicious. Sauté or steam them as you would spinach.

Quick Tip

When working with red and pink beets, be prepared for beet-red stains on your hands and countertops. The color is difficult to remove from wood or plastic surfaces; you may want to work on waxed paper and wear gloves.

Selecting Beets are available all year, but are at their best in late summer and autumn. While most beets are about the size of small lemons, much smaller beets, about the size of large marbles, are in the markets now. Regardless of the size, look for firm, rounded vegetables with smooth skins and no noticeable bruising. Fresh beets, sold in bunches, should have the greens attached and 1 to 2 inches of root end, which looks like a tail. Do not buy beets with wilted, browning leaves—the leafy greens indicate the freshness of the beets. If the greens have been trimmed, look for bunches with at least 2 inches of stem still attached.

Storing Cut the greens from the root vegetable as soon as you get home, leaving 1 to 2 inches of stem attached. The beets will not spoil if left at cool room temperature for a few days, but they do best when refrigerated for up to 10 days. If they turn soft, discard them. Beet greens should be washed and cooked on the day they are bought. They do not keep well; if necessary, however, they may be put unwashed into a perforated plastic bag and refrigerated overnight. Canned and pickled beets should be refrigerated after opening. Canned beets will keep for 1 week after opening; pickled beets will keep for at least twice this period of time. Fully cooked and cooled whole beets can be frozen in zippered plastic freezer bags or rigid containers for up to 10 months.

Preparing Beets are best when cooked whole and unpeeled, then peeled and sliced, chopped, or mashed afterward. Roasting beets will help intensify their flavor and color, and you should wrap them in aluminum foil first, so you won't have to clean a pan. If boiling, leave about 1 inch of the stem and the root end intact to keep the beets from "bleeding" into the cooking water. Once they are fork-tender, let them cool and then slip off their skins.

For more information, see BOILING; ROASTING; STEAMING.

BELGIAN ENDIVE See CHICORY.

BELL PEPPER Also called sweet pepper. Bell peppers may be green, red, yellow, orange, brown, or purple. Some are blunt ended, while others are tapered, but the shape does not make any difference in the flavor.

Bell peppers are available all year long. Green bell peppers are usually sharper flavored, more plentiful, and less expensive than peppers of other colors. They are immature and do not ripen once picked. Red bell peppers are simply a more mature (and sweeter) stage 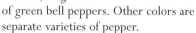 of green bell peppers. Other colors are separate varieties of pepper.

Use bell peppers raw in salads and for crudités. They often appear in sauces, stews, soups, relishes, and baked dishes. Large bells are excellent for stuffing and roasting, and any size pepper can be grilled. Bell peppers, particularly red ones, are delicious roasted and peeled, at which point they can be refrigerated in plastic bags or rigid containers—as is or covered with olive oil—for 3 to 4 days.

Selecting Buy firm, smooth, bright-colored peppers.

Storing Refrigerate the peppers as soon as you get them home, storing them loosely in a perforated plastic bag. Green peppers keep for at least 1 week, while red, yellow, orange, and purple peppers are best used within 5 or 6 days.

Preparing Cut the pepper in half at the equator or lengthwise. Remove a pepper's stem with your hands or a knife. Trim away the seeds and white membranes, or ribs, and cut to desired size and shape.

Stemming.

HOW TO *Roast and Peel Bell Peppers*

1. Using tongs or a large fork, hold the pepper over the flame of a gas burner, turning as needed, until the skin is blistered and charred black on all sides, 10 to 15 minutes. This may also be done in a broiler; watch the peppers carefully to prevent burning their flesh.

2. Once the skin is blackened and puffy, transfer the peppers to a paper bag and close loosely. This allows the peppers to steam as they cool and helps the skins to loosen.

3. When cool, peel or rub away the charred skin. Do not worry if a little stays on the flesh. Don't rinse the peppers under running water, or you will wash away some flavor.

4. Lay the peppers on a cutting board. Using a small, sharp knife, slit each pepper lengthwise. Some liquid will run out, so have paper towels handy. Open the pepper and spread it on the cutting board. Cut around the stem end, then remove the stem, seeds, and membrane.

Quick Tip

When roasted whole, bell peppers accumulate sweet juices inside their cavities. If you like, peel and seed them over a bowl to catch those juices, then strain the juices to eliminate any seeds or bits of charred skin. If the roasted peppers will be used in a salad, add the juices to the dressing; or reserve them for adding extra flavor to a marinade or sauce.

HOW TO *Prepare Peppers for Stuffing*

Most recipes for stuffed bell peppers require parboiling the peppers first. Even if not specified, parboiling will make the peppers more tender.

1. Cut a slice ½ inch thick from the stem end of each pepper, leaving an opening like the top of a bowl. Remove the seeds and membrane.
2. Bring a large pot three-fourths full of water to a boil. Place a bowl of cold water nearby. Drop the peppers into the boiling water and cook until slightly softened, about 5 minutes.
3. Using tongs, transfer the peppers to the cold water to halt the cooking, then drain, cut side down, on paper towels.
4. When cool, stuff the peppers and cook according to individual recipes.

BERRY Berries are small, succulent fruits that grow on bushes, vines, or canes. They are available year-round, although they are more flavorful, plentiful, and affordable in the spring and summer months (except for

cranberries, which are in season in the autumn, and raspberries, which have a second harvest in fall).

Owing to their delicacy, many varieties must be hand-harvested, which contributes to their expense. Berries can be served raw or cooked into sauces, pies, relishes, and other sweet and savory preparations. They also make wonderful ice creams, sorbets, and preserves.

BLACKBERRY The blackberry is sweetest when completely black. When immature, blackberries are green or red. Blackberries are in season from late spring to early autumn and are best in high summer. Among the most fragile berries, blackberries should not be refrigerated for more than a day. Olallieberries are a kind of blackberry, and boysenberries and loganberries are blackberry hybrids. They may be freely substituted for one another or combined in recipes.

BLUEBERRY Blueberries are in season from late spring to late summer. They are dark blue and should have a powdery white bloom. When the bloom is gone, the berries are too old. Blueberries can be refrigerated for up to 1 week. Wild blueberries from Maine are legendary and, while they do not travel well, are increasingly available frozen. These wild berries (which are now domesticated as well) are smaller and darker than ordinary blueberries and usually very sweet.

BOYSENBERRY This blackberry hybrid is a little larger and more purple to red hued than other cultivated blackberries. Boysenberries are preferred by some because of their sweet-tart flavor, juiciness, and large size.

CRANBERRY Native to North America, the cranberry is an integral part of American cooking, from the cranberry relish served with the Thanksgiving turkey to the healthful glass of bottled cranberry juice. The berries are harvested throughout the fall, with most of the crop finding its way to commercial food processors for sauce and juice. Cranberries are too tart to eat raw on their own but lend themselves to savory and sweet preparations, marrying nicely with other fruits, such as apples and pears, and with nuts and grains. Fresh cranberries should be plump, firm, and dry and range from deep scarlet to light red. Both fresh and

b

frozen whole cranberries are usually packaged in plastic bags rather than sold loose. Refrigerate the berries for up to 1 month, or freeze them for up to 10 months.

CURRANT The red currant is grown in the United States, while both red and black currants are available in northern Europe, where they enjoy great popularity. Since they are both high in pectin, a natural jelling agent, most currants find their way into jams, preserves, jellies, and syrups. Although perfectly ripe currants are pleasing to anyone who likes slightly tart fruit, they are usually sweetened before they are eaten. Fresh currants are in season from early July through early August but are difficult to find in markets. If you locate them, buy small, firm berries and refrigerate them for no longer than 2 days. So-called dried currants are actually dried grapes, or raisins.

GOOSEBERRY This small berry, resembling a white-striped grape, is pale green and quite tart when underripe and gold, red, pink, white, or dark burgundy when ripe. Ripe gooseberries can be eaten straight from the plant, although they are sometimes very tart. Underripe berries are cooked and sweetened for making preserves, sauces, and pies. The berries are not readily available in markets in the United States but are popular in Europe. If you find them for sale, choose large, firm berries and refrigerate them for up to 3 days.

HUCKLEBERRY Close relatives of the blueberry, huckleberries, also called whortleberries, tend to be seedier and a little tarter and are not cultivated. One variety grows on the East Coast and another on the West Coast, with the latter being a true berry and the former a drupe, or a fruit with a center seed.

LOGANBERRY A blackberry hybrid developed in California and named after a Santa Cruz judge, James Logan. Loganberries are large and cone shaped, more purple than black, and decidedly juicy.

MARIONBERRY Another blackberry hybrid, often sold simply as "blackberries." Marionberries are sweet and firm enough to hold up in baking and in desserts.

MULBERRY These fragile berries with a sweet-sour flavor are rarely sold commercially. When ripe, they fall from the bush or tree and are gathered off the ground—mostly in home gardens. They look much like blackberries but come in white and red as well as black.

OLALLIEBERRY A large, fragrant blackberry hybrid that grows in California and is sweet and juicy. Because they are fragile and do not travel well, olallieberries are not usually available outside their region. They are most commonly found at farmers' markets, or at pick-your-own farms.

RASPBERRY For many people, this is the ultimate berry. Fragrant and subtly sweet-tart, raspberries, which grow on low, thorn-laden shrubs and have been cultivated for hundreds of years, can be red, black, or golden. All taste similar and all are extremely delicate, with hollow centers. Eat them as soon after purchase as possible. Raspberry season extends from June through October.

STRAWBERRY Bright red berries bursting with sweet flavor and blessed with a heady fragrance, strawberries are available all year, although they are best in the spring and early summer. Some large berries can taste good, but most giant supermarket berries do not. Shop for strawberries at farmers' markets, looking for smaller berries, preferably organic, with a rich, glossy red color and shiny green leaves. Avoid berries with white or green shoulders and brown or limp leaves. Tiny strawberries called wild or wood strawberries or *fraises des bois* are especially sweet. Hull strawberries before freezing them or using them for most preparations. To do so, use a small paring knife or a strawberry huller to carve out the white center core from the stem end of each berry.

Quick Tip

To bring out the flavor of lackluster berries, put them in a bowl (hull and slice strawberries first) and sprinkle with a little sugar, a tablespoon or two for every pint. Let them sit at room temperature for at least 15 minutes. The sugar draws moisture from the berries to make a sweet natural syrup.

Selecting Berries should be selected with care. Never buy them if they are moist, overly soft, pale colored, or show signs of mold. Do not buy berries if their cartons are leaking and wet, a sure sign that unseen fruits will be moldy. In fact, a quick check of the underside of the carton may very well let you see any mold that is growing on bruised fruit at the bottom; put

that carton back. As a rule, berries are best in their natural season. Seek them out at large food stores, farmers' markets, and pick-your-own farms.

Frozen berries are often good. They are sold coated in sweet syrup or unsweetened. For recipes that call for fresh berries and require sugar to be added, use unsweetened frozen berries. If you plan to spoon the berries over ice cream, pound cake, or yogurt, sweetened berries are a fine choice, forming their own syrup as they thaw.

Storing Berries are fragile and should be handled with care. All require refrigeration, and they freeze well. Don't wash berries until just before you plan to eat them, as the moisture will encourage mold. If you don't plan to eat the berries within 1 to 2 days, rinse and dry them completely and then freeze them. Frozen berries will keep for 8 to 10 months.

HOW TO *Freeze Berries*

1. Put cranberries in the freezer in their original plastic bag packaging. Pack blueberries in rigid plastic containers and freeze. Spread more delicate raspberries, blackberries, and hulled strawberries in a single layer on a baking sheet and then freeze them. When firm, transfer to rigid plastic containers or zippered plastic freezer bags.

2. There is no need to thaw frozen berries for many recipes, including most sauces or ice creams. If a recipe calls for thawed berries, let them sit at room temperature for an hour or so. If necessary, transfer them to a colander to drain. You may capture the juice and use it for flavoring drinks or for other recipes.

Preparing While all fresh berries should be rinsed, they should not be soaked for any length of time, since they will absorb the water and turn mushy. For eating on their own, all berries—even the largest strawberries—should be left whole.

b

BEURRE BLANC See SAUCE.

BISCUIT Small, raised quick breads, bis-cuits are usually unsweetened and served piping hot. They are most readily associated with Southern cooking and generally are made from white flour, butter, a leavener, and milk or buttermilk. The most desirable qualities of a biscuit are tenderness, flaki-ness, and rich yet delicate flavor.

Add sugar to biscuit dough and it be-comes shortcake, which can be split and topped with sweetened strawberries, peaches, or another fruit and sweetened whipped cream. Sweet biscuit dough is also used as a topping for fruit cobbler.

Biscuit cutters.

Like all quick bread batters, biscuit bat-ter should be baked soon after mixing. As they bake, biscuits rise straight up, rather than spreading as many cookies do, and their tops turn golden brown. Once baked, they should be served hot from the oven, split and spread with butter, which will begin to melt immediately. They are also delicious with preserves or filled with ham or turkey. Biscuits spread with honey and served with fried chicken are old-fashioned comfort food.

Biscuit Savvy

- When cutting the butter or other fat into the flour, work quickly so it does not melt too much before you put the dough in the oven. If the butter or fat becomes soft, it prevents the flakiness that characterizes good biscuits.

- Biscuit dough can be mixed in a food processor. Take care not to overmix, using only on-off pulses. The fat should remain in discrete, flour-covered chunks the size of small peas.

- When pouring the liquid (usually milk or buttermilk) into the flour-fat mix-ture, do it all at once. If it's added in small amounts and stirred after each addition, the dough will be overworked and the biscuits will not be flaky.

- Do not overknead biscuit dough, or the biscuits will be tough. Gently knead just until the dough is smooth and cohesive but still soft and a little sticky.

- Dip your biscuit cutter in flour to slice more easily through sticky dough.

- When stamping out biscuits, do not twist the cutter. Lift straight up to prevent the sides of the dough from pinching together or twisting, which can inhibit rising or make misshapen or tough biscuits.

- After cutting out as many biscuits as you can from the initial patting or roll-ing out, gather the dough remnants together, pat out, and cut out one more batch. Do not reroll scraps more than once, or your biscuits will be tough.

- If you like a crisp crust, lightly brush the tops with water before baking. For soft biscuits, brush them with milk.

Quick Tip

If you don't have a biscuit cutter, use a cookie cutter or an inverted thin water glass. Another option is to pat the dough out into a square and cut out square-shaped biscuits with a chef's knife.

See also CUTTING IN.

BISCUIT CUTTER See BAKING TOOLS.

BLACK BEAN See BEAN, DRIED.

BLACKBERRY See BERRY.

BLACKENING A technique in which food, usually whole fish, fish fillets, or steak, is cooked in an extremely hot skillet, usually cast iron. The heat chars the exterior of the food so that it literally turns black. The quick cooking leaves the interior of the food tender and moist. Blackening is associated with Cajun cooking and was made popular by chef Paul Prudhomme of New Orleans. In traditional recipes for blackened food, the fish or meat is rubbed with a spice mixture before it is cooked. This forms a full-bodied blackened crispy crust that imparts extra aromatic flavor to the flesh beneath.

True blackening produces billows of smoke, so do not attempt this technique at home unless you have a well-ventilated kitchen. Most blackening is done in restaurant kitchens that are equipped with professional stoves capable of producing extremely high heat.

BLACK-EYED PEA See BEAN, DRIED; PEA, FRESH.

BLANCHING To submerge food—usually vegetables or fruits—in a generous amount of boiling water for a few seconds or for up to a minute or two before plunging it immediately into very cold water, preferably ice water, to stop the cooking process. The immersion in boiling water does not cook the food but just softens its texture. Plunging it into cold water sets a bright color as well. (This technique is also known as refreshing or shocking.) Blanching also makes some thin-skinned fruits, such as peaches or tomatoes, easier to peel, while leaving the inner flesh firm. Strong flavors—such as those of onions

and garlic—may be mellowed by blanching, and sometimes cured meats—bacon, ham, salt pork—are blanched to reduce their saltiness.

Blanching is also necessary before freezing certain vegetables in order to disable the enzymes that would otherwise ruin their bright color and firm texture. Broccoli, Brussels sprouts, carrots, cauliflower, corn, green beans, okra, and English peas should all be blanched before they are frozen for this reason.

Tongs, large strainers with handles, pasta pots with perforated inserts, slotted spoons, and mesh skimmers may all be used for blanching. They allow you to move the food quickly from the hot water to the cold water so that it does not continue cooking longer than desired.

Foods may be blanched up to a day ahead of time and refrigerated until they are needed.

Quick Bite

The term *blanching* can also refer to cooking food partially in hot oil as a preparatory step in a recipe. French fries, for example, are often blanched in hot fat, drained, and then finished in fat at a higher temperature.

HOW TO *Blanch Vegetables for Freezing*

1. Plunge the vegetables into a large pot of boiling water for 20 seconds to 2 minutes. (Blanching time will depend on the recipe or on the size and hardness of the vegetables.) Begin counting from when the water starts to bubble again.
2. Using tongs, a strainer, or similar utensil, immediately transfer the vegetables to ice water. The water must be as cold as possible to ensure that they retain their bright color. Let the vegetables cool, but do not leave them soaking in the water.

HOW TO *Blanch Fruits for Peeling*

1. First cut out the stem and then score, or shallowly cut, an X in the blossom end of the fruit. This will help you remove the skin quickly.

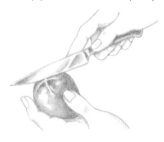

2. Plunge the fruit into a large pot of boiling water for 20 to 60 seconds. (Blanching time will depend on the recipe or on the size and hardness of the fruit.) Begin counting from when the water starts to bubble again. The fruit is ready when the skin begins to wrinkle. Remove it quickly—any longer and it may begin to cook.

3. Using tongs, a strainer, a fork, or a similar utensil, transfer the fruit to very cold water, preferably ice water.

4. As soon as it is cool, remove the fruit from the water and peel away the skin, using your fingers or a small paring knife.

Quick Bite

In agriculture, blanching refers to covering a vegetable, such as asparagus, with straw or soil as it grows to prevent sunlight from activating its chlorophyll and turning it green.

BLENDER Also called liquefiers, blenders are excellent for puréeing soups and blending cold drinks such as milk shakes or fruit smoothies. Basic blenders can also be used to chop bread for fresh bread crumbs and to chop herbs. They can usually handle more liquid volume than food processors and are good complements to them. (Blenders do not aerate liquid well and they quickly overbeat delicate mixtures, so do not use them for whipping cream or beating egg whites.) When buying a blender, choose a sturdy, powerful model with a reliable motor that will last for years.

Standing Blenders These blenders have heavy metal or plastic bases that encase electric motors. A widemouthed, lidded canister, called a jar, is designed to fit on the base, permitting the motor to spin a small propeller-type blade inside the jar. Jars generally hold 5 to 8 cups, and most have lids fitted with removable center caps that double as 2-ounce measures. The removable cap also allows you to pour liquid into the blender while the motor is running without stopping to remove and replace the entire lid. Be sure to put the lid on while you're blending at higher speeds, and never stick a spoon or anything else into the jar while the blade is moving. Invest in a blender with a glass jar, as plastic retains odors. You don't want garlic-scented milk shakes or margaritas. Blenders can have as many as 16 or more speeds, although some, including many super-powered bar blenders, have only 2 speeds. Others have special ice-breaking capabilities. Don't try to break ice in your blender unless the instruction booklet assures you that your machine is up to the job.

Immersion Blenders Also called hand or handheld blenders, immersion blenders have an extended blade that is immersed in a food or mixture to blend or purée it. Immersion blenders are great for puréeing food in the container in which it is mixed or cooked. This means that they can blend larger amounts of food than will fit in the jar of a standing blender. Immersion blenders also tend to incorporate more air into a liquid and as such can be used to make frothy foam on creamed soups. These blenders usually have only 2 speeds, and the blade must be completely immersed in the food to prevent spattering. Many are designed to hang in a wall mount for easy storage. Some have whisk attachments or small containers for blending smaller amounts of food.

BLENDING To mix at least two ingredients so that they combine thoroughly and evenly. Chopped or minced vegetables and meat can be blended as well as liquid ingredients or dry ingredients. Blending differs from beating because its purpose is only to combine the ingredients, not to incorporate air into the mixture. It can be accomplished by spoon, fork, whisk, rubber spatula, electric mixer, food processor, blender, or your bare hands.

See also BEATING; BLENDER; CREAMING; MIXER; MIXING.

BLIND BAKING Also called prebaking, blind baking means partially or completely baking a pie or tart shell before filling it. Some very juicy pie fillings, such as berry and other fruit fillings, can make a bottom crust soggy, but partially baking a crust prevents the crust from absorbing too much liquid. Other pie and tart fillings, such as custard, are cooked separately from the crust or require no baking, and in these cases the crusts must be fully baked before they are filled. Follow the instructions given in your recipe.

HOW TO *Blind Bake*

1. After the dough is rolled out and fitted into the pans, carefully lay a sheet of aluminum foil or parchment paper over the dough and weight it down with a layer of raw rice, dried beans, or pie weights, small metal or ceramic balls designed specifically for this use. If using rice or beans, discard them after a couple of bakings.

2. Bake according to the instructions in the recipe. If partially prebaking, this is usually until the sides of the crust are just set but still pale. If completely prebaking, it's until the crust is a deep golden brown. In either case, the recipe will instruct you to remove the weights and foil or paper after several minutes and continue cooking until the crust is ready. At this point, some recipes will instruct you to prick the crust with the tines of a fork to permit steam to escape before continuing.

3. If the filling is not baked in the crust, set the pan on a wire rack and let cool completely before filling, to prevent sogginess.

Blind baking generally takes from 25 to 40 minutes, depending on whether the shell is to be partially or fully baked, and on the ingredients, the size and thickness of the pastry, and the size of the pan.

Tiny tartlet shells, baked in individual tartlet molds, are nearly always blind baked. Because it is awkward to line small molds with foil, spray the outsides of same-shaped molds with cooking spray and set them inside the pastry-lined molds. Weight these with beans, rice, or pie weights and proceed as directed above.

See also BAKING; PIE & TART; ROLLING OUT.

BLUEBERRY See BERRY.

BOILING Heating liquid to its hottest point before it evaporates. At sea level, water boils at 212°F. (For boiling at high altitude, see HIGH-ALTITUDE COOKING.) When water, or any other liquid, boils, it moves rapidly and large air bubbles break through the surface in rapid succession. When this bubbling cannot be halted by stirring, cooks refer to it as a rapid, full, or rolling boil. When the bubbles are smaller and cling to the edges of the cooking pot so that the surface of the liquid gently undulates instead of rolls, the liquid is said to be simmering (about 185°F). A moderate boil is the state between these two: larger air bubbles rise to the surface than at a simmer, but at a slower pace than during a rolling boil. Simmering and moderately boiling liquids temporarily stop bubbling when stirred.

Boiling causes the liquid to convert to gas, which, in the case of water, takes the form of steam. (This steam can scald you just as boiling water can, so use caution!) Any liquid that is allowed to boil for a length of time will eventually disappear, with all the water in it converting to steam.

Solids, even those that have liquefied, will be left behind. When used deliberately in stock and sauce making, this process is called "reducing" or "cooking down" the liquid, allowing it to thicken and combine with the solids into a sauce or gravy.

Boiling is an intense method of cooking and should be used only for certain sturdy vegetables and dried pastas. Dried pasta is a particularly good candidate because a large pot of boiling water can disperse the starch that naturally comes off pasta as it cooks; as a result, the pasta will be neither gummy nor sticky. Even though the names of some meat dishes suggest that they are boiled, such as New England boiled dinner, the meat is actually gently simmered (called braising) or poached. Boiling any meat would in fact render it tough and tasteless.

Boiling Times for Various Foods

Artichoke, medium	30 to 40 minutes
Asparagus	
Thin spears	4 to 6 minutes
Thick spears	7 to 10 minutes
Beets	
Medium	30 to 35 minutes
Large	45 to 60 minutes
Broccoli	
Florets	3 to 5 minutes
Spears	7 minutes
Cauliflower	
Florets	3 to 5 minutes
Head	10 to 15 minutes
Corn on the cob	1 to 2 minutes
Pasta	
Strand pasta	6 to 8 minutes
Shaped pasta	8 to 12 minutes
Peas	3 to 5 minutes
Potatoes, cut into 1½- to 2-inch chunks	20 to 25 minutes

Use times only as a guideline when boiling food, relying on other tests to determine when the food is done. Taste the pasta and peas; pierce the potatoes and broccoli with a sharp knife to test for tenderness. Cooking times start when the water returns to a boil after the food is added.

Quick Tip

Boiling green vegetables in a lot of water helps retain their color but results in lost nutrients. Boiling them in smaller amounts of water retains nutrients but not as much color.

See also BLANCHING; HIGH-ALTITUDE COOKING; REDUCING; SIMMERING.

BOK CHOY Also called pak-choi, Chinese white cabbage, or white mustard cabbage, this common Asian vegetable is one of the best-known members of the extended Chinese cabbage family. Bok choy has long, white stalks with dark green leaves; a mild, chardlike flavor; and a crunchy texture. Baby bok choy is about half the size and more tender. Cut-up bok choy can be stir-fried, sautéed, or used raw in salads. Whole baby bok choy is good braised or steamed.

Selecting The stalks and leaves should be crisp, firm, and brightly colored. Avoid stalks with brown spots, bruising, or cracking or wilted leaves.

Storing Refrigerate bok choy in a plastic bag for up to 4 days.

Preparing Stalks and leaves may be used together or separately. Trim the stalks before using, removing the tough ends. If using leaves only, separate the leaves from the stalks and chop or shred as desired.

BONING Some recipes require removing the bones, sinews, and excess fat from meat or poultry. The terms *debone* and *fillet* also mean to bone. Many beginning cooks feel boning is too difficult to tackle, although with the right knife and a little practice it is an easy matter to bone a chicken breast or thigh. It is economical, too, because boneless cuts are pricier than bone-in cuts. Boning a tiny quail, a leg of lamb, or a whole fish, however, takes more skill, and you'll probably want to leave these tasks to the butcher or fishmonger.

Boned food cooks more quickly than bone-in food. It is well suited for poaching, sautéing, frying, and quick grilling.

A boning knife has a 6- or 7-inch-long, narrow blade that cuts through tendons and cartilage, slips easily between the flesh and bones of the meat or poultry, and is flexible enough to follow the contours of the bones.

HOW TO *Bone a Chicken Breast*

1. Skin the breast, if desired; pull off the skin and use a boning knife as needed to cut it free.
2. If starting with a whole breast, place the breast bone side up and slit down the center of the thin membrane covering the breastbone. Grasp the breast firmly at each end and flex it upward to pop out the breastbone. Pull out the bone, using a boning knife if needed. Cut through the center of the breast to split it in half, cutting away the tough sinews between the halves.

continued

3. To bone each breast half, starting along the rib side, insert a boning knife between the bones and meat. Following the curve of the bone with the knife and lifting the meat with your other hand, gradually cut the meat away from the bone. When you come to the wishbone, make a slit to remove the meat.

4. When the meat is free of the bone, trim away the tough membrane from the rib edge of the breast meat. Find the white tendon on the underside and remove it by scraping the meat away from it with your knife until it detaches from the breast. Trim the breast of any large bits of fat or skin.

HOW TO *Bone a Chicken Thigh and Leg*

1. Skin the chicken, if desired; pull off the skin and use a boning knife as needed to cut it free.

2. Without separating the thigh and leg, cut along the thigh bone to expose it. Cut down the length of the leg to expose the leg bone.

3. Using your fingers, push the meat away from the bones. Holding the thigh bone, let the thigh meat and the leg meat and bone hang from it.

4. Lay the meat on the cutting board, spreading it out as much as possible. Following the line where the meat is still attached, carefully cut the meat from the bones.

5. Carefully cut the leg meat from the thigh meat, if desired. For a more attractive presentation, trim away rough edges.

BORAGE See HERB.

BORLOTTI BEAN See BEAN, DRIED.

BOUILLON See BROTH.

BOUQUET GARNI (boo-KAY gahr-NEE) This French term refers to a bundle of herbs added at the start of cooking to a soup or stew to perfume it with flavor. A traditional bouquet garni includes parsley, thyme, and bay leaf and is most often tied in cheesecloth to make the herbs easier to retrieve and discard at the end of cooking. Other herbs and aromatics also may be added. Some rustic bouquets garnis are enclosed within pieces of celery or the dark-green leaves of a leek, the whole bundle securely tied with kitchen string.

BOWL See BAKING TOOLS; MIXING BOWL.

BOYSENBERRY See BERRY.

BRAISING To simmer food slowly in a moderate amount of liquid. Relatively tough cuts of meat, such as chuck roast and brisket, and fibrous vegetables, such as carrots, celery, and leeks, are excellent candidates for braising. Braising liquid can be water or more flavorful liquid such as broth, stock, wine, or beer. Onions, garlic, herbs, or other ingredients are often added to braising liquid for flavoring. Braising and stewing are closely related, although stews are made with more liquid and smaller pieces of food.

Meat to be braised is generally browned first in fat to give it color and add to its flavor. It is then cooked in a relatively small amount of liquid (usually only 1 to 2 inches deep) in a tightly closed pot or baking dish on the top of the stove over medium-low to medium heat or in a moderate (325° to 350°F) oven. The lid prevents liquid from evaporating, and the food is quickly surrounded by steam.

Quick Tip

In classic French-style braising, the vegetables that are cooked with the meat or poultry to impart their aromatic flavors are not necessarily served. Instead, fresh vegetables may be added toward the end of cooking for the benefit of their fresher color, texture, and flavor.

Braising results in tender, full-flavored dishes. Braised dishes are typically hearty, cold-weather fare. Some favorite braised dishes are pot roast, coq au vin, and lamb shanks. The braising times in the chart at right are based on braising in a tightly lidded pot in a 325°F oven or on top of the stove over medium heat, maintaining the liquid at a gentle simmer.

See also BROWNING.

BRAN See FLOUR.

BRAZIL NUT See NUT.

Braising Times for Various Foods

Beef flank steak, 1¼ to 1¾ inches thick	1½ to 1¾ hours
Beef pot roast, 3 to 4 pounds	2 to 3 hours
Beef rump roast, 3 to 5 pounds	3½ to 4 hours
Beef short ribs	1½ to 2 hours
Belgian endive, halved lengthwise	40 to 45 minutes
Cabbage, shredded	20 to 25 minutes
Chicken, 3½ pounds or less	35 to 40 minutes
Chicken, 3¾ to 4 pounds	50 to 60 minutes
Chicken, 5 to 6 pounds	1¾ to 2 hours
Fennel bulb, quartered	20 to 25 minutes
Lamb shanks, 1 pound each	1½ to 2¼ hours
Lamb shoulder, 3 to 5 pounds	2 to 2½ hours
Lamb shoulder chops, ¾ to 1¼ inches thick	35 to 45 minutes
Pork chops, 1 to 1½ inches thick	35 to 50 minutes
Pork ribs, country style	1½ to 2¼ hours
Radicchio, cut into wedges	3 to 5 minutes
Veal shanks, 1 pound each	2 to 3 hours
Veal shoulder, 4 to 5 pounds	2 to 2½ hours

b

Bread

The most basic bread is made of flour, water, and a leavener, usually yeast. From this elemental triad come all breads, some of them made with specialty flours, others with sweeteners such as honey and molasses, and still others with fruits and nuts.

Breads can be formed into traditional or free-form loaves or into rolls or buns. Although most are leavened with yeast and thus dubbed yeast breads, others known as quick breads are raised with baking powder and baking soda or, in a few cases, eggs. See QUICK BREAD for more information.

Most people buy bread in the supermarket, where the selection is slowly but surely getting better. Today, large supermarkets may have in-store bakeries that sell fresh-baked European-style or rustic breads. These loaves tend to have a soft crumb (interior) and crisp 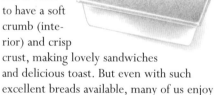 crust, making lovely sandwiches and delicious toast. But even with such excellent breads available, many of us enjoy baking bread at home whenever we can.

Nearly all flour used for bread baking is milled from wheat. Wheat flour contains glutenin, the protein in the bread that expands into elastic strands known as gluten to capture the gases released by the yeast during kneading, rising, and baking. Other flours, such as rye, corn, and rice, do not have glutenin, or they have such a tiny amount that it is not capable of raising bread. For this reason, recipes for breads made with other flours include wheat flour, too. Cake and pastry flours are rarely appropriate for breads because of their small amounts of glutenin.

Some recipes call for making a sponge, which is a very wet version of the bread dough and acts as a kind of head start for the yeast. The sponge, left at room temperature for an hour or longer (up to 36 hours), will swell as the yeast interacts with the flour and water. When it's time to make the bread, the sponge is mixed with more flour and other ingredients for a loaf with good texture and boosted flavor.

Water is the liquid used for most breads. Some recipes call for milk, which produces a very tender crumb. Except for the warm water used to activate the yeast, the water used in the recipe should be at room temperature. Tap water is generally fine, although some bakers think bottled or filtered water makes better-tasting bread. If your tap water tastes heavily of chemicals, you might want to consider buying water.

As a rule, breads contain very little fat, although some are rubbed with oil or softened butter before baking to encourage browning. A few recipes call for incorporat-

Quick Tip

To refresh a stale loaf of bread, sprinkle it with water, wrap it in aluminum foil, and bake it at 350°F until it is warm and soft. It will be good for one more use.

ing oil into the dough. Salt, on the other hand, is crucial to the taste of bread. A generous sprinkling brings out the flavor of the bread as nothing else will. Salt should be added to the dough with the bulk of the flour—never to the yeast and warm water mixture or to a sponge, as it inhibits the development of the yeast. See YEAST for further details.

Quick Tip

A little mold on a loaf of bread is not harmful. Cut it off and use the remaining bread. If numerous patches of mold are visible, however, discard the loaf.

In many bread recipes, a sprinkling of sugar or 1 teaspoon of honey is added to the yeast and water mixture to give the yeast a boost as it bubbles and swells. This small amount makes no significant contribution to the final flavor of the bread, and while the sweetener feeds the yeast, using it for proofing is not necessary. Of course, doughs for sweet breads, such as coffee cakes, dessert breads, muffins, cinnamon buns, and so on, are sweetened intentionally. Granulated and brown sugar, honey, and molasses are the most commonly used sweeteners, although some recipes call for maple syrup, barley malt, rice syrup, and organic cane sugar syrup.

Selecting Bread is a supermarket staple, and regular turnover is not usually a problem. Most stores stock fresh bread, but you should check the sell-by date to make sure it hasn't passed. Presliced soft-crusted loaves should feel relatively heavy and soft. Fresh-baked bread is generally better in quality than presliced, but it won't last as long. Crusty breads and rolls should feel firm but not rock solid.

Storing Store bread at room temperature, on a cupboard shelf or in a bread box or drawer. Fresh-baked bread may last only 1 or 2 days before going slightly stale (but perfect for fresh bread crumbs, stuffing, or French toast), while presliced bread should still be good 2 days after its sell-by date. Storing crusty bread in plastic bags will keep it fresh longer but will compromise the crust by making it soft.

Refrigeration can dry out bread, although pita bread and tortillas should be refrigerated. If you must refrigerate bread, put it in a zippered plastic bag to hold in moisture. Bread also freezes well enclosed in a zippered plastic freezer bag. Let frozen or refrigerated loaves come to room temperature in their packaging. Slices from a frozen loaf can be toasted without thawing, although they will defrost in a matter of minutes on the countertop.

Quick Tip

Don't be tempted to defrost bread in the microwave. Even a short stint in the microwave will dry it out. If you must defrost a muffin, roll, or slice of bread in the microwave, wrap it first in a paper towel to hold in moisture and microwave it for only a few seconds at a time.

Toasting Bread Breakfast fanciers almost always make toast part of their morning ritual. And while some eaters may opt for honey, others may reach for butter and cinnamon-sugar, and still others may insist on strawberry preserves. But the topping is not the only variable. Toasting may be a simple process, but the results vary greatly depending on the approach. Some people like to start with a slightly stale loaf, which produces more firm-textured toast, while fresh bread yields toast that is crisp on the outside while still tender within. Toasting at a higher heat has a similar effect. For more uniformly crisp toast, prepare the bread at a lower heat, which will dry it more before it turns golden.

continued

b

Bread, continued

Yeast Bread Savvy

- Yeast and gluten thrive in warmth, so bread benefits from a warm kitchen, warm hands, and a good, hot oven.
- After mixing the yeast and warm water together, stir in the minimum amount of flour called for in a recipe to achieve the right consistency. More can be added, but it can't be removed.
- When mixing the dough, use your hands and a sturdy spoon (many bread bakers like wooden spoons and earthenware bowls for mixing bread) until the dough holds together in a cohesive mass. It will not be smooth. This can be also done in a stand mixer fitted with the paddle attachment or a food processor fitted with a steel blade.

Mixing by hand.

- For instructions on kneading, see KNEADING.
- A good test to determine if you have kneaded the bread long enough is to insert your fingertips into the dough. If the indentation springs back, the dough is well kneaded. The dough should also have a shiny look to its surface.
- Some heavy-duty stand mixers have dough hooks for kneading. Watch for the same indicators of properly kneaded dough as when kneading by hand.
- Kneaded dough is allowed to rise in an oiled or buttered bowl, after turning the dough to coat the surface. This coating prevents the dough from sticking to the bowl as it rises, allowing for a smooth and unimpeded leavening.

Placing in oiled bowl.

- Keep rising dough in a warm environment and allow ample time for the dough to rise. Most recipes call for dough to double in bulk.

Risen dough.

- Some breads benefit from second or even third risings, which help them develop finer texture and even more flavor. When repeated risings are called for, do not shape the dough into the desired loaf form until it has risen at least once.
- Bread will develop a finer texture and flavor if its rising is slowed by the cold of refrigeration. When time and your schedule allow, place the bowl of dough on a refrigerator shelf and leave it to rise slowly overnight.
- See PUNCHING DOWN and RELAXING for information on that step.
- Before baking, many bread recipes call for the top of a loaf to be slashed with a razor blade or sharp knife. These slashes enhance and increase crust area and promote more even rising in the oven.

- Most loaves are baked until they are well risen and lightly browned and sound hollow when tapped on the bottom. Take the bread from the oven, but do not turn the oven off. Turn the loaf from the pan into your hand (protected with an oven mitt) and literally knock on the bottom of the loaf with your bare knuckles. If it does not sound hollow, return it to the still-hot oven, checking it again after 5 to 7 minutes. If it does sound hollow, let it cool.
- Cool bread on wire racks to allow air to circulate. Allow the bread to cool completely before cutting—although it is tempting to cut it while warm and try a slice with butter melting on the hot crumb. However, the crumb will have the best flavor and texture if the bread is permitted to cool completely.

HOW TO *Shape Yeast Bread*

Following are simple instructions for shaping dough into the three basic loaf styles. In all cases, the dough should be allowed to rise after it has been shaped into a loaf, according to a recipe's instructions.

ROUND LOAF

The most basic of bread shapes, the round loaf nonetheless requires some technique to ensure an even, well-risen form.

1. After pressing the risen dough flat, form it into a ball. With both hands, stretch the sides of the dough downward and under, rotating the ball as you do so to form a tight, compact shape.

2. Pinch the seam closed to seal.

RECTANGULAR LOAF

All kinds of basic doughs may be baked in a loaf pan. Rolling up the dough and pinching its seams closed ensures a uniform, well-risen shape and even texture.

1. With a rolling pin, roll out a ball of dough into a flat, even rectangle of size specified. Starting at a short side, roll up the rectangle.

2. With your fingertips, pinch together the long seam and the spiral seams on both ends to seal them. Place the dough in a greased loaf pan with its long seam down.

BRAIDED LOAF

Braiding, a traditional form for an egg loaf, is one of the easiest ways to prepare bread dough for a festive presentation.

1. Start with 3 ropes of dough of the length specified and braid them from the center to one end by alternately twisting the left- and right-hand ropes over the center rope. Pinch them together at one end. Braid from the center to the other end and pinch together to seal.

continued

Bread, continued

The Bread Basket Glossary

BAGEL A traditional, chewy Jewish bread made by forming dough into individually portioned doughnut shapes and then boiling them before baking. See BAGEL.

BAGUETTE A long, narrow loaf; also called French bread.

BOULE A rounded, free-form loaf with crisp crust.

BREADSTICKS Long, very narrow, crispy loaves of yeast bread, often coated with seeds. Also called *grissini*.

BRIOCHE Bread made from rich egg dough and traditionally baked in a mold so that it has a crowned top.

CHALLAH A high-rising, egg-rich yeast bread that is served at traditional Jewish holidays. The bread may be formed into elaborate loaves.

COUNTRY STYLE Any rustic, full-bodied, usually free-form yeast bread.

CROISSANT A flaky, buttery, half-moon-shaped bread made from a yeast dough similar to puff pastry. Croissants are often flavored with almond paste or filled with chocolate or cheese.

DANISH PASTRY A buttery pastry related to the croissant but sweeter and more breadlike.

FOCACCIA Yeast dough that is flattened, stretched, and dimpled before baking so that the finished loaf has a bumpy surface.

PITA A flat, round bread from the Middle East made with white or wheat flour and very little leavening. Known also as pocket bread or pita pockets, the bread forms a large hollow at the center as it bakes.

ROLL A wide variety of individual-portion breads, including the descriptively named clover-leaf and knot.

RYE A robust dark bread made from rye and wheat flour. See also FLOUR.

SODA BREAD In general, any bread leavened with baking soda, but more specifically, a traditional Irish loaf combining white and whole-wheat flours, buttermilk, baking soda, and salt.

SOURDOUGH Yeast bread with a tangy flavor, the result of a sourdough starter, or fermented mixture of flour, water, and yeast. Starters are kept for long periods of time, even passed from generation to generation. Atmospheric conditions contribute to the starter's flavor, which is why sourdoughs made from starters originating in a particular region (notably San Francisco) have a distinctive flavor.

STOLLEN Sweet yeast dough mixed with raisins, candied fruit, and citrus peel and juice and then folded into an oval shape before baking. Stollens are traditional holiday breads, particularly in Germany.

WHITE Refers specifically to those breads made from a dough of white-wheat flour.

WHOLE-GRAIN A general term applying to any bread that includes significant amounts of unrefined flour from any grain typically used in bread doughs.

See also BAGEL; BREAD CRUMBS; BREAD MACHINE; CORN BREAD; FLOUR; KNEADING; POPOVER; PUNCHING DOWN; QUICK BREAD; RISING; TORTILLA; UNMOLDING; YEAST.

BREAD BOARD See BAKING TOOLS.

BREAD CRUMBS Bread crumbs, fresh or dried, are the good cook's secret weapon, bestowing a crisp topping on casseroles and a crunchy coating on pan-fried meats. Dried bread crumbs, sold in canisters and cellophane packages, may be plain or seasoned and generally are finely ground. Seasoned dried crumbs, sometimes called Italian-style bread crumbs, often contain salt, herbs, and dried cheese and thus can interfere with other flavors in a dish. Be careful not to buy seasoned crumbs for a dessert preparation. Japanese-style dried bread crumbs, called *panko,* are sold in some supermarkets and in Asian food markets. They are delicate crystal-shaped crumbs that deliver an especially light, crisp texture to fried foods.

Fresh bread crumbs are almost always homemade (a few bakeries sell them), ground from slightly stale bread. About 2 ounces of bread, or 1 slice, makes about $\frac{1}{2}$ cup bread crumbs. Making bread crumbs is a good way to use up the last few pieces of a loaf going stale.

Selecting When a recipe calls for bread crumbs, it usually means dried crumbs unless otherwise specified. Do not substitute one for the other, as fresh crumbs contain more moisture than dried and the two will behave differently in recipes.

Look for crumbs in a market with good turnover, checking their sell-by date before purchase. Even though packaged crumbs are dry, they will eventually become stale and contribute an "off" flavor to a dish. This is especially true of seasoned crumbs. If the crumbs are packed in clear cellophane, make sure they look fresh and dry.

Storing Store commercial dried bread crumbs in a cool, dry cupboard. They will keep for about 1 month after the sell-by date. Store homemade bread crumbs in a rigid plastic container or zippered plastic bag in the refrigerator for up to 1 month for dried and for 3 or 4 days for fresh. Freeze them for up to 1 year.

HOW TO *Make Bread Crumbs*

FRESH CRUMBS

1. Lay bread slices flat on the countertop and leave overnight to dry out, or "stale." Or use any bread a few days past its peak of freshness. Baguettes, whole-wheat breads, and egg breads make good crumbs.
2. Tear the bread into large pieces and process in a blender or food processor fitted with the metal blade to the texture you want.

3. To season fresh crumbs, toss them with a teaspoon of olive oil for every cup, spread the crumbs on a baking sheet, and bake at 325°F, tossing once or twice, until crisp, 10 to 12 minutes. Add minced garlic, herbs, or spices to the olive oil for your flavor of choice.

DRIED CRUMBS

1. Let the bread dry out in a 200°F oven for about 1 hour. A hotter oven will brown the bread.

2. Break the bread into large pieces and then process in a blender or food processor into fine crumbs.

b

BREADING A crust or topping made primarily of bread crumbs, cracker crumbs, or another dry coating such as cornmeal. Breading is typically applied to foods that will be deep-fried or panfried. The crumbs, sometimes mixed with seasonings, grated cheese, or other ingredients, adhere to the food, such as a fritter, chicken breast, or fish fillet, and help it stay moist and tender during frying.

Breading is also the process by which these crumbs are applied to the food. Most often, the breading mixture is spread in a shallow dish, such as a pie dish, and the food is rolled in it, or the crumbs are patted on it. To help the crumbs stick, the food may first be dipped in beaten egg or another wet medium.

HOW TO *Bread Food*
Food should not be breaded until shortly before cooking. If allowed to sit too long with the coating, it will become gummy.
1. Dredge food in flour, turning to coat all sides and shaking off excess.
2. Dip food in beaten egg or another liquid, according to a recipe.
3. Place food in bread crumbs, patting in crumbs and again turning to coat all sides before shaking off excess.

BREAD MACHINE Bread dough is mixed, kneaded, raised, and baked in a bread machine. The process can be conveniently timed so that the bread is ready exactly when you want it—after work or first thing in the morning. Loaves baked in bread machines are shaped like the canister in which they are mixed and baked. Some people choose to mix, knead, and raise the dough in the machine but then shape it by hand and bake it in the oven.

See also BREAD.

BRIE See CHEESE.

BRINE A strong saltwater solution, a brine can be flavored with herbs, spices, or sugar, depending on its purpose. Brine is used to preserve or flavor food. Pickles are packed in brine; so is corned beef. The term "brining" means to immerse foods in brine or inject them with brine to preserve or flavor them, or both.

Caution!

Be sure to note that brine-cured meat is only partially cured and must still be cooked.

Soaking meat or poultry in brine to enhance its juiciness is an old-fashioned cooking technique that is now regaining popularity. Chefs and home cooks alike are discovering that a good brine bath adds flavor and juiciness to pork, chicken, turkey, even shrimp. Brining frozen shrimp for 15 to 20 minutes will refresh their texture after thawing. Depending on the food, brining can take from 30 minutes (for shrimp) to 2 days (for pork loin) to 2 weeks (for some pickles).

The brine must contain salt—for meat and poultry, use about a cup of kosher salt for every gallon of water—but other flavorings can be added, such as garlic, herbs, peppercorns, red pepper flakes, sugar, or honey. The brine can also include liquids other than water, such as cider, vinegar, beer, or wine. The salt should be kosher salt, which is free of additives. The liquid is brought to a boil to pick up the flavor of the herbs and spices, then thoroughly chilled before the food is added. The brine must cover the food completely. As the meat soaks, the salt will penetrate it, drawing in moisture and any other seasonings. The result is juicy, flavorful cooked meat and poultry that won't necessarily taste salty—just delicious.

See also CURING.

BROAD BEAN Another name for fava bean. See BEAN, DRIED; BEAN, FRESH.

BROCCOLI Broccoli is a cruciferous vegetable and is part of the cabbage family, as is cauliflower. In early stages of cultivation, these two vegetables resemble each other, and for hundreds of years, cooks made no distinction between them. Nowadays, we are perhaps more likely to cook broccoli than cauliflower. With its clusters of green florets topping thick stalks, broccoli is popular largely because it is readily available fresh all year long, is easy to cook, and is high in vitamins A and C and in iron.

Broccoli is at its best when briefly cooked. Although it can be eaten raw, too much of it can cause gastric distress. When cooked until soft, its flavor is strong and its texture unappealing. Consider steaming or stir-frying just until crisp-tender.

Selecting Buy heads with tightly clustered dark green or purplish florets and with no signs of yellowing or flowering. Stalks should be firm and fresh looking with healthy green leaves. Do not buy broccoli with tough or woody stems. The stalks of young, tender broccoli are slender, while those of older broccoli are thick and have hollow cores. Fresh broccoli, at its best from the fall through the spring, is available all year and usually is inexpensive.

Quick Bite

The small leaves on the broccoli stalk are higher in vitamin A than the florets, making them well worth eating.

Frozen broccoli is also readily available. Many markets sell only the florets, fresh or frozen, and these can be convenient for a quick weeknight dinner.

Storing Refrigerate broccoli as soon as you get it home. It will keep for 5 days in a perforated plastic bag. To freeze broccoli, trim the leaves and peel the stalks if they look a little woody. Cut the stalks and florets into small strips 1 to 3 inches long. Blanch the broccoli for about 5 minutes, plunge into cold water, drain, and freeze in freezer bags. Frozen broccoli keeps for about 1 year.

Preparing Trim the leaves on the broccoli stalk only if they appear discolored or unhealthy and cut away any tough portions on the bottoms of the stalks. If the stalk seems tough, peel it with a vegetable peeler or paring knife. Cut the broccoli lengthwise into manageable spears, usually about 3 inches long. Both the stalks and florets can be precooked by blanching or parboiling, particularly if you will be stir-frying or sautéing the vegetable. Florets cook more quickly than stalks, so split the stalks lengthwise only to the flower heads to cook them intact. Broccoli that is cooked until soft does not reheat well, but broccoli cooked until crisp-tender can be reheated.

Peeling broccoli stalks.

See also BLANCHING; BOILING; STEAMING.

b
—

BROCCOLI RABE Also called broccoli raab, rape, *rapini,* or Italian broccoli, broccoli rabe is a relative newcomer to the vegetable section of the average American market. The bright green vegetable, with its slender stalks and small florets, resembles a stunted head of broccoli, although it has many more leaves, which are small and jagged. Like broccoli, broccoli rabe is a cruciferous vegetable and is related to cabbage, turnips, and mustard. Chefs and home cooks alike appreciate its mild, pleasantly bitter taste with overtones of sweet mustard.

Broccoli rabe is popular in Italian cooking, where it may be sautéed in olive oil and garlic and served alongside meat or used as the basis of a pasta sauce. It can also be steamed, lightly braised, or blanched before sautéing, which reduces its bitterness. It is excellent cooked and chilled in salads or used to top pizzas.

Selecting Choose broccoli rabe with bright green florets and leaves and some open yellow flowers. Pass it up if the florets are yellowing. The stalks should be firm and can be slightly flexible. Some of the bottom leaves may appear slightly wilted, which is acceptable. Broccoli rabe is at its best during the autumn and winter.

Storing Refrigerate broccoli rabe in a perforated plastic bag for up to 3 days.

Preparing Trim any wilted leaves and any tough stem ends. As noted, some cooks blanch more mature broccoli rabe to reduce bitterness before sautéing it.

BROILING To cook relatively thin, tender cuts of meat, poultry, fish, or other food by placing them beneath and close to a high heat source. A broiler can be part of an oven or a separate unit. In general, foods are placed between 4 and 8 inches away from the broiler element. The best way to regulate the temperature is to move the food closer to or farther from the heat. Thicker cuts of meat and fish must be placed farther away from a broiler in order to cook properly. Otherwise, the outside will char before the inside cooks. During broiling, the food is set on a broiler pan, which has a perforated upper pan, or rack, that allows the fat to drip into the lower, deeper pan. To prevent sticking and for easy cleanup, spray the upper pan with nonstick cooking spray and line the lower pan with heavy-duty aluminum foil.

Broiler pan.

Broiling is a fast and efficient means of cooking foods without the addition of fat or liquids. The dry, radiant heat browns the surface of the food as it cooks it. Most meat or poultry should be turned at least once during broiling. Use tongs or a spatula, not a fork, to prevent juices from escaping. Fish, which is more delicate than meat and poultry, should not be turned during broiling unless it is very firm fleshed.

If using an electric broiler, let it preheat for about 5 minutes. Gas broilers do not require preheating—and as a rule do not reach the same high temperatures as electric broilers. When using an electric broiler, most manufacturers recommend keeping the oven or broiler door ajar to prevent the oven from overheating, which would cause the thermostat to turn off

Broiling Times for Various Foods

BEEF

Hamburger	1 inch thick	3 to 5 minutes for rare* 9 to 11 minutes for medium* 13 to 15 minutes for well done
Flank steak	1 inch thick	4 to 6 minutes for rare 7 to 9 minutes for medium
Club steak Porterhouse steak Sirloin steak T-bone steak	1 inch thick	4 to 6 minutes for rare 8 to 11 minutes for medium 12 to 16 minutes for well done
Filet mignon	1 inch thick	3 to 5 minutes for rare 6 to 8 minutes for medium

LAMB

Loin and rib chops	1 inch thick	5 to 7 minutes for rare 8 to 10 minutes for medium 12 to 14 minutes for well done

PORK

Loin and shoulder chops	1 inch thick	8 to 10 minutes for medium 12 to 15 minutes for well done
Tenderloin		10 to 12 minutes for medium 14 to 17 for well done

POULTRY

Small chicken (3 to 3½ pounds), split		30 to 35 minutes
Bone-in chicken parts		20 to 25 minutes
Turkey tenders or fillets		5 to 10 minutes

VEAL

Loin and rib chops	1 inch thick	8 to 10 minutes for rare 12 to 14 minutes for medium

FISH

Salmon	1 inch thick	5 to 6 minutes for medium-rare 7 to 10 minutes for medium
Tuna	1 inch thick	4 to 5 minutes for rare 6 to 7 minutes for medium-rare 7 to 10 minutes for medium

*Although many cooks enjoy a touch of pink in their burgers, the U.S. Food Safety and Inspection Service recommends that ground beef be cooked to an internal temperature of 160°F to avoid all risk of bacterial contamination; see BEEF and DONENESS for more information.

b

the broiler. High-end gas stoves are often equipped with infrared broilers that heat very quickly to approximately 1500°F, about twice the temperature of other broilers. Food cooks nearly twice as quickly in these highly efficient units.

Most grilling recipes can be accomplished in a broiler instead. Broiling is also used to brown the top of casseroles, open-faced sandwiches, and gratins.

In the chart on page 71 are estimates of the total time it will take various foods to cook on a broiler pan positioned 4 to 6 inches from the heating element. Figure on turning meat or poultry once during cooking. Use these times as general guidelines. If you have an industrial stove, the broiler will be hotter than the broiler in a conventional home stove. Testing the temperature of the interior of the meat and poultry with a meat thermometer is the best gauge of doneness. Fish is done when it is opaque and the flesh is just beginning to flake when prodded with a fork.

About Pan Broiling Pan broiling is cooking rapidly in a skillet or sauté pan over high heat, without the addition of liquid or the use of a cover and very little or no fat. Similar to cooking on a grill or griddle, this dry-heat method develops flavor by browning the exterior of the food. Using a heavy pan and preheating it until very hot *before* adding the food are the two keys to successful pan broiling. This method works best for thin cuts of meat such as flattened boneless chicken breasts, veal scallops, or fish fillets that do not rely on long cooking or additional moisture for tenderness. One of the best-known variations of pan broiling is blackening.

BROTH Any commercially made and packaged stock made by cooking vegetables, chicken, beef, or fish in water is called a broth. These convenient products can be used as a base for soups, sauces, stews, braises, and pan gravies. Vegetable, chicken, beef, and fish broths are available in cans, in aseptic packaging, or frozen, or can be

Quick Bite

The term *broth* is sometimes also used to refer to a fortified homemade stock or soup, such as a Scotch broth.

made from bouillon cubes or powdered bouillon. Some commercial broths, like bouillon, are condensed and must be mixed with water. All of these products can be used in place of homemade stock, although they tend to be more salty, particularly bouillon cubes and powdered bouillon, and not as fresh tasting. Low-sodium and low-fat canned broths are available and allow more control in seasoning.

Selecting Choose a major brand, trying several until you find one you like best. Some cooks prefer the frozen or canned broths in health-food stores because they tend to be lower in sodium and additives.

Storing After opening, unused broth should be transferred to glass or plastic containers; do not store it in the can, or the broth will take on an unpleasant flavor. Refrigerate for up to 1 week. Store bouillon cubes and powdered bouillon at cool room temperature for up to 1 year. Broth in aseptic packaging can be held at cool room temperature for up to 1 year, but once opened should be refrigerated; it will keep for up to 1 week. Broth may be frozen for up to 3 months.

Preparing Use broth in any recipe calling for stock. Use it in place of water when cooking rice or beans for a flavor boost. Add it to stir-fries to reduce the amount of fat needed for cooking and to add flavor. But be careful with any recipe that calls for reducing or boiling down broth, since its sodium will become more concentrated as the liquid boils away. Use low-sodium broths for these dishes.

See also STOCK.

BROWNIE See COOKIE.

BROWNING When meat, poultry, or another food is cooked over high heat in an oiled or dry pan, the surface of the food quickly darkens and takes on an appealing brown color. It also gives the food a corresponding deeper flavor. For this reason, browning is often the first step in many braises and stews. It should be done quickly so as not to dry out the meat.

Quick Tip

Before browning, wipe meat or poultry dry with a paper towel and brown food in batches if necessary to prevent crowding in the pan. This keeps the food from steaming in the hot pan and results in a crisp, brown exterior.

Keeping the heat high and not overcrowding the pan are keys to successful browning. It also helps to understand that browning cannot occur in the presence of liquid or excessive moisture. This is why many recipes instruct you to dry meat or poultry before browning. Browning occurs at temperatures upward of 310°F, and, since water and other liquids cannot heat beyond 212°F, proper browning will never occur when water is present. Liquid fat, unlike water, can hold temperatures far above 310°F and is therefore an ideal medium for browning. And, since sugars and proteins brown readily, foods with a high amount of either will brown quickly.

Foods also brown in the oven during roasting. The skin of turkeys and chickens in particular will become brown, especially if you baste the birds with pan juices.

Cookies, cakes, and breads brown in the oven as their outer crusts cook.

See also BASTING; SEARING.

BROWN SUGAR See SUGAR.

BRUISING In its most familiar sense, this term refers to damaged spots or sections on fruits and vegetables. Once a fruit is bruised, a brownish discoloration starts to spread as cell walls break down, but this discoloration may be slowed down slightly by refrigerating the food.

Some foods are purposefully bruised so that their flavor is released. The aroma and flavor of herbs, spices, and garlic and onions are carried by their essential oils. When these foods are bruised, the oils are released and the flavor better infuses a dish. To bruise fresh or dried herbs, roll them between your fingers and thumb. To bruise hard spices, garlic, and onion, place them under the flat side of a chef's knife and carefully strike the flat side of the knife with the heel of your palm or your fist.

See also CRUSHING; SMASHING.

BRUSH See BAKING TOOLS; COOKING TOOLS.

BRUSSELS SPROUT Members of the cabbage family, Brussels sprouts grow on long, curving stalks as small, tightly closed heads that resemble tiny cabbages. The tops of the stalks have spreading leaves, making these impressive-looking plants when in the field. Brussels sprouts grow best in cool, coastal regions and are in season in the fall and winter. They may be boiled, braised, or steamed or parboiled and then sautéed.

Selecting Buy fresh Brussels sprouts that are heavy for their size and bright green, with leaves clinging tightly to the heads. Avoid any with yellowing leaves, which indicate aging. They may be pale green at the base. Check that the stem ends are freshly cut. Also avoid soft heads with loose leaves. Small heads, about 1 inch in diameter, are usually preferable to large ones, which can be almost twice that size. If the large heads are dark green and firm, however, they should taste good. Fresh Brussels sprouts are sold loose or packed in pint baskets or small tubs, although at some farmers' markets you can buy them on the stalks. Brussels sprouts freeze well, so if fresh are not available, buy them frozen.

Storing Store in plastic bags or the original packaging in the refrigerator for up to 4 days, but try to eat them as soon as possible after purchase. To freeze, rinse and dry the heads, blanch for 4 to 5 minutes, depending on their size, refresh in cold water, drain, and freeze in sturdy freezer bags or rigid containers.

Preparing Rinse and dry the heads. Trim any brown outside leaves and trim away the stem ends. Cut a shallow X into the stem end before cooking so that the heads will cook quickly and evenly. Larger heads can be halved or quartered before cooking.

Quick Tip

If you are faced with loose-leafed Brussels sprouts, simply take apart the heads and separate and steam the individual leaves.

See also STEAMING.

BUCKWHEAT See GRAIN.

BUFFALO See GAME.

BULGUR See GRAIN.

BUNDT PAN See Tube Pan in BAKE-WARE.

BUTTER This essential dairy product is made by churning, or agitating, cream until the fats separate from the liquids, producing a semisolid fat. Butter is most often made from the 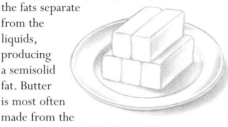 cream of cow's milk, although it can be churned from the milk of sheep, goats, and other mammals as well.

Butter is 80 to 85 percent milk fat. The rest is made up of milk solids (proteins) and water. Most commercially packaged butter has wrappers marked with tablespoon increments. Butter is sold in two

Quick Tip

When butter is heated, it will first melt, then begin to foam. When the foam is just beginning to subside, but before it begins to brown, the butter has reached the right temperature for cooking food.

basic styles. More familiar is salted butter, although many cooks favor unsalted butter, also called sweet butter, for two reasons. First, salt in the butter adds to the total amount of salt in a recipe, which can interfere with the taste. Second, unsalted butter is likely to be fresher, since it has no salt, which acts as a preservative and prolongs its shelf life. (If you're not planning to use it soon, you should freeze it.) If you have no choice when shopping, salted butter will work in most cooking recipes (you may want to taste and adjust other salt in the recipe), but it is not recommended as a substitute for unsalted butter in baking.

Storing Salted butter, if left wrapped and stored in a cold section of the refrigerator, will keep for about $2\frac{1}{2}$ months, while wrapped unsalted butter will store well for about $1\frac{1}{2}$ months. After that, the butter may begin to pick up refrigerator odors, thus losing its delicate flavor. Both types freeze well for up to 6 months in their original packaging. Once unwrapped, salted and unsalted butter should be eaten within 3 weeks. Even if wrapped, do not keep butter longer than 1 week beyond its sell-by date, unless you freeze it.

Buttering a Pan Buttering a pan means rubbing it with a thin film of softened butter. This can be done with a brush, your fingers, a wadded paper towel, or the wrapper from the butter. Or you can just grasp the stick of partially wrapped butter and use it to paint butter over the pan. In most cases, if a recipe instructs you to "grease" or "oil" the pan, you can use butter, margarine, or another fat. The layer of fat prevents food from sticking to the pan. Because butter burns at lower temperatures than refined vegetable oils, it is not recommended for greasing pans headed for very hot ovens.

As a general rule, when recipes call for buttering a pan, the relatively small amount of butter used is not listed but is in addition to any amount of butter called for among the actual ingredients.

Quick Tip

To soften butter in the microwave, put the butter in a microwave-safe glass dish and cover with waxed paper. Microwave on Defrost for 15 to 30 seconds. Check the butter and repeat if necessary. The larger the measurement, the longer the time in the microwave (1 cup, which is 16 tablespoons or 2 sticks, may take up to a minute to soften). Do not melt.

Butter Equivalents

1 cup	= 16 tablespoons	= 8 ounces	= 2 sticks
$\frac{3}{4}$ cup	= 12 tablespoons	= 6 ounces	= $1\frac{1}{2}$ sticks
$\frac{1}{2}$ cup	= 8 tablespoons	= 4 ounces	= 1 stick
$\frac{1}{4}$ cup	= 4 tablespoons	= 2 ounces	= $\frac{1}{2}$ stick

HOW TO *Clarify Butter*

Clarified butter keeps about three times as long as other butters because the milk solids, which can become rancid, have been removed. It is used for cooking but not as a spread, as it turns grainy when it cools and solidifies.

1. Melt at least 1 cup unsalted butter over low heat in a small pan or skillet.

2. Let the butter simmer undisturbed for about 10 minutes. The water will evaporate and the white milk solids will collect at the bottom.

3. Skim any foam off the top of the butter.

4. Remove the butter from the heat and carefully pour the clear, golden liquid through a fine sieve into a glass jar, leaving the white milk solids in the pan or sieve. Discard the solids.

5. Cool the clarified butter completely, cover, and then refrigerate. It will keep for about 3 months.

BUTTER BEAN Another name for lima bean. See BEAN, DRIED; BEAN, FRESH.

BUTTERFLYING The technique of cutting a food nearly all the way through so that, instead of being split into two pieces, it can be opened up to lie relatively flat—like a book or, more poetically, a butterfly. Butterflying also allows fast, even cooking when the food is spread out flat and cooked, such as a boned leg of lamb on a charcoal grill. Butterflying also allows meat to be stuffed, rolled up, and tied before cooking. While most cooks think only of meat as a candidate for butterflying, the technique can also be applied to vegetables and fruits such as bell peppers and pears.

Butterflying a chicken breast.

HOW TO *Butterfly Jumbo Shrimp*
1. After shelling and deveining (see SHRIMP), cut through the shrimp on the outside curve without slicing all the way through, so that the shrimp can be opened flat.

HOW TO *Butterfly and Stuff a Pork or Beef Tenderloin Roast*
1. Using a chef's knife, carefully cut a lengthwise slit along the center of the meat. As you cut, open the flaps of meat like a book, leaving them attached to each other and cutting to within about 1/2 inch of the opposite side.

2. Place the slit tenderloin on a work surface with its cut side up and flaps opened flat. Using the smooth side of a meat pounder, pound the tenderloin evenly all over until it has the uniform thickness called for in the recipe.

3. Evenly arrange the prepared stuffing lengthwise along the center of the butterflied tenderloin. Wrap both sides around the stuffing and, using lengths of kitchen string, securely tie the stuffed tenderloin at regular intervals.

HOW TO *Butterfly a Whole Chicken*

1. Place the bird breast side down on a cutting board. Cut along one side of the backbone with kitchen shears or a large knife. Pull open the 2 halves of the bird and cut down the other side of the backbone to free it. Discard the backbone or save it for making stock.

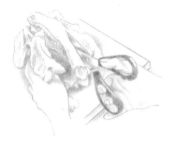

2. Turn the chicken breast side up, opening it as flat as possible. Cover it with plastic wrap and, using your hands, the smooth side of a meat mallet, or a rolling pin, press and pound it to break the breastbone and flatten the bird.

3. Make a small incision in the loose skin between thigh and breast, near the bottom of the breast, and push the ends of the drumsticks through the incisions to tuck them away neatly during cooking.

BUTTERMILK Traditionally, buttermilk is the liquid left behind when butter is churned from cream. Today, most buttermilk is a cultured product made by adding bacteria to skimmed milk (or sometimes whole milk) to convert the sugars to acids. Cultured buttermilk is thick—sometimes even bits of butter are added to give it more body and an old-fashioned appearance—and it tastes tangy. Your great-grandmother would never recognize it as the buttermilk she remembers from the days when she was a young girl.

Some people like to drink a tall glass of icy cold buttermilk. Perhaps more common, however, are buttermilk pancakes or waffles for weekend breakfasts. Buttermilk is also is used in various baking recipes, from cakes to scones, where it acts as a leavener when the acid in the buttermilk reacts with alkaline baking soda to create gas bubbles.

Storing Buttermilk will keep refrigerated for up to 10 days past its sell-by date. Use only what you need and return the carton to the refrigerator immediately. Do not let it sit out at room temperature, as buttermilk spoils easily.

Quick Tip

If a recipe calls for buttermilk and there's no time to go to the market, substitute sour milk. To make sour milk, add 1 tablespoon cider vinegar, distilled white vinegar, or lemon juice for every cup of whole, low-fat, or skim milk and let it sit at room temperature for about 10 minutes. The milk will curdle and is then ready to use. Likewise, buttermilk can be substituted for sour milk in a recipe.

See also BAKING POWDER & BAKING SODA; MILK.

*everything from cabbage
to cutting in*

CABBAGE Like broccoli and cauliflower, cabbage is a cruciferous vegetable, a group believed by some scientists to safeguard against certain forms of cancer. Fresh cabbage leaves may be pale green or red, with green cabbage (also called Dutch white) the most plentiful.

Green cabbage.

Red cabbage has thicker leaves, a faintly peppery taste, and a slightly higher price tag but is used in the same way. Another variety, savoy, has crinkled green leaves.

Savoy cabbage.

Chinese cabbage, also called napa or celery cabbage, is elongated and has wrinkly, light yellow-green leaves and a pearly white core. Cabbage is sold fresh all year long.

Cabbage is the primary ingredient in two popular preparations, coleslaw and sauerkraut. Whole leaves can be boiled or blanched until pliable and then stuffed and steamed. Whole cabbages can be stuffed as well, with a flavorful mixture tucked between the leaves. Chopped cabbage is added to soups and braises.

Chinese cabbage.

Selecting Buy firm, heavy heads of green, red, and savoy cabbage with closely furled leaves. An average head weighs about 2 pounds. Color is an indication of freshness. For example, green cabbages stored for too long lose pigment and look almost white. To ensure freshness, check the stem ends of cabbage heads to make sure the stem has not cracked around the base, which indicates undesirably lengthy storage. Chinese cabbage leaves should be crisp and unblemished and pale green with tinges of yellow and white.

Storing Refrigerate heads of green and red cabbage for up to 2 weeks, savoy and Chinese cabbage for 5 or 6 days. If you want to eat the cabbage raw, do so within

Quick Tip

Nothing combats the odor of cooking cabbage, despite old wives' tales about dropping a whole walnut or a chunk of bread into the cooking pot. Cooking it quickly helps, but a kitchen exhaust fan is the best defense.

3 or 4 days. Do not cut or shred cabbage until you are ready to use it. Store the unused portion intact, wrapped in plastic, and use within 2 days.

Preparing Pull off and discard any wilted outer leaves and cut the core from the head, either by cutting the head in half or quarters and slicing the core from the center, or by cutting around the core from the base.

Coring cabbage.

Shred or slice cabbage for salads (a food processor makes quick work of the task).

Cutting cabbage shreds.

See also BRAISING; SAUERKRAUT.

CAKE See page 80.

CAKE PAN See BAKEWARE.

CAKE ROUND See BAKING TOOLS.

CALAMARI See SQUID.

CALZONE The term *calzone,* Italian for "pantaloon," charmingly describes the shape of this pizza transformed into a turnover to be baked or deep-fried. Virtually any pizza

can be made into a calzone. Essentially, pizza dough rounds are folded in half to conceal a filling. The technique is best suited to abundant fillings that will not sit well atop a pizza.

HOW TO *Shape a Calzone*

1. Prepare a pizza dough. Form the risen dough into individual-serving balls. On a lightly floured surface, roll each ball into a neat round about 10 inches in diameter or flatten and stretch the dough with your hands.

2. Prepare the filling. Mound it on the rolled-out dough, covering roughly half of it and leaving a generous rim.

3. Using a brush dipped in water, lightly moisten the edges of the dough. Fold the uncovered portion over the filling, gently stretching it to cover the ingredients completely. Press and crimp the edges together to seal securely.

Cake

Most celebrations, whether large or small, planned or spontaneous, elegant or casual, call for a cake. Indeed, at weddings and birthdays, a festively decorated cake is the culinary star. In other instances, it transforms an ordinary meal into an occasion.

Cakes are usually made from batters composed of flour, milk (or another liquid), sugar, eggs and often another leavener as well, butter (or sometimes oil or shortening), and flavorings. The batter is baked until its interior sets and becomes a crumb and a firm exterior crust develops. As is the case with all baked goods, the exact proportion of ingredients makes a significant difference in the texture, flavor, and quality of the finished cake. (The term *cake* also may refer to any round, flat disk of food, such as a crab cake, a pancake, or even a yeast cake. In fact, the earliest cakes, which date back at least as far as ancient Egypt, were nothing more than sweet breads; cake recipes featuring beaten eggs only began to be popularized some time around the 17th century.)

Cakes are divided into two main types: foam cakes and butter cakes. Foam cakes have a high proportion of eggs, sugar, and liquid to flour, and the air trapped in the beaten eggs is the primary leavener. They contain very little if any fat, such as butter or oil, and so have a relatively dry and spongy texture. Popular foam cakes include angel food cake and sponge cake.

Butter cakes are richer and more velvety and rely on the chemical leaveners, baking powder and baking soda. They are made with a comparatively high percentage of butter. Typical butter cakes are American layer cakes and pound cakes.

Some cakes, such as chiffon cake and the classic French génoise, combine elements of both types of cake.

Equipment Having the right equipment makes cake baking easier, and for most home baking needs, the basics are few. Measuring cups and spoons, a mixing bowl and spoon, a whisk for beating egg whites, and a pair of round cake pans or a tube pan are all you'll need for many recipes. Batters can always be mixed by hand, but are more easily whipped up with a handheld electric mixer or in a stand mixer. For more details, see BAKEWARE; BAKING TOOLS.

Ingredients Begin with the freshest ingredients possible. When making cakes, this pertains mainly to the butter, eggs, and milk. If your baking powder or soda is more than 6 months old, replace it to guarantee effectiveness. Be sure to use the right kind of flour called for in a recipe, and never use high-protein bread flour to make a tender cake. For more detail, see FLOUR.

Preparing the Pans Properly prepared pans are a crucial part of cake baking. A poorly prepared pan can mean a cake will stick to it and refuse to emerge without tearing. Most recipes say to "grease (or butter) the pan," and some say to flour it as well. Regardless of what the recipe says, when a recipe requires greasing a pan, it is always a good idea to line and flour the pan as well. (Note that some cakes, such as angel food cakes, are baked in dry pans.)

HOW TO *Prepare a Cake Pan*

1. Cut a waxed or parchment paper round or rectangle that will fit snugly in the bottom of the pan. Use the pan as a guide for tracing the right shape and size.

2. Rub the inside bottom and sides of the pan with butter, margarine, or vegetable shortening, or spray it lightly and evenly with un-flavored cooking spray.

3. Lay the paper form in the pan and rub it with a little butter, margarine, or vegetable shortening, or spray it with a little cooking spray.

4. Sprinkle some flour on the paper form and on the sides of the pan. Holding the pan over the sink or work surface, turn and tilt the pan to distribute the flour evenly. Gently tap the excess flour from the pan and discard it. If you are baking a chocolate cake, use cocoa powder in place of flour, to avoid a contrasting white dusting on the brown cake.

Mixing the Ingredients Every recipe is slightly different, but for most cakes the following techniques are recommended.

Before mixing, measure out and prepare all ingredients according to the ingredient list. Unless the recipe directs otherwise, the ingredients should be at room temperature. Start preheating the oven.

Quick Tip

Butter contributes good flavor but may burn if used for preparing cake pans for batters that bake at very high temperatures. Margarine and vegetable oil are better at high temperatures because they don't burn as readily. Unflavored cooking spray is convenient, too.

Stand mixers are valuable tools for making large quantities of cake batter or cakes that call for prolonged and vigorous beating to incorporate maximum air. If using a stand mixer, fit it with the paddle attachment to cream the butter (see CREAMING) and to mix the batter, and the whisk attachment for whisking egg whites or cream. If using a stand or handheld mixer, use a rubber spatula to scrape the flour up from the bottom of the bowl several times during mixing as well as from the sides.

Paddle and whip attachments.

Do not overmix the batter. Mix it just until the flour is no longer visible or, if folding egg whites into batter, until only a few streaks of egg white remain.

continued

C

Cake, continued

Filling the Cake Pans When making layer cakes requiring two or more pans, pour equal amounts of batter into each, using a rubber spatula to smooth the surface. To ensure an equal amount of batter in each pan, use a kitchen scale. Weighing each filled pan and evening them out is the only way to end up with perfectly even layers. (Be sure also to account for any difference between the weight of the pans when empty.)

Once the pans are filled with batter, handle them gently. Though some cooks tap them once on the counter to release any large air bubbles, banging them roughly can release too much air from the batter and cause a cake to "fall," or sag in the center.

Baking the Cake Set the pans on the center rack in the preheated oven. Use an oven thermometer to check the accuracy of your oven, and adjust the temperature knob to compensate. If baking more layers than will fit on one oven rack, place the racks as close to the center of the oven as possible.

Do not open the oven door during baking until it's time to check for doneness. A considerable amount of heat escapes every time the oven door is opened. Also, banging an oven door shut can cause a cake to fall. Begin checking 8 to 10 minutes before the cake is supposed to be done.

Cooling the Cake Set the pan on a wire rack and let the cake cool for about 5 minutes. Place the wire rack on top of the cake and carefully invert the cake in its pan.

Inverting the cake pan.

If the pan doesn't lift easily from the cake, give it a slight shake. The cake should fall from the pan.

Removing the pan.

If necessary, before inverting the cake, loosen the sides of the cake with a table knife or tap the bottom of the pan, or both.

Loosening the cake.

Peel the waxed or parchment paper from the bottom of the cake and discard. Let the cake cool completely before frosting and serving. See FROSTING, ICING & GLAZE for more information.

Storing and Freezing Cakes Wrap cooled, unfrosted cakes in plastic wrap, place in an airtight container or under an airtight cake dome, and store at room temperature for up to 2 days.

Store frosted cakes in the same manner as unfrosted cakes unless the frosting contains cream, in which case it should be refrigerated immediately; if it contains butter it should be left at room temperature for no more than 2 hours.

If a cake requires refrigeration, cover it loosely with plastic and refrigerate it for up to 3 days. Let most cakes come to room temperature before serving. To keep the plastic wrap from sitting directly on the frosting, insert evenly spaced toothpicks in the cake and rest the plastic on them.

To freeze cooled, unfrosted cakes, wrap them in freezer-weight plastic and freeze for up to 2 months for foam cakes and others with little fat. Butter cakes, which contain more fat, will keep for 6 months.

To freeze frosted cakes, put the frosted cakes in the freezer until the frosting hardens. Wrap them carefully in freezer-weight plastic and freeze for up to 1 month.

Let frozen cakes, still wrapped, defrost in the refrigerator or at room temperature. When they are partially defrosted, unwrap and let them come to room temperature.

Butter Cake Savvy

- Start with room-temperature ingredients. Eggs should be large, unless otherwise specified.

- When creaming the butter with sugar, start by thoroughly creaming the butter before adding any sugar. Then beat the butter and sugar together well. Be patient: it takes several minutes of beating for the butter and sugar mixture to become light and fluffy. See CREAMING for more details.

- When mixing eggs into the batter, add them one at a time, incorporating each fully to create an emulsion.

- Combine the dry ingredients (flour, salt, baking powder), whisking them 8 to 10 times, before they are mixed with the wet ingredients. This ensures that salt and leavening are evenly distributed in the batter.

- Butter cakes are done baking when the top is lightly browned, the edges begin to pull away from the sides of the pans, and the surface springs back when you press the center with a fingertip. Another test: insert a toothpick, kitchen knife, or cake tester into the center. It should come out clean and dry, or, as some cakes require (check your recipe), with just a few crumbs clinging to the tester, showing that the center remains a bit more moist.

Foam Cake Savvy

- Eggs separate more easily when cold but whip up better when room temperature. Separate the eggs as soon as you take them from the refrigerator, then let the whites sit out in a bowl for about 30 minutes to come to room temperature before beating them. See EGG for instructions on separating eggs.

- If a recipe calls for whisking the eggs or egg whites over hot water, do not let the bottom of the bowl touch the water, or the eggs will cook.

- Be sure to use a spotlessly clean bowl and beaters or whisk for beating egg whites. Any spot of grease or fat (including egg yolk) will prevent the whites from expanding to their full volume.

- Lift the beaters or whisk from the whites and turn them upright to determine the state of their peaks. Soft peaks will gently fall over onto themselves, while stiff, dry peaks will stand straight up.

Soft peaks.

Stiff peaks.

- Overbeating eggs will cause them to clump and look somewhat chalky, and the cake will not rise as successfully.

- Before baking, gently run a kitchen knife or small rubber spatula through the batter to deflate any large air bubbles.

continued

Cake, continued

- A foam cake is done when the top is golden and the cake springs back when gently pressed with a fingertip.
- For more about working with eggs, see EGG; FOLDING.

Cake Blues Got a problem with your cake? Find the explanation here.

BATTER CURDLES AND SEPARATES. Eggs were not added one at a time and beaten thoroughly after each addition; an electric mixer was set at too high a speed; and/or the eggs were too cold. Try adding 1 tablespoon of flour per egg and reducing the speed of the electric mixer.

CAKE DIDN'T RISE. Too much or not enough fat or liquid in the batter; batter was overbeaten; and/or oven temperature was too high.

CAKE IS TOUGH. Butter and sugar were underbeaten in the early stages of mixing; batter was overbeaten after the flour was added; not enough sugar; not enough baking powder; and/or not enough fat. Try brushing cake layers with sugar syrup or filling and frosting cake layers with a generous layer of moist frosting.

CAKE CRUMB IS STICKY. Too much sugar in the batter or sugar was too coarse.

TOP CRUST IS HARD. Oven temperature was too high; cake was overbaked; and/or cake was baked too close to the top of the oven. Try slicing off the top of the cake layer before frosting.

CAKE SINKS IN THE CENTER. Too much fat and/or sugar or leavening; batter was overbeaten; cake pan was too small; the filled cake pan was tapped too roughly on the countertop; the oven door was banged shut; or the oven temperature was too low. Try cutting out the fallen center and treating the cake like a tube cake; or, fill the depression with fruit or extra frosting.

CAKE PEAKS IN THE CENTER. Wrong type of flour was used (contained too much gluten); batter was overbeaten; too little fat and/or sugar in the batter; and/or oven temperature was too high. Try slicing the peaked center off the cake and frosting it.

TUNNELS RUN THROUGH THE CAKE. Not enough fat in the batter; batter was overbeaten; or wrong type of flour was used (contained too much gluten).

CRUST IS UNEVENLY COLORED. Too much leavener and/or sugar in the batter; not enough fat in the batter; oven temperature was too high or too low; oven heats unevenly. Try camouflaging with frosting.

CAKE ROSE UNEVENLY. Cake layers were crowded on the oven rack and heated unevenly. Bake each layer on its own rack. Trim the layers to even them out and camouflage with frosting.

Cake Styles There's a different type of cake to suit every taste. The following are some of the most popular choices:

AMERICAN LAYER CAKE A basic butter cake flavored with whatever suits the baker, from vanilla to coffee to strawberry, and usually frosted.

ANGEL FOOD CAKE Tall, single-layer, butterless white cake leavened with egg whites and baked in a tube pan. Seldom frosted.

CHIFFON CAKE This moist, light American classic falls somewhere between a foam cake (also contains lots of separated eggs) and a butter cake (although it uses oil rather than butter).

DEVIL'S FOOD CAKE Rich chocolate cake made from a mix of acidic and alkaline ingredients that produce a reddish hue.

GÉNOISE A delicate French sponge cake leavened by eggs only. Lends itself to layered and rolled cakes such as jelly rolls.

POUND CAKE Old-fashioned cake usually baked in a loaf pan and rarely frosted. Its name comes from the weight of each ingredient—butter, sugar, eggs, flour—traditionally needed to make one cake.

See also BAKING; BATTER; FLOUR; FROSTING, ICING & GLAZE; UNMOLDING.

CANADIAN BACON Cut from the loin of the hog, and cured but not always smoked, Canadian bacon, also called back bacon, is generally sliced thick. Many people appreciate its mild flavor and lean, meaty texture, which are closer to that of ham than bacon. It is used for eggs Benedict, the popular brunch dish that combines it with English muffins, eggs, and hollandaise sauce. Fully cooked, it can also be baked and fried.

Selecting Canadian bacon is widely sold in butcher shops and most food markets in both whole and presliced pieces.

Storing Canadian bacon should be refrigerated in its original packaging or carefully wrapped in plastic until ready to cook. Sliced Canadian bacon will keep for 3 to 4 days, while unsliced chunks will keep for up to 1 week. The bacon can also be frozen for up to 2 months.

Preparing Panfry Canadian bacon in a little fat over medium-high heat or broil it until lightly browned and fragrant. Drain on paper towels. Depending on the thickness of the slices, cooking can take as few as 3 minutes or as long as 10 minutes.

CANDY MAKING Most candy making involves working with sugar and a thermometer. With a little diligence and understanding, anyone can make toffee, caramel, fudge, and other candies.

The first step is often to make a sugar syrup by heating sugar and water together over high heat. The sugar dissolves easily, and the clear liquid goes through a number of stages as it rises in temperature and the water evaporates, increasing the syrup's concentration. The stages are defined progressively as thread, soft ball, firm ball, hard ball, soft crack, hard crack, light caramel, and dark caramel (see chart, page 86). Those terms refer to the syrup's appearance and behavior, but they are best determined with an accurate candy thermometer, and candy recipes usually specify both the stage and the temperature, such as hard-ball stage and 265°F. The best kind of candy thermometer has a mercury bulb and column mounted on a protective metal casing fitted with a clip that attaches to the side of a pan.

Using a candy thermometer.

While crystallization (the formation of very small crystals, not large ones) is desirable when making fudge or fondant, it should be avoided when making most other candies. In other words, the goal is usually to prevent crystals from forming. Otherwise, the resulting candy will be unpleasantly grainy. A little corn syrup or an acid such as cream of tartar or lemon juice added to the syrup impedes the development of crystals, but the best defense is to let the syrup boil undisturbed without jostling or stirring. Also, when first mixing the sugar and water, use a wooden rather

Caution!

Because the sugar gets very hot, burns can be severe. Always exercise extreme caution when cooking with sugar, protecting your hands and forearms with heavy oven mitts. And always keep a bowl of ice water next to the stove to cool down the bottom of a pan of sugar syrup quickly if it overheats.

than a metal spoon to prevent crystals. Sugar crystals do not adhere as readily to wood as they do to metal. Brushing down the sides of the pan with a pastry brush dipped in hot water as the sugar boils also prevents crystallization.

Sugar Syrup Savvy

■ To test a thermometer for accuracy, bring water to a boil. Submerge the thermometer in the water for 1 or 2 minutes. If it does not register 212°F, adjust the temperature in the recipe accordingly.

■ Before using a thermometer, put it in warm water to raise its temperature a little, particularly if the kitchen or storage drawer is cool.

■ Cook sugar syrup on dry, cool days, if possible. If high humidity cannot be avoided, cook the syrup to the highest temperature for its stage—or even a few degrees higher. As the syrup cools, it will absorb humidity and may soften.

■ Sifting lumpy granulated sugar after measuring will help it dissolve and prevent crystallization.

■ Cooking the syrup in a heavy pan smaller than the burner lets the sides of the pan heat as well as the bottom.

■ Once the sugar dissolves and the syrup boils, do not stir it.

■ Use a clean brush dipped in hot water to brush sugar crystals down the sides of the pan into the syrup as it cooks.

■ Soak pots and other utensils used for cooking sugar in hot tap water soon after use. The water will dissolve the sugar and facilitate washing. To loosen stubborn sugar, boil water in the pot.

■ After removing a thermometer from hot syrup, submerge in hot water for easy cleaning. Cold water may crack it.

Sugar Syrup Stages

STAGE	TEMPERATURE	TEST
Thread	230° to 234°F	Syrup breaks into 1- or 2-inch threads when lifted from the pan and again when dropped into ice water. The threads do not form a ball.
Soft ball	234° to 240°F	When dropped into ice water and rolled between the fingers, the syrup forms a soft ball.
Firm ball	244° to 248°F	When dropped into ice water and rolled between the fingers, the syrup forms a ball that holds its shape.
Hard ball	250° to 265°F	When dropped into ice water and rolled between the fingers, the syrup forms a ball that holds its shape and also offers resistance when lightly squeezed.
Soft crack	270° to 290°F	When dropped into ice water, the syrup can be stretched into flexible strands.
Hard crack	300° to 310°F	When dropped into ice water, the syrup forms a mass that can be easily broken into two or three pieces.
Light caramel	320° to 338°F	When poured onto marble or a white dish, the syrup looks clear amber.
Dark caramel	350°F	The syrup turns dark brown or caramel color.

Checking the Stage Using a candy thermometer is the only foolproof way to determine when the syrup has reached a desired stage. However, the time-honored method used by many cooks is to drop a little of the syrup in ice water and then to try rolling it between the fingers to judge its stage by its appearance.

Caution!

Never touch hot syrup directly, as it will burn you badly!

Thread stage.

Soft ball stage.

Hard ball stage.

Soft crack stage.

Hard crack stage.

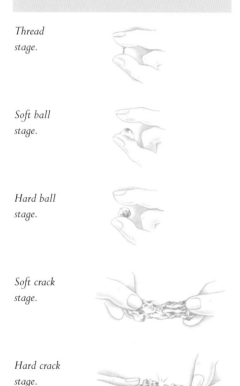

Take care: a sugar syrup will continue cooking off the heat, and when cooked beyond the dark caramel stage, 350°F, it burns and will taste bitter.

See also CARAMELIZING; CHOCOLATE.

CANNELLINI See BEAN, DRIED.

CAN OPENER See COOKING TOOLS.

CANTALOUPE See MELON.

CAPER The small unopened flower buds of a shrub native to the Mediterranean, capers are unpleasantly bitter when raw. Once dried and packed in brine or salt, however, they add a pleasantly pungent flavor and a light crunch to meat, fish, and egg dishes and to various sauces. The smallest capers, called nonpareils, are from Provence, in southern France, and many culinary authorities consider them to be the finest capers. But how these edible flower buds are treated has more to do with their quality than does their size. If large pea-sized capers are packed in a mild brine or properly salted, they can add delicious flavor to any number of dishes.

Selecting Capers are usually sold in a vinegar brine and sealed in glass jars. Salted capers are harder to find, but they are usually carried in well-stocked Italian markets in bulk or in jars. Try a few brands before deciding which one you prefer.

Quick Bite

Caper berries are the fruit of the same shrub that produces capers. Popular throughout southern Europe, they are now finding their way into shops beyond the Continent. Olive shaped and with long stems, they are pickled or salted and, like capers, must be rinsed. They are especially delicious with firm, full-flavored cheeses.

Storing Unopened capers will keep for up to 1 year in a cool, dark cupboard. Once opened, they should be refrigerated, still covered with brine, and used within 9 months. Salted capers, packed in an airtight container, can be stored at room temperature for 6 months.

Preparing For capers in brine, drain them before using and gently blot dry with paper towels. For salted capers, thoroughly rinse and drain them. Blot them dry and taste them to be sure you have rinsed them enough to your taste. Do not soak them or they will lose flavor. Large capers may require chopping.

Quick Tip

Capers keep a long time, so if you spot a forgotten half-empty jar on your refrigerator shelf, consider pulling it out, taste-testing one, and using the capers to enliven sliced tomatoes, tuna salad, or stuffed eggs.

CARAMELIZING To heat sugar until it turns light to dark brown, or to cook other foods until natural sugars in them caramelize. Sugar becomes less purely sweet and develops a more complex flavor as it caramelizes. Sugar is considered caramelized when it registers between 320° and 350°F on a candy thermometer.

Caramelizing can be done in two ways: the sugar can be dissolved in water to make liquid syrup, or it can be sprinkled in a heavy pan and heated over a high flame. White or brown sugar, sprinkled over food and then heated under a broiler, is considered caramelized when it melts and darkens to form a crunchy, sweet crust, such as the topping on classic crème brûlée. (In restaurants, the sugar is caramelized with a standard-sized butane torch; home cooks can use miniature versions.) Caramelized sugar often lines serving dishes or custard cups for flan or crème caramel, too. Finally, when a mixture of sugar, corn syrup, and cream is caramelized to the soft-ball stage on a candy thermometer, and then butter and vanilla are added, you have cooked up a batch of chewy tan caramels.

Caution!

As with any sugar cooking, use great caution when caramelizing sugar, as any burns can be serious. Handle pans and utensils with heavy pot holders to avoid injury. Keep a bowl of ice water next to the stove to cool down the pan bottom quickly if the sugar syrup overheats.

HOW TO *Caramelize Sugar*

1. Put 2 parts granulated sugar to 1 part water in a heavy saucepan with a light-colored interior that lets you judge the color of the caramel. Enameled cast iron is a good choice.
2. Set the pan over medium-high heat and cook the mixture, shaking or tilting the pan in a circular motion, until the sugar dissolves.
3. Watching carefully and shaking or tilting the pan in a circle from time to time, bring the mixture to a boil and boil until the syrup begins to turn amber, about 3 minutes; the color will continue to darken slightly. Do not let it turn dark brown, or it will taste burned.
4. Immediately remove the pan from heat and use the caramel, as it thickens quickly. If necessary, remelt over low heat. Take care, as both caramel and pan will be very hot.

Other foods, such as onions, beets, and carrots, can be "caramelized" by cooking for a long time in a moderate oven or over medium-high to high heat so that their natural sugars, which caramelize during cooking, are accentuated. While this type of caramelizing is not precisely the same thing as caramelizing granulated cane sugar, it refers to a cooking method that emphasizes the sugar naturally occurring in many foods

C

that are not ordinarily considered sweet. Although not always necessary, some cooks encourage caramelizing by sprinkling on a little extra sugar. This has become a popular way to prepare vegetables, particularly in recent years.

"Caramelized" is also used to refer to the darkened, flavorful drippings left on the bottom of a roasting pan after roasting meats and poultry.

See also CANDY MAKING; DEGLAZING; SUGAR.

CARAWAY SEED See SPICE.

CARDAMOM See SPICE.

CARROT Moms have long told kids that eating carrots guarantees good eyesight, so it is not surprising that nearly every kitchen has a few of these healthful root vegetables in the refrigerator bin. They turn up raw in lunch boxes and cooked in soups, stews, braises, salads, stir-fries, and vegetable side dishes. A favorite role is in moist carrot cake topped with cream cheese frosting. Another popular role—and one that is especially good for you—is bright orange carrot juice. Small carrots, already trimmed and peeled and packaged in 8- or 16-ounce plastic bags, have become popular as a quick and easy snack food.

Quick Tip

Carrots that have become slightly limp from overlong storage can be revived by a refreshing 30-minute soak in ice water.

Carrots, which are members of the parsley family, are among the least expensive of all vegetables. They are a good source of vitamin A, which actually accumulates during the months of storage after the carrots have been harvested. Their sweetness intensifies, too, during storage. Only beets have a higher sugar content among root vegetables.

Quick Tip

Carrot juice is deliciously sweet and refreshing and packs a wallop of vitamins and other nutrients. It attracts bacteria and so should never be stored for more than a day—unlike whole carrots. For the best taste and benefits, drink it immediately after juicing.

Selecting Look for smooth, firm, brightly colored carrots without cracks or any green, whitening, or sprouting around the stems. Larger carrots tend to have woody cores; baby carrots are tender but not especially sweet. Smaller, slender, mature carrots are the tastiest. Those with the feathery greens still attached, indicating freshness, generally are more expensive. They are not necessarily a better buy, however. The greens draw moisture and nutrients from the orange carrot roots and should be removed and discarded as soon as you get the carrots home (in many markets, the greengrocer will chop off the greens for you). Already trimmed carrots can be just as flavorful as those with their tops attached.

Storing Store carrots in plastic bags in the refrigerator for up to 2 weeks. They like both cool temperatures and high humidity. Do not store carrots near fruit such as bananas or apples, which emit ethylene gas and can give carrots a bitter flavor.

Preparing Trim off the root and stem ends. If the carrots are organic and on the small side, simply scrub them under cold running water with a soft vegetable brush and use without peeling, since many nutrients will be lost if the peel is removed. If the carrots are not grown organically, peel them and trim at least an inch from the stem end, where pesticides concentrate. If the carrots have a woody core, remove it by halving the carrots lengthwise and cutting out the center with a small sharp knife.

See also STEAMING.

CARVING The art of removing meat or poultry from the bone and cutting it into attractive, serving-sized pieces. While some people are better at carving than others—and everyone improves with practice—performing this necessary task should not intimidate anyone. A good-quality sharp knife and a degree of confidence (as well as a healthy appetite!) facilitate carving as nothing else does.

A two-pronged carving fork to steady the roast is also very helpful.

Carving knife and fork.

While an all-purpose slicing knife may be used for carving any type of roast, different knives are better suited to some roasts than to others. One with a long, flexible, but still sturdy blade is best for following the contours of a large turkey. A shorter, sturdier knife makes quick work of the smaller chicken. Long, straight blades with scalloped sides cut more readily through red meats. Whatever knife you use,

make sure it is well sharpened for easier, safer carving. A sturdy, slip-resistant carving board also facilitates the process by keeping the meat firmly in place.

Before carving roasted meat or poultry, let the roast rest, that is, sit at room temperature, for 10 to 25 minutes, depending on its size. This allows the juices time to settle and permits the internal temperature to stabilize. Some cooks suggest tenting a piece of aluminum foil over the meat to hold in the heat a bit, but this is generally ineffective unless the kitchen is very cold. It may also turn crispy poultry skin irretrievably soggy. Roasts are not meant to be served piping hot. Steaks, too, should be allowed to sit for 5 to 10 minutes before being sliced.

Carving board.

Meat should be carved across the grain. This produces a more handsome slice and avoids long strands of tough meat that can lodge in one's teeth. Also, the tougher the meat to be carved, the thinner the slice should be, again for ease of chewing. Finally, do not change the direction of the knife blade in midslice, or the pieces will be ragged and uneven.

Carve only the meat that will be consumed at the meal. The leftover meat will stay juicier if it remains uncarved. Once carved, the meat should be arranged attractively on a platter, usually in evenly overlapping slices, or placed directly on individual plates.

HOW TO *Carve a Turkey*

Generous in size, a turkey offers each diner an ample amount of dark leg meat and white breast meat. Carve only as much as you need to serve at one time, completing one side before starting the next.

1. With the turkey breast up, cut through the skin between leg and breast. Move the leg to locate the thigh joint, then cut through the joint to sever the leg. In the same way, remove the wing, cutting through the shoulder joint where it meets the breast.

2. Cut through the joint to separate the drumstick and thigh. Carve both the drumstick and thigh, cutting thin slices parallel to the bone.

3. Just above the thigh and shoulder joints, carve a deep horizontal cut toward the bone, creating a base cut on one side of the breast. Starting near the breastbone, carve thin slices of breast meat vertically, cutting parallel to the rib cage and ending at the base cut.

HOW TO *Carve a Chicken*

The basics of carving a chicken are similar to those for turkey. But because of the bird's smaller size, the drumstick and the thigh can be served whole and, depending on the number of mouths to feed, the entire chicken may be carved at once.

1. With the chicken breast up, cut through the skin between thigh and breast. Move the leg to locate the thigh joint, then cut through the joint to sever the leg. In the same way, remove the wing, cutting through the shoulder joint where it meets the breast.

2. If the chicken is small, serve the whole leg as an individual portion. If it is larger, cut through the joint to separate the drumstick and thigh into 2 pieces. You may want to slice a large thigh into 2 pieces.

3. Starting at the breastbone, cut downward and parallel to the rib cage, cutting the meat into long, thin slices.

HOW TO *Carve a Bone-in Ham*

Whether you are carving a whole ham or a butt or shank end, the carving process is basically the same: cutting parallel slices perpendicular to the bone, which are then freed by cutting along the bone.

1. Starting at the widest end of the ham, cut a vertical slice about ¼ inch thick and perpendicular to the bone. The slice will remain attached to the ham.

2. Continue making cuts of the same width and parallel to the first, cutting as many slices as you wish to serve.

3. Free the slices from the bone: cut horizontally through the base of the slices, with the knife blade parallel to the bone. When all the meat has been removed from the first side, turn the ham over and repeat on the second side.

HOW TO *Carve a Boneless Roast or Ham*

1. Set the roast on end, leaving the twine in place to hold the roast together. Remove the twine as you reach it.
2. Hold the roast steady by inserting the fork below where you are slicing. Cut horizontal slices ¼ to ½ inch thick; arrange on a platter.
3. For a smaller roast, set the roast on its side and make vertical slices.

HOW TO *Carve a Prime Rib of Beef*

A prime rib of beef is fairly simple to carve, provided you have a long, sharp knife and a sturdy fork to steady the roast. You may wish to leave some slices attached to the ribs, for anyone who likes gnawing the meat on the bone.

1. Place the roast bone side down and steady it by inserting a carving fork. Using a long, sharp, sturdy blade, cut a vertical slice across the grain from one end of the roast down to the rib bone, much like slicing a loaf of bread. Then, holding the knife parallel with the rib bones, cut along the bone to free the slice.

2. Cutting parallel to the first slice, continue to carve ¼- to ¾-inch-thick slices. As individual rib bones are exposed, cut between them and the meat to remove them, or leave them attached to meat slices if preferred.

HOW TO *Carve a Leg of Lamb*

Shaped like an irregular, elongated pear, a leg of lamb presents a challenge. The keys to successful carving lie in cutting parallel to the bone and providing guests with slices from both sides of the leg.

Before cooking a bone-in leg of lamb, be sure to ask the butcher to remove the hip bone, to save you work.

1. Firmly grasp the protruding end of the shank bone with a kitchen towel and tilt it slightly upward. Using a long, sharp knife, carve a first slice from the rounded, meaty side of the leg at its widest point, cutting away from you and roughly parallel to the bone.

2. Cutting parallel to the first slice, continue carving the meat in thin slices until you have as many slices as you need.

3. Grasping the bone, rotate the leg of lamb to expose its other, flatter side—the inner side of the leg, which is slightly more tender. Still cutting parallel to the bone, carve slices.

CASHEW See NUT.

CASSEROLE The casserole, a savory baked dish that mixes two or more ingredients and can be eaten with a fork alone, is an American culinary standard—a preparation that gained popularity with busy cooks in the 1950s and has never lost its appeal. The same term is used for the deep oven-proof dish in which the food is cooked. Such dishes often have lids and may be round, oval, rectangular, or square. They can be made from any number of materials, ranging from tempered glass to earthenware to porcelain to stoneware to enameled cast iron. A popular material for casserole dishes is the familiar heat-resistant glass that is often referred to by its trade-marked name: Pyrex.

Quick Tip

Casseroles are soft and often creamy and therefore may be complemented well by a crunchy topping. A mixture of buttered bread crumbs and grated Parmesan cheese sprinkled over the top and allowed to brown during the final minutes of baking adds texture.

Noodles and rice are common casserole ingredients and are often combined with a creamy, thick sauce. Classic casseroles include tuna noodle and macaroni and cheese. Lasagne is also a casserole. These and many other dishes are baked in casserole dishes that can go directly from the oven to the table for serving.

Casseroles are great favorites with cooks who like or need to plan ahead, since many freeze well. They should be cooked thoroughly, allowed to cool just to room temperature, covered with foil or the casserole lid, and frozen. Most can be reheated directly from the freezer in a moderate (350°F) oven for about an hour, or until bubbling hot. If you want to brown the top, uncover the dish during the final 10 to 15 minutes of cooking.

Many baking dishes can be used for cooking casseroles. Most casserole dishes are relatively deep and have handles or lips and a noticeable heft to them. The most popular sizes hold from 2½ to 5 quarts, although some dishes hold as little as 1½ quarts, while others hold up to 7 quarts.

All casserole dishes are oven safe, but not all are meant to be used on top of the stove. Make sure you know which are flame resistant, either by reading the tags when you buy them or by using common sense: pottery casseroles usually are not meant for stove-top cooking, while shock- and heat-resistant glass ones, such as Pyrex, are. Many casserole dishes, particularly those made by large commercial companies, can go directly from the refrigerator or freezer into a hot oven without cracking. These are usually dishwasher safe, too. Those made by artisan potters tend to be more fragile.

See also COOKWARE.

CAULIFLOWER Mark Twain once described cauliflower as "cabbage with a college education." A member of the cabbage family, cauliflower is akin to broccoli, which it closely resembles.

Firm, compact, creamy white florets form a head, which is the primary edible portion of the cauliflower. The inner leaves are edible, too, and taste somewhat like collard greens. Unfortunately, they are rarely sold with the cauliflower, and even the green leaves near the stem end are usually removed. If you grow cauliflower, don't discard the leaves.

Cauliflower has a mild flavor that marries nicely with cheese and with vegetables such as green beans and carrots. It can be cooked and then puréed for soup. The florets are also good raw or blanched in salads or served on a crudité platter.

Quick Tip

Adding a few drops of lemon juice or a little milk to the cooking water helps cauliflower retain its creamy white color. As with cabbage, there is no way to prevent an odor's emanating from the cauliflower during cooking. Cut cauliflower into small florets, cook them quickly, and turn on exhaust fans and open windows to disperse any odor.

Selecting Cauliflower is in season in the fall, although it is available throughout most of the winter. Look for firm, tight heads without bruises or brown spots, with evenly colored ivory or cream florets. A few varieties of cauliflower have a green or purple tinge, which is natural and does not change the taste. If any leaves remain, they should be green and fresh looking. Avoid cauliflower with loosely packed or spreading florets. It is acceptable if a few green shoots are showing among the florets, or if the florets look a little grainy or bristly.

Storing Store cauliflower in a loose, perforated plastic bag in the refrigerator for up to 1 week. If you do not use the entire head, plan to eat the remaining florets within a day. Or, you may freeze them, first blanching them in lightly salted water for about 3 minutes, draining, and then putting them in rigid containers or plastic bags in the freezer for up to 1 year. Once cooked, cauliflower keeps for only 1 or 2 days in the refrigerator.

Preparing Remove any leaves from the stem end of the head, separate the head into florets, and rinse under cold running water. Trim off any brown spots. Cauliflower can be cooked whole as well and the florets separated after cooking. Steam or boil cauliflower until tender and toss with a little butter or lemon juice, or other vegetables, before serving.

See also BOILING; STEAMING.

CAVIAR Nearly synonymous with elegance, fresh, icy-cold caviar is one of history's most enduring luxuries. It is the roe (eggs) of various members of the sturgeon family, and although the roe of other fish such as salmon, whitefish, trout, and lumpfish also are sold under the name, they are not "true" caviar.

The best and most expensive caviar is from the three types of sturgeon that swim in the Caspian Sea and its tributaries: beluga, osetra, and sevruga. American sturgeon, most of which are farmed in California, also produce good caviar. Another good-quality caviar, called kaluga, is exported from China.

Beluga, considered the finest, has the largest grains, ranging from light gray to inky black. The grains have a firm, crisp texture and a clean, fresh, pleasingly salty flavor. Some caviar lovers prefer osetra. It has a bolder, nuttier flavor, and the grains, which may be quite small, can be inky or very pale. The grains of sevruga caviar are

Quick Bite

The "caviar" sold at room temperature in vacuum-packed jars is not true caviar but rather less-desirable lumpfish roe that has been dyed black, gray, or red. Many people use it for hors d'oeuvres.

smaller and saltier than those of beluga or osetra. Many prefer sevruga's more pronounced flavor, and of the three classic caviars, it is the least costly.

Selecting Buy caviar from a reputable merchant in a shop with good turnover. It should be fresh packed in jars or tins that are stored at temperatures between 28° and 31°F. The eggs should be plump and whole and covered with a sheen of oil but not drenched in it. They should be light to dark gray (almost black), depending on the variety. Ideally, these grains pop when pressed against the roof of your mouth with your tongue, releasing their light, intoxicating flavor. Choose caviar labeled *malossol,* Russian for "lightly salted." When the tin or jar is opened, the grains should smell only slightly fishy or of the sea. Some manufacturers pasteurize the caviar to extend its shelf life, although aficionados avoid this, dismissing the resulting slightly softer texture and diminished flavor.

Storing A good caviar merchant will pack your purchase in an insulated bag for transportation home. Even so, do not make any stops. Store the caviar in the coldest part of the refrigerator, which is usually at the back of the bottom shelf or in a meat drawer. If it is already opened, serve the caviar within 24 hours. If not, it will keep in the refrigerator for up to 2 weeks.

Quick Tip

Although some people who indulge in caviar may have been born with silver spoons in their mouths, silver and caviar do not mix. The silver interacts with the caviar grains, giving them a metallic taste. Serve this delicacy with mother-of-pearl or bone caviar paddles, antique ivory spoons, or gold spoons. Small plastic spoons are fine, too.

Preparing The traditional way to serve caviar is ice cold, scooped straight from the tin or jar into a bowl on a bed of shaved ice. Many caviar lovers like it simple—no adornments—but others pair it with such accompaniments as thin toast points, chopped hard-boiled eggs, crème fraîche, sour cream, lemon slices, and chopped onions. Caviar also marries well with potatoes, blinis, and eggs. Chilled Champagne or vodka is a good partner.

CAYENNE PEPPER See SPICE.

CECI BEAN See BEAN, DRIED.

CELERIAC See CELERY ROOT.

CELERY This bland yet satisfyingly crunchy vegetable is so commonplace, we seldom think of it when pondering the vegetable kingdom. Yet nearly every refrigerator contains a head, and countless recipes list celery as an ingredient. Everyday celery is Pascal celery. A northern European variety of white celery (also called golden celery) is sometimes grown under cover to keep it from turning green. It is far rarer than Pascal celery.

A head of celery consists of several pale or darker green leafy ribs attached at a lighter-colored base. The inner section of this base is the celery heart, the tender, light-colored ribs in the center of the head, prized as an ingredient in some salads and braised dishes. These ribs are smaller than the outer ribs, but they are not always significantly smaller.

Celery is frequently matched with onions and carrots as the base for soups, stews, casseroles, and other savory dishes. Its mild flavor easily blends with others and its crispness disappears during cooking. The ribs can be served raw, either plain or filled with soft cheese or peanut butter, or chopped and added to tuna or chicken salads.

Celery hearts.

Selecting Buy firm, crisp heads with few blemishes and healthy-looking green leaves. Pass on any heads with ribs that do not look as though they will snap decisively when broken. Some heads are trimmed of leaves and bagged in plastic; these may be called "celery hearts," although they also include a good portion of the ribs.

Storing Refrigerate whole heads of celery in a perforated plastic bag in the vegetable crisper for up to 2 weeks.

Preparing Separate the ribs from the head only as needed. Wash them thoroughly under cold running water and trim off both ends. With few exceptions, new celery varieties have eliminated the need for

Quick Bite

Mirepoix, a classic French mixture of diced onions, carrots, and celery, flavors stocks, stews, and sauces and serves as a bed for roasting meat. Once they have given up all their flavor, the vegetables are generally strained from the stock or sauce.

removing strings from the ribs. Refresh slightly tired celery ribs with a 30-minute soak in ice water.

CELERY ROOT If you have ever ordered *céleri-rave rémoulade* in a Paris bistro, you will have tried this tough-looking vegetable in one of its most sophisticated guises: julienned raw and tossed with mustard mayonnaise. Also called celeriac, celery knob, or turnip-rooted celery, celery root is the root of a celery plant (not the same variety that produces the familiar supermarket celery bunches) grown specifically for its root, although both the leaves and stalks are edible. The gnarled, knobby brown root bulb may look impenetrable, but once the outside is peeled, the tender ivory flesh is delicious either raw (usually shredded in salads) or cooked. Celery root tastes similar to common celery but has a more pronounced nutty, earthy flavor and a softer, denser texture. Boil it as you would a potato, then mash; add it to stews or soups; or chop or shred it raw and add it to salads.

Selecting Buy firm, medium-sized roots, about the size of small grapefruits, that feel heavy for their size and are free of bruising and soft spots. Tangled root ends are acceptable, as are any green stalks growing from the top. Celery root is available from early fall through early spring.

Storing Trim any greenery and root ends from the celery root and store the unwashed roots in a perforated plastic bag in the vegetable crisper of the refrigerator for 3 to 5 days.

Preparing Scrub the celery root with a stiff bristle brush under cold running water. Trim the root further if it appears tough or particularly fibrous and then use a vegetable peeler or small, sharp knife to peel the brown skin. Immediately sprinkle the root with lemon juice to prevent discoloring. For cooking, cut, chop, or shred the root using a knife, food processor, or shredder.

CELERY SEED See SPICE.

CHANTERELLE See MUSHROOM.

CHARBROIL To broil meat or poultry over charcoal to the point where its surface begins to turn black and char.

CHAYOTE (chy-OH-tee) Also called vegetable pear, mirliton, or christophine. A soft-skinned, large, pear-shaped squash with light green or white skin and pronounced ridges running from top to stem end. The skin is not edible, and while many preparations suggest discarding the large, flat seed, it is perfectly edible in smaller, younger chayotes and can be cooked along with the chayote and eaten as a snack. The chayote has a somewhat mild flavor, not unlike zucchini, and is popular in Mexico and Central America, where it is indigenous. The flesh is cut into pieces and steamed, boiled, baked, or braised. Chayotes can also be split and cooked like a squash, or the flesh can be eaten raw in salads.

Selecting Buy firm, heavy-feeling chayotes with healthy-looking skin. Avoid those with soft spots or wrinkling, which indicate age. They should also look clean, with no trace of soil. Soft bristles on the skin are acceptable.

Storing Store in a perforated plastic bag in the refrigerator for up to 2 weeks.

Preparing Wash the chayote under cold running water. Like a potato's, a chayote's skin can be cut away before cooking or slipped off the vegetable after cooking, depending on what makes the most sense for a recipe. If a slimy substance escaping from the skin of the uncooked vegetable irritates your skin, peel the chayote under running water. (This is a common irritant, not harmful, and it disappears during cooking.) Discard the skin and single seed, unless you decide to cook it. You can also cut the flesh into pieces and steam, boil, bake, or braise it as you would zucchini or summer squash.

CHEDDAR See CHEESE.

CHEESE See page 100.

CHEESECAKE Most home bakers appreciate cheesecake for two reasons: it lends itself to advance preparation, and it generally gets rave reviews. This classic indulgence is irresistible to nearly everyone, even the most dedicated dieter.

American-style cheesecakes, commonly made with cream cheese, are so satiny smooth they melt in your mouth. Italian-style cheesecakes, made from lightly grained cheese (usually ricotta) mixed with flour, have drier textures but make equally impressive desserts.

Fillings Cheesecakes can be either sweet or savory. While they traditionally are made with cream cheese or ricotta, they can also include cottage cheese, Cheddar cheese, Swiss cheese, and farmer cheese. The cheese is blended with eggs, sugar or another sweetener (for sweet cheesecakes), and flavorings, poured into a pan, and baked. Flour and cornstarch are common thickeners, although too much cornstarch, in particular, will toughen the cake. Cream, sour cream, or yogurt adds smoothness and lightens the texture while adding richness. Chocolate is a popular flavor addition, but other crowd pleasers are ginger, citrus zest, espresso powder, chopped nuts, nutmeg, cinnamon, raisins, extracts, and candied fruit. Fruit and chocolate glazes are favorite toppings.

Unbaked cheesecakes generally rely on gelatin to stabilize them. Follow the recipe carefully and never use more than is called for, or the cake will be rubbery.

Crusts Cheesecake crusts typically are crumb crusts made with graham crackers, crumbled chocolate wafers, gingersnaps, or soda crackers. Other ingredients such as nuts, coconut, or citrus zest may be added to the crumbs to enhance the taste or texture. Cheesecakes also may be baked in traditional pastry crusts or shortcake crusts, or they can be baked without a crust in a buttered pan.

HOW TO *Form a Crumb Crust*
1. Put the crust ingredients in a food processor fitted with the metal blade. Process until the mixture forms fine crumbs that begin to stick together.
2. Drape plastic wrap over your hand to form a glove and press the crumb mixture firmly and evenly into a springform pan or other pan as directed in the recipe.

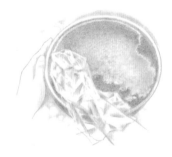

3. If directed, bake the crust for about 10 minutes to firm it up. Let the crust cool before filling it.

Cheesecake Savvy

- Beginning with all ingredients at room temperature ensures the creamiest, most easily blended batter.
- Before you start to mix the ingredients, beat the cream cheese by itself until it is completely free of lumps, light, and smooth. Trying to rid the batter of lumps later won't be successful.
- For perfect creaminess, never overbake a cheesecake. Baking the cheesecake in a water bath will help. (See WATER BATH.) If using a springform pan, wrap it in aluminum foil before placing it in the water, to avoid seepage.
- Take the cheesecake from the oven when the center still quivers; it will continue to cook outside the oven and will firm up. Overbaked cheesecakes will crack as they cool.
- To unmold a crustless cheesecake baked in a solid pan, run a flexible knife around the inside edge of the pan when the cake is taken from the oven, and then let the cake cool completely. Unmold the cake by putting a flat platter or plate over the pan and inverting it. Shake very gently or tap the bottom of the pan to release the cheesecake. If it is still reluctant to unmold, put the pan over a low flame or in a heated cast-iron frying pan for a few seconds and try again. To avoid this problem, bake cheesecakes in a springform pan. (See BAKEWARE.)
- To freeze a cheesecake, let cool completely in the pan, chill in the refrigerator for several hours, then carefully wrap the cheesecake, still in the pan, with freezer-weight plastic and freeze for up to 3 months. Thaw in the refrigerator and, when it is still very cold, release the sides of the pan or unmold the cake. Bring the cheesecake to room temperature before serving.

Quick Tip

While most cheesecakes are eaten cold, Italian-style cheesecakes based on ricotta are also delicious warm. Let them cool for about 20 minutes before slicing and serving; briefly reheat leftover slices in a low oven.

CHEESECLOTH Also called butter muslin, cheesecloth is lightweight, 100 percent cotton gauze, free of dyes and finishes. It is primarily used for straining and filtering, as it does not fall apart when wet or submerged in boiling water and never imparts any flavor to the food.

Cheesecloth is perhaps best known as the material used to hold the herbs for a bouquet garni or any bundle of herbs or spices. It is useful for holding a whole fish, such as salmon, during poaching. Cheesecloth is also employed for straining stocks, sauces, and jellies and for draining the whey from curds in fresh cheeses (hence its name) and the excess liquid from yogurt. Some cooks soak cheesecloth in melted butter or oil and drape it over turkey or chicken during roasting to add fat and flavor and promote browning.

Fine-mesh cheesecloth, preferred for jelly making and other fine straining needs, is generally found in kitchenware shops. Standard coarse-mesh cheesecloth is sold with other kitchen equipment in supermarkets, general houseware stores, and hardware stores, and while it is suitable for making bundles of herbs and poaching fish, it may be too coarse for straining fine liquids such as consommé or fruit jelly. Many sauce recipes recommend using a double layer of coarse-mesh cheesecloth to imitate a finer mesh. Handy cheesecloth bags for herbs are sold in many specialty-food stores, too, although making your own from hand-cut squares is less costly.

Cheese

Hundreds of cheeses with unique tastes and textures are enjoyed throughout the world, but they are all created from the same basic ingredients and by the same basic process.

The fresh or pasteurized milk of cows, sheep, or goats is first treated with enzymes, such as rennet, to separate it into creamy curds and watery whey, and then the curds are concentrated by various methods. The nuances of each unique cheese develop from the most minute variations in what the animals eat, the time of year the cheese is made, the method used to make the cheese, and how and where the cheese makers store and age the cheese.

Jack, mozzarella, and Swiss cheeses.

Cheeses can be divided into two basic categories: fresh and ripened (aged). Most fresh cheeses are simply curds separated from and drained of their watery whey, while ripened cheeses undergo aging to develop an infinite variety of textures and complex flavors. The longer a cheese ages, the drier and more flavorful it becomes. The same cheese may be eaten when young and soft or later after it is transformed by aging and drying. Fresh and ripened are, however, only the two most basic categories. Cheeses are grouped by a number of distinctive qualities, and these categories overlap in many cases.

Fresh Cheeses Very mild and soft, unripened fresh cheeses are used often in desserts and in some main-course recipes, breakfast dishes, and sandwiches. Some have a slightly acidic taste.

COTTAGE CHEESE A mild-flavored fresh cheese characterized by large or small curds mixed with a little milk or cream. Also called pot cheese. Unlike creamed, or regular, cottage cheese, dry-curd cottage cheese is not mixed with milk or cream.

CREAM CHEESE A mild, tangy fresh cheese made from whole milk and extra cream. Most commercial brands contain stabilizers and other additives. Cream cheese blends deliciously with other ingredients, such as herbs, chutneys, jellies, chocolate, and fruit. It is the primary ingredient in many cheesecakes and various hors d'oeuvres dips, and bagels are hardly bagels without a generous smear of cream cheese.

Quick Tip

Many baking recipes have been developed using full-fat, block cream cheese such as Philadelphia brand. Do not substitute light, whipped, or natural cream cheese for block cream cheese, and never use fat-free cream cheese in these recipes.

CRÈME FRAÎCHE Not everyone agrees that this cultured cream product is a fresh cheese, although many cheese makers say it is. Its silken texture and pleasing sour, mildly nutty flavor make it similar to sour cream, but sweeter and even more indulgent. See CRÈME FRAÎCHE.

FARMER CHEESE Similar in flavor to cottage cheese but with no curds. Instead, it is pressed into a block that can be sliced.

FROMAGE BLANC A mild fresh cheese made from skim or whole milk, with or without cream added. It is eaten flavored with sugar as a simple dessert and also used in cooking.

MASCARPONE A very soft, rich, smooth fresh Italian cheese made from cream, with a texture reminiscent of sour cream. Sold in plastic tubs.

NEUFCHÂTEL A mild, creamy, spreadable yellow cheese made in Normandy, France. In the United States, low-fat cream cheese is often called Neufchâtel and is used in recipes that attempt to cut calories and fat.

PROVOLONE Most commonly made from cow's milk, provolone is sold when young and mild and as a sharper, tangier aged cheese. Also available smoked.

QUESO FRESCO A Mexican cow's milk cheese made from fresh curds pressed into round molds. The result is a soft, crumbly, slightly grainy cheese similar in taste to ricotta or farmer cheese.

RICOTTA A whey-based cheese made by heating the whey left over from making sheep's, goat's, or cow's milk cheeses. Most Italian ricotta is made from sheep's milk. It takes no solid form but is sold in plastic containers. Fresh Italian ricotta is superb. See also Ricotta Salata, page 102.

Stretch-Curd Cheeses The mild Italian cheeses in this category, known in Italy as *pasta filata,* are made by immersing the curds in hot water and then kneading and stretching (or "stringing") them. In general, the cheeses melt smoothly over bread, pasta, vegetables, or poultry and also are good for slicing and using in sandwiches.

MOZZARELLA Mild, creamy cheese made from cow's or water buffalo's milk curd formed into balls. It may be salted or not. If possible, seek out fresh mozzarella, which is sold surrounded by a little of the whey, rather than the rubbery products made in large factories.

STRING CHEESE A popular snack food, particularly with children, string cheese is mozzarella cheese that has been pulled into strings, or strands, and then packaged in plastic so that it is shaped like short, fat sticks. It is also called Armenian-style string cheese, rope, or braided cheese. String cheese is rarely, if ever, used in cooking.

Soft-Ripened Cheeses Uncooked and unpressed (that is, the curds are left to firm naturally), these cheeses are aged for a very short time after being transferred to molds. Their texture is usually soft enough to spread, and they have an edible rind that is powdery white or orange in color. Some of the rinds of the stronger-flavored cheeses have been washed in brine, brandy, or even beer to add flavor during aging. Since the flavors of these cheeses are easily lost when heated, they are rarely used in cooking (except for Brie, which is sometimes baked in a pastry or almond crust).

BOURSAULT A rich, nutty French cheese with a creamy texture. Made from pasteurized or unpasteurized cow's milk. Most aficionados prefer the unpasteurized cheese, but it is rare outside Europe.

BRIE A sublimely smooth, ivory cheese with an edible rind, made from cow's milk, pasteurized or unpasteurized (again, rare outside Europe). Brie should be served only when ripe and so soft it is almost—but not quite—runny. It is sold in flat rounds of various sizes.

CAMEMBERT This cow's milk cheese, similar to Brie, has a yellow interior and edible rind. Camembert should be as soft as bread dough when ripe and ready to eat.

continued

Cheese, continued

LIMBURGER A soft, slightly salty, full-flavored cow's milk product with a powerful aroma that dissuades some from trying the tasty cheese. The rind is washed in brine during ripening, which contributes to the development of the cheese's smell.

PONT L'ÉVÊQUE A full-flavored French cow's milk cheese similar to Brie and Camembert but with a stronger flavor. The cheese, with its light brown crust and pale yellow interior, is packed in square wooden boxes.

RICOTTA SALATA A mild, pure white, rindless sheep's milk cheese with a smooth texture and pleasantly sweet flavor. Ricotta salata is most readily associated with Sicily, Sardinia, and the southern part of Italy. The cheese is aged for at least 3 months, although in Sicily it may be aged far longer, until firm and appropriate for grating. It is served in much the same way as feta cheese (rather than as fresh ricotta cheese) or used to top pasta.

TELEME Resembling a tangy Brie and aged for about 3 weeks, this cheese of northern California is made from extra-rich milk.

Semisoft Cheeses Cooked but not pressed, these cheeses are soft but can be sliced. They are ideal for melting on sandwiches and on baked dishes.

HAVARTI An extremely mild cow's milk cheese sold in blocks and without rind, peppered with small indentations. It is as mild as Monterey jack and just as adaptable for sandwiches and melting. Originally from Denmark but now made in the United States and elsewhere.

MONTEREY JACK A soft, white, mild cow's milk cheese that originated in California, either with tiny "eyes" or smooth, depending on where it is made. Jack is often sold infused with hot red chiles and called "pepper jack." A dry version is also made, which was used by West Coast Italian

Americans to replace Parmesan when it was in short supply during World War II.

MUENSTER When made in America, this cheese is very mild and smooth with great melting properties. French Muenster is fuller flavored with an odiferous rind and nutty overtones. German and Danish Muensters (or Münsters) fall between the two in terms of flavor and are formed into rounds, rather than rectangles.

PORT-SALUT A mild French cow's milk cheese with a creamy, yellow interior.

TALEGGIO An aromatic Italian cow's milk cheese with a pale brown rind and ivory interior and a bold, nutty, fruity flavor.

Semifirm (or Semihard) Cheeses These uncooked, pressed, and aged cheeses are dense in texture and ivory to pale yellow in color. They are popular for eating with bread and fruit, for sandwiches, and for cooking, as they melt nicely.

Semifirm cheese with plane.

ASIAGO An Italian cow's milk cheese sold in wheels and, when semifirm, pleasantly sharp tasting and covered with an inedible rind. Also available fresh (mild) and aged (sharper). American Asiago is very mild.

CHEDDAR This cow's milk cheese is appreciated for its sharp, salty flavor, which ranges from mild to sharp. Farmhouse Cheddars are stronger tasting than other American Cheddars.

EDAM Mildly tangy cow's milk cheese with a smooth interior covered with red wax, traditionally produced in the Netherlands in a town of the same name.

EMMENTHALER A cow's milk cheese produced in the mountains of Europe, most notably Switzerland, and distinguished by its random holes, which range in size from small to quite large. Ivory colored and mildly nutty in flavor.

FONTINA A mild, fruity Italian cow's milk cheese with a pleasing firmness and light but heady aroma.

GOUDA A mild cow's milk cheese encased in red wax that is similar to Edam, above, although less tangy. Also made from goat's milk.

GRUYÈRE This smooth, creamy cow's milk cheese is produced in Switzerland and France and revered for its nutty yet mild flavor.

JARLSBERG A cow's milk cheese made from partially skimmed milk and characterized by its hole-filled interior and mild, slightly nutty flavor.

MANCHEGO A Spanish sheep's milk cheese with a mild, pale yellow interior dotted with holes and tasting mild and a little salty.

RACLETTE A sweet, fruity cheese with an inedible rind and pale beige interior. This cheese, produced in Switzerland and France, melts beautifully and is used for the classic Swiss melted cheese and potato dish of the same name.

REBLOCHON Very smooth, sweet, fruity French cheese sold formed into disks and sandwiched between two paper-thin wooden rounds. Reblochon is made with pasteurized or unpasteurized milk, the latter difficult to find outside of France.

SWISS A generic term for a variety of cheeses typified by Switzerland's Emmenthaler, above. Swiss cheeses are noted for their mild, nutlike flavor, semifirm texture, and network of holes or "eyes."

Firm (or Hard) Cheeses These cheeses are cooked, pressed, and aged for a firm, compact texture. Perfect for grating, some have a granular texture and a hard rind. Fine examples of these same cheeses are sometimes enjoyed as part of a cheese course at the end of a meal.

Grating cheese.

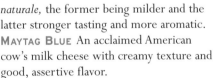

PARMESAN A wonderful grating cheese, Parmesan is an ivory-colored cow's milk cheese with a distinctive, salty flavor. See also PARMESAN.

PECORINO ROMANO A pleasantly salty Italian sheep's milk cheese with a grainy texture. Primarily used for grating.

Blue-Veined Cheeses These cheeses are inoculated with the spores of special molds to develop a fine network of blue veins for a strong, sharp, peppery flavor and a crumbly texture. Most blue cheeses can be crumbled, diced, spread, and sliced. Depending on the cheeses' moisture content, however, some hold their shape when sliced better than do others.

DANISH BLUE A cow's milk cheese with bold, straightforward flavor and smooth, creamy, moist texture.

GORGONZOLA An exceptional cow's milk cheese from Italy with a moist, creamy texture and complex flavor. May be marketed as *dolce* or *naturale,* the former being milder and the latter stronger tasting and more aromatic.

MAYTAG BLUE An acclaimed American cow's milk cheese with creamy texture and good, assertive flavor.

ROQUEFORT A sheep's milk cheese from France with a moist, crumbly interior and true, clean, strong flavor. Some Roqueforts are rather salty.

STILTON A cow's milk cheese from England with firm texture and an assertive flavor.

continued

C

Cheese, continued

Goat's Milk Cheeses Made from pure goat's milk or a blend of goat's and cow's milk. Mild, creamy, and only slightly tangy when fresh, goat cheeses become distinctly sharp in flavor as they age and harden. They are molded in a variety of shapes, such as logs and wheels, and may be coated with dried herbs, leaves, or ash. The French term for goat cheese is *fromage de chèvre,* which is often shortened to "chèvre" (SHEV).

BANON A soft, flavorful, somewhat spicy French goat cheese formed into disks and traditionally wrapped in chestnut leaves. Banons may sometimes be sprinkled with herbs or spices instead.

BÛCHERON Aged French goat's milk cheese sold in logs.

CROTTIN French goat's milk cheese shaped into thick rounds or short logs. Most have soft, mild, pure white interiors of young goat cheese; others are made from stronger, aged goat cheese.

FETA Sometimes made from goat's milk, but more generally from sheep's. See Sheep's Milk Cheeses, below.

MONTRACHET Mild, young French goat's milk cheese sold in logs with bright white interiors and spreadable texture. The term has become a generic designation for any young, fresh goat's milk cheese.

Sheep's Milk Cheeses

FETA A young cheese, traditionally made in Greece, Bulgaria, and Corsica (France) of sheep's milk. It usually has a crumbly texture that, in some cases, may be creamy as well. The pleasant, salty flavor of the white cheese is accentuated by the brine in which the cheese is pickled. American, Australian, Danish, and German feta cheeses are often made from cow's milk but taste very like sheep's milk feta. The cheese may also be made from goat's milk.

Double- and Triple-Cream Cheeses

Cow's milk cheeses with cream added to increase the fat content for an extremely soft, smooth texture and a rich, slightly sweet flavor. By law, double-cream cheeses must have at least 60 percent milk fat, while triple-cream cheeses must have 75 percent or more. They can be either fresh or ripened.

BOURSAULT See Soft-Ripened Cheeses, page 101.

BOURSIN A creamy cheese flavored with herbs or garlic, or both.

BRILLAT-SAVARIN A buttery, very rich and creamy French cheese sent to market while still young and light.

EXPLORATEUR A full-flavored, creamy French cheese with a pale ivory interior and a bloomy edible rind.

PETIT-SUISSE A bright white, fresh French cheese sold in small logs with a very soft texture and sweet-tart flavor. Sometimes sold mixed with fruit.

Selecting A specialized cheese dealer with a rapid turnover will offer the best-quality cheeses. Look for cheeses with uniform color and veining, avoiding any with cracks or color changes near the rind. Although they may smell strong, cheeses should not have a sour or ammoniated odor. Wedges freshly cut from a larger wheel will retain more flavor. Before buying, ask for a small piece to sample. Because cheese stales quickly after grating, buy grating cheese in a single piece and grate it at home. When substituting another cheese for one specified in a recipe, try to use a cheese from the same general category for similar results.

Storing Because of their high moisture content, soft and fresh cheeses do not keep as long as aged firm and semifirm cheeses. Refrigerated, softer cheeses will keep for 1 week to 10 days, while harder ones can be stored for 2 to 4 weeks. Some very hard ones, like Parmesan, will keep for up to 10 months. Wrap cheese first in waxed paper to hold in the moisture and then double wrap it with a tight seal of plastic wrap or aluminum foil.

Preparing Cheese meant to be enjoyed as an appetizer, as a first course, or at the end of a meal is at its best served at room temperature. Remove the cheese from the refrigerator about an hour before serving.

In order to keep it moist and flavorful, grate or shred cheese just before serving or using in a recipe. Perforated metal cheese graters come in a variety of shapes and sizes, from the familiar box grater to the rotary grater. For more details, see GRATING; SHREDDING.

Rotary cheese grater / shredder.

The most popular devices for cutting cheese (other than a knife) are the cheese slicer, fitted with a taut wire that glides through a block of cheese, and the cheese plane or shaver. The plane, with its rounded or triangular blade, has a slot near the handle that has a sharp edge capable of shaving cheese as it is pulled across its surface. This device works well for semifirm cheeses, but should not be used for soft cheeses.

Cheese slicer.

Small cheese cleavers resemble larger butcher cleavers and are good for cutting cheese—and not much more.

The Cheese Course An array of quality cheeses may be served as an elegant alternative to dessert. To highlight a good selection of cheeses, present them simply on a tray, platter, or small marble or wooden cutting board, lining the surface with grape leaves (if you like). Make it easy for guests to help themselves by including appropriate cutting instruments, such as a sharp, broad-bladed knife for hard cheeses, a sharp knife with a pronged tip for semihard cheeses, a blunt-bladed knife for cutting and spreading soft cheese, and a cheese plane for shaving slices from blocks. Provide bread or crackers, fresh fruit (apples, pears, grapes) or dried fruits (apricots, nectarines, dates), and/or nuts, and wine.

Three or four cheeses is adequate. More will confuse the palate. When composing the tray, pick cheeses with contrasting textures and flavors. For example, try pairing Stilton, a mild goat cheese, and Fontina; or serve a wedge of Cheddar, Explorateur, and Gruyère with fresh fruit, slices from a baguette, and some walnuts or pecans. Some classic combinations are Cheddar with apples and Burgundy; Port-Salut with grapes and sweet Riesling; Stilton with pears, walnuts, and Port; and fresh goat cheese with dates. Remember, too, even a single delightful cheese can make a memorable impression.

Quick Bite

Dry natural cheese rinds occur as the cheese air-dries; they are generally not eaten. Soft white rinds, such as that on Brie, are a bloom of white mold; these are edible. Yellow to dark red washed rinds result from the cheese's being washed with one of a variety of liquids; these are not usually eaten. Artificial rinds may be produced from wax, ashes, or leaves and are not eaten.

CHERIMOYA Also known as the custard apple. This large tropical fruit has pale green skin and is slightly flattened and heart shaped. But the most distinctive visual clues to its identity are the overlapping leaf imprints that make the fruit look like an upside-down artichoke. The interior is white and creamy and studded with black seeds. Its texture is like firm custard, and while some say its flavor is a combination of bananas and mangoes, with a hint of strawberries, others declare it reminds them of pineapple. Cherimoyas are ripe when their leathery skin turns a brownish green and they give slightly when gently pressed, much like a peach or an avocado.

Selecting These fruits transport well and usually arrive at the market unripe. Buy firm, heavy cherimoyas with even-colored green skin. Avoid fruit with brown spots, although one or two are acceptable. Cherimoyas are sold in some supermarkets as well as Asian and Latin markets. Their season runs from November through April.

Storing If not yet ripe, let cherimoyas ripen at cool room temperature out of direct sunlight. If ripe, eat the fruit or wrap it in plastic and refrigerate for up to 3 days.

Preparing Cherimoya is best eaten chilled with a spoon. Cut the fruit in half and scoop out the flesh. Discard the seeds. Unless eating immediately, sprinkle a little lemon or lime juice on the flesh to prevent browning. Serve with citrus fruits or heavy cream, or cube and add to fruit salads. Cherimoyas are never cooked. But their tender, fragrant, and flavorful flesh is sometimes puréed for use in refreshing tropical punches or fruit sauces or as an ingredient in frozen desserts.

CHERRY Even if life isn't always just a bowl of cherries, a bowl of cherries can make anybody's life a little sweeter. Perfectly ripe cherries are a nearly unrivaled treat. Their short season is anticipated by all but the most jaded eaters.

Cherries are related to other one-seeded stone fruits, called drupes, most closely to plums, but also to peaches and nectarines. Two primary types exist: sweet and sour (or tart). Sweet cherry varieties include the deep red, plump Bing, the bright red, late-blooming Lambert, and the light-colored Royal Ann. Sour cherries need to be cooked and are usually processed for canned pie filling, preserves, and juice.

Selecting Cherries are harvested when ripe; they do not ripen significantly off the tree. Their season runs from late May to very early August, peaking in June and early July. When buying sweet cherries, make sure they are large, plump, smooth, and dark colored for their variety (golden cherries such as Royal Anns are meant to be pale) and have firm stems. The darker the cherry, the sweeter its flavor. Avoid any that are pale colored (again, for their variety) and rock hard, which indicates immature fruit, or those that are wet, sticky,

Quick Tip

Cherry pits, which should not be eaten, have the flavor of almonds, which explains the fruit's affinity for dishes that include almonds and other nuts. A drop of almond extract added to cherry pie or cobbler filling or to cherry sauce enhances the cherry flavor.

bruised, excessively soft, or have shriveled stems, all signs of age. Cherries with the stems attached are desirable; once the stem is removed, the cherries spoil more rapidly.

Sour cherries are rarely sold fresh. If they are available, however, buy them following the same guidelines as for sweet cherries. Most taste too tart for pleasant eating out of hand, but they are good when sweetened for pies or preserves and other baking or cooking uses. Morello and Montmorency are two well-known varieties.

Quick Bite

Maraschino cherries are made from light-colored or white cherries such as Royal Anns or Rainiers, which are pitted and macerated in sugar syrup to preserve them. The cherries are then dyed red or green (unlike in the past, dyes used nowadays are considered safe) and packed in syrup. They are used as a garnish—the cherry on top of the ice cream sundae or in cocktails such as whiskey sours and old-fashioneds. Maraschino cherries are so named because they once were soaked in maraschino liqueur, a now-rare practice.

Both sweet and sour cherries are available pitted and canned, packed in water or syrup, or frozen. The latter generally have a better texture and taste than canned. Whenever you can, substitute fresh sweet or sour cherries for canned. A pound of fresh cherries can replace a 1-pound can of sour cherries. Once they have been pitted, the fresh cherries will yield the same 2 cups the can holds.

Storing Put fresh cherries in a plastic bag and refrigerate immediately. Eat them within 3 days. Canned cherries will keep for 1 year unopened in a cool, dark cupboard. Once opened, transfer the cherries to a covered glass, plastic, or ceramic container and refrigerate for up to 1 week.

Preparing If using fresh cherries in pies or the like, pit the fruit with a cherry pitter or small, sharp knife.

Pitting with a cherry pitter.

If the recipe calls for canned sour cherries and you wish to use fresh sweet cherries, reduce the amount of sugar and add a little lemon juice to taste. This works very well for cherry pie, cherry sauce for ice cream, or cherry topping for cheesecake.

CHERVIL See HERB.

CHESTNUT See NUT.

CHÈVRE Goat's milk cheese; see CHEESE for information.

CHICKEN Long gone are the days when Sunday dinner meant roast chicken. Everyone still loves a good roasted chicken, but modern cooks are just as likely to skin it, bone it, or cut it into parts, then bake, broil, braise, stir-fry, or grill it.

Chicken forms the perfect canvas for both sweet and spicy flavorings, marrying as successfully with apples, onions, or orange marmalade as with chiles and ginger or tomatoes, garlic, and wine. Its bones make a flavorful stock that can be used as a base for soups, sauces, and gravies.

Chicken Labeling Poultry can be labeled as "fresh" only if it has never been held at temperatures below 26°F. If chicken has been frozen and then thawed for sale, the label will say "previously frozen." Buy

C

fresh chicken when possible. If given a choice between frozen and previously frozen, pick frozen, as chicken deteriorates quickly after thawing.

The terms *natural, free-range,* and *organic* are used to indicate a higher-quality chicken that also costs more in most cases. These terms have specific and different Food and Drug Administration (FDA) definitions and are not synonymous.

Natural is the broadest of these terms and simply means that the chicken contains no artificial ingredients and was minimally processed. It gives no indication of how or where the chicken was raised and may be only a limited indication of quality.

Free-range refers to a chicken that was allowed access to the outside. While this label is designed to invoke the image of a bird that has spent its time pecking and scratching in fresh air and developing meaty, leaner muscles, this is not always the case. Some free-range poultry is decidedly better quality than others, but it is important to judge for yourself rather than just following the label.

The final and most stringent category is *organic.* This means that the chicken producer has undergone a lengthy certification process to prove that the chickens have been raised in free-range conditions, without hormones or antibiotics, and on exclusively organic feed.

Before deciding to spend money for natural, free-range, or organic chicken, talk with the butcher or, if possible, a local chicken farmer at the farmers' market. Ask how the chicken was raised and what it was fed. This kind of knowledge is the best defense against buying mass-produced chicken that is misleadingly sold under the "free-range" or "natural" label.

Selecting Buy Grade A chicken, which is the grade most readily available to consumers. The bird should have even coloring, whether pale yellow or ivory. The color reflects the type of food the chicken was fed. Look for plump birds with well-defined breasts and legs. Press gently on the meat (through the plastic); it should be firm and resilient. Any visible fat should be white to light yellow. The skin should be unbroken, clean, and dry looking. Be sure to buy chicken before the sell-by date, which is a week after the bird was processed. If a chicken smells "off," you probably will be able to detect it even through plastic wrap. If you don't notice anything wrong at the store and the chicken smells bad when you open the package at home, return the poultry to the place where you bought it. If in doubt, do not eat it.

Storing Chicken is highly perishable and a potential haven for salmonella bacteria. Refrigerate raw chicken as soon as possible after purchase. Plan to cook chicken no more than 2 days after purchase, or else freeze it as soon as you get it home.

If you're planning to cook them soon, store chicken parts in the original packaging in the coldest part of the refrigerator, which is usually at the back of the bottom shelf or in a meat drawer. (A refrigerator thermometer will tell you for sure.) If the chicken is leaking, wrap the package in another layer of plastic, slip it into a plastic bag, or place it in a bowl or on a plate.

Chicken freezes well. Unwrap it from its original packaging and rinse the chicken under cool water. Remove any giblets and use within 24 hours. Pat the chicken dry and wrap in freezer-weight plastic or a zippered plastic freezer bag. Freeze for up to 6 months. Thaw the chicken in the refrigerator, which is the safest and surest way to do it. If time is a consideration, thaw plastic-wrapped chicken (or chicken parts) in a bowl of cool water, but tend it carefully and cook it as soon as it is thawed. Leaving thawed chicken at room temperature for any length of time is dangerous. You can also defrost chicken parts in the microwave on a low setting. Watch these carefully, however, to prevent them from cooking on the surface before they are completely thawed, and cook them immediately upon defrosting.

Preparing Trim the chicken or chicken parts of excess fat, skin (if desired), and tough gristle, if any. Wash it (inside the cavity as well, if preparing whole chicken) with cold running water and pat dry. Be sure to wash hands, utensils, and working surfaces in hot, soapy water after working with chicken.

Cutting up a whole chicken or boning a breast or thigh is not as difficult as you might think; see BONING and DISJOINTING. Reserve the bones and trimmings for making stock.

Many recipes call for browning the chicken as the first step. This gives the bird an appealing color, especially if it is going to be braised in liquid afterward. Chicken can also be sautéed, stir-fried, broiled, roasted, grilled, and used in stews, casseroles, and soups and to make stock.

Regardless of how you prepare chicken, be sure to cook it thoroughly. There are a few old-fashioned tests for determining when it is done: cook until the meat is no longer pink at the bone, the juices run clear when a thigh is pierced with a knife, or the breast meat is opaque throughout. The best way to determine doneness, however, is to insert an instant-read thermometer into the thickest part of the thigh, making sure it doesn't touch the bone.

Doneness Temperatures for Chicken

Thigh	165° to 175°F
Breast	150° to 160°F*

Although these temperatures yield what many cooks feel are the optimum taste and texture for breast meat, a temperature of less than 160°F is lower than that suggested by the U.S. Food Safety and Inspection Service guidelines; see Chicken Safety, below, and DONENESS.

Chicken Safety It's important to handle chicken—and all poultry—safely. Raw chicken may harbor bacteria such as salmonella that can make a healthy adult very ill and may kill small children, elderly people, or anyone with a compromised immune system. Safe handling means:

■ When preparing raw chicken, use a cutting board reserved only for flesh foods.

■ Make sure no raw chicken or chicken juice comes in contact with other food. Wash the countertop, cutting board, knives and other utensils, and your hands with hot, soapy water immediately after working with chicken. Try to prepare the chicken before or after preparing other ingredients or dishes to avoid cross-contamination. See also FOOD SAFETY.

■ Never serve marinade that was used for raw chicken without first bringing it to a boil and cooking it for at least 5 minutes to kill any bacteria.

■ For more information about the doneness temperatures suggested by the U.S. Food Safety and Inspection Service, see DONENESS.

■ Don't let raw or cooked birds sit at room temperature for more than 1 hour—or ½ hour in hot weather.

■ Stuff whole birds right before cooking. After cooking, test the stuffing with a thermometer; it should reach a temperature of 165°F. If it does not, transfer it to a baking dish and return it to the oven until the temperature is reached.

■ After the meal, remove the stuffing from the bird and store it separately in a tightly covered container in the refrigerator for no more than 2 days.

See also BONING; BUTTERFLYING; CARVING; CORNISH GAME HEN; DISJOINTING; GIBLETS; STOCK; TRUSSING; individual cooking methods.

Quick Tip

Whether it has been roasted, broiled, grilled, braised, stewed, or poached, chicken is one of the most versatile of leftovers. Use large slices of cooked chicken for sandwiches. Smaller scraps from a whole bird are ideal for tossing together with mayonnaise, thinly sliced celery, fresh herbs, and other embellishments such as nuts or raisins to make a chicken salad.

Chicken Glossary

Most chickens in the market weigh between 3 and 4 pounds. They are classified as broiler-fryers, a combination of what used to specify two different sizes of bird. These all-purpose birds can be broiled, fried, grilled, roasted, or, when on the large side, braised or stewed. While you can find the other chicken types listed here, they are not as readily available in supermarkets as they once were. If you want a specific size, you may need to ask a butcher for help. Weight and size are determined by age and are therefore an indication of tenderness—the smaller the bird, the more tender the meat.

POUSSIN The youngest chicken, weighing about 1 pound and also known as spring chicken. These tiny birds are tender and sweet tasting. They can be broiled, grilled, roasted, or sautéed. Substitute Cornish game hens.

BROILER Very young chicken weighing between 1 and 2¾ pounds. Broilers have fine-textured meat and delicate flavor. Excellent for broiling, grilling, roasting, or sautéing. Unfortunately, most chickens this size are sold to restaurants and are hard to find in the supermarket.

FRYER Very young chicken weighing from 1½ to 2¾ pounds. The parts from a fryer are small enough to cook all the way through during deep-frying before the skin becomes too crisp. Chickens are rarely sold as plain fryers anymore; instead they are sold as broiler-fryers and weigh up to 4 pounds.

BROILER-FRYER Young chicken weighing between 2¾ and 4 pounds. Its flavorful meat with good texture is recommended for broiling, frying, grilling, roasting, braising, and even stewing.

BROILER HEN Also called stewing chicken or fowl, this older bird weighs between 4 and 6 pounds and is recommended for stewing, braising, or making stock. The meat is full flavored but dry and benefits from these moist cooking methods.

ROASTER Chicken weighing between 3 and 5 pounds and with more meat than a broiler, which makes this tender bird ideal for roasting, although it can also be braised or stewed.

CAPON A plump chicken created by castrating a male bird, capons weigh between 5 and 8 pounds and are sweet, juicy, and great for roasting.

CHICKPEA See BEAN, DRIED.

CHICORY Members of this family of pleasantly bitter greens have a range of uses, from salads to braises to grilled side dishes. One is even made into a beverage. There is a good deal of name confusion, however, which includes Belgian endive, curly endive, escarole, frisée, and radicchio.

BELGIAN ENDIVE This chicory is grown in two steps. First, it is planted in a field and harvested, and the tops are cut off and thrown away. The roots are then placed in a dark room for a few weeks, where they sprout and are carefully tended to produce the torpedo-shaped shoots we know as Belgian endive. The leaves of this tender, white cylindrical green have a pleasingly mild, bitter flavor that is a desirable addition to salads, and they can be stuffed with mild fillings for hors d'oeuvres, while the whole head is sometimes braised or even grilled. Red-tipped Belgian endive, which has the same flavor and adds pretty color to a salad or cold platter, is appearing in specialty markets these days. Buy firm, fat, crisp heads (usually about 6 inches long) with tight, unblemished white leaves ending in yellow (or red) tips. Green tips indicate that the endive is not fresh. The cut end should look fresh, with no browning. Refrigerate wrapped in plastic, a soft kitchen towel, or paper toweling to prevent bruising. Belgian endive keeps for 3 to 5 days, but it is best if used on the same day you buy it. Rinse gently, first separating the leaves if called for in the recipe.

CURLY ENDIVE A close cousin of escarole (see below), this frilly, somewhat bitter green is also known as chicory or curly chicory. It has narrow, spiky, finely curled leaves and a creamy white heart. It is used primarily in salads, tossed with olive oil and lemon juice. Available year-round; select crisp heads with good color. Slip into a perforated plastic bag and refrigerate for up to 4 days.

ESCAROLE Also known as common chicory, broad chicory, or Batavian endive, escarole has loose, broad, green, tangy outer leaves, wide white stalks, and a yellow-green heart. The leaves can be chopped and mixed with other salad greens, cooked as a green, or added to soups or pasta sauces. Buy crisp, green heads with no browning. If too many of the leaves look thick or tough, pass on that head—those leaves will taste unpleasantly bitter. Escarole is most plentiful in the early spring and fall, although it is available year-round. Store in the refrigerator in a perforated plastic bag for up to 4 days.

Quick Bite

Since the late 18th century, certain types of chicory have been cultivated specifically for their large tap roots, which, when roasted, ground, and steeped in water, produce a dark brown, bitter beverage resembling coffee. Chicory is traditionally added to coffee in New Orleans to produce the familiar local brew.

FRISÉE French cooks have long used this flavorful green in salads—it is especially nice with pears and walnuts or as a bed for grilled chicken or fish. It is basically slightly immature curly endive, with smaller heads and a more delicate and tender leaf. Select and store in the same way. It is available year-round.

RADICCHIO A variety of chicory native to Italy and characterized by its variegated purplish red leaves and bitter taste. The sturdy raw leaves hold up well in a salad, and their assertive flavor is nicely matched with cheeses, cured meats, anchovies, olives, and capers. The leaves, which darken when cooked, can be sautéed with garlic and anchovies for a side dish, a pasta sauce, or a pizza topping, or the heads can be grilled. Winter through early spring is the peak season for radicchio, although it is available most of the year in many locales. Look for

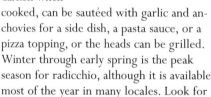

Quick Tip

Salads are rarely made with chicories alone. They would taste far too bitter, unless wilted with a warm dressing. Try mixing the bitter greens with milder butterhead varieties, such as Bibb or Boston, or oakleaf. Chicories are also good in salads containing nuts and fruits.

a head with a white core that is firm and has no holes or blemishes. Avoid those with moist leaves. Store in the refrigerator in a perforated plastic bag for up to 1 week.

See also GREENS, SALAD.

CHILE See page 114.

CHILE OIL Used extensively in Asian cooking and now finding its way into Western kitchens, chile oil is a red-hued vegetable oil whose color and heat are derived from steeping hot red chiles in oil. Drizzle a small amount in stir-fries and sautés to add a bit of fire.

Selecting Buy chile oil in small quantities from a store with good turnover. Asian markets and specialty-food stores are the best sources.

Storing Store at room temperature in a cool, dry cupboard for up to 4 months. Chile oil will keep for up to 8 months in the refrigerator, but like all oils, it will turn cloudy when chilled.

CHILE PASTE A very hot condiment made of chopped or ground chiles and (usually) vinegar and salt, used extensively throughout Southeast Asia, China, and Korea. Depending on the place of origin, different seasonings, such as garlic, ginger, soybeans, sesame oil, and even sugar, are added. Use it with caution. There are numerous brands and types for sale in Asian markets, which may be labeled "chile paste" or "chile sauce." (These should not be confused with the relatively benign commercial American product called chile sauce, a tomato-based sauce that is only slightly spicier than ketchup and is commonly used to make cocktail sauce to serve with shrimp and other seafood.)

Selecting Look for chile paste in Asian markets and specialty-food shops. Try several kinds to find what you like best. Those labeled chile-garlic sauce, a condiment with roots in Vietnam, are usually the hottest. Other pastes, which may include soy oil, are usually a little milder.

Storing Once opened, chile paste should be stored in the refrigerator, where it will keep for up to 1 year.

CHILI A thick, robust stew native to the American Southwest and also beloved elsewhere, seasoned with fresh or dried chiles, dried chile powder, or the spice blend known as chili powder. Traditional chilis may feature simply chiles and small pieces of pork or beef; other popular embellishments include tomatoes, herbs, pinto beans or black beans, and a little cornmeal as a thickener. Chili cook-offs are widespread, with devotees developing secret recipes based on rare chile types or blends and a wide range of other seasonings, meats, poultry, or game.

See also CHILE; CHILI POWDER.

CHILI POWDER A commercial spice blend that usually combines dried chiles, cumin, oregano, garlic, cloves, and coriander. It is used to season chili, as well as any other dishes that benefit from its distinctive, slightly spicy flavor, such as eggs, cheese dishes, and even tuna salad.

Some cooks prefer to season their pots of chili with pure ancho chile powder, claiming it provides excellent flavor and a good level of heat.

Selecting Most supermarkets will carry one or two standard brands of chili powder in jars or packets in the seasonings section. Look in specialty-food stores for chili seasoning mixes from smaller, regional labels, which may offer the more authentic flavor some chili aficionados are seeking.

Storing Store both types of powder in tightly capped containers in a cool, dry cupboard for up to 6 months.

CHILLING The cooling of food to below room temperature but above freezing is known as chilling. Recipes often instruct the cook to chill such items as custards, salads, gelatin-based dishes, fruit soups and desserts, and pâtés and terrines before serving.

Because food is most vulnerable to bacteria growth between the temperatures of 40°F and 140°F, chilling food to below 40°F keeps it safer. While it's a good idea to let food cool down before you put it in the refrigerator (otherwise it will heat up the entire refrigerator), don't let it sit at room temperature for more than 2 hours at most. Thick stews and soups, particularly dishes like chili, are the most difficult to cool down since they hold heat so effectively. Stirring foods as they cool redistributes the heat and makes them cool faster. Some recipes—in particular those for meat stocks—instruct you to set the pot in ice water, lowering the temperature of the food quickly before refrigerating.

Quick Tip

Divide large pots of food into smaller, shallower containers to expedite chilling.

HOW TO *Chill Food*

1. Let hot food cool slightly on the kitchen counter or carefully plunge the pot or saucepan into an ice-water bath. For the bath, put a stopper in the sink drain and fill the sink with cold water and ice cubes. Be careful not to swamp the food with water. Stir the food occasionally to expedite cooling.

2. As soon as it is no longer hot—but not completely cool, either—transfer the food to the coolest section of the refrigerator, usually the back of the bottom shelf. Do not cover.

3. When it is cold, cover it, and keep it refrigerated until ready to use.

See also COOLING.

C

Chile

From Sumatran saté to Sichuan stir-fry, Kashmiri red korma to Angolan *piri-piri* sauce, Mexican chiles rellenos to Jamaican jerk seasoning, chiles deliver heat, add color, and deepen the flavor of dishes around the globe.

Familiar sights to travelers from Luong Prabang to Lima, Biarritz to Bangkok are strings of bright red chiles drying in the summer sun.

Over centuries of domestication, hundreds of chile varieties have been developed. Requiring hot summers, they grow well in tropical areas. Diverse and versatile, chiles can be large or tiny, mild or fiery, sprinkled as a seasoning or cooked as a vegetable. They are left whole for stuffing, sliced for pickling, diced into salsa, puréed into sauces, dried and roasted for smoky flavor, and ground finely for seasoning. Hot sauces and salsas have helped to make chiles immensely popular.

Chile Varieties Many chile varieties, both fresh and dried, are widely available. Among the most popular are the following:

ANAHEIM A mild fresh green chile measuring 6 to 10 inches long. Anaheims are classically used for chiles rellenos. Anaheims have a tough skin and are often roasted or charred to remove the skin before using. They also are the chiles you find cooked and chopped in cans labeled "green chiles." Use them in place of poblanos. When dried, Anaheims, which turn a deep burgundy, are typically called California chiles.

ANCHO A mild, dark reddish brown or brick red, squat-looking dried poblano chile. About 4 inches long, anchos can pack a bit of heat along with their natural sweetness. Ancho chile powder is available in Latin markets and is generally considered to make the best pure ground chili powder. Use California chiles (see Anaheim, above) or mulato chiles when anchos are not available.

ÁRBOL About 3 inches long, narrow, and very hot. These chiles are bright orange when fresh and red to orange when dried.

BANANA Long yellow fresh chile, 5 to 6 inches, with a mild flavor. When allowed to mature, these turn red.

CASCABEL Globe-shaped, deep red, medium-hot dried chile usually no more than 1½ inches in diameter. Its toasted flavor is appreciated in sauces and soups.

CAYENNE A tapered, bright red chile, about 3 inches long, pleasingly hot and smoky tasting. Most of the cayenne chile crop is ground into the familiar red powder.

CHIPOTLE A dried and smoked jalapeño chile, with lots of flavor and lots of heat. These dark brown chiles are about 3 inches long and may be bought either dried or in cans or jars, packed in an oniony tomato mixture called adobo sauce.

Fresno A mild-to-hot fresh chile about 3 inches long. Usually red, but sometimes a less ripe one may be yellow or green. The red ones are sometimes mistaken for jalapeños.

Guajillo Narrow, dark red dried chile with a lot of heat and bold flavor. The guajillo is 5 to 6 inches long and resembles the New Mexico chile. When fresh, it is called the *mirasol* and is difficult to find outside of Mexico. The guajillo is interchangeable with the dried árbol.

Habanero Some consider this small (1½ to 2 inches long) fresh chile the hottest—and certainly its heat exceeds those of virtually all those commercially available—but it also has a lovely citrusy bouquet and flavor. Closely related to Scotch bonnets, they are most often green, but can also be red or orange.

Hungarian Cherry Pepper A small, sweet, bright red, round chile measuring about 2 inches or less in diameter. This pleasant-tasting chile does not pack much punch and often is pickled.

Jalapeño Ranging from mildly hot to fiery, the fleshy jalapeño is usually green but can also be red. Jalapeños measure from 2 to 4 inches long and are widely cultivated and available in most of the world. Jalapeños are also sold canned, whole or sliced, and pickled. Use in place of any hot chile—serranos or Thai in particular. Substitute 2 or 3 jalapeños for 1 habanero or Scotch bonnet.

Mulato Sweet mild-to-hot dried chile that is so dark it almost looks black; it is 5 to 6 inches long. Similar in taste and heat to the ancho but with sweet undertones.

New Mexico Large red or green fresh chile (6 to 8 inches long) with moderate-to-hot bite. Also available dried. New Mexicos can be substituted for guajillos and are at their best when roasted.

Pasilla Also called *chile negro*. Dark, narrow, and wrinkled, this 6-inch-long dried chile is sweet and hot. A good substitute for ancho.

Pequín A very small, very hot fresh or dried chile, measuring no more than ½ inch across, which may be round or tapered. This is not a variety of chile but instead a term for any tiny, hot chile and may be any one of a number of different kinds.

Poblano Large and fairly mild, the dark green fresh poblano is about 5 inches long and has broad shoulders. Poblanos have a nutty flavor and are often stuffed for chiles rellenos. They usually should be roasted and peeled. Substitute Anaheims for poblanos if necessary. When dried, these are called ancho chiles.

Scotch Bonnet Smaller than the habanero, only 1 to 1½ inches long, the Scotch bonnet is extremely hot. The little round fresh chiles are green, yellow, orange, or red. Use Scotch bonnets interchangeably with habaneros or 3 or 4 jalapeños.

Serrano Similar to jalapeños in heat intensity, the serrano is sleeker and tends to have more consistent heat. About 2 inches long, serranos may be green or red and can be used in place

continued

Chile, continued

of jalapeños in any recipe. Although they are most often available fresh, occasionally you may find dried serrano chiles, which are called *serranos secos*. They are hot.
THAI Small, thin green or red chiles, usually only about 1 inch long. Also known as bird chiles. Thai chiles are very hot.
Selecting It is not always necessary to use the exact chile called for in a recipe. In fact, many recipes simply use phrases such as "small hot chiles" or "hot red chiles," rather than identify a specific type. Choose

Quick Tip

To impart just a little of a chile's warmth to a dish, sauté a fresh or dried pepper in the cooking oil and then remove it before adding other ingredients.

a chile based on how it is described in a recipe, what's available in your local market or on hand in your pantry, and your own taste buds.

When buying fresh chiles, select firm, bright chiles that are free of blemishes, moldy stems, soft spots, or wrinkling. In general, the smaller and more pointed the chile, the hotter it is. If you want heat, select small, green, pointed chiles, such as serranos or jalapeños. Small red chiles pack a punch, too, so don't go by color alone. Larger or rounder chiles, such as Anaheim or poblano, tend to be milder. But don't take this as gospel: although habaneros and Scotch bonnets are both relatively broad-shouldered chiles with blunt tips, they are considered among the hottest varieties known to humankind.

In the Southwest, some of the chile harvest is also frozen. Check in markets of the region, in mail-order catalogs of regional foods, or on the Internet. They make excellent replacements for fresh chiles.

When buying dried chiles, look for flexible pods rather than brittle ones. They will be wrinkled and perhaps a little twisted, but should have good, uniform color. Dried chiles may be sold loose or packaged in plastic or cellophane. They also may be woven into colorful, attractive wreaths and sprays. These are wonderful while fresh, but beware of letting them stay too long on the kitchen wall, as the heat of the room will dry them out and they will collect dust and possibly harbor insects.

Chiles are at their peak in late summer to early fall. Visit Asian and Latin American markets for specialty chiles, and look for whole dried chiles and canned chiles in sauce at Mexican markets and in the ethnic-foods aisle in major grocery stores. Ground cayenne and chile flakes, also known as red pepper flakes, appear in the spice section of supermarkets, while pickled peppers and hot sauces are in the condiment aisle.

Storing If you plan to use fresh chiles within 2 days of purchase, you can keep them at room temperature. For storage of up to 1 week, refrigerate them in perforated plastic bags to prevent molding. Alternatively, wrap the chiles first in a paper bag or paper towel to absorb excess moisture, then place them in a plastic bag. Refrigerate for 1 week or freeze for 6 months. Although dried chiles can be hung in the corner of your kitchen, they will fare better if stored in an airtight container away from light and moisture. Keep ground chiles in a cool, dry place for no longer than 6 months.

Quick Tip

If you are not sure about a chile's heat level, add a little at a time; you can always add more. If preparing a dish in advance, remember that the heat chiles impart to a dish increases with time.

Preparing The compound that gives chiles their heat, known as capsaicin, is concentrated in the white membranes, or ribs, inside the chile. The heat is transferred from these membranes to the attached seeds. To lessen the heat of a chile, trim off the membrane and scrape away the seeds.

Caution!

Wear gloves when working with hot chiles to prevent burns to your fingers. The heat of chiles can linger for hours on your skin, so thoroughly wash your hands, the cutting board, and the knife with hot, soapy water as soon as you have finished working with them. Avoid touching your face, especially your eyes and lips, or other sensitive areas before you complete this thorough washing process.

HOW TO *Toast Dried Chiles*

Dried chiles are toasted in Mexican and other cuisines to make them flexible and intensify their flavor. This step is especially necessary if the chiles are dried out and brittle. Toasted chiles are either ground dry or soaked and ground.

1. Place the chiles on a griddle or in a heavy cast-iron frying pan over medium heat.
2. Turn the chiles frequently with tongs until they are fragrant and lightly toasted.
3. Transfer to a plate to cool.

HOW TO *Roast and Peel Fresh Chiles*

1. Preheat the broiler.
2. Lay whole chiles on an aluminum foil–lined broiler pan and broil about 6 inches from the heat, turning as needed, until the skin is blistered and charred black on all sides, 10 to 15 minutes. Watch the chiles carefully to avoid burning their flesh.
3. Once the skin is blackened and puffy, transfer the chiles to a paper bag and close loosely. This allows the chiles to steam as they cool and helps the skins to loosen.

4. When cool, peel or rub away the charred skin. Do not worry if a little stays on the flesh. Don't rinse the chiles under running water, or you will wash away flavor.

5. Lay the chiles on a cutting board. Using a small, sharp knife, slit each pepper lengthwise.

Some liquid will run out at this stage, so have paper towels handy. Open the chile and spread it on the cutting board.

6. Cut around the stem end, then remove the stem, seeds, and membrane.

Quick Tip

If your mouth is aflame from eating chiles, drink milk or eat a slice of bread or a mouthful of cooked rice. Dairy products and starches will help neutralize the burning sensation.

See also BELL PEPPER; PIMIENTO.

CHINESE LONG BEAN See BEAN, FRESH.

CHINESE PARSLEY Another name for cilantro; see HERB.

CHINESE WHITE CABBAGE See BOK CHOY.

CHINOIS See STRAINER.

CHIPOTLE See CHILE.

CHIVE See HERB.

CHOCOLATE For many, it is the ultimate indulgence of choice. Never mind Champagne and caviar; bring on the rich, elegant Belgian chocolate or, in a pinch, the mass-produced chocolate bar.

We all know how wonderful it is, but defining chocolate is elusive. Chocolate is an ingredient, a flavor, a candy. It begins with cocoa beans, originally harvested in Central America but now cultivated in equatorial regions around the world. The beans are fermented, roasted, shelled, and crushed into bits called nibs. The nibs, which are more than 50 percent cocoa butter, the fat of chocolate, are ground and compressed into a mass called chocolate liquor—which with only a little further refining becomes unsweetened chocolate. Or, depending on the amount of sugar added, the chocolate liquor becomes bittersweet, semisweet, or sweet chocolate, all called dark chocolate. The addition of milk solids results in milk chocolate. When about three-fourths of the cocoa butter is removed and the remaining chocolate liquor is pulverized into powder, it becomes cocoa powder.

Much like coffee, chocolate manufacturing starts with beans or blends of beans. How the beans are harvested and fermented, how they are roasted, and then how the chocolate liquor is processed and how much extra cocoa butter is added (for smoothness and richness) all contribute to the end product. This explains why some chocolates are quite inexpensive, while others are remarkably pricey.

From unsweetened to the finest bittersweet, all chocolate has culinary uses. Because sugar and fat content vary from one variety to another, it is unadvisable to substitute one type of chocolate for another in a recipe. Take the time to find the right chocolate to suit your needs.

Selecting Buy chocolate from a store with good turnover. The packaging should be clean and neat. Avoid any that looks old, shopworn, or dusty. Acceptable baking and cooking chocolate is sold in supermarkets, while specialty shops sell better, more expensive, often imported brands. Better chocolate often produces a better baked good or candy. But for many chocolate aficionados, "better" is a matter of personal taste and experimentation. Most of all, buy the kind you like. Just make sure it's the right type of chocolate (unsweetened, bittersweet, cocoa powder, and so on).

Storing Store chocolate, well wrapped in aluminum foil and plastic wrap, at cool room temperature. Do not keep chocolate, especially milk and white chocolates, near foods with strong odors or flavors. If you refrigerate or freeze chocolate, wrap it very carefully in a double layer of plastic (freezer weight for the freezer) and allow it to come to room temperature before unwrapping it. When properly stored, dark chocolate keeps for up to 1 year; milk and white chocolates keep for up to 8 months.

Preparing Chocolate is nearly always melted for cooking and baking purposes. While this can be done over direct heat, you'll risk burning the chocolate. Better to do it in a double boiler or a microwave.

Chop the chocolate coarsely before melting it to speed the process. Do this carefully on a cutting board, using a large knife.

Chopping chocolate.

HOW TO *Melt Chocolate on the Stove Top*

1. Chop the chocolate into large chunks and transfer it to the top pan of a double boiler.
2. Set the top pan of the double boiler over barely simmering water in the bottom pan. Make sure the water does not touch the bottom of the pan holding the chocolate. Do not let the water boil. Any moisture or steam that comes in contact with the chocolate could cause it to seize, or stiffen.
3. As it melts, stir the chocolate every now and then with a wooden spoon. When the chocolate is liquefied, remove the top of the double boiler from the bottom and set aside to cool slightly, unless otherwise instructed in a recipe. Do not cover the chocolate as it cools.

HOW TO *Melt Chocolate in a Microwave Oven*

1. Chop the chocolate into large chunks and transfer it to a microwave-safe dish.
2. Heat the chocolate on Medium (50 percent power) and check it after the first minute.
3. Keep checking it every 30 or 40 seconds to prevent scorching.
4. When the chocolate looks shiny and softened, remove it from the microwave. It will not melt completely in the microwave but will become smooth and liquid upon stirring.

HOW TO *Make Chocolate Curls*

1. Slightly soften a 3- to 4-inch chunk of chocolate in the microwave oven on Medium (50 percent power). Use a vegetable peeler to pare pretty, delicate curls from the softened chocolate. Refrigerate the curls until ready to use.

HOW TO *Make Chocolate Shavings*

1. Use a vegetable peeler or knife to shave flat, thin shavings from a room-temperature block of chocolate.

What Is Tempering? When cocoa butter crystals in chocolate harden into a stable crystalline pattern, the chocolate is said to be in temper. All chocolate leaves the manufacturer in temper, but when stored incorrectly, it may go out of temper. When melted, it goes out of temper, too. A process called tempering restabilizes the crystals, so that when the chocolate cools and rehardens, it is smooth and glossy and breaks with a satisfying snap. When untempered chocolate cools, it is dull, grainy, and may even remain soft or sticky.

Tempering is done by heating and cooling the chocolate to particular temperatures. Different chocolates require different temperatures. Chocolate that is to be used in cakes, cookies, brownies, and mousses does not need to be tempered. Candy makers, however, must temper chocolate for dipping or enrobing.

Quick Tip

To use chocolate for dipping without tempering it, melt the chocolate with 2 teaspoons of vegetable shortening for every 8 ounces of chocolate. The shortening will keep the chocolate looking shiny and smooth after it cools.

Chocolate Blues Got a problem with your chocolate? You can find the simple explanation here.

CHOCOLATE LOOKS PALE, POWDERY, AND BLOTCHY. The appearance, called bloom, is the result of storage at too warm a temperature or in too humid an environment. The chocolate can still be used; the flavor and texture are only slightly altered.

MELTED CHOCOLATE IS HARD, STIFF, AND LUMPY. Chocolate has seized, or come into contact with a bit of moisture during melting and stiffened up. To salvage it, remove from the heat and work in a bit of water, a tablespoon at a time. This restored chocolate will be smooth and shiny and fine for use in icings and fillings, but will not work in recipes where the chocolate must set up, such as for candies. See SEIZING for more information.

Chocolate Glossary

Many kinds of chocolate are created by adding ingredients such as sugar or milk to chocolate liquor. Some general variations and additions are described below.

BAKING CHOCOLATE See Unsweetened Chocolate, below.
BITTER CHOCOLATE See Unsweetened Chocolate, below.
BITTERSWEET CHOCOLATE Made from chocolate liquor sweetened with sugar and blended with additional cocoa butter. This chocolate is at least 35 percent chocolate liquor, with sugar making up about 40 percent of its weight. In general, European dark chocolates are called bittersweet, while American dark chocolates are called semisweet. For everything but the most specialized confectionery, the two can be used interchangeably in baked goods, frostings, sauces, and candies. Bittersweet chocolate also has devoted fans who eat it right out of the wrapper.
CHOCOLATE CHIPS These small droplets of semisweet, milk, or white chocolate let you incorporate the confection evenly into batters or doughs, of which a favorite example is chocolate chip cookies. Although their slightly lower cocoa butter content helps them keep their shape when baked, chocolate chips also melt easily and evenly, eliminating the need to chop blocks or bars of chocolate for melting.

✎ Chocolate Glossary, continued ✎

COCOA POWDER Made by removing nearly all the cocoa butter from chocolate liquor and then grinding it to an unsweetened powder. While less fatty than other chocolate, it still contains about 22 percent cocoa butter. Do not confuse this unsweetened powder with sweetened cocoa drink mixes.

Alkalized, or Dutch-processed, cocoa powder is treated with an alkali to make it milder and more soluble than nonalkalized cocoa powder. Nonalkalized or natural cocoa powder is lighter in color but bolder in flavor than the alkalized powder. Both types of cocoa powder have their roles in baking and cooking, and one is not better than the other. Nonalkalized cocoa powder is always used for devil's food cake, because when the mildly acidic cocoa powder reacts with the baking soda in the recipe it gives the cake crumb its characteristic reddish hue. Use the kind of cocoa powder specified in the recipe. If none is specified, use either.

COUVERTURE CHOCOLATE High-quality dark chocolate used for specialty candy making. Because of its relatively high percentage of cocoa butter, it melts smoothly, making it easier for enrobing, dipping, and molding chocolate. When properly tempered and cooled, it forms a thin, glossy shell. You will find couverture chocolate in some specialty-food shops and in mail-order catalogs.

DARK CHOCOLATE A term to describe any sweetened chocolate without milk solids, usually referring to bittersweet and semisweet chocolates.

MILK CHOCOLATE This familiar chocolate contains milk solids, cocoa butter, and sugar. Milk chocolate is most often eaten out of hand in the form of a candy bar, although it appears in recipes from time to time. It should not be substituted for bittersweet or semisweet chocolate, except in the form of chips for chocolate chip cookies.

PLAIN CHOCOLATE In the United States, the term *plain chocolate* refers to unsweetened chocolate, while in Great Britain the term commonly refers to bittersweet chocolate. See Unsweetened Chocolate, below.

SEMISWEET CHOCOLATE This dark chocolate is at least 35 percent chocolate liquor. Semisweet chocolate is what Europeans call bittersweet; the terms are interchangeable.

SWEET CHOCOLATE Sweet chocolate is dark chocolate that is sweeter than semisweet but is not milk chocolate. It is an ingredient rarely called for in recipes, except for German chocolate cake, named for the chocolate's inventor.

UNSWEETENED CHOCOLATE Chocolate liquor that is refined but not sweetened. Also called baking, plain, or bitter chocolate. This product is used only for baking and cooking—never for eating out of hand.

WHITE CHOCOLATE A mixture of cocoa butter, sugar, and milk solids but no chocolate liquor. Some manufacturers market a product called confectionery coating, which is like white chocolate but contains vegetable fat instead of cocoa butter and is less expensive.

C

CHOPPING Cutting food into irregular pieces that are small enough that they require no further cutting at the table, or are easy to mix or otherwise work with. *Chopping* is a general term; some more specific ways of cutting include dicing, cubing, julienning, and mincing. See the Chopping Glossary, below.

HOW TO *Chop*

Chopping is a common kitchen chore. For many chopping tasks, a knife is used in a specific way for efficiency.

1. Make sure that any large pieces are roughly cut into manageable pieces and that herbs—thick stems removed and discarded—are piled into a neat, fairly compact mass.
2. Grip the knife handle close to the blade, extending your thumb along the side of the blade if you wish, and rest the fingertips of your other hand on top of the knife's tip to keep it in contact with the cutting board.
3. Move the knife heel up and down rhythmically, trying not to lift the tip from the board.

4. Use a graceful, rolling motion, pushing the knife down and forward, rather than jerking the knife straight up and down.

5. As the mass of food is chopped smaller, use the knife occasionally to gather the food again into tight, mounded piles. Try not to chop too much at a time, or it will spill off the board.

To chop carrots, peppers, onions, or other larger vegetables coarsely, grip the knife handle as described above and with the other hand hold the item being chopped. While keeping the tip of the knife on the board, lift the heel of the knife and cut down through the food in a smooth, even stroke. Adjust the position of the food as you cut, sliding it closer to the blade of the knife, while being careful to keep your fingertips well away from the cutting edge.

Chopping Glossary

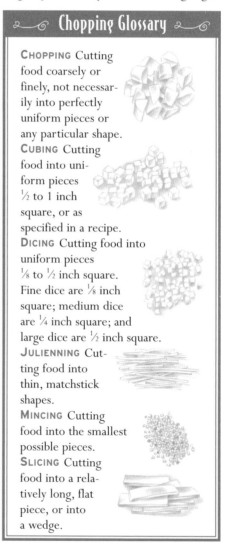

CHOPPING Cutting food coarsely or finely, not necessarily into perfectly uniform pieces or any particular shape.

CUBING Cutting food into uniform pieces ½ to 1 inch square, or as specified in a recipe.

DICING Cutting food into uniform pieces ⅛ to ½ inch square. Fine dice are ⅛ inch square; medium dice are ¼ inch square; and large dice are ½ inch square.

JULIENNING Cutting food into thin, matchstick shapes.

MINCING Cutting food into the smallest possible pieces.

SLICING Cutting food into a relatively long, flat piece, or into a wedge.

Heavy knives and cleavers are the most common tools for chopping. Although the food processor makes quick work of sizable amounts of ingredients, it generally does not offer the kind of precision required when certain recipes call for food to be cut into uniform cubes or dice. In such cases, a chef's knife usually works best.

Cutting boards and sharp knives facilitate chopping. Cutting boards provide traction so that food will not slip away as you work. Dull knives are actually more dangerous than sharp ones, as you have to work harder, pressing the knife into the food, and there is more chance it will slip. The Italian mezzaluna (a curved blade with a wooden handle at each end) can also make quick work of chopping tasks.

See also CUBING; CUTTING BOARD; DICING; KNIFE; MINCING; SLICING.

CHOPSTICKS Arguably the most indispensable tool in both the Asian kitchen and dining room, chopsticks make perfect sense when eating dishes such as stir-fries in which the food is cut into bite-sized pieces before cooking. Chopsticks are held in one hand, between the thumb and forefinger. The bottom stick is held stationary, while the top one is moved up and down by the forefinger to grasp the food in a pincerlike grip. Chopsticks are also used for scooping rice and noodles into the mouth from a bowl held close to the face. Long chopsticks, useful in the kitchen for stir-frying and deep-frying and at the table for serving, are available in Asian markets.

Using chopsticks.

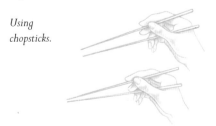

CHRISTOPHINE See CHAYOTE.

CHUTNEY A condiment that originated in India but is now made in a number of countries, chutney comes in countless styles, offering taste sensations ranging from sweet, hot, and tart to bitter. Most commonly served alongside curries and other savory dishes, chutneys may be raw or cooked mixtures of fruits or herbs, and usually also include vinegar, sugar, chiles, and spices. They may be used to cool the mouth when eating spicy foods or to add punch to milder ones. Some are thin enough to serve as dips, while others are chunky and thick and can be spread on bread or crackers or spooned onto a plate. Chutney can also be stirred into tuna or chicken salad for a flavor boost.

Selecting Most supermarkets carry the classic mango chutney called Major Grey's and may have some others, too. For a wider variety, look for bottled chutneys at Indian or Pakistani markets or specialty shops. Some of these markets may sell their own freshly prepared chutneys as well.

Storing Bottled chutneys, like jams and similar preserves, will keep unopened for up to 1 year in a cool, dark cupboard. Once opened, they will last 3 months or longer in the refrigerator. Fresh chutneys containing sugar will keep for up to 1 week in the refrigerator. Most others will keep for up to 2 days in the refrigerator.

Quick Bite

The name *chutney* derives from the Sanskrit word *chatni*, "for licking."

CILANTRO See HERB.

CINNAMON See SPICE.

CITRUS See individual fruits; ZESTING.

CLAM The clam is one of the most versatile members of the shellfish family. While clams are most often steamed, tender hard-shelled clams can be eaten raw, like oysters, with a squeeze of lemon juice and perhaps a dab of cocktail sauce. Clams are also terrific tossed with pasta in cream or tomato sauce, stuffed, and in the classic rice-based dish from Spain called paella. They also turn up in seafood stews, dips, and other dishes that benefit from their fresh, clean, sweet flavor. Clam chowder, whether white (milk or cream based) or red (tomato based), is a classic soup along the Atlantic coast. Deep-fried clams are another Eastern seaboard classic.

In addition to belonging to the broad category of shellfish, clams are classified as mollusks, along with abalone, scallops, mussels, and oysters. They are also bivalves, which is a general term referring to any creature with a soft body enclosed between two hinged shells.

Clams are either hard shelled or soft shelled, and different varieties are found in the Atlantic and the Pacific. Atlantic hard-shelled clams are called quahogs and come in various sizes, from small little-necks to large chowder clams. On the Pacific coast you'll find unrelated hard-shelled little-necks. Soft-shelled clams have shells slightly softer than those of hard-shelled clams, although still firm. They also have thin, elongated shells and visible necks, or siphons, a portion of the clam's filtering system that extends from the shell. On the East Coast, look for soft-shelled steamer clams. On the West Coast, razor clams are the common soft-shelled variety.

Selecting Buy the freshest clams you can find from a reputable fish merchant. They are sold live in the shell or freshly shucked and packed in pint and quart containers that usually contain clam liquor (or liquid), too. Hard-shelled quahog clams should have firm, finely textured gray shells with no yellowing; other hard-shelled clams should have even-colored, firm shells. The clams

Quick Bite

Soft-shelled clams are known as steamers on the East Coast, due to a simple and favorite way of preparing them. The clams are steamed open, and the steaming liquid is served with the clams, along with melted butter.

should not be open—if one gapes a little, prod it gently. If it does not close immediately, do not buy it. An open shell is the sign of a dead clam. Shucked hard-shelled clams should be plump and moist with clear liquor and a fresh and briny aroma.

Soft-shelled clams should be oval and evenly colored, with a neck, or siphon, protruding from the shell. To check for freshness, tap the neck. It should pull back toward the shell. The shells will not close as tightly as those of hard-shelled clams.

If you cannot find good fresh clams, you may be able to substitute frozen or canned ones. They will provide good flavor in pasta sauces, clam dips, and seafood broths but will not be as plump and juicy, so don't try them in paella or fried clams. Quick-frozen clams, available in some fish markets, are your best bet after fresh clams. Bottled clam juice, usually shelved near the canned seafood in supermarkets, can be substituted for fish stock or broth in recipes.

Storing Fresh clams in the shell should not be suffocated by being enclosed in a plastic bag or submerged in water. Instead, lay them on a flat tray or in a shallow bowl, cover them with a damp cloth, and refrigerate. Or put them in a mesh bag in a large bowl and refrigerate. Serve them the same day you buy them for the best flavor and texture, and certainly within 2 days.

Ready-shucked clams will also keep in the refrigerator for up to 2 days, although they are best eaten as soon after purchase as possible. Keep them in a tightly lidded container and push them to the back of the refrigerator where it is coldest.

Store canned clams in a cool, dark cupboard for up to 1 year and use them as soon as they are opened. If you can't use them immediately, transfer them to a plastic or glass container with a lid and refrigerate for no more than 2 days. Keep frozen clams in the freezer until ready to use, and use within 1 month of purchase.

Preparing Check over clams for any open shells. If their shells do not quickly shut tight after prodding, discard them.

Scrub clam shells well under running water with a soft-bristled brush to get rid of sand and grit. Soft-shelled clams, because of their slightly gaping shells, tend to be sandier than hard-shelled.

Scrubbing clams.

Clams may be cooked in the shell, which will open as they cook, or a recipe may require you first to shuck them, removing them from their shells. Opening hard-shelled clams calls for some dexterity, but the meat is easy to free from the open shell by scooping the knife around the perimeter. Briefly steaming clams to open them is easier than shucking them before cooking.

HOW TO *Purge Clams*

The traditional method of cleaning clams includes the step of soaking them in salt water to encourage them to purge any sand caught in their shells. This is not necessary unless you have very sandy soft-shelled clams. If the clams look clean and tightly closed, simply scrub them under cold running water before shucking or steaming them open. If you find sand in the clam liquor from the shell or steaming liquid, you can strain it through a coffee filter or doubled fine-mesh cheesecloth before using it. Alternatively, let the sand sink to the bottom and don't pour off the last few drops of sandy liquid.

1. Place the clams in a large bowl or pot and cover with fresh seawater, if available. If not, mix up a batch of cold, salted water. To create an approximation of the salinity of the ocean, dissolve 5 to 6 tablespoons of salt per gallon of tap water.

2. Discard any clams that do not sink to the bottom. Let the other clams soak for 3 or 4 hours.

3. Drain and rinse with cool water.

Caution!

Clams and other bivalves filter the shallow coastal waters in which they live through their shells. If the water is contaminated, eating the clams can result in illness. Most clams sold in stores and restaurants are purchased from wholesalers who vouch for the safety of the waters in which the clams were harvested. Other outlets, such as small roadside stands or pickup trucks parked near the beach, are not as reliable. If you gather clams yourself, ascertain that the waters have been tested and deemed safe for harvesting. Pay close attention to any posted signs. If there is any question, contact local officials or the state's department of agriculture, the agency that monitors local offshore waters.

C

Clam Glossary

BUTTER Small, sweet Pacific clam, also called moneyshell. Can be eaten raw when small—2 to 3 inches in diameter—but toughens as it grows and is then best cooked.

CHERRYSTONE A small hard-shelled Atlantic clam, measuring up to a maximum of 3 inches in diameter. Cherrystones are delicious raw or cooked.

GEODUCK Pronounced "gooeyduck," this large clam (weighing as much as 3 pounds) calls the Pacific home, where it is best gathered during very low spring tides. These strange-looking soft-shelled clams have a long neck that can measure up to 3 feet and are delicious eaten raw or lightly cooked once their tough outer skin is removed. The interior meat is good in soups and stews.

LITTLENECK There are two kinds. The smallest of the hard-shelled clams, Atlantic littlenecks measure from $1\frac{1}{2}$ to $2\frac{1}{4}$ inches in diameter. These are particularly sweet and delicious raw or very gently cooked. Pacific littlenecks are not related. Because they are a little tough, they should be steamed.

MAHOGANY A hard-shelled clam from Atlantic waters with a dark, reddish brown shell and pinkish meat. Also called ocean quahog, it has a flavor similar to that of large quahogs.

MANILA Also called Japanese clam. A small, sweet clam farmed off the Pacific coast of the United States, although it is not native. Most are harvested when they are barely 1 inch in diameter. Great favorites among chefs, they can be served raw or very lightly steamed.

PISMO A hard-shelled Pacific clam, quite rare and prized, is now most abundant in Baja California. Pismo clams are harvested when about 5 inches in diameter. Their tender, sweet adductor muscle is eaten raw, while the body meat is added to chowder or deep-fried.

QUAHOG Pronounced "coe-hog." A large hard-shelled clam from the Atlantic, measuring more than 3 inches in diameter. The flavor is sweet, but not quite as sweet and salty as smaller hard-shelled clams.

RAZOR A soft-shelled Pacific clam with a neck extending from its dark, narrow sharp shell. This clam is shaped like an old-fashioned straight razor, which explains its name and also explains its fairly sharp edges. Handle these clams with care. Razor clams require relatively long cooking and are good simmered in soups, stews, or sauces. They are found in both the Atlantic and the Pacific.

STEAMER A soft-shelled clam from the Atlantic Ocean. Also known as long-neck, fryer, or maninose clam. Its thin, oval shell measures 3 to 4 inches long. The meat is sweet and mild.

SURF This large hard-shelled Atlantic clam represents a big harvest along the Eastern seaboard. Also known as the skimmer, sea, or bar clam, it is good added to sauces and soups.

HOW TO *Shuck Clams by Hand*

A clam knife, with a squat, wide blade and thick handle for easy gripping, will make the job of prying open clam shells a much easier task.

1. For protection from a slip of the knife, use a folded cloth or oven mitt to hold the clam in one hand. (Hold the clam over a bowl to catch any clam liquor that might escape, and if it is sandy, strain the accumulated liquor through a coffee filter before using.)
2. Slide the clam knife sideways into the crack between the shells. When the knife penetrates the clam shell, sever the muscle at the hinge end of the shell and pry the shell open.

3. Run the knife around the clam meat to free it and then remove it. If serving the clam on the half shell, remove and discard the top shell.

HOW TO *Shuck Clams by Steaming*

Another, easier method of extracting clams from their shells is to steam them for a brief period of time. If using the clams in a recipe, make sure you pull them out of the pot just as soon as they open, and be careful not to overcook them.

1. Using a steamer rack in a large pot, steam clams over simmering water just until their shells barely open, not more than 5 minutes.
2. Run a knife around the clam meat to free it and then remove it.

Canned clams lend themselves to various preparations. Because they are already cooked, they require only gentle heating or no cooking at all. Frozen clams should thaw completely in the refrigerator and then be treated as fresh clams (they are not already cooked). Use them as soon as they defrost; do not refreeze them, or their texture will be destroyed.

CLARIFYING See BUTTER; STOCK.

CLAY POT Clay has been a material used to fashion cooking pots since ancient times. Today, most cookware is made from metal alloys or treated ceramic, but many loyal cooking enthusiasts still praise unglazed clay pots. The porous properties of these pots promote slow, moist, even cooking. And when the food is done, it can be served in the handsome clay pot. These pots are also known as terra-cotta bakers, Römertopfs, or Roman pots.

The most popular food for cooking in a clay pot is chicken. The pots, usually oval in shape with a domed lid, are designed to hold a whole chicken along with accompanying vegetables and, usually, broth. As it bakes, the food simultaneously steams and braises for deliciously succulent meat. Other meats, fish, and vegetables are cooked in unglazed clay pots, too.

Clay pots are meant for oven cooking, not stove top. Most are microwave safe. They should be soaked in cold water before every use to trap water in the porous clay, which forms steam during cooking. As a rule they are not dishwasher safe and should be cleaned carefully after each use. Be sure to follow the manufacturer's instructions for overall care.

See also COOKWARE.

CLOUD EAR See MUSHROOM.

CLOVE See SPICE.

COCOA See CHOCOLATE.

COCONUT Growing on palm trees in tropical climates, the coconut is the world's largest nut. Its nutmeat is firm, creamy, and snowy white, while its hollow center is filled with a sweet but watery liquid called coconut water or, erroneously, milk.

Coconut is a rich and generous nut, giving us not only coconut meat, but also coconut sugar and oil and the makings for coconut milk and cream. Coconut is a favorite ingredient for sweet baked goods, such as cakes, pies, and cookies, and for savory dishes, such as curries, often added in the form of coconut milk.

Selecting Hard, green outer shells are removed from coconuts before they are sent to market. The smaller, rounder brown shell, covered with hairy fibers, is left intact. Choose heavy coconuts filled with liquid. Shake the coconut near your ear, listening for the liquid inside. The more water sloshing around inside the nut, the fresher it is. Coconuts are available all year around but are more plentiful in the fall and winter months.

Shredded coconut.

Bags or cans of grated, shredded, and flaked dried coconut are sold in the baking-supply aisles of supermarkets and smaller grocery stores. This processed coconut is nearly always sweetened, although it is possible to buy unsweetened coconut in some supermarkets, in health-food stores, and in specialty-food stores. The bags contain dry coconut flakes or shreds, while canned flakes usually are moister. Check your recipe to be sure you buy the correct type.

Quick Tip

The coconut "milk" you drain from the nut is more correctly called coconut water. It is different from the coconut milk often used in curries or sweetened coconut cream, which is mostly used to make tropical drinks such as the piña colada. For more detail, see COCONUT MILK.

HOW TO *Crack a Coconut*

1. Drive a long nail, ice pick, or other sharp spike through one of the three smooth "eyes" at one end of the coconut.
2. Drain the liquid and drink it immediately or refrigerate it for up to a few hours.
3. Put the nut on a hard surface—the floor or porch—and hit it with a hammer until it cracks.
4. Break the shell apart using your hands, the hammer, or another sturdy tool.

5. Very carefully cut the white meat from the shell with a knife. Peel the brown skin from the coconut meat.

6. Grate or chop the meat using a box grater, rotary grater, food processor, or small, sharp knife, depending on how you will be using it.

Storing Store the unopened nut in the refrigerator for up to a month. Once the water is drained, drink it within a few hours. The coconut meat will keep, wrapped in plastic and refrigerated, for 5 days. Dried or canned coconut will keep in the refrigerator, covered with plastic wrap, for up to 1 month.

Quick Tip

Coconut shells can be easier to crack if they are heated or frozen first. These steps make the shell brittle, making it easier to crack. After draining the liquid, bake the coconut in a 375°F oven for about 15 minutes. Hit it with a hammer as soon as it is removed from the oven. Alternatively, put the coconut in the freezer for 2 or 3 hours beforehand. Both methods also work for removing meat once the coconut is open. Heating or freezing the broken shell makes it easier to pry the meat from it.

See also COCONUT MILK.

COCONUT CREAM See COCONUT MILK.

COCONUT MILK With its rich and nutty flavor, coconut milk, made by soaking grated coconut in water, is an essential ingredient throughout the tropics. It thickens sauces, turns rice dishes creamy, flavors desserts, smoothes out soups, and is a perfect foil for the heat of chiles. Coconut milk should not be confused with canned sweetened coconut cream, sometimes labeled "cream of coconut," which is used primarily for desserts and tropical drinks.
Selecting Good-quality coconut milk is available in cans or frozen in Asian and Latin markets.
Storing Store opened coconut milk in a lidded glass or plastic container for up to

Quick Tip

When using coconut milk for a Thai curry, avoid shaking the can. Instead, skim off the thick coconut cream that has settled on top, and heat it in place of oil for cooking the curry paste and aromatics. Later, stir in the remaining coconut milk to make the sauce.

3 days in the refrigerator. Unopened canned coconut milk can be kept for up to 1 year.
Preparing The solids in coconut milk separate and rise as cream does in cow's milk. For coconut cream, spoon the cream from the top of the opened can and reserve the remaining milk for another use. For recipes calling for coconut milk, shake the can vigorously before opening. If need be, whisk to remove the more stubborn lumps.

HOW TO *Make Your Own Coconut Milk*

1. Soak freshly grated coconut or dried, unsweetened coconut flakes in an equal amount of hot water (that is, 1 cup flakes to 1 cup water) until the coconut has softened.
2. Process briefly in a blender or food processor just until barely smooth.
3. Pour the mixture onto a large double layer of cheesecloth or a linen dishtowel draped over a bowl.
4. Gather the cloth around the coconut mixture and squeeze tightly to extract as much of the fluid as you can.
5. Repeat steps 1–4 up to two times, if desired. The subsequent pressings will yield thinner coconut milk. Use the batches separately, or mix them for uniform flavor and consistency.

CODDLING An exceedingly gentle form of cooking. Coddled eggs have been cooked just so that they are no longer raw but still extremely soft. They are sometimes cooked in a lidded porcelain dish called an egg coddler. The eggs are cracked into the coddler, covered, and then lowered into a pan of simmering water. Note that coddling does not raise the temperature of an egg above 160°F, which is necessary to kill salmonella bacteria. See also EGG.

COFFEE For many of us, a day without coffee (and its caffeine boost) is a day when we are  destined to feel sluggish and dull. Luckily, coffee is a ready staple in most kitchens, and specialized coffeehouses have proliferated in recent years, so that cappuccino, latte, and espresso are ours for the asking, any time of the day or night.

Coffee is brewed from beans harvested from trees that grow in tropical regions. After processing to remove the pulp and skins that enclose them, the beans are roasted and mixed to produce various blends—some so distinctive they practically announce themselves, and others quite ordinary but still unmistakably coffee. Coffee is also a favorite flavoring, starring in ice cream, cream pies, cakes, and candies, and often costarring with chocolate. Coffee-flavored liqueurs such as Kahlúa are delightful, too, as an ingredient in dessert recipes and on their own.

Most ordinary coffee is made from robusta beans, which grow at lower altitudes and are widely cultivated, primarily in Brazil and Indonesia. Coffee of distinction is more likely to be brewed from arabica beans, which thrive at high altitudes. Some of the best-tasting arabica beans are grown in Kenya, in Africa, and Sumatra and Sulawesi (formerly Celebes), in Indonesia. Beans from Costa Rica, Guatemala, and Colombia also can be exceptional. The famous Jamaican Blue Mountain beans produce remarkable coffee, but the harvest is small. Although Hawaiian coffee makes up only a small percentage of the world's crop, it is of high quality.

Origin alone does not determine the quality of the coffee. Coffee beans must be roasted to bring out their rich, heady flavor and, depending on the producer, this process differs. There is good reason coffee is often referred to by its roast, since this is perhaps the single most important process in coffee production. After roasting, the beans may or may not be combined for blends.

Essentially, various roasts produce darker or lighter cups of coffee. Standard American roast is a medium-light roast. It also is called breakfast roast and produces coffee that is neither particularly strong nor dark. This is the brewed coffee most often sold at convenience stores, diners, fast-food outlets, and many restaurants. Medium-dark roasted beans produce darker, richer coffee. A good example is Viennese roast, but the brewed coffee, while full flavored, does not have the full body of darker roasts. Dark-roasted coffee beans, usually dubbed French or Italian roast, produce a black, full-bodied cup of coffee and are used for making espresso.

Quick Bite

A good rule of thumb: "tropical" names—Sumatra, Jamaica, Kenya—refer to the source of beans, while European names—French, Italian, Viennese—describe the roast.

All coffee contains some amount of the stimulating compound known as caffeine. Caffeine, as much as flavor, is what attracts many of us to coffee. It perks us up in the morning and increases mental acuity. It also prevents some of us from falling asleep at night, and its sudden absence from our daily diet can bring on headaches and crabbiness. Some people are minimally affected by caffeine; others feel better overall when they drink only decaffeinated brew. Caffeine is removed by two methods, the water process and the solvent process, with the former resulting in a better-tasting cup. Decaffeinated coffee is approximately 97 percent caffeine-free.

Quick Tip

Different coffeemakers call for different grinds. French presses, for example, need coarse grounds. Consult your owner's manual or a good coffee merchant.

Selecting Buy coffee beans from a reputable merchant with good turnover. There are many roasts and blends, so experiment until you find those you prefer.

A coffee merchant will grind beans for you. While coffee beans do start to lose flavor once they are ground, if you drink a lot of coffee and can replenish your supply regularly, this is not a bad option.

Home bakers rely on instant coffee and espresso for flavoring. Instant coffee is sold as powder, freeze-dried crystals, or dehydrated granules. Instant espresso is commonly dehydrated granules and produces a slightly darker cup than instant coffee.

Storing Store the coffee beans you use every day in a cool cupboard, sealed in an airtight container, for up to 2 weeks. Beans can also be refrigerated for up to 1 month if you don't think you will use them up in a couple weeks' time. Well wrapped in plastic, coffee beans freeze for up to 3 months, which is useful if you like to buy your beans in bulk or like to store them in a weekend house. If you buy preground coffee, store it in an airtight container in a cool, dark place for up to 2 weeks.

Preparing Coffee tastes best when brewed from freshly ground beans. As soon as they are ground, coffee beans begin to lose essential oils and flavor. Check your local kitchenware or coffee stores for a small, efficient coffee grinder. Grind only as many beans as you need at the time. All coffee must be brewed with hot water. The optimum water temperature for brewing is 200°F (not quite boiling). When making coffee manually, bring the water to a boil and then let it cool briefly before brewing.

Coffee-Making Methods Most people make drip coffee, the method in which hot water passes through the ground coffee and then drips through a filter into a waiting pot. Electric drip coffeemakers are convenient, but a pot of well-made manual drip coffee probably tastes better. The latter allows you to heat the water to just the right temperature and also to moisten and stir the grounds as you begin to brew, which releases the flavor more evenly.

Drip pot.

Quick Tip

Keeping coffee warm in an electric coffeemaker or on the stove will soon result in a burnt flavor. Pouring freshly made coffee into a thermos (or making drip coffee directly into a thermos) will keep coffee flavorful for hours.

French press or plunger coffeemakers, in which a plunger fitted with a screen is pushed through a mixture of grounds and water, are another option. This method is easy and quick, but the coffee often contains sediment and cools quickly.

Plunger pot.

The percolator, in which boiling water passes through the grounds over and over during brewing, does not result in a good-tasting cup. When coffee is brewed for too long—more than a few minutes— more bitter-tasting elements of the beans are extracted and affect the coffee's flavor.

Whichever method you use, coffee should be served promptly after brewing for the best-tasting cup.

Coffee Savvy

- Begin with freshly ground beans, and grind only as much coffee as you need for a pot.
- For best results, use a manual drip pot fitted with a paper filter. Make sure the pot is scrupulously clean and free of soapy residue.
- Measure 2 level tablespoons (one coffee measure) of ground coffee for every 6 fluid ounces (¾ cup) of water.

Quick Tip

Coffee does not reheat well. Discard cold, left-over coffee or use it to make iced coffee.

- Start with cold tap water. Often, hot tap water has been sitting in a water heater and may taste stale or slightly metallic. If the water tastes of chemicals or is otherwise unpleasant, use bottled water.
- Bring the water to a boil, remove from the heat, and let cool slightly. The water should be 200°F, just below boiling, when it blends with the coffee.
- Before pouring the water into the grounds, moisten them with a little of the hot water and stir to distribute it.
- Once the coffee is brewed, serve it immediately. Pour the remaining coffee into a thermos to keep it warm.
- Do not let coffee boil. Boiling destroys its flavor.

COLANDER See STRAINER.

COLLARD See GREENS, DARK.

CONDENSED MILK See MILK.

CONFECTIONERS' SUGAR See SUGAR.

CONFIT When meat or poultry is cooked slowly in a large amount of its own fat until very tender and then stored in a pot or other container and completely covered with fat, it is called confit. This French method was developed originally as a way to preserve salt-cured meat and fowl, most notably pork and goose. Today, duck or goose confit is found on menus of upscale restaurants. Both are key ingredients in classic cassoulet. The poultry or meat for confit no longer is cured, although it usually is well seasoned. Some chefs cook vegetables such as green onions, yellow onions, and garlic slowly in oil and call the preparation a confit.

CONVERSION See MEASURING.

COOKIE See page 134.

COOKIE CUTTER See BAKING TOOLS.

COOKIE SHEET See BAKEWARE.

COOKING Home-cooked meals are more than simple sustenance: just as they nourish our bodies, so do they nourish our spirits. Nearly miraculous transformations in flavor, aroma, texture, and appearance take place when heat is applied to ingredients. Basic strategies will make the task of cooking easy and pleasurable, regardless of your level of expertise.

- Read through the recipe twice to make sure you have the ingredients, equipment, and time required. Make a shopping list based on the recipe, first checking the cupboard and refrigerator.
- Determine substitutions for any hard-to-find ingredients. See SUBSTITUTIONS & EQUIVALENTS.
- Decide which dishes or recipe steps can be prepared ahead of time.
- Allow sufficient time for foods to defrost or reach room temperature.
- Prepare the ingredients according to the ingredient list before you move on to the method of a recipe. This may involve chopping, dicing, slicing, or measuring ingredients; separating eggs; or letting ingredients soften at room temperature.
- Use the correct size pot, pan, or skillet. Good recipes will specify or will simply presume a medium-sized pan.
- Cook at the suggested temperatures. Use an oven thermometer to make sure your oven is accurate, adjusting the temperature dial accordingly.
- Use all your senses in the kitchen. Well-written recipes will give you visual, tactile, taste, and aromatic cues, as well as timing instructions.
- Taste dishes as you cook, adding such ingredients as herbs, spices, wine, vinegar, citrus juice and zest, chiles, sugar, and salt and pepper as needed. Long cooking, such as stewing and braising, alters the flavors of foods more so than stir-frying and sautéing do. Add seasonings with a measured hand, keeping in mind that you can always use more, but it's difficult to disguise an overused herb or spice. Always taste just before serving and adjust the seasoning accordingly.
- Clean up as you go. Put jars and bottles away as you finish with them. Wash bowls and utensils when you have a spare minute or soak them in the sink.
- When you run out of an ingredient, make a note of it. Don't trust your memory to kick in a few days later.

As much as many of us would like a large, spacious, well-designed kitchen with yards of shelving, few of us have one. Instead, we have to make adjustments and use space carefully. Following are some common-sense approaches to organizing your kitchen to make cooking more efficient.

- Plan your cupboard contents so that the foods you use often (oil, sugar, spices) are easy to reach. Store infrequently used items on higher or lower shelves.
- Put more perishable foods, such as chocolate and dried herbs, in cupboards distant from heat and light.
- Arrange the refrigerator so that frequently used foods, such as butter, milk, and juice, are easy to reach.
- Keep countertops clutter free. You'll be less eager to cook if you have to clear a space before you can begin.
- Make use of space-saving devices such as racks hung inside cupboard doors, below-cabinet shelving, pot racks, drawer organizers, and stacking bins.

See also HIGH-ALTITUDE COOKING; LOW-FAT COOKING.

C

Cookie

Chocolate chip. Gingersnap. Spice. Peanut butter. Cookies come in just about every flavor you can imagine. They are wonderful tucked into lunch boxes for a midday lift or dipped into milk while you watch the 11 o'clock news.

Cookies can be made from dough that is dropped onto baking sheets; rolled and cut out, and then placed on sheets; piped with a pastry bag; pushed through a cookie press; or molded by hand; and then baked. Some cookie doughs must be refrigerated to firm them up before baking. Others, such as those for bar cookies like brownies, are made from soft batter that is smoothed into a square or rectangular pan and cut into squares or bars after baking and cooling. Even no-bake versions of both cookies and bars exist, too.

Using a cookie cutter.

Equipment Cookies and bars are simple to make with the equipment most home bakers have. A mixing bowl, wooden spoon, and two baking sheets (or a pan for bars) will suffice in many cases. Recipes can be mixed by hand but are more easily assembled with a handheld electric mixer or in a stand mixer. The rapid beating also incorporates more air and lightens the batter. See also BAKEWARE; BAKING TOOLS.

Ingredients Cookies and bars rarely require expensive or hard-to-find ingredients. Most are simple mixtures of flour, butter, sugar, eggs, and flavorings. Nearly all recipes call for all-purpose flour, unsalted butter, granulated sugar, and large eggs. The flour may require sifting before measuring; the butter usually is softened or melted; and the eggs should be at room temperature. Most cookies and bars are leavened with small amounts of baking powder or baking soda.

General simplicity aside, a home cook setting out to make a batch of cookies should also bear in mind that they are a form of pastry. As in pastry making and other forms of baking, precise measuring of ingredients and following of recipe instructions will help ensure success.

HOW TO *Make Drop Cookies*
1. With a tablespoon, scoop up a spoonful of batter and use a second spoon to push it off onto a baking sheet, spacing the cookies at least 2 inches apart on all sides.

HOW TO *Roll Dough for Refrigerator Cookies*
1. Spoon the dough down the center of a sheet of waxed paper. Roll the dough up inside the paper, forming a log of whatever shape you desire—cylinder or rectangular block.
2. Refrigerate until firm. Unwrap, slice, and bake as directed in the recipe.

HOW TO *Use a Cookie Press*

Cookie presses work best with fairly firm, pliable dough. For opening the tube and pressing the cookies, consult your owner's manual, as models vary.

1. Roll the dough into a log with a diameter slightly smaller than that of the cookie press cylinder and about the same length. See How to Roll Dough for Refrigerator Cookies, above, step 1.

2. Unwrap the dough (no chilling is necessary) and slip it into the cookie press.

3. Select a design plate. Fit the plate into its holder and screw it securely onto the press.

4. Hold the press upright, securely grasp the handle, and, applying even pressure, press out the dough to form cookies.

Cookie Savvy

Recipes vary, but for most cookie baking, the following techniques are useful:

■ If a recipe simply says to grease the baking sheet or pan, use softened butter or margarine, vegetable oil, or unflavored cooking spray. Butter, which burns at lower temperatures than oil, is not recommended for cookies that bake at high temperatures. Alternatively, line the baking sheets with parchment paper or nonstick liners, available in cookware shops. This eliminates some cleanup.

■ Stir cookie batter just until the flour disappears, or your cookies may be tough.

■ When rolling out cookie dough, work on a lightly floured surface, start at the center of the dough disk, and use gentle strokes. See also ROLLING OUT.

■ If using a cookie cutter, dust it lightly with flour to avoid sticking. Press the cookie cutter straight into the dough and then lift it up without twisting.

■ After cutting out as many cookies as you can from the initial rolling out, gather the remnants of dough together, pat out, and cut out one more batch of cookies. Do not reroll scraps more than once unless you're working with a very rich and buttery dough; if you do, your subsequent cookies may be tough.

■ If cookie dough softens too much during rolling and becomes limp and sticky, refrigerate it for 10 or 15 minutes, until firm enough to roll and cut.

■ Be sure to leave ample room for spreading between dropped cookies. Don't try to crowd too many cookies on a sheet for each batch.

■ Set the timer for the least amount of time if a range is given in a recipe. Use an oven thermometer to gauge the accuracy of your oven.

■ If baking more than one sheet of cookies at a time, switch the baking sheets from

continued

Cookie, continued

the upper to lower rack and rotate them halfway through the baking time to ensure even cooking.

■ Let baking sheets cool completely between batches, or, to save time, get each new batch ready on a piece of parchment paper, then slide it onto the sheet and move them directly into the oven. If you drop dough onto baking sheets still hot from baking the last batch of cookies, the dough will begin to cook, softening and spreading, before you've dropped all the cookies.

■ For bar cookies, line the baking pan with aluminum foil for easy removal of the bars after baking.

Lining the baking pan.

Removing from the pan.

■ If you can't bake all the cookies at once, refrigerate the dough for up to 24 hours, even if it is not called refrigerator dough. Cover the bowl with plastic wrap or aluminum foil before refrigerating. There is no need to bring the dough to room temperature before continuing with baking. The exception is bar cookies, which nearly always should be baked immediately after mixing. Their batter will deflate if left to sit for any length of time.

Storing Many cookie doughs can be frozen, particularly those designed for rolling into logs and slicing. Other good candidates include stiff, buttery doughs. See FREEZING for more details.

Most baked cookies and bars can be stored at room temperature for up to 3 days. Soft cookies with lots of fat, such as chocolate chip, will not keep as long as crispier ones, such as biscotti. When fully cooled, cookies or cut bars should be transferred to an airtight container, such as a cookie tin or rigid plastic container. Bars that have not been cut and removed from the pan can be covered with foil and set aside at room temperature for up to a day. For longer storage, the bars should be transferred to an airtight container.

Most cookies and bars can be frozen for long storage. Let them cool completely and then wrap them individually or in small stacks in plastic wrap. Pack the wrapped cookies snugly in rigid plastic containers, or in zippered plastic freezer bags, pressing out as much air as possible. Label the packages with their contents and date. Most can be frozen for up to 3 months.

Defrost frozen cookies, still wrapped, at room temperature or in the refrigerator. The choice depends on when you want to serve them. It also depends on whether the cookies or bars are to be served cold (in which case, defrost them in the refrigerator) or at room temperature. Most cookies will defrost within 2 hours, although some very thin, crisp cookies will defrost in 30 minutes or less. Serve cookies as soon as possible after they are defrosted. They are not as moist as fresh baked and therefore tend to go stale faster.

Do not store crisp and cakey cookies together. The crisp cookies will absorb moisture from the others and soften. Store frosted or topped cookies in single layers, separated by waxed or parchment paper to prevent them from sticking together.

Cookie Blues Got a problem with your cookies? Find the simple explanation here.

DOUGH RIPS AND TEARS WHEN ROLLED OUT. Hot, humid weather makes rolling tricky. Bake on cool, dry days, or chill the dough before rolling and be sure to rub the rolling pin and work surface with ample flour. If the dough softens so that it rips and tears, refrigerate it for about 20 minutes and rub the rolling pin with a little more flour.

SOME COOKIES BROWN TOO QUICKLY. Sugar-rich doughs brown more than do other types of dough. Use insulated baking sheets (see BAKEWARE) or line the sheets with foil. Check your oven temperature with a thermometer and lower the heat if necessary. Also, note that dark-colored sheets promote more rapid baking and may require lowering the heat by 20° to 25°F.

COOKIES SPREAD TOO MUCH IN THE OVEN. Dough was placed on a hot baking sheet; allow sheet to cool or prepare each batch on parchment paper, transfer it to the sheet, and place sheet directly in the oven.

COOKIES ON ONE BAKING SHEET BURN AND THOSE ON THE OTHER DON'T. One sheet may be too close to the bottom of the oven, so the cookies are baking more quickly. Bake the cookies a sheet at a time on a rack in the top third of the oven, or switch and rotate the sheets as the cookies bake.

COOKIES STICK TO THE BAKING SHEET. You may have left the cookies on the baking sheet too long. Lift them off with a spatula 2 to 3 minutes after they are removed from the oven and transfer them to wire racks to let them cool completely.

Quick Tip

For most home baking, two baking sheets and two or three large cooling racks are adequate. If you often bake large batches of cookies, however, consider stocking more of both for the most efficient use of time.

The Cookie Jar Cookies come in nearly every shape, size, and flavor.

BISCOTTI In Italy, all cookies are *biscotti*. Here, the term refers to Italian cookies that are baked twice—first in loaf form, then sliced and baked a second time.

BROWNIE The quintessential bar cookie, made from chocolate and sometimes containing nuts. Some brownies are fudgy and dense, while others are more cakelike.

GINGERBREAD MAN Children love this spice cookie made from a molasses-rich dough easily cut into figures, baked, and decorated with piped icing.

MACAROON A light cookie made from almonds pounded to a moist paste, then mixed with beaten egg whites and sugar and baked until the edges are golden.

MADELEINE Traditionally baked in distinctive shell-shaped molds, this delicate French cookie has a consistency reminiscent of sponge cake.

OATMEAL A chewy drop cookie made from a dough of rolled oats, flour, sugar, eggs, and butter. Raisins and nuts are often added.

SHORTBREAD A crumbly, rich bar cookie made from dough composed of flour, sugar, and a generous measure of butter.

SPRITZ A buttery German cookie made by pressing a rich dough through a cookie press fitted with any one of a variety of plates, from rosettes to ribbons to ropes.

TOLL HOUSE The ultimate American cookie. Created by a Massachusetts innkeeper in 1939, who discovered that small pieces of chocolate mixed into dough stay firm when baked.

TUILE A thin, fragile cookie made from an egg white–rich batter that is piped or dropped onto baking sheets. While still hot from the oven, the cookies are gently shaped over a rolling pin to recall Mediterranean roof tiles. The same batter is used to make cornets, "cigarettes," and cups.

See also BAKEWARE; BAKING; BAKING TOOLS; MEASURING; ROLLING OUT.

C

COOKING METHODS A good cook will learn to master all the varied methods by which foods are cooked, namely, baking, braising, grilling, roasting, sautéing, steaming, stewing, and stir-frying. More important still, a good cook will develop a sound knowledge of which cooking methods work best for particular types of foods.

In general, tender and small food items such as shrimp and scallops or thin slices of boneless poultry must be cooked quickly to keep them from toughening or drying out. Foods with a chewy, dense texture, such as stew meats, need long, slow cooking with moisture to achieve tenderness. Some foods, such as squid and flank steak, are tender only if cooked either very briefly or for a long time.

Foods intended to be quickly sautéed or stir-fried should be inherently tender or should be cut up into pieces that will cook quickly. Some vegetables also benefit from blanching to soften them slightly before they are sautéed. Meat destined for roasting should be a tender cut with some marbling or interior fat, or it can be barded (see BARDING). Tougher or very lean cuts, such as veal and pork, are often braised rather than roasted.

Dry vs. Moist Cooking Methods

Dry Methods	Moist Methods
Baking	Boiling
Frying	Braising
Grilling	Poaching
Roasting	Steaming
Sautéing	Stewing
Stir-frying	

See also individual cooking methods; individual foods; TECHNIQUES.

COOKING SPRAY Also called vegetable oil spray, baking oil spray, canola oil spray, or olive oil spray, cooking spray is canned oil packed under pressure, dispersed by a propellant, and used to grease pots and pans. Cooking spray also is handy for lubricating the racks on charcoal and gas grills. Food, too, can be sprayed to prevent sticking during cooking, although the sprays are not recommended as substitutions for liquid oils in recipes. Using cooking spray is healthful as well as convenient because in general you use less oil than if you were pouring or brushing it over a surface.

Caution!

Never aim cooking spray toward an open flame, and use caution with it when grilling or cooking on a gas burner. The flame can travel back up the stream of spray and seriously burn you or cause an explosion.

Selecting Most cooking sprays are mixtures of soybean or canola oil, lecithin, water, and a propellant. Select the contents best suited for the type of cooking you do. Some contain flour as well, which is convenient for use on cake pans but undesirable for coating a sauté pan; others contain olive oil, which, because it burns at lower temperatures than soybean and canola oils

Quick Tip

Look for refillable spray bottles that use a pumping mechanism to build enough pressure to propel oil with about the same intensity as a can of commercial cooking spray. These devices allow you to spray high-quality olive oil or your favorite balsamic vinegar over salad greens, or to use peanut or canola oil from your own bottles to grease pans.

and because it imparts a distinct flavor, is not recommended for baking. Olive oil spray does add a little nice flavor when cooking onions, garlic, peppers, and other savory foods.

Storing Store the cans at cool room temperature in a dark cupboard. Do not refrigerate and do not let the cans reach temperatures exceeding 120°F, or they may explode. Manufacturers suggest using the sprays at temperatures between 68° and 75°F and not keeping them for more than 6 months after purchase.

Preparing Aim the spray nozzle at the pan or food and press it quickly several times, moving the stream across the surface of the pan or grill. In a short time the surface will be covered with a thin, even coating. If cooking on top of the stove, let the coated pan get hot before adding food.

Quick Bite

Approximately eight 1-second spritzes of oil from a can of commercial cooking spray equal ½ teaspoon oil.

COOKING TOOLS See page 140.

COOKWARE See page 146.

COOLING A loose term that can mean anything from allowing a pan to cool until you can comfortably hold it to letting food cool to room temperature. Cakes and other baked goods are set on racks to cool so that air can circulate around them, while soup and coffee are allowed to cool only until they don't burn the tongue. Many recipes call for cooling cooked foods "just until cool enough to handle"—that is, until you can just comfortably hold them—before peeling or slicing.

There's no trick to cooling. Simply remove the food from the heat source and let

it sit. Once cool, any moist, protein-based food should be served or chilled. Leaving food at room temperature too long invites bacterial growth. Never let perishable protein-based food (meats, poultry, soups, stocks, casseroles, custards, and the like) sit out for more than 2 hours at most.

See also CHILLING.

COOLING RACK See BAKING TOOLS.

CORIANDER When fresh, another name for cilantro; see HERB. For dried, see SPICE.

CORING To remove the central core of a fruit or vegetable. Heads of cabbage and lettuce usually require coring, as do apples, pears, and quince. Tomatoes, zucchini, and pineapples frequently are cored, too. Unless a recipe calls for the food to be kept whole, as for stuffing, you can simply cut it into halves or quarters and cut out the core from each piece.

Coring apple half with knife.

Coring whole apple with corer.

If you core a lot of fruit and vegetables, consider buying specialty corers. If the task comes up only now and then, you might want to save drawer space for other tools.

Cooking Tools

Stocking a kitchen with a selection of useful cooking tools is a lifelong process—and one you cannot begin too soon. Some gadgets may quickly lose their initial appeal, while others will wear out, get lost, or break; but if you invest in high-quality cooking tools they will last for decades. Good knives, sturdy bowls, and well-made pots and pans will never let you down.

THE BASIC COOK Following are the tools every home kitchen should have.

BRUSHES Natural-bristle brushes suitable for brushing foods with marinades, sauces, glazes, and other liquids should be firmly rooted in the handle. Handles can be made of wood or heavy-duty plastic and must be easy to grasp and long enough to allow dexterity. Wash the brushes after each use in hot, soapy water, flick them to remove excess water, and then air dry. Keep brushes used for savory foods separate from those used for dessert making.

Other useful brushes include soft- to medium-bristle vegetable brushes, good for cleaning potatoes, carrots, and other firm vegetables, and soft brushes appropriate for cleaning mushrooms.

CAN OPENER It can be frustrating to use a can opener that doesn't work well, so choose a high-quality one. The most popular can openers are manual geared ones. Variations on this style include those that remove tops from cans without producing sharp edges and those that mount on the wall. Electric can openers can stand on the countertop or be mounted.

COLANDER A bowl-shaped metal device perforated with small holes. Ideal for draining boiled foods such as pasta or vegetables. See also STRAINER.

CORKSCREW A simple metal spiral or other device designed to pull corks from wine bottles. See also CORKSCREW.

CUTTING BOARD A portable work surface. Cutting boards of various sizes and materials are used for knife work in the preparation or serving of food. See also CUTTING BOARD.

EGG BEATER Precursor of the handheld electric mixer, this convenient old-fashioned device quickly turns two bladed beaters by means of a hand-cranked ratchet wheel, easily whipping up egg whites, cream, or batters.

FORK Not just for eating at table, forks are used while cooking or serving to pierce, pick up, or steady foods. Large two-pronged carving forks steady roasts during carving; smaller ones turn steaks on the grill, or, smaller still, spear pickles from a jar. Large forks with 3 or more tines may be used for picking up and serving foods as varied as bacon, spaghetti, or sauerkraut. Even ordinary table forks may be used for many of the above-mentioned tasks.

GRATER A device used to grate food into fine particles with the aid of sharp, pointy rasps arrayed on a flat surface. (The same term is also sometimes used erroneously to refer to a shredder, since a box grater, a common kitchen tool, includes both shredding sides and a rasp-surfaced grating side containing sharp-edged holes.) See GRATING for details.

KNIFE Good, sharp knives in a few basic styles are kitchen essentials. See KNIFE for more information.

LADLE At least one ladle is essential in every kitchen. The bowl should be made of stainless steel or rigid, heat-resistant plastic and large enough to scoop up a good measure of soup, stew, or chili. The handle should be heat resistant as well and long enough for easy use. Small ladles are useful for saucing foods and skimming stocks.

MEASURING SPOONS AND CUPS Measuring spoons, sized from ⅛ teaspoon to 1 tablespoon, are fashioned from metal or plastic and usually bundled together. Liquid measures are made from clear tempered glass or plastic and generally measure up to 1 or 2 cups. This allows the cook to set the cup on the counter and view the liquid amount at eye level to get an accurate reading. Dry measures generally range from ¼ to 1 cup, are made of metal or rigid plastic, and are sold in nesting sets. See MEASURING for details on using measuring cups correctly.

MIXING BOWL Every kitchen should have an assortment of bowls in a range of sizes. Larger bowls contain mixtures as you stir and toss, while smaller-sized bowls are good for holding ingredients that have been prepared for a recipe. Bowls come in a range of sizes and materials; see MIXING BOWL for more information.

PEPPER MILL So many recipes nowadays call for pepper freshly ground from whole dried peppercorns that a pepper mill is an essential for even basic kitchens. Look for a sturdy model made from either wood or plastic, with a hardened-steel grinder that adjusts by the turn of the screw at the top of the mill to provide ground pepper of varying degrees of coarseness or fineness.

POTATO MASHER A handheld tool with a handle attached to a perforated or bent wire grid, used to mash cooked potatoes by pressing down on them repeatedly. Choose a sturdy masher made of stainless steel. Some ingenious models include two parallel grids, the lower one of which is attached to a spring in the handle, making the mashing action more efficient. See also Potato Ricer, page 145, and MASHING.

POT HOLDERS AND OVEN MITTS Essential for taking pots from the stove and pans from the oven, pot holders and oven mitts should be thickly padded and large enough to perform their designated tasks with safety. Do not skimp on these. Square potholders should be generous in size, and glovelike oven mitts should reach above the wrist and be well insulated. Mitts designed to reach nearly to the elbow are especially useful for taking large pans from the oven and for working over a hot grill.

Oven mitt.

SCISSORS AND SHEARS Every kitchen should have at least one pair of scissors in the drawer to cut parchment paper, kitchen string, cheesecloth, fresh herbs, fruits, and even pickles. Basic kitchen scissors should have stainless-steel blades and one serrated edge. Heavier and longer poultry shears are useful for cutting chicken pieces and trimming fat and skin. Specialized scissors— shellfish shears, grape shears, pizza shears—can be acquired as the need arises.

Poultry shears.

continued

Cooking Tools, continued

SPATULA Most people think of metal spatulas, hamburger or pancake turners, when they think of spatulas. These measure from 2 to 4 inches wide, have thin edges for slipping under food, and may have short or long handles. Flexible rubber spatulas, excellent for blending ingredients and scraping bowls, can have blades of varying sizes, heatproof or not. Wooden spatulas are good for lengthy stirring and for sautéing, as they won't heat up and burn your hands. Use heatproof silicone rubber and wooden spatulas on nonstick surfaces to avoid scratches; metal spatulas are fine for grills and heavy-duty frying pans. Long, narrow frosting (or icing) spatulas make quick work of frosting cakes.

*Frosting spatula
(top) and
rubber spatula
(bottom).*

SPOON An assortment of wooden, plastic, and metal spoons, both solid and slotted, is useful. See SPOON for more details.

*Slotted
spoon.*

STEAMER BASKET Also known as vegetable steamer or folding steamer. Steamer baskets are collapsible contraptions made of perforated metal with fanned sides that allow them to adjust to fit into a number of different-sized pans. They sit on small feet so they hold food above the boiling or simmering water, ensuring that the steam will circulate around the food to yield the best results. See also STEAMING.

STRAINER Also called a sieve. Strainers are used to separate out lumps or larger particles from ingredients, drain off liquid from solids, or purée soft foods. Made of fine or coarse wire mesh, they come in a variety of sizes. See STRAINER for details.

STRING Kitchen string, also called kitchen twine, is used for trussing chicken and tying roasts, as well as numerous other tasks. The string should be soft and pliable, and preferably linen—which won't burn.

THERMOMETER Every kitchen should have a meat thermometer. There are two kinds: a probe type, which is inserted into the meat at the beginning of cooking and left there until the proper temperature is reached, and an instant-read type, which is inserted toward the end of the cooking period to test for doneness. Most cooks prefer instant-read thermometers. They are more accurate and make a smaller hole in the meat, thus releasing fewer juices.

*Instant-read
thermometer.*

You can also use an instant-read thermometer to test different sections of the same piece of food, as well as more than one piece of food, and they are more convenient for grilled and panfried foods. Insert a meat thermometer in the center of a piece of meat or a roast, or on the inside of the thickest part of the thigh of a bird; make sure the thermometer is not touching bone. See BAKEWARE for information on oven thermometers and SAFETY for information on refrigerator thermometers. See also CANDY MAKING; DONENESS; and individual meats.

TIMER This invaluable little gadget is your best friend if you're cooking several dishes at once, are cooking in the midst of company, or are doing other tasks at the same time as cooking. Timers range in complexity from the simple spring-activated ones to digital timers that can time three different recipes at once. Most new stoves now have built-in oven timers. A clip-on timer that attaches to your apron is helpful when grilling outdoors.

Quick Tip

Always use a portable timer when you've put anything on a burner or in the oven but you are not staying in the kitchen. Take the timer with you so you'll hear it, and you'll save yourself the heartache of a burned pot.

TONGS These scissorlike tools, with their blunt ends capable of grasping food, are extremely useful. Some are fitted with finger loops, similar to scissors; others have a V-shaped holding end, which allows a bit more control. Most are 10 to 12 inches long; longer tongs are available for grilling. Tongs are useful for handling hot food, picking up pieces of meat without piercing them (and losing juices), tossing salads, checking pasta for doneness, and arranging food on plates. Many longer tongs are outfitted with a locking device

that keeps them closed during storage—a real space saver for a crowded utensil drawer.

VEGETABLE PEELER Sharp-edged blades and easy-to-hold handles define good vegetable peelers. Swivel-bladed peelers are more maneuverable, hugging the curves of vegetables and lessening your work. They will dull after several years of use and usually are replaced, not sharpened.

WHISK With a head of looped thin metal wires, a whisk is used to rapidly beat or whip ingredients. Also known as whips, whisks are made in various sizes and shapes for various uses. Elongated sauce whisks are the basic model, used to mix ingredients thoroughly without adding excess air. See also WHISKING.

THE WELL-STOCKED COOK

Specialty tools make particular tasks easier and cooking more pleasant. Once you have stocked the basics, you may want to add a few extras.

BULB BASTER Also called a turkey baster, this plastic, glass, or metal tube with a squeezable bulb at one end resembles a giant eyedropper. It is used to baste turkeys and other meats. See also BASTING.

CHERRY PITTER A tool that speeds the process of pitting cherries. The pitter has a hollowed-out cradle in which a single cherry is placed, and then a rod is pushed through it, forcing out the pit and leaving the fruit whole. This simple device doubles as an olive pitter. See CHERRY.

CHINOIS A fine cone-shaped strainer used for making stock, jellies, or purées. See also STRAINER.

continued

Cooking Tools, continued

EGG SLICER This tool is used to achieve uniform slices of hard-boiled eggs for salads, hors d'oeuvre platters, and other uses. The egg is placed on a rounded, slotted base attached to a frame composed of about 10 fine wires. The frame is pushed down through the egg, slicing it perfectly.

FUNNEL Metal and rigid plastic are the most common materials for funnels. Make sure they are not too large for your storage space and that the working ends fit easily in bottles and jars.

GARLIC PRESS Tool capable of mincing a peeled clove of garlic, so that it can be mixed more easily with other ingredients. The hinged tool is fitted with a perforated hopper and a plunger that squeezes the garlic through the perforations. Some have a third arm accessory with small teeth that fit through the perforations to push out the garlic waste. Others have plastic tubes for storing pressed garlic. The most useful are the simplest, made of metal rather than plastic. If you like garlic and use it a lot, look in specialty cookware shops or catalogs for oversized garlic presses capable of holding and pressing several cloves at a time.

HEAT DIFFUSER A disk that sits directly on a stove burner to shield fragile pots or delicate contents—hollandaise sauce, chocolate—from direct heat by diffusing it through two sheets of perforated metal with an air space between them. A second type of diffuser is a thick steel disk that stands about ¾ inch above the burner, the air space between the two modifying the intensity of the heat. The most popular brand of the latter type is the Flame-Tamer, a name that has become nearly synonymous with the tool itself.

ICE CREAM SCOOP Two styles of scoop are popular for spooning frozen ice cream and sherbet from containers: the dipper scoop and the half-sphere scoop. The dipper has a thick handle and a rounded, shallow bowl. The handle is hollow and transmits heat from your hand to the dipper. The half-sphere scoop has a full, deep bowl and a trigger-released metal wire that pushes the ice cream from the scoop. Some specialty shops and catalogs also carry electrically heated scoops that cut through ice cream more easily.

MEAT MALLET A mallet is useful for pounding boneless meat and poultry pieces until thin for quick and even cooking. Also called a meat pounder, although pounders tend to have one smooth side for flattening only, while mallets often have two sides, one with blunt teeth that help break down fibers in the meat, thus tenderizing it.

MELON BALLER Also known as a vegetable scoop, potato baller, or melon-ball scoop, this hand tool has a small bowl about 1 inch in diameter at one end used for making decorative balls from melon or other semi-firm foods. It is useful for coring some foods, such as pears, or preparing them for stuffing. Some scoops have a second, slightly smaller bowl at the opposite end of the handle.

MORTAR AND PESTLE This primitive pair of tools used for pounding and grinding ingredients consists of a sturdy bowl-shaped mortar and a heavy, cylindrical pounder or pestle. While their work is often replaced nowadays by such mechanized tools as spice mills and food processors, the duo remains an excellent way to grind up spices or nuts, or to pound garlic together with fresh basil and pine nuts for pesto sauce at its most rustic. The best material for a mortar is marble, which is heavy, sturdy, and will not absorb food odors; heavy-duty ceramic models are also good. Pestles may be made from wood, metal, marble, or ceramic.

PIZZA WHEEL Although pizzas and open tarts can be cut with serrated knives, using a rotating pizza wheel, or pizza cutter, is more efficient. The sharp-edged wheels are from 2 to 4 inches in diameter; the metal or wooden handles are short and sturdy and are fitted with a protective thumb guard. Buy the sturdiest pizza wheel you can find, making sure it has a strong handle and a large thumb guard.

POTATO RICER A useful device for making smooth mashed potatoes and similar dishes. A plunger pushes potatoes through a perforated basket, reducing them to the consistency of grains of rice that are then stirred into a fluffy mass. See also RICING.

REAMER A handheld or freestanding tool designed to squeeze the juice from lemons, usually by means of a mound-shaped ridged surface pressed and twisted against and into a cut lemon half to help squeeze out the juice. See also JUICING.

SALAD SPINNER Also called a salad washer, this plastic device allows you to dry greens quickly and efficiently. Most salad spinners are 3-piece plastic contraptions with a perforated inner basket that is spun so that the water is removed from the washed greens by centrifugal force.

SALT GRINDER With the growing popularity of various types of coarse salt and sea salt, this handheld mill makes it possible to use them at table, reducing the flavorful salts to finer particles for seasoning individual portions of food. Unlike pepper mills, whose steel mechanisms would corrode with prolonged exposure to salt, these feature hardwood or heavy-duty plastic grinding mechanisms that crush the salt with the turn of a key, dispensing it from below.

SKEWERS Also called kabob or brochette skewers. Made of metal, wood, or bamboo, skewers have sharp points for pushing them through food. Metal skewers sometimes have looped handles to prevent food from sliding off. See also GRILLING.

SKIMMER Designed to skim frothy scum or foam from the tops of simmering stocks and other liquids, with a long handle and a large, shallow bowl of wire mesh or perforated metal. May also be used to remove pieces of food from hot fat when deep-frying. See also STRAINER.

STRAWBERRY HULLER Tweezerlike tinned steel tool with broad blades used to pluck the green stem from a strawberry without bruising the fruit. Also handy for picking out small bones that often remain in fish fillets.

ZESTER The citrus zester's metal blade at the end of a short handle is fitted with a row of 4 to 6 sharp-edged holes that allow for the removal of thin strips of the colorful outermost part of the peel while leaving behind the bitter white pith. See also ZESTING.

See also BAKEWARE; BAKING TOOLS; COOKWARE; GRILLING; KNIFE.

Cookware

The most important long-term investment the home cook makes is in cookware. Some would argue that it is more crucial to successful cooking than stove tops or ovens, as the kind and quality of cookware greatly affects the final outcome of a dish.

Peek into the cupboards of the best cooks you know and you likely will find an eclectic assortment of pots and pans of varying sizes, shapes, materials, and hefts.

Many beginning cooks, or those setting up a new kitchen, want to buy a complete set of pots and pans, all made by the same manufacturer and with the same design. While this is a convenient idea—and surely the matching pots and pans look handsome hanging from a pot rack—this is not the ideal way to buy cookware. Instead, select a few pieces at a time, building your stock over time as you learn more about cooking in general and your own cooking style in particular. As with all kitchen equipment, look for solid equipment that will last a lifetime. Lower-quality pots and pans tend to warp and dent easily, often do not hold heat well, and will probably end up needing to be replaced.

COOKWARE MATERIALS Different metals and alloys and different gauges (thicknesses) work most effectively for different cooking tasks.

ALUMINUM Heats rapidly and evenly, is durable and relatively inexpensive, but reacts with acidic foods and can impart a metallic taste. It also tends to warp if not of sufficient gauge. Select anodized aluminum, which has been treated with an electrolytic process to make it harder, denser, and resistant to corrosion.

CAST IRON Heats more slowly than some other materials but holds the heat extremely well and uniformly, even at high temperatures, making it good for frying and searing. It reacts with acidic foods and can impart a metallic taste. By the same token, it imparts a little iron into the food, which is beneficial. Regular cast iron is heavy and should always be dried after washing to prevent rusting. Enameled cast iron holds heat extremely well and is good for long, slow cooking but is prone to chipping and staining. See also SEASONING.

COPPER Heats and cools rapidly and evenly. Many cooks feel copper is the preferred metal for cookware. Copper cookware must be lined to avoid reactions with foods. Copper pans with stainless steel interiors and alloyed-aluminum and aluminum cores, which are durable and handsome, are a good compromise. They have good heft and heat quickly and evenly.

ENAMELED STEEL A good choice. Today's enameled steel is heavy and durable. It will not react with acidic foods.

GLASS Tempered to withstand both stove-top cooking and baking. It holds heat well and is noncorrosive, but heat conduction is not as uniform as with metal and there is the danger of breaking and cracking if glass cookware is mishandled.

NONSTICK SURFACES These popular coatings have steadily improved over the years. Unlike in the past, coatings today do not

C

affect the metal's ability to conduct heat. In addition, they are durable and very easy to clean. Keep in mind that although nonstick is helpful for making omelets, oatmeal, and rice, it will interfere with browning meat.

STAINLESS STEEL Does not react with acidic ingredients and will not corrode, but it is a poor absorber of heat. Cladded stainless steel, that is, stainless steel exterior with a carbon core, boasts rapid and uniform heat conduction. Stainless steel with a layered alloyed-aluminum and aluminum core or an aluminum disk bottom also heats quickly and evenly, does not corrode, and is durable.

THE BASIC COOK Following are the pots and pans every kitchen should have.

BAKING DISH A shallow, rectangular dish made of tempered glass, porcelain, earthenware, or a pan made of metal, this all-purpose item works well for roasting meat or vegetables and baking brownies, gratins, or bread pudding.

BROILER PAN Also called a broiler tray, this rectangular pan is made to fit under a broiler's heat elements. Standard size is 9 by 12 inches and 1½ to 2 inches deep. Broiler pans come with a removable slotted tray to hold the food and allow drippings to fall into the bottom of the pan. Many oven manufacturers supply a broiler pan with their ovens.

CASSEROLE Deeper than your average baking dish, a casserole may be made of metal, porcelain, or stoneware, and usually comes with a fitted lid.

DUTCH OVEN Large, round or oval pots with tight-fitting lids and two loop handles used for slow cooking on top of the stove or in the oven. Most are made of enameled cast iron, although some are

made of regular cast iron or other uncoated metals. They range from 4 to 12 quarts; 8 or 9 quarts is recommended for most home kitchens. Also called heavy casseroles and stew pots.

FRYING PAN See Skillet, page 148.

ROASTING PAN AND RACK A large rectangular pan with handles that is sometimes fitted with a removable rack to hold the meat or turkey above the bottom of the pan. Roasting pans should be made from metal heavy enough to prevent them from warping or denting.

SAUCEPAN A simple round pan with either straight or sloping sides. In general, saucepans range in size from 1 to 5 quarts. Most useful is the 2-quart size. Traditional saucepans are twice as wide as they are high. This facilitates rapid evaporation, so that a sauce thickens and cooks efficiently. Straight-sided saucepans with high sides are ideal for longer cooking, since the liquid will not boil away so quickly. Slant-sided saucepans, commonly called chef's pans, with outwardly flaring sides, promote rapid evaporation, making them excellent for sauce making. The best materials for saucepans are anodized aluminum or aluminized steel.

SAUTÉ PAN Also known as a straight-sided frying pan. Sauté pans have a high, angled handle and relatively high sides so that the food can be flipped inside the pan and won't bounce out. The sides are 2½ to 4 inches high, with 3 inches being the height preferred by many cooks. Sauté pans are also very nice for braised dishes or any stove-top recipe that uses a lot of liquid. They may measure from 6 to 14¼ inches in diameter, and volume capacities generally

continued

Cookware, continued

range from one 1 to 7 quarts, with 2½ to 4 quarts being the most useful for the home cook. Sauté pans often have lids.

Sauté pan (top) and skillet (bottom).

Skillet Also called a frying pan, this broad pan is often confused with a sauté pan, but traditionally differs in that it has sides that flare outward, making it useful for cooking foods that must be stirred or turned out of the pan. Most kitchens should have both a smaller one, 9 or 10 inches across the bottom, and a larger one, 12 or 14 inches. Skillets do not have lids. The best materials are anodized aluminum or cast iron; if you buy two, make one of them nonstick.

Stockpot Also known as a spaghetti pot or soup pot, a stockpot is a high, narrow pot designed for minimal evaporation during long cooking. Stockpots are fitted with two looped handles for easy lifting and tight-fitting lids. They should be made of heavy-gauge metal with good heft. The smallest stockpots have an 8-quart capacity. Most home cooks find stockpots with 10- to 12-quart capacities to be the most useful.

THE WELL-STOCKED COOK You may eventually want to acquire these more specialized pots and pans, depending on the types of cooking you do.

Clay Pot Also known as clay cooker, terra-cotta baker, clay chicken pot, Römertopf, or Roman pot. Unglazed clay pots are meant for oven cooking, not stove top. Most are microwave safe. Because they are porous and because they are saturated with water before every use, they promote especially moist, succulent food. Chicken and other poultry are the most popular foods to cook in the pots, which are handsome enough to carry to the table for serving. See also CLAY POT.

Crepe Pan A small, shallow pan with flared sides that permit crepe batter to cook quickly and evenly. Its relatively long, flat handle is shaped so that the pan can be rotated easily during cooking. See also CREPE.

Deep and Double Roaster This extra-deep roasting pan effectively creates a smaller oven within the environment of your kitchen's oven, speeding cooking time and promoting browning by holding in heat all around a roast. Most double roasters come with lids that transform them into large-sized dutch ovens. Some lids are mirror images of the bottom pans and offer the added convenience of effectively providing you with an additional roasting pan.

Double Boiler A set of two pans, one nesting atop the other, outfitted with one lid that fits both pans. A small amount of water is barely simmered in the lower pan, while ingredients are placed in the top pan to heat them gently, keep them warm, or melt them. See also DOUBLE BOILER.

Fish Poacher Specifically designed to fit whole fish (and can be used for large fillets), this deep, lidded poaching pan comes in a range of shapes and sizes. The most classic of these is a long, rectangular pan that fits across two burners, perfect for holding a side of salmon or even a whole salmon; a perforated rack fits inside, on which the fish may be easily lowered into or lifted from the poaching liquid. Smaller, oval poachers are ideal for whole flatfish such as sole, while a traditional rectangular French pot called a *turbotière* is made expressly for the cooking of whole turbot.

GRATIN DISH Shallow baking dish designed to maximize surface area for the formation of a well-browned, crisp crust. Gratin dishes of varying sizes may be made from metal, enameled metal, porcelain, or earthenware. See GRATIN.

GRIDDLE Flat rectangles or rounds of cast iron or cast aluminum, often with a nonstick finish, griddles sit flat on the stove top and are designed to be heated over one or two burners. They are used to

cook pancakes, eggs, bacon, thin steaks, cheese sandwiches, and more. Most have depressed rims to catch grease.

GRILL PAN A cast-iron skillet with ridges across the bottom for "grilling" meat or fish indoors. Some grill pans are designed for use in the broiler, others on top of the stove, fitting over one or two burners. Made of cast iron or anodized aluminum.

KETTLE In the old days, a kettle was any large pot used to boil water. Today, the word more specifically refers to teakettles designed to boil water quickly and to pour

Quick Tip

Not all pots and pans are made to sit on a burner, just as many are not made to go in the oven. Some can go from burner to oven, but not all. Be sure to read the instructions carefully that come with your pots and pans to determine if they are flameproof, ovenproof, or both. Flameproof means the pot or pan can go on a burner, whether it heats with gas flames, electric coils, or thermal induction. Ovenproof means the pot or pan can go into the oven.

it safely from an angled spout. Teakettles hold from 2 to 5 quarts and should have a removable lid for filling and cleaning and a stay-cool handle. A stockpot is often referred to as a soup kettle.

MULTIPURPOSE POT This tall pot with a tight-fitting lid is fitted with a perforated insert that cooks up to 2 pounds of pasta, which can be lifted from the pot for easy draining, as well as a steamer insert. Multipurpose pots usually have 6- or 8-quart capacities. They are useful for blanching.

OMELET PAN A shallow pan with rounded sloping sides, a long handle, and, preferably, a nonstick surface, for easy cooking and folding of omelets.

PASTA POT See Multipurpose Pot, above.

WOK This ingenious Chinese pan is a versatile cooking device ideal for stir-frying, deep-frying, and steaming. Traditionally made of plain steel, a good retainer of heat, the wok has a rounded bottom that allows small pieces of food to be rapidly tossed and stirred, while the gradually sloping sides help to keep the food inside the pan.

CORKSCREW Designing the perfect corkscrew is as challenging as designing the perfect mousetrap, but this has not stopped equipment designers from trying. Numerous devices for getting the cork out of a wine bottle are on the market, and in most cases which one you choose is a matter of personal preference. Most work well after a bit of practice, although a few are better than others. It is always a good idea to try out a new corkscrew on a bottle of inexpensive wine.

Corkscrews.

Corkscrews are no longer simply hefty screws topped with a perpendicular wooden handle. The twin-bladed cork puller consists of two slim metal shafts designed to grab the cork on either side while you pull it from the bottle. This style is especially useful for brittle older corks. Some find it tricky to use, but after a bit of practice, you'll be glad never to shred another cork. The double-screw corkscrew relies on two screws, one to invade the cork, the other to pull it from the bottle. When the screw on the double-wing corkscrew is twisted into the cork, two side handles are forced up; when they are pushed down, the cork rises from the bottle. Once you get the hang of the waiter's knife, tucked into the pocket of nearly every good waiter, it works beautifully. The tool has a handle that hooks onto the side

of the bottle while the screw enters the cork. The cork is then levered from the bottle—and can be levered back into the bottle, too. Professional vintners and serious hobbyists often use a professional lever corkscrew, which effortlessly pulls corks from the bottles and just as effortlessly pushes them back. The tools are large and expensive. Finally, a device called a Screwpull is popular with many wine lovers. The specially engineered screw easily enters the cork as a levered handle is turned in one direction, and then, when the handle is turned in the other direction, the cork is pulled from the bottle.

CORN One of the joys of summer in temperate climates is eating freshly picked sweet corn. The briefly cooked kernels are sweet and crisp and usually need no more than a sprinkling of salt and pepper, or perhaps a pat of butter. The season for this golden grain, which many people erroneously consider a vegetable, is fleeting, and corn lovers anticipate it just as happily as they do the tomato crop, frequently pairing the two at meals. But corn plays an important role in our culinary universe year-round, not just during its short season.

Corn, whose true name is maize, is one of the world's most important crops. It is used to make oil, corn syrup, cornstarch, cornmeal, breakfast cereal, bread, and tortillas. In addition, field corn is fed to cattle and hogs, which is perhaps its most expansive role. Not all corn is yellow. Some types are white or a mixture of white and yellow kernels. Blue corn, grown in the

Southwest and Mexico, is used mainly for chips, cornmeal, and flour. Popcorn, a sizable crop, is used for only one thing.

See also BOILING; CORN BREAD; CORNMEAL; POLENTA.

Selecting Sweet corn is sold fresh, canned, and frozen. When fresh, it is sold on the cob, usually still in its outer green husk. It is at its best when just picked, with the freshest ears usually found at farmers' markets. Choose ears with green husks with no signs of browning or drying. They should feel cool, never noticeably warm. The silk, or tassels, should be pale yellow and moist, showing no signs of drying or rot. Whether the kernels are yellow or white, or a combination of the two, they should be tightly packed in even rows and look plump and juicy. Freshness is more crucial than the color of the kernel. If shopping in a supermarket, buy corn only if it is displayed in a refrigerated section. The ear may be partially husked and wrapped in plastic, revealing the kernels.

Quick Bite

When you tear back the husk to view the corn in the market, you are shortening its shelf life. Once the husk is removed, the corn begins to lose moisture and freshness more quickly.

Corn kernels are sold frozen, and you can sometimes find frozen corn on the cob. Frozen corn retains much of its good flavor and texture and can be used in place of fresh corn in many recipes.

Storing Fresh sweet corn should be kept wrapped in its husks in a cool place—a cooler or the refrigerator—until you are ready to cook it, preferably for no longer than a day. The natural sugar in corn begins to turn to starch the minute the ear is picked, so corn should be consumed as soon as possible after harvest. But this time-

Corn Glossary

CORN HUSKS, DRIED Dried corn husks (outer leaves) used to wrap tamales, sold packaged in specialty and Mexican stores. Corn husks are not meant to be eaten, but they give the tamales a deeper corn flavor.

CORNMEAL Any meal ground from dried corn, whether made from yellow, white, or blue corn; fine, medium, or coarse in texture; ground by millstones or steel rollers; and with or without the corn's husk and germ included. See CORNMEAL; POLENTA.

GRITS A ground meal of yellow or white hominy, cooked like cornmeal to a thick porridge. See also GRAIN.

HOMINY Mildly sweet-tasting, firm-textured kernels of dried white or yellow corn that have been soaked in a lye solution to slough off their hulls. See also GRAIN.

POLENTA Italian-style cornmeal, cooked in either water or stock until it becomes thick and porridgelike. See GRAIN; POLENTA.

POPCORN A type of corn that, because of its composition and ratio of protein to starch, "pops" through its outer skin and expands when heated.

SAMP Dried hominy that has been broken into large pieces or pounded into coarse meal, less refined than grits. Grits can be used in place of samp in most recipes.

honored admonishment about corn is not as true as it once was. Growers have developed new supersweet and sugar-enhanced varieties that make longer storage (and, consequently, long-distance shipping) possible. This means that some fresh in-season corn will keep for more than a day, and that out-of-season corn on the cob now may be quite delicious, although traditional summertime feasts of golden fried chicken and butter-slathered ears of corn seldom taste as good on a blustery fall day.

Preparing Strip the husks and silk from the ears, snapping the leaves off the bottom along with any remaining stem (unless you want to keep it as a handle for eating). Stubbornly clinging strands of corn silk can be removed by scrubbing the corn under cold running water with a vegetable brush.

To cut kernels from the cob, uncooked or cooked, break the cob in half and hold each cob half upright, flat end down. Using a sharp knife, slice straight down between the kernels and the cob, but not too deeply, to avoid the kernels' fibrous bases. If you want the corn milk for a recipe, place the cob's flat end in a shallow bowl as you cut. Run the back of the knife blade along the length of the ear after removing the kernels to squeeze every drop into the bowl.

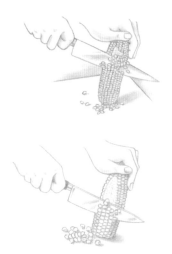

To get creamed corn or just the corn pulp and not the kernels, first score the individual rows of kernels by running the tip of your knife down each row. Then, stand-ing the ear on one end, run a spoon or the back of a knife blade along the kernels with enough pressure to express the milk and pulp but leave the skin behind.

You can drop fresh corn into boiling water and cook it quickly, or grill it or roast it in the oven or on a barbecue, usu-ally brushed first with oil or butter and wrapped in foil. Four or five ears may be cooked successfully in the microwave. The kernels can be cut from the cob and sautéed, steamed, boiled, or added to soups, fritters, puddings, stews, casseroles, salads, and fresh relishes.

See also BOILING.

CORN BREAD An American favorite, corn bread is a quick bread made with cornmeal. Because of the inclusion of flour and sugar, corn bread in the North tends to be cakier and sweeter than Southern corn bread, made with just cornmeal, liq-uid, salt, leavener, and a little fat. Corn bread can be made with any type of corn-meal. Stone-ground cornmeal gives the bread fuller flavor and better texture, but corn bread is still good made with ordinary steel-cut cornmeal. Commercial mixes yield acceptable breads, although they tend to be sweet. Like all quick breads, corn bread should be baked immediately after the batter is mixed.

Corn bread usually is baked in a square or rectangular pan or, more traditionally, a cast-iron skillet, and sometimes in a loaf pan, muffin cups, or corn-stick pans, for bread shaped like ears of corn. While most modern recipes call for baking the bread in the oven, skillet corn bread can be "baked" on top of a stove, over a campfire, or nes-tled in the hot ashes of a fireplace. Many recipes, particularly those from the South, call for melting butter or bacon fat in the pan and then pouring the batter into the hot pan, resulting in a crisp, tender crust.

A lightly sweetened corn bread, split and spread with an aromatic honey, is good for breakfast, while a more savory version is wonderful with stews, soups, and chili. In recent years, making corn bread with roasted peppers or hot chiles such as jalapeños, and sometimes with Cheddar cheese as well, has become popular, especially as an accompaniment to chili.

See also CORNMEAL; QUICK BREAD.

CORNED BEEF See BEEF.

CORNISH GAME HEN Also known as a rock Cornish game hen or Cornish hen. This diminutive bird is a hybrid of two kinds of poultry, the Cornish game cock and the white Plymouth Rock hen. The Cornish game hen weighs from 1 to 1¼ pounds and is large enough to serve one or two people. Sold frozen in almost every supermarket, Cornish hens are available fresh, or fresh hens may be ordered. They may be substituted for poussins, chicken, and squabs and are usually roasted or grilled, either halved or whole. They may also be braised. Because of their delicate flavor, these birds pair well with mild marinades and sauces.

Selecting Choose fresh hens when possible; they should smell fresh and have no discoloration. The flesh should be firm and resilient. Packaged birds should not have accumulated liquid in the package. Frozen birds should not have pink-tinged ice.

Storing Store in the refrigerator in the original packaging, adding a layer of plastic to birds wrapped only in butcher paper. Use within 2 days of purchase.

Preparing One Cornish hen will feed one or two people. Prepare as for any poultry: remove the innards, wash and pat dry, and pluck any remaining feathers with a pair of tweezers or needle-nosed pliers.

See also CHICKEN; SQUAB.

CORNMEAL Made from yellow, white, or blue corn, cornmeal can be ground fine, medium, or coarse, and any one of these grinds can be used in recipes requiring cornmeal, unless otherwise specified. There is no difference between yellow and white cornmeal in terms of taste and usage, although yellow cornmeal has more vitamin A. Blue cornmeal is considered a specialty food and produces pleasingly nutty, full-flavored baked goods.

Stone-ground cornmeal is preferred by many home cooks because it contains the germ of the corn, giving it a fuller, slightly nutty flavor and more nutrients. It is literally ground between stones, often powered by water (for water-ground cornmeal), rather than steel-cut by more modern, industrialized equipment. Stone-ground cornmeal is softer, moister, and more perishable than steel-cut. Other cornmeal, labeled "enriched degerminated," contains only the starchy endosperm and has a longer shelf life. Cornmeal is used to make cornbread, polenta, corn pudding, spoon bread, Johnnycakes, and batter bread. It is also sprinkled on baking stones to keep pizza and focaccia doughs from sticking.

Selecting Buy stone-ground cornmeal if possible. Health-food stores and farmers' markets often sell cornmeal ground by small mills. These meals tend to be tastier than others, so try them if you can. Otherwise, buy the cornmeal available at the market, checking the sell-by date, particularly if the cornmeal is one of the more perishable stone-ground varieties.

Storing Stone-ground cornmeal will become rancid and stale with age. It must be stored in the refrigerator, where it will keep for up to 4 months. Degerminated cornmeal in an airtight container can be stored at cool room temperature for up to 1 year.

See also CORN; CORN BREAD; POLENTA.

C

CORNSTARCH A highly refined, silky powder made from the endosperm of the corn kernel and used to thicken sauces, puddings, fruit fillings and glazes, and stews. Sauces and glazes thickened with cornstarch have a glossy sheen, unlike those thickened with flour, which are opaque. Cornstarch has nearly twice the thickening power of flour.

Selecting Buy any commercial brand of cornstarch in the size of box suited to your cooking needs.

Storing Store cornstarch in a cool, dry cupboard for up to 1 year after its sell-by date. In humid climates, enclose the box in a plastic bag.

Preparing Cornstarch should be whisked with a small amount of cold water (1 part cornstarch to 3 parts liquid) to make what is called a slurry before it is added to a dish. It is then cooked gently for a minute or so to eliminate any starchy taste. Take care not to let the liquids boil once the cornstarch has been added, or the sauce will thin out.

See also THICKENING.

CORN SYRUP This syrup, made from cornstarch, is used to sweeten everything from commercial candies and jams to snack cakes and cookies. It also is used in home cooking and baking. Available in dark and light versions, corn syrup does not crystallize when heated, which makes it desirable for candy making. It also adds moisture and chewiness to cakes and cookies. Dark corn syrup has more flavor than light syrup. Imitation pancake syrups are made by adding maple flavoring to corn syrup.

Selecting Corn syrup is sold in glass bottles. Buy either dark or light, depending on your cooking needs or recipe.

Storing Store unopened corn syrup in a cool, dark cupboard for up to 6 months after the sell-by date. Once opened, it should be stored in the same cupboard for up to 6 months. To discourage spoiling, keep the syrup tightly capped and wipe any spillage from the outside of the bottle.

Preparing Use as directed in individual recipes. Light corn syrup can be used in place of dark, although it's generally best to use what a recipe directs. The reverse is not always true because dark corn syrup might add too much flavor to some dishes. Dark or light corn syrup can be used in place of honey in recipes, although you should expect it to be sweeter than honey, with a less interesting flavor. Light corn syrup can be substituted in equal measure for granulated sugar in many instances, although not in baking. Dark corn syrup can be substituted for molasses, although it is not as sweet.

CORRECTING THE SEASONING See ADJUSTING THE SEASONING.

COTTAGE CHEESE See CHEESE.

COURT-BOUILLON (KOOR bwee-YAWN) A stock requiring only short cooking (*court* means "short" in French) and used most often to cook fish, seafood, and vegetables. Court-bouillon may be used as a poaching or braising liquid and then discarded, or can become the base for a sauce. It is made from water and aromatic vegetables such as onions, celery, and carrots, along with a bouquet garni.

Court-bouillon also contains an acidic ingredient, such as vinegar, lemon juice, or wine, useful for keeping fish firm during poaching. Vegetable stock can be used in place of court-bouillon, although if using it to cook fish, add a dash of lemon juice.

See also BOUQUET GARNI.

COUSCOUS Couscous is a pasta made from semolina flour, which is coarsely ground from the hulled berries of durum wheat. The semolina is mixed with water and salt, formed into tiny, round pellets, and then steamed and dried. Some couscous also contains plain whole-wheat flour, or it also may be made from ground millet, corn, or barley.

Like other pastas, couscous does not have much flavor on its own but takes well to combining with other, stronger-flavored foods. Couscous is a staple throughout North Africa, where it is cooked in a double-tiered pot called a *couscousière*. For the hearty, traditional dish, also known as couscous, lamb or chicken, vegetables, and spices cook in the lower tier while the small grains of couscous steam in the perforated top tier, where they are flavored by the aromatic vapor produced below.

Selecting Buy regular or instant (quick-cooking) couscous, regular or large-grained, depending on the recipe and your needs. Regular couscous takes a little longer to cook than instant and is a little lighter and fluffier. Most recipes can be made with either, however, and instant couscous is often easier to find in the market. Couscous is available in most supermarkets and health-food stores and also in Middle Eastern markets and specialty stores. It usually is sold in packages but is sometimes available in bulk.

Storing Once its package is open, couscous should be stored in a cool, dry cupboard and will keep very well for at least 3 months and far longer in the refrigerator. A sealed package keeps indefinitely in a cool, dry place.

Preparing When cooking couscous, the goal is to let the grains absorb moisture and swell as much as possible. Many cooks feel regular couscous, not instant, does a better job of this, and steaming is the best way to cook it. Steam regular couscous in a perforated basket or sieve above boiling water for 20 to 30 minutes, or cook it in boiling liquid for about 10 minutes and then let it stand for 15 to 20 minutes until softened and swelled. Stir instant couscous into boiling water, remove from the heat, and let it sit for 5 to 10 minutes to soften and expand. Using a fork, be sure to fluff the couscous to separate the grains before serving.

COWPEA See BEAN, DRIED.

CRAB Crabs, like lobsters and shrimp, are crustaceans. Hundreds of varieties of crabs live in the world's waters. In the United States, a crab's popularity is determined by its local availability: along the Atlantic and Gulf coasts, blue crabs are eaten most often; in southern Florida, stone crabs are considered delicacies; along the Pacific coast from southern California to Washington, the Dungeness is the crab of choice; and in Alaska, king crab and snow crab reign supreme.

Like lobsters, crabs must be kept alive until cooking, after which their shells turn bright red. They are a little more tricky to eat than lobster, although in crab-eating regions such as Charleston and Maryland's eastern shore, folks think nothing of the messy task. In other parts of the country, many people prefer buying the sweet, velvety crabmeat out of the shell and already cooked, although you'll have better flavor if you extract the meat yourself. On the West Coast, Dungeness crab is usually sold cooked but still in the shell, although it is possible to buy the giant shellfish live for cooking at home. Alaskan king crab and snow crab are nearly always sold cooked and frozen except in Alaska, where they can be bought fresh.

Selecting Live hard-shelled crabs should move their claws with some vigor when poked. Live soft-shelled crabs should look moist and soft, with no hint of hardening shell. When you lift a crab, if its claws drop, reject it. Ideally, buy them immedi-

ately before you plan to cook them, and go directly home from the market. The only exception is if a fishmonger will pack the crabs in seaweed and then in special boxes for transport.

Cooked crabmeat usually is pasteurized and sold in cans or vacuum-packed plastic bags. It is commonly served cold, in salads or with cocktail sauces, as heating diminishes its flavor, although it is also used to

✦ Crab Glossary ✦

The following entries describe the characteristics and uses of the six types of crab most widely available in North America. Thousands of other edible crab species exist, however, leading to the possible availability of other local types in coastal areas. Feel free to substitute any variety of crabmeat that appeals to you for another in a recipe.

ALASKAN KING CRAB The best meat found in this type of crab is located in the long, spindly legs. The legs are cooked and frozen before being shipped.

BLUE CRAB Plentiful and popular on the Atlantic and Gulf coasts, these pleasant, mild-flavored crabs have dark green to black shells. They are used for much of the pasteurized crabmeat sold across the country, although they are also served whole. See also Soft-Shelled Crab, below.

DUNGENESS CRAB Large and delicious, the Dungeness is usually sold cooked in markets on the West Coast—and with increasing frequency elsewhere across the country.

SNOW CRAB A type of spider crab found in Alaskan waters with skinny legs and flavorful meat. The claws are available frozen, already cracked for easy eating, but most of the catch is used for crabmeat.

SOFT-SHELLED CRAB Before they reach their full maturity, blue crabs shed their hard shells several times. When they do, they are known as soft-shelled crabs during the days before they grow new, larger hard shells. Available from the spring to early autumn, they are meant to be eaten whole, soft shell and all.

STONE CRAB The only part of the stone crab that is eaten is the claws. When a crab is caught, a claw is pulled off the live crab. The crab is then returned to the sea where it will eventually grow a new one. The claws are usually sold cooked and eaten cold—except in southern Florida, where they are cooked and served hot.

make crab cakes. Some fishmongers sell crabmeat freshly cooked and unpasteurized, packed in plastic tubs. This is usually meat from blue crabs. Lump crabmeat, also called backfin or jumbo, is the most desirable, as it is white meat taken from the center of the body and is in the largest pieces. Flake crabmeat is light and dark meat from the center and legs and is in smaller pieces; it's still tasty. If possible, avoid cooked crabmeat that has been frozen.

Storing Although it is always best to cook live crabs on the day you purchase them, properly packed live crabs can be refrigerated for up to 2 days. Lay them in a shallow bowl and nestle the bowl in a larger one containing ice. Cover the crabs with a damp kitchen towel or with wet seaweed, if it came with the crabs. Replace the ice as needed. Properly stored, the crabs should still be alive after a day or so. Discard any that are no longer living.

Freshly cooked crabmeat will keep in the refrigerator for 2 days; if the crabmeat has been frozen and thawed, eat it on the day you buy it. Pasteurized crabmeat packed in vacuum-sealed bags will keep in the refrigerator for 3 to 4 weeks. Frozen crab will keep in the freezer for 4 months; thaw in the refrigerator.

HOW TO *Clean Hard-Shelled Crabs*

Blue crabs can be cleaned while still alive or after they are cooked. For eating whole, they are cleaned after cooking; for soups and stews, they are cleaned first.

1. Rinse the crab under cold running water and scrub it with a small brush to remove any sand and grit.
2. Plunge the crab into boiling water for about 30 seconds and then rinse it under cold water to halt the cooking. (If it is already cooked, ignore this step.)
3. Using your hands, twist off the crab's legs and claws and set them aside.

4. Turn the crab upside down, and use your thumb to peel back and twist the apron off the body. The apron is the small triangular shell flap on the underside of the crab.

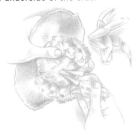

5. Insert your thumbs into the small crevice between the underside of the crab's body and its top shell. Pull them apart, lifting the top shell off the body and keeping the body intact.

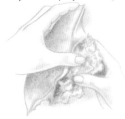

6. Pull or scrape out the liver and dark gray intestines from the center of the body, along with any roe you might find (the roe is dark before cooking and orange afterward). Scrape and rinse out the top shell if it is to be used in serving the crab. When the shell of Dungeness crab is removed for eating, underneath are its edible organs and fat called "crab butter" or "crab mustard." This yellow mass should be saved and eaten with the crab.

continued

7. Using a spoon or your fingers, scrape or pull off the spongy, feather-shaped white gills, known as "dead man's fingers," from either side of the body.

8. In blue crabs, remove the sand sac in the head behind the eyes. For Dungeness crabs, lift out the white intestine that runs along the back and remove the small mouth section as well.
9. If the crab is uncooked, cut the center section of the body in half or quarters using a sharp knife. Use the crab in soup or stock. If it is already cooked, break the crab's body in half to reveal the meat. Using your fingers, a knife, or a lobster pick, remove the meat from all the body cavities.

10. Using a mallet or lobster cracker, crack the shells of the claws in several places, as well as any legs large enough to contain a good amount of meat. Break away the shell pieces and remove the meat with your fingers or a lobster pick.

HOW TO *Clean Soft-Shelled Crabs*

1. Rinse quickly under cold water.
2. Turn the crab over and pull off and discard the apron, the small triangular shell flap on the underside of the crab.

3. With a small knife or sharp scissors, cut off the crab's eyes—but not the entire head—by making a straight cut about ¼ inch behind the mouth and eyes.

4. Squeeze the body gently and use the point of a knife to pull out the small bubblelike sand sac that hides behind the mouth.
5. Fold back the points of the top shell on either side of the crab to expose the spongy, feather-shaped white gills and pull off the gills from either side of the body.

6. Cook immediately.

Quick Tip

Female blue crabs, identified by their rounded aprons, are called "she-crabs" when young and "snooks" when mature. They are greatly prized for their roe, or eggs, which are an integral part of most recipes for the renowned she-crab soup. Male blue crabs, identified by their narrow, pointed aprons, are called "jimmies." Jimmies have more meat, although she-crab fans argue that the meat of jimmies is not as sweet. There are laws regulating the harvesting of she-crabs in some waters to protect the species.

CRANBERRY See BERRY.

CRANBERRY BEAN See BEAN, DRIED; BEAN, FRESH.

CRAYFISH A small freshwater crustacean, which abounds in the South (where it is called crawfish). Crayfish resemble tiny lobsters. They are prized for their sweet, succulent tail meat. Usually cooked by steaming or boiling, they are eaten hot or cold on their own or shelled in gumbos or other Cajun and Creole dishes.

Selecting Crayfish should be bought alive or frozen.

Storing Store live crayfish in the refrigerator covered with a damp kitchen towel for no more than 1 or 2 days. Keep frozen crayfish for up to 3 months. Once defrosted, they should not be refrozen, or their texture will deteriorate. Cooked crayfish may be refrigerated for up to 3 days.

Preparing Before cooking, discard any dead crayfish. Like lobster and crab, crayfish will turn red when they are cooked, usually within 5 minutes. Take care not to overcook them.

CREAM People of a certain age may remember the days when the milkman left glass bottles of milk on the back stoop every morning. The unhomogenized milk naturally separated, with the cream rising to the top, hence the vernacular expressions that compare cream and excellence. These days, nearly all commercial milk is homogenized, a process that uniformly disperses the fat throughout the milk, so that the cream cannot separate from it.

Fresh milk contains fat, and it is this fat that makes cream sublime. Cream is sold according to the amount of milk fat it contains, with heavy cream containing the most and half-and-half the least. In between are light whipping cream and light cream. Cream is also used to make sour cream, cream cheese, and ice cream.

Nearly all cream sold by large dairies today is ultrapasteurized, which involves heating the cream to 300°F to kill certain microorganisms and extend shelf life, but which gives it a mildly cooked taste and makes it a little harder to whip.

Quick Tip

Whipped cream can be sweetened with confectioners' or granulated sugar added during whipping. The confectioners' sugar will blend a little more smoothly with the cream. A little vanilla extract is another nice addition.

Selecting Buy the kind of cream called for in a recipe. To make whipped cream, buy heavy cream (whipping cream) or light whipping cream. Light cream and half-and-half will not whip. Some specialty stores and farmers' markets sell minimally processed cream that has not been put through the ultrapasteurization process. This cream whips better but is more perishable. For most sauce-making purposes, buy heavy cream.

Storing Cream should be kept in the coldest part of the refrigerator, usually the back of the bottom shelf. Unopened ultrapasteurized cream will keep for about a month, or 3 or 4 days past the sell-by date. Once opened, it will keep for up to 4 days. Other cream will keep for 2 or 3 days after its sell-by date. Heavy cream can be frozen for up to 4 months and used for baking, frostings, and sauces, but once frozen and defrosted, it will not whip. When using cream, pour just the amount of cream you need from the carton and return the carton to the refrigerator as quickly as possible. Do not pour room-temperature cream back into the carton; instead, store it separately in a lidded glass jar.

Quick Tip

Cream that is reaching the end of its life will form flecks in hot coffee, a result of its interacting with the acid in the beverage. It is still fine to use at this point, but it also is time to put cream on your shopping list. When cream is spoiled you will know it by a single whiff.

Preparing Whip chilled heavy or light whipping cream in a metal bowl with a whisk, an egg beater, a handheld mixer, or in a stand mixer fitted with a whisk. For the best results, put the bowl and whisk or beaters in the refrigerator for an hour or more to chill them. Blenders are not recommended, as they don't aerate the cream properly and are apt to whip it into butter, but large amounts of cream can be whipped

in a food processor fitted with a specially designed whipping attachment. The cream will not, however, ever reach the same billowing heights it will in a bowl. Process the cream just until it rises in the bowl and thickens. Still, beware of overbeating, which can happen quickly in a food processor. For most uses, whip cream just until it forms soft peaks. When the whisk is lifted from the cream, the cream should form a peak that gently falls to one side. For piping, cream should be whipped to

Cream Glossary

HEAVY CREAM This cream has the most milk fat, containing between 36 and 40 percent but averaging about 36 percent. Whips up to a very dense and stable whipped cream, less voluminous than light cream, which can be useful for piped cake decorations. Also can be labeled heavy whipping cream or just whipping cream.

LIGHT WHIPPING CREAM Contains only slightly less milk fat than heavy cream, from 30 to 36 percent. Whips up to a softer, slightly more voluminous whipped cream than heavy cream does.

LIGHT CREAM Similar to half-and-half, this product is also known as coffee cream or table cream and contains 15 to 20 percent milk fat. It cannot be whipped.

HALF-AND-HALF A mixture of milk and cream, containing from 10 to 18 percent milk fat. It is used for coffee, to pour over cereal and berries, and in many creamed soup recipes. You can make your own, in a pinch, by combining equal parts milk and heavy cream. It cannot be whipped.

stiff peaks, which hold their shape and stand upright when the whisk is lifted.

Whipped cream, soft peaks.

Whipped cream, stiff peaks.

See also MILK; SOUR CREAM.

CREAM CHEESE See CHEESE.

CREAMING A recipe for cake batter or cookie dough typically starts with instructions to "cream the butter" or "cream the butter with the sugar."

Creaming means beating fat, or fat plus another ingredient, until it becomes soft and smooth. You should first whip or beat softened (not melted) butter alone until it expands, lightens in color, and is as soft and smooth as possible. This can be done using an electric mixer or by hand with a wooden spoon or wire whisk. Give the butter a little time to cream—it may take 3 or 4 minutes with an electric mixer, or longer by hand, to reach the desired stage. Do not rush this step; thorough creaming aerates the butter and contributes to the lightness of the final product.

Once the butter is creamed, add the sugar, again beating until the mixture is fluffy and light. At this point, the mixture may be referred to as batter. Creamed batter is often described as soft, smooth, and pale yellow or ivory. The grains of sugar should be fully incorporated into the butter. If you rub a little creamed batter between your fingertips, it should not feel gritty. Besides sweetening the batter, the sharp, crystalline edges of the sugar actually cut into the butter and create many tiny air bubbles. In fact, the creamed mixture has almost twice the original volume of its two components when sufficient time has been taken to do it correctly.

When adding other ingredients such as flour and eggs to creamed batter, be sure not to overwork it, or you may destroy the air bubbles and the resultant lightening effect of creaming.

CREAM OF TARTAR This powdery white substance, found in every supermarket and most kitchens, is potassium tartrate, a by-product of wine making. Once a common leavening agent for breads made without yeast, today cooks use it to stabilize egg whites so that they whip up well. (The common ratio is $\frac{1}{8}$ teaspoon cream of tartar for each egg white.) Also used in candy making, cream of tartar inhibits sugar from crystallizing. Some cake recipes, such as angel food cake, include cream of tartar for whiter, finer crumbs and greater loft. It also contributes to the creaminess of frostings. Cream of tartar, an acid, is mixed with baking soda, an alkaline, to make commercial baking powder.

Selecting Buy any reliable brand of cream of tartar, which usually is packaged in a jar or can with a tight-fitting lid.
Storing Store it in a cool, dry cupboard for up to 1 year.

CRÈME BRÛLÉE (KREM broo-LAY)

A rich, satiny egg custard topped with a thin caramel crust. This dessert is a standard on restaurant menus, and a growing number of home cooks are attempting it in their own kitchens. The juxtaposition of textures—creamy custard and brittle caramel—has sent this indulgence to the top of many dessert lovers' lists of all-time favorites.

In restaurants today, the caramel topping usually is made by scattering granulated white or brown sugar over cold custard and passing a very hot butane torch over the sugar to melt and caramelize it. Such devices are now being made in miniature size for the home cook, but most nonprofessionals rely on hot broilers to melt the sugar.

Alternatively, one can pour hot, liquid caramel over cold custards and allow it to harden to a shiny crust. The advantage of this latter method is that the dessert can be assembled 10 to 12 hours ahead of time; the disadvantage is that the caramel crust will soften as the dessert sits. The ultimate crème brûlée has a still-warm, brittle, dark caramel crust on top of a cool, creamy custard.

Caramelizing the sugar.

Crème Brûlée Savvy

■ If using an electric broiler, preheat it for at least 5 minutes so that it is very hot (gas broilers require no preheating). Position the broiler pan 2 to 3 inches from the heat to cook the sugar quickly without heating the custard.

■ Do not take the custard-filled ramekins from the refrigerator until the last minute. The interaction of the cold custard and hot sugar is crucial to forming a good crisp topping.

■ If using brown sugar, sift it to remove any lumps before sprinkling it evenly over the custards. Or use granulated brown (or white) sugar, which requires no sifting.

■ Place the custards in a water bath to keep them from heating up. For more details, see WATER BATH.

■ Turn the ramekins during broiling if necessary to help the sugar melt and caramelize as evenly as possible.

■ For the best effect, serve crème brûlée immediately after preparing it.

See also CARAMELIZING; CUSTARD; WATER BATH.

CRÈME FRAÎCHE (KREM FRESH)

A soured, cultured cream product, originally from France, crème fraîche is similar to sour cream. The silken, thick cream is tangy and sweet, with a hint of nuttiness, and adds incomparable flavor when used as a topping for berries and pastry desserts. It is also delicious paired with smoked salmon and trout, and lends a velvety smoothness and rich flavor to soups and sauces. Crème fraîche, which is 30 percent fat, is not always easy to find, and many home cooks make their own (see below).

Selecting Crème fraîche is sold in some supermarkets as an ultrapasteurized cream product. It is far more expensive than cream or sour cream. Because it loses flavor as it sits on the refrigerator shelf, buy it as fresh as possible. It is also sold in gourmet markets and cheese shops, often made by the purveyor or a local supplier. No two are exactly the same.

Storing Refrigerate for up to 2 weeks. Homemade crème fraîche will keep in a covered container for 1 week.

HOW TO *Make Crème Fraîche*

1. To make 1 cup crème fraîche, combine 1 cup heavy cream and 1 tablespoon buttermilk in a small saucepan over medium-low heat. Heat to lukewarm. Do not allow it to simmer.
2. Remove from the heat, cover, and allow to thicken at warm room temperature, which can take from 8 to 48 hours, depending on your taste and recipe needs.
3. Once it is as thick and flavorful as you want it, refrigerate to chill well before using.

CREMINO See MUSHROOM.

CREPE (KREP or KRAPE) A very thin pancake made from a pourable batter. Anyone who has stopped at a sidewalk crepe stand in France wants to try to duplicate that experience back home. Crepes are filled or sauced with creamy, savory mixtures and served for brunch or light suppers or with sweet mixtures for dessert. Crepes can be folded around a filling into halves, quarters, or envelopes.

Filled and folded crepes.

They can also be rolled into open-ended rolls, or stacked with filling between the layers and cut into wedges like a cake. The term *crepe* applies both to the pancakes and to the final dish. The pancakes can be made well ahead of time, stacked, and refrigerated and then filled and reheated. They also freeze well. Unlike other pancakes, crepes are not leavened, so they do not puff up when cooked.

Crepe batter must be made ahead of time, since it needs to chill for at least an hour (and will keep as long as 12 hours). During chilling, the flour expands and absorbs the liquid, a step that is essential for tender crepes. Crepes destined for dessert are often made from a slightly sweetened batter, while those for savory fillings are made with an unsweetened batter.

Crepes should be cooked in a small skillet or in a crepe pan, which is a small, shallow pan with flared sides and a long, flat handle, just large enough to cook one crepe at a time. Its configuration makes it easy to rotate the pan, first to spread the melted butter over its surface, and then the batter. The shape also makes it easy to flip the crepe during cooking.

Crepe pan.

Crepe Savvy

- Crepe batter should be very smooth and free of lumps. Whip the batter in a blender or food processor, or use a whisk if mixing by hand. Beat the eggs into the batter one at a time and add the milk gradually while stirring to ensure a smooth batter. Some cooks recommend straining the whisked batter to eliminate even the tiniest clumps of flour.

C

- Before adding melted butter to the batter, let it cool down for 1 to 2 minutes to avoid curdling the eggs.
- When putting butter in the heated crepe pan, use only enough to film the bottom. Brush on the fat as you need it before starting a new crepe. It averages out to about $\frac{1}{2}$ teaspoon butter per crepe. If using a nonstick pan, it is not necessary to grease it, although the butter also adds good flavor.
- Ladle in only enough batter to spread in a thin layer as you tilt the pan. This is usually 3 to 4 tablespoons batter for a 7-inch crepe.

*Swirling
batter.*

- If needed, run a knife around the edge of the crepe after it has set a bit to keep it from sticking.
- If you cannot flip the crepe by shaking the pan, slip a small knife or spatula under the pancake and turn it, using the tool or your fingers.

*Flipping
a crepe.*

- Placing a square of waxed paper atop each crepe as you stack them will prevent them from sticking together.

CREPE PAN See COOKWARE.

CRIMPING To seal together the edges of two pieces of pastry dough by pressing the dough with the tines of a kitchen fork, the side of a knife, or a pastry crimper. Crimping differs from fluting in that you press down the dough with a tool in order to seal it, while fluting means to make a decorative shape with your fingers. Crimping is a good way to seal together securely the uncooked crusts of a double-crust pie, which may then be fluted if desired. See also BAKING TOOLS; PIE & TART.

CROCKPOT Ranging in size from 1 to 6 quarts, these handy covered electric pots slowly cook moist dishes such as stews, soups, and braises, allowing safe, unattended slow cooking. Sometimes known as slow cookers, they can be filled in the morning with soup or stew ingredients and left for the day. While generally favored for their convenience, some older models may cook foods unevenly. Newer appliances have resolved this problem and work extremely well. When using, follow instructions carefully to avoid overcooking and to ensure that food is cooked at the correct temperatures for safety.

CRUDITÉ (krew-dee-TAY) Crudités are trimmed whole or sliced vegetables served raw or lightly blanched or steamed and accompanied with a dip. A crudité platter is a colorful and healthful addition to a buffet table or cocktail party menu. For a festive touch, scoop out a large bell pepper or small pumpkin and serve the dip in it.

CRUMBLING To break food into small bits between your fingertips. Semisoft cheeses such as feta and Roquefort frequently are crumbled, as are dried herbs to bring out their flavor.

CRUSHING To turn a larger piece of food into many small particles, using your fingers, a rolling pin, a mortar and pestle, a mallet, or a tool specifically designed for the job. A garlic press crushes whole cloves of garlic; a rolling pin crushes crackers enclosed in a plastic bag. See also BRUISING; SMASHING.

CRUST See CHEESECAKE; PIE & TART.

CRYSTALLIZING Forming sugar crystals during cooking, which turns a syrup or other preparation gritty. Crystallizing is desirable in some instances, as with fudge, but unacceptable for most other candies. See also CANDY MAKING.

Fruits and edible flowers may be crystallized, or dipped or cooked in sugar syrup. This makes them into an elegant decoration. Also called candied or iced fruits or flowers, they can be found in specialty stores and mail-order catalogs.

CUBING To cut food, often meat and poultry, into small, uniformly sized pieces $\frac{1}{2}$ to 1 inch square. This helps them cook evenly, and the bite-sized configuration makes them ready for use in stir-fries, soups, and stews. Smaller cubes, $\frac{1}{8}$ to $\frac{1}{2}$ inch square, are generally called dice. See also CHOPPING; DICING.

CUCUMBER This watery, mild-flavored, crunchy green vegetable shows up in green salads, on crudité platters, and as a garnish on cold plates. Chilled cucumber soup is a summer delight, and a cucumber sandwich is the darling of the afternoon tea lover. While fresh cucumbers can be steamed or lightly sautéed, they are most often consumed raw. Perhaps the best thing to happen to cucumbers is pickling. This versatile vegetable takes famously to long soaks in flavorful brines.

Slicing cucumbers.

Although numerous varieties of cucumbers are grown in home gardens, most supermarkets, greengrocers, and farmers' markets carry only two basic types: slicing varieties and pickling varieties. Slicing cucumbers are further divided into outdoor and hothouse, or English, varieties. Nearly all of the small, finger-length gherkin cucumbers, used to make little pickles called cornichons, are sold directly to food companies. Occasionally, however, they show up at farmers' markets and specialty greengrocers, and pickle makers snap them up. They are easy to grow, too, and many backyard gardeners harvest bumper crops.

Pickling cucumbers.

Selecting When choosing slicing cucumbers—the type used in salads and other cold preparations—look for slender, dark green vegetables without yellowing or shriveling. Outdoor varieties should be 8 to 10 inches long and 1 to $1\frac{1}{2}$ inches in diameter at the center. Many are coated with wax, which makes them shiny and helps preserve them. Avoid these if you can, as waxed skin must be peeled, and with the skin goes the vitamin A. Hothouse

Quick Tip

For pretty cucumber garnishes, use a vegetable peeler to create alternating stripes of dark green peel and light green flesh, and then slice the cucumber into thin disks.

cucumbers, usually sold wrapped in plastic, should be 12 to 16 inches long and have thin, smooth skin.

Storing Store cucumbers in a perforated plastic bag in the refrigerator for 5 days. Do not put cucumbers in the coldest part of the refrigerator; they prefer temperatures just above 40°F (the temperature of most refrigerators). Sliced cucumber will keep refrigerated in a covered container for 2 days.

Preparing Unless the skin is waxed, there is no need to peel cucumbers. Check for wax by scraping the cucumber with a fingernail. Pickling cucumbers should be scrubbed with a vegetable brush under cold running water to remove loose spines.

Cucumbers may be seeded for stuffing or before slicing crosswise for a salad.

HOW TO *Seed a Cucumber*
1. Slice the cucumber in half lengthwise.
2. Use a melon baller or spoon to scoop out the seeds and the surrounding pulpy matter.

3. Proceed with stuffing or place the cucumber flat side down on a cutting board and slice crosswise.

CUMIN See SPICE.

CURDLING When eggs get too hot, their proteins react and they clump and expel moisture, a condition called curdling. When hollandaise sauce "breaks" or when custard separates, it is curdled and considered spoiled, or at least in need of salvage. On the other hand, when cream mixed with an acid such as buttermilk thickens and lumps, it becomes crème fraîche, a happy situation indeed but curdling nonetheless. Scrambled eggs are curdled eggs and are, of course, delicious. Cheese is made with milk and cream that have been allowed to curdle as one of the early steps in the cheese-making process.

Scrambled eggs.

As desirable as curdling may be in some instances, for the home cook it usually spells disaster. The best way to avoid curdling is to monitor the heat. When cooking mixtures containing eggs, heat them gently and slowly, just to the point of thickening. Eggs to be added to hot liquids should be "tempered" first, by mixing a little of the hot liquid into them to warm them up. Then they can be stirred into the larger amount of hot liquid without curdling. See EGG for more detail.

Fat also prevents curdling, so when making recipes involving milk or cream plus an acidic ingredient, be wary of substituting a lower-fat version of the milk or cream called for in the recipe. It may cause curdling, whereas the full-fat version would have worked beautifully.

CURING Any process that preserves fresh food, usually meat or fish, by salting, brining, or smoking. Salting, which usually involves mixing the salt with sugar and/or herbs and spices, is used for gravlax (cured salmon) and other fish and for some hams such as prosciutto, which is salted and then left to cure in the open air. Brining, which is curing in a salt solution, is used for corned beef, pickles, and sauerkraut, among other foods. Smoking is used for everything from fish to whole chicken to cheese to nuts. Some, but not all, smoked foods are cured by dry salting or brining before smoking. There are two kinds of smoking: cold smoking, used for foods to be eaten raw (salmon) or later cooked (bacon); and hot smoking, used for foods that require no further cooking (chicken, certain sausages).

See also BRINE; SMOKING.

CURLY CHICORY See CHICORY.

CURLY ENDIVE See CHICORY.

CURRANT See BERRY; DRIED FRUIT.

CURRY Curry is a distinct flavor, immediately recognizable, but made from a mixture of seasonings and not dependent on any one ingredient. It is also a stewlike dish flavored with curry powder or curry paste. Curry is most readily associated with Indian cooking, although bold and pungent curries are made in Southeast Asia, most notably in Thailand; in Jamaica and other parts of the Caribbean; and in Mozambique and other countries in Africa. Curry leaves, which resemble small lemon leaves, smell of curry and are used in a number of Southeast Asian and Indian recipes and, not surprisingly, are components of many commercial curry powders.

Quick Bite

The best curry powders and pastes are made with whole spices that are first roasted and then ground. Cooks select the individual spices depending on the kind of curry they plan to cook, then grind the spices by hand in a mortar to ensure they are not overground.

In many Indian and Pakistani home kitchens, curry powder is made fresh daily or at least every few days. In other countries, it generally is sold already mixed and may be mild or spicy. Although numerous spices are ground together to make the powder, and the mixtures vary from region to region, and house to house, among the most common ingredients are cumin, curry leaves, cardamom, coriander seeds, fennel seeds, mustard seeds, mace, fenugreek, red and black peppers, and turmeric.

Curry paste, made throughout Southeast Asia, usually includes fresh ingredients such as lemongrass, galangal, garlic, onions, green or red chiles, and cilantro. Curry pastes are often classified as green, red, or yellow, depending on their ingredients. (Indian and Pakistani cooks also make curry paste, but curry powder is more widely used in Indian cooking.)

Selecting Curry powder is sold in supermarkets. The flavor of the widely distributed commercial brands may pale in comparison to those sold in specialty stores and from mail-order catalogs specializing in spices. Try a few different curry powders

Quick Tip

In most recipes, curry powder is cooked in a little oil to release its flavors. Curry paste, too, is cooked with a little fat, such as oil or coconut milk or cream, in a hot wok as the first step for many Southeast Asian dishes.

C

before selecting a brand you like. Curry paste is sold in Southeast Asian and Indian markets and in some specialty-food markets. Some are far hotter than others, so choose with discretion. Look for it in plastic tubs, jars, and cans. Curry leaves are available fresh and dried in Indian markets. They are 1 to 2 inches long and about ½ inch wide.

Quick Tip

Madras curry powder, a blend popular in southern India, is the most common type of curry powder sold commercially in countries where curry powders are not made at home. When a recipe calls for generic curry powder, it is acceptable to use Madras curry powder.

Storing Curry powder loses flavor after 2 months of storage in a cool, dry cupboard. Curry paste will keep in the cupboard for 6 months and once opened should be refrigerated, where it will keep for 2 or 3 months. Fresh curry leaves, often sold on the stalk, can be stored in the refrigerator for several days and freeze well for up to 6 weeks. Dried leaves will keep for 2 or 3 months, although their flavor dissipates as they age.

CUSTARD Custard is a mixture of eggs and milk or cream cooked just until the proteins in the ingredients thicken to form a soft, smooth, satiny dish that slides smoothly over the tongue. Both sweet and savory custards are among the world's most enduring comfort foods.

Sweet baked custards can be as simple as a *pot de crème* (vanilla cup custard) and as elegant as a crème brûlée or crème caramel. Spain's national dessert, flan, is made with sweetened condensed milk for richness. Savory baked custards are made following the same basic principles as those for sweet custards.

Custards are served in their ramekins, spooned from larger molds, or unmolded and plated. Those to be unmolded, such as crème caramel, contain whole eggs and a higher ratio of egg to milk or cream. This produces a firmer custard. Sleek, softer custards served in molds tend to be less stable. These may be made with egg yolks alone, as the proteins in egg whites are not needed to add stability.

Custard sauces, or stirred custards, are made from milk or cream, eggs, and sugar. They are cooked on the stove top, resulting in a different consistency: they are pourable. Perhaps the best-known custard sauce is English custard, or crème anglaise. This is the most basic of custard sauces and greatly appreciated by chefs and home cooks alike. From this basic sauce, you can make chocolate-, coffee-, mocha-, or almond-flavored custard sauces. Many ice creams are simply frozen English custard.

Pastry cream, or crème pâtissière, is yet another type of custard. Cornstarch and flour are added to the eggs, milk, and sugar for a firmer mixture and more stable custard. It is used to fill cream puffs, eclairs, fruit tarts, and cakes. Pastry cream can be flavored with chocolate, fruit, coffee, or crushed nuts.

Some home cooks fear making custards, concerned that they will curdle and clump or that they will toughen up and "weep," exuding water. The way to guarantee success is to control the heat, cooking the custard slowly and evenly, and to avoid overcooking it. This is necessary both during initial cooking on top of the stove and baking in the oven.

Baked Custard Savvy

■ Because milk may develop a skin when it has boiled, it should not boil or even simmer. Cook the milk or cream and sugar only until the sugar dissolves and the liquid is hot.

- Before eggs are added to hot milk or cream, "temper" them by whisking in just a little of the hot liquid to warm them up. This heats them up gradually to prevent curdling. The mixture can be returned to the pan and whisked into the hot liquid.
- Many custard recipes call for cooking the mixture until it is thick enough to "coat the back of a spoon." To test if the density is correct, carefully run your finger along the custard coating the spoon. If the path it makes stays in place and does not flow back onto itself, the custard is ready to be removed from the heat. To avoid overcooking custard, cook it just until it reaches this stage.

Testing the thickness.

- Strain the custard into its baking container(s). Straining dissipates air bubbles and any lumps, producing a smooth consistency.
- Bake the custard in a water bath for gentle, even cooking. See WATER BATH.
- Don't let the custard's center set fully in the oven. It should still wiggle slightly, or a knife inserted in the center should come out moist. Carefully remove the custard from the oven and let cool, still in its water bath. Since the custard continues to cook for a few minutes outside the oven, taking it out just before it is firm prevents overcooking and tough, weeping custard. When the water bath is lukewarm, remove the custard and let it cool to room temperature.
- If the custard's center cooks through in the oven and an inserted knife comes

out completely clean and dry, remove the custard dish from the water bath and carefully submerge it halfway in a shallow pan or sink filled with cold water and ice cubes. This will quickly arrest the cooking.

Custard Sauce Savvy

- Cook the custard ingredients in a heavy saucepan, keeping the heat very low. The custard should hover between 160° and 170°F. As an extra precaution, use a heat diffuser; see COOKING TOOLS.
- Use a wooden spoon or silicone rubber spatula to stir custard. Both are more efficient at scraping the bottom of the pan than metal spoons.
- Stir the custard very carefully and gently. Hard, fast stirring can break the sauce and make it runny.
- Be patient. The custard sauce will thicken slowly, and slow cooking is the best safeguard against curdling. Don't raise the heat to hurry it up.
- To test for correct thickness, allow the custard to coat the spoon or spatula and carefully run your finger across the tool. A trail should remain that does not immediately run together.
- When custard sauce settles (any bubbles have dissipated), looks glossy, and feels noticeably thicker as you stir it, it's ready to remove from the heat.
- Once it is off the heat, continue to stir the sauce for a few minutes until completely thickened.
- Even if the sauce does not come out perfectly smooth, it will still taste good. Strain it to rid it of lumps.

Storing To chill custard, let it cool on the countertop and then place in the refrigerator until cold. Once it is cold, lay a piece of parchment or waxed paper directly on the surface of the custard to prevent a skin from forming and refrigerate. Custard will keep for 2 days.

C

Reheat custard sauce by setting it in a container in a larger saucepan of hot, but not simmering or boiling, water. Stir the custard until warm.

See also CRÈME BRÛLÉE; CURDLING; PUDDING; TEMPERING.

CUTTING BOARD Among the most indispensable pieces of kitchen equipment, a cutting board is frequently a built-in feature of contemporary kitchens. But even the simplest kitchen should have at least one portable cutting board.

Wood and polyethylene boards.

Portable cutting boards are most commonly made of wood or polyethylene, a soft but rigid plastic. Marble and tempered glass boards, less familiar in many kitchens, are not recommended for cutting, as they will dull your knives, but they are appreciated by pie and pastry cooks for rolling out dough because they stay cool. Cutting boards made of very hard rubber, which once were reserved for chefs, are now available in limited supply to everyday home cooks.

Portable cutting boards may measure only 6 by 10 inches, although larger ones are more useful. For most kitchen work, boards should measure at least 12 by 18 inches and be ¾ to 1½ inches thick.

Cutting boards are used to chop meat, vegetables, herbs, and fruit; to knead bread; and to roll pastry. Using one protects the countertop and also is easier on knives. The sharp blade holds its edge longer when used on a cutting board.

Whether to buy wooden or polyethylene cutting boards is mainly a question of personal preference. In past years, controversy raged over which material was better in terms of safety. Polyethylene was believed to harbor fewer microorganisms and so was touted as being more sanitary than wood. More recently, wood was found to be safer, although these findings did not declare polyethylene unsafe. Whichever material you choose, it is a good idea to keep one cutting board for meat and chicken only and another for vegetables and other uses. This will limit the possibility of cross-contamination, or transferring flesh-borne bacteria to other foods in the kitchen. See also FOOD SAFETY.

The best wooden cutting boards are made of maple, oak, cherry, birch, and walnut and are all hardwoods with a long life. Cutting boards are traditionally made by laminating end-grain or edge-grain pieces of the wood, which naturally have some give. A wooden carving board with depressed grooves around the perimeter and a shallow well is preferred for slicing cooked meats and poultry, as escaping cooking juices are captured in the grooves. This board may be smooth on the reverse side and so is doubly useful.

As a rule, polyethylene cutting boards are lighter in weight than wooden boards. Most have rough, pebbly surfaces, which prevent food from slipping. Some have small feet on the underside; others are designed to be used on both sides.

Caring for Cutting Boards Carefully clean all cutting boards after each use and store away from heat, which can cause even heavy wood to warp and split. Every month or two, rinse both wooden and polyethylene boards with a mild solution of bleach and warm water, 4 cups of water to 1 teaspoon of bleach, to sanitize them. After bleaching them, rinse well with hot water.

Wooden Board Savvy

- Before using a new wooden board, rub it with tasteless, odorless mineral oil to season it. Use a wadded-up paper towel or small brush to spread a thin layer of oil over the wood. Rub it with fine steel wool and then let the oil soak in for 5 or 10 minutes. Wipe it dry with a soft cloth or paper towel and store. Repeat this seasoning process once a month for 10 to 12 months. After this time, oil the board periodically, particularly if the wood appears dry.
- After each use, wash the board with dishwashing liquid and a soft brush. Rinse well with hot water and dry completely before storing.
- For caked-on food, use a dough scraper to remove it and then wash the board. See BAKING TOOLS.
- If a board absorbs odors, clean it with lemon juice or salt, or a mixture of the two. Rinse well and dry before storing.
- Never let a wooden board soak in a sink of water or put it in the dishwasher. It will absorb water and warp.

Polyethylene Board Savvy

- After each use, wash the board with dishwashing liquid and a soft brush. Rinse well with hot water and dry before storing.
- Many of these boards are dishwasher safe. The heat of the dishwasher sanitizes them, although it may also warp some boards over time.
- These boards can be soaked in a sink of water, but it is rarely necessary and best avoided, as they could warp slightly.

CUTTING IN The technique of combining flour and fat for flaky pastry. Cutting in is accomplished by systematically working the flour and fat with a pastry blender, two table knives, or a fork until it resembles coarse crumbs. A food processor also is an effective and fast way of accomplishing the same thing. Cutting in differs from rubbing in only in that you do not use your fingertips exclusively. Using utensils instead of warm hands keeps the mixture cooler and is preferred for flaky pastry.

HOW TO *Cut Fat into Flour*

1. Measure out and whisk together the flour and other dry ingredients in a large bowl, then chop up the chilled fat called for in a recipe—usually butter, vegetable shortening, or a combination—before putting it into the flour. Toss the chunks of fat in the flour until they are coated.
2. Using a pastry blender or fork, preferably chilled, repeatedly slice through the fat as you turn the bowl quarter turns with your other hand. To use two knives, hold a knife in each hand and draw the knife blades across each other in a scissoring motion. (You can also use your fingertips to break down the fat to smaller pieces, but try not to handle it too much or you risk warming and melting the fat.) If using a food processor, fit it with the metal blade.

Using a pastry blender.

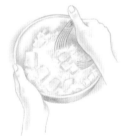

3. Keep tossing the fat in the flour as you slice, and wipe the fat off the blade occasionally to keep from mashing it. Continue slicing until the fat resembles small peas or coarse crumbs.

For flaky pie crust, take care that the flour and fat do not become too finely mixed or pasty. Small chunks of flour-coated fat result in light, flaky pastry; pieces that are too small or partially melted ones result in dense, crumbly pastry. See also BISCUIT; PIE & TART; RUBBING IN.

everything from date to dusting

DAIKON See RADISH.

DANDELION GREENS See GREENS, DARK.

DASH See MEASURING.

DATE Sweet, sticky, splendid dates grow in heavy profusion on towering date palm trees that flourish in the desert climates of North Africa and the Middle East. They are also grown domestically, mainly in California's arid Coachella Valley. Nearly all dates are sold fresh, although because of dates' naturally tacky consistency, many date lovers believe they are eating dried fruit. Another reason for this misconception is the dates' high sugar content and concentrated flavors, which, in terms of taste, make them more akin to dried fruits. Dates are also dried (see also DRIED FRUIT).

Dates are classified as being soft, semi-dry, or dry. Soft dates have a high moisture content and soft texture. They must be harvested by hand because of their fragility and then refrigerated to prevent deterioration. Medjool, Khadrawy, and Halawy are common varieties of soft dates. Semidry dates have a lower moisture content and firmer texture. They can be mechanically harvested and are packed in moisture-proof packages that are stocked on shelves rather than refrigerated. Deglet Noor (the most popular date sold in the United States) and Zahidy are the best-known semidry dates. Finally, dry dates, known also as bread dates, have an extremely high sugar content and low moisture content. Thoory is the most common variety. Home cooks frequently pit dates, stuff the cavities with savory or sweet fillings, and serve them as hors d'oeuvres or after-dinner sweets. Dates are also tossed into stuffings for pork and duck and baked into cookies, breads, and cakes.

Selecting Dates are available year-round, although their peak season is from October through January, making them favorite holiday treats. Look for dates in the produce section of markets, usually in moisture-proof packages. Choose plump, shiny dates, and avoid any that are excessively sticky or covered with crystallized sugar. The exception is Medjool, which may have a dusting of natural sugar. Some dates are sold pitted.

Quick Tip

To prevent dates for baked goods from sticking to the knife as you chop them, dust the knife blade with flour.

Storing Tightly wrap soft and semidry dates in plastic and refrigerate for up to 3 weeks. Dry dates, well packaged, will keep refrigerated for 10 to 12 months.

Preparing All dates have pits, which must be removed before using the fruits in cooking or eating out of hand.

DEBEARDING Removing a mussel's beard, which looks like a little tuft of stringy dark hair extending from some shells, as part of the cleaning process. See MUSSEL.

DEBONING See BONING.

DECANTING Pouring wine from its original bottle into a glass container called a decanter. Before the advent of modern wine-making practices, wines were decanted as a matter of course to separate the liquid from the sediment that naturally collected in the bottles. Today, unless one is serving an older red wine or vintage Port, it rarely is necessary to decant wine for this or any other reason, as wines now are generally quite clear and can be served from the bottle with no danger of the wine drinker's imbibing bitter sediment. A very young or tannic wine may be decanted and allowed to "breathe" and soften for up to several hours before serving. This period of breathing is not recommended for older wines, as their bouquet fades rather quickly after pouring.

See also WINE.

DECORATING COMB See BAKING TOOLS.

DECORATING TURNTABLE See BAKING TOOLS.

DEEP-FRYING See FRYING.

DEFROSTING See FOOD SAFETY; FREEZING; THAWING.

DEGLAZING Using liquid to dislodge and dissolve the browned bits of meat, poultry, or other sautéed or fried food that become stuck to the pan bottom as a result of cooking. The liquid, usually wine, stock, or water, is added to the pan after the food has been removed. The liquid is heated over medium-high or high heat, and the cook stirs it with a wooden spoon or spatula and scrapes the pan bottom at the same time to free the browned bits. Before long, the flavorful liquid is reduced, meaning it partially cooks away or evaporates. The resulting sauce is often called a reduction sauce or pan sauce. See also REDUCING; SAUTÉING.

DEGREASING As stocks and pan drippings simmer and as they cool, the fat in them rises to the top. Degreasing means removing this fat for a clearer soup or sauce.

During stock making, the liquid should be kept at a gentle simmer so that the fat extracted from the meat and bones rises to the surface rather than becoming an integral part of the stock, which would happen if it was boiled. When the fat rises to the surface, the simmering stock can be degreased by skimming off the fat with a spoon or mesh skimmer (see COOKING TOOLS). Then, as the stock cools, any remaining fat separates from the liquid and also rises to the top. As the fat gathers, you can blot it up gently with a wadded paper towel.

If the liquid is chilled, the fat solidifies in a layer on top, which easily can be lifted off the surface with a large spoon or spatula.

Degreasing chilled stock.

This same technique can be applied to the fat left in a roasting pan with the drippings. Use a spoon or mesh skimmer to remove excess fat from the surface of the drippings before making gravy.

See also GRAVY; SAUCE; SKIMMING; STOCK.

DEVEINING To remove the dark intestinal vein in a shrimp or lobster, which can be bitter, gritty, and unsightly. Once it is cooked, the intestinal vein is harmless—its removal is simply a matter of aesthetics. See LOBSTER; SHRIMP.

DICING Cutting food, often vegetables or fruit, into small, uniform cubes, usually ⅛ to ¼ inch square, which ensures that they will cook evenly and makes them easy to eat. Food cut into larger uniform pieces is considered cubed.

Cutting dice.

See also CHOPPING; CUBING.

DILL See HERB.

DIRECT HEAT See GRILLING.

DISCOLORING When some fruits and vegetables are peeled and exposed to the air, oxygenation causes them to darken, or turn brown, which is referred to as discoloring. This happens most commonly in low-acid fruits (such as apples and bananas) and vegetables (such as artichokes and eggplants). While the browning does not cause

any harm, it does cause the food to lose some of its visual appeal.

A little acid, usually lemon juice or vinegar, slows the discoloring. It may be sprinkled over or rubbed on the cut apples, avocados, or bananas. Or, to avoid adding an acidic bite, the food may be submerged in acidulated water, which is water that has been mixed with a little lemon juice, vinegar, or another acid. The proportion of acid to water is fairly low—about 1 tablespoon per quart of water—so the flavor of the acid is not imparted to the food. Exact

Quick Tip

Fruits and vegetables that discolor when cut and exposed to air: apple, artichoke, avocado, banana, cauliflower, celery root, cherry, eggplant, fig, Jerusalem artichoke, lotus root, mushroom, nectarine, parsnip, peach, pear, potato, rutabaga, yam.

measurements generally are not important, however, except in the case of recipes that call for cooking vegetables and fruits in properly acidulated water. But remember, acid does not *prevent* discoloration; it simply slows it down. Over time, the cut surface will brown.

On the other hand, acid actually causes browning of some green vegetables. Acidic dressings and sauces will darken or discolor broccoli, green beans, and asparagus if the vegetables are allowed to stand in the liquid. For this reason, most recipes suggest tossing cold vegetable salads just before serving. Also, cooking green vegetables with acidic ingredients such as tomatoes or corn will cause them to turn a drab green.

See also ACID.

DISJOINTING The availability of precut chicken pieces has made disjointing—cutting up a whole, uncooked chicken—an endangered art. Yet, it is a simple process, and a whole chicken not only will cost you less than an equivalent weight of already-cut pieces, but also will yield backbones and other trimmings for the stockpot.

HOW TO *Disjoint a Chicken*

1. Place the chicken, breast up and drumsticks toward you, on a cutting board. With a sharp, heavy knife, cut through the skin between the thigh and body. Locate the joint by moving the leg, then cut through the joint to remove the leg. Repeat on the other side.

2. Move the drumstick to locate the joint connecting it to the thigh. Cut through the joint to separate the 2 pieces. Repeat with the other leg.

3. Move a wing to locate its joint with the body. Cut through the joint to remove the wing. Repeat with the other wing.

4. Starting at the neck opening, cut along both sides of the chicken, separating the breast section from the remainder of the bird.

5. Holding the breast skin side down, slit the thin membrane covering the breastbone along its center. Grasp the breast firmly at each end and flex it upward to pop out the breastbone. Pull out the bone, using the knife if necessary to help cut it free.

6. Place the breast skin side down on the cutting board. Cut along the center of the breast to split it in half.

Disjointed and neatly trimmed, a whole chicken yields 8 serving-sized pieces ready for cooking: 2 each of thighs, legs, breasts, and wings. Before cooking, be sure to rinse the pieces with cold water and pat dry with paper towels.

d

DOLLOP A generous spoonful of a substance, usually a smooth, soft one such as whipped cream or sour cream. A dollop is not a precise measurement but generally signifies the amount of topping spooned atop a bowl of soup or a dessert, such as the swirl of sour cream that floats on a serving of borscht or the whipped cream that crowns strawberry shortcake.

DONENESS The degree to which food is cooked or baked so that it is ready to eat. Do not rely on a recipe's cooking time alone to judge a dish's doneness, a common pitfall for inexperienced cooks. Good recipes provide tests in addition to time for doneness. For example, you might be instructed to sauté onions "until translucent," toast spices "until browned and fragrant," or bake a cake "until a toothpick inserted into the center comes out clean." Pay attention to these cues as you follow a recipe; in time, you may rely more on your senses than on stated cooking times.

However, you should note that because of safety issues, internal temperature is the best way to judge when meat or poultry is done. Use an accurate meat thermometer and insert it into the meatiest part of the roast or bird, such as the thigh of a chicken or the heart of a pork loin, making sure it does not touch bone. (Bone conducts heat, skewing the reading.) See individual foods, or the guidelines below.

U.S. Government Doneness Guidelines The U.S. Food Safety and Inspection Service suggests temperatures for cooked meat and poultry to ensure the maximum degree of safety for consumers. A minimum temperature of 160°F is needed to destroy bacteria. Many people choose to cook food to a lower temperature for juicier flesh and fuller flavor. If you are pregnant or older, are cooking for young children or older people, have a compromised immune system, or want to limit your exposure to bacterial risk as much as possible, you may want to observe these guidelines:

Safe Doneness Temperatures	
Whole beef cuts (roasts, steaks)	160°F
(For rare meat, 145°F in the center is safe, except for rolled roasts or mechanically tenderized cuts.)	
Whole pork cuts (roasts, chops)	160°F*
Whole poultry	160°F*
Ground meat or poultry	160°F
Poultry stuffing	165°F
Casseroles with meat or egg	165°F

Some pork and poultry cuts will still have traces of pink at this temperature and can be cooked longer for a more appealing appearance of doneness.

See also FOOD SAFETY.

DOTTING Topping fruit pie fillings, gratins, or other foods with small slices or dabs of butter before baking. The butter should be scattered evenly over the food, so that it will seep consistently throughout the food as it melts during baking. Dotted butter provides richness and moisture and assists in browning.

DOUBLE BOILER A double boiler is a set of two pans, one nested atop the other with room for water to simmer in the pan below. Delicate foods such as chocolate, custards, mousses, and cream sauces are placed in the top pan to heat them gently, or to melt them in the case of chocolate. Double boilers are also good places to keep foods warm without cooking them further, or at least not too quickly. The top pan should not touch the water beneath it, and the water is not meant to boil. A tight fit between the pans ensures that no water or steam mixes with the ingredients, which can cause melting chocolate to stiffen, or seize.

You can easily create your own double boiler by placing a heat-resistant mixing bowl or slightly smaller saucepan over a larger one, although it may not be as steady or the fit as tight.

Melting chocolate in a makeshift double boiler.

DOUGH An unbaked, pliable mixture of flour and liquid, which may also include eggs, fat (such as butter), sugar, salt, and leaveners. Doughs, which are thicker and firmer than batters, do not require containment in a bowl. Bread and biscuit doughs, for example, are scraped from the bowl and worked, or kneaded, on a work surface. They are softer than cookie and pastry doughs, which have a higher ratio of flour to liquid and are rolled (with a rolling pin) or patted (with fingertips) into smooth, thin rounds or rectangles. See also BAKING; BATTER; BISCUIT; BREAD; COOKIE; PIE & TART; QUICK BREAD.

DOUGH BLENDER Another term for pastry blender; see BAKING TOOLS.

DOUGH SCRAPER See BAKING TOOLS.

DRAINING Foods cooked in water or other liquid until tender and edible may be drained before they are served. Pasta, potatoes, vegetables, and other foods are drained in colanders. Foods soaked in liquids, such as raisins that are plumped or clams left in salt water to purge sand, are also drained before cooking. Foods with a high moisture content, such as yogurt or ricotta cheese, may be drained in a strainer or through cheesecloth, thus thickening as the liquid seeps from them. Watery vegetables, such as eggplant·and cucumbers, benefit from being cut, salted, and left to drain in a colander or on paper towels.

Draining differs from straining in that you reserve the liquid when you strain, and usually discard it when you drain.

DREDGING To coat with flour or another dry ingredient, such as cornmeal or bread crumbs, often seasoned. Food is sprinkled with the dry ingredient, dragged through it, or shaken with it.

Dredging in flour.

Turning to coat.

Alternatively, the food and coating may be placed in a plastic bag and shaken together.

Dredging in a plastic bag.

After dredging, the food should be shaken to remove excess coating. Do not dredge food too far in advance of cooking, or the coating will absorb moisture from the food and become gummy. Laying dredged food on a wire rack also helps avoid gumminess.

Dredged food is usually sautéed, fried or deep-fried, or baked. The coating helps it brown nicely and retain moisture, and adds a nice crispiness.

DRESSING A light sauce used to moisten and flavor salad greens and other raw vegetables. Classic salad dressings are variations of vinaigrettes—mixtures of oil, vinegar, and seasonings such as salt, pepper, fresh herbs, garlic, and mustard. Other dressings are mayonnaise based.

When tossing a salad with dressing, use a light hand. Mix the greens or other vegetables with a relatively small amount of dressing, distributing it with numerous tossings. Do not drench the greens, and dress salad greens just before serving to keep them crisp.

Dressing can also refer to the bread-based mixture used to accompany turkey, chicken, and other poultry. Practically speaking, the terms dressing and stuffing are interchangeable, but with regional preferences. In the East and the South, dressing may be cooked in or out of the bird, while elsewhere, stuffing is cooked inside the bird and dressing is baked in a separate buttered casserole alongside it.

See also GREENS, SALAD; STUFFING; VINAIGRETTE.

Quick Tip

Mix a salad dressing in the bottom of the serving bowl up to an hour or so before dinner. Lightly pile greens on top, cover, and refrigerate, then toss just before serving.

DRIED FRUIT Using sunshine or the heat of kilns, many fruits are dried for prolonged storage and to give them an intense flavor and chewy texture. Some fruits, such as sticks of papaya or disks of cored pineapple, are candied to help preserve them and enhance their flavor.

Selecting Look for more recently dried and packaged fruits, which have a softer texture than older dried fruits. Health-food stores and farmers' markets, which often have more rapid turnovers of stock, are good places to shop.

Storing Store dried fruits in airtight containers at room temperature for up to 1 month or refrigerated for up to 6 months.

Preparing Depending on the recipe, dried fruits may be used whole or cut up, and are sometimes soaked in hot water, liqueur, or another liquid for about 20 minutes to "plump" or reconstitute them.

See also LIQUEUR; PLUMPING.

DRIPPINGS The liquid that collects in the roasting pan when large cuts of meat or poultry are roasted or fried is called drippings or pan drippings. Once degreased (the fat skimmed from the surface), the flavorful drippings are used to make gravy or sauces. The term *drippings* also applies to bacon drippings, namely, the melted fat rendered from bacon during cooking, which is used to cook other foods in turn. This fat could clog drains, and should be collected in an empty can and then discarded with the trash if not used for cooking purposes. See DEGLAZING; DEGREASING; GRAVY.

Dried Fruit Glossary

APPLE Typically sold in thin rings, dried apples may be sweet or tart, depending on the variety.

APRICOT Pitted whole or halved fruit, sweet and slightly tangy.

CHERRY Dried sour cherries have lovely sweet flavor and are increasingly available. Pitted before drying, they resemble raisins in shape and may be used in the same way.

CURRANT While fresh currants are berrylike fruits grown and used widely in Europe, dried currants are actually Zante grapes, tiny raisins with a distinctively tart-sweet flavor. If they are unavailable, substitute raisins.

DATE The sugars of this desert-grown fruit become even more concentrated when dried, though they are generally eaten fresh.

FIG The dried form of this compact and succulent black, green, or golden fruit is distinguished by the slightly crunchy texture of its many tiny seeds.

PEACH Halved or quartered, pitted, and flattened fruit; sweet and slightly tangy.

PEAR Halved, seeded, and flattened fruit, retaining the fresh pear's distinctive profile.

PRUNE Variety of dried plum, with a rich, dark, fairly moist flesh.

RAISIN Variety of dried grapes, popular as a snack on their own. For baking, use seedless dark raisins or golden raisins.

DRIZZLING To dribble a liquid, such as olive oil, melted butter, or chocolate sauce, lightly and irregularly over food. Sliced tomatoes are drizzled with olive oil, corn on the cob is drizzled with melted butter, and sliced strawberries are drizzled with chocolate sauce. For extra sweetness and a pretty pattern, drizzle melted white chocolate over a cake or other baked good.

To drizzle, put the liquid in a small ladle or cup and gently swirl it over the surface of the food. Or, dip a fork in the liquid and drizzle the liquid from the ends of the tines. Drizzle olive oil by placing your thumb over the mouth of the bottle, leaving just a tiny gap, and shaking it back and forth over the food. Specialized spouts that allow drizzling are also available for olive oil and other bottles. A plastic squeeze bottle can be used to drizzle mustard over a hot dog or caramel sauce over a bowl of ice cream.

DRY INGREDIENTS Flour, sugar, salt, baking powder, baking soda, cocoa, and cornmeal are all examples of dry ingredients. They are mixed with fats and wet ingredients—butter, eggs, water, milk, cream—to make batters and doughs. Many baking recipes suggest mixing the dry ingredients together before combining them with the wet ingredients. Depending on the recipe, this may be done by whisking or sifting them together. Not all recipes require sifting, but it is never a bad idea to spoon the dry ingredients into a shallow bowl and mix them with a large wire whisk, using 8 or 9 strokes. This aerates the dry ingredients, which helps with rising, and also distributes salt or leavening evenly throughout the mixture.

See also BAKING; MEASURING; SIFTING; WET INGREDIENTS; WHISKING.

DRY RUB See RUB.

d

DUCK Similar in size (but not shape) to a chicken, a duck is a treat many people order only in restaurants, rarely thinking to cook it at home. This is a shame because duck is rich and full flavored and no more difficult to cook than other poultry.

Duck is hunted recreationally during the fall. None of this game can be sold commercially. Only farm-raised duck is

Quick Bite

Although traditionally a wild duck, the mallard is now sometimes farm raised. It has pleasantly gamy meat.

available to the consumer, and most of this reaches the market frozen. If you can find fresh duck, buy it, as it is tastier than frozen. Duck is marketed when only months old and is often labeled as duckling.

With its mild, tender, lean meat, White Pekin is the most commonly available type of duck. Over the years, Long Island, New York, has become the leader in the breeding and raising of this delicious bird, and so today White Pekin is often referred to as Long Island duckling. A Muscovy reaches market slightly older than other ducks (nearly 3 months old), which results in mature, especially flavorful breast meat. The prized breasts may be marketed as *magrets*. The Muscovy is raised for excellent foie gras, too.

Quick Bite

Moulards are a cross between a male Muscovy and a female White Pekin duck. Most of them are raised for foie gras.

Selecting Most likely the duck you buy at the supermarket or from a butcher will be frozen; it should be solidly frozen with no signs of thawing. If it is fresh, look for smooth skin without discoloration. Duck breast is considered the finest part of the duck and often is sold separately.

Storing Store fresh duck in the cold rear section of the refrigerator in its original packaging and cook it within 2 days. Store duck tightly wrapped in the freezer for up to 6 months.

Preparing Let frozen duck defrost in the refrigerator for a day. To avoid the growth of harmful bacteria, do not let it defrost on the countertop. If time is an issue, it can be defrosted in cool water. Submerge the duck, still in its plastic packaging, in cool water for 2 to 3 hours, changing the water every 30 minutes or so to keep it cold. Once thawed, the duck can be kept in the refrigerator for another day but should not be refrozen. Bring to room temperature before cooking, then cook it promptly.

Remove any lumps of duck fat from the cavity before cooking a whole duck, or strain the rendered fat left in the pan after cooking and use it to cook potatoes or eggs.

See also FOIE GRAS; GAME.

DUMPLING WRAPPER See NOODLE.

DUSTING To sprinkle food with a light layer of a powdery ingredient such as confectioners' sugar or cocoa, usually for decorative purposes. To dust food (or to garnish plates), use a small, fine-mesh strainer. Put the sugar in the strainer and gently tap the side of it as you move it over the food, leaving a fine, even coating.

Cake pans may be dusted with flour or cocoa after being greased, which helps to prevent the batter from sticking.

See also BAKING.

DUTCH OVEN See COOKWARE.

_everything from egg
to extract_

EGG See page 183.

EGG NOODLE See NOODLE; PASTA.

EGGPLANT Native to Africa and Asia, eggplants are commonly associated with the cooking of the Mediterranean, as illustrated by the many Italian and French dishes that feature them, such as eggplant parmigiana, caponata, and ratatouille. But eggplant turns up with equal, if not more, frequency in Chinese, Indian, Southeast Asian, and Middle Eastern cuisines.

The most familiar eggplant, called a globe eggplant, is usually large, egg or pear shaped, with a thin, shiny, deep purple skin that looks almost black.

Globe eggplant.

Asian eggplants, also purple skinned—some lavender, some deep purple—are smaller, longer, and narrower.

Other varieties may be slightly smaller and have white, rose, green, or variegated skin. The color of the skin does not determine the flavor of the vegetable.

Asian eggplants.

Mild, meaty eggplant flesh lends itself to countless simple, everyday preparations. In many countries, it is served in place of meat (which is saved for special occasions).
Selecting Eggplants are available year-round but are at their best from July through September. Choose smooth, firm, glossy-skinned eggplants with green caps and stems. Avoid any that are torn, bruised, or scarred, or that have brown, dried caps. Smaller eggplants are generally sweeter than large ones, and the vegetables should feel heavy for their size.
Storing Refrigerate eggplants in perforated plastic bags in the vegetable crisper for 4 or 5 days. They are best if cooked sooner rather than later, and if cooking on the day of purchase, let the vegetable sit at room temperature until ready to cook.
Preparing Large eggplants can be bitter, which explains why so many recipes suggest salting the cut-up vegetable, a step that draws out the bitterness. Salting also extracts excess moisture, which may interfere with the success of some recipes. As eggplants have become more commonplace in supermarkets, growers have been offering smaller, sweeter vegetables, which rarely

_e_

need salting. If the eggplant is large or old, or if the flesh looks dark and watery, however, you'll want to salt it after slicing. If frying eggplant, it's always a good idea to salt it, or at least press it gently to remove excess moisture. If the vegetables appear firm and quite dry, you can skip this step. Simply rinse the whole vegetable under cold running water and proceed with a recipe. Peeling is needed only if the skin seems thick and tough.

HOW TO *Salt Eggplant*

Salt an eggplant to remove bitterness or excess moisture that can interfere with the finished dish.

1. Cut the eggplant as directed in a recipe, and sprinkle pieces with coarse salt on all sides.
2. Put the pieces in a stainless steel or plastic colander set in the sink or over a plate and let drain for about 30 minutes.
3. Spread the eggplant on a double thickness of paper towels and, using a clean kitchen towel or more paper towels, gently press to squeeze out excess moisture.
4. Wipe with paper towels to remove excess salt. Do not rinse under running water, as the eggplant will absorb the water.

The flesh of an eggplant will discolor when exposed to the air for any length of time. To prevent this, sprinkle with a little lemon juice. Do not submerge in acidulated water, as the eggplant will absorb the water and turn soggy.

Quick Tip

A chemical reaction is produced when eggplant is cooked in aluminum, resulting in a metallic taste.

When sautéing or panfrying eggplant, be careful not to use more oil than needed. The eggplant will absorb nearly any amount of oil you pour into the pan. To combat this tendency, quickly cook the vegetable in a little oil over high heat.

Quick Bite

In Europe, an eggplant is called an aubergine, a word that also is used to describe its distinctive purple color.

EGG WASH Beaten whole eggs, yolks, or whites mixed with water, milk, or cream and used as a glaze on baked goods.

EMULSION An emulsion is a stabilized mixture that contains two or more liquids that would ordinarily not combine, such as oil and vinegar. While some emulsions are temporary, such as vinaigrette, others are more stable, such as mayonnaise. All emulsions require vigorous blending, such as shaking or whisking. When you shake a bottle of vinaigrette dressing and the ingredients mix together, you've created a temporary emulsion.

Whisking together an emulsion.

A stable emulsion also requires an agent known as an emulsifier to help hold the other ingredients together. Egg yolks are popular emulsifiers in the kitchen for recipes such as mayonnaise, hollandaise sauce, and Caesar dressing. Other emulsifying agents include mustard (which helps explain its presence in many vinaigrettes) and cream.

See also MAYONNAISE; VINAIGRETTE.

Egg

A common kitchen ingredient, the egg is as much a staple as sugar, flour, salt, and milk. But eggs are small miracles. They can be eaten by themselves—fried, boiled, scrambled, poached, baked—or added to numerous other dishes, both sweet and savory, to provide flavor, color, and consistency.

Cookies, cakes, soufflés, omelets, custards, and quiches cannot be made without breaking a few eggs.

Eggs are nutritional powerhouses, supplying protein; vitamins A, D, and E; and minerals such as phosphorus, manganese, iron, calcium, and zinc. Egg whites, also known as albumen, are among the most healthful of foods, being low in fat and high in protein. The yolks, on the other hand, contain the fat and cholesterol—and the most flavor.

Selecting Chicken eggs, by far the most commonly marketed and eaten eggs, are graded according to quality and size. Quality refers to freshness rather than nutrition. The highest-quality eggs, determined at time of packing, are AA, which have thick whites and firm, plump yolks. Grade A eggs fall only shortly behind in terms of quality. (Grade B eggs are low quality and rarely make it to the retail market.) In terms of size, eggs are labeled jumbo, extra-large, large, medium, small, and peewee. Most recipes are developed for large eggs, and while other sizes may

be substituted, you may have to adjust the recipe. For more details, see SUBSTITUTIONS & EQUIVALENTS. Fertile eggs from hens that have mated are considered a delicacy in some cultures, but these eggs offer no difference in nutritional value and do not keep as well.

Buy large AA eggs if possible. Look for those without cracks and with clean shells. All eggs destined for the commercial market have been carefully washed and coated with a natural mineral oil to prevent the introduction of bacteria.

Check the sell-by date, which should be as distant as possible.

Storing Store eggs in a cold area of the refrigerator where the temperature is below 40°F. Do not leave eggs at room temperature: a day on a countertop ages them as much as a week in the refrigerator.

Store eggs in their cartons. Don't transfer them to the egg racks found in some refrigerators. They may not stay cold enough, as the door exposes them to changing temperatures as it opens and closes. The carton helps keep them cold and less likely to pick up refrigerator odors. Additionally, eggs should be stored with the broad ends up, which is how they are packed. This keeps the yolk centered.

Unbroken eggs refrigerated in their carton will keep for 5 weeks past their sell-by

continued

Egg, continued

date. As they age, the whites will thin and become more transparent and the yolks will flatten, but the nutritional value of the eggs will not diminish. Use older eggs for baking, reserving the fresher ones for other cooking. Older egg whites are easier to whip up into voluminous meringue than absolutely fresh eggs, while fresh eggs are best for emulsified sauces such as hollandaise and mayonnaise.

Recipes will sometimes call for egg whites or egg yolks only, leaving you with leftover parts of eggs. Refrigerate uncooked egg whites in a tightly lidded glass or plastic container for up to 5 days. Refrigerate uncooked egg yolks in a glass or plastic container covered with a little water and tightly lidded for up to 2 days. Uncooked whole eggs removed from the shell can be stored in the same way and for the same length of time as egg yolks, but without the layer of water floated on top.

Quick Tip

If you find yourself with an excess of egg whites because a recipe used yolks alone, use them to make meringue, angel food cake, or egg-white omelets, or add them to whole eggs for more healthful scrambled eggs. If, on the other hand, you have an excess of egg yolks, get ready to make ice cream, mayonnaise, or chocolate mousse.

Freezing Eggs Remove whole eggs from their shells and place in a rigid container. (Never freeze eggs in the shell.) Stir lightly to break the yolks; do not stir briskly, or air bubbles may be incorporated. Cover, leaving only ½ inch of headroom, and freeze for up to 9 months. To freeze egg whites only, combine them in a rigid container, cover, and freeze for up to 1 year. To freeze egg yolks only, combine

them, as with whole eggs, add a pinch of salt or sugar, seal, and freeze for up to 9 months. When thawed to room temperature, frozen egg whites will whip up more easily than fresh whites. Use thawed, frozen whole eggs and egg yolks as you would fresh, for baking or omelets.

Preparing The best way to crack an egg is to tap it sharply against a flat surface such as a countertop—not a bowl rim. Holding the egg lengthwise over a container, break it in half, letting the white and yolk plop into it. If any shell gets into the bowl, use another piece of egg shell, a spoon, or a fork to remove it. (See also Egg Safety, below.)

HOW TO *Separate an Egg*

Cold eggs separate more easily than room-temperature eggs. If possible, take the eggs from the refrigerator immediately before separating them.

1. Position 2 small bowls side by side: 1 for the whites, the other for the yolks.
2. Crack the egg sharply on its equator, making a clean break.

3. Pour the yolk and whites into your clean cupped hand, letting the whites run through your fingers into one of the bowls, or use an egg separator in place of your hand. Slide the remaining yolk into the other bowl. (An egg separator is a small, bowl-shaped device with a center depression made to hold the yolk while the egg white slides through slots on the side into a waiting bowl.) Or, pass the egg yolk back and forth from one shell half to the other, letting the whites slip into the bowl. (See also Egg Safety, below.)

Egg separator.

4. If any yolk gets into the whites, they will not beat properly. Whites in the yolks will make no difference to the recipe. If separating more than 1 egg, you may want to use 3 bowls to avoid any risk of yolks getting into egg whites. Crack each egg over an empty bowl and transfer the whites to the egg white bowl, the yolks to the yolk bowl.

Egg Whites Savvy

■ When beating egg whites, start with a spotlessly clean bowl and whisk. Any spot of grease or fat (including egg yolk) will prevent egg whites from expanding to their full volume. A ceramic or glass bowl with slippery sides is not the best choice, and plastic tends to be a bit oily; stainless steel works better. The best choice is copper, which chemically interacts with the eggs whites to make them more stable and beautifully satiny. If using a copper bowl, cream of tartar may be omitted from a recipe.

■ Egg whites may be beaten with a hand-held electric mixer or stand mixer, fitted with the whisk attachment, or by hand with a whisk. (Some cooks think hand-beating incorporates the most air, yielding a very stable foam.) Food processors and blenders do not aerate well.

■ Beat egg whites thoroughly, according to the directions given in a particular recipe, in order to incorporate plenty of air. Once the whites foam, they will begin to increase in volume and will become opaque white rather than translucent. Lift the whisk or beaters from the whites to determine the state of their peaks. When the eggs are beaten to soft peaks, they will gently fall over to one side, while eggs beaten to stiff, dry peaks will stand upright.

Soft peaks.

Stiff peaks.

■ Do not overbeat egg whites, or they will become clumpy and grainy and act less effectively in delicate baked goods.

■ Fold beaten egg whites into a batter gently to avoid deflating them. See also FOLDING.

Egg Safety In recent years, raw eggs have been at the center of a controversy over their safety, namely, the incidence of salmonella bacteria present in some eggs. Recipes using raw eggs disappeared from the pages of newspapers, magazines, and cookbooks for years, but some are gradually reappearing in print now that the risk is better understood.

Salmonella bacteria can be found in a number of organisms, including poultry, meat, fish, and eggs. According to the American Egg Board, the incidence of salmonella in eggs is low, about 1 chance out of 20,000 overall. If an infected egg is properly stored so that the bacteria cannot

continued

Egg, continued

multiply, a healthy person probably will not get sick from eating it. Risk increases when a number of eggs are mixed together and

a single contaminated egg infects the entire batch, as could happen in restaurant kitchens. If you are pregnant or older, are cooking for young children or for pregnant or older people, have a compromised immune system, or want to limit your exposure to bacterial risk as much as possible, you may want to observe these guidelines:

- Buy eggs only from refrigerated cases.
- Keep all eggs refrigerated, whether they are in the shell or out.
- Do not leave eggs at room temperature for longer than 30 minutes.
- Make sure your hands, work surfaces, and utensils are clean.
- Refrigerate leftovers containing eggs as soon as possible. Put them in shallow containers so that they cool quickly.
- Use only clean, unbroken eggs. Discard cracked eggs.
- To be especially cautious, do not let the shell come into contact with the egg after it is broken, either by passing the yolk back and forth between the shell halves as

you separate the egg or by scooping other broken shell out of the egg.

- Cook eggs so that they are held at 140°F for at least 3½ minutes or reach a temperature of 160°F. Soft-boiled, poached, and coddled eggs do not reach 160°F.
- Avoid foods made with raw eggs, such as hollandaise sauce, béarnaise sauce, mayonnaise, and Caesar dressing.

A Basket of Breakfast Eggs

FRIED Cooked in butter or other fat, fried eggs can be finished "sunny-side up," that is, never flipped and with the yolk a bright yellow; or "over easy," that is, flipped and cooked briefly to set the yolk further.

OMELET Beaten eggs are cooked in a shallow pan, producing a firm exterior and soft interior, then typically folded over or rolled around a savory filling.

POACHED A classic topping for corned beef hash, poached eggs are cooked in simmering water or other liquid until the whites are set and opaque.

SCRAMBLED Whole eggs beaten, preferably with a little water, and then cooked slowly and stirred gently until thickened but still soft and moist.

SOFT-BOILED Eggs cooked in the shell until the whites are opaque and the yolks are hot and runny. Traditionally eaten directly from the shell in an eggcup.

Egg Substitute Made mainly of egg whites and thus lacking rich flavor, egg substitute is recommended for anyone avoiding the fat and cholesterol in egg yolks. Use in some baking, such as brownies and cookies, for scrambling, or in sauces.

See also CURDLING; FOOD SAFETY.

ENDIVE Also known as Belgian endive or witloof, this member of the chicory family is widely grown in Belgium, the principal source of the endive sold in North American markets. It relies on a painstaking, nonmechanized cultivation method (the reason for its high price) that calls for forcing chicory roots to sprout in a darkened, humid room, to yield small, white (or sometimes red-tipped), tightly furled, bullet-shaped heads. These carefully tended vegetables are fragile, and, while they travel well to foreign markets, they should be handled carefully at every step, including once you get them home. See also CHICORY.

ENOKI See MUSHROOM.

EPAZOTE See HERB.

ESCAROLE The robust, slightly curled leaves of this chicory relative are, like all chicory varieties, slightly bitter, but pleasingly so. The ruffled-leafed heads are particular favorites of Italian cooks, who add the leaves to a light broth for a simple soup or sauté the leaves quickly in olive oil with garlic and red pepper flakes and then toss them with pasta. See also CHICORY.

EVAPORATED MILK See MILK.

EVAPORATING A liquid heated to a certain temperature will boil, and agitating molecules will escape into the air, or evaporate. When water evaporates, it escapes in the form of a vapor called steam. The steam remains at a constant temperature just above the boiling point (212°F or 100°C for water at sea level). For this reason, steaming is a gentle, stable way to cook food and keep it moist.

Boiled long enough, a liquid will be reduced to only dry solids or trace residue.

Cooks take advantage of this process of evaporation to concentrate flavors and thicken sauces. In candy making, the water in boiling sugar syrup gradually evaporates, changing the temperature, density, and color of the syrup. See also BOILING; CANDY MAKING; DEGLAZING; HIGH-ALTITUDE COOKING; REDUCING; SAUCE.

EXTRACT Concentrated flavorings made from plants such as vanilla beans or almonds. Extracts, which are commonly used to flavor sweet dishes, are created by evaporating or distilling the plant's essential

Quick Tip

Because fats hold essential oils particularly well, add extracts while creaming the butter and sugar in a cake or cookie recipe to get the best flavor dispersion. As a general rule, use 1 teaspoon extract to flavor each 2 cups of food.

oils, which give it its distinctive flavor, and then suspending these oils in alcohol. In the United States, an extract labeled "pure" must contain only essential oils distilled from natural plants. Imitation flavorings, such as imitation vanilla extract, try to replicate the flavor of natural foods, sometimes using synthetic compounds. Artificial flavorings mimic foods that do not exist naturally, such as root beer or butterscotch. **Selecting** Use pure extracts whenever possible. They may cost more, but they have stronger, more complex flavors than either imitation or artificial products. **Storing** Store in a cool, dark cupboard. Extracts will keep for up to 1 year.

Quick Bite

In Britain and Australia, extracts are referred to as *essences*.

e

*everything from fat
to fudge*

FAT & OIL Too often demonized nowadays, fats and oils (the latter being fats that are liquid at room temperature) play an essential role in the kitchen. In sautéing, stir-frying, and panfrying, they lubricate food and cooking vessel alike, preventing sticking, and they transfer heat efficiently, promoting browning. In deep-frying, they become the cooking medium itself. In baking, they are used to grease pans, preventing batters and doughs from sticking. As part of those same batters and doughs, they give tenderness to the crumbs of breads and cakes and flakiness to pastries of all kinds. In dressings and sauces, and as spreads for bread, they add a smooth consistency. Particular fats and oils also contribute their distinctive and satisfying flavors to any recipe in which they appear.
Fats and Health With 9 calories per gram, fat is a concentrated calorie source, yielding two and a quarter times the energy by weight that a protein or carbohydrate offers. As a result, eating a high-fat diet without getting enough exercise can lead to weight gain and illnesses associated with obesity.

All fats from animal sources contain some cholesterol. This substance plays important roles in our bodies, helping to build cell membranes, nerve fibers, and hormones, for example. But because our livers actually manufacture all the cholesterol we need, diets high in animal fats introduce excess cholesterol, which can be deposited on arterial walls and lead to high blood pressure, heart disease, or stroke.

Different types of fat in food affect our bodies in different ways. Saturated fats, namely, those from animal sources, coconut and palm oils, and cocoa butter, bring excess levels of cholesterol to the blood. Another saturated fat is the trans fat that results when vegetable oil is hydrogenated to form margarine or solid shortenings. By contrast, the polyunsaturated fats found in most ordinary vegetable oils tend to lower blood cholesterol levels. But they are prone to oxidation, which can increase the buildup of plaque on arterial walls. Monounsaturated fats, such as olive and canola oils, not only lower blood cholesterol but also resist oxidation and are considered the healthiest choices of all.

Medical researchers generally recommend that we get no more than 30 percent of our daily calories from fat. No more than one-third of those should come from saturated fat, and as much as possible should come from monounsaturated fats.
Selecting Apart from the health-related issues already discussed, your choice of fat or oil for cooking will depend on three factors. One is whether a solid fat or liquid oil is required. Some baking recipes, for example, rely for their consistency on the ability to cut solid cubes of butter into little pieces covered in flour, or on the ability of solid fat to "cream" to a smooth, fluffy consistency when mixed with sugar. Another factor is whether or not the particular flavor of a fat or an oil is desired, an especially important question with flavorful olive oil. Finally, the temperature to which an oil or

Oil Glossary

In most markets, the shelves devoted to cooking oils display a wide range of choices, from vegetable oils to nut oils to seed oils. The following, including notes on their uses, are the most common.

CANOLA OIL Bland oil pressed from rapeseed, a relative of the mustard plant. High in monounsaturated fat. Good for general cooking and baking, but can smell unpleasant at high frying temperatures.

COCONUT OIL Popular as a deep-frying oil in Indian and Malaysian kitchens, imparting rich flavor. High in saturated fat.

CORN OIL Deep golden, relatively flavorless all-purpose oil largely used for general cooking and deep-frying.

GRAPESEED OIL Pressed from grape seeds and mild in flavor. Heats to very high temperatures and is suitable for frying. Also popular in salad dressings and marinades.

HAZELNUT OIL Highly flavorful oil, usually imported from France, pressed from toasted hazelnuts and used sparingly to enrich dressings and to flavor savory and sweet dishes. With its low smoke point, it is not used for cooking.

OLIVE OIL Prized oil produced in Mediterranean countries, California, and Australia from the fruit of the olive tree. Extra-virgin olive oil, a term applied to products pressed without the use of heat or chemicals, has a clear green or brownish hue and a fine, fruity, sometimes slightly peppery flavor, and is low in acidity. Use it in dressings or as a seasoning or condiment. Those olive oils labeled "mild," "light," "pure," or simply "olive oil" will have less fragrance and color than extra-virgin and are better suited to light cooking such as sautéing. All olive oils, and especially extra-virgin oils, are high in healthful monounsaturated fat.

PEANUT OIL Pressed from peanuts, which give it a hint of rich, nutty flavor, unless it is a refined version. Popular in Chinese cooking for stir-frying or deep-frying, it also may be used in salad dressings and dipping sauces.

SAFFLOWER OIL Widely available, flavorless oil pressed from safflower seeds, with a high smoke point. High in polyunsaturated fat.

SESAME OIL Deep amber–colored oil pressed from toasted sesame seeds and used as a seasoning in Chinese and Japanese kitchens. A pale golden, fairly flavorless cold-pressed sesame oil, sold in health-food stores, may be used for sautéing but is not a suitable substitute in recipes that call for Asian oil.

SOYBEAN OIL Bland oil pressed from soybeans, with a high smoke point suitable for deep-frying.

SUNFLOWER SEED OIL Pale, light, flavorless oil high in poly- and monounsaturated fats. Good all-purpose oil, used for everything from deep-frying to sautéing to salad dressings.

VEGETABLE OIL Commercial term applied to general-purpose oils that may be composed of corn, safflower, canola, or other oils, blended and filtered to have a pale color, neutral flavor, and high smoke point.

WALNUT OIL Rich-tasting, deep brown nut oil imported from France or Italy and used as a seasoning on its own or blended into dressings or sauces. Walnut oil is not good for frying because of its low smoke point.

f

189

Fat Glossary

The well-stocked kitchen always has a good range of solid cooking fats on hand for sautéing, frying, and baking.

BUTTER Imparts the rich, creamy flavor of cow's milk. Used for brief, lower-heat sautéing (it tends to burn) or to enrich sauces or baked goods. See also BUTTER.

LARD Pure pork fat rendered from back and kidney fat, very rich in flavor and with the finest known as leaf lard. Favored by some bakers for the flaky texture and rich taste it gives to pastry. Has a high smoke point, making it suitable for deep-frying.

MARGARINE Butter substitute made from hydrogenated vegetable oil. With the exception of reduced-fat margarine, may be used for baking or frying. See also MARGARINE.

SCHMALTZ A rich, flavorful ingredient used in traditional Jewish cooking, schmaltz is rendered chicken fat, sold in Jewish delis and some well-stocked food stores. Used for brief sautéing and to enrich savory dishes such as matzo balls.

SHORTENING This term applies in general to any solid fat used in baking. More specifically refers to vegetable shortening, a type of hydrogenated solid vegetable fat manufactured for use in baking or deep-frying. See also SHORTENING; VEGETABLE SHORTENING.

SUET Pure beef fat rendered from solid white fat from the kidney and loin, particularly prized in Europe for the rich taste it gives to pastries and deep-fried dishes.

a fat can be heated before it begins to break down and smoke, called its smoke point, will determine the use to which it can be put, from no-heat use in dressings to high-temperature deep-frying. See the Oil Glossary on page 189 for a few tips.

With some oils, you'll have a choice of refined and unrefined. Asian sesame oil is a good example of an unrefined oil, which contains some flavorful solids in suspension. Peanut and corn oils also are found in both forms. Unrefined oils are generally not best for cooking, as their smoke points are fairly low, but they are full of flavor and good for dressings. Refined oils are better for cooking but are largely flavorless.

Storing The enemies of fat are light, water, and heat. Exposure to any of these will promote rancidity. Store solid animal fats such as butter or lard in the refrigerator in their original packaging or, after

Quick Tip

When oil being heated becomes fragrant and shimmers, it is hot and ready to cook with.

opening, in a covered container. Unopened packages also may be frozen for up to 6 months. You can keep shortening still sealed in its original packaging in a cool, dry place indefinitely. Once opened, it will keep for up to 1 year. Store oils in airtight containers away from light and heat. Flavorful nut oils, which go rancid more quickly, should be bought in small quantities and kept refrigerated, which will likely turn them solid. Bring to room temperature before use.

See also BUTTER; COOKING SPRAY; FRYING; LOW-FAT COOKING; MARGARINE; SMOKE POINT; VEGETABLE SHORTENING.

FAVA BEAN See BEAN, DRIED; BEAN, FRESH.

FENNEL Also known as sweet fennel or finocchio. The fennel plant's leaves, seeds, and stems all have a sweet, faintly aniselike flavor. The stems of fennel swell and overlap at the base of the plant to form a bulb with white to pale green ribbed layers that are similar to celery in appearance and texture. The pretty green leaves are light and feathery and slightly resemble fresh dill. Use them as a bed for steaming fish or in small amounts as a garnish. 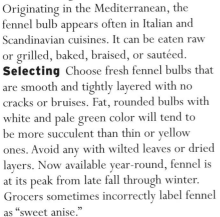 Originating in the Mediterranean, the fennel bulb appears often in Italian and Scandinavian cuisines. It can be eaten raw or grilled, baked, braised, or sautéed.

Selecting Choose fresh fennel bulbs that are smooth and tightly layered with no cracks or bruises. Fat, rounded bulbs with white and pale green color will tend to be more succulent than thin or yellow ones. Avoid any with wilted leaves or dried layers. Now available year-round, fennel is at its peak from late fall through winter. Grocers sometimes incorrectly label fennel as "sweet anise."

Storing Keep fennel bulbs in a perforated plastic bag in the refrigerator for up to 5 days. If kept too long, they will lose their flavor and toughen.

HOW TO *Trim and Cut Fennel*

1. Remove the green stems and leaves, saving them to flavor or garnish other dishes such as soups or fish.
2. Discard the outer layer of the bulb if it is tough and cut away any discolored areas.
3. Cut the bulb in half lengthwise and remove the base of the core if it is thick and solid.
4. Gently separate the layers with your hands and rinse well to remove any grit between them.
5. Slice or cut as directed in a recipe.

Quick Tip

While grilling, toss a handful of dried or fresh fennel stems onto the charcoal to infuse meat or fish with a light anise flavor.

See also BRAISING; SPICE.

FENUGREEK See SPICE.

FERMENTATION Some of the most important and most flavorful foods in the world, from bread, buttermilk, yogurt, cheese, and chocolate to beer and wine, depend on fermentation. Complex flavors emerge and textures change as yeast and bacteria are allowed to multiply in the food and break down large sugar or starch chains into smaller molecules, creating carbon dioxide and alcohol in the process. In some cases the gas produced during fermentation is trapped, making bread dough rise and Champagne bubbly. In other cases, it is released, as with still wine and cheese.

FETA See CHEESE.

FIG Among the world's oldest known foods, the fig was immortalized by the ancient poets, offered to early Olympic athletes during training, and long ago used in place of expensive or nonexistent sugar. The trees flourish in warm climates, where they can live for over a century and grow to a height of more than 100 feet. The soft, pear-shaped "fruit" is, in fact, a flower  swollen and turned in on itself, while the many tiny "seeds" are the actual fruit of the tree.

f

There are more than 150 varieties of figs, with skin that can be purple, green, yellow, brown, or white and flesh that ranges from pale gold to deep, rich red. Among the best-known varieties are green-skinned, white-fleshed Adriatic; the small, dark purple, sweet-tasting Mission (also known as Black Mission and California Black); the gold-skinned Calimyrna; the yellow-green, virtually seedless Kadota; and the nutty, amber-hued Smyrna. When dried, figs become delightfully chewy and even sweeter.

Fresh figs are delicious when poached or baked in tarts or paired with poultry or game. Use dried figs like raisins, chopping them and adding them to muffins, quick breads, cookies, couscous, or rice pilafs.

Selecting Fresh figs are available twice a year. The first crop, which is the smaller of the two, arrives in the market in June and lasts through July, but the fruits themselves are larger and more flavorful than the harvest from the second crop. The second crop begins in early September and runs through mid-October. Because they do not ripen off the tree, figs must be picked ripe and are quite fragile. They must be handled exceedingly carefully, which accounts for their usually high price tag.

Choose figs that are soft to the touch but not wrinkled, mushy, or bruised. Look for plump figs with firm stems and good color free of gray or tan spots. Figs with a webbing of delicate fissures, stretch marks revealing particularly moist and sweet fruit, are highly prized—a classic farmers' market treat. A sour aroma indicates an over-ripe fig that has begun to ferment.

Figs are widely available dried. Often sold in blocks or rounds, they lose their shape if packed too tightly. For better quality, buy dried figs in bulk at specialty markets or health-food stores. Dried figs should still be slightly soft.

Storing Fresh figs are highly perishable and should be eaten as soon after purchase as possible. If need be, they can be refrigerated for 1 to 2 days, arranged in a single layer on a tray lined with paper towels. They do not ripen if left at room temperature, but if they are just a little too firm to enjoy right away, they will soften enough to eat in a day or so.

Dried figs will keep in a cool, dry place for 1 or 2 months or in the refrigerator or in an airtight container or plastic bag for up to 6 months.

Preparing Rinse fresh figs and pat dry gently just before serving. Some recipes call for peeling them, a step that is purely aesthetic and generally unnecessary, since the entire fruit is edible. Overhandling will bruise the delicate fruit.

Quick Tip

Slit whole dried figs, stuff them with walnuts, and serve with a glass of tawny Port for an elegant after-dinner nibble.

FILBERT Another name for hazelnut; see NUT.

FILLET (fil-LAY) As a noun, the term *fillet* (sometimes spelled *filet,* especially when the subject is beef) signifies a piece of boneless fish, meat, or poultry. As a verb, "to fillet" means to remove the bones from fish, meat, or poultry, thus producing a fillet. With a little practice and a good narrow-bladed, rigid, sharp boning knife, home cooks can bone fish, chicken, or meat, but most people leave the job to the fishmonger or butcher. See also BONING.

FILO (FEE-loh) Also spelled "phyllo." These large, paper-thin sheets of dough create the flaky layers of many Middle Eastern and Greek sweet and savory pastries.

Honey-sweet baklava, cinnamon-infused *bisteeya,* and rich *spanakopita* all depend on filo for their delicate crusts. Filo also replaces more time-consuming puff pastry and tart doughs in recipes that highlight convenience and light texture.

Selecting Traditionally stretched into expansive nearly transparent sheets by master bakers, commercially produced filo is now widely available. The machine-rolled and frozen filo in major grocery stores is a good alternative to the fresh sheets sold at Middle Eastern markets. A 1-pound box will generally have 20 to 24 sheets, each measuring about 12 inches wide and 18 inches long. Try to buy them from a source with a high turnover. Long-frozen filo sheets will tend to stick together in clumps and break easily once thawed. Fresh sheets may be slightly smaller than frozen ones.

Storing Well-wrapped filo can be frozen for up to 6 months. Once thawed, an unopened box will keep in the refrigerator for up to 3 weeks. Defrosted filo should not be frozen again. You can wrap unused sheets in several layers of plastic wrap and return them to the refrigerator for up to 1 week; however, they may lose some of their pliability. Seal fresh filo in plastic wrap and refrigerate for up to 3 days.

Preparing For pliable sheets that do not stick or tear, thaw frozen filo in the refrigerator for 24 hours. Before beginning to layer or shape the sheets, be sure your work surface is clean and dry, your filling is cool, and all your ingredients and equipment are ready at hand. Although more fat between the layers means richer flavor and flakier texture, you can use as little as 1 teaspoon melted butter or olive oil for each layer. Clarified butter (see BUTTER) results in the crispiest pastry, but simple melted butter or a healthier butter-oil mix will work as well.

Quick Tip

With moist fillings, keep the filo layers dry and crisp by sprinkling a teaspoon of bread or cookie crumbs on each sheet after spreading the butter or oil. Sprinkle additional crumbs on the layer just beneath the filling.

Carefully unwrap the filo sheets from their packaging and spread them flat on a large tray or baking sheet. Cover the stack with plastic wrap or waxed paper, and then drape the whole tray with a damp cloth. Working with filo is not nearly as difficult as many believe. The most important points to remember are to bring the filo to room temperature, to work quickly, and to keep the sheets covered to prevent them from drying out. Filo layers can be used in place of homemade strudel dough or as a variation for pie or tart pastry.

HOW TO *Butter and Layer Filo*

1. Lightly coat a pan or baking sheet with melted butter or olive oil.
2. Remove only 1 sheet of filo at a time, using both hands to lift it up straight by 2 corners. Lay the sheet of filo down in the pan.
3. Dot the filo with the butter or oil, and then brush outward to the filo's edges to spread the fat evenly.

4. Repeat with the desired number of layers.
5. Coat the outside surfaces of the completed pastry with fat to encourage a golden brown color. Bake as directed.

fish

As the old saying goes, "There are a lot of fish in the sea." And that's not to mention the fish found in oceans, gulfs, lakes, rivers, reservoirs, streams, ponds, and bayous.

With the growing awareness of the benefits to be derived from eating this generally low-fat source of protein, more and more kinds of fish are turning up on menus and in markets, to be enjoyed as appetizers or main courses, on their own or in a wide range of salads, soups, sandwiches, pastas, and other preparations.

Selecting Use your eyes and nose to help you discern quality and freshness. All fish should look moist and bright and have a fresh, clean scent. Steer clear of products with discoloration, dryness, or even the slightest hint of an "off" aroma. Whole fish, in general, should look almost alive, with clear eyes; bright, intact scales and skin; and red, moist gills.

To find the best-quality fish, start with a reliable fishmonger or the seafood department of a well-stocked food store with frequent turnover. The staff should be readily able to tell you the origin of a fish and whether it is fresh or defrosted frozen. They should also willingly clean, scale, skin, fillet, or otherwise prepare the fish to your specifications.

Because fish tend to spoil more quickly than other animal proteins at normal refrigeration temperatures, all products at a fishmonger or seafood department should be displayed on crushed ice or in refrigerated cases with thermometers that clearly display a temperature of 33°F or lower.

Frozen fish also can be excellent if they were frozen on board the ship, soon after being caught. Avoid any that look dry, indicating freezer burn, or that come in packages containing liquid that has frozen, a sign of defrosting and refreezing—and of damage to the fish's texture.

Several popular kinds of fish are also commonly sold in other forms, including smoked, canned, pickled, and salted.

Storing Refrigerate fresh fish the moment you get it home and, ideally, cook it the day you buy it. To keep it in optimum condition for use on the following day, refrigerate the wrapped package in a baking pan—or any container large enough to hold it—and cover it with ice. Do not let the flesh of fish come in contact with ice, or it will cause freezer burn and leach out flavor. Always protect the flesh with plastic or some kind of barrier. Whole fish may sit directly in ice with no deterioration.

Frozen fish will keep well for 1 to 2 months in a freezer with a maximum temperature of 0°F. To defrost frozen fish, leave it on a tray or plate in the refrigerator for 24 hours, then store in a pan or tray of ice until ready to cook.

Preparing Hundreds of different types of fish, each with its own unique characteristics, are caught and eaten around the world. Most fish, however, can be classified in several simple ways that provide guidance on how to prepare, cook, and eat them.

LEAN FISH VS. OILY FISH Many fish, such as cod, sea bass, sole, and snapper, have mild-tasting, very lean flesh that calls for cooking with liquid or some fat to keep it moist. They are best when cooked by moist-heat methods, such as braising, poaching, or steaming, or when cooked in fat, as in frying or sautéing. When cooked by grilling, broiling, or roasting, they need to be either diligently basted or wrapped up to contain their juices. By contrast, more distinctively flavored, oily-fleshed fish, such as salmon, tuna, mackerel, and eel, do well when cooked by nearly all dry-heat methods—sautéing, frying, grilling, roasting, baking—virtually basting themselves, although they also can be good when cooked by moist-heat methods. See also COOKING METHODS.

FIRM FISH VS. DELICATE FISH Some fish, such as cod, snapper, sole, and trout, have fairly delicate flesh that requires careful cooking. Their fillets, for example, may fall apart during grilling, so the fish should only be grilled whole. Other varieties, such as swordfish or tuna, have a meaty texture, almost akin to steak, that can stand up to almost any cooking method.

FLATFISH VS. ROUND FISH Fish that are flat and narrow, such as sole or flounder, cook quickly, whether they are left whole or boned to yield 4 thin fillets. They do well with rapid methods, such as sautéing, but can disintegrate or dry out if cooked too long. Large fish with a rounded body, such as salmon, swordfish, or tuna, yield a wider variety of cuts—including large fillets, boneless medallions, and cross-sectional bone-in steaks—that adapt well to a wide range of cooking methods.

Testing for Doneness Common kitchen wisdom holds that, whatever cooking method is used, any piece of fish should be cooked for a total of 10 minutes for each inch of thickness at its widest point. As the moistness and texture of fish vary widely from species to species, however, it is wise to start checking for doneness after 8 minutes have elapsed.

To test for doneness, use the tip of a small, sharp knife to separate the flakes of the fish or otherwise cut into it at its thickest point. Unless you are deliberately cooking to medium or medium-rare, as some contemporary recipes for salmon and tuna indicate, the fish should be just opaque but still moist at its center and easy to flake. If it is already flaking without being prodded, it is likely overdone.

Testing fish for doneness.

A School of Fish

ANCHOVY This small, strong-tasting, oily saltwater fish is generally sold as fillets, either packed in salt or canned in oil. See also ANCHOVY.

BLUEFISH A rich-tasting, oily-fleshed saltwater fish found in Atlantic waters that is best cooked by a dry-heat method such as broiling or grilling.

CARP The mild taste and moist, meaty texture of this pale-fleshed, slightly oily freshwater fish is best highlighted by moist cooking such as braising or frying.

CATFISH This fairly firm-textured, white-fleshed freshwater fish can be cooked any way you like: fried, grilled, broiled, steamed, sautéed, or braised. Farm-raised specimens will have the mildest flavor.

COD Mild tasting, delicate, and lean, this white-fleshed saltwater fish takes well to any method but grilling.

EEL Found in both fresh- and saltwater, this long, slithery fish has rich-tasting, meaty, oily flesh that is good when broiled, grilled, braised, or stewed. Smoked eel, occasionally found in specialty-food stores, is especially delicious.

FLOUNDER A family of lean, delicate flatfish requiring quick cooking by any method.

continued

Fish, continued

HADDOCK Lean, mild, delicate saltwater fish similar to cod that may be cooked by any method.

HALIBUT Mild-flavored, lean, fairly firm-fleshed saltwater fish that may be cooked by any method.

HERRING Oily, flavorful, tender saltwater fish that is usually pickled, although fresh herring may be grilled or broiled.

MACKEREL Oily, flavorful, tender saltwater fish similar to herring that is likewise usually pickled, although the fresh fish may be grilled, broiled, or braised.

MONKFISH A white-fleshed saltwater fish, sometimes called the "poor man's lobster" for its meaty texture and mild, sweet flavor. May be cooked by any method.

PERCH Lean, mild, firm-fleshed freshwater fish that may be cooked by any method.

PIKE Mild-tasting and sweet, very lean, firm-fleshed freshwater fish that takes well to any cooking method.

ROCKFISH Delicate, mild-flavored, lean saltwater fish that takes well to any cooking method except grilling.

SABLE Rich, oily saltwater fish that is suitable for cooking by any method.

SALMON A firm, meaty, oily fish that may be poached, baked, roasted, panfried, steamed, broiled, or grilled. See SALMON.

SARDINE Small, slender, oily saltwater fish usually sold in cans. Fresh sardines are excellent cooked by dry heat. They are also good for pickling.

SEA BASS Lean, tender but meaty, white-fleshed saltwater fish suitable for cooking by any method.

SHAD Oily freshwater fish with a mild, sweet taste and tender texture best complemented by dry-heat cooking or sautéing. Shad roe, the delicate egg sac, is a springtime specialty, cooked by brief sautéing.

SHARK A family of lean, meaty-textured saltwater fish, of which some of the most commonly eaten varieties are the shortfin mako, the black tip, and the spiny dogfish. Shark may be cooked by any method.

SMELT Small, slender, oily saltwater fish with tender texture and mild, sweet flavor. Best quickly cooked by dry heat. Also known as whitebait in its smallest form, which is fried and eaten whole.

SNAPPER A family of tender but firm, lean, mild saltwater fish, of which red snapper and yellowtail snapper are the most popular varieties. Snapper may be cooked by any method.

SOLE A family of lean, delicate ocean flatfish, among which common varieties are Dover, lemon, petrale, and rex. May be cooked by any method, but only briefly.

STURGEON Very firm-textured, oily, rich-tasting salt- or freshwater fish, may be cooked by any method.

SWORDFISH Firm-textured, somewhat oily, rich-tasting white-fleshed ocean fish that may be cooked by any method.

TROUT Delicate, somewhat oily freshwater fish that may be cooked by dry heat. Excellent when smoked.

TUNA Meaty, flavorful, oily saltwater fish that is good cooked by any method and is excellent raw as sashimi or sushi. Also commonly available canned. See TUNA.

TURBOT Mild, tender white-fleshed saltwater flatfish that can be cooked by dry- or moist-heat methods.

WHITEFISH Oily, tender, flavorful freshwater fish that can be cooked by any method and is a favorite smoked fish.

See also CAVIAR; FILLET; FLAKING; individual cooking methods.

Quick Bite

Oily-fleshed fish, especially herring, anchovy, salmon, tuna, sardine, mackerel, and swordfish, are rich in a type of healthful polyunsaturated fat called omega-3 fatty acids.

FISH SAUCE Southeast Asians use fish sauce in much the same way Westerners use salt, both as a cooking seasoning and at the table. It is a clear liquid, ranging from amber to dark brown, and famous (or infamous) for its pungent aroma and strong, salty flavor.

The best-quality fish sauce is pressed from small fish, commonly anchovies, that have been salted, packed in barrels, and fermented for several months under the steady heat of the tropical sun. Fish sauce is called *nam pla* in Thailand, *nuoc mam* in Vietnam, *tuk trey* in Cambodia, and *patis* in the Philippines. In the Southeast Asian kitchen, these add depth to almost every savory dish, and at the table, fish sauce is mixed with various seasonings, such as lime juice, rice vinegar, sugar, black pepper, and chiles, and then used as a dipping sauce. Not surprisingly, the sauce is also high in protein.

Selecting The first pressing of the salted and fermented fish produces liquid with the clearest color and the most balanced flavor. A lighter color indicates a more subtle flavor, best as a table condiment and in dipping sauces. The darker fish sauces, which are used more often in cooking, tend to taste stronger and saltier.

Storing Fish sauce will keep indefinitely if stored in a cool, dark place.

FLAGEOLET See BEAN, DRIED; BEAN, FRESH.

FLAKING To separate food, especially cooked or canned fish, into its natural layers. Typically a fork is used to ease the layers apart. Sometimes the purpose of flaking is to break up the food sufficiently for easy mixing; other times larger flakes are desired for an attractive appearance, such as for a composed salad. Flaking can also be a test for when fish is done cooking: if a fork inserted vertically into a piece of fish separates the layers easily and reveals the flesh to be opaque throughout, the fish is done.

FLAMBÉING To pour warmed liquor over food and ignite its fumes. Flambéing, or flaming, is often used to prepare sauces and desserts at tableside for a dramatic presentation, but it also has a culinary purpose. Liquor is often used to flavor dishes, and burning off the alcohol tempers its harshness and accentuates the flavor. Not all the alcohol actually burns off; anywhere from 5 to 85 percent may remain in the dish, an important consideration for anyone avoiding alcohol. Flambéed dishes are not as popular as they once were, but flambéing is an essential element in coq au vin, bananas Foster, crêpes Suzette, cherries jubilee, baked Alaska, and the traditional English plum pudding served at Christmastime.

Restaurant chefs usually tilt their pans slightly over a gas burner to ignite the fumes. Don't try this professional technique at home; it is easier and safer to use a long kitchen or fireplace match. If you have a chafing dish or a portable burner, you can flambé at the table.

Caution!

- Brandy or an 80-proof liquor is best for flambéing. Higher-proof alcohol is too volatile, and anything lower in proof won't flame as effectively.
- When using a gas stove, always pour alcohol from a bottle into a pan that is well away from the heat. The flame from a gas burner can follow the alcohol into the bottle and cause it to burst.
- Be careful not to let long hair or loose sleeves catch fire, and don't lean your face too close to the pan as you ignite the alcohol fumes.

f

HOW TO *Flambé*

1. Have the dish with its sauce gently simmering over very low heat.
2. Warm the liquor in a small pan just until it is hot but not boiling. It can also be warmed in a microwave, allowing 15 to 20 seconds for every ¼ cup of liquor. The liquor must be warmed first in order to flambé successfully.
3. Remove the pan holding the food to be flamed from the burner, or turn the burner off. Pour the warmed liquor evenly over the food.
4. Without stirring, return the pan to the heat or turn the burner back on. Light a long match and hold it 1 to 2 inches above the food to light the fumes. Do not touch the match to the food or the liquor itself.
5. Wait for the flames to subside completely, or shake the pan gently or cover it with a lid if necessary to smother them. The longer you let the flames burn, the more alcohol you will burn off. Alcohol carries flavor, some of which you may wish to retain in the dish.

Quick Tip

To garnish with flames: Just before serving a dish, soak sugar cubes with liquor, arrange them decoratively on or around the food, and then ignite the fumes rising from the cubes.

FLAME-TAMER A brand-name heat diffuser; see COOKING TOOLS.

FLATTENING See POUNDING.

FLOUR The product that results from grinding grains, dried vegetables, or nuts into a fine powder. Flours provide the body and substance of breads, noodles, cakes, and cookies. They also thicken sauces and serve as coatings for fried meat and vegetables. One of the oldest and most important foods in the human diet, the first flour was ground over 14,000 years ago.

In common usage, the term *flour* generally refers to ground wheat grain. Stone-ground flour retains more nutrients and flavor than flour milled with steel rollers, which heat the grain, changing its flavor. The first milling breaks the wheat grain and separates its three components. The outer hull, or bran, is rich in nutrients; the wheat germ contains the seed's embryo that will later sprout; and the endosperm, which makes up most of the grain and provides most of its starch, will become white flour. Since bran and germ contain oils that spoil quickly, they are removed to extend the shelf life of white flour, which is then fortified with vitamins and minerals to replace the lost nutrients. It will lighten naturally as it ages, but much of the flour sold is bleached chemically. Although not as white as chemically bleached flour, unbleached flour has a better flavor.

Storing Try to buy flour in amounts that you can use in 4 to 6 months. It will keep longer but is best used fresh. Transfer flour to an airtight container and keep it in a cool, dry place away from light. Because the bran and germ contain oils, whole-wheat flour will go rancid quickly if stored at room temperature. Wrap it tightly and keep it in the refrigerator for up to 6 months or in the freezer for up to 1 year.

About Sifting Passing flour through a fine mesh filters out lumps and creates a lighter, smoother texture. Although many flours come presifted, it is still a good idea to sift flour before you use it for cakes, cookies, and other tender baked goods. Read a recipe closely to see if it asks you to sift before or after measuring.

About Wheat Flour There are two general types of wheat grown. Soft wheat, found in milder climates, has less protein and more starch. Hard wheat generally grows in colder areas and is ground into bread and pasta flour. These natural variations in wheat, plus different kinds of processing, make for several different styles of wheat flour. For a baker, the most important difference to understand is the protein content, which can range from 5 to 15 percent. The varying levels of protein help determine the difference between tender cupcakes and chewy bread. A higher protein content in the flour used in bread baking allows a dough to form a strong, elastic network of interlocking strands, called gluten, to capture the gases needed to raise the bread. If low-protein cake flour is used in a bread recipe, the gluten structure will not be strong enough and the bread will not rise properly or attain a chewy texture. If high-protein bread flour is used in a cake recipe, it will have a tough, sturdy texture that no one wants in a cake. The following types of flour are arranged by protein, from highest to lowest, to help you choose the right one for a particular use.

HIGH-GLUTEN FLOUR High-protein flour, milled from hard wheat and treated to remove a relatively high percentage of its starch. It is commonly mixed with flours that are very low in protein, such as rye.

BREAD FLOUR An unbleached, hard-wheat flour. Its high protein content creates an elastic dough for higher rise and more structure in breads, pizza crusts, and pastas. Some bread flours include malted barley flour to feed the yeast.

ALL-PURPOSE FLOUR A mixture of soft and hard wheats, with the bran and germ removed. This is the popular general-use flour that is good for a wide range of foods, from sauces to cookies to quick breads to pancakes to fritter batters.

WHOLE-WHEAT FLOUR Milled from whole grains of wheat. Since it still contains the bran and germ, whole-wheat flour has

more flavor, higher nutritional value, and darker color than white flour. It also absorbs more liquid, is denser after baking, and contains more fat. Because it contains more parts of the whole grains, whole-wheat flour has a lower protein content than all-purpose flour.

SELF-RISING FLOUR A relatively soft, or lower-protein, all-purpose flour mixed with baking powder and salt, intended as a convenience when making biscuits, quick breads, and cookies. Its leavening power decreases gradually after 2 or 3 months, which is one reason that many bakers prefer to use all-purpose flour and add rising agents themselves for consistent results.

PASTRY FLOUR With slightly more protein than cake flour, pastry flour offers the additional structure needed for puffed and layered pastry dough but is still more tender than all-purpose flour.

CAKE FLOUR Milled from soft wheat and containing cornstarch, cake flour is low in protein and high in starch. It gives cakes a light crumb. Cake flour has also undergone a bleaching process that increases its ability to hold water and sugar, so cakes made with cake flour are less likely to fall.

f

About Specialty Flours Flour is generally understood to be basic wheat flour, but there are other grains, vegetables, and nuts that can be ground into flour as well. The term *meal* refers to other coarsely ground grains.

BUCKWHEAT FLOUR A dark flour with a nutty, slightly sweet flavor and firm texture. Used to make soba noodles in Japan, crepes in Brittany, and pancakes and blini throughout Eastern Europe and Russia.

CHESTNUT FLOUR A flavorful, extremely fine flour ground from dried chestnuts. Used in desserts in Italy and Hungary.

CHICKPEA FLOUR Called *farinata* in Italy and *besan* in India. Ground from dried chickpeas, a rich flour used to make flat breads, dumplings, and fritters.

CORN FLOUR Finely ground white or yellow cornmeal. In Great Britain, the term *cornflour* refers to cornstarch.

MASA HARINA Literally "dough flour" in Spanish, a form of cornmeal used in Mexico to make tortillas and tamales. Whole corn kernels are cooked in a caustic mineral lime solution to remove their hulls, then dried and ground into flour.

OAT FLOUR Sweet, earthy flour made from finely ground groats. It makes particularly soft and moist baked goods.

Quick Tip

Gluten-forming proteins are plentiful in wheat but appear in much smaller amounts in rye and oats. Gluten-free grains include buckwheat, corn, and rice. Flours ground from vegetables or nuts such as chickpea and chestnut also do not form gluten, so these flours are traditionally used to make unleavened, or flat, breads. Replace no more than one-third of a recipe's wheat flour with oat or rye flour. You may substitute up to one-fourth of the wheat flour with gluten-free or nongrain flours.

POTATO FLOUR Ground from steamed and dried potatoes. Used to thicken delicate sauces and to make tender cakes and cookies. Also called potato starch.

RICE FLOUR Ground from white rice. Long-grain rice flour is used as a wheat substitute in baked goods and to obtain a light, crispy texture in crackers and cookies. Short-grain, or glutinous, rice flour gives Asian sweets their soft, chewy texture. In Japan, the flour is ground from cooked rice and then mixed with water and cooked to make the familiar sticky national sweet known as *mochi*. Neither should be confused with rice powder, which is exceedingly fine. Flour ground from brown rice has a nutty flavor and darker color.

Quick Tip

Both fat and acid will inhibit the development of gluten strands, which is good for pastry (and bad for bread). Less gluten will help make a dough easier to roll out and more tender after baking. When making pastry, for every cup of flour, add 1 teaspoon of lemon juice or 2 tablespoons of oil to the wet ingredients called for in a recipe.

RYE FLOUR A slightly bitter and tangy flour, second only to wheat flour in the world of bread baking, that makes a dense, heavy bread. Dark rye flour retains more of the bran than medium rye.

SEMOLINA FLOUR Ground from a particular variety of wheat, called durum wheat, that is especially hard (that is, high in protein) and used primarily for making dried pasta. High-quality pasta will be made from 100 percent durum semolina. Semolina flour is also used to make desserts such as cake and pudding.

See also BREAD; KNEADING; MEASURING; QUICK BREAD; SIFTING; SUBSTITUTIONS & EQUIVALENTS; THICKENING.

FLUFFING To make a mixture or dish light and airy, usually by gently stirring and lifting with a fork. Grains of rice, for example, are compact after cooking, but fluffing will separate them and lighten the overall texture of the rice.

FLUTING Decorative shaping of the edge of a pie crust. The edge of a single-crust pie can simply be pressed into gentle curves with fingertips or pinched into a ropelike pattern. The edges of double-crust pie are generally  crimped with a fork both to seal the top and bottom crusts together and to make a decorative pattern. See also CRIMPING; PIE & TART.

FOCACCIA A moist, rustic flat bread from northern Italy, traditionally made from a soft yeast dough that is spread into a pan, dimpled deeply with fingertips, and then generously drizzled with olive oil and sprinkled with sea  salt before baking. Contemporary focaccia may also be sprinkled with other ingredients, such as fresh rosemary, shredded basil, olives, grated cheese, paper-thin tomato slices, or caramelized onions.
Selecting Look for rounds or rectangular sheets in the bakery sections of grocery stores or in Italian bakeries or delis.
Storing Best eaten as soon after baking as possible. To keep focaccia longer, wrap well with plastic and foil and freeze for up to 1 month.

FOIE GRAS (FWAH GRAH) specialty of the Gascony, Alsace, and Périgord regions of France, foie gras is a luxurious delicacy. Literally "fat liver" in French, foie gras is the greatly enlarged liver of a goose or duck that has been force-fed a special diet, usually of corn. Foie gras is silky in texture, creamy beige to light yellow with tinges of pink, and buttery rich in flavor, lacking the assertive flavors usually associated with liver. Good-quality foie gras is produced in countries other than France, including Israel, Poland,  Hungary, Canada, and the United States, although supplies everywhere are limited.
Selecting Foie gras from geese has a mellow flavor and rich texture. Livers from ducks will have a more intense, almost winy flavor. Color is not a good indicator of quality, but the highest grade of livers will be large and firm—never spongy. Buy foie gras from gourmet markets or specialty meat shops. It is available year-round. Cooked whole foie gras, foie gras mousse, and purée are available in cans.

Foie Gras Grades

FOIE GRAS GRADE A Weighs no less than 14 ounces and has no imperfections. Smooth and buttery, it is ideal for sautéing.
FOIE GRAS GRADE B Softer than Grade A and with slight imperfections. Weighs 11 to 13 ounces. Can be sautéed or baked.
FOIE GRAS GRADE C Meaty though small. Weighs 7 to 10 ounces. Rarely available to the consumer.

f

Storing Since fresh foie gras is highly perishable, use it as soon as possible after purchase. If necessary, wrap well in plastic and refrigerate for up to 2 days. Whole uncooked livers packaged in heavy plastic Cryovac can be kept refrigerated for 3 to 4 weeks. A whole foie gras can be frozen for up to 2 months, but its texture may suffer. Store canned foie gras in a cool, dry place for up to 1 year.

Preparing Whole, fresh foie gras has two lobes that must be carefully trimmed of all traces of green bile and white fat. Let the liver come to room temperature before preparing. Separate the lobes and pull out all veins.

Duck foie gras is often simply sautéed quickly only until still pink. (Cooked for a long time or at temperatures higher than 195°F, it will melt into a pool of fat.) Goose foie gras, which is fattier and even more likely to melt, is better chopped or ground into pâté, which is slowly cooked in a dish called a terrine. When pâté is served in a terrine, it is called a terrine; when it is unmolded, it is called pâté.

Quick Bite

What happens to the rest of the bird? These meaty specimens are used to make confit and other rich poultry dishes. Duck breasts, called *magrets*, are particularly large and tasty.

FOLDING This mixing technique is used to combine two ingredients or mixtures with different densities. Light, airy mixtures, such as beaten egg whites or whipped cream, will lose their loft if incorrectly folded into heavier batters, and your cake or soufflé won't rise properly. It is a simple but crucial technique. Use a firm but light hand when folding, and don't overdo it: stop folding once the mixtures are just blended.

HOW TO *Fold*

1. Spoon one-fourth of the lighter mixture, such as beaten egg whites, atop the heavier mixture, such as batter.
2. With a long-handled rubber spatula, slice down through both mixtures and sweep the spatula along the bottom of the bowl. Bring the spatula with a gentle circular motion up and over the contents. The goal is to lift up some of the heavier batter from the bottom of the bowl and gently "fold" it over the top of the lighter mixture without deflating the lighter mixture.

Folding in egg whites.

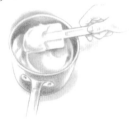

3. Rotate the pan or bowl a quarter turn and repeat the down-across-up-over motion. Continue in this manner, rotating the bowl each time, until the lighter mixture is incorporated. This initial folding of just one-fourth of the lighter mixture allows the rest of it to be folded in more easily.
4. Add the remaining lighter mixture. Fold as explained above, quickly but gently, just until the mixtures are evenly incorporated. A little streaking is fine. Overmixing will deflate the lighter mixture.

FONTINA See CHEESE.

FOOD GUIDE PYRAMID In 1992, the United States Department of Agriculture (USDA) and the Department of Health and Human Services unveiled the official Food Guide Pyramid. Studies had linked high-fat and high-salt diets to heart problems, high blood pressure, and cancer and other degenerative diseases, and the pyramid was designed to illustrate which foods in which quantities were considered most beneficial to overall good health.

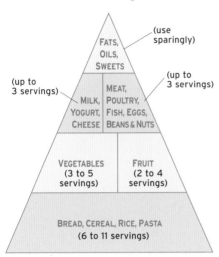

A refinement of the old-fashioned "four basic food groups," the pyramid's shape reflects current nutritional recommendations. Grains and cereals are the pyramid's wide foundation. Fats, oils, and sweets should be eaten "sparingly," illustrated by their placement in the narrow tip.

The recommended number of servings each day may seem high. Keep in mind, though, that the USDA's definition of 1 serving is less than what the average person might eat at one sitting. For example, a single serving in the bread group is just 1 slice of bread or ½ cup pasta. In the meat group, a serving might be 3 ounces of lean beef, 1 tablespoon of peanut butter, or 1 egg, while the average person might eat at least twice that in a sitting.

FOOD MILL Used to purée cooked or very soft foods, usually fruits or vegetables, a food mill looks like a stainless-steel or sturdy plastic saucepan with a perforated bottom and an interior crank-shaped handle. It also may have arms that extend for fitting it securely over a bowl. At the bottom of the mill is a circular, paddle-shaped blade that rotates against a disk perforated with small holes. As you turn the handle, the blade forces food through the holes and into a bowl or other receptacle, trapping any seeds, peels, or fibers in the mill. Some mills have interchangeable disks with holes of varying sizes for creating purées of various consistencies, while others have a single fixed disk. Food mills treat food more gently than food processors and produce more even-textured purées.

FOOD PROCESSOR Efficient, powerful, and capable of performing a wide variety of functions in the kitchen, food processors have become so popular in the past quarter century or so that recipe writers often assume they are as readily available as blenders and electric mixers.

Most models consist of a straight-sided work bowl that sits on a motorized base. Various disks and blades fit on a rotating shaft at the center of the bowl. The all-purpose, S-shaped metal blade chops, blends, mixes, and purées. Other attachments include disks for shredding, grating, or slicing; a plastic blade for kneading dough; and a disk for julienning. (See page 204.) A feed tube allows you to add ingredients while the food processor is running.

Despite their popularity, food processors are not capable of performing every kitchen task. Their powerful motors can easily overwork foods, sometimes making a mush if you are not careful. They are not recommended for mashing potatoes (it makes them gummy), nor can they normally be used for beating egg whites or whipping cream. Sometimes a whip attachment is available, but generally the machine is incapable of aerating these ingredients sufficiently for good loft. If you plan to mix very dense dough, make sure your processor motor is powerful enough, or the motor may dangerously overheat.

Metal blade and dough blade.

Slicing and shredding disks.

Grating and julienne disks.

Food Processor Savvy

■ To avoid having to wash the bowl when chopping several ingredients in succession, start with the driest and mildest ones and finish with the stronger, moister ingredients, such as onions. If needed, wipe out the work bowl with a dry paper towel between ingredients.

■ For easier cleanup after processing sticky foods, lightly coat the blades, disks, and work bowl with flavorless vegetable oil before use.

■ If the work bowl leaks between the blade and the shaft or under the lid, it is probably holding too much liquid. Process smaller batches, or strain the liquid out first and purée the solids separately.

■ Chopping large amounts of chocolate or stale bread will dull the blade. Crushing ice cubes may damage it.

■ Because the blade crushes ingredients as it chops, some cooks avoid using the food processor with ingredients that are easily bruised, such as onions, garlic, or fresh basil.

■ When scraping foods out of the work bowl, prevent the blade from falling into the bowl or pan with the food. Hold the bowl with your thumb inserted in the blade port on the bottom, pressing against the blade to keep it in place, with your fingers resting on the side.

FOOD SAFETY A few simple precautions and smart cooking habits will help safeguard you from the possibility of illness caused by the small amounts of bacteria naturally present in food.

Safe Shopping

■ Always check sell-by dates printed on food packaging.

■ When buying fresh meat or poultry, make sure that the package is not leaking. If there is any moisture, slip the package into a plastic bag so that it does not drip onto other fresh foods.

■ Buy eggs, meat, poultry, and fish only from refrigerated cases and only in good condition. Avoid those with "off" odors or discoloration.

- Put perishables into your shopping cart last, and put them away first as soon as you get home.
- Avoid packaged foods in cans or jars with dents or bulges.

Safe Storage

- Check and follow use-by dates printed on food packaging.
- See food safety and general storage guidelines given in the individual ingredient entries of this book as well as under DONENESS.
- Use your physical senses, along with common sense, in judging whether any ingredients are in good condition. If you have any doubt, throw it out.
- In the refrigerator, place any packaged raw or defrosting frozen meat, seafood, or poultry on a dish or rimmed tray to catch any juices that might leak out.
- When recipes state to store food in the coldest part of the refrigerator, this usually means the back of the bottom shelf or in a meat drawer. (A refrigerator thermometer will tell you for sure.)
- Large quantities of hot food should be allowed to cool to room temperature before refrigerating; otherwise, the heat of the food can lower the internal temperature of the refrigerator, compromising the safety of the other food stored there. Spoon it into several small, shallow containers, stir it occasionally, and don't cover it. This will speed the cooling process. Refrigerate within 2 hours.
- Don't keep your refrigerator jammed full of food. Air needs to be able to circulate around the stored food to keep it at the correct temperature. At the same time, an empty refrigerator (or freezer compartment) is not as efficient as one with a good amount of food. The cold food helps maintain the temperature.

- Buy a refrigerator thermometer to make sure your food is refrigerated safely. The thermometer should be placed on the top shelf close to the door. Leave it overnight, then check to make sure the temperature is no more than 40°F.

Safe Food Preparation

- Before and after you handle any ingredients, especially raw seafood, poultry, and meat, wash your hands thoroughly with lots of warm water and soap.
- After preparing any foods, thoroughly wash all the kitchen tools, cutting surfaces, and dishware that touched them with lots of warm water and soap.
- Before cooking poultry, use cold running water to rinse off the bird, outside and inside the cavity.
- Before you cook fruits and vegetables or eat them raw, rinse them thoroughly with cold running water, scrubbing them as needed. Some fruits and vegetables are waxed to enhance appearance and lengthen storage. These commercial waxes are not toxic, but they can trap pesticide residues, so scrub them off thoroughly before eating.
- Rinse lettuce, spinach, and other greens thoroughly, even those bought in sealed plastic packages.
- Always use separate cutting boards for animal products and for produce. Thoroughly wash the boards after each use. Periodically sterilize polyethylene boards in the dishwasher at its hottest setting, or wash wooden or polyethylene boards with a solution of 4 cups warm water and 1 teaspoon household bleach.
- In preparation for cooking, do not leave perishable food out of the refrigerator for more than 2 hours. In warm weather, reduce this time to no more than 1 hour. As soon as possible, and no more than 2 hours after serving, refrigerate or freeze leftovers.

f

Caution!

If you are pregnant or older, are cooking for young children or older people, have a compromised immune system, or want to limit your exposure to bacterial risk as much as possible, you may want to observe even stricter guidelines for leaving out any perishable food, limiting it to 30 minutes.

Safe Cleanup

- Wipe up spilled foods quickly and thoroughly from counters and floors to avoid the growth of bacteria.
- Use fresh, clean kitchen towels, replacing them frequently, especially if they get soiled or damp.
- Run sponges, scrubbing pads, and brushes through the dishwasher every week or so to sterilize them. Alternatively, boil or microwave them for 2 minutes.

See also BEEF; CHICKEN; DONENESS; PORK; SAFETY.

FREEZING Freezing is one of the easiest and most nutritious ways to preserve food. Meats, fish, fruits, vegetables, breads, and many finished dishes all freeze well if certain guidelines are followed.

Understanding what happens in the freezer will help make sense of the rules. When food is frozen, the water in the food freezes, thus stopping (or slowing) the normal cell activity that would otherwise cause deterioration and spoilage. When foods are frozen quickly at extremely low temperatures (as is the case in commercial food manufacture), the ice crystals in the frozen water are tiny and do very little to disrupt the food's cell structure. When food is frozen at higher temperatures (for example, the temperature of a home freezer), it freezes more slowly and larger ice crystals

form. These larger crystals are actually sharp enough to puncture the food's cell walls. When the food thaws, there will be far greater deterioration than is the case with commercially frozen food.

In the interest of keeping cell damage and water loss to a minimum, try to freeze food as quickly as you can. Fluctuations in temperatures that allow partial thawing and then refreezing lead to extensive damage and textural degradation.

Food that is not well protected from the dry, cold air of the freezer will suffer freezer burn, extreme drying that ruins both texture and flavor. Freezer burns appear as dried, white, or darkened areas on the surface of the food. When preparing foods for freezing, wrap them carefully and expel excess air from their packaging to limit their exposure to air.

The most common form of freezer spoilage after freezer burn is rancidity. Fats can eventually turn rancid in the freezer, and the freezer life of frozen foods is directly correlated to their fat content. Exposure to air promotes rancidity, so again careful wrapping before freezing helps slow the process.

Freezer Savvy

- Maintain the freezer temperature as close to 0°F as possible.
- Cool all foods completely before transferring to containers and freezing.
- If possible, remove excess air from containers: fold down bags to squeeze out all the air you can.
- Divide large batches into the smaller quantities that you would be using at one time, such as portions of pesto in ice-cube trays, tomato sauce in pint containers, chicken breasts in pairs.
- Be sure to mark the date and contents on packages with a permanent marker, and mark containers the same way using tape or another removable label. It may

seem obvious to you at the moment, but 3 months from now you'll be hard-pressed to remember what is in that well-wrapped package at the back of the freezer.

- Don't try to freeze too much food at once, as this may lower the freezer temperature. When putting unfrozen food into the freezer, leave plenty of space between the packages or containers. Once completely frozen, the food can be closely stacked.

- Once the food is frozen, a full freezer is the most efficient freezer.

- When buying frozen food at the grocery store from open freezer cases, be sure that the entire package of food is sitting well below the indicated freeze line, marked on the side of the case, and that the contents are completely frozen. Return home as quickly as possible to prevent any thawing before transferring the food to your own freezer.

About Freezer Materials and Containers

ALUMINUM FOIL Aluminum foil is not the best material for cold storage. It creates mysterious little bundles in the refrigerator, unless you take the time to label. It also turns brittle under freezing temperatures and does not form the most secure seal. If you want to wrap food for the freezer in foil, wrap it first in waxed paper or plastic wrap. Use only heavy-duty freezer foil, not the lightweight version that can tear easily and disintegrates quickly. And do not use foil for highly acidic foods, since they may react and create "off" flavors and dark colors.

FREEZER PAPER Laminated with foil, glassine, cellophane, or rubber latex to provide protection against freezer burn. Be sure to seal completely with freezer tape. Freezer paper can be used over cardboard, plastic, or foil for additional protection.

PLASTIC

- Bags: Look for zippered bags made of heavy-duty plastic that are specially made to withstand freezing temperatures. Place the bag in a container to keep it upright and open for easy filling. Once full, eliminate excess air (to help prevent freezer burn and rancidity), seal closed, and then freeze it on a flat surface. When the contents are hard, stack the bags for efficient storage.

- Wrap: Heavy-duty plastic wrap is a good alternative. It seals out more air than bags do and does not waste space in the freezer. Wrap foods with at least two layers for the best protection.

- Containers: In addition to liquid foods such as soups and stews, fragile foods such as berries are best frozen in plastic containers to prevent bruising or squashing. Do not use a container larger than 2 quarts, or the food will take too long to freeze. The best containers are airtight, resist water and grease, and are made of materials that will not crack at low temperatures. Fairly rigid containers made of heavy plastic are ideal. Clean milk cartons can be cut down to fit specific foods, then tightly sealed in freezer bags. Leave ½ inch of headroom for dry foods and 1 inch for liquids, to allow for expansion during freezing. Square containers stack easily and use freezer space most efficiently. If using glass, look for dual-purpose glass jars specifically treated to withstand the cold temperatures of the freezer. A wide mouth allows easier removal of frozen food. Cardboard will eventually allow flavors to enter and moisture to escape. Check that lids in every case seal tightly.

- Vacuum-sealed: Vacuum-sealed plastic requires a machine or a special valve to suck out as much air as possible before sealing food in heavy-duty plastic.

f

TRAY FREEZING This method is ideal for berries, shrimp, ravioli, individual pastries, or other small foods that you want to keep distinct. Spread foods in a single layer, preferably not touching, on a baking sheet or tray. Freeze until the individual pieces are firm, transfer to a plastic bag (or a rigid plastic container if the food is particularly fragile), and return to the freezer.

About Freezing Foods

VEGETABLES Certain enzymes that break down vegetables, changing their color, flavor, texture, and nutrient content and shortening their shelf life, continue to work in the freezer. Blanching destroys these enzymes and helps to halt deterioration. Unblanched freezing is acceptable for onions, peppers, and herbs.

Frozen vegetables will have better texture and flavor if they are cooked without thawing. (An exception is corn on the cob, which should be partially thawed before cooking.) Steaming is the ideal method for cooking frozen vegetables.

FRUITS Select only fully ripe, but slightly firm, fruits for the freezer. Those with more delicate textures, such as papayas, mangoes, pears, watermelons, and avocados, do not generally freeze well. Although not usually blanched, most fruits, especially sliced ones, benefit from a light coating with granulated sugar or mixing with a light sugar syrup before they are frozen, to keep them firm, improve their flavor, and prevent oxidation. Berries and other small fruits are best kept whole, but larger ones should be peeled and cut as you would to the point of cooking. Sprinkle lemon juice over fruits that tend to brown when cut. See also DISCOLORING.

The higher the water content, the mushier the fruit will be upon thawing. Berries are a good example. Thaw fruits only partially and serve them while still slightly firm. Once thawed, frozen fruit tends to have more juice than an equal measure of fresh fruit. Cut back on the liquid called for in recipes. Adjust also for any sugar added before freezing.

MEATS, POULTRY, AND FISH Fresh meat and poultry freeze well, and fish freezes less well. Remember that fat can turn rancid in the freezer, so lean cuts freeze better and last longer than fatty ones. Also, unsaturated fats (in fish, chicken, and pork) turn rancid more quickly than saturated fats (in beef). Finally, ground meat and poultry have the shortest shelf life of all, because grinding increases the meat's exposure to oxygen, which promotes rancidity. Cured meats, such as bacon, ham, and sausage, fare less well, lasting no more than 1 to 2 months. The salt and other additives used in curing promote deterioration.

Reduce the amount of air in contact with the meat to prevent rancidity and freezer burn. Rancid meat will have an "off" odor and flavor, and freezer-burned meat will have a tough texture and "off" flavor.

Meats lose water as they thaw, making them drier when cooked. Those thawed too quickly will lose more liquid. Thaw meat in the refrigerator for the best quality and for safety. Immerse plastic-wrapped meat in cool water for faster thawing. Cook thawed meat or fish promptly.

BREADS Yeast breads and quick breads (banana bread, muffins, biscuits) freeze well, both before and after they are baked. Cooked batter breads like waffles also freeze well.

For unbaked breads, freeze wet batters in their containers and firm doughs on a baking sheet or in their pans until hard. Remove and wrap well. When ready to bake, return the bread, unthawed, to its pan and proceed with baking, allowing 15 to 20 minutes extra cooking time.

For baked breads, wrap and freeze as soon as they have cooled completely. To reheat, unwrap them, sprinkle lightly with water for a crispier crust, and heat, unthawed, at 325°F until warmed through.

CAKES For unfrosted baked layers, cool cakes completely. Return them to their pans to give support while freezing. Once firm, remove the layers from the pans and wrap them well with freezer-weight plastic wrap. Thaw in the refrigerator, keeping them well wrapped. For frosted layers, freeze the entire cake unwrapped, then wrap and return to the freezer.

COOKIES For unbaked dough, form even logs of dough, then wrap in freezer-weight plastic and freeze. Slice the logs as instructed in a recipe and bake while still frozen. For drop cookies, form them on a baking sheet, freeze them on the sheet, and then transfer drops to a plastic bag. To bake, arrange them on the baking sheet again and bake as directed. Allow about 5 minutes extra cooking time in both cases. For baked cookies, use a plastic container or wrap the cookies in short stacks. Thaw at room temperature or in the microwave.

COOKED DISHES Stews, casseroles, sauces, and filled breads and pastries usually freeze well. (The exceptions are wheat flour–thickened sauces and stews that contain pasta or potatoes.) For best texture, do not overcook dishes that you plan to freeze, and do not thaw before reheating. If you freeze them in an ovenproof container, thawing is simple. For stews and casseroles, cover and reheat in a 350°F oven. Filled pastries and pies should be reheated at 375° to 400°F.

For soups, use less liquid, stop cooking 10 minutes before the soup is finished, and omit any potatoes for freezing. Add cooked potatoes or raw pasta and additional liquid while reheating over very low heat until completely thawed. For soups containing milk, cream, or egg yolks, it is best to whisk after thawing to prevent curdling. Reheat cream soups in a double boiler.

FRIED FOODS Some hardier fried foods, especially yeast breads and battered or breaded food, can be frozen. Those with a denser, sturdier structure fare better.

- Freezing before cooking: Once the food is breaded or battered, arrange it on a parchment-lined baking sheet and freeze until firm. Transfer to plastic freezer bags and freeze for up to 3 months.
- Freezing already-fried food: Once the food is completely cooled, spread it in a single layer on a rack-lined baking sheet and place it in the freezer until firm. Transfer to heavy plastic freezer bags and freeze for up to 3 months.
- To reheat: Arrange the food, without the pieces touching, on a rack-lined baking sheet. Bake at 325°F just until crisp and hot. Serve immediately. Once the food is rewarmed, do not refreeze it.

FOODS THAT DO NOT FREEZE WELL

- Cream sauces, custards, and creamy fillings thickened with wheat flour.
- Cooked rice, unless incorporated into a casserole.
- Meringue, cooked egg whites, or icings made from egg whites.
- Cheese.
- Cooked potatoes (the exception being half-cooked french fries).
- Delicate fried foods such as fritters.
- Salad greens, celery, cabbage, cucumbers (unless already brined and pickled).
- Emulsified sauces, like mayonnaise.

See also THAWING; individual foods.

FRISÉE See CHICORY; GREENS, SALAD.

FRITTATA This Italian dish resembles a crustless quiche, a mixture of eggs, cheese, and other ingredients cooked slowly in a skillet until firm. Its preparation differs from a French omelet in that ingredients are mixed into the uncooked egg, rather than used as a filling.

Frosting, Icing & Glaze

For every great cake, there is a sweet, rich, silky coating that complements it perfectly. Although just about anything spread on the outside of a cake goes by the name frosting, it is actually only one of three ways to cover a cake: frosting, icing, or glaze.

Thick, fluffy, and sweet, frostings hold their shape, lending themselves to dramatic swirls and high peaks. Popular frostings include buttercream, seven-minute, white mountain, and simple whipped cream.

A fine line divides frostings and icings. In general, icings are slightly shinier and thinner than frostings. The two terms are frequently interchanged. Royal icing is the most common icing.

Thinner than either frostings or icings, glazes are poured, drizzled, or brushed on cakes, tarts, and pastries. As they cool and dry, they become smooth and shiny. Glazes can be as simple as confectioners' sugar mixed with lemon juice, or apricot jelly melted with liqueur. Ganache and poured fondant are also glazes.

Glazing a bread loaf.

Ingredients Bring all the ingredients to room temperature and always sift the sugar first to get rid of lumps. Sugar is the base of virtually all frostings, icings, and glazes. Eggs, butter, milk, and cream add necessary richness and body.

Equipment For frosting or icing a cake, have on hand the following equipment:

waxed paper, a straight or offset stainless-steel frosting spatula to spread frosting quickly and smoothly, a cake round or a decorating turntable to rotate the cake, toothpicks, a serrated knife, and a decorating comb or pastry bag (if desired).

HOW TO *Cut a Cake Round*
Professional bakers use cardboard cake rounds to carry, arrange, and frost cake layers without any cracking or breaking. They are also excellent for supporting the layers in the freezer. Cake rounds are available at baking supply stores, but you can make them easily yourself.

1. Trace the bottom of the cake pans on heavy, corrugated cardboard.
2. Cut out the rounds. Making them the same size as the pan is easiest for decorating. A round can be slightly larger if it will be used under the bottom layer for serving the cake.
3. If you plan to reuse them, cover the rounds with aluminum foil.
4. Transfer cooled cake layers onto the rounds to frost them.

Preparing the Cake Layers Gently curved tops on the cake layers are fine. If you need to even out sharply peaked layers, hold a large serrated knife flat against the top, with the blade parallel to the work surface, and gently saw off the dome. Frosting will spread more easily and cleanly if you place any trimmed layers cut side down.

Cake layers can be cut in half for thinner, more elegant layers. Mark the halfway point on the side of a layer with toothpicks, sticking them in partway. Hold a long, serrated knife parallel to the work surface and cut from the outside edge of the cake toward its center, using the toothpicks to guide the knife. Turn the cake as you cut. Use a cardboard round or a plate to lift away the top layer. If the crust seems tough or if it is darker than both the interior of the cake and the frosting, you can trim it away with a serrated knife. The cut surfaces will shed crumbs readily, however, interfering as you frost. To help seal in crumbs, brush the cake surface with melted jelly or simple syrup and let set.

Cutting
cake layers.

HOW TO *Frost a Layer Cake*

A cake must be completely cool before you begin frosting. If it is still even slightly warm, the frosting or glaze will melt and not adhere. A decorating turntable will make the job easier.

1. To keep the cake plate clean while frosting, arrange 4-inch-wide strips of waxed paper in a square to cover the edges of the plate. Center the cake on the plate, making sure the strips are under the edge of the cake. After you finish, pull the strips away.

2. Lightly brush away all the loose crumbs from the surface of the cake. If your cake layers are just slightly domed on top, to ensure a well-balanced cake, place the first layer with its top side down.

3. Spread $\frac{1}{2}$ to $\frac{3}{4}$ cup frosting on the top of the first layer. If you are using a filling different from the outer frosting, leave a $\frac{1}{2}$-inch unfrosted border around the edge, to allow for its spreading from the weight of the next layer.

4. Place the second layer over the first layer, checking that the edges of the layers are even with each other. Tap the top of the cake gently to set the second layer. (If the second layer is not the top layer, place it domed side down. If it is the top layer, it may be set either way.)

Quick Bite

The top of a cake can be rounded or flat, depending on how the layers are placed. Facing the flat sides of two layers together will reveal a straight line of filling when the cake is sliced.

5. Apply the crumb layer, a very thin layer of frosting on the top and sides of the cake. This will trap crumbs and keep them from appearing on the finished surface of the cake. If you find the frosting too stiff to spread easily, thin it with a tiny amount of milk or water.

6. Frost the sides, sweeping up and creating a rim above the edge of the cake. It should be $\frac{1}{4}$ to $\frac{1}{2}$ inch thick. Do not apply too much frosting. Keep in mind the richness of the frosting and the relative amount of cake.

continued

Frosting, Icing & Glaze, continued

7. Drop the rest of the frosting at 3 or 4 points on the top layer of the cake. Using a frosting spatula, spread the frosting, sweeping out from the center and meeting the rim of frosting at a clean right angle. Use gentle pressure and smooth back-and-forth strokes.
8. Smooth the top and any excess frosting that may have fallen down the sides.

9. If desired, use a decorating comb or pastry bag to decorate the cake. For information on using a pastry bag to decorate a cake, see PIPING.

How Much Frosting Will I Need?

For thinner frostings, you will need the lesser amounts. When filling and covering a cake with light, fluffy frosting, plan on using the larger amounts.

Frosting Amounts	
8- or 9-inch cake, 2 layers	2½ to 3 cups
8- or 9-inch cake, 3 layers	3 to 3½ cups
10-inch tube cake	3 to 3½ cups
13 x 9-inch sheet cake	3½ to 4 cups
12 large cupcakes	1½ to 2 cups

Quick Tip

You can fill layers with the same frosting, or use another mixture with contrasting flavor, texture, and color. Lemon curd, custard, chopped nuts, fresh fruit, and fruit purées make excellent fillings.

HOW TO *Glaze a Cake*

You must work quickly with warm glaze, so have everything at hand.

1. Set the cake or filled and stacked cake layers on a rack placed over a baking sheet.
2. Pour the glaze over the cake all at once, aiming at its center and letting the glaze flow down the sides. For a tube cake, pour in a steady stream as you circle the top of the cake.

3. Immediately spread the glaze over still-exposed areas with a spatula. Work quickly. Ease the glaze gently, but do not swirl or press with the spatula. Let the glaze cool until set.

4. Resist the temptation to fix spots or smears. If needed, however, you can moisten the spatula and carefully smooth out imperfections.

See also BAKING TOOLS; GANACHE; PIPING.

FRUIT, DRIED See DRIED FRUIT.

FRUIT, FRESH See RIPENING; individual fruits.

FRYING French fries, fish and chips, crispy chicken, clam strips, spring rolls, tempura, doughnuts, and beignets—frying undeniably produces some of the world's most delectable foods. Grilling and sautéing may be the focus of more modern recipes, but frying, especially deep-frying, gives food a light, crisp texture and deep golden color difficult to achieve with any other method.

Ordinary frying, also called panfrying, means to cook food in a pan with a moderate amount of fat or oil over medium heat. Panfrying is similar to sautéing, but generally requires more fat, more time, and less heat. It is a good method for larger pieces of meat, such as thick pork chops, bone-in chicken parts, and hefty hamburgers. Firmer vegetables, such as pearl onions or potatoes, may also be panfried. (Very soft, juicy foods, such as ripe tomatoes, are not suitable for frying since they tend to liquefy at high temperatures.) In deep-frying, the food is immersed in a greater amount of fat and cooks for a shorter amount of time than in panfrying.

Stir-frying, a frying technique developed in Asia, uses a special bowl-shaped pan, small cuts of food, and very little oil. See STIR-FRYING.

Coatings for Frying Although some sturdy foods, such as potatoes or doughnuts, do not need coatings to protect them from the heat, most benefit from a coating that provides a crisp crust and a buffer from the hot fat. Food is sometimes dredged with flour first to help the coating adhere. Coat delicate or particularly moist foods, including fish, shellfish, chicken, zucchini, onions, and cheese.

BATTER Since batters are thin, they are best suited to foods that will keep their shape and are easily dunked, such as crisp vegetables, dry fruits, and firm fish. Different ingredients in batters have different effects. Eggs and flour provide protection from the hot oil. Milk encourages deep browning, sugar in a batter causes quick browning, and water or club soda makes light batters. Beer gives batter sweet flavor and airiness. Yeast adds additional lightness, and butter adds richness.

CRUMB COATING Crumb coating helps hold together flaky mixtures and provides a crisp crust for such foods as soft cheeses, delicate fish, and crab cakes. Coatings include cracker crumbs, bread crumbs, cornmeal, rice flakes, and ground nuts.

WRAPPER In Asia, thin wrappers enclose whole shrimp, small pieces of meat, or mixed fillings. Spring rolls and fried wontons are examples of these fried tidbits.

Fat and Oil for Frying Use refined fats and oils with high smoke points. Peanut, soybean, corn, safflower, and grapeseed oil, as well as vegetable shortening, will easily withstand the high heat of frying. Clarified butter and coconut and palm oils give crisp texture and incomparable flavor but are less used now because of their high amounts of saturated fat. Also less used today by home cooks are animal-rendered fats such as lard, beef fat, or duck fat, but they do contribute wonderful flavor. Extra-virgin olive oil and toasted sesame oil will quickly smoke and burn, while canola oil can give off an unpleasant odor. See also FAT & OIL.

f

Quick Tip

The secret to Japanese tempura is using thinly sliced foods, cold batter, and a light hand in stirring the batter.

Deep-frying Accessories and Equipment Glossary

BIRD'S NEST BASKETS A nesting pair of small, round, scoop-shaped baskets with long handles. Smaller potato nest baskets are used to form potato slices into basket shapes, while larger tools are made for shaping tortillas and wonton skins.

DEEP FRYER Also known as a deep-fat fryer. Stove-top deep fryers are fitted with a fry basket that fits comfortably in a heavy bottom pan. Both basket and pan have long handles. When frying in stove-top fryers, use an accurate thermometer. Electric deep fryers are cased in metal and stay-cool plastic and are fitted with a control panel and built-in thermometer, making them easier to use. Although fryers with capacities of 2½ quarts are available, a 4- to 5-quart fryer is more practical, and many home cooks prefer an even larger one.

FRYING PAN A large pan with straight or slightly flared sides, preferably made of a heavy material such as cast iron, to retain heat and prevent temperature fluctuations. For deep-frying, it must be deep enough for the sides to extend several inches above the surface of the oil, while for panfrying, 4 inches is the minimum height.

MESH SKIMMER Used to skim off bits of batter and food in oil to prevent burning and a bitter flavor from forming.

PAPER TOWEL Used to absorb grease when draining fried foods.

RACK Draining fried foods on a sturdy wire rack set on a baking sheet produces crispier, less soggy results than paper towels. Also used to keep fried foods warm in the oven.

SLOTTED SPOON A spoon with perforations that allow fat to drain away when lifting out food. A second slotted spoon may be used to transfer food from batter to oil.

SPATTER GUARD Also called a splatter screen. A large, round, flat mesh lid with a long handle that is placed over frying food to prevent oil spatters.

SPIDER Small, wire-netted, basketlike skimmer used for removing foods from hot oil and draining them.

THERMOMETER Large, high-temperature thermometer that clips to the side of the pan. Be sure the tip does not touch the bottom of the pan.

TONGS For adding, turning, and removing food from hot oil quickly and easily.

WIRE BASKET LINER Wire basket with a long handle that nests inside a pan of oil, placed there before the food is added. Lift the basket gently to remove a whole batch of food at once.

WOK The wok is a good choice for deep-frying, as it will hold a large amount of oil and is responsive to rapid changes in temperature.

About Deep-frying Although deep-frying has received a bad health rap in recent years, proper frying actually results in minimal oil absorption. Food is immersed in oil at 350° to 375°F, which causes the water in a food to evaporate instantly, converting it to steam that will push out any oil trying to seep into the food. If the temperature of the oil is too low, there will be no outward push of steam and the food will absorb the oil instead, becoming greasy. The key to deep-frying is maintaining the oil at the proper temperature.

Taking Precautions Hot fat or oil is dangerous. If allowed to get too hot (400°F or beyond, where most will reach their smoke points), it can burst into flame. A few commonsense precautions will help avoid any accidents:

- Use thick oven mitts that reach well beyond your wrists when frying to avoid spatter burns.

- Make sure the pot's handle is turned away from the front of the stove.
- Use a deep-frying thermometer when frying, and do not let the fat heat to 400°F or beyond.
- Gently lower the food into the oil with tongs or a slotted spoon. Do not drop it into the oil and allow it to splash.
- Clean any oil drips on the outside of the pan, which could catch fire.
- Hold the fried food above the oil for a few seconds to let any excess drip back into the pot, rather than onto the burner.

Frying Savvy

- In panfrying, the oil should reach no more than halfway up the sides of the food; the depth will depend on what type of food is being cooked. For deep-frying, use oil at a depth of at least 2 inches, and use enough oil to cover the food by at least ¾ inch. Use a large, deep pan, however, and never fill it more than one-third full of oil.
- For deep-frying, use a deep-frying thermometer. Adjust the heat to maintain the oil at the temperature specified in the recipe (350° to 375°F), keeping its temperature as constant as possible. Adding food in small batches will prevent large drops in temperature as well as ensuring even immersion in the oil.
- Having foods at room temperature prevents a drop in oil temperature. (Exceptions are recipes that call for chilling to keep a delicate dough or soft food firm.)
- Remove excess moisture from the surface of food before cooking, and keep liquids away from the hot oil. Liquids can cause spatters and explosions when they come in contact with hot oil.
- Use a slotted spoon to lower food into hot fat. If you drop it in, the fat may spatter and burn you.
- Fry a small amount of food at a time. Overcrowding the pan will quickly

lower the temperature, causing the food to absorb the oil, to stick together, and to cook unevenly.

■ Fry more mildly flavored foods first, then cook successively stronger-flavored foods, as the oil will carry the flavors of the foods. Fry vegetables before meat, and meat before fish.

■ Use a fine-mesh skimmer to remove small bits of batter or food from the fat during frying and between batches. This will keep the oil from obtaining a bitter, scorched flavor.

■ When deep-frying in batches, let the oil regain its correct frying temperature between each batch of food.

■ Drain fried foods on a rack set on a baking sheet. If no rack is available, drain food on several layers of paper towels or a clean brown paper bag.

■ Salt just before serving. If salted too far in advance, the food will become tough and soggy.

■ Always try to serve food as soon after frying as possible. If it must be held, arrange the food on a rack on a baking sheet and place it in a 225°F oven for up to 30 minutes.

Quick Tip

When the surface of the oil shows expanding circles and small bubbles, it is very hot, or almost smoking.

Serving Fried Foods To help soak up any excess oil, fold a cloth or heavy paper napkin on the serving plate before arranging the food on it.

Serve savory fried food with lemon wedges, fruity vinegars, spicy dips, or other tart, fresh sauces that will temper the richness.

Reusing Oil If oil is used to deep-fry a small amount of food and the food was not

Quick Tip

Foods containing relatively high amounts of sugar, such as beets, sweet potatoes, doughnuts, and fritters, require a slightly lower deep-frying temperature (350°F). Otherwise the sugar in them will burn before the food cooks thoroughly.

strongly flavored and none of it burned, you can reuse the oil after straining it carefully. Let it cool completely, strain it through a coffee filter, and store it in an airtight container in the refrigerator for up to 3 months. Add at least one-fourth of its volume in fresh oil the next time that you use it. Do not fry with the same oil more than three times. Every time you heat oil, it deteriorates a bit and its smoke point is lowered. Eventually, the oil will no longer be able to hold temperatures sufficient to fry food properly. If needed, you can fry thick slices of fresh potatoes in the oil to clarify it before cooking. Oil should not have any "off" or rancid smell.

See also BATTER; BREADING; DREDGING; FAT & OIL; SMOKE POINT; STIR-FRYING.

FRYING PAN Also known as a skillet; see COOKWARE.

FUDGE An old-fashioned, rich, smooth confection made from chocolate or cocoa, butter, sugar, corn syrup, and other ingredients such as milk, half-and-half, and cream. This traditional American candy, a favorite of New England cooks, usually contains walnuts and vanilla extract, and sometimes citrus zest, dried fruits, or marshmallow is added.

6

everything from galangal to guava

GALANGAL (GAH-leng-gall) An aromatic seasoning with a hot, peppery, somewhat resinous flavor, galangal looks like a root but is actually an underground stem called a rhizome. Used throughout Southeast Asia, it resembles its relative ginger and is sometimes called Thai ginger. It has pink shoots, cream-colored fibrous flesh, and pale yellow skin with thin, dark stripes circling the rhizome. In Thailand, galangal is crushed with lemongrass, garlic, and chiles in the mortar as the base for curries. Thin slices of the rhizome infuse soups throughout Southeast Asia, while in Indonesia it replaces common ginger. If galangal is unavailable, some cooks recommend substituting ginger and black pepper with a bit of bay leaf to mimic the flavor.

Selecting Dried slices and sometimes the fresh or frozen rhizome can be found in Southeast Asian markets. When buying it fresh, look for firm specimens with smooth skins. Also sold are dried slices packaged in plastic and a less flavorful powder available in bottles.

Storing Keep fresh galangal in the refrigerator, wrapped in a paper towel inside a plastic bag, for up to 2 weeks. Store dried and powdered galangal away from air, light, and heat for up to 6 months.

Preparing Soak dried slices in warm water for 10 minutes before using.

If fresh galangal is used in chunks or slices and is not eaten, no peeling is necessary. If it will be consumed, peel and cut as directed before adding to a recipe.

GAME Our definition of game has changed considerably in recent times. Not so long ago, the term applied specifically to the meat of animals hunted in the wild, from birds such as wild turkey and duck, pheasant, and quail to animals such as deer, antelope, moose, and elk. All such meats are characterized by their robust flavor and relatively dark flesh, the result of their varying diets and active lives. Today, while such game still has its devotees and is available not only to hunters but also through specialty mail-order catalogs and websites, many more people are enjoying farm-raised game that is processed to uniform standards and has a milder flavor than its wild counterparts. Among the most popular types, available in well-stocked food stores and butcher shops, are buffalo, the meat of the American bison, leaner and slightly stronger tasting than beef; quail, small, flavorful birds with dark meat; squab, a type of pigeon, with dark, meaty breasts; and venison, the lean meat of deer, with dark red color, fine-grained dense texture, and a robust flavor.

GANACHE A smooth mixture of melted chocolate and cream. While still barely warm, it is poured over cakes and tortes to form a smooth glaze. Once cooled, it is whipped to become the filling for chocolate truffles and various pastries.

g

GARBANZO BEAN Also known as chickpea; see BEAN, DRIED.

GARLIC An edible bulb, garlic is a pungent member of the *Allium* genus, along with the onion. Each bulb, or head, of garlic is a cluster of 12 to 16 cloves, individually covered and collectively wrapped with papery, white to purplish red skin. Garlic is fundamental to cuisines around the world. Few kitchen staples arouse as much interest as humble garlic—revered for its therapeutic 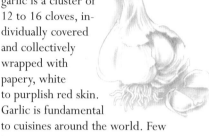 properties, endowed with both divine and devilish power, and reviled for its persistent odor. Shortsighted rulers in ancient Rome stayed clear of it, while suggesting that the peasant class should consume it for strength and good health.

Selecting Choose plump heads with smooth, firm cloves. Pass up those with soft, withered spots or green sprouts. The largest crop of garlic is harvested in midsummer, but garlic is widely available year-round. The strongly flavored, white-skinned American variety peaks in the middle of summer; milder, purplish red Mexican or Italian garlic comes to market in spring. Commercially prepared garlic paste, chopped garlic in oil, and peeled whole cloves are available as well, as are minced, flaked, and powdered forms.

Storing Keep whole garlic heads in an open container in a cool, dark, well-ventilated place for up to 2 months. To help prevent the heads from drying out, leave the papery skin on and break off individual cloves only as needed. Once separated, unpeeled cloves will keep for up to 1 week. Chop only as much garlic as you will use right away. Although chopped garlic can be refrigerated, sealed in an airtight container to prevent the transfer of odor and flavor to other foods, the volatile oils in garlic that give it its flavor begin to break down as soon as it is crushed or chopped. It will discolor, and the flavor will take on unpleasant tones. Commercial garlic paste and commercial chopped garlic will keep in the refrigerator for up to 3 months.

Garlic Glossary

ELEPHANT GARLIC With heads as large as a small orange, elephant garlic is not a variety of garlic, but instead a close relative to the leek. The flavor of its enormous cloves is much milder than that of ordinary garlic.

GARLIC SHOOTS Resembling chives, garlic shoots are the tender stems and flowers of an immature garlic plant, with a hint of garlic's flavor. Sprinkle raw over green salads, fold inside omelets, or add to light pasta dishes.

GREEN GARLIC Harvested just before the garlic plant begins to form cloves and available in the spring at farmers' markets, green garlic resembles large green onions with a tinge of pink at the bulb. Grill to accompany meat or fish.

Quick Tip

Sprinkle garlic cloves with a little salt to prevent them from sticking to the knife blade as you chop. Just be sure to allow for the salt when seasoning the dish.

Preparing Some recipes call for whole garlic cloves, while others specify sliced, chopped, minced, or crushed garlic. Garlic added to long-cooking recipes can be left in larger pieces so its flavors can be coaxed out over time, imbuing the dish with a mellow garlic flavor. Minced garlic has a hotter, more volatile flavor that will disperse quickly but is good for uncooked or quickly cooked foods where you want a pronounced garlic flavor. Crushing garlic will release much more of its aromatic oils than simply slicing or chopping it. Garlic presses make short work of mincing garlic, although some cooks believe their pressure creates bitterness. Some presses do not require you to peel the garlic cloves first.

Many cooks believe that even the beginnings of a green shoot spoil the sweet flavor of garlic. If you spy a green shoot starting to emerge, halve the clove and cut out the shoot.

Garlic is often sautéed as a first step in a recipe. Sauté garlic just until it is golden. If it scorches, it becomes unpleasantly bitter. To prevent burning, cook garlic over low heat, or add it to a pan after onions have been cooked slightly, in order to cook it for a shorter period of time. You can also cook crushed cloves briefly in hot oil to flavor it and then discard them before adding other ingredients.

HOW TO *Peel Garlic*

When you're faced with a heap of garlic cloves to peel, any one of the following will help loosen the skins:

- Crush cloves gently with the flat side of a knife blade.

- Heat separated cloves in a dry skillet over medium-low heat for 30 seconds to 1 minute.
- Microwave a whole head of garlic for 1 minute and individual cloves for 5 seconds. Let cool slightly before peeling.

- Blanch in boiling water for 1 minute and drain.
- Roll the cloves 1 or 2 at a time in a flat sheet of rubber such as a jar-lid gripper. Kitchenware stores sell special rubber tubes specifically designed for this task.

HOW TO *Roast Garlic*

Roasted garlic purée is excellent spread on warm bread, whisked into sauces and soups, or mashed into potatoes.

1. Peel away the loose, papery outer layers of a whole head of garlic, leaving just enough skin to hold the cloves together. Cut off just enough of the top to expose the garlic cloves.
2. Center the head of garlic on a square of aluminum foil. Drizzle with olive oil or water. If desired, sprinkle with dried thyme or oregano. Wrap the foil tightly around the garlic.
3. Roast at 425°F degrees until soft, for about 30 minutes. Let the cloves cool slightly before unwrapping them.
4. Squeeze the head of garlic from base to top, like a tube of toothpaste, to extract the purée. Or, serve it whole at the table and let each diner squeeze his or her own cloves.

GARNISHING A slim slice of melon or a delicately fanned strawberry can add appealing color and freshness to an otherwise plain plate of food. Asian chefs train for years to learn the art of carving intricate flowers and animals to adorn dishes and platters. More casual American cuisine may call for only a sprig of flowering thyme on the rim of a dinner plate or a few vegetables propped against a roast. More and more chefs believe that garnishes should be edible and complement the flavor and appearance of the serving platter or composed plate. Remember, simpler is better. You don't want to detract from what should be the main focus of the dish—the food itself.

GELATIN Refrigerate homemade stock, and you will see the effect of natural gelatin: the stock will thicken and turn into a loose jelly. Gelatin is an odorless, colorless, tasteless thickener derived from collagen, a protein extracted from the bones, cartilage, and tendons of animals. Without gela-

tin, many fillings, mousses, puddings, and molded desserts, as well as marshmallows and jellied candies, would lose their shape. Although many cooks may not use it from one season to the next, gelatin is a common kitchen staple.

Quick Tip

Raw pineapple, papaya, fig, guava, kiwifruit, and fresh ginger contain enzymes that inhibit the setting of gelatin. Cook these foods first or use canned versions when adding them to any gelatin mixture.

Selecting Look for powdered unflavored gelatin packaged in small paper envelopes in the baking section of grocery stores. Clear, paper-thin sheets of unflavored leaf gelatin are available at gourmet and specialty baking stores. Leaf gelatin is not as convenient to use, but many bakers prefer it to the powdered form because it results in a smoother and clearer consistency. Although powdered and leaf gelatin can be used interchangeably in any recipe, their thickening powers may vary slightly.

Fruit-flavored gelatins are sold in small boxes in supermarkets. Do not confuse flavored gelatins with desserts such as Jell-O.

Storing Unflavored gelatin will keep for up to 3 years if sealed in an airtight container and stored in a cool, dry place. Flavored gelatin will keep for 1 year.

Quick Tip

Do not put a hot gelatin mixture into the freezer, as it can turn chewy and the surface will crack.

Preparing One envelope or 4 sheets of unflavored gelatin will jell 2 cups of liquid. Each ¼-ounce envelope of unflavored gelatin contains 1 scant tablespoon powder.

Softening gelatin first in a small amount of cold liquid will help it dissolve evenly when combined with the rest of the ingredients in a recipe. Once softened, gelatin then must be warmed with liquid to activate the protein. Finally, it must be allowed to cool and jell. Once this process is begun and the gelatin is softened, it should be used immediately. Do not boil gelatin, or it will lose its setting power. Although you should not stir gelatin while it soaks to avoid forming strings, be sure to stir it thoroughly into other mixtures.

Gelatin can set almost any liquid, from stock or tomato juice to Champagne or cream. Flavored gelatins are easy to use and generally require nothing more complicated than being stirred into very hot water; follow the package directions.

Keep homemade jelled foods cold to retain their shape. Prepared foods containing gelatin, such as marshmallow or jellied candies, do not require refrigeration.

HOW TO *Use Unflavored Powdered Gelatin*

1. Sprinkle 1 envelope (1 tablespoon) powdered gelatin over ¼ cup cold liquid and let it soften for about 5 minutes. Do not stir. It will swell slightly and develop a spongy consistency.
2. Stir the softened gelatin mixture directly into about 1¾ cups hot liquid.
3. Before stirring it into cold liquid in a recipe, heat the softened gelatin in a double boiler over hot water, swirling the pan until the gelatin is completely dissolved.
4. Proceed as directed in the recipe.

Quick Bite

Agar-agar, a tasteless, dried seaweed extract used in Asian kitchens, is prized by vegetarians as a replacement for animal-based gelatin. See also SEAWEED.

HOW TO *Use Unflavored Leaf Gelatin*

1. Soak the sheets in cold water for 15 to 20 minutes. They will resemble wet plastic wrap.
2. Transfer the sheets to a small saucepan, leaving behind the soaking liquid. Heat gently over very low heat until liquefied completely. Shake or swirl the pan, but do not stir.
3. Stir the melted gelatin into about 2 cups of hot liquid and proceed as directed in the recipe.

GIBLETS The small paper package tucked inside the cavity of most purchased whole birds, such as chickens and turkeys, contains the giblets, a term usually referring to the heart, gizzard, and liver of the poultry. Except for the liver, these parts can be used to make gravy, stock, or soup. The liver can be cooked separately and is often considered a delicacy. Giblets also make a nice addition to bread stuffings.

What Do I Do with Giblets?

1. Rinse the giblets well.
2. Simmer them (minus the liver, which would cloud the stock and may be cooked separately) in water with herbs and chopped aromatics such as garlic or onion for about 30 minutes, or until cooked through completely, to make a little stock for a sauce.
3. Finely dice the cooked giblets and stir into gravy or stuffing. Gravy made this way is called giblet gravy.

GIN See SPIRITS.

GINGER The brown, gnarled, knobby appearance of fresh ginger belies its refreshing and slightly sweet flavor. It also packs a fair amount of spiciness. Although mistakenly called a root, ginger is actually a rhizome, or underground stem. A kitchen staple throughout Asia, ginger is an essential aromatic in countless dishes. It adds a fresh note to rich dishes.

The cream- and pink-colored shoots of the rhizome, known as young ginger, are available during the summer in Asian grocery stores. They are more delicate in texture and flavor than mature ginger, the more fibrous,  commonly found ginger with the papery brown skin. Crystallized ginger, candied in sugar syrup and then coated with granulated sugar, adds sweet-spicy flavor to dessert fruit fillings, cake batters, ice cream, or fruit salad. Familiar to anyone who loves sushi, pickled ginger is used in Japan as a palate cleanser. Ground dried ginger adds a delightful fragrance and flavor to many breads, cookies, and cakes.

Selecting Look for ginger that is hard and heavy, with an unbroken peel that is thin, light colored, smooth, and shiny. As ginger ages, it becomes darker and more flavorful but also drier and more fibrous. Avoid wrinkled ginger or pieces that give to moderate finger pressure. Young ginger should be a creamy pink color and have smooth, paper-thin skin. Fresh ginger is sold all year long in supermarkets and green grocers. Choose or break off the size piece that best accommodates your needs. Look for crystallized ginger sold in bulk at health-food stores or in small jars in specialty-food stores or grocery stores. Pickled ginger is available in Asian markets.

Storing Store ginger in a cool, dry place for up to 3 days or in the refrigerator for up to 3 weeks. To keep ginger from developing mold in the refrigerator, wrap it first in a paper towel or small paper bag and then in a plastic bag. Ginger freezes relatively well. Cut off slices as needed from the still-frozen rhizome. Store powdered ginger, often called ground ginger, in an airtight container in a cool, dark cupboard and replace every 6 months.

Preparing When a recipe calls for gingerroot, it simply means fresh ginger. If the ginger will be eaten (rather than just used to flavor a dish), peel it with a vegetable peeler or paring knife before using. Like garlic, ginger will have a more intense flavor when crushed or grated rather than simply sliced or chopped. Crush ginger slices with the flat side of a knife blade. To "mince" ginger quickly, crush a small, peeled chunk in a garlic press.

Quick Tip

When a recipe calls for a knob of ginger, it means a chunk of ginger usually about an inch long. Remove before serving the dish.

A ginger grater is a small, flat ceramic tool with tiny, very sharp teeth covering its surface. A knob of peeled ginger rubbed across the notches will fall away in tiny bits, leaving the fibers behind.

Ginger grater.

GLAZE See FROSTING, ICING & GLAZE.

GLUTEN See BREAD; FLOUR.

GOOSEBERRY See BERRY.

GORGONZOLA See CHEESE.

GOUDA See CHEESE.

GRAIN See page 224.

GRANITA See SORBET.

GRAPE Grapes come in many sizes and colors, from tiny ones that look like peppercorns to giants that could be mistaken for plums, from sparkling silver-green to deep purple-black. They reflect the specific local conditions of soil and climate in which they were cultivated, developing what the French call *goût terroir,* or "the taste of the land."

Nearly 90 percent of the grapes grown for wine and table belong to the European species *Vitis vinifera.* This includes seedless table grapes like red Emperor, crunchy Flame, and the oblong green Thompson, as well as famous wine varietals such as Chardonnay, Merlot, and Cabernet Sauvignon.

Native to North America, *Vitus labrusca,* or slip-skin grapes, have easily removable peels that make them ideal for jams, jellies, and juice. The Concord grape, starring in such childhood favorites as peanut butter and jelly sandwiches, is the best-known example of this type of grape species.

Whatever their species, grapes find themselves more popularly divided into two broad color categories, red or green, although some countries see things differently and classify grapes as black or white. Grape eaters, and thus grape growers, also further define their fruits by whether they have seeds or are seedless.

Grape leaves, primarily used as wrappers (for appetizers such as rice-stuffed dolmas, or for encasing cheeses or meats for grilling), are also edible. Use young, fresh leaves (blanch to soften), or purchase jars of brined leaves (rinse before using).

Selecting Choose grape bunches with plump, firm fruits, passing over those with fruits that are soft, withered, bruised, or easily brushed from their stems. Green grapes with a hint of yellow or amber are the ripest and sweetest. Red grapes should have no tinge of green in their skin. Darker grapes tend to have tougher skins than the lighter varieties. Bloom is a naturally occurring white powdery substance that covers freshly harvested grapes. Each of the many varieties of grapes peaks during different months, but most come to market between May and September, with a few arriving later into February. Grapes do not become sweeter once harvested.

Storing Remove and discard any bruised or spoiled grapes. Keep grape bunches in a perforated plastic bag in the refrigerator for up to 1 week. To freeze whole grapes, spread small clusters or individual fruits on a baking sheet. Freeze completely and then transfer them to an airtight container and keep in the freezer for up to 6 months.

Preparing Since they are highly susceptible to pests and molds, most grapes have been treated with chemicals, so be sure to rinse well. Let drain on paper towels to dry. Since they are most flavorful at room temperature, remove grapes from the refrigerator at least 30 minutes before serving.

HOW TO *Seed Grapes*

1. Grapes are more easily seeded if halved first, but if you need to keep them whole, use a clean bobby pin to remove the seeds. Holding the two prongs of the pin, insert the crook into the stem end of the grape, hook the seeds, and pull them out.

Quick Tip

Freeze a cluster of grapes and eat them on a hot day to cool off.

Grain

Quite literally, a world of grain awaits the adventurous cook eager to journey beyond such tried-and-true staples as rice and oats. In all their various forms, these edible seeds of cultivated grasses or other plants are outstanding sources of carbohydrate, fiber, protein, and other nutrients.

Grains may be used in virtually every course of the meal and at any time of day: as breakfast cereals or savory side dishes; to add both flavor and texture to salads, soups, stews, casseroles, and stuffings; and as the foundation of or embellishment to a wide array of desserts and baked goods. In addition, of course, many grains are finely ground to make flours.

Bulgur and wheat berries.

Selecting Most well-stocked food stores carry a wide assortment of grains. Look in their specialty or ethnic-foods sections for less common types. For the widest selection, go to a large health-food store, where you will most likely find such un-usual varieties as quinoa and triticale.

Storing Any whole grains, or cracked grains made from whole grains, will still contain their germ, which is rich in oil. For this reason, they are prone to turning rancid relatively quickly. Buy in small quan-tities, no more than you will use in a few months. Store in an airtight container in the refrigerator for up to 6 months. By contrast, polished grains—that is, those that have been hulled and de-germed—generally keep well in an airtight container at cool room temperature for up to 1 year.

A Cornucopia of Grains

BARLEY This ancient grain was probably the first one cultivated. Despite a long his-tory of sustaining humankind, its primary uses now are in soups and to make Scotch whisky. It should not be forgotten by the home cook, since its nutty flavor and chewy texture lend themselves to delicious prepara-tions. Barley can be cooked as a risotto-style dish, added to stews, and used cooked cold in salads. It can be bought whole and hulled, flaked, and pearled. Most recipes call for it in the common pearled form, meaning hulled and polished to a pearl-like shape and sheen.

BUCKWHEAT A grain probably native to Mongolia or Siberia. Kasha, the tan-colored, pyramid-shaped seeds of buckwheat, has a pleasantly sour, nutlike taste and robust texture. A popular choice for side dishes in eastern Europe and Russia, the grains are usually pan-toasted before being cooked to tenderness in boiling water.

BULGUR Made from wheat that has been steamed, dried, and cracked, nutty-tasting bulgur is most commonly found in Middle Eastern and Balkan cooking, used much as other cuisines use rice. Tabbouleh, a salad with parsley, onion, tomatoes, and lemon juice, is a well-known dish based on bulgur. Cracked wheat is sometimes mistaken for bulgur. See Wheat, page 227.

CORNMEAL Finely or coarsely ground, dried, whole or polished kernels of yellow or white corn. See also CORNMEAL.

COUSCOUS Not a grain but a pasta. See also COUSCOUS.

GRITS Also known as hominy grits, this is a ground meal of yellow or white hominy. Cooked to a thick porridge, grits, a favorite throughout the American South, is served as a side dish at breakfast, lunch, or dinner. The grain is available in three forms: regular coarsely ground, slow-cooking grits; finer quick-cooking grits; and precooked and dried instant grits, which reconstitute with the addition of boiling water.

HOMINY Dried corn kernels that have been soaked in an alkali such as lime or lye, washed to remove the outer skin, and boiled for several hours. In the end, the kernels resemble soft, white, rather puffed-up kernels of corn. Hominy is sold as either whole kernels or cracked into coarse bits that are cooked in boiling liquid. Whole-kerneled hominy is called samp. Served with butter or cream as a side dish.

KAMUT (ka-MOOT) Kamut is an ancient Egyptian grain. It is an unhybridized relative of durum wheat, similarly high in protein, with a sweet almost buttery taste.

KASHA See Buckwheat, above.

MILLET A common ingredient in birdseed mixtures, these pale yellow, spherical, bland-tasting grains are also cooked in liquid, swelling considerably to make a side dish or breakfast cereal popular in southern Europe, northern Africa, and Asia.

OATS Rich, robust, and flavorful, this favorite grain of northern Europe, Scotland, and Ireland is enjoyed in many forms: whole hulled oats; rolled or old-fashioned oats; quick-cooking rolled oats; and quick-cooking instant oats. Whatever their form, oats are most commonly eaten as a breakfast cereal or used in baking.

POLENTA The Italian name for cornmeal and the Italian dish made from it. See also POLENTA.

QUINOA (KEEN-wah) An ancient staple of the Incas of Peru, these highly nutritious grains look like spherical sesame seeds. When steamed, quinoa has a mild taste and light texture that lends itself well to pilafs, casseroles, salads, or breakfast dishes. Quinoa must be rinsed before cooking because the grain has a natural residue that is very bitter tasting.

RICE Many different types of this most widespread of cereal grains are sold for use in a broad variety of different preparations. See also RICE.

RYE Soft-textured, slightly sour grain native to eastern Europe. Rye is sold either as whole berries, the round seeds seen in rye bread, which can be cooked in soups, stews, casseroles, or stuffings; as cracked unpolished kernels, excellent in pilafs or as a morning cereal; as rolled flakes, to be cooked for breakfast; or as a fine flour for baking. See also FLOUR.

TRITICALE (trih-tih-KAY-lee) A hybrid of wheat and rye first cultivated in Scotland in the late 19th century, triticale has a full, nutty flavor. Like both its parent grains, the berries may be cooked whole and used in a wide ranges of dishes. Low in gluten, triticale flour may be used as a supplement to wheat flour in baking.

continued

225

Grain-Cooking Timetable

This chart provides basic cooking directions for 1 cup grain. Add ½ to 1 teaspoon salt if desired.

TYPE	LIQUID	METHOD	YIELD
Barley, pearl	4 cups	Add to boiling liquid. Simmer 45 minutes. Drain.	3 to 3½ cups
Bulgur	2 cups	Add to cold water. Bring to a boil, then simmer, covered, 10 to 12 minutes.	2½ to 3 cups
Cornmeal (polenta)	3 to 4 cups, depending on desired consistency (thick or thin)	Add to cold liquid, amount to vary with desired consistency. Bring to a boil, then simmer, stirring frequently, 20 to 45 minutes.	3 to 4 cups
Grits, regular	See Cornmeal, above.		
Hominy	See Cornmeal, above.		
Kamut	3 cups	Add to boiling liquid. Bring to a boil for 2 to 3 minutes, then simmer, covered, for 1½ to 2 hours. Drain if necessary.	3 cups
Kasha	1½ cups	Add to cold liquid. Bring to a boil, then simmer, covered, 10 to 12 minutes.	2 cups
Millet	2 cups	Add to boiling liquid; simmer, uncovered, 15 minutes. Remove from heat, cover, and let stand 10 minutes.	3 cups
Oats, quick-cooking	2 cups	Add to boiling liquid; simmer, covered, 1 minute. Remove from heat and let stand, covered, 3 minutes.	2 cups
Oats, rolled	2 cups	Add to boiling liquid; simmer, uncovered, 5 to 8 minutes.	1¾ cups
Oats, steel-cut	2½ cups	Add to boiling liquid; simmer, covered, 20 to 25 minutes.	3 cups
Quinoa	2 cups	Rinse thoroughly. Add to boiling liquid; simmer, covered, 12 to 15 minutes.	3 cups
Rye berries	3 cups	Add to boiling liquid; simmer, covered, until tender, about 1 hour, adding more liquid as needed. Drain if necessary.	3 cups
Triticale	See Rye berries, above.		
Wheat berries	See Rye berries, above.		
Wheat, cracked	2 cups	Add to cold liquid. Bring to a boil, then simmer, covered, 30 to 45 minutes, depending on coarseness of grain.	3 cups

WHEAT Source of the flour we use for most of our baked goods and pasta, wheat also may be enjoyed like other grains. Dark brown, chewy, and rich-tasting whole wheat berries are boiled in water for use as a breakfast cereal, a side dish, or an enhancement for stuffings or baked goods. So, too, are particles of coarse to finely ground cracked wheat. Cracked wheat may look like bulgur, but it has not been steamed, so it requires boiling to soften fully. See also Bulgur, page 224, and FLOUR.

Preparing The chart at left provides basic cooking directions for 1 cup of any listed grain. Please note that specific recipes may call for other cooking techniques or times.

Grain Terminology The following terms apply to the structure and processing of grains:

BERRIES Plump individual whole grains, particularly of wheat and rye.

ENDOSPERM The soft inner portion of a grain, loaded with nutrients; often the only part of it that is eaten.

FLAKE Flat pieces of grain formed either by pressing between high-pressured rollers or by fine slicing.

GERM The embryo contained within every whole grain, which would grow if the grain were planted and watered. The oil-rich germ is often removed during milling to prevent flour from going rancid. It is nutritious, however, and is often sold separately.

HULL The tough outer husk of some grains such as barley, oats, and rice.

PEARL A term for polishing grains, like barley, to remove their tough hulls.

ROLLED Applies particularly to oats that are hulled and then steamed and flattened between rollers into quick-cooking flakes.

See also CORN; CORNMEAL; COUSCOUS; FLOUR; POLENTA; RICE.

GRAPEFRUIT The grapefruit is a relative newcomer in culinary history. It didn't come on the scene until the 18th century, when it was bred from a cross between oranges and pomelos. It is the second largest citrus fruit, after the pomelo, and is grown primarily in the United States. It has a tart, refreshing flavor and a wealth of juice. Depending on the variety, the pulp ranges in color from white to pale pink to ruby red. The peel is always yellow, although some varieties sport a pinkish blush. Many seedless varieties are available.

Selecting Choose grapefruits that are firm and heavy for their size. Avoid fruits that have soft spots or a puffy appearance. Small blemishes on the peel are generally not indicative of a poor interior.

Storing Grapefruits can be left out at room temperature for 1 week or kept in the refrigerator for up to 3 weeks. They will be juicier and sweeter if brought back to room temperature before serving.

Grapefruit spoons.

Preparing Cut grapefruits in half along their equators. Specially designed grapefruit spoons and angled grapefruit knives, both with serrated edges, permit the drowsy morning grapefruit eater to free the juicy sections easily from the tough membranes. There are even grapefruit bowls armed with sharp points to hold the grapefruit in place. Lacking any of these accoutrements, use a small, sharp knife to cut all the way around the circumference of the halved grapefruit, loosening the segments from the peel, and then cut along either side of each section to separate it from the membrane.

Cutting grapefruit segments.

Quick Bite

Although some food historians attribute the grapefruit's name to the grapelike clusters in which it grows, others insist that it originated with an early recorder of horticultural finds in the West Indies who likened the grapefruit's taste to that of a grape.

GRATIN Any recipe with the term *gratin, gratinée,* or *au gratin* in its name refers to a dish covered with a browned and crisp crust, usually of bread crumbs (sometimes mixed with bits of butter), cracker crumbs, finely ground nuts, grated or shredded cheese, or similar topping. The dish, usually some form of seafood, meat, poultry, or vegetable bound with a white sauce, is slipped into an oven or under a broiler to brown the crust. Specially designed shallow, usually oval heavy gratin dishes allow for a particularly large surface area, which increases each diner's share of the desirable crispy crust.

Gratin dish.

GRATING This term turns up in a wide variety of recipes. It calls for transforming a food into tiny particles, usually by rubbing it over sharp, pointy rasps on a flat grater surface.

Quick Bite

Although "grating" is commonly used interchangeably with "shredding," the latter is the proper term for reducing food to thin, narrow strips. Medium-soft cheeses, such as Cheddar and Monterey jack, and vegetables, such as carrots and zucchini, are shredded on the largest holes of a box grater.

Among likely candidates for grating are Parmesan cheese for pasta, lemon zest for cookie dough, bread crumbs for a meat loaf, or nutmeg for a pumpkin pie. The objective of grating is often to make foods cook, melt, dissolve, or blend more quickly and easily.

Grating and shredding cheese.

Different types of graters are available. The box grater, a common kitchen tool, includes both a rasp-surfaced grating side and

Quick Tip

When grating, try using a clean, thin, green scrubbing pad to help grip the food securely and to prevent any nicks and cuts on your fingers and knuckles.

one or more shredding sides (medium or large holes with one raised edge).

Rotary graters, in which food is fed through a small hopper and grated by a rotating drum or disk, speed the job; they include handheld types and hand-turned countertop models.

Rotary cheese grater.

Food processors also come with grating disks among their other attachments.

Fine-rasped nutmeg graters are designed for freshly grating whole nutmegs and include a small compartment for storing the spice. Although most graters are made of stainless steel, small porcelain ginger graters, a standard tool in Asia, easily grate the fibrous rhizome—and can also be used for citrus zest.

Quick Tip

Use a pastry or vegetable brush to clean between the holes of graters.

See also CHEESE; GINGER; NUTMEG; SHREDDING.

GRAVY A sauce that accompanies roasted or panfried meat and is prepared with the meat's own drippings and juices. Traditional gravies call for briefly cooking flour in the drippings to make a light roux. Some cooks, however, use cornstarch or the reduction method as a thickener instead. Gravy can be enriched and flavored with stock, milk, cream, wine, bacon fat, butter, herbs, or tiny pieces of meat or giblets.

HOW TO *Make Gravy*

1. While the roast rests before carving, carefully pick up the roasting pan and pour off all but 3 to 5 tablespoons of the fat.

2. Place the roasting pan over medium heat. Sprinkle in 1 to 3 tablespoons all-purpose flour, stirring rapidly to incorporate it with the fat and pan juices and to break up any lumps. Cook briefly, stirring, until lightly browned.

3. Raise the heat to high and, stirring vigorously, pour in hot stock or water and bring to a boil. Reduce the heat to medium and simmer, stirring often, for 5 minutes. Stir in more stock if necessary to achieve a saucelike consistency.

4. Season the gravy to taste with salt and pepper. Pour through a fine-mesh sieve into a warmed gravy boat, stir in a tablespoon of minced fresh herb (if desired), and serve hot.

See also DEGLAZING; GIBLETS; REDUCING; SAUCE; THICKENING.

GREAT NORTHERN BEAN See BEAN, DRIED.

GREEN BEAN See BEAN, FRESH.

GREEN ONION Also known as a scallion; see ONION.

GREENS, DARK Hearty in flavor and high in nutrients, dark greens, also known as cooking greens, are no longer limited to the braising pot. Young, tender leaves can replace lettuce on sandwiches or be added to the salad bowl. Represented by several different vegetable families, they range in flavor from lemony sorrel to peppery turnip greens. See also CABBAGE; GREENS, SALAD.

Selecting Look for fresh, crisp leaves free of blemishes, yellowed spots, or tiny insect holes. Do not buy greens if they are wilted or dried out. Small, young leaves will have a milder flavor, and more and more greens are now available as tender "baby" leaves. Look for greens tied in bunches or washed, chopped, and sealed in plastic bags. (Even though the latter are prewashed, they should be rinsed well again before using.) Baby greens are sold in bulk or in plastic bags. Greens are available year-round in large markets, but most are at their peak from late winter to early spring. Exceptions are turnip greens, in late fall; spinach, spring and fall; beet greens, during the summer and early fall; and Swiss chard, arriving in early spring and lingering through the fall.

A Guide to Dark Greens

BEET GREENS Closely related to chard, beet greens have smooth, thin leaves and an earthy flavor. See also BEET.

BROCCOLI RABE Long, slender, sometimes tough stems with dark green, rippled leaves. Bright yellow broccoli rabe flowers are also edible. See also BROCCOLI RABE.

COLLARD GREENS Large, thick, dark green leaves, each branching from a thick central stem. The flavor is mild, but the tough texture calls for long cooking. A favorite in the American South.

DANDELION GREENS Although unwelcome on most lawns, the pale green, sharply saw-toothed leaves of the dandelion have a pleasantly bitter flavor. The larger and older the leaves, the stronger and tougher they will be. Dandelion cultivated specifically for eating grows longer leaves and is more tender than its wild cousin. (Do not pick greens from lawns that have been treated with chemicals or from busy roadsides.)

ESCAROLE A slightly bitter member of the chicory family with broad, ruffled leaves. Eaten cooked or raw. See also CHICORY.

KALE A member of the cabbage family, with firm, tightly crinkled leaves on long stems. Sturdy kale is dark green in color, has an earthy flavor similar to cabbage, and holds its texture well in cooking.

MUSTARD GREENS Light green, with hints of yellow. Different varieties range in size, shape, and sharpness. Large-leafed mustards tend to be sweeter than those loosely formed into heads, which have a pungent bite. Small, curled mustards have the hottest, spiciest flavor.

SORREL Delicate, triangular leaves with a strongly tart flavor similar to that of rhubarb. The paler the leaves, the more delicate the flavor. Sorrel discolors with cooking, but it lends a bright, pleasantly sour flavor when puréed into soups and sauces.

SPINACH Dark green leaves and earthy, faintly bitter flavor. There are several varieties of spinach: some have thick, crinkled leaves, while others are smooth and flat. Small, immature leaves, marketed as baby spinach, are sold in bulk in many markets and are an excellent salad green.

SWISS CHARD Also known as chard. Large, crinkled leaves on fleshy, ribbed stems. There are two varieties: one with red stems and another with pearly white stems. Red chard, also marketed as rhubarb or ruby chard, has a slightly earthier flavor, while chard with white stems tends to be sweeter.

TURNIP GREENS Among the most assertive of the dark greens. Rarely eaten raw, turnip greens have rich flavor when slowly braised. Often mixed with collard and mustard greens. See also TURNIP.

Storing Since greens will continue to draw nutrients and moisture from their roots after harvesting, trim off the greens and store them separately if you plan to eat the roots as well. Wrap unwashed greens in a clean, damp kitchen towel or damp paper towels, then cover them loosely with a plastic bag. They will keep in the refrigerator for 3 to 5 days. Generally, the sturdier greens will keep for a longer period of time than the delicate ones, although their flavor may become stronger—and perhaps unpleasant—with age.

Preparing The textured leaves of greens often trap large amounts of dirt and sand, especially the leaves of darker varieties. Wash well just before using: Fill the sink or a large bowl with cool water, immerse the greens, then lift them out, letting the grit settle at the bottom. Repeat a few times until no grit is left behind.

Washing spinach.

HOW TO *Remove Stems*

When stems are fibrous and leaves are tender, you'll want to remove the stems before cooking. Use a paring knife to cut away the wide, thick stems of tougher greens such as chard or mustard. For thin stems of tender greens:

1. Gently fold a leaf in half lengthwise along the stem with the vein side out.

2. Holding the folded leaf in one hand, quickly tear the stem away along with the tough center vein.

Most tender greens, such as spinach and broccoli rabe, can be simply sautéed. Tougher greens, such as kale and chard, may need a quick blanch to tenderize them and remove some of their bitterness.

GREENS, SALAD Once upon a time, a wedge of iceberg drizzled with thick dressing qualified as the ultimate in salads. But a quick glance today down any produce aisle will reveal that greens have come a long way. From pale romaine hearts to tender baby spinach, from frilly tufts of frisée to elegantly tapered heads of Belgian endive, there is an endless variety of color, flavors, and textures that you can toss in your salad bowl. Mesclun, a mix of baby greens, is now a staple in markets and restaurants, while imports from Europe and Asia have added zip and flair to the salad course. The French believe that anything added to greens beyond a sprinkle of fresh herbs spoils a salad, but Americans love to combine vegetables, greens, and other ingredients in explosions of color and texture. Europeans traditionally follow the main course with refreshing, palate-cleansing greens, while Americans serve salads as an opening course to stimulate the palate. Whatever your preferences (and iceberg lettuce has even made a comeback!), explore the steadily expanding world of greens and make salads a delicious part of every meal.

Selecting Choose heads that are densely packed and heavy for their size. Avoid any wilted or browned greens. If you are buying greens sealed in cellophane bags, check their freshness date and look closely, especially at the bottom of the bag, for any leaves that are discolored or wet. Baby greens are available in bulk and packaged in cellophane bags. Grocery stores stock lettuce greens year-round, but during the cool months of spring and fall, look for locally grown young greens, especially at the farmers' market.

Select greens from the different groups and don't hesitate to experiment with colors, textures, and flavors to make a salad that suits your taste.

A Salad Bowl of Greens

DELICATE LEAVES WITH SWEET FLAVOR:

BIBB LETTUCE Also called limestone. Very tender, pale green leaves loosely gathered in a small, rosettelike head.

BUTTER LETTUCE Also called Boston lettuce. Loose head with soft, "buttery"-textured, light green leaves. Similar to Bibb, but larger.

GREEN-LEAF OR RED-LEAF LETTUCE Large, ruffled leaves gathered at their stems to form an open, loose head. Mild and delicate in flavor, it is a popular all-purpose salad green. Red-leaf variety has a deep red blush on the leaf edges.

MÂCHE Also called field salad, corn salad, or lamb's lettuce, for it appears in early spring with the lambs. Very delicate and mild, with oval leaves that grow in small, loose bunches.

MESCLUN A varied mixture of young, tender greens. Mesclun, which is a Provençal word for "mix," is traditionally a salad consisting of the first greens and herbs of spring, hence its other name, spring mix. The mixes vary greatly but usually include a wide range of color and textures.

OAKLEAF LETTUCE  Tender, mild lettuce with notched leaves resembling those of the oak tree, sometimes fringed in red. Also sometimes applies to red-leaf lettuces.

CRISP LEAVES WITH MILD FLAVOR:
ICEBERG LETTUCE Also known as crisp-head lettuce. Bland, crisp, thick leaves are good for adding crunch to salad mixes and sandwiches. Very pale green, blending nearly to pale yellow or ivory at the center. The sturdy leaves from the tightly layered, round heads can serve as cups to hold minced salads or other appetizers.

ROMAINE An elongated head of crisp, sturdy leaves that are juicy and sweet. The traditional lettuce for Caesar salad, it can hold up well to strongly flavored dressings and firm garnishes. The pale and crunchy inner leaves of romaine hearts are sometimes sold separately.

SPINACH Slightly bitter-tasting dark green leaves. For use raw in salads, it is best to select small baby spinach leaves, often sold already washed and prepackaged; they have the mildest flavor and best texture.

LEAVES WITH NUTTY AND SWEET FLAVOR:
MIZUNA Originally from Japan, now grown domestically. Long and feathery leaves with a sweet, mild cabbage flavor.

SALAD SAVOY An ornamental variety of kale, tasting faintly of cauliflower. Has small ruffled leaves with stems and leaves streaked in pinkish purple or creamy white.

LEAVES WITH BITTER OR PEPPERY FLAVOR:
ARUGULA Also called rocket. Its dark green, deeply notched leaves resemble small, elongated oak leaves. Nutty, tangy, and slightly peppery in flavor. Larger leaves are more pungent. See also ARUGULA.

BELGIAN ENDIVE Crisp leaves in a small, cylindrical head. See CHICORY; ENDIVE.

CURLY ENDIVE Also known as curly chicory. Loose, bushy head of narrow, frilly leaves with long stems. Pale yellow center leaves have a milder taste. See also CHICORY.

ESCAROLE A green with broad, ruffled leaves and a slightly bitter flavor, similar to curly and Belgian endive. Popular green for wilted salads. See also CHICORY.

FRISÉE Young curly en-dive. Lacy leaves gathered loosely, with tender, pale green outer leaves and a pale yellow to white heart. See also CHICORY.

WATERCRESS Small, round, dark green leaves on short, delicate stems. Its refreshing, peppery flavor can turn bitter with age. See also WATERCRESS.

CRISP AND BRIGHTLY COLORED LEAVES:
RADICCHIO Grows in round or elongated heads. Complements other greens with its deep ruby red color and pleasantly bitter flavor. See also CHICORY.

RED CABBAGE Thinly sliced into strips and tossed into salads for color and texture. See also CABBAGE.

RED ENDIVE A reddish purple variety of Belgian endive. See also CHICORY; ENDIVE.

Storing Store greens unwashed in plastic bags. Although best if eaten the day of purchase, soft-leaved greens will keep for up to 4 days in a plastic bag in the crisper of the refrigerator. Firmer lettuces such as romaine will keep for up to 10 days.

Preparing Immerse greens in a large bowl or sink filled with cool water. Discard any wilted or yellowed leaves. Lift out the greens gently, and repeat the washing until the water is clear. A salad spinner is ideal for drying greens, but shaking them gently in a clean kitchen towel will also absorb excess moisture. Be sure to dry the greens as much as possible, for excess water will dilute the dressing and prevent it from coating the leaves. If you have time, put the washed greens in the refrigerator to crisp.

To prevent discoloration and bruising, tear leaves instead of cutting them. (Romaine leaves, however, are traditionally cut.) Do not dress salad greens until just before serving them; acid and salt in the dressing will quickly wilt the leaves. The lighter and softer the leaf, the more quickly it will wilt. Milder greens are best in simple salads with few ingredients and less acidic vinaigrettes. More strongly flavored greens, such as the chicories, can stand up to other ingredients, including thinly sliced fruit and vegetables, citrus segments, cheese, and toasted nuts.

HOW TO *Wash Greens in Advance*
Washed lettuce can stay crisp in the refrigerator for up to a day. This is also a convenient way to transport lettuce for a picnic or a potluck.
1. Rinse the greens well, then shake off most but not all of the water.
2. Spread a clean kitchen towel flat and arrange the leaves in a single layer on the towel.
3. Gently roll up the towel with the leaves, jelly-roll fashion, being careful not to crush the leaves. Loosely cover the roll with a large plastic bag or plastic wrap.
4. When ready, unwrap and unroll the lettuce and continue as needed.

See also DRESSING; GREENS, DARK; SALAD; VINAIGRETTE.

GRIDDLE See COOKWARE.

GRILLING Nothing defines summer like grilling in the backyard. Cooking food on a grid placed over a fire, from fanning the charcoal to relishing the burnt ends, is a favorite pastime on leisurely August weekends. And now, with the steadily growing manufacture of sophisticated gas grills for the outdoors and simple grill pans for the indoors, grilling has become a way to cook in every season, for every occasion.

Direct vs. Indirect Heat Cooking food directly over smoldering coals or gas flame is called direct-heat grilling. It is an intense, high-heat method ideal for thin cuts of meat, fish, and vegetables that require less than 25 minutes to cook. On a gas grill, direct heat can be achieved by turning all the burners beneath the food to medium-high or high.

On the other hand, some recipes call for cooking by indirect heat. For charcoal grills, this means piling up charcoal opposite where the food will be placed, allowing for slower cooking. Gas grills simply need to be turned to very low or completely off beneath the food. This method works well with whole poultry, roasts, and other large cuts that would not cook all the way through over direct heat before their surfaces burned. Indirect-heat cooking, which is similar to roasting, also eliminates the flare-ups caused by fat dripping directly onto hot coals or flame, which can scorch food.

Indirect-heat grilling.

If you will be cooking only by indirect heat, you can arrange the coals on either side of the grill and cook the food at the center. If you will be using both methods or direct heat only, pile the charcoal on one side of the grill.

Before placing food on the grill, nestle a drip pan in the area of low heat, to catch juices and to reflect heat toward the food. **Types of Grills** Despite the wide variety of grill styles, only three basic different kinds of grills exist, classed according to their source of heat. In charcoal grills, charcoal is burned until heated through, then spread into a single layer for flavorfully smoky heat. With charcoal, the heat level can be difficult to control.

A gas grill, commonly fueled by propane, emits gas flames that in turn heat ceramic briquettes or lava rocks. Once hot, the rocks cook the food. With gas burners and knob controls like a stove, the heat of gas grills can be adjusted. (Even set to high, a gas grill can never achieve the high temperatures of hardwood and charcoal, and purists claim that the food never acquires the flavor delivered by a good charcoal fire. Nonetheless, for most backyard cooks, the convenience of the gas grill more than makes up for any difference.)

Lastly, for indoor use, there are various models of electric grills. Some can cook enough food for up to six people. Powered by electricity, these tabletop appliances rarely reach the high temperatures of outdoor gas or charcoal grills. Open tabletop grills are shaped like hibachis; closed tabletop grills resemble large waffle makers with plates that may be grooved or smooth. The two sides close, sandwiching and cooking food that is placed between them. When using an electric grill, be sure to cook near an open window or exhaust fan.

One of the most common designs for an outdoor grill is the kettle grill, a spherical, covered design intended for promoting good heat circulation. A kettle grill has a domed lid that efficiently directs heat back down to the food and may be high enough to accommodate a whole turkey. Most kettle grills use charcoal, but gas models are also available.

Kettle grill.

Hibachis are small, inexpensive uncovered square-cornered grills. Although good for picnics and grilling in tight spaces, they can hold only a few servings at a time. They are available as portable charcoal grills or electric tabletop appliances.

Double hibachi.

Range-top grills are sometimes an option, too. Some stoves include a dedicated grill section, while others offer a grate as an accessory to replace two of the burners. Range-top grills require powerful exhaust fans to avoid filling a room with smoke. **Fuel** An array of fuels offers varying levels of flavor, convenience, and cost. The basic fuel for gas grills is liquid propane, which is sold in large, metal tanks. Be sure to keep track of the propane level so that you don't run out midway through cooking steaks at your next party. Color-coded magnetic patches attached to the side of the tank will clearly display the fuel's level.

With charcoal grills, you can use briquettes or natural hardwood charcoal. Briquettes are charcoal and sawdust pressed together in small, square-shaped coals. They are more widely available and less expensive than hardwood charcoal, but additives can impart unwanted flavors. Avoid briquettes that contain petroleum, nitrates, sand, or clay as fillers. Some contain starter for instant lighting and bits of wood for hints of hardwood flavor. Natural hardwood charcoal—mesquite, hickory, oak—is well worth its higher price. Virtually all carbon, these hardwood chunks light quickly, burn cleanly and slowly, and produce higher heat than either briquettes or gas.

Fuel choices.

Wood chips add excellent flavor to grilled foods. Fruit woods such as apple, cherry, almond, grape, or olive have subtle aromas, while stronger woods such as mesquite or hickory give off more assertive smoke. For the best flavor, use them during slow cooking. You can use the chips dry for strong, smoky flavors, or soak them in water, beer, or wine for steamy, moist heat.

FOUR WAYS TO USE WOOD CHIPS

- Fill a drip pan with chips.
- Seal chips in a sheet of heavy-duty aluminum, forming a flat envelope. Poke holes in the package and place on coals.
- Scatter chips directly on the coals. For a subtler flavor, soak the chips in water

for at least 30 minutes before throwing them on the coals.

- Use them in the smoker box of a gas grill. Follow manufacturer's instructions.

Quick Tip

To infuse food quickly with fragrant smoke, soak a handful of woody herbs such as rosemary or thyme, spices such as cinnamon sticks or star anise, fresh fennel fronds, or grapevine cuttings in water for at least 15 minutes (to prevent burning), then drain and toss onto hot coals.

Starters The challenge of starting and maintaining a fire lends outdoor grilling much of its mystique. Gas grills were designed to bypass the difficulties and, for some, the fun. You need simply open the fuel valve of the propane tank, light the flames as directed by the manual, and then turn the knobs to adjust the heat level. Allow 15 to 20 minutes for a gas grill to heat completely.

Charcoal chimney starter.

Charcoal grills, on the other hand, call for more finesse. If you grill frequently, consider purchasing a charcoal chimney. Resembling a large coffee can with a handle and holes circling the bottom, it lights coals quickly without the use of lighter fluid. Place crumpled newspaper in the bottom section, center the chimney in the grill, pour charcoal into the top compartment, and light the paper below. The flames burning upward inside the chimney will heat the charcoal. When they are ready, pour the coals from the chimney into the grill. If you need to add more preheated coals for extended cooking, add them to the grill on top of the burning coals as needed to continue grilling. Always let fresh coals burn down a bit before grilling food over them.

If you do not have a chimney, pile charcoal in a neat heap at the center of the grill. Soak the coals with lighter fluid and then light them. Although inexpensive and popular, lighter fluid gives off chemical flavors, especially if too much is used. Allow it to burn off completely before beginning to cook. Nontoxic solid cubes of odorless and smokeless paraffin lighter (or paraffin-soaked corn cobs), tucked into a pile of charcoal, can replace newspapers or liquid starter. An electric starter, basically an iron coil attached to a handle, requires an outlet, but it will heat your charcoal quickly and easily. Keep it away from high-traffic areas, however, since the combination of a cord and a bare element is a potential hazard.

৶ Grilling Accessories and Equipment ৶

Buy utensils with extra-long wooden handles to keep your fingers away from the heat.

BASTING BRUSH Use a wide natural bristle brush, and avoid plastic bristles, as they will melt.

DRIP PAN Use a small, shallow metal pan to place under the meat during indirect cooking. You can also fill it with water for slow-cooking ribs or with wood chips for smoking.

HINGED BASKET Folding, two-part rectangular or oval baskets that enclose whole fish, hamburgers, or mixed vegetables.

MITTS Look for thick, flame-retardant materials and extra-long cuffs.

SKEWERS Invest in sturdy, stainless steel skewers if you grill brochettes fre- quently. Bamboo skewers are simple and inexpensive, but they tend to burn even with presoaking. Wide, flat skewers and double-pronged ones provide additional support for turning food. Long rosemary sprigs, stripped of their lower leaves and soaked for an hour, make beautiful and aromatic skewers.

SPECIALTY GRIDS Variously shaped mesh sheets and baskets to hold small, odd shaped, or delicate foods on top of the grill's standard grid or grill rack.

THERMOMETER For long cooking with lower heat, insert an instant-read thermometer in the vent opening to monitor the temperature inside the grill without opening the lid. See also COOKING TOOLS.

TONGS Extra-long tongs make turning and removing foods quick and easy without piercing them and losing juices.

WIRE BRUSH Stiff wire bristles scrape residue off the grill rack.

When Is the Charcoal Ready?

- After the flames die down, wait until a fine layer of white ash covers all of the charcoal pieces before spreading them. When using briquettes, wait until all traces of red are gone before cooking, to ensure that the food does not take on chemical or coal flavors.
- For a low-tech way to gauge the heat level of coals, hold your hand about 4 inches above the fire, or at the point where the food will be cooking. Keep your hand there as long as you comfortably can and count: 1 to 2 seconds is a hot fire, 3 to 4 seconds is a medium-hot fire, and 5 seconds or more is considered a low fire.

Grill Savvy

- If the grill rack is not clean when you're ready to cook, let the residue burn off while the charcoal is burning down to the point at which it is covered with white ash. Then scrape the rack clean before placing food on it.
- Be sure to preheat the grill rack, which helps keep food from sticking to it. Oiling it will also help. See FAT & OIL for more details. When grilling delicate foods such as fish, cut a large potato into thick slices and rub it on the grill rack before grilling. Its starch will coat the metal and help prevent sticking.
- For cooking most foods, place the rack 4 to 6 inches from the charcoal.
- Cover the grill to increase the heat level and the intensity of the smoky flavor. For a crispier char, leave the lid off.
- Adjust the vents as needed to keep the desired heat level. Opened wide, they will allow more air in for a hotter fire. Closed slightly, they will dampen the heat. Do not close them all the way unless you want to put out the fire.
- To keep a charcoal fire hot for extended cooking times, scatter 10 to 15 unlit, chemically untreated charcoal pieces at 30-minute intervals, or add a large number that have been lit separately in a chimney placed in a heatproof container, such as an old roasting pan or disposable aluminum pan.
- To prevent burning, brush on glazes or sauces, especially those containing sugar, toward the end of cooking.

Cleaning Up

- After cooking, cover the grill and allow the heat of the dying coals or gas flames to burn off the residue.
- Clean the cooled grill rack with a stiff wire brush or scrubbing pad.
- Clean the grill after every use, so the food does not dry on the rack.
- If your grill doesn't have an ash collector or a way for ashes to drop into a pan below, wait until the ash is completely cool, scoop it out, and discard it in a nonflammable container.
- Make sure all the vents are clear.
- To clean lava rocks, let cool completely, place in a heavy paper bag, and shake to knock off any bits of food. Do not wash the rocks with detergent.

Caution!

- Never spray liquid starter on already-lit charcoal.
- Do not leave a grill unattended, especially if children or pets are present.
- Do not grill indoors (except with an indoor grill pan).
- Place the grill away from foliage, dry grass, or other highly flammable material.
- Keep a water hose ready in case of fire.
- Store starter in a safe, secure place away from the grill.

See also BARBECUING; MARINATING; RUB.

GRILL PAN See COOKWARE.

GRINDING To crush foods such as grains, spices, nuts, seeds, or coffee to a fine texture. Various kinds of equipment are employed to grind ingredients, from large mill stones and industrial steel rollers to countertop electric appliances and old-fashioned mortars and pestles. Because they are not subjected to the heat of steel rollers, stone-ground products retain more flavor and tend to have more distinctive textures. Although grinding your own spices or coffee at home just before using them takes time, they will boast fuller flavors than already-ground ones, as their aromatic components will not already have dissipated upon exposure to air.

See also COFFEE; NUT; SPICE.

GRITS See GRAIN.

GRUYÈRE See CHEESE.

GUAVA Long enjoyed in Central and South America, the delicious and sweet-smelling guava is popular in tropical countries around the world. Vaguely pear shaped, guavas can be as small as a walnut or as large as an apple, depending on the variety. Their skin may be pale yellow or light green, while their flesh may be white, pink, yellow, or red. The flavor of the flesh can bring to mind strawberries, bananas, pineapple, or all three. Some varieties are seedless, but others have numerous small edible seeds, especially toward the center. The best varieties have a creamy texture and a soft rind that can be eaten as well.

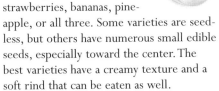

Enjoy ripe guavas out of hand, peeling and seeding them if needed. Slice them and toss gently with starfruit and kiwifruit for a colorful tropical salad. Puréed and strained guavas can thicken a fruity sauce for poultry or pork or flavor mousses, ice cream bases, whipped cream, or custards for desserts. They won't hold up to long cooking but can be gently simmered or poached briefly in sugar syrup.

Selecting Like avocados, guavas should yield to gentle pressure. Although small scuffs and scars are natural, avoid any fruit with discolored, soft spots. Sniff the fruit and choose one with an especially floral bouquet. When unripe, they may have a slight musky fragrance but should emit hints of sweetness. Since they do not survive shipping well, most guavas found in markets are grown domestically and are available from September to February.

Latino markets and some specialty supermarkets sell guava paste in firm, dark red blocks. In Latin America, it is typically sliced and served paired with a mild white cheese as a dessert, or is sometimes eaten alone, much like a candy bar. Check supermarkets for guava jelly, jam, nectar, and frozen purée, as well as cans of the whole fruit. In general, these products lack the fresh fruit's delicate, distinctive flavor but are convenient to use.

Storing Unripe guavas have an astringent bite, but they ripen quickly if stored at room temperature, especially in a paper bag. Once guavas are fully ripe, keep them in a plastic bag in the refrigerator for no more than 3 to 4 days.

Guava paste can be stored indefinitely in a sealed container at room temperature. Store guava purée in the freezer and the jellied or canned fruit in a cool, dark place for up to 1 year.

Preparing Peel and seed guavas if desired or called for in a recipe.

GUGELHOPF PAN See BAKEWARE.

H

everything from ham to husk

h

HABANERO See CHILE.

HALF-AND-HALF See CREAM.

HAM Ham is a portion of the lean hind leg of a pig that has been cured, or preserved, and flavored, often by smoking. The curing is done by various methods, depending on the style of ham. Traditional European hams, like Italian prosciutto and Spanish serrano, are dry-cured in salt and air-dried. In the United States, the hind leg of the pig is traditionally dry-cured or cured in brine (which is known as pickle curing), then smoked and aged for months to become country ham, the best-known version of which is the Smithfield ham of Virginia. Some country hams are sugar-cured, which means that the brine used for curing includes sugar, and other variations exist in other regions of the United States. American country hams must be soaked, simmered, and then baked before eating. Most European dry-cured hams and American country hams are highly flavored and fairly

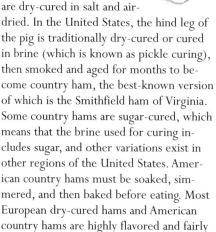

salty and are usually eaten in thin slices. European dry-cured hams may be used as an ingredient in cooked dishes but are not otherwise cooked before eating.

Aside from traditional ham, there is mass-produced ham. Most such hams are cured by injection, which takes considerably less time. A solution of brine is introduced into the pork through a needle. These hams may be smoked at this point (or given another injection, this time with liquid smoke) and then partially or fully cooked. Mass-produced hams are usually given only a "light cure," using a less-salty brine than country hams; they are also generally only lightly smoked or not smoked at all. The result is a milder tasting ham that is juicier and more tender than country ham, but with less distinctive flavor and texture. It is the type of ham with which many Americans are best acquainted.

Selecting Mass-produced hams are sold either fully or partially cooked. Fully cooked are labeled "ready to serve" or "heat and serve" and may be baked again before serving, but only to heat them through. Partially cooked require additional cooking. They are available with or without the bone, although bone-in hams are generally more flavorful. Sometimes the hams are sold spiral sliced for convenience.

Avoid hams labeled "with natural juices," "water added," or "ham and water product," which means that they have retained some of the water used in the brine-injected curing process. Instead, reach for those marked "no water added" or simply "ham." These latter hams are aged longer—for

Quick Bite

Picnic hams are made from the picnic shoulder, or front leg, of the pig; they are fattier and less expensive than hams from the hind leg.

at least a year—to create a more complex flavor and denser meat than their water-logged counterparts. However, some people prefer the moister, milder meat of shorter-aged hams.

Storing Whole or half hams will keep for no longer than 1 week in the refrigerator. Ham, because of its high salt content, is not a good candidate for long-term freezing; the flavor suffers.

HOW TO *Bake a Fully Cooked Ham*
1. If there is a rind, cut it off and trim away all but about ½ inch of the outer layer of fat.
2. For a ham to be presented whole at the table, score the remaining coat of fat diagonally in two directions to make diamond shapes; stud the center of each diamond with a whole clove.
3. Bake in a preheated 325°F oven until a meat thermometer registers 140°F at the center of its thickest part, which, depending on the size of the ham, will take 1 to 1½ hours. If desired, glaze with marmalade; a mixture of brown sugar, mustard, and honey; or melted cranberry sauce during the last 30 minutes of cooking.

HOW TO *Bake a Partially Cooked Ham*
1. Trim and score the ham as directed above.
2. Bake in a 350°F oven until a meat thermometer registers 155°F at the center of its thickest part, allowing 10 to 12 minutes per pound. If desired, glaze the ham during the last 30 minutes of cooking, using one of the glazes suggested for a fully cooked ham, above.

See also CARVING; PORK; PROSCIUTTO.

HAMBURGER Although the term sometimes refers to ground or chopped beef, it usually evokes the American favorite, a beef patty slipped into a bun. The hamburger's ancestral namesake is the pounded beefsteak served in 19th-century Hamburg, Germany, but it was in the United States that countless diners and fast-food chains immortalized this humble meal. The standard burger comes on a round bun, topped with some favorite combination of cheese, mayonnaise,

Quick Tip

Ground chuck, 80 to 85 percent lean, is ideal for juicy, tender, and flavorful burgers. You can use ground round or sirloin, but the leaner meat will have less flavor.

ketchup, mustard, onion, pickle, tomato, and lettuce. In recent years, however, a new class of gourmet burgers has introduced such up-to-date adornments as arugula and blue cheese, and burgers of tofu, poultry, grains, or vegetables now appear as menu options alongside their meaty cousins on many restaurant menus.

HARICOT VERT See BEAN, FRESH.

HAZELNUT See NUT.

HEAPING Describes a measure that is slightly more full than level, such as "1 heaping tablespoon." See also MEASURING.

HEART OF PALM The tender, edible core of a young cabbage palm tree is a delicacy in tropical countries. Hearts of palm are slender and white, with many thin, concentric layers, like a leek. They resemble thick stalks of white asparagus, have a taste reminiscent of artichokes, and are tossed with vinaigrette and served as part of a salad, or are included in lightly cooked dishes.

Selecting Fresh hearts of palm are rarely seen in markets outside of tropical regions,

h

but they are commonly available canned in water in well-stocked food stores. If you do come across fresh ones, buy stalks that are not dried, split, or separated in layers.

Storing Since they are highly perishable, store fresh hearts in a perforated plastic bag in the refrigerator and use them within 2 days. Once opened, canned hearts should be transferred to a glass, plastic, or ceramic container, covered with water, and refrigerated for up to 1 week.

Preparing Blanch fresh hearts for 30 seconds to remove bitterness. To remove any tinny taste from canned hearts, soak them in water and a little lemon juice for 10 minutes before using.

HEAT DIFFUSER See COOKING TOOLS.

HERB See page 244.

HIGH-ALTITUDE COOKING At high altitudes, cooks must adjust cooking times and temperatures. Due to the decrease in air density and air pressure, water molecules turn to steam more readily, thus boiling at lower temperatures than at sea level. Foods require longer cooking to compensate for this heat loss. The higher the altitude, the greater the difference.

Small adjustments will correct most of the effects of low pressure. Trial and error will determine exact changes for each dish. For best results, however, follow recipes written specifically for high altitudes.

Adjusting Time and Temperature Cook food at higher heat or for a longer amount of time.

- Increase oven temperature by 25°F.
- Expect to boil or simmer food for a few minutes more.
- Starting at 4,000 feet, expect to simmer stews 1 hour more for every additional 1,000 feet.

- When deep-frying, decrease the oil temperature 3°F for every 1,000 feet above sea level, to prevent food from overbrowning on the outside while undercooking inside.

Adjusting Liquid Since liquids evaporate more rapidly at higher elevations, ingredients will become drier. The higher the elevation, the greater the loss of liquid.

- Increase the amount of liquid in recipes, adding 2 to 4 tablespoons to every 1 cup of liquid.
- Add several cups more liquid for boiling pasta and legumes.
- Double-wrap already baked breads and cakes to prevent drying out.

Boiling Point at High Altitudes

ELEVATION	FAHRENHEIT	CELSIUS
Sea level	212°	100°
2,000 feet	208°	98°
5,000 feet	203°	95°
7,500 feet	198°	92°
10,000 feet	195°	90°
15,000 feet	185°	85°

Adjusting Ingredients

LEAVENING At 3,000 feet above sea level, bread baking takes on new dimensions— literally. Baking powder, baking soda, and even yeast produce gas more quickly at high altitudes. And with less air pressure for baked goods to rise against, they can tower to greater heights. Unfortunately, they collapse more quickly, too, because they lack the time necessary to develop the structure to support themselves.

- Decrease leavening by one-fourth the amount required at sea level.
- Watch yeast dough carefully as it rises. Punch it down and let rise a second time

until doubled. With recipes that call for two risings, add a third rising.

OTHER INGREDIENTS

- Reduce every 1 cup of sugar by 1 to 2 tablespoons.
- Do not beat egg whites beyond soft peaks for meringues or cake batters. They will dry out too much, collapse easily, and add too much unstable air.
- Add an additional whole egg to delicate, airy batters (popovers, sponge cakes) to provide additional leavening.

HOISIN SAUCE A thick, sweet, reddish brown sauce made from soybeans, sugar, garlic, Chinese five-spice powder or star anise, and a hint of chile. It can be thick and creamy or thin enough to pour. Used throughout China, hoisin sauce is rubbed on meat and poultry before roasting to give them a sweet flavor and red color. It sometimes appears as a condiment but should be added with caution, as its strong flavor can easily overpower most foods.

Selecting Hoisin sauce is available in large cans, but smaller jars are more practical and are usually of better quality. Look for it in Asian markets or the ethnic-food aisle of major grocery stores.

Storing The sauce keeps indefinitely in the refrigerator. Once opened, transfer canned hoisin sauce to a glass jar or an airtight plastic container.

HOMINY See GRAIN.

HONEY The old adage "busy as a bee" has its basis in reality. A hive of bees must fly over 55,000 miles and visit 2 million flowers to produce a single pound of honey, the sweet, syrupy liquid that bees make from flower nectar to feed their hive, and that children, tea drinkers, and bakers love.

Honey arrives at market in three basic forms. Most common is liquid honey, extracted from the honeycomb by centrifugal force, gravity, or straining. Liquid honey is usually pasteurized and filtered. Sold in a crystallized state, spun honey, also called granulated or crème honey, can be spread like butter at room temperature.

Comb honey comes just as the bees produced it—still in its wax comb, which is edible as well. Cut comb honey, a variation, contains small chunks of the honeycomb.

Selecting Depending on the source of the nectar, honey ranges from almost white to deep, rich brown. The flavor changes according to the plants that surround any given hive. In general, the lighter the honey's color, the more delicate its flavor.

LIGHT AND MILD HONEYS Acacia, alfalfa, clover, lavender, orange blossom, rosemary.

DARK AND STRONG HONEYS Basswood (pale color but assertive flavor), buckwheat, chestnut, eucalyptus, tupelo, wildflower.

Caution!

Do not feed honey to children younger than 1 year old. The honey may contain bacterial spores that can cause infant botulism.

Storing Liquid and spun honey will keep for 1 year or more if stored in an airtight container at room temperature. Liquid honey may crystallize at colder temperatures; this is harmless. Comb honey will keep in a cool, dark cupboard for 6 months.

To reliquefy honey that has crystallized, remove the lid and set the jar in a pan of very hot water for 10 to 20 minutes, or microwave it in 30-second intervals, stirring after each one, until clear.

h

Herb

An Italian roast lacking rosemary, a Thai salad in need of cilantro, Scandinavian gravlax missing dill, Lebanese tabbouleh minus mint—without fresh and fragrant herbs, cuisines around the world would lose their heart and soul.

As immigrants share their traditional dishes and as travelers explore the tables of distant countries, cooks everywhere are discovering the power of herbs. Grocery stores now offer an ever-expanding selection of fresh herbs: alongside curly parsley appear bouquetlike bunches of delicate chervil, heady oregano, velvety sage, and perhaps three different varieties of thyme. Whether simmered in a simple broth, stirred into a sauce, or sprinkled over a fruit tart, fresh herbs enliven dishes with their perfume and infuse them with their distinct flavors. Although leafy and delicate herbs may lose significant flavor when dried, many other herbs, such as rosemary, dill, and thyme, dry well. Convenient to use and handy for last-minute inspirations, quality dried herbs are an important part of any kitchen's basic pantry. Since dried herbs have more concentrated flavors, use about one-fourth the amount of the dried form in place of fresh.

Herb or Spice? Although the two are used for similar purposes, herbs and spices actually refer to distinct categories of seasonings. Herbs are the fragrant leaves and tender stems of green plants, having an almost floral bouquet and more delicate flavors. Spices, on the other hand, generally come from woody plants, many of them native to the world's tropical regions. Most familiar in their dried forms, spices can be taken from the rhizomes, stems, buds, seeds, or bark of the plants, where concentrated amounts of their complex aromatic components result in significantly stronger flavors. Cinnamon, nutmeg, ginger, and clove all display the intense aromatic qualities of spices.

Selecting Choose fresh herbs that look bright, fragrant, and healthy. Avoid those that have wilted, yellowed, or blackened leaves or moldy stems. Herbs may be packaged in plastic bags or thin plastic containers, or simply gathered with rubber bands. Young, tender hothouse herbs make delicate garnishes but have less flavor than larger, hardier field-grown herbs. Although herbs with blossoms make attractive edible garnishes, leaves picked from plants without buds or flowers will have more flavor. When buying dried herbs, buy small amounts from a reputable specialty market that sells them in bulk with a high turnover or choose small glass jars containing large bright green flakes. A higher-priced brand usually ensures higher quality.

A Bouquet of Herbs

BASIL Traditionally used in kitchens throughout the Mediterranean and in Southeast Asia, basil is one of the world's best-loved herbs. Although related to mint, basil tastes faintly of anise and cloves. Italians use it in pesto, often pair it with tomatoes, and consider it essential to a classic minestrone. In Thailand and Vietnam, basil is often combined with fresh mint for seasoning stir-fries, curries, and, in the case of Vietnam, salads.

Quick Bite

More than 60 varieties of basil exist. Familiar green basil, also called sweet basil, has a mild anise flavor. Purple basil, also known as opal basil, has smaller leaves and tastes a little spicier than sweet basil. Lemon basil has a mild and pleasing citrus flavor.

BAY Elongated gray-green leaves used to flavor sauces, soups, stews, and braises, imparting a slightly sweet, citrusy, nutty flavor. Usually sold dried, bay leaves should be re-moved from a dish before serving, as they are leathery and can have sharp edges.

Quick Tip

Use fresh bay leaves as you would dried leaves, but add them with a light hand and ex-pect more flavor in the finished dish. Milder French bay (called laurel in Europe) can be used in greater quantities than California bay.

BORAGE Fresh or dried leaves that, when finely chopped, impart a light flavor remi-niscent of cucumber to vegetables, salads, soups, stews, and other dishes. Purple borage flowers may be used as a garnish.

CHERVIL A spring-time herb with a taste reminiscent of parsley and anise. It goes particularly well with poultry and seafood, with carrots, and in salads.

CHIVE These slender, bright green stems are used to give an onionlike flavor without the bite. The slender, hollow, grasslike leaves can be snipped with a pair of kitchen scissors to any length and scattered over scrambled eggs, stews, salads, soups, tomatoes, or any dish that would benefit from a boost of mild oniony flavor. Chives do not take well to long cooking—they lose flavor and crispness and turn a dull grayish green.

CILANTRO Also called fresh coriander and Chinese parsley, cilantro is a distinctly flavored herb with legions of loyal followers—and some emphatic detractors. Used extensively in the cuisines of Mexico, the Caribbean, India, Egypt, Thailand, Vietnam, and China, as well as in numerous others, cilantro asserts itself with a flavor that can't be missed. Some describe its taste as being citrusy or minty; others find hints of sage and parsley; others describe it as soapy. It is used fresh, as it loses flavor when dried. The herb is best added at the end of cook-ing; its flavor disappears during long expo-sure to heat.

Quick Tip

Cilantro and flat-leaf (Italian) parsley look somewhat similar and can be mistaken for each other. Check each bunch carefully. If in doubt, give it a sniff or taste a leaf.

DILL Fine, feathery leaves with a distinct aromatic flavor. Often used in savory pas-tries, baked vegetables, and, of course, in the making of pickles.

continued

Herb, continued

EPAZOTE A pungent herb, possibly indigenous to Mexico, that has no substitute for its unusual flavor. Although seldom available commercially outside Mexico or India, it is easily grown from seed and is self-sowing. It can be used dried, after the twigs are discarded, but its flavor is greatly diminished.

LAVENDER Highly perfumed blossoms, leaves, and stalks of a flowering plant that grows wild in southern France, where it is a signature seasoning. Use sparingly to season lamb or poultry, or infuse syrups for use in dessert making.

Quick Bite

Lavender is a signature ingredient in *herbes de Provence*, a traditional French herb blend that often also contains marjoram, rosemary, sage, and summer savory.

LEMON BALM A sweet, lemon-scented herb used with fresh fruit and in egg dishes, soups, and salads.

LEMON VERBENA A strongly lemon-scented herb, native to South America. Use sparingly, fresh or dried, to flavor fruit or custard desserts or herbal teas.

MARJORAM This Mediterranean herb, which has a milder flavor than its close relative oregano, is best used fresh. Pair it with tomatoes, eggplant, beans, poultry, and seafood.

MINT Refreshing herb available in many varieties, with spearmint the most common. Used fresh to flavor a broad range of savory preparations, including spring lamb, poultry, and vegetables, or to garnish desserts.

OREGANO Aromatic, pungent, and spicy herb, also known as wild marjoram, used fresh or dried as a seasoning for all kinds of savory dishes. Especially compatible with tomatoes and other vegetables.

PARSLEY Adds vibrant color and pleasing flavor to almost any savory dish. The two most popular varieties are curly-leaf parsley and flat-leaf, or Italian, parsley. Both have a refreshing and faintly peppery flavor, but flat-leaf parsley's flavor is stronger and more complex and is preferred in cooking. The hardier curly-leaf parsley garnishes many a dinner plate, and although not as flavorful, it can be substituted for the flat-leaf variety.

Flat-leaf (Italian) parsley.

ROSEMARY Used fresh or dried, this Mediterranean herb has a strong, fragrant flavor well suited to meats, poultry, seafood, and vegetables. It is a particularly good complement to chicken and lamb.

SAGE Soft, gray-green sage leaves are sweet and aromatic. Used fresh or dried, they pair well with poultry, vegetables, or fresh or cured pork.

SORREL Delicate, triangular leaves with a highly tart flavor. Lends bright, pleasantly sour flavor when puréed into soups and sauces.

SUMMER SAVORY More delicate than its cousin winter savory, summer savory has a scent reminiscent of thyme and a faintly bitter, almost minty flavor. Add in small amounts to stews, beans, and meat dishes or use to infuse vinegar.

TARRAGON With its distinctively sweet flavor that recalls anise, tarragon is used to season salads, egg and vegetable dishes, and fish and chicken dishes.

THYME One of the most important culinary herbs of Europe, thyme delivers a floral, earthy flavor to all types of food, including vegetables (especially roots and tubers) and poultry. One variety, lemon thyme, adds a subtle citrus note.

WINTER SAVORY This shrublike Mediterranean evergreen herb has a strong, spicy flavor that some cooks liken to thyme. It complements dried beans and lentils, meats, poultry, and tomatoes.

Storing Wrap in damp paper towels, then wrap in a plastic bag and refrigerate for 3 to 5 days. Take care with fragile herbs, such as chives and basil, for they bruise and discolor easily. To keep long-stemmed herbs, such as parsley, basil, and cilantro, for up to 10 days, trim off the ends of their stems, remove any yellowed leaves, and place the bunch in a container of water, like a bouquet of flowers. Drape a bag loosely upside down over the leaves, secure with a rubber band around the mouth of the jar, and refrigerate. Remove sprigs as needed. To prepare a large amount of herbs in advance with little loss of flavor, chop them up to 24 hours ahead. Then, place them in an airtight container, cover them with a damp paper towel, seal the lid, and store in the refrigerator.

Quick Tip

At many farmers' markets you can find herbs with roots still attached. Immersed in a glass of water, they will keep fresh for weeks.

Store dried herbs in airtight containers away from both light and heat. Buy in small amounts, replacing them after 4 to 6 months, as they fade in color, fragrance, and flavor. Although cork tops and prominently displayed racks add decorative touches to your kitchen, they only allow herbs to lose their flavor more quickly.

Quick Tip

Forgot about that bunch of thyme at the bottom of the vegetable bin? Herbs that are a little weary can be redeemed by a soaking in vinegar. Crush the herbs gently in a nonreactive container, pour in just enough warm vinegar to cover, and refrigerate overnight. Use in a flavorful vinaigrette or a cooked sauce.

continued

Herb, continued

Preparing Since fresh herbs can be sandy, rinse them well under cold running water, or dunk them gently in a bowl filled with water. Do not wash them until needed, however, to preserve their flavor and lengthen their storage life. To release their aromatic oils, crush dried herb flakes before using. Before searing or roasting meats, try to remove any herbs clinging to the surface of the meat, to prevent them from scorching.

As a general rule, fresh herbs are best added toward the end of cooking, for the better appreciation of their lighter flavors, which can dissipate rapidly. Dried herbs, more concentrated in flavor, are usually added earlier in the preparation of a dish, so that their aromas may permeate it and mingle with other ingredients. For more complex flavor, add herbs at two different points in cooking: dried at the beginning to intermingle with the other ingredients, and then fresh at the end of cooking to deliver a bright burst of flavor.

About Crushing Dried Herbs

Recipes using dried herbs often call for them to be crushed before adding to a dish. Crushing reduces the herbs to finer particles and helps release their aromatic oils, increasing the flavor they impart. To crush a small amount of herbs, place them in the palm of one hand and press down with the thumb of the other, twisting your thumb as you do so. Large quantities of herbs may also be crushed using a mortar and pestle.

Crushing dried herbs.

About Mincing Fresh Herbs Begin with dry herbs; otherwise, they will stick to the knife. Rinse them far enough ahead of time for them to dry fully, or use a paper towel to pat them dry. Remove the leaves and discard the thick stems (or reserve for adding to the stockpot). Then, keeping fingers safely clear, chop the leaves with a good-sized chef's knife, holding down the knife tip with one hand so that it never leaves the cutting board and moving your chopping wrist and hand rhythmically. Gather the herb repeatedly into smaller and tighter clumps and chop until it is as fine as you want it. As a rule, herbs are finely chopped. A pair of scissors or a mezzaluna also comes in handy for mincing.

Chopping parsley tops.

Mincing parsley.

Quick Tip

A food processor minces large amounts of herbs quickly, but it also crushes and bruises them. Mince fresh herbs by hand if you have the time. See also MINCING.

See also BOUQUET GARNI.

HONEYDEW See MELON.

HORSERADISH A thick, gnarled root of a plant in the cabbage family that is native to Europe and Asia. The root has a refreshing, spicy bite that perks up everything from beef brisket to boiled beets. It is blended into sour cream to accompany smoked fish, into whipped cream to partner a rib roast, or into cocktail sauces to eat along with shellfish. It is available fresh but is more commonly used already grated, mixed with vinegar or beet juice, and packed in glass bottles labeled as prepared or commercial horseradish. It is also dried and sold as powder. Getting into the habit of using fresh horseradish pays off, for the flavor is purer and cleaner.

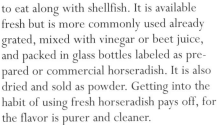

Selecting Fresh horseradish appears in markets from late fall to early spring. Look for firm roots free of wrinkles, soft spots, and mold. Prepared horseradish is available bottled in jars with white vinegar, but since some brands can be quite vinegary, a better

Quick Tip

Do not cook horseradish. While strong and biting when raw, the root is easily tamed by heat.

alternative is to reconstitute dried horseradish powder with water just before using—or at least try several brands and decide which you prefer. The horseradish packed in white vinegar is called white horseradish, while the horseradish packed in beet juice is called red horseradish.

Storing Keep the fresh root wrapped first in a paper bag or paper towels, then in a plastic bag. Store in the refrigerator for up to 3 weeks. The root freezes well and will grate easily into small flakes while frozen. Once opened, bottled horseradish should be refrigerated; it will keep for up to 4 months. Longer storage will not cause the horseradish to spoil, but it will lose its punch. Powdered horseradish may be stored in a cool place for up to 1 year.

Preparing Wash fresh horseradish roots, then peel. Trim away any green areas, for they will be unpleasantly bitter. Like parsnip, a large horseradish root will have a tough, fibrous core that should be removed and discarded. Horseradish quickly turns brown once cut. Prepare it just before serving, sprinkle it with a little lemon juice or vinegar to prevent discoloring, and use nonreactive containers.

HOT PEPPER See CHILE.

HUCKLEBERRY See BERRY.

HULL The dry outer covering of a fruit, seed, or nut. The term also refers to the leafy base where a stem connects to a fruit, as in a strawberry. Generally, both types of hulls are removed from food, either during processing or by the cook.

HUSK The dry papery sheath found on certain vegetables and fruits, the best known example of which is the corn husk. In Mexico—and wherever Mexican food is served—dried corn husks are used as wrappers for the ubiquitous tamale. Another common husk-covered market item is the tomatillo, a sour, green tomato-like vegetable that is a popular base for salsas.

h

I·J

*everything from ice cream
to julienning*

ICE See SORBET.

ICE CREAM See page 252.

ICED TEA See TEA.

ICING See FROSTING, ICING & GLAZE.

INDIRECT HEAT See GRILLING.

ITALIAN BEAN Another name for
romano bean; see BEAN, FRESH.

ITALIAN BROCCOLI See BROCCOLI
RABE.

JALAPEÑO See CHILE.

JAM & JELLY Most of us use these
two terms interchangeably, and if pressed
to explain the difference between them, we
are likely to struggle. In truth, the distinction is quite simple. While both are sweet
preserves (so called because added sugar
slows spoilage), usually of fruit but sometimes of vegetable-fruits such as chiles or
herbs such as mint, jams contain the edible
portion of the fruit in its entirety and are
therefore chunky, while jellies have been

strained to achieve a perfectly smooth consistency and often a crystalline clarity. In
certain recipes, your choice can make a
significant difference. Jams, for example,
may serve as a simple filling for tartlets,
having sufficient body to partner a crisp
pastry shell. Jellies, by contrast, are sometimes employed as a glaze for sweets such
as pastries or even for cooked meats: they
are melted (sometimes with a little liqueur)
and then spooned over the food.

JARLSBERG See CHEESE.

JELL To become firm or gelatinous,
especially from a mostly liquid state. Jelling
is usually a controlled process, using ingredients such as gelatin, pectin, or sugar
to thicken food or to form it into specific
shapes. It can also refer to protein-rich
stocks or sauces that naturally jell as they
cool. See also GELATIN; PECTIN.

JELLY See JAM & JELLY.

JELLY-ROLL PAN See BAKEWARE.

JERUSALEM ARTICHOKE Not
from Jerusalem and not an artichoke,
this delicate vegetable owes its name to
the Italian word for sunflower, *girasole*—
although admittedly it is a leap from there
to *Jerusalem artichoke*.
Also known
as sunchokes,
these are the
small tubers of
a sunflower plant
native to North
America. Knobby
and beige skinned, they resemble fresh
ginger in appearance. Their crisp, ivory
flesh has a sweet, slightly nutty flavor
that is delicious raw, thinly sliced in salads,
as well as steamed, sautéed, or baked.

Selecting Look for Jerusalem artichokes that are small and firm, with smooth, unblemished skin. As with potatoes, do not buy them if they have sprouts or a green tinge. They are in season from midautumn through early spring and are at their best when harvested a few weeks after a frost.

Storing Jerusalem artichokes will keep at room temperature for 4 days. Or wrap first in a paper bag or paper towels, then in a plastic bag, and store in the vegetable bin of the refrigerator for up to 2 weeks.

Quick Tip

To prevent discoloring, avoid cooking Jerusalem artichokes in reactive pans made of aluminum or cast iron.

Preparing Wash Jerusalem artichokes well, scrubbing gently to remove dirt and grit. They will darken when cut and exposed to air. Sprinkle pieces with lemon juice to prevent discoloring. The tubers also bruise easily, so handle them with care. They do not need to be peeled, but their thin skin peels off easily after cooking.

JICAMA (HICK-uh-muh) A large, round tuber shaped like a turnip with golden beige skin and crisp, juicy, sweet white flesh. Jicama is also known as yam bean, and for good reason: like beans, it is a member of the legume family. It is eaten both fresh and cooked in Mexico, the American Southwest, and throughout Asia. Jicama is at its best raw or very briefly cooked, but you can also steam, fry, roast, or boil and purée it much like potatoes. It pairs especially well with citrus fruits and chiles. Peel a jicama's thick skin before using. Cut it into thin, wedge-shaped slices and toss with olive oil, fresh lime juice, and a pinch of chili powder for a healthy snack or a refreshing accompaniment to Mexican dishes. Because it does not discolor, jicama is perfect for crudité platters, coleslaws, hors d'oeuvres, and both green and fruit salads. Its crunchy texture makes it a convenient substitute for water chestnuts in stir-fries.

Selecting Choose a jicama that is firm and heavy for its size. Jicamas arrive at market in a range of sizes, from a convenient ½ pound to a rather unwieldy 5 or 6 pounds. Buy the size you need; girth does not indicate toughness or starchiness, although the thickness of the skin does. The skin should be thin and smooth, with no cracks or soft spots. Scratch the skin to check that it is thin and the flesh is juicy. The tuber is widely available year-round but is at its best from late fall to late spring.

Storing You can leave an uncut jicama at room temperature for 2 to 3 days. It will keep for up to 3 weeks in the refrigerator if stored unwrapped in the vegetable bin. Once cut, wrap the unused portion with plastic wrap and refrigerate for up to 1 week longer. To keep peeled, cut pieces fresh, cover them with water and refrigerate for no longer than 4 days.

HOW TO *Peel Jicama*

Cut a large jicama in half if you do not plan to use all of it.

1. If needed, cut it into manageable wedges.
2. With a sharp paring knife, trim both the stem and root ends.
3. Cut and lift up a small piece of the peel near the stem end, then tear a wide strip of the peel down. Repeat in segments with the remaining peel. The skin is too tenacious to be removed with a vegetable peeler.
4. If the jicama has another tough layer beneath the peel, repeat step 3 to remove it as well.

Ice Cream

Ancient Romans carried snow down from the Alps to fashion some of the earliest ice creams, and the Chinese reportedly were serving flavored ices as early as 1100 B.C.

The Turks were busy, too, whipping up fruit ices and fruit drinks, concoctions that some historians believe are the forerunners of today's sherbet. Italians invented the first machine-made ices, however, and perfected commercial freezing. Once enjoyed only by the wealthy, who could afford the pricey transport of ice and snow, ice cream is now enjoyed by all, young and old alike, in winter and summer.

Ingredients Ice cream has several essential ingredients or components, and each plays a carefully balanced role. Fat from cream and milk imparts richness, smoothness, and flavor. Too much fat, however, will cause the mixture to curdle and form small lumps.

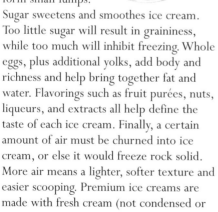

Sugar sweetens and smoothes ice cream. Too little sugar will result in graininess, while too much will inhibit freezing. Whole eggs, plus additional yolks, add body and richness and help bring together fat and water. Flavorings such as fruit purées, nuts, liqueurs, and extracts all help define the taste of each ice cream. Finally, a certain amount of air must be churned into ice cream, or else it would freeze rock solid. More air means a lighter, softer texture and easier scooping. Premium ice creams are made with fresh cream (not condensed or powdered milk), real eggs, and natural flavorings. They have very little air added.

Other Frozen Treats

FROZEN YOGURT Made from either low-fat or nonfat yogurt, along with skim milk or a mixture of milk and cream. Although the amount of fat in frozen yogurt can vary widely, in general it tends to have lower amounts than ice cream. Stabilizers take the place of most of the fat.

GELATO Contains only a minimal amount of air that is incorporated naturally in the mixing process. Gelato (and some premium ice cream) is so dense that it requires a slightly lower serving temperature, a perfect point at which the scoop is firm but not hard, yet not so soft that it melts immediately. Recipes usually include more egg yolks, more milk, and less cream than regular ice cream. In the end, gelato actually has less fat than its more conventional kin. Its low percentage of air, however, makes for an extremely creamy treat.

GRANITA A grainy-textured ice made by continued scraping and refrigerating of the mixture. See SORBET.

ICE Similar to a sorbet. A frozen mixture of ice and liquid, typically coffee, fruit juice, wine, or an herbal infusion. See SORBET.

ICE MILK With less fat than ice cream, ice milk tends to have a lighter texture.

SHERBET Made with fruit or fruit juice and (in some places) a small amount of milk. Sherbets tend to be coarser in texture than ice cream, with a slightly tarter flavor. See SORBET.

SORBET Contains no milk, cream, or eggs, only ice, sweeteners, and flavoring such as fresh fruit. See SORBET.

Equipment There are two basic kinds of ice-cream makers. A hand-operated maker consists of a hand-cranked bucket with a smaller canister inside and a dasher, or stirrer. A combination of ice and rock salt fills the gap between the bucket and the canister to chill down the ice-cream base. A popular variation involves a canister filled with liquid coolant that does not require ice; the liquid-gel canister simply needs to prefreeze for at least 1 day. Electric ice cream makers all have motors but range from wooden buckets that still require ice to large, imported gelato churners with self-contained refrigeration that make rich gelato with the touch of a button.

Homemade Ice Cream Savvy For best results when making homemade ice cream, follow these guidelines:

- If making a custard-based ice cream, cook the base gently in a double boiler to prevent scorching. Straining will remove all lumps.
- Be sure to refrigerate the base overnight, or for at least 4 hours. This helps bring together the flavors and prevents ice crystals from forming as the ice cream is churned, improving the final texture. Also, if you're using a machine that requires ice, less ice will be required later to cool the base and thus churning time will be reduced.
- Expect the base to taste sweeter than you would like the finished ice cream to. Food tastes less sweet when it is cold.
- Do not use only heavy cream if you want fine texture. The ice cream will be quite dense. Add condensed milk or half-and-half to lighten the consistency.
- If using a machine that requires ice, crushing ice increases its surface area. The cold will transfer more efficiently to the ice cream base.
- If using a machine that requires salted ice, use coarse salt, not table salt, since it dissolves more slowly.
- Continuous stirring, especially once the base begins to thicken, will decrease the size the of ice crystals that form and result in a smoother ice cream.
- Ice cream can be served immediately from the ice cream freezer while still somewhat soft, not unlike a frozen custard or fast-food soft-serve products. Or it can be transferred to your refrigerator freezer to set and harden for at least 3 hours before serving for a more familiar thick, solid consistency.
- Add fruit after freezing but before hardening. Or stir it in just before serving the ice cream.
- Berries can be used raw, but fruits such as peaches, pears, and plums should be poached in syrup for better flavor and texture. Poaching fruits such as kiwifruit and pineapple will also deactivate enzymes in them that would break down the ice cream.
- Be careful when adding alcohol to ice cream, since it lowers the freezing point. Too much alcohol will prevent ice cream from setting properly.
- Rinse salt well from all parts of the ice cream maker to prevent corrosion.

Ice Cream Blues Got a problem with your homemade ice cream? Find the simple explanation here.

MY HOMEMADE ICE CREAM IS LUMPY. The base was not strained, the egg coagulated; the base was not stirred evenly; or the paddle didn't scrape the sides of the canister enough to incorporate all the ingredients.

MY HOMEMADE ICE CREAM IS GRAINY. Too much water or alcohol in the base; not enough fat or sugar in the base; the cream curdled from too high of a fat content or from the base's being too acidic; the base churned too slowly; or the container was overfilled.

i·j

JUICING Various gadgets have been designed for juicing, from a handheld wooden reamer for squeezing out some lemon juice to large machines for extracting a drink from the hardest beet. The simple, classic citrus juicer resembles a shallow bowl with a deeply fluted, inverted cone that fits into a citrus half and a spout for pouring freshly squeezed orange or grapefruit juice into breakfast glasses. Fancier versions may include a mechanized cone or a perforated base for catching seeds and pulp.

Juicing citrus with a reamer.

Tall, mechanical presses have a small, domed compartment for holding citrus halves. Press down on the lever, and juice drains into a cup set below. If you're ready to move on to carrot juice, then you'll need a big, heavy juice extractor. These machines grind and then separate the juice from the pulp, seeds, and peels of denser fruits and vegetables.

Mechanical citrus press.

JULIENNING Refers to cutting food into long, thin strips, which in turn are called a "julienne." Vegetables are most commonly julienned, although meats and cheeses may be prepared this way, too.

HOW TO *Julienne*

1. Cut the vegetable, here a carrot, into pieces the length of the desired julienne strips.

2. Cut each piece lengthwise into slices as thick as the desired julienne.

3. Stack the slices and cut them lengthwise into the julienne.

Alternatively, you can use a mandoline or the julienne-cutting disk of a food processor, especially for large quantities.

Quick Tip

To julienne basil or other leaves, stack several together, roll up lengthwise into a compact bundle, and thinly slice crosswise. These thin ribbons are also called a chiffonade.

JUNIPER BERRY See SPICE.

i·j

Quick Tip

Thread shrimp to be grilled on 2 parallel soaked wooden skewers to keep the shrimp from twisting.

K

everything from kabob to kumquat

KABOB The term *kabob* comes from the Turkish *siskebabi,* or "spit-roasted meat." On streets throughout the Middle East, vendors sit by narrow metal braziers, fanning charcoal and tending to a multitude of skewers. In recipes that date back to ancient Greece, chunks of lamb absorb flavor from a mixture of olive oil, lemon juice, and herbs such as oregano, cumin, or rosemary. The marinated meat is threaded onto skewers, grilled, and then tucked into warm pita bread along with salad and pickles to make tasty sandwiches. At a Middle Eastern kabob house, the meat might be drizzled

Quick Tip

When grilling lamb kabobs, consider using twigs or branches of rosemary as fragrant skewers. Select sturdy, straight twigs at least 6 inches long. Strip off all leaves except for a tuft at one end. Use a kitchen knife to trim the other end into a point that can pierce the lamb cubes.

with paprika oil and served over broken pita with tomato and yogurt sauces.

While lamb is the traditional kabob meat, beef, veal, fish, chicken, vegetables, and even tofu also appear on skewers. If you prepare kabobs at home, remember always to leave a little space between the pieces to allow for flavorful browning. If packed together too tightly, the pieces will steam and cook unevenly. Flat, metal skewers hold chunks of food more securely in place and also conduct heat to aid in quick and even cooking. Some cooks like to serve kabobs that combine meat and vegetables. This can be done one of two ways: by either threading them together on the same skewer or slipping them onto separate skewers. The former method creates a wonderful exchange of flavors and textures, while the latter better allows for different cooking times and guarantees that the meat browns well. See also GRILLING.

Chicken and mushroom kabobs.

KAFFIR LIME A large, slightly pear-shaped citrus fruit grown throughout Southeast Asia, with a thick, bumpy, yellow-green peel and distinctive double leaves attached in pairs, end to end. The lime's juice is rarely used in the kitchen, but its highly aromatic peel and leaves add a fresh, tart flavor and flowery perfume to soups, curries, and grilled fish. The kaffir lime is traditionally used in the cuisines of cooks in Indonesia and Thailand.

Kaffir lime leaves.

Selecting You may find the fresh fruits or their leaves in a Southeast Asian market, but more common are frozen leaves and dried or powdered peel. Look in the freezer section for the leaves, packaged in small plastic bags. They are also available dried, like bay leaves. Dried peel, sold in small bags, offers more flavor than powdered.

Storing Keep the frozen leaves wrapped tightly in freezer-weight plastic in the freezer for up to 1 year and use as needed. The dried peel will keep for 3 to 4 years and the dried leaves for up to 1 year if sealed in an airtight container and kept away from heat and light.

Preparing When adding the leaves to a curry, sauce, or soup, partially tear the fresh and frozen leaves lengthwise to release more of their flavor. Or cut a fresh or frozen leaf crosswise into very thin strips to sprinkle over stir-fries, salads, or grilled fish or chicken. If using dried peel, soak it briefly in warm water first and then mash it before using.

KALE See GREENS, DARK.

KAMUT See GRAIN.

KASHA See GRAIN.

KETTLE See COOKWARE.

KIDNEY BEAN See BEAN, DRIED.

KIWIFRUIT A relatively recent import from New Zealand, kiwifruit was once called the Chinese gooseberry. The small, egg-shaped fruit has a distinctive fuzzy brown peel and lime green flesh with a sunburst pattern of tiny black seeds. Early on, kiwifruit's bright color, unique sweet-tart flavor, and exotic pedigree made it the darling of restaurant chefs. After appearing for years as garnishes on dramatic nouvelle cuisine plates, kiwifruits have now joined apples, bananas, and oranges as standard fare in fruit bowls and salads. They can also be puréed and used as a sauce for desserts or frozen in a sorbet.

Selecting Choose fruits heavy for their size and free of bruises. Like peaches, kiwifruits are ready for eating when they give to gentle pressure. Handle them with care, for they bruise easily. They are widely available year-round. California's crop peaks from winter to spring, while the New Zealand fruits appear in our markets in summer and fall.

Quick Tip

Kiwifruit contains the same powerful tenderizing enzymes as papaya. Rub or marinate meats with kiwifruit before grilling or roasting.

Storing Leave kiwifruits at room temperature until they soften. Accelerate the ripening by enclosing the fruits in a paper bag with an apple or a banana. Once ripe, keep kiwifruits in a plastic bag in the refrigerator for up to 1 week.

Preparing Peel off the fuzzy skin with a vegetable peeler, using a gentle sawing motion. Or, if the fruit is soft and ripe, simply cut it in half and scoop out the flesh in one piece with a spoon. Slice a kiwifruit crosswise to highlight the pattern of its seeds.

KNEADING Folding and pressing dough repeatedly, to develop the structure of bread and other baked goods. During kneading, the gluten in flour interlocks to create an elastic network that captures gases and stretches as the bread rises. The rhythmic, tactile nature of kneading accounts for much of the meditative mystique of bread baking.

HOW TO *Knead by Hand*

A bread dough may require 5 to 20 minutes of kneading, with most taking about 10 minutes. (Scones and biscuits should be kneaded only 5 to 10 turns.)

1. Gather the dough in a ball and place it on a hard, stationary work surface that has been lightly dusted with flour.
2. Flour your hands to prevent sticking. Push firmly into the center of the dough with the heel of your hand.

3. With your other hand, fold the dough in half toward you, and then rotate it a quarter turn.

4. Repeat, adding more flour as necessary to keep it from sticking and working it into the dough as you knead. Do not add more flour than necessary, using any measurements in the recipe as a guide. Continue until the dough is smooth and elastic, or as directed in the recipe.

Kneading Savvy

- Many bakers prefer kneading on a wood surface; it holds in warmth and creates a hospitable environment for the yeast.
- Use a dough scraper to gather and turn a particularly soft, moist dough.
- Some doughs such as brioche or rye breads are slightly sticky. To knead these, lightly coat your hands or the machine kneading attachments with oil.
- If you end up adding too much flour during kneading, sprinkle the dough lightly with warm water and continue kneading until the dough is soft again.
- Scrape off and discard any dried bits of flour that stick to your palm. If incorporated back into the dough, they will bake into hard, pebblelike lumps.
- Some recipes call for adding more flour during the kneading process. If a recipe calls for a range of flour amounts, mix the dough first with the smaller measure and then slowly incorporate more while you continue to knead. The dough should remain soft enough to work but not be wet or too sticky.
- A good test to determine if you have kneaded long enough is to push your fingertips into the dough. If the indentation springs back, the dough has been kneaded sufficiently. The dough should also have a satiny surface.
- To take a break, cover the dough and leave it for 5 to 10 minutes.

Many bakers are happy to let a machine knead the dough. Food processors come with a plastic kneading blade, and heavy-duty stand mixers have dough hooks. When using either, keep an eye on the dough. While it is almost impossible to overknead a bread dough by hand, it can happen easily in a machine. An overkneaded dough will suddenly turn gooey and inelastic.

See also BREAD; FLOUR.

k
—

KNIFE No good cook can accomplish much without this most fundamental and versatile of tools. With a well-made, keenly sharpened kitchen blade of the right size and shape, you can easily and efficiently do everything from paring a few small fruits for a salad or garnish to cutting enough for a big batch of jam, from removing bones from a single chicken breast to carving and serving a large holiday roast for a dozen family members.

Basic kitchen knives.

Knife Materials The sharpness of the knife is the secret to efficient, safe cutting. A dull blade cuts reluctantly, leading to excessive force, possible slippage, and a threat of injury. Knives with blades made of carbon steel, which could be honed to razor sharpness, were once the sharpest available; harder stainless steel simply could not hold an edge as well. That, however, is no longer the case, as today's best knives are made of carbon–stainless steel alloys that combine the best of both metals. They sharpen well and are easy to maintain, yet offer stainless steel's resistance to rusting or pitting from humidity or acidic ingredients.

For secure, durable construction and good balance, look for knives with full tangs—that is, those in which the metal of the blade visibly extends through the entire length of the handle. Most knife handles are made of wood, resin-impregnated wood, plastic, or rubber. Whatever the material, they should be securely attached to the tang, usually with visible metal rivets. In addition, the entire knife should feel well balanced in your hand.

Knives are sold in a wide variety of shapes and sizes, both individually and in sets that might include a sharpening steel and a knife block as well.

HOW TO *Use a Knife*

1. The knife handle should feel comfortable and secure in your grip.

2. Hold the food to be cut with your fingertips curled away from the knife blade.

Knife Storage and Maintenance Knives should never be stored loose in kitchen drawers or in receptacles with other utensils. Such practices can result in injuries or a dull or nicked blade. Always store your knives in a knife block, rack, or

Quick Tip

Some experienced cooks say that all they need in their kitchens are a chef's knife and a paring knife. Start with the best-quality examples of those you can find that fit your budget and feel good to you. Add others from the list as dictated by your cooking habits and by the kinds of foods you like to prepare.

special drawer insert containing slots for blades, or on a magnetic bar mounted somewhere safely away from casual reach.

To safeguard the edges of your blades, always work on a resilient surface made of wood or soft plastic, avoiding hard or slick surfaces. Never use the blade for scraping.

Wash knives individually and carefully by hand with hot, soapy water, drying them immediately. Never immerse them in a sinkful of water. Prolonged soaking can loosen handles, and the knives could also accidentally be picked up by their sharp blades. Do not clean them in dishwashers, which can dull the blade.

Before you put a knife away after use, it's a good idea to sharpen it briefly. The best home tool to use is a sharpening steel, available wherever good-quality knives are sold. Swipe each side of the cutting edge a few times across and along the length of the steel, alternating sides and holding the blade at about a 15-degree angle to the long metal rod. This process will realign the sharp cutting edge.

When your knives seem to be cutting at anything less than their best, and your sharpening efforts no longer seem to have an effect, check with the shop where you bought them or with a local butcher shop or food-store meat department. The personnel should be able to hone the blades to keen new edges or recommend a professional who can do it at a reasonable cost.

k
—

✥ Basic Knife Styles ✥

CHEF'S KNIFE A larger, evenly proportioned, tapered blade, of which the most useful usually averages 8 inches long. Most often used for chopping as well as for slicing, dicing, julienning, or mincing of ingredients.

PARING KNIFE A small, evenly proportioned, tapered blade usually 3 to 4 inches long. Used for paring and slicing fruits and vegetables and for chopping small quantities.

BREAD KNIFE A straight, serrated blade at least 8 inches long. The serrated edge cuts easily through the tough crusts of breads or through the delicate skins of tomatoes that might otherwise be crushed by an ordinary knife.

CARVING KNIFE A long, sturdy blade for slicing through and serving roasted meats such as beef or ham.

SLICING KNIFE A long, slender, fairly flexible blade, well adapted to carving roast poultry and whole fish.

UTILITY KNIFE Similar to a paring knife but slightly larger, with a blade 6 to 8 inches long. Used for peeling and slicing or for carving small cuts of meat.

BONING KNIFE About the length of a utility knife, this tool has a very narrow, curve-edged blade that maneuvers more easily around the bones of raw poultry or meat.

KOSHER Derived from *kashruth,* Hebrew for "proper" or "fit," *kosher* refers to food that accords with the strict dietary laws of Judaism. The laws originate from the Bible but have been expounded and refined by rabbinic legislation into a complex code on preparing and eating food.

Diverse Jewish communities have creatively adapted their local cuisines to the dietary laws, but the same basic tenets are followed throughout the world. Most of the guidelines concern meat, fish, and dairy, since all fruits, vegetables, and grains in their natural state are pareve, or neutral.

An Overview of Kosher Laws

MEAT An animal used for meat must both chew its cud and have split hooves. Beef, veal, lamb, and goat are kosher, but pork is not. Wild game is not kosher. Animals must be slaughtered quickly and painlessly. In kosher slaughtering, a specially trained butcher uses a sharp knife to kill the animal in a single stroke without stunning or maiming it. Afterward, the meat must be drained of all blood by salting. Because nerves and lobes of fat are also forbidden, large cuts of beef, veal, and lamb require the complete removal of these tissues.

NO MEAT WITH DAIRY The Bible's prohibition against boiling a calf in its mother's milk, out of respect for life and death, led to an absolute division between meat and dairy ingredients. The two cannot be mixed together in the same dish or even served within the same meal. The utensils, equipment, and dishware used to prepare and serve meat and dairy dishes must also be kept completely separate from each other. In addition, cheese cannot contain the coagulating agent rennet, an enzyme derived from an animal's stomach.

POULTRY Wild game birds, such as pheasants, are forbidden. Like meat, poultry must be slaughtered and prepared according to kosher law. It cannot mix with dairy.

FISH Only fish with fins and scales are allowed. Thus all shellfish such as shrimp, lobster, and squid are not kosher. Fish does not require special preparation, and some followers consider it neutral, meaning it can be served with meat or dairy.

WINE Because of their importance in the Sabbath meal, all wines, including brandies and other grape products, require strict rabbinic supervision during preparation.

KUGELHOPF PAN See BAKEWARE.

KUMQUAT No other member of the citrus fruit family may be popped into the mouth whole and chewed up, peel, seeds, and all. Resembling a miniature orange and measuring little more than 1½ inches long, this Asian native takes its name from the Chinese *kam kwat,* meaning "gold-orange." Two main species exist: the oval kumquat *(Fortunella margarita)* and the round kumquat *(F. japonica).* The tender peel is sweet and contrasts pleasantly with the slightly tart, juicy pulp within.

Selecting Choose kumquats that are firm and free of blemishes. Avoid fruit with wrinkled or dull skin. Available from November to June, kumquats are at their peak during the winter months.

Preparing In addition to being eaten whole (be sure to remove any stems first), kumquats are canned, candied, preserved in brandy, cooked in syrup, and used in jams, marmalades, and pickles. Try dipping fresh kumquats in chocolate, or slice them crosswise as a decoration for cakes, pastries, or other desserts.

everything from label terms to low-fat cooking

LABEL TERMS Mouthwatering photographs, colorful logos, and catchy names help push foods off grocery-store shelves and into our shopping carts. A stroll down any aisle will also uncover those food-company phrases designed to seduce increasingly health-conscious shoppers: "low fat," "fat free," "low sodium," "low cholesterol." To protect consumers and to standardize labels, the Food and Drug Administration (FDA) has strictly defined an entire vocabulary of health claims. The FDA has also staked out precious space on food packaging to provide accurate, easy-to-read information on the nutritional content of processed foods.

Nutrition Labeling Since the Nutrition Labeling and Education Act of 1990, most processed and prepackaged foods in the United States must display nutrient information. The Nutrition Facts panel, in a standard format, is now a familiar sight on the back of most bags, boxes, bottles, and cans in a grocery store.

All foods that have more than one ingredient must declare a complete list of ingredients, presented in descending order of their amount in the food. In addition to using consistent serving sizes, package labels must clearly state the amount of total calories, calories from fat, total fat, saturated fat, cholesterol, sodium, total carbohydrates, dietary fiber, sugars, protein, vitamin A, vitamin C, calcium, and iron. A second column of numbers, the Percent Daily Values, shows how the food's nutritional content compares to the National Academy of Science's recommended daily allowances (RDA). These guidelines suggest minimum quantities of certain nutrients that are necessary to good health, such as vitamins and minerals. It also suggests maximum amounts of nutrients that may be detrimental to one's health in large quantities, such as fat, cholesterol, and sodium.

What's in a Word? The FDA has strict definitions of certain descriptions that are commonly used on food labels.

FREE Used in conjunction with fat, saturated fat, cholesterol, sodium, sugars, or calories, indicates that the food contains none at all or only a "physiologically inconsequential" amount of the component.

LOW Regulated, along with "little," "few," and "low source of." Foods labeled "low" in any particular component can contain, per serving, no more than a designated amount of that component.

    Low Fat: 3 g fat
    Low Saturated Fat: 1 g saturated fat
    Low Sodium: 140 mg sodium
    Very Low Sodium: 35 mg sodium
    Low Cholesterol: 20 mg fat, with 2 g
      of saturated fat
    Low Calorie: 40 calories

LEAN Indicates meat, poultry, and seafood with less than 10 g fat, 4.5 g saturated fat, and 95 mg cholesterol per serving.

EXTRA LEAN Indicates meat, poultry, and seafood with less than 5 g fat, 2 g saturated fat, and 95 mg cholesterol per serving.

LIGHT Designates a food that contains two-thirds of the calories or half of the fat contained in the regular version of the food. However, it can also describe the color or texture of a food, not just its caloric or fat content.

FRESH Used for preservative-free foods that have never been heated or frozen.

Freshness Dating Milk and other dairy products have long been date-stamped, but now cereal, soda, beer, even batteries and film boast freshness dates. The sell-by date on food packaging indicates when the food is past its prime. Stores will pull a product from its shelves by the sell-by date. This does not mean the food has spoiled, but since there are no standards for freshness coding, the exact number of days the food can still be eaten varies. Milk tends to last no longer than 5 days after the sell-by date, while eggs can be good a month later. "Best if used by" recommends the last day for preparing or serving the food; it does not refer to selling or safety. In general, avoid buying food on or near its freshness date if you will not be using all of it immediately.

Some egg packers in the United States stamp cartons with a "Julian date," so-called for the Roman name of the calendar we all use, on the day they are packed. These dates begin with number 1 on January 1 and end with 365 on December 31. The eggs can be stored for up to 5 weeks beyond this date. It may take a little calculating to decipher the Julian date, but it's worth examining the carton for it.

LADLE See COOKING TOOLS.

LAMB Mild and tender lamb, the meat of a young sheep, is a far cry from the tough, gamy flesh of adult sheep, or mutton. Today, nothing helps define an upscale restaurant menu like a rack of lamb; and as kabobs, *tagine,* and *korma* enter our national lexicon, lamb is finding a new following in places far from the rugged terrain trod by the shepherds who originally dined on such dishes.

The lamb sold in supermarkets and at butcher shops is graded "prime" or "choice," United States Department of Agriculture (USDA) grades indicating quality and tenderness. For special occasions, splurge for the superior marbling (intermuscular fat that gives meat delicious flavor, tenderness, and juiciness) of prime meat. Spring lamb, sometimes called genuine lamb or simply lamb, specifies, by USDA regulation, a lamb less than a year old. The term once referred to the much-anticipated young, tender meat of the early season, but year-round production has largely diluted the term's significance. Most of the lamb that comes to market now is between 5 and 7 months old, thereby falling into the category of spring lamb. Baby lamb is 6 to 10 weeks old, and milk-fed or hothouse lambs drink a strict diet of milk only. Both have delicate flesh that cooks to a nearly white color. Lamb raised in the United States tends to be larger, meatier, and milder in flavor than lamb from Australia and New Zealand.

One-year-old, or yearling, lamb has darker, gamier flesh. Two-year-old mutton has an especially assertive flavor. Although many Europeans prefer the older, more flavorful mutton, it is nearly impossible to find in the United States and is increasingly difficult to locate even in Europe.

Selecting Fresh, young lamb will have rosy, fine-grained flesh and firm, white fat. Avoid cuts with yellowed fat. When buying trimmed racks, look for slender, pale bones.

Storing Store fresh lamb in the refrigerator for 2 to 3 days. Use ground lamb within 1 day of purchase. If sealed in heavy-duty plastic or placed in a zippered plastic freezer bag, lamb will keep in the freezer for 4 to 6 months. Do not freeze ground lamb or cooked lamb dishes for more than 3 months. Thaw frozen meat and cooked dishes slowly in the refrigerator.

❧ Lamb Glossary ❧

Lamb cuts.

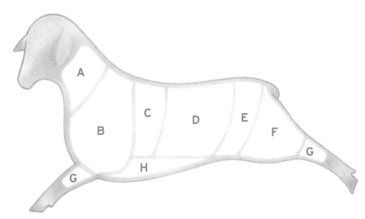

amb destined for the market is divided into large primal, or wholesale, cuts that butchers divide into smaller cuts, individual portions for cooking and serving. Understanding the recommended cooking techniques for primal cuts will help you decide what to buy for dinner.

NECK (A) Meat from the neck section, rich in flavor but tough, is most commonly sold as ground lamb for lamb burgers and casseroles.

SHOULDER (B) This large cut contains firm, flavorful meat streaked with a moderate amount of fat. It yields shoulder chops for grilling or broiling; cubes of stewing meat for braising and kabob meat for grilling; ground lamb; and convenient rolled boned roasts for roasting or braising.

RIB (C) With its tender, rich meat, the rib section is one of the better sections of the lamb. It yields rib chops for sautéing, broiling, or grilling, as well as the whole roast composed of the chops left intact, known as rack of lamb or, when formed into a circle, a crown roast. For

the best flavor, use high heat to roast, broil, or grill racks of lamb just until they are done medium-rare or medium.

Rib chop.

Rack of lamb.

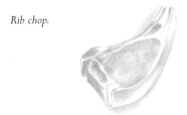

LOIN AND FLANK (D) Little-used muscles in the loin make for some of the most tender cuts of lamb. The loin is the source of compact tenderloin and loin chops, best broiled, grilled, or sautéed, as well as whole loin roasts, often boned and tied. Tough but flavorful flank meat is most often sold ground.

continued

Lamb Glossary, continued

SADDLE (E) The lamb's saddle portion contains the tender, well-marbled sirloin, which may be roasted whole or cut into sirloin chops and steaks for grilling, broiling, and sautéing. For grilled kabobs, chunks of boneless sirloin are ideal.

LEG (F) The firm, flavorful leg meat may be roasted whole or cut into cubes for kabobs or stew. If buying a bone-in leg, look for

a French-style or three-quarter leg of lamb, with its upper pelvic bones removed, allowing for easier carving. Boned, butterflied, and marinated, a small leg is succulent when grilled or broiled. See boning and butterflying instructions at right.

SHANKS (G) This is the lower, shin section of the leg. Hearty, economical, and full flavored, the tough shank meat requires long, gentle braising. A few hours of gentle simmering will result in rich, moist, spoon-tender meat. The small, lean foreshank is usually braised as an individual-serving cut. The hind shank may be cut into thick, crosswise slices, or it may be boned and cut into stew meat for slow braising.

BREAST (H) This thin cut runs along the belly. The fatty, flavorful meat, with its many tiny rib bones, may be boned and cooked whole by braising, which results in tender meat, or it may be cut up and braised or grilled as lamb riblets. The breast is also sold ground for making grilled lamb burgers.

HOW TO Bone and Butterfly a Leg of Lamb

1. If possible, start with a leg that is still cold from the refrigerator and thus firm. Gripping the surrounding white skin with a cloth or paper towel, tear away the outer membrane. With a thin, sharp boning knife, trim away tough skin and excess external fat.

2. The large, rounded hipbone at the broad end of the leg and the S-shaped aitchbone attached to it form the pelvic bone. Making short, shallow cuts with the tip of the knife, outline the pelvic bone.

3. Slowly cut deeper and scrape away the meat, uncovering the bone down to where it meets the leg's ball-and-socket joint. Cut the tendons attached to the pelvic bone and remove it.

4. Holding the shank bone at the narrow, pointed end of the leg, sever the tendons connecting the meat to the base of the bone. (At this point, the leg can be trussed and roasted as a French-style leg of lamb.) Keeping the knife angled close to the bone, cut the meat away from the shank bone down to its joint. Sever the tendons and remove the shank bone.

5. Cutting into the muscle, trace the leg bone with the tip of the knife. Ease the leg bone out, carefully scraping and cutting away the meat under it as well as the tendons at both ends. Remove the leg bone.

6. To butterfly the boned leg, holding the knife blade parallel to the work surface, cut into the thickest part of the leg meat from the center outward toward the edge to open it out in a flap. Take care not to cut completely through the meat. The result should be a large, flat piece of meat of relatively uniform thickness.

Preparing For the most succulent, tender meat, serve grilled, broiled, roasted, or panfried lamb slightly pink in color. If cooked to well done, the meat will be tough and dry, and it will take on a gamy flavor.

Quick Tip

Lamb fat has an assertive, unpleasant flavor. On roasts, leave no more than a ¼-inch-thick layer. Take care not to remove the thin, translucent membrane, which serves to hold the meat together.

Check the internal temperature of the meat with an instant-read thermometer. Since meat continues to cook and rise in temperature as it rests, remove the lamb when it registers 5° to 10°F less than the desired finished temperature.

Internal Temperatures for Lamb

Rare	125°F*
Medium-rare	130°F*
Medium	140°F*
Ground lamb	140°F*

*Although these temperatures yield what many cooks feel are the optimum taste and texture for these foods, they are lower than those suggested by the U.S. Food Safety and Inspection Service guidelines; see DONENESS.

See also CARVING; ROASTING.

LARD See FAT & OIL.

LARDING To insert strips of fat into a lean cut of meat to add flavor and moisture during dry-heat cooking, such as roasting. The strips are inserted using a special tool called a larding needle. For a simpler technique with similar effect, see BARDING.

LEAVENING The formation of gas bubbles in batters or doughs that will expand during cooking, to lighten baked goods and give them an airy texture. Chemical substances such as baking powder and baking soda react with liquids and heat to create carbon dioxide. Yeast also gives off carbon dioxide, a natural by-product created as the microorganisms digest sugar and starches. When whipped, the proteins of eggs, especially the whites, create a foamy network of tiny air bubbles. The gases created by all these leaveners will expand when heated, causing foods to rise. By the time the gases dissipate, the structure provided by the starches and proteins of other ingredients, such as flour and sugar, will have set into a solid that is stable enough to hold itself. For more details, see BAKING POWDER & BAKING SODA; YEAST.

LEEK Resembling a giant green onion, with its bright white stalk and its long, overlapping green leaves, the leek is the mildest member of the onion family. Native to the Mediterranean region and essential to classic French cuisine, leeks bring a hint of both garlic and onion to the dishes they flavor. They can serve as a component of *mirepoix,* a classic French seasoning mixture; meld with other ingredients such as potatoes in standard preparations like vichyssoise; or star in a gratin or quiche. Raw leeks can also be sliced and added to salads.

Selecting Choose smaller leeks with dark green leaves that are crisp, firm, and free of blemishes. Check to make sure that the roots are light in color and still pliable. Avoid darkened, dried roots and wrinkled, wilted leaves.

Storing Keep leeks in a plastic bag in the refrigerator for up to 5 days.

Preparing Because leeks grow partly underground, grit is often lodged between the layers of their leaves. Wash them thoroughly before cooking.

HOW TO *Clean Leeks*

1. Trim off the roots and the tough, dark green tops of the leaves. If the outer layer is wilted or discolored, peel it away and discard.
2. Quarter or halve the stalk lengthwise. If using the leek whole, leave the root end intact.

3. Rinse well under cold running water, separating the layers and rubbing the leaves to remove any silt between them.

4. If a recipe calls for sliced leeks, slice the white and lighter green parts crosswise.

LEGUME See BEAN, DRIED; BEAN, FRESH; PEA, FRESH.

LEMON Although too sour to eat alone, lemons are an important seasoning in the kitchen and appear at the table in an endless parade of dishes. This small but versatile fruit was cultivated in tropical regions of Asia and India for centuries before the Moors introduced it to Europe. In refreshing dishes such as Latin America's seviche and Southeast Asia's lemon beef, the acidity in the juice turns seafood and thinly sliced meat opaque and firm, much as cooking does. Lemon is also a popular flavoring for pastries, cakes, and other baked goods.

Many dishes benefit from a grating of fragrant lemon peel or a squeeze of its tart juice. Lemon serves as a healthful substitute for salt in low-sodium diets, and its juice is used in place of vinegar to add fruity zing to almost any dressing.

Quick Tip

Add lemon juice or oil at the end of cooking for the freshest flavor.

Selecting Choose lemons heavy for their size and free of blemishes or soft spots. Lemons with smooth, glossy rinds offer the most juice, but buy lemons with thick, bumpy skin only when you need their zest. Although available year-round, lemons peak during the winter months.

Fresh lemons are so widely available that it shouldn't be difficult to avoid commercially packaged lemon juices, whether in glass bottles or in faux lemons fashioned out of squeezable plastic. The fresh will always supply a better flavor. In an emergency, frozen pure lemon juice is a good substitute. Look for it in the freezer section next to juice concentrates, thaw it, and store it in the refrigerator for up to a month. Natural lemon oil is another way to add lemon flavor to recipes. To preserve its flavor, store the oil in the refrigerator for up to 2 years.

Quick Bite

The Meyer lemon, a hybrid, was discovered by a man named Frank Meyer in 1908. Although the exact derivation of the Meyer lemon is disputed, many believe it is a cross between a lemon and a mandarin orange, as hinted at by its rounder shape, yellow-orange color, sweeter flavor, and flowery fragrance. Its peak season is November to May.

Storing Lemons can stay at room temperature for around 1 week. For longer storage, up to 1 month, keep them in plastic bags in the refrigerator.

Putting the Squeeze on Lemons

Like most citrus fruits, lemons release their juice more readily if you try the following:

■ Store them at room temperature. If a lemon is still cold from the refrigerator, microwave it on High for 20 seconds.

■ Roll them firmly against a hard, flat surface or between your palms to crush some of their inner membranes.

■ Use a reamer. Its fluted ribs will extract every last drop. Take care not to rub too hard, though, or you will crush the pith and infuse the juice with some of its bitterness. A fork inserted into the cut surface of the lemon then rotated back and forth will work almost as well as a reamer.

If you have extra lemons, squeeze their juice and freeze it in an ice cube tray. Once hardened, transfer the lemon juice cubes to a plastic bag and add as needed during cooking.

See also ACID; DISCOLORING; JUICING; ZESTING.

LEMONGRASS An aromatic herb used throughout Southeast Asia, lemongrass flavors soups, curries, and grilled dishes from Myanmar to Malaysia. Resembling a green onion in shape, lemongrass has long, thin, gray-green leaves that meet and overlap along a woody, ivory-colored stem with bits of pale pink coloration.

Selecting Once found only in Asian markets, fresh lemongrass is now widely available in supermarkets. Look for firm stalks with no sign of fading or drying. In Asian stores, you can find small containers of finely minced lemongrass in the refrigerator or freezer sections. The herb is also available as dried shreds or a powder; avoid both forms, as they have none of the herb's fresh, lemony aroma. Lemongrass is traditionally paired in Asia with chicken, pork, seafood, tofu, tomatoes, and chiles, and is used in preparations ranging from soups to stir-fries to stews. The leaves make a refreshing infused tea.

Quick Tip

Simmer finely chopped lemongrass in equal parts sugar and water to make a fragrant syrup with an appealing lemony flavor. Store in an airtight container in the refrigerator. Uses include sweetening iced tea, drizzling over orange slices, glazing grilled chicken, and poaching fruit.

Storing Trim away the green leaves and refrigerate lemongrass in a plastic bag for up to 2 weeks. For convenient use, shred lemongrass stalks in a food processor or blender, and then freeze in a zippered plastic freezer bag for up to 6 months.

Preparing Only the pale bottom part of the stalk is used in cooking. Crush the stalk with a pestle or the side of a knife blade before chopping. Since its fibers are tough, lemongrass needs to be minced finely or removed from a dish before serving, much like a bay leaf. To infuse stock, slice lemongrass thinly on a sharp diagonal or cut it into 2-inch lengths and pound lightly. Both methods will help release more of the herb's flavor, while the latter allows a more easy removal of the pieces later.

LEMON VERBENA See HERB.

LENTIL See BEAN, DRIED.

LETTUCE See GREENS, SALAD.

LICHEE Or lichi. See LITCHI.

LILY BUD Also called golden needle or, mistakenly, tiger lily bud, lily bud is the dried, unopened blossom of the Chinese lily. Long, thin, golden, and earthy in flavor, lily buds measure 2 to 3 inches in length and appear 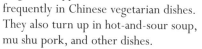 frequently in Chinese vegetarian dishes. They also turn up in hot-and-sour soup, mu shu pork, and other dishes.

Selecting Lily buds should be a rich burnished gold and still soft and pliable. Pass up any that are dark and brittle. Look for lily buds in Asian markets, packaged in 4- or 8-ounce plastic bags.

Storing Transfer the buds to an airtight, glass jar and store in a cool, dark place for up to 6 months.

Preparing Before cooking, soak the dried lily buds in warm water for about 20 minutes until softened. Do not leave them longer, or they may lose flavor. Drain and then trim off the hard stems. Knot the buds at their centers, individually or in small bundles, to keep them intact in stir-fries and braises. For delicate soups, tear the buds lengthwise into 3 or 4 shreds. This will also release more of their flavor.

LIMA BEAN See BEAN, DRIED; BEAN, FRESH.

LIME Smaller and more delicate than lemons, their yellow-skinned cousins, limes are tart with a hint of sweetness. They are an essential ingredient in the cuisines of Southeast Asia, Latin America, Africa, the West Indies, and the Pacific Islands. Lime can be used in place of lemon in nearly any recipe. Twist a bit of the zest into cocktails or add thin slices to a summery punch. In tropical countries, fresh lime juice deepens the flavor of sweet, musky fruits like papaya and guava. Lime pickles accompany Indian curries, fresh lime juice infuses Cuban chicken soup, and lime wedges accompany Mexican beer.

Familiar grocery store limes are Persian limes. Smaller, rounder Key limes grow in southern Florida. With thin, leathery skin and an abundance of seeds, highly tart Key limes lend their name to the famous pie. They appear fresh only occasionally in specialty produce markets, but look for good-quality bottled Key lime juice in gourmet shops. They are also known as the Mexican or West Indian lime.

Key lime.

Selecting Buy smooth, glossy limes that are plump and heavy for their size. Avoid any with dull skin or soft spots. Pick Persian limes with dark green rind. Fully ripe Key limes have a yellowish rind and green flesh. Although available year-round, fresh limes peak from May to October.

Quick Tip

Look for small bottles of natural lime oil. Add a few drops to any recipe for instant lime fragrance and flavor.

Storing Limes can be stored at room temperature for 3 to 5 days. More perishable than lemons, limes fare better in a plastic bag in the refrigerator. Exposure to light and air will rapidly diminish the amount and tartness of their juice. Store lime oil in the refrigerator.

Preparing See LEMON for basic information on juicing citrus fruits.

Quick Tip

Bartenders use a lemon stripper to get the perfect citrus zest twists that grace cocktails.

See also JUICING; KAFFIR LIME; LEMON; ZESTING.

LIQUEUR See page 270.

LIQUID INGREDIENTS See MEASURING; WET INGREDIENTS.

LITCHI Also spelled lichi, lichee, and lychee. With pearly white, translucent flesh encased in a roughly textured, bright red shell, this fragrant tropical fruit is a luxury even in its native land of southern China. In Western countries, litchis are most commonly found packed in syrup. When dried, the fruit shrivels and looks and tastes similar to a raisin. Pour canned litchis over a shallow dish of cracked ice for a refreshing, simple dessert, or over vanilla or coconut ice cream.

Selecting Fresh litchis appear in Asian markets in late spring to early summer.

Fresh litchis.

Look for fresh fruit with shells that are still rosy red or pink. Hardened, brownish fruits are old, dry, and flavorless. Litchis are also available canned in syrup, dried and packaged in plastic bags, or candied.

Canned litchis.

Look for them in Asian markets and well-stocked supermarkets.

Storing Fresh, whole litchis will keep in a plastic bag in the refrigerator for up to 2 weeks. Store canned or dried litchis in a cool, dark place for up to 2 years.

Preparing If you are lucky enough to find fresh litchis, enjoy them as a dessert on their own. With a paring knife, split open the thin shell. You can scoop out the flesh with a small spoon, pinching or cutting away the smooth seed at the center.

Quick Tip

To add a tropical twist to a glass of iced tea, drop in a whole canned litchi and stir in a spoonful of its syrup.

Liqueur

Often called crèmes, liqueurs are spirits flavored by natural extracts, essential oils, pure fruit syrups, sugar syrups, or, in the case of liqueurs of lesser quality, chemical extracts.

The flavors can come from fruits, nuts, spices, herbs, coffee, or chocolate.

A liqueur may be sipped in small quantity as an after-dinner drink or used to flavor desserts and sauces. Sometimes a fruit brandy, or eau-de-vie, may be served as a liqueur; see SPIRITS.

Cooking with Liqueurs Take care not to add too much liqueur to a dish, for the concentrated sweet flavor can easily

Liqueur Flavors

FLAVOR	LIQUEUR
Almond	amaretto; crème d'amandes; crème de noyaux; Noyau de Poissy
Anise	anisette; ouzo; pastis; Pernod; sambuca
Apricot	crème d'abricot; Abricotine; Apry
Banana	crème de banane
Cherry	crème de cerise; maraschino (sweet); Cherry Rocher; Peter Heering; Wishniac
Chocolate	crème de cacao; Chocolat Suisse; Chéri-Suisse (chocolate-cherry); Vandermint (chocolate-mint); Sabra (chocolate-orange)
Coffee	Kahlúa; Kona; Pasha; Tía Maria
Currant, black	crème de cassis
Hazelnut	Frangelico
Herbs & Flowers	Chartreuse (herbs); Chartreuse verte (herbs); Bénédictine (herbs); Liquore Galliano (herbs); crème de rose (rose); crème de violette (violet)
Melon	Midori
Orange	Cointreau; Curaçao; Grand Marnier; mandarine; Triple Sec
Pear	Birnengeist
Peppermint	crème de menthe; peppermint schnapps
Pineapple	crème d'ananas
Plum	prunelle; sloe gin
Vanilla	crème de vanille
Walnut	nocello; nocino

become cloying. The alcohol level of liqueurs tends to be relatively high, most fall between 50 and 100 proof, and their flavors are intense. As a general guideline, add no more than 2 tablespoons of liqueur to every 1 cup of sauce or batter. Remove a pan from the heat before stirring in a liqueur, and avoid letting the mixture sit too long before serving, since the flavors of liqueurs dissipate quickly when exposed to heat and air.

Pair liqueurs with dishes to accentuate the same flavor, such as adding almond-flavored amaretto to whipped cream that you plan to serve with an almond-crust tart; or to provide a pleasing complement to another ingredient, such as tart orange-flavored Grand Marnier with sweet strawberries. Food that combines well with a certain fruit will also match a liqueur derived from that same fruit, such as duck and cherries with kirsch. When soaking dried fruit for a recipe, try replacing the water or fruit juice with a related or contrasting liqueur, such as cherries in maraschino or dried cranberries in orange-flavored Cointreau. Liqueurs are also a nice touch in cream fillings, soufflés, ice creams, fruit compotes, and dessert sauces. Pour a little into hot drinks like hot chocolate or coffee.

Quick Bite

Bénédictine, which was developed in 1510 by Dom Bernardo Vincelli, a monk resident in the French Abbey of Fécamp, is believed to be the world's oldest liqueur. He reportedly poured his "elixir" for the resident monks, who sipped it as a cure for fatigue.

See also SPIRITS.

LOAF PAN See BAKEWARE.

LOBSTER On a candlelit table or in a clambake on the beach, a bright orange lobster is one of the undisputed icons of special occasions. Although once so plentiful that American colonists dismissed it as food for the poor, lobster now demands royal treatment in upscale restaurants and commands equally majestic prices.

Lobsters can be divided into two broad categories: clawed lobsters and spiny lobsters. Clawed lobsters are what most of us think of when we think "lobster." This includes orange and black American lobsters, also called Maine lobsters, which live in

American lobster.

the cold waters off Newfoundland and New England. (Orange lobsters are blue-black when uncooked, turning orange when cooked.) They appear at market from July through November. Although similar to the American lobster, blue-black European lobsters are now scarce and extremely expensive. Some believe European lobsters have more delicate flavor and texture, but others can detect no significant difference.

Spiny lobsters, also known as rock lobsters or *langoustes,* lack large claws but are easily recognized by their extra-long antennae and the thin spines covering their hard shell. Cold-water spiny lobsters found near South Africa and Australia boast better quality meat than the warm-water species from Florida and the Caribbean. California spiny lobsters are rarely found beyond the markets of southern California and western Mexico. Actually sea-dwelling crayfish, live spiny lobsters arrive only at local markets from August to March. Their tails, however, with flesh slightly tougher and not as sweet as that of the American lobster, are widely available frozen.

Although New England purists insist that only drawn butter and corn should appear next to lobster on the dinner table, the sweet, rich flavor of this popular crustacean pairs well with a wide range of flavors, from dill, tarragon, basil, parsley, and saffron to mustard, lemongrass, and lime. Avocado, cucumber, citrus fruits, white wine, brandy, cream, coconut milk, chiles, and eggs are just a handful of the ingredients that are often matched with lobster.

Selecting When buying a live lobster, choose one that proves especially feisty. Hold a lobster up, grasping its sides safely behind its claws, to check that it quickly snaps its tail tightly under its body. Any that are sluggish and apathetic have been in the tank too long. Captured lobsters are not fed, so their meat will shrink away with time. Likewise, when purchasing a whole cooked lobster, make sure that its tail curls, an indication that it was still alive when it was dropped into the cooking pot.

A lively debate rages between those who prefer the firmer flesh of male clawed lobsters and those who like the sweet flesh of females. Also hotly contested are the merits of succulent 1-pound "chicken" lobsters versus fleshy 3-pound "jumbos." Those who have braved 10-pounders swear that the giants are just as sweet and tender. Most lobsters sold at markets fall between 1¼ and 2 pounds.

Quick Tip

How to subdue live lobsters: Place them in the freezer for 5 to 10 minutes before cooking.

He or She?

- Male lobsters have somewhat larger claws, and female lobsters grow slightly wider tails.
- Females have thin, soft, feathery swimmerets on the underside of their tails; these will later hold their eggs. Male lobsters have long, hard, spiky swimmerets.
- The red roe inside a female lobster may be a delicacy, but strict laws require that all females with eggs on their swimmerets be returned to the water.

Although missing one or both claws, less expensive "culls" taste just as good in soups, stews, or salads. If you lack a reliable local source for live lobsters, numerous companies can ship them to you overnight. Frozen lobster tails, usually from spiny lobsters, and already cooked whole lobsters can give you a head start on recipes.

Quick Tip

Lobster tails will curl during cooking. For a straight tail, stretch a live lobster flat and tie it firmly to a wooden spoon, ruler, or stick before boiling or steaming. If cooking the tail only, insert a skewer just beneath the shell.

Storing If not cooking them immediately, cover live lobsters with a damp cloth or wet newspaper, place them in a small cardboard box or large, heavy paper bag, and refrigerate. Although best if prepared as soon as possible after purchase, you can keep them in the refrigerator for up to 2 days, if needed. Expect the quality of the meat to diminish significantly with each day. Leave the rubber bands on in order to prevent mishaps with snapping claws. Do not immerse lobsters in tap water, for they will quickly die. Uncooked tails can be kept in the freezer in a zippered plastic freezer bag for 3 to 4 months, but cooked lobster will turn mushy and flavorless if frozen.

HOW TO *Halve and Clean Lobster*

These steps can be followed to prepare an uncooked lobster for grilling, roasting, or broiling.

1. If you have purchased a live lobster, plunge it into boiling water for about 30 seconds and then rinse it under cold water to halt the cooking. (If it is already cooked, ignore this step.) Alternatively, set the lobster on a firm surface and securely hold the lobster's tail with a folded cloth to prevent slipping. Insert the tip of a large chef's knife straight down through the back of the lobster to the board, piercing the cross mark in the area between the first and second pairs of thin legs.
2. Cut the lobster's head in half lengthwise. If desired, hold an uncooked lobster over a bowl to catch the juices.

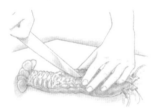

3. Turn the lobster around, hold its head, and cut the rest of the lobster sharply in half.
4. Lift away and discard the sand sac near the head. Using the tip of the knife, carefully remove the gray intestinal vein that runs along the lobster's back.
5. With a small spoon, scoop out the liver, known as the tomalley, which will be black if uncooked and green if cooked, and any coral, or eggs, which will be black if uncooked and bright red if cooked. Reserve both for sauce as needed.

6. For a neater look, cut away the legs and claws. Crack claws in a few places with a lobster cracker or mallet, so diners can easily reach the meat inside.

7. Before serving cooked lobsters, remove the pale, feathery gills along the sides of the lobster's body. If desired, loosen the cooked tail meat from its shell for easier eating. If you have them, provide lobster picks, small two-pronged forks designed specifically for the purpose.

HOW TO *Boil Lobster*

Serve boiled lobster with a dipping sauce such as melted butter, tarragon mayonnaise, chile-lime sauce, extra-virgin olive oil and lemon juice, or melted butter flavored with a touch of vanilla.

1. Bring a large pot of water to a full boil. To ensure quick cooking, use 1 gallon for 1 lobster; add 1 quart for each additional lobster.
2. Drop a live lobster in headfirst, taking care to avoid any splashing from its tail. Once the water returns to a boil, reduce the heat to maintain a gentle simmer.
3. Cook a lobster 8 minutes for the first pound plus 2 minutes for each additional ¼ pound. Remove with tongs and let the lobster cool slightly before serving.

Quick Tip

Traditionally, lobsters are boiled, but they can be steamed over 1 to 2 inches of water.

HOW TO *Remove Meat from Cooked Lobsters*

1. Drain any residual water from boiled or steamed lobsters by making a small cut between the eyes on the lobster head. Hold the lobster by its tail over a sink to drain the excess cooking liquid from underneath the shell.
2. Firmly twist off the claws from the body. With a lobster cracker or mallet, break the hard shell of each claw in several places. Pull away the shell pieces, taking care not to damage the claw meat if a recipe calls for it to be left whole.
3. Insert the tip of a large, sharp, sturdy knife into the point where the tail and body sections meet, and carefully cut lengthwise through the tail. Turn the lobster around and continue to cut from the center through the head, cutting the lobster into 2 equal halves.
4. Pull out and discard the black vein that runs the length of the body meat, as well as the small sand sac at the base of the head. Remove the white meat from the shell. If you like, reserve the green tomalley, or liver, and any bright red roe, which can be added to lobster dishes for extra flavor.
5. Firmly grasp the fins of a tail half with one hand. With the other, firmly pull out the tail meat in a single piece, using a fork to pry it loose if needed. Repeat with the other tail half.

What to Do with All Those Shells

- Simmer them with aromatics and herbs to make a rich lobster stock.
- Crush the shells and heat gently with butter for 15 minutes. Ladle through a fine-mesh strainer, pressing down to extract as much flavor as possible. Add small amounts of the intensely flavored butter to sauces, spread on sandwiches, or use to top fish. Store covered in the refrigerator for up to 1 month or freeze for up to 1 year.

LOGANBERRY See BERRY.

LOTUS While its spectacular blossoms appear in water gardens from India to Japan, other parts of the lotus plant play flavorful roles in the kitchen.

Lotus leaf.

Dried and used as wrappers, the large leaves lend their subtle fragrance and flavor to small bundles of savory and sweet fillings to be steamed. The ivory-colored roots have a crisp texture and sweet flavor. Thin slices are excellent stir-fried or deep-fried as tempura, while thick ones are good braised with other vegetables. Lotus seeds are one of the celebrated "eight treasures" of Chinese dishes, adding their nutty flavor to many festive preparations.

Selecting Look for lotus in Asian markets or in the specialty produce section of major supermarkets. When selecting lotus roots, look for smooth, unblemished specimens and check at the trimmed ends for flesh that is still pale and moist. They may also be found cut in slices and vacuum packed in heavy plastic bags. Both the leaves and the pale, round seeds are available dried and packaged. Lotus seeds are also available canned or in bulk.

Storing Keep whole roots in the vegetable bin of the refrigerator for no longer than 1 week. Once cut or peeled, the unused portion should be immersed in lightly acidulated water to prevent darkening (see DISCOLORING) and returned to the refrigerator for up to 2 days. The dried leaves and seeds will keep indefinitely in an airtight container in a cool, dark place. Drain the canned seeds, transfer them to a container, add fresh water to immerse them completely, cover, and refrigerate them for up to 5 days.

Preparing Snap off whole sections of lotus root as needed. Peel the streaked, buff-colored skin with a vegetable peeler. Cut the roots crosswise into thick or thin slices according to a recipe, keeping them in acidulated water to prevent browning. Soften the dried leaves in boiling water. To prepare the seeds for cooking, drain them, remove the bitter green bud at their center, and boil until softened.

LOW-FAT COOKING In recent years, low-fat cooking has become enormously popular. Cookbooks and magazines promoting ways to cut fat and calories abound; supermarket shelves bulge with reduced-fat and fat-free products; an ever-growing list of restaurants are putting heart-safe or low-fat dishes on their menus; and even fast-food chains, long-standing bastions of high-fat foods, have cut the fat by offering such healthful alternatives as grilled chicken sandwiches and salad bars.

Quick Tip

Nonfat or reduced-fat products such as sour cream, cream cheese, cottage cheese, and mayonnaise don't always work in a recipe the way their regular counterparts do. Rather than simply substituting, seek out recipes specifically created for these products.

Low-fat cooking experts often disagree on how much protein and total fat to consume daily, and self-proclaimed gurus promising rapid weight loss if you follow a certain diet are everywhere. But a few commonsense guidelines on how to trim fat from cooking have emerged from the proliferation of literature and research.

Unless your doctor tells you otherwise, do not try to eliminate all the fat from your cooking. Fat contributes to flavor, texture, and overall satisfaction. If you don't feel satisfied, you might eat more. When you want a smear of cream cheese on a bagel or a dollop of mayonnaise on a tomato, go for the real thing if doctor's orders allow. Eat in moderation and make the food you eat enjoyable.

Ways to Reduce the Fat

- Use cooking spray in place of liquid cooking oil to grease pans.
- Use nonstick cookware.
- Steam, broil, grill, or bake food to avoid the fat used for sautéing and frying.
- Rely on chicken and beef stock, wine, and water to moisten and baste foods while they cook, instead of additional oil or butter.
- Use herbs and spices to flavor foods, instead of additional butter or cream.
- Learn about fat-cutting techniques such as replacing whole eggs with egg whites and using applesauce and puréed prunes in baked products in place of some of the butter.
- Skin poultry before or after cooking.
- Use water-packed tuna instead of the oil-packed version.
- Use ground turkey breast instead of ground beef.
- Trim meat and poultry of external fat before cooking.
- Substitute flavorful fat-free spreads such as jams, jellies, chutneys, or mustards for butter or margarine.

LYCHEE See LITCHI.

*everything from macerating
to mustard*

m

MACADAMIA NUT See NUT.

MACE See SPICE.

MACERATING To soak fruit in juice, sugar, liqueur, or other flavoring and tenderizing mediums. Although similar to marinating, macerating applies specifically to fruit. To meld fruit flavors, let them soak together. On the other hand, to keep delicate flavors distinct, to prevent bleeding of bright colors, or to protect soft fruits from the crush of heavier, firmer fruits, soak each fruit separately. Always use a nonreactive bowl, as the acid in fruits can react with certain metals to create "off" flavors.

MÂCHE See GREENS, SALAD.

MADELEINE PAN See BAKEWARE.

MALT Malt is produced by first allowing soaked barley grains to germinate and then drying, roasting, and grinding them to a powder. When malt is mentioned, most of us think of ice cream and chocolate syrup blended with it into a frosty treat. But malt plays a quiet, yet important, role in foods from vinegar to beer to bagels.

Pure malt powder is used in the production of beer and whiskey and in bread making to boost yeast growth; improve flavor, structure, and crust color; and extend shelf life. Malted milk powder is a mixture of malt sugar and powdered milk. Malt syrup can replace honey or maple syrup, resulting in a subtler flavor and lighter color.

MANDARIN ORANGE Named after officials in the Chinese emperors' courts who wore orange robes and headpieces with distinctive buttons resembling the fruit. Mandarin oranges are less acidic and smaller than oranges, with a slightly flattened shape. They are distinguished by delicate strands of pith that lie beneath thin, loose skins. Their classification, *Citrus reticulata,* refers to this netlike filigree that encloses the sweet, juicy segments.

In the United States, mandarin oranges are commonly known as tangerines, although in the citrus trade this term actually designates specific varieties with a darker, red-orange peel. Mandarins grown in Florida, where they were first introduced from Tangier, Morocco, by way of Spain, generally carry the name *tangerine*. In Great Britain, *tangerine* identifies mandarin varieties from the Mediterranean region that are pale in color and mild in flavor.

Popular members of the whole mandarin group include the sweet Satsuma from Japan; the smooth, juicy Clementines from Algeria, Spain, and France; the ubiquitous red-orange Dancy tangerine from Florida; and the large, knobbly-skinned King mandarin from Southeast Asia. Tangors, such as the tart Temple orange, are a hybrid of mandarins and oranges. Tangelos result from a cross between a mandarin and a pomelo or grapefruit. The honey-flavored Minneola, with its distinctive stem-end neck, is perhaps the most recognized of the tangelos.

Easy to peel, mandarin oranges make appealing snacks for eating out of hand. While many do have seeds, the most common ones in markets tend to have few or no seeds. As festive in appearance as they are delicious, they are traditionally part of the celebrations at Christmas and Chinese New Year. See also ORANGE.

Selecting Choose fruits that are deep in color, heavy for their size, and free of dull or soft spots. Although some will have loose skins, avoid those that appear overly bumpy or puffy, for they are most probably old and overripe. Although the specific peak months vary according to variety and origin, mandarin oranges are generally at their best from November to March. They are also available in cans, their segments preserved in sugar syrup.

Storing Display colorful mandarin oranges at room temperature for up to 1 week. For longer storage of up to 1 month, keep them in a plastic bag in the refrigerator. Store canned segments in a cool, dry place for up to 2 years; once opened, they should be transferred to a nonreactive container and refrigerated for up to 1 week.

Preparing Although at their best simply eaten out of hand, mandarin oranges also are good in light sauces for poultry, fish, and pork, infusing them with subtle citrus flavor. They should be added at the end of cooking and just heated through to preserve their delicate flavor.

MANDOLINE A flat, rectangular tool ideal for cutting food quickly and easily. Mandolines usually come with an assortment of smooth and corrugated blades, so food can be sliced, julienned, or

waffle-cut. The advantages of using a mandoline are precision and regularity. It takes time to acquire the knife skills to transform a mountain of potatoes into the uniform pieces needed to make *frites* or into paper-thin slices for chips, or to trim a knobby celery root into perfect julienne strips, but once armed with a mandoline, even a novice cook can easily cut vegetables like a seasoned cooking professional.

> ### Quick Tip
> A mandoline makes short work of thinly slicing a dozen zucchini, but hang on to your knife for cutting that half carrot or single shallot. The minutes saved cutting with a mandoline may not make up for the time spent assembling and washing the tool and its blades.

> ### Quick Bite
> The strumming motion of food on the mandoline reputedly inspired the tool's name.

Mandolines are available in a variety of designs. Some must be steadied by hand or placed over a bowl, while others have foldaway legs that permit you to stand them up at an ergonomic angle. You can choose a high-quality stainless-steel commercial model or a simpler plastic version. Look for one with a hand guard that keeps your fingers clear of the cutting edge as you move the ingredient across the extremely sharp mandoline blade.

MANGO This highly aromatic fruit was first cultivated in India. Now, mangoes are among the most commonly eaten fresh fruits in the world. Diced ripe mangoes are excellent in chutney to accompany pork, chicken, or fish. Mangoes complement coconut, pineapple, raspberries, and smoked chicken; puréed mango, strained and mixed with lime juice, makes a delectable dessert sauce for cakes, ice cream, or pastries. The brightly flavored mango chutneys of India depend on underripe green fruits, and the crisp, unripe fruit is shredded for popular salads in Southeast Asia.

Selecting The best mangoes are in the markets from May through September, but fresh fruits are available all year long, since different varieties are imported from around the world. When shopping for ripe mangoes, choose ones that emit a full aroma at their stem end, give slightly to gentle pressure, and have perfectly smooth skin. Mangoes will also ripen after purchase, although those picked too early will be particularly fibrous near the pit. Depending on the variety, they can range in color from all green to all red, with blushes of every shade of yellow and orange in between. Those with yellow in their skin tend to be the most flavorful, but do not buy any that are wrinkled or have soft spots. Most fruits sold in supermarkets weigh about ¾ pound each. For convenience, look for already peeled and cut mangoes packaged in jars or in plastic containers in the refrigerated section of the produce aisle.

Mango nectar, mango purée, and dried mango spears are available in health-food stores, supermarkets, and Indian markets.

Storing Keep not-quite-ripe mangoes at room temperature for a few days until ripened. You can place them inside a paper bag to speed up the ripening process. Like other tropical fruits, mangoes do not fare well when exposed to cold temperatures for long periods of time. After they are ripe, refrigerate them for no more than 2 or 3 days—or preferably not at all. Puréed mangoes can be frozen for up to 1 year. Keep unopened cans of mango nectar in a cool, dry place, but refrigerate them after opening. Store dried mango in an airtight container in the refrigerator for up to 6 months.

Preparing Always peel the fruit before serving. Slit the thick, sometimes leathery skin with a knife tip and pull it off in strips.

Caution!

Because the mango is a distant cousin of poison oak and poison ivy, some people will have allergic reactions to its skin. If you have any irritation or simply suspect that you are allergic, use gloves while peeling mangoes. Be sure to remove all of the skin before serving.

HOW TO *Eat a Mango*

In the tropics, where mangoes are as common as apples are in Washington, the locals have developed distinctive ways to eat the fruits. If you try either of the following methods, be prepared for a bit of a mess.

1. Score the skin so the fruit can be partially peeled, and then eat the mango similar to the manner in which one consumes a banana.
2. Roll an unpeeled ripe mango on a tabletop so the pulp almost liquefies, and then suck the pulp out of the stem end using a straw.

HOW TO *Cut a Mango*

The large, flat pit at the center of a mango can present a challenge when slicing and dicing the fruit.

1. Peel the mango.
2. Stand the mango up on one of its narrow edges, with the stem end pointing toward you.
3. With a large, sharp knife, cut down about 1 inch to one side of the stem, just grazing the side of the pit. You should have 1 large mango "half." Repeat with the other side of the fruit.
4. Place the mango halves cut side down on the cutting board and slice as desired.
5. Trim off the flesh left encircling the pit.

HOW TO *Make Quick Mango Cubes*
1. With the peel still on, cut the mango in halves as above.
2. Following a crisscross grid pattern, carefully score the cut side of the mango halves just down to the skin. Do not pierce the skin.

3. Using your thumbs to press against the skin side, turn the halves inside out. The cubes of mango will pop out.

4. Cut across the bottom of the cubes, along the peel, to release the cubes. Trim off the flesh left encircling the pit.

Quick Bite

In India, where mangoes are revered for their sweetness, versatility, and abundance, giving a basket of the fruit is a gesture of friendship.

MAPLE SYRUP Pure maple syrup is made from the boiled sap of the sugar maple tree. The caramel-colored, maple-flavored corn syrup commonly drizzled on waffles and pancakes and called "pancake syrup" has no relation to the real thing. In early spring, throughout Canada and the northern United States, most notably in New York and New England, taps for collecting sap appear on the trunks of maple

Making the Grade

GRADE A Grade A Light or Fancy, sometimes called Grade AA, is clear gold and has a wonderfully subtle flavor. The most expensive of the maple syrups, its delicate character does not hold up in cooking. It is usually made into maple candies and is a favorite topping for pancakes, waffles, and ice cream. Grade A Medium is also used as a topping for the same familiar breakfast items and ice cream. Dedicated maple-syrup lovers will buy Grade A Dark, which is similar to Grade B.
GRADE B This maple syrup is produced only in Vermont. Preferred by some for its depth of flavor and pronounced caramel notes, others find it rather too strong and dark.
GRADE C Develops a robust, molasses-like flavor. Used primarily in making commercial table syrups.

trees. Sugaring season, as it is called, lasts for a month or so, as long as the nights are cold and the days are warm enough to get the sap rising. A long boiling reduces the clear, fresh sap to a rich, aromatic, amber syrup. Good-quality maple syrup will taste of vanilla and caramel. To make a single gallon of maple syrup, up to 40 gallons of fresh sap must be boiled down.
Selecting Blended maple syrups contain anywhere from 2 to 15 percent real maple syrup. Pure maple syrup is expensive, but it is so flavorful that less is needed. Maple syrup is graded according to its quality and color. In general, the lighter the color, the milder-tasting the syrup.
Storing Smaller amounts that can be used within 2 months can be kept in an airtight container in a cool, dry place. Store large

m

amounts of syrup in an airtight glass container in the refrigerator indefinitely.

Preparing Use maple syrup much as you would honey. Add it to barbecue sauces, muffins, quick breads, frostings, glazes, fresh fruit salads, and salad dressings. And, of course, drizzle it generously over pancakes and waffles.

MARGARINE This century-old substitute for butter is made from hydrogenated vegetable oil. Hydrogenation is the process by which food manufacturers transform liquid oil into solid fat. Margarine has less saturated fat than butter and no cholesterol, but because of the trans fatty acids it contains, it is not the healthful alternative to butter it once was believed to be.

Quick Bite

The hydrogenation of oils creates compounds known as trans fatty acids, now believed to be more harmful to your health in high amounts than regular saturated fats. The more an oil is hydrogenated, the stiffer it becomes and the more trans fats are created. This explains the increasing popularity of softer tub margarine, which has 50 to 80 percent less trans fat than the firmer stick form.

Because hydrogenated oils have a higher melting point than butter, they will scorch less readily when heated, which makes margarine useful for panfrying and browning or for greasing cake pans destined for hot ovens. For the same reason, margarine does not melt at body temperature, which is part of the reason it lacks butter's nutty flavor and "melt-in-your-mouth" richness. Manufacturers sometimes add vitamins, food coloring, and milk or cream to create a more butterlike product. Blending dairy butter or cream into margarine makes it more flavorful but also adds cholesterol.

Quick Tip

Because reduced-fat margarine contains a high proportion of water, do not use it in place of regular margarine in baking or frying. The results will be disappointing.

Selecting Margarine is widely available in the refrigerated dairy section of supermarkets, molded into firm sticks like butter, or packaged as a soft spread in plastic tubs. Reduced-fat and fat-free margarine also are available. Other forms of margarine, such as liquid squeezed from a plastic bottle and a powder that may be sprinkled on food at the table, help make it even more convenient.

Storing Keep margarine in the refrigerator for up to 2 months or in the freezer for up to 18 months. Store margarine to be frozen in a zippered plastic freezer bag or wrapped in freezer-weight plastic.

MARINATING A marinade is a highly flavored, acid-based liquid mixture in which meat, fish, or vegetables soak for a set amount of time. Marinating flavors the food and has some tenderizing effect on the surface of meat and fish. Research has shown that the flavoring and tenderizing effects are relatively slight, as the acid can penetrate only the surface of any food. Its effects are greatest on smaller, thin cuts.

Marinating meat.

Marinades usually contain three types of ingredients: oil to help keep meat moist, acid to tenderize protein, and flavorings such as spices and herbs. Marinades that do not have a significant liquid component are sometimes called dry marinades or, more often, rubs. The combinations are endless, but choosing an appropriate oil or acid will add depth to the mix. Some basic examples include sesame oil and rice vinegar for an Asian flair, citrus juice and a light oil for a refreshing, subtle flavor with seafood, or a robust red wine vinegar and olive oil for roasted meats.

Marinating Savvy

- Always use containers made of non-reactive material such as glass, stainless steel, or plastic. See NONREACTIVE.
- Place spices and aromatics in cheese-cloth or a mesh tea ball for easy removal from a marinade.
- If you plan to baste meat, fish, or poultry with some of its marinade during cooking, reserve a portion of the marinade at the beginning, before adding the food to it.

Caution!

Never use a meat's or poultry's marinade as a sauce for serving without first bringing it to a boil and letting it boil for 5 minutes, as it contains raw juices from the meat.

- Use heavy-duty zippered plastic bags to coat food evenly and neatly with wet marinades. Place the food in a bag and pour in the marinade. Fold down any excess plastic at the top, press out as much air as possible, and then seal.

Placing poultry in a bag to marinate.

- The thicker or bigger the food, the longer it will need to marinate. Thin slices of chicken may need only 15 minutes, while a large roast may require several days. Scoring a thick cut of meat will help a marinade to penetrate it. Use a small, sharp knife to make shallow cuts in the meat's surface.

Scoring poultry to help it marinate.

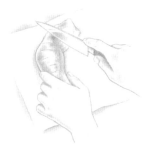

- Do not marinate meat or poultry at room temperature for more than 2 hours. For longer marinating, always refrigerate.
- Drain food and pat dry before cooking, especially if you want to sear and brown meat. Small pieces of onion, garlic, and fresh herbs from a marinade still clinging to meat will scorch over high heat.
- Take care when marinating delicate fish and shellfish. If left in acids too long, they will become firm and opaque. This is fine for seviche, but not for seafood that needs further cooking. See also RUB.

MARIONBERRY See BERRY.

MARJORAM See HERB.

MASA HARINA See FLOUR; TORTILLA.

MASCARPONE See CHEESE.

MASHING Starchy vegetables such as potatoes, parsnips, squash, and beans can be cooked until soft, then mashed to a smooth purée. Mash a small amount of cooked vegetable solids (potato, turnip, carrot) in a soup or stew to thicken it. A masher, a special tool with a sturdy handle connected to a wavy thick wire or a round cutout grid, is an age-old tool for crushing food.

Potato mashers.

Potatoes can become unpleasantly gummy if they are whipped rather than mashed, so avoid using a food processor.

See also RICING.

MATZO Also spelled matzoh. A flat, brittle bread baked without any leavening. It is traditionally eaten during Passover, a holiday commemorating the flight of the Jews from Egypt, when, in their haste, they did not have time to let their bread rise. Matzo meal, ground from the bread, gives bulk to matzo balls and replaces flour in baked goods. Like bread crumbs, matzo meal can also be used to bind, thicken, and coat other foods. Matzo meal cake flour, made from matzo ground to a fine powder, is used primarily for cakes.

MAYONNAISE A creamy, cold sauce of egg yolks, oil, and lemon juice or vinegar blended into a thick emulsion. Whipping together mayonnaise was once the test of a dedicated cook, but now making it at home is simple with a food processor, a blender, or an electric mixer.

Recently, homemade mayonnaise has raised concerns because of the slight possibility of salmonella bacteria in raw eggs. If you wish to limit your potential exposure to bacteria as much as possible for health reasons, avoid making mayonnaise with raw eggs. Store-bought mayonnaise, which is made with pasteurized eggs, can be customized with the addition of any number of ingredients, from minced fresh herbs to curry powder to mustard.

Selecting Prepared real mayonnaise and its popular imitation version labeled "mayonnaise-type salad dressing" are widely available in jars. Mayonnaise is sold in low-fat and low-cholesterol versions. Prepared mayonnaises are good and inarguably convenient, but homemade mayonnaise will have a superior flavor.

Storing Once opened, jars of prepared mayonnaise should be kept in the refrigerator for no longer than 6 months. Refrigerate homemade mayonnaise as well, but do not keep it for more than 3 days. Do not leave salads that contain mayonnaise unrefrigerated for more than 2 hours.

Preparing Be extremely careful not to contaminate mayonnaise. Always use clean utensils for scooping it out of the jar, and never return leftover mayonnaise to the original batch.

Quick Tip

Don't worry if your homemade mayonnaise separates into a mess of curds as you are making it. The rescue is easy. Simply beat another egg yolk in a clean bowl. Then, gradually add the broken mayonnaise, whisking steadily until it reforms. Balance the additional egg with more oil and seasonings.

See also EGG; EMULSION.

MEASURING See opposite page.

MEASURING CUP AND SPOON See COOKING TOOLS; MEASURING.

Measuring

Although experienced cooks have learned to add "a little of this" or "a lot of that" without bothering to measure, understanding the fundamentals of measuring helps prevent problems in baking or when trying new recipes. Certain ingredients require special attention to ensure accurate measurement.

Reading the Recipe Read the ingredient list of a recipe closely to check whether an item is measured *before* or *after* some form of preparation. For example, "1 cup walnuts, chopped" calls for measuring the walnuts *before* chopping, while "1 cup chopped walnuts" directs you to measure the nuts *after* chopping. Preparing an ingredient before or after measuring can make a big difference in the amount actually used. Using the same example, 1 cup chopped walnuts is actually more walnuts than 1 cup walnuts, chopped, because you can fit more chopped walnuts into a measuring cup than unchopped ones. Although the differences are sometimes not visible to the eye, they can seriously affect the outcome of recipes, especially when you are engaged in the exacting chemistry of baking.

Measuring Equipment Every kitchen should have both dry and wet measuring cups, which are not interchangeable. For accurate measuring, use the correct type of measuring cup.

Dry measuring cups are graduated cups in a standard set ranging from $\frac{1}{4}$ cup to 1 cup. Sometimes a $\frac{1}{8}$-cup measure is also included. They are usually made of heavy-duty plastic or stainless steel. Each cup, when leveled at its brim, measures a specific amount. Look for a 2-cup dry measure; recipes frequently call for this amount.

Measuring a dry ingredient.

Liquid measuring cups look like pitchers with rulers printed vertically on the side. They are clear glass or plastic, have pour spouts, extra room at the top for sloshing liquid, and continuous markings for fluid ounces and cups. The two most common sizes are 1 quart and 1 cup, and some manufacturers include metric markings as well. Although a 2-cup size is less common, seek one out, as it is convenient to have on hand. When measuring a liquid, place the cup on a flat surface, let the liquid settle, then read it at eye level.

Measuring a liquid.

continued

Measuring, continued

Measuring spoons come in a set of ¼ teaspoon, ½ teaspoon, 1 teaspoon, and 1 tablespoon. The occasional set will include ½ tablespoon or ⅛ teaspoon. You can use them for both dry and liquid ingredients. As with the dry cups, after filling a measuring spoon, level off the dry ingredient with a flat edge.

PLASTIC, STAINLESS STEEL, OR GLASS? Plastic dry measures are light and can be strong, but plastic can also absorb oils and strong flavors. Metal ones are generally more durable, but avoid aluminum spoons, which will react with acidic ingredients such as lemon juice and vinegar to create an "off" flavor.

Plastic and glass liquid measures allow you to heat ingredients in the microwave, but Pyrex glass measures can even be used on gas stoves to scald liquids.

Whatever the material, look for measuring cups with comfortable handles securely attached, easy-to-read numbers that won't wear away, and the ability to nest for compact storage.

Quick Tip

If you don't have a ½ tablespoon measure, measure out 1½ teaspoons.

How to Measure If a measure includes no adjective, such as 1 tablespoon sugar or 1 cup sugar, then a level measure, that is, one that is even with the rim of the tablespoon or cup, is understood. A "heaping" measure, such as 1 heaping tablespoon sugar, is generously rounded above the rim. A "rounded" measure, such as 1 rounded tablespoon sugar, calls for a slightly rounded dome above the rim, or slightly less than "heaping." Finally, 1 scant tablespoon sugar means slightly less than full. In other words, the ingredient is not level with the top of the measuring spoon but just below it.

BROWN SUGAR Pack moist brown sugar into the measuring cup firmly enough for it to retain its shape when it is tapped out of the cup.

CORN SYRUP Lightly coat the measuring cup with oil or butter before pouring in corn syrup, and it will slip out easily and cleanly. This also works for honey, molasses, and other sticky ingredients.

FLOUR Weighing flour is the most accurate way to measure it, but most American recipes are not written this way. There are two ways to use volume measures for flour. For the spoon-and-sweep method, lightly fill the measuring cup with a separate scoop or spoon. Level off the flour with the back of a knife, making it flush with the edge of the cup. Do not tamp down the flour. For the scoop-and-sweep method, fluff up the flour with a fork or whisk, dip the cup into the flour to scoop it up, and then sweep the top level. With the latter method you will end up with slightly more flour in the cup. Unless a recipe indicates which to use, pick a method and use it every time for consistent results in your baking.

Although all-purpose flour is commonly sold presifted, check the ingredient list of your recipe. If it specifically states sifted flour, sift it again for accurate measuring, since volume varies greatly between sifted and unsifted flour.

SHORTENING Fill a large measuring cup with cold water to the 1 cup level. Add shortening in large spoonfuls until the water registers the required amount plus 1 cup. Dump the water and you will have the exact amount of shortening needed. (Gently pat the shortening dry before using it in a mixture or for panfrying.)

Measurement Equivalents

3 teaspoons = 1 tablespoon	= $\frac{1}{2}$ fluid ounce					
2 tablespoons	= 1 fluid ounce					
4 tablespoons	= 2 fluid ounces	= $\frac{1}{4}$ cup				
5 tablespoons plus 1 teaspoon		= $\frac{1}{3}$ cup				
16 tablespoons	= 8 fluid ounces	= 1 cup				
	16 fluid ounces	= 2 cups	= 1 pint			
	32 fluid ounces	= 4 cups	= 2 pints	= 1 quart		
	128 fluid ounces	= 16 cups	= 8 pints	= 4 quarts	= 1 gallon	

Metric Conversions

VOLUME

U.S. to Metric	
1 teaspoon	5 milliliters
1 tablespoon	15 milliliters
$\frac{1}{4}$ cup	59 milliliters
1 cup	236 milliliters
1 pint	473 milliliters
1 quart	946 milliliters
1 gallon	3.8 liters

Metric to U.S.	
10 milliliters	2 teaspoons
30 milliliters	1 fluid ounce
100 milliliters	$\frac{1}{2}$ cup minus 1 tablespoon
500 milliliters	2 cups plus 2 tablespoons
1 liter	$4\frac{1}{4}$ cups, or 1 quart plus $\frac{1}{4}$ cup
2 liters	$8\frac{1}{2}$ cups, or $\frac{1}{2}$ gallon plus $\frac{1}{2}$ cup

WEIGHT-MASS

U.S. to Metric		
1 ounce	28.4 grams	
1 pound	454 grams	0.45 kilogram

Metric to U.S.	
100 grams	3.5 ounces
500 grams	1.1 pounds
1 kilogram	2.2 pounds

LINEAR

1 centimeter	0.4 inch
1 inch	2.5 centimeters
1 meter	39.4 inches

continued

Measuring, continued

Temperature Temperature is a key factor in good cooking. Every well-equipped cook should have three types of thermometer: a meat thermometer, a candy thermometer, and a deep-fat thermometer. Meat thermometers come in two varieties: one that remains in the meat throughout the cooking and the instant-read type, which is inserted at the presumed moment of doneness and gives an accurate reading within several seconds. The latter kind is also handy for testing water temperature for activating yeast and similar tasks. Thermometers that work equally well for both candy making and deep-frying are available (those designed solely for frying measure slightly higher temperatures). An oven thermometer is also handy, used to calibrate your oven so it can be set precisely to required cooking temperatures. See also COOKING TOOLS.

TO OBTAIN FAHRENHEIT:
Multiply the Celsius figure by 9, divide by 5, then add 32. After 65°F, Celsius figures are often rounded off.

$$F° = 9C°/5 + 32$$

TO OBTAIN CELSIUS:
Subtract 32 from the Fahrenheit figure, multiply by 5, then divide by 9.

$$C° = 5(F° - 32)/9$$

Key Temperatures in Cooking

FAHRENHEIT	CELSIUS	DESCRIPTION
0°	−17°	
32°	0°	Freezing (water)
100° to 110°	38° to 43°	Yeast activation
130°	54°	Scalding
160°	71°	Safe internal temperature for meat, poultry, and eggs
160° to 180°	71° to 82°	Poaching
185° to 205°	85° to 96°	Simmering
212°	100°	Boiling (at sea level)
234°	112°	Soft ball (sugar)
244°	117°	Firm ball
250°	121°	Hard ball
275°	135°	
300°	149°	
350°	177°	
400°	204°	
450°	232°	
500°	260°	

MELON Long enjoyed only by aristocrats, sweet and fragrant melons now tumble from piled-up pyramids at every neighborhood market. Thin wedges of cantaloupe are ubiquitous inclusions on brunch plates, icy melon sorbets are refreshing desserts, and many agree that the essence of summer is a big wedge of watermelon with plenty of seeds to spit. Many melon varieties exist, but they can be divided into two broad categories: muskmelons and watermelons. Winter melon and bitter melon are members of the squash family.

Muskmelons A single ripe muskmelon can fill an entire room with its fragrance. Depending on the variety, rinds range in color from cream to yellow to pale green, with various patterns and combinations of streaks. Inside, the flesh can be white, pale orange, or the lightest of greens. They have a hollow center where all their seeds are connected in a fibrous mass. Two general types of muskmelons exist, distinguished by the texture of their skin. Netted melons, such as cantaloupe, have fine, raised ridges and are generally at their peak from midsummer to early fall. Smooth-skinned melons, such as honeydew, have less aroma, juicier flesh, more delicate flavor, and a longer storage life. Belonging to a category of muskmelons known as winter melons (not related to the winter melon squash mentioned above), they are at their best—full of flavor—during the cooler months of autumn.

CANTALOUPE Popular in the United States. Beige netted skin, with undertones of green. Flesh is orange, moist, and fragrant. Cantaloupes are best in July and August.

CASABA Golden yellow, slightly wrinkled and ridged rind and creamy, pale yellow flesh. Any green in the skin indicates an unripe specimen. Peak season is September and October.

CHARENTAIS One of the true cantaloupes of France. The flesh is orange, while the skin is smooth, gently ribbed, and very pale green with radiating streaks of darker green. Best in July and August.

CHRISTMAS Also know as Santa Claus melon. Elongated and resembling a small, dark green watermelon with bright yellow streaks. Creamy white flesh tinged with pale green is similar in taste to honeydew. Peaks in December.

CRENSHAW Large, smooth-skinned, and slightly pointed at the stem end. Bright yellow rind mottled with dark green spots. Very fragrant flesh, cream to salmon colored, with a rich, spicy flavor. Best in August and September.

HONEYDEW Smooth skin that ripens from pale green to creamy yellow. Its pale green flesh is sweet and juicy. A hybrid with pink flesh is sometimes available. Peak season is from June to October.

PERSIAN Fine, brownish netting over dark green skin. Firm, sweet flesh is orange with faint pink tones. At its best in August and September.

Selecting Ripe muskmelons have a strong, sweet fragrance and give slightly when pressed at both ends. Muskmelons allowed to ripen on the vine will break away cleanly, leaving only a shallow, symmetrical indentation. A melon picked while unripe, in order to facilitate shipping, will have a

m

green stem, ragged fibers, or an irregular scar where the stem once was. For varieties with a netted skin, look for netting that is pronounced and evenly distributed. Smooth-skinned melons should be just that, smooth. A fully ripe melon may have tiny cracks at the stem end. Choose a melon heavy for its size and free of blemishes, shriveled peel, or soft, moldy areas.

Storing Although it will not obtain the flavor of a vine-ripened melon, an unripe melon will sweeten slightly if left in a paper bag at room temperature for a few days. An exception is the honeydew, which will stay only as sweet as it was when harvested. Once ripe, melons will keep for up to 5 days in the refrigerator or a dark, cool place. Seal whole and cut melons in plastic wrap or an airtight container, as they readily absorb the odors and flavors of other foods while they transfer their own.

Preparing Cut muskmelons in half and scoop out their seeds with a large spoon. To keep the melon moist, peel and cut off slices only as needed.

Quick Tip

Muskmelons will taste sweeter if served at room temperature or only slightly chilled. Remove from the refrigerator about 30 minutes before cutting and serving.

Watermelons The flesh of watermelon, true to its name, is almost 95 percent water. Native to West Africa, watermelons were and are crucial sources of water in arid areas and in countries with polluted waterways. Lovingly tended, they can grow to 100 pounds, but most come to market at a comfortable armful of 10 to 15 pounds. Unlike muskmelons, watermelons belong to a small, simple family. The choices are basically round or oblong, solid green or striped, with or without seeds. Watermelons have deep pink to bright red flesh that is crisp, juicy, and sweet. Yellow- and now orange-fleshed hybrids are sometimes available. Dark, shiny seeds are scattered throughout their flesh. Melons labeled seedless may still harbor a few soft, white, perfectly edible seeds. Watermelon seeds, roasted and dyed red, are served in Asia as a symbol of abundance during the Lunar New Year, and the rinds are made into pickles around the world.

Selecting Judging the ripeness of a whole watermelon is an inexact science, but a few indicators can point toward a sweet and juicy specimen. Look for a large, pale yellow (but not white, soft, or moldy) patch on one side, showing that it was left on the vine longer and may be sweeter than others. Shoppers knocking on watermelons in the produce section are listening for a particularly resonant thud that reveals the melon is juicy and full of water. Check cut watermelons for firm flesh with a deep red color and no white streaks. Watermelons are available year-round, but they are at their best during the summer months.

Storing Keep whole and cut watermelons in the refrigerator, because after they are picked from the vine, their flesh becomes increasingly dry and fibrous in warm temperatures. Although best eaten as soon as possible, a whole watermelon can stay in the refrigerator for up to 1 week. If it is too big, store it in a cold, dark place for no more than 3 days. Seal cut pieces in plastic wrap or an airtight container.

MELTING When certain solid ingredients must be incorporated into a mixture, melting them is often the best way to achieve uniform texture. Although solid at room temperature, foods such as butter, chocolate, gelatin, peanut butter, and sugar will become liquid if heated. Generally, melting calls for gentle heating in a double boiler or a microwave and frequent stirring.

MERINGUE One of the wonders of the kitchen is sweet, white, fluffy, delicate meringue, produced by beating a simple mixture of egg whites and sugar. Meringue can be either soft, glossy and smooth for spooning onto pies and other desserts, or hard, made with more sugar and baked until crisp, light, and dry. In Europe, hard meringues are important components in many classic desserts. Soft meringues are more popular in the United States.

Meringue Savvy A bowl and a whisk are all you need for whipping up meringue, but it helps to know a few secrets. Here are some tips that will keep your meringue up and your frustration down:

- While older egg whites will whip up more easily and to higher proportions, fresh egg whites have stronger proteins that hold air better and remain more stable once whipped.
- Separate eggs while they are still cold from the refrigerator, but set the whites aside for at least 30 minutes before whipping them. Room-temperature egg whites are easiest to whip.
- Make sure no egg yolk gets into the whites, which would prevent them from whipping up.
- Make sure your bowl and beaters are absolutely clean and free of fat.
- If possible, use a copper bowl. A harmless chemical reaction increases the beaten whites' volume and makes them more stable.
- If you do not have a copper bowl, add a small amount of cream of tartar or lemon juice before whipping the egg whites to increase their stability and volume.

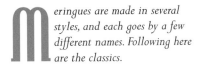
Meringue Glossary

meringues are made in several styles, and each goes by a few different names. Following here are the classics.

DACQUOISE A Swiss meringue with finely chopped almonds or hazelnuts folded into it. Also known as a japonaise meringue, dacquoise is traditionally piped into spiraled rounds and then baked to form cake layers.

FRENCH MERINGUE Also called cold or simple meringue. After the egg whites are whipped to soft peaks with a small amount of sugar, the remaining sugar is folded in gently. French meringue is the lightest and most fragile of all meringues and must always be baked or incorporated into a batter and then cooked. Excellent for lightening batters and topping desserts.

ITALIAN MERINGUE A dense, stable meringue that is extremely smooth and shiny, created by slowly pouring hot sugar syrup into the egg whites during whipping. When baked, it has a more melting texture than the others. Since the meringue has been cooked by the hot sugar syrup, Italian meringue may be served with no further cooking. Ideal spread on filled pies and folded into puddings.

SWISS MERINGUE Also known as warm or cooked meringue, since the sugar (usually confectioners') and egg whites are beaten over hot water to dissolve the sugar completely and increase the height of the egg foam. It is a sturdy meringue and can be stored in the refrigerator for several days. Used in icings and decorations.

m
—

- Superfine sugar is ideal for making meringue, since it dissolves more quickly and completely than regular granulated sugar.
- Use the back of a spoon to swirl meringue peaks atop a pie.

- Use or bake meringue immediately after preparing it.
- To avoid even the slightest discoloration, do not leave egg whites sitting in either aluminum or copper bowls.

Meringue Blues Got a problem with your meringue? Find the simple explanation here.

THERE ARE BEADS OF MOISTURE ON MY SOFT MERINGUE TOPPING. Meringue was overcooked. Use an oven thermometer to check your oven temperature, and don't cook your meringue topping on a cold filling, as the top can overcook before the meringue is cooked through.

MOISTURE IS OOZING FROM THE BOTTOM OF MY MERINGUE TOPPING. "Weeping" is caused by undercooking meringue. Cooking meringue topping on a cold filling can cause the bottom of the meringue to undercook.

Quick Tip

Serve meringue desserts soon after preparing. Soft meringue will begin weeping in warm, humid weather, and hard meringue will become soggy after it comes in contact with moist ingredients.

MESCLUN See GREENS, SALAD.

MEZZALUNA Meaning "half-moon" in Italian, the mezzaluna has a curved, crescent-shaped blade that chops herbs and small vegetables more quickly, safely, and easily than a chef's knife. With a wooden handle at each end, it is held with both hands and used with a rocking motion. Also known as a crescent cutter, it may be used on a cutting board or in a shallow wooden bowl designed for this purpose. See also KNIFE.

MICROWAVE OVEN Teenagers everywhere know microwave ovens are handy for making popcorn, and even the most traditional cook will admit there's no faster, easier way to melt butter or soften petrified brown sugar. Even better, many vegetables cooked in a microwave oven retain more nutrients and achieve perfect crisp-tenderness. Microwave ovens quickly defrost frozen meat or reheat leftovers.

Microwaves work by heating the moisture in a food. Anything that contains moisture can be cooked in a microwave; the less moist a food is, the longer it will take to cook. Lacking dry heat, microwave ovens do not brown meat, but for dishes that are normally steamed, simmered, or poached, they provide excellent moist cooking.

The appliance has been much maligned, yet nearly every kitchen boasts one and they do come in handy. Microwaves come in all shapes and sizes, some small enough to hang from a cupboard, others large and imposing. The technology has developed over the years so that today microwaves are easy, efficient, and safe. Most cooks think of them as another timesaving device or kitchen tool, rather than a replacement for conventional ovens and stove tops.

Microwave Savvy

- Microwaves of different wattage will produce varying results. The standard for most published microwave recipes is 700 watts. If yours has a different wattage (check your owner's manual), here is a general formula for converting cooking times in recipes: add or subtract 10 seconds for every 50 watts that your oven is below or above 700 watts, respectively. Experiment until you have a good sense of the power levels of your particular appliance.

- Since corners concentrate microwave energy, use round pans and plates to promote even cooking, and arrange appropriate foods in a circle.

- If your microwave does not have a turntable or a fan, be sure to rotate the dish and stir food frequently, especially thick liquids and chunky mixtures.

- Although microwaves do not heat up containers, they do heat up the food, which in turn makes the containers hot. Be sure to use pot holders when taking them from the microwave.

- Cut food into uniform-sized pieces for even cooking.

- Do not arrange whole foods or large pieces too snugly in the dishes. Allow a little space around each food so that the microwaves can reach it on all sides.

- It will take about twice as long to cook 2 potatoes as 1 potato, and nearly three times as long to cook 3 potatoes. For this reason, when cooking large amounts of food, it soon becomes just as efficient to use the conventional oven.

- If covering food with plastic wrap, turn back a corner or cut a small hole in the wrap to vent the dish. Don't let the plastic touch the food directly.

- Do not put metal in the microwave. (This includes foil wrappers and the shiny trim on dishes.) Use only plastic, glass, or ceramic containers that are specified microwave-safe.

- Pierce foods sealed in skins or membranes (egg yolks, sausages, tomatoes, potatoes) with a toothpick or fork to vent steam and prevent explosions.

- When melting chocolate, do not expect it to melt to a liquid pool. Remove it when it is soft and shiny and then stir the chocolate to liquefy fully.

- Food continues cooking after removal, so undercook dishes slightly in the microwave for perfect doneness.

See also OVEN.

MIE(N) See NOODLE.

MILK The milk of cows, goats, sheep, oxen, buffaloes, and yaks has been part of the human diet for thousands of years. Today, the term *milk* commonly refers to cow's milk. High in nutrients, milk and its products compose one of the fundamental food groups. Whether simply poured into a glass or transformed into béchamel sauce, cultured into nutritious yogurt or frozen into ice cream, milk is essential to the cuisines of many countries.

Quick Tip

Milk loses vitamins and flavor when exposed to sunlight or fluorescent light. If you buy your milk in glass bottles, keep it in the dark as much as possible or transfer it to a clean, airtight container that blocks out light.

The rich flavor of milk comes from its emulsified fats; its distinctive white color derives from casein protein; and its faintly sweet flavor reveals the presence of lactose, a type of sugar found only in milk. Most processed milk is fortified with vitamin D, which helps the body absorb calcium, and vitamin A.

✒ Milk Glossary ✒

The corner grocery store carries a wide range of cow's milk products—in cartons, in cans, in bottles, in boxes, on the shelf, in the refrigerated case. Here are the basic choices.

ACIDOPHILUS MILK Contains beneficial bacteria, *Lactobacillus acidophilus*, which aid in the digestion of milk.

BUTTERMILK Traditionally the liquid drained from churned butter. Today, milk is commercially cultured to develop the tangy flavor and creamy texture of buttermilk. For more details, see BUTTERMILK.

CONDENSED MILK Also known as sweetened condensed milk. Basically, condensed milk is evaporated milk with a high proportion of sugar (40 percent). It is also high in fat, at around 8 percent. Condensed milk has an ivory color, a syrupy consistency, and a glossy surface. It is sold in cans and used mainly in confections and desserts. After opening, transfer the milk to an airtight container and refrigerate for up to 2 weeks.

EVAPORATED MILK Has had about 60 percent of its water removed by heat. The process darkens the milk's color slightly to a pale ivory and gives it a faint caramelized flavor. Evaporated milk is sealed and sterilized in cans or cartons. Stable when heated, it is sometimes used in thick sauces and puddings that might otherwise curdle. It can be reconstituted with an equal amount of water, although it will taste a bit sweeter than fresh milk. Once you open a can, transfer the milk to an airtight glass or plastic container and keep it in the refrigerator for up to 1 week. Also available in low-fat and nonfat forms.

HALF-AND-HALF A mixture of milk and cream. It will not whip up but can be used in any recipe calling for a pouring cream. See also CREAM.

HOMOGENIZED MILK Forced through tiny holes to break its fat globules into small particles that will remain suspended evenly throughout the milk. Nonhomogenized milk will have cream that rises to the top. Almost all of the milk sold today is homogenized.

LACTOSE-REDUCED MILK Low-fat or nonfat milk with at least 70 percent of its lactose, or milk sugar, converted to more easily digested simple sugars. Over half of the world's population lacks the enzyme required to break down lactose, but adding the enzyme directly to milk reduces the amount of indigestible sugar. Breaking down the complex lactose sugar molecule into two simple sugars with higher sweetening power creates a milk that is sweeter in flavor as well as easier to digest.

LACTOSE-FREE MILK Low-fat or nonfat milk in which 99 percent of its lactose has been broken down. See Lactose-Reduced Milk, above.

LOW-FAT MILK Also known as partially skimmed milk, low-fat milk may contain either 1 or 2 percent fat. It has fewer calories and less fat than whole milk, but otherwise provides the same nutritional value.

NONFAT MILK Nonfat, or skim, milk must contain less than 0.2 percent fat.

PASTEURIZED MILK Heated briefly and then quickly cooled, a process that destroys most of the harmful bacteria in raw milk and extends its shelf life. Almost all milk sold in the United States has been pasteurized.

m

Milk Glossary, continued

POWDERED MILK Also called dry milk, this is pasteurized milk that has been dehydrated. It can be whole, low fat, or nonfat. To reconstitute, mix the powder with water. Although considered stable, the flavor of dry milk will deteriorate if the powder is exposed to light or air. Transfer dry milk powder to an airtight glass container, and keep it in the refrigerator for longer shelf life. Once reconstituted, the milk must be refrigerated; it will keep for up to 1 week. Powdered milk is used to boost the nutritional value of foods and to thicken sauces, and it is used in baking as well.

RAW MILK Has not been pasteurized. Many countries have banned raw milk, since bacteria can easily contaminate it. Stringently regulated (certified herds and hygienic premises), it is available in some health-food stores in the United States.

ULTRAPASTEURIZED MILK Heated to a higher temperature for a shorter period of time than pasteurized milk. It has a longer shelf life but also less flavor.

ULTRA HEAT PASTEURIZED (UHT) MILK Undergoes an extra-high heat treatment that effectively destroys all organisms present in the milk. Packed into aseptic containers, it can be stored unopened at room temperature for up to 3 months. Once opened, however, it should be stored in the refrigerator and should not be kept longer than 36 hours.

WHOLE MILK Contains around 3.5 percent fat. If not homogenized, it will have a layer of cream.

Selecting Choose cartons with the latest sell-by date for the freshest milk. The dates are conservative, so milk is usually still good for up to 5 days afterward, although it may have lost flavor by then.

Storing Unfortunately, bacteria also benefit from milk's abundant nutrients. To avoid contamination, keep milk in the refrigerator (no higher than 40°F) as much as possible. Buy milk at the end of your grocery shopping, avoid leaving the whole carton out on the table or counter for more than a few minutes, and do not pour milk that has been left at room temperature back into a carton of chilled milk. Since milk easily absorbs other odors and flavors, close cartons and bottles securely.

See also BUTTER; SCALDING; YOGURT.

Quick Tip

Milk curdles when mixed with acidic ingredients, such as lemon juice. To prevent curdling, mix a small amount of cornstarch into the acidic ingredient or the milk before combining them, then heat gently.

MILLET See GRAIN.

MINCING To chop food as finely as possible. Herbs and aromatics such as garlic are commonly minced to help release their flavor and meld them texturally into a mixture. The gently curved blade of a chef's knife allows for the two-handed rocking motion that makes quick work of mincing a pile of garlic or parsley. Be sure the knife is sharp, for a dull blade will crush and bruise ingredients instead of cleanly mincing them.

See also CHOPPING; GARLIC; HERB; KNIFE; MEZZALUNA; ONION.

MINT See HERB.

MIREPOIX See CELERY.

MIRLITON See CHAYOTE.

MISO See SOY FOODS.

MIXER Two basic types of motor-driven electric mixers are available, stand or standing and handheld or portable, and each has its place in the kitchen. Stand mixers are stationary machines good for large amounts and heavy batters.

Stand mixer.

The basic set of attachments usually includes a wire whisk for beating egg whites or whipping cream, a paddle for creaming together butter and sugar and mixing batters, and a dough hook for kneading bread.

Attachments for stand mixer.

Handheld mixers are small, light portable machines. Lacking the power and special attachments of stand mixers, these appliances are adequate for most batters and soft doughs but they do not work well for stiff doughs. For long mixing tasks, such as making buttercream or beating large volumes of egg whites, handheld mixers can become tiring to hold. However, they can be used with nearly any bowl or pan, even those set over a pan of simmering water on the stove top.

Handheld mixer.

MIXING Mixing is the simple combining of two or more ingredients or mixtures. Some delicate batters require only a few turns of a spoon, leaving visible lumps but maintaining tenderness and airy height. Other recipes specify complete blending of ingredients until evenly distributed. A variety of equipment, from wooden spoons to whisks, mixers to blenders, allows a cook to obtain exactly the consistency needed. See also BEATING; BLENDING; MIXER; WHIPPING; WHISKING.

MIXING BOWL The well-equipped kitchen includes bowls in a range of materials, shapes, and sizes suitable for a variety of cooking and baking tasks. For example, whipping egg whites and creaming butter call for deep bowls. Some useful features include a turned rim or a beak for mess-free pouring, cup measurements marked

Materials for Mixing Bowls

CERAMIC Earthy and sturdy and standard in kitchens for centuries. Ceramic bowls change temperature slowly, keeping hot contents warm and cold ingredients cool. Be sure the glaze is food-safe.

COPPER For mixing egg whites. The moving whisk actually scrapes up minute amounts of copper ions that bond to the egg whites' unraveling proteins and stabilize them in the airy foam. Never mix acidic ingredients in copper; the food will react, taking on an unpleasant color and flavor. See NONREACTIVE.

GLASS Attractive for showing off colorful foods at the table, but not the most practical for mixing. Glass can be heavy and fragile, and its slippery surface can keep beaten egg whites from climbing and foaming up properly. Specially tempered heat- or flameproof Pyrex is available, fashioned either into bowls or into large measuring cups that can double as mixing bowls.

PLASTIC Light and convenient, and useful for storing or transporting foods when lidded. Avoid mixing delicately flavored ingredients or batters in them, however, since plastic can retain odors, flavors, and oils even after washing. In particular, residual oil can prevent egg whites from properly foaming.

STAINLESS STEEL There should be at least one stainless-steel bowl in every kitchen, if not a nesting set of various sizes. Stainless steel won't react with food, as copper or aluminum will, and is lighter and more durable than ceramic or glass.

on the side, airtight covers for storing prepared ingredients, rubber rings on the bottom for nonskid mixing, and the ability to nest, thus keeping storage space to a minimum. Knowing the advantages of certain materials, though, is the most important part of deciding which bowl to use.

MIZUNA See GREENS, SALAD.

MOLASSES A syrup used to sweeten baked goods, top breakfast dishes, and flavor sauces. Widely available in jars, molasses is a by-product of sugar refinement, a process that requires repeated boiling of cane syrup.

Selecting Each step in the molasses-making process produces a different type of molasses. Mixed with pure cane syrup, light molasses has the lightest flavor and color of any molasses and can be used as a topping for pancakes or waffles. Dark molasses is thicker, darker, stronger in flavor and less sweet than light molasses. It may be used interchangeably with light molasses and gives a distinctive flavor to baked beans, barbecue sauces, certain cookies, and gingerbread.

Quick Tip

Both light and dark molasses may be bleached with sulfur dioxide. Processed without sulfur, unsulfured molasses has a milder flavor.

Blackstrap molasses, also known as black treacle, is darker still than dark molasses and has a pronounced bitter flavor that some find overly strong. Considered healthier because it contains a high amount of minerals, it can sometimes be found in health-food stores. It should not be substituted for light or dark molasses in recipes.

Storing All styles of molasses can be kept in a cool, dark place for up to 1 year.

MOLDING Forming food into a specific shape, with special containers or simply by hand. Molded foods—fanciful terrines, rainbow gelatin salads, bright-colored ice-cream bombes, icy punch rings—recall a time when cooks regularly allowed hours for the preparation of meals.

Molds come in a wide range of sizes, shapes, and materials. Although today's more natural approach to food presentation has helped to banish large molds to decorative outposts on kitchen walls, many cooks still depend on ramekins, timbales, terrines, and rings to create dinner party fare. See also UNMOLDING.

MONTEREY JACK See CHEESE.

MOREL See MUSHROOM.

MORTAR & PESTLE Before electricity and food processors revolutionized the kitchen, a cook needed a mortar and pestle to grind, purée, and blend ingredients. Purists still eschew electrically powered machines for making a pesto, mole, or curry, insisting that such preparations require a mortar and pestle to crush the spices and herbs in a way that best releases their flavors and to give the cook better control over the end texture.

A bowl-shaped mortar holds the ingredients, while the club-shaped pestle crushes and grinds them. Mortars vary in magnitude and material, from palm-sized porcelain bowls etched with decorative ridges to substantial marble vessels to huge stone blocks that serve as permanent fixtures in many Indian homes. Although a pestle is often made of the same material as the mortar, it can also be carved from hardwood. Either the mortar or pestle must have an abrasive surface to work effectively.

MOUSSE A mousse is an airy, rich concoction of sweet or savory ingredients. It may be a suspension of fruit or chocolate in whipped cream served as an elegant dessert; or finely ground seafood lightened with cream and gelatin; or puréed chicken livers enriched with butter and seasonings. Some chilled mousses, also known as cold soufflés, contain beaten egg whites for extra height and lightness. A mousse that includes egg yolks, such as a classic chocolate mousse recipe, has a dense and creamy texture. Most mousses are served chilled, but both hot and frozen variations exist. Although closely related, molded Bavarian creams and chiffons, the fillings for ever-popular chiffon pies, have firmer textures that allow them to hold their shape.

MOZZARELLA See CHEESE.

MUENSTER Or Münster. See CHEESE.

MUFFIN Straddling the line between cake and bread, a muffin can be as healthful as bran studded with fresh or dried fruits or as decadent as a chocolate-chip variation topped with streusel and drizzled with a glaze. Although once a yeast bread, the modern muffin is usually leavened with baking powder or baking soda and is baked in distinctive pans with cup-shaped compartments. Muffin flavors range from apple and blueberry to banana-walnut and lemon-poppyseed. Muffins can be savory—such as cornmeal or oat muffins to accompany meals—as well as sweet.

Muffin Savvy

- There are two kinds of muffin batter. Some batters are made by adding all the dry ingredients into the wet ones and mixing quickly; others are made like cakes, where butter and sugar are creamed together and dry and wet ingredients are alternately added. For the first style of batter, the ingredients should be mixed quickly with only a few turns of a spoon, just enough to bring the wet ingredients and dry ingredients together into a rough, lumpy mix. Any more stirring will create tough muffins.

- Toss fruit and nuts with a little flour to coat them lightly before stirring them into the batter with the last few strokes of mixing. The thin layer of flour will help suspend them evenly throughout the muffins.

- Fill any empty muffin cups halfway with water to ensure even cooking of the batter-filled cups and to prevent the pan from warping.

- If you do not have a convection oven, turn the pan 180 degrees halfway through cooking for even browning.

- Speed pan cleanup by using paper or foil muffin-cup liners.

HOW TO *Prepare Muffins in Advance*

1. Prepare pans and batter and fill pans, adding any nut or crunch toppings.
2. Place unbaked pans of muffin batter into the freezer. When firm, transfer the muffins to an airtight container or zippered freezer-weight plastic bag and freeze for 2 to 4 weeks.
3. To bake, preheat the oven and grease the same pan. Place the frozen batter back in the cups and bake without thawing, allowing about 15 minutes extra baking time.

Muffin Blues Got a problem with your muffins? Find the simple explanation here.

MUFFINS BROWN ON TOP BEFORE COOKING THROUGH. Oven heat was too high; pan was placed too close to top of oven.

MUFFINS DON'T RISE HIGH ENOUGH. Batter was allowed to sit for too long before baking; oven heat was too low.

MUFFINS HAVE CRATERS OR UNEVEN TOPS. Oven heat was too high.

MUFFINS HAVE HARD, SHINY TOPS AND LONG, VERTICAL INTERIOR TUNNELS. Batter was overmixed, developing the gluten and toughening the muffin.

MUFFINS STICK TO THE PAN. The pan was not greased sufficiently, or the muffins were left sitting too long in the pan after its removal from the oven.

MUFFINS TOPS HAVE A CENTER KNOB AND A SPREADING BASE. Too much batter was put into each muffin cup.

See also BAKEWARE.

MULBERRY See BERRY.

MULLING To sweeten and infuse a drink with spices and fruit. Mulled wine or cider, heated gently with such flavoring ingredients as sugar syrup, cinnamon sticks, cloves, allspice, and orange peel makes a comforting treat in the wintertime. Whole spices may be placed in a tea ball to save the trouble of straining the wine or cider. A mulled drink is often fortified with spirits.

MUNG BEAN See BEAN, DRIED.

MUNG BEAN NOODLE See NOODLE.

MÜNSTER Or Muenster. See CHEESE.

MUSHROOM See page 298.

MUSLIN See CHEESECLOTH.

Mushroom

Almost 40,000 varieties of mushroom exist in the world, but only a fraction of them make it to the table, where they are enjoyed for their rich, earthy flavor. For culinary purposes, mushrooms are divided into two categories: cultivated and wild.

Today, as demand for different varieties increases, mushroom growers are able to cultivate more and more types, and the line between cultivated and wild is blurring. The most flavorful—and most expensive—mushrooms, however, are still gathered by foragers in forests under trees or on old stumps. Highly prized mushrooms, such as the matsutake and the morel, have eluded all attempts at cultivation. Around the world, mushroom hunting after the rains of spring or during the cool mornings of autumn is still a thriving—and ultimately delicious—tradition.

Although mushrooms can be cooked by almost any method, they taste wonderful when simply sautéed in olive oil, with a little garlic, over high heat. Mushrooms are also good tossed with olive oil (be judicious; these little sponges can soak up a lot of oil) and seasonings, then roasted or grilled gill side up to retain their juices. To grill small mushrooms, thread them on skewers.

Caution!

Some wild mushrooms are fatally toxic, and they can closely resemble edible varieties. Do not pick or eat wild mushrooms unless a trained expert collector familiar with local varieties identifies them. Supermarket "wild" mushrooms generally are farmed and certainly not poisonous.

A Guide to Mushrooms

BUTTON MUSHROOM See White Mushroom, page 300.

CHANTERELLE Also known as girolle. Bright golden yellow and shaped like a trumpet, this distinctive mushroom is appreciated for its apricot-flavored overtones. A less-common black variety, called black trumpet or trumpet of death, is close in flavor but has a more delicate texture. Chanterelles are not cultivated to date.

CHINESE BLACK MUSHROOM Always sold dried. The best are actually beige to brown with cream-colored cracks radiating over the caps. See also Shiitake, page 300.

CLOUD EAR MUSHROOM Ruffled, brown-black Chinese mushroom with almost no flavor. Its crunch stands up to heat, however, and it adds texture to soups, vegetable stir-fries, and fillings. Almost always sold dried, they expand a great deal after soaking. (For example, 3 heaping tablespoons dried cloud ears will swell to 1 cup softened and chopped.) After reconstituting, trim off the tough, flat stems.

CREMINO MUSHROOM The common brown mushroom. Cremini (the Italian plural) are closely related to common white mushrooms and can be used whenever white mushrooms are called for, but they have a light brown color, firmer texture, and fuller flavor. Cremini mature to become portobellos.

ENOKI Tiny, white Asian mushrooms with long, thin stems and caps shaped like pinheads, enoki are crisp and delicate in flavor. Available fresh during the winter or water-packed in cans or plastic tubs, they make beautiful garnishes for salads and clear soups.

MATSUTAKE A delicacy in Japan, the matsutake appears beneath pine trees for a brief period in midautumn. It has a slightly pointed, thick, dark brown cap and a meaty stem. Not cultivated and difficult to find, the matsutake appears in the northwest region of the United States, but the most flavorful ones come from Japan. Sauté them or wrap in foil and place on the grill.

MOREL Considered the king of mushrooms, the morel has an intense, musky flavor that makes it highly sought after. The uncultivated mushroom has a dark, elongated, spongelike cap and hollow stem. The crevices tend to fill with sand and insects, so you may want to treat them as an exception to the no-washing rule: immerse them briefly in a large bowl of water and agitate to dislodge all the sand. You can halve them lengthwise for easier cleaning.

Morels are especially delicious in cream sauces or scrambled eggs.

OYSTER MUSHROOM Cream to pale gray mushroom, with a fan shape and a subtle flavor of shellfish. They used to be wild only but are now cultivated. Look for smaller, younger oysters, since they become tough and bitter as they grow older. They weep a great amount of liquid, so are best grilled, roasted, or stir-fried. Cook oyster mushrooms just until heated through to preserve their silken texture.

PORCINO MUSHROOM Also known as cepe and bolete. Porcini (Italian for "little pigs")

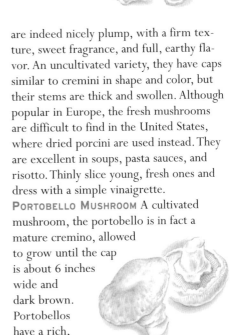

Dried porcini.

are indeed nicely plump, with a firm texture, sweet fragrance, and full, earthy flavor. An uncultivated variety, they have caps similar to cremini in shape and color, but their stems are thick and swollen. Although popular in Europe, the fresh mushrooms are difficult to find in the United States, where dried porcini are used instead. They are excellent in soups, pasta sauces, and risotto. Thinly slice young, fresh ones and dress with a simple vinaigrette.

PORTOBELLO MUSHROOM A cultivated mushroom, the portobello is in fact a mature cremino, allowed to grow until the cap is about 6 inches wide and dark brown. Portobellos have a rich,

continued

Mushroom, continued

smoky flavor and meaty texture. Leave the caps whole for grilling or roasting, or slice and sauté them to top pasta or polenta. Food mixed or cooked with portobello mushrooms will take on some of their color, turning an unpleasant gray, so prepare the mushrooms separately and add just before serving. The thick, tough stems should be removed (and may be saved for stocks, soups, or sauces).

SHIITAKE The most popular mushroom in Japan and now widely cultivated. Buff to dark brown, they are available fresh and dried. Fresh shiitake should have smooth, plump caps, while better-quality dried ones will have pale cracks in the cap's surface. Dried shiitake and Chinese black mushrooms are interchangeable. Shiitake take well to grilling, roasting, stir-frying, and sautéing. Remove their thin, tough stems before using.

STRAW MUSHROOM Grown on straw left in rice paddies after harvest. These small, globe-shaped mushrooms have a distinct earthy flavor and a color ranging from beige to brown. Only available canned outside of Asia, they are a common addition to soups and stir-fries.

TREE OR WOOD EAR MUSHROOM Smaller, more delicate variety of the cloud ear, resembling crinkled black flakes. They are used much like cloud ears.

WHITE MUSHROOM The cultivated, all-purpose mushroom sold in grocery stores. Sometimes called button mushrooms, although the term refers specifically to young, tender ones with closed caps. For general cooking, use the medium-sized mushrooms with little or no gills showing. The large ones are excellent for stuffing.

Selecting Fresh mushrooms should be firm and have smooth, unblemished caps. Avoid any that are broken, limp, wrinkled, soggy, or moldy. Stems with gray, dried ends indicate that the mushrooms have been stored too long. Some mushrooms have closed caps, like the common button mushroom. For these varieties, if the caps are open so that the gills are exposed, the mushrooms are too old. For varieties where the gills are exposed, like portobellos, check that the gills are unbroken. As mushrooms age, they dry out, so the heaviest mushrooms should be the freshest. If you plan to cook mushrooms whole, select those with caps of the same size for even cooking. Check that packaged, presliced mushrooms are not wrinkled or discolored. Mushrooms are also available whole or sliced in jars, preserved in a brine or marinated with oil and herbs.

Storing Refrigerate fresh mushrooms for no more than 3 or 4 days, keeping them in a paper bag to absorb excess moisture. Spread delicate varieties in a single layer on a tray and cover them with a damp cloth. If sealed in plastic, mushrooms will become slimy and mold quickly.

Preparing Mushrooms absorb water readily, becoming soggy and flavorless if left to soak. While some cooks insist that you should not wash mushrooms at all, a quick rinse and a thorough drying with paper towels immediately before cooking will not hurt them. If you have time or plan to cook only a few mushrooms, wipe them clean with a damp cloth or brush. Special mushroom brushes are available for gentle removal of dirt, or a toothbrush with soft bristles will work. Trim the dried end of tender stems; but if the stems are tough, remove them completely (and save them for soup or stock).

Brushing a mushroom.

When mushrooms are sautéed, they will at first give off a great deal of liquid when they hit the hot pan. Continue to cook them until they have reabsorbed all their flavorful juices and the pan is almost dry. Some mushrooms will shrink to less than half their original size.

HOW TO *Reconstitute Dried Mushrooms*

Reconstituted, or rehydrated, dried mushrooms may be substituted for fresh ones in most cooked dishes, although they may take longer to become tender. Cooks love dried mushrooms for their intense flavors and firmer textures.

1. Cover dried mushrooms with warm water or stock, letting sliced ones or pieces soak for 30 minutes and whole ones for 1 hour. Or for fuller flavor, reconstitute them in cold liquid overnight in the refrigerator.

2. Do not discard the flavorful soaking liquid. Strain it through cheesecloth or a coffee filter and use it in the same recipe as the mushrooms, or add it to other soups or sauces.

Quick Bite

Duxelles, a classic French mixture of finely chopped mushrooms and aromatics, is cooked until rich and flavorful. It is used primarily in sauces and fillings.

Mushroom Savvy

■ Toss raw white mushrooms, whole or sliced, with lemon juice to prevent discoloring.

■ To keep white mushrooms snowy white, rub them with a paper towel that has been dipped in acidulated water.

■ Cooking pale mushrooms in a pan of aluminum or cast iron will darken them, although it won't affect their flavor.

■ For the best flavor and texture in a finished dish, sauté mushrooms before adding them to a soup, sauce, or risotto.

■ For a more complex flavor, try replacing a small portion of the fresh mushrooms called for in a recipe with rehydrated dried ones.

■ To stretch wild mushrooms, mix them with less expensive cremini or white button mushrooms. Experiment with different combinations, but avoid mixing highly flavored ones with delicate varieties, or the flavors will not be balanced.

HOW TO *Make Duxelles*

1. Finely chop mushrooms—any variety will do—along with tender stems. (Because they will shrink significantly, use about twice the volume of fresh mushrooms as you will need cooked for the dish.) Wrap them in a kitchen towel, a handful at a time, and squeeze to remove as much moisture as possible.

2. In a skillet over medium-high heat, briskly sauté the mushrooms with finely chopped shallots or onion in unsalted butter, stirring occasionally, until the mushrooms and shallots or onion are lightly browned and the mushrooms begin to separate. The timing will depend on the type and quantity of mushroom used.

3. When the mushrooms are dry and tender, season with salt and freshly ground pepper. (Sometimes ground nutmeg is added as well.) Remove from the heat and use immediately or let cool, cover, and refrigerate.

See also TRUFFLE.

MUSSEL A saltwater mollusk with slightly pointed shells ranging in color from blue-green to yellowish brown to inky black. Mussels have cream to orange-colored meat that is sweeter than that of oysters or clams. Mussels are an excellent buy, too, since they generally are less expensive than other shellfish.

The majority of the mussels available in the marketplace today are cultivated. Although there are dozens of different species, the two mostly widely available are the Atlantic blue or common mussel and the Pacific green-lipped or New Zealand mussel. The blue mussel, which is actually quite black, is 2 to 3 inches long. The green-lipped mussel is larger, 3 to 4 inches long, but its meat is also tougher.

Selecting Buy live mussels from a reputable fishmonger. They should have a fresh sea smell, with no trace of ammonia. Tap the mussels, and do not buy them if they stay open, indicating a dead or at least dehydrated mussel. To cut preparation time, look for already-shucked and cooked mussels chilled in the seafood section or freezer case of your supermarket. Already-shucked mussels are also available frozen, and occasionally mussels can be found frozen on the half shell. Mussels are also available smoked and canned.

Storing Remove live mussels from their packaging, place them in a bowl, cover them completely with a moist kitchen towel, and refrigerate. Dampen the towel if it dries out during storage. Since they also need air, do not cover mussels with water or seal them in a plastic bag. Fresh mussels are best if used as soon as possible; keep them for no more than 1 day. To freeze, place live mussels in a zippered plastic freezer bag and store for no more than 3 months. Defrost frozen mussels slowly in the refrigerator before cooking.

Preparing Scrub grit off the shells of fresh mussels with a stiff-bristled brush, then debeard each mussel, as needed.

Scrubbing a mussel.

HOW TO *Debeard a Mussel*

1. Remove the beard, the little tuft of fibers the mussel uses to connect to rocks or pilings, by cutting and scraping it with a knife or scissors. You may also pull it sharply down toward the hinged point of the shells with your fingers, but this does tend to pull away a bit of the meat, so many cooks prefer to cut it.

Do not debeard mussels more than an hour before cooking, since doing so kills them. All mussels used to come with a very tough beard, but today farm-raised ones have hardly any beard, making cleaning them less of a chore.

While cleaning them, discard any mussels that are very light, as they are likely dead, or any that are heavy with sand. Remember that live mussels will close tightly, if a little slowly, when touched. If in doubt, try twisting the shells sideways in opposite directions, as if unscrewing a bottle cap. The shells of dead mussels will break apart easily. The mussels should open up again after cooking. Check cooked mussels and discard any that failed to open.

Caution!

Since mussels are susceptible to water contaminants and "red tides" of poisonous plankton, be sure to read posted signs and check with local health or game agencies before collecting your own mussels.

To shuck mussels, or remove the shells, steam them with 1 inch of liquid for 2 to 3 minutes, just until they loosen and open slightly. With a small knife—preferably one designed for shucking clams—pry open the shells and cut the meat away. Reserve the steaming liquid to use in the sauce.

Smaller mussels are best for steaming, while the larger ones lend themselves to stuffing, broiling, or grilling.

See also DEBEARDING; SHELLFISH.

MUSTARD, PREPARED At its simplest, prepared mustard is a mixture of ground mustard seed and water. But this basic paste has been refined around the world by the addition of everything from wine, beer, vinegar, fruit juice, and honey to a multitude of herbs and aromatics. 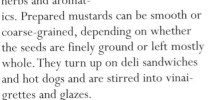 Prepared mustards can be smooth or coarse-grained, depending on whether the seeds are finely ground or left mostly whole. They turn up on deli sandwiches and hot dogs and are stirred into vinaigrettes and glazes.

Selecting Finer mustards are available in glass jars, while the popular American style

Prepared-Mustard Glossary

AMERICAN MUSTARD The classic ballpark mustard. Made from yellow seeds, it is mild, yet with an edge of sharp pungency. Its bright yellow color comes from the addition of ground turmeric.

CHINESE MUSTARD Hot, pale yellow mustard served in Chinese restaurants, made by mixing powdered mustard with water.

DIJON MUSTARD Silky smooth and slightly tangy. Originating in Dijon, France, the mustard contains brown or black seeds, white wine, and herbs.

ENGLISH MUSTARD Very hot. Made from a combination of brown or black seeds and yellow seeds that have been ground very finely, along with wheat flour and turmeric. Usually mixed from powder.

GERMAN MUSTARD Mild or hot, hearty, and slightly sweet, to complement German sausages. It can be coarse or smooth. It has a dark color since the whole seed is used.

is found in convenient squeeze bottles. As with other condiments, experiment with different mustards, finding those you like.

Storing Since naturally occurring compounds effectively inhibit the growth of bacteria in prepared mustard, it will keep indefinitely in a tightly lidded glass or ceramic container in the refrigerator.

See also SPICE.

MUSTARD GREENS See GREENS, DARK.

MUSTARD SEED See SPICE.

everything from nonreactive to nutmeg

NAVY BEAN See BEAN, DRIED.

NECTARINE See PEACH.

NONREACTIVE Every cook who regularly reads recipes has seen the following phrase, "combine the ingredients in a nonreactive bowl or pan." The meaning behind this instruction is quite simple: acidic ingredients such as tomatoes, citrus juice, vinegar, wine, and most vegetables will react with certain metals, resulting in a chemical reaction that creates an "off" flavor and unappealing (though harmless) dark color. A nonreactive pan or bowl is one made of or lined with a material—most commonly stainless steel, enamel, glass—that will not react with acidic ingredients. Reactive materials include nonanodized aluminum, unlined copper, or cast iron. Cast iron is the least problematic reactive material, however, and it can generally be used for preparing acidic food if the food is not left in the pan for an extended period of time.

NONSTICK See BAKEWARE; COOKWARE.

NOODLE See opposite page.

NOPAL CACTUS The nopal, also known as the prickly pear cactus, is grown both for its succulent, oval, flat pads, or paddles, and its sweet, egg-shaped fruits called prickly pears. The thorn-covered paddles, or *nopales* in Spanish, have a taste reminiscent of green beans, and the cleaned pads are cut up, cooked, and served as a vegetable, in salads, or in scrambled eggs. The fruits, also known as Indian figs and, in Spanish, *tunas,* appear in late summer on the mature joints of the plant. They range from pale yellow to magenta to red and are eaten out of hand or puréed and used as a dessert sauce or for making sorbet.
Selecting Look in Latin markets and well-stocked supermarkets for firm, slim paddles that are free of wrinkles and blemishes. They should have a fresh, bright green color. Fresh paddles are occasionally sold, both whole and cut up, with the spines removed, a real time-saver. Cactus pieces are also sold in cans or jars. Choose firm prickly pears that have a slight sheen.
Storing Refrigerate fresh paddles or fruits in plastic bags for up to 4 days. Once opened, canned cactus pieces should be refrigerated for no more than 1 week. If left on a countertop, underripe prickly pear fruits will soften within a few days.
Preparing To remove nopal spines, don heavy gloves or use a thick towel to hold the paddle, then pare away the bumps that conceal the tiny thorns and trim off the tough, fibrous base. Do not peel away all the green skin that sheaths the paddle. Cut as directed in individual recipes, then cook in boiling salted water until tender, 10 to 20 minutes, depending on the freshness and age of the cactus; drain, rinse well to rid the pieces of sliminess, and use as desired.

Prickly pears are usually sold with the spines removed (watch out for overlooked ones) but must be peeled and seeded before eating.

Noodle

Stemming perhaps from the perennial debate between those who believe the Chinese noodle predated spaghetti and those who insist Italians made pasta long before the time of Marco Polo, the terms *noodle* and *pasta* refer more to geographic distinctions than culinary classifications.

For details about the most popular and widespread Western-style noodles, see PASTA. Of course, pasta is not the only noodle story in the West. German, Dutch, and Eastern European noodle dishes like spaetzle and kugel are some of the world's most enduring comfort foods.

In Asia, where noodles symbolize long life, they are eaten throughout the day. A big bowl of noodle soup is a standard breakfast, stir-fried noodles from the corner vendor make a quick lunch, and seafood-crowned crisp fried noodles are served at formal dinners. Noodle uses vary, but most can be served with stir-fried meats, seafood, and vegetables. Try tossing your favorite stir-fry dish with cooked noodles in place of serving it over rice. They are also refreshing served cold, with simple sauces and thinly sliced vegetables.

Oodles of Noodles The flour, whether bean, rice, or wheat, used to make Asian noodles generally also categorizes them.

BUCKWHEAT NOODLES Popular in Japan, where they are known as soba, these grayish beige noodles have square-cut edges and a nutty, faintly sweet flavor. They are available fresh and dried, and are used in soups or chilled and accompanied with a dipping sauce during summer. Cook dried buckwheat noodles in boiling water until al dente.

CELLOPHANE NOODLES See Mung Bean Noodles, page 306.

DUMPLING WRAPPERS Rolled into thin sheets from the same dough as wheat noodles and then cut into squares or rounds, dumpling wrappers vary in size and thickness. Paper-thin squares are shaped into tender wontons for soup, slightly thicker rounds encase pot stickers, and larger sheets make crisp, golden brown egg rolls. Packaged in plastic, fresh wrappers keep for up to 1 week if sealed well and refrigerated. You'll find them in the refrigerator cases of Asian markets. When selecting them, thumb the stack of wrappers to check that their edges are firm and separate easily.

EGG NOODLES Much like Italian egg pasta, egg noodles are cut or extruded from a dough of wheat flour, eggs, and salt. The noodles can be narrow or wide, thin or thick, round or square, and are available dried or fresh, in tangled skeins or neat bundles. Check the packaging carefully; some noodles labeled "egg flavored" are artificially flavored. Asian egg noodles can be boiled and added to soups, braised with sauces, fried into a crisp cake, or stir-fried with meat and vegetables. Shrimp- and crab-flavored Asian egg noodles contain roe

continued

Noodle, continued

from the shellfish to complement seafood dishes. Boil fresh egg noodles for 2 to 3 minutes until al dente. See also PASTA.

MIE(N) See Wheat Noodles, below.

MUNG BEAN NOODLES Also called cellophane noodles, transparent noodles, glass noodles, or bean thread noodles, mung bean noodles are dried noodles made from ground mung bean flour and water. They resemble thin, white wires when dry but become soft and transparent after cooking. They are usually bundled in 1½-ounce skeins. Soften in warm water for 20 minutes before using in thin soups and stir-fried noodle dishes. If you wish to cut the noodles into shorter lengths, do so with scissors after soaking. Deep-fried without soaking, they expand into a nest of puffy, white crisps.

RICE NOODLES Made from rice flour and water, rice noodles vary in size from very thin dried rice sticks to wide, ribbonlike noodles. They appear in pad thai, spring rolls, and Vietnamese soups. Soak dried rice noodles in warm water for 20 minutes, cook them for 2 to 3 minutes just until al dente, and then rinse them in cold water. Soak but do not precook if you plan to stir-fry them; the sauce will soften and cook them just enough. Unlike mung bean noodles, dried rice noodles can overcook easily and turn to mush. Look for them in clear plastic packages, most often sold dried either as loose skeins or tightly tied into bricklike bundles. Fresh rice noodles, sold cut into ribbons usually about ¾ inch wide or in sheets to be cut as desired by the cook, are available in Asian markets. They are served hot or at room temperature. Wider versions generally are used in stir-fried dishes, while narrower ones are added to soups. Cook them for 1 to 2 minutes in boiling water to heat them through and make them pliable.

RICE VERMICELLI Often confused with rice noodles, dried rice vermicelli are more creamy in color, very straight, and packaged in small, ribbon-tied bundles. They cook extremely quickly, often needing only a soaking in hot water before being drained. They are delicate in texture and flavor and are used in both sweet and savory dishes, from Indonesian soups to Indian desserts. Like mung bean noodles, they expand to feathery, crisp threads when deep-fried.

SOBA NOODLES See Buckwheat Noodles, page 305.

SOMEN NOODLES See Wheat Noodles, below.

UDON NOODLES See Wheat Noodles, below.

WHEAT NOODLES Called *mie* or *mien,* a term derived from Chinese, in many Asian countries, wheat noodles are made from wheat flour, water, and salt and are sold fresh and dried. Without eggs, they tend to be lighter in color than egg noodles but come in the same variety of sizes and shapes. In Japan, thin wheat noodles are called *somen,* and thick, hearty wheat noodles are known as *udon.* After they have been boiled, wheat noodles may be fried into crisp pancakes, braised in a thick sauce, or added to soups.

WONTON WRAPPERS See Dumpling Wrappers, page 305.

Selecting Noodles are available dried, fresh, and frozen, with the last two primarily found in Asian markets. In general, fresh noodles are the best. Check packages for firm noodles that separate easily and avoid any that look soft, gray, or clumped. Dried noodles should not have pale spots or many broken pieces.

Storing Keep fresh noodles sealed in plastic in the refrigerator for up to 3 days. Fresh noodles freeze well, but defrost them completely before cooking. Store dried noodles in a cool, dark place for up to 6 months.

Preparing See specific noodle entries above for special instructions. Fresh and dried noodles are usually boiled before they are used. In general, cook noodles in a large pot of unsalted boiling water, stirring gently from time to time to separate the noodles while they cook. They should be cooked briefly, just until they are al dente. Once the water has returned to a boil and depending on size, fresh or thawed noodles require only 1 to 2 minutes, while dried noodles may need 2 to 3 minutes, or longer. Drain noodles in a colander and rinse them with cold water, tossing constantly, to stop the cooking and wash away excess starch that would cloud stocks and overthicken stir-fries and braises. Use as directed. (Not all cooks agree that noodles should be rinsed with cold water. Follow the recipe or use your own judgment.)

If coated with a tiny amount of oil and wrapped well, cooked noodles can be refrigerated for a day. Although not traditionally done in Asian cooking, some Westerners like to cook fresh egg noodles directly in soups without precooking, so that the extra starch coating the noodles will thicken the stock into more of a sauce consistency.

See also AL DENTE; PASTA.

NORI See SEAWEED.

NUT See page 308.

NUTMEG Although long prescribed as medicine and burnt as incense, nutmeg did not enter the kitchen until the 16th century. It is the seed of a tropical evergreen tree: brown, oblong, and closely wrapped in a brilliant red, lacy membrane. (The membrane, or aril, becomes the similarly flavored spice known as mace.) Whole nutmegs resemble unshelled pecans. The spice's warm sweetness complements creamy sauces, egg and cheese dishes, spiced cakes and cookies, fruit desserts, vegetables, and hot drinks. In France, a pinch of ground nutmeg is the secret ingredient in many spinach dishes.

Selecting Both whole and ground nutmeg are widely available, but nutmeg you grind or grate yourself from the whole spice far surpasses the packaged powdered spice.

Storing Keep ground and whole nutmeg in airtight containers away from light and heat. Whole nutmeg will keep for up to 2 years, but the flavor of ground nutmeg will dissipate after 6 months.

Preparing Grate whole nutmeg on specialized nutmeg graters, which have tiny rasps and usually a small compartment for storing a nutmeg or two. The finest rasps of a box grater may also be used. Nutmeg is powerful; even a tiny pinch will flavor an entire dish. Add it at the start of cooking to allow its flavor to mellow and meld with other ingredients.

See also GRATING; SPICE.

NUTRITION See FAT & OIL; FOOD GUIDE PYRAMID; LABEL TERMS; LOW-FAT COOKING.

n

Nut

Nuts find favor in kitchens the world over. Almonds thicken romesco sauce in Spain, cashews add crunch to curries in India, pecan halves generously fill pies in the American South, and rose-scented pistachios nestle among filo layers in Greece.

An essential ingredient in virtually every cuisine, nuts provide richness, flavor, body, crunch, and vital nutrients in dishes both sweet and savory. In their purest form, with their varied shapes and hues, unshelled nuts piled high in a festive bowl help mark the autumn season.

Most nuts have a hard shell, a protective coating developed by plants to shield their seeds from hungry animals. Inside each shell is usually one edible kernel. Once a staple in the diets of early hunter-gatherers, nuts are dense in nutrients, especially potassium, iron, vitamin E, and the B vitamins. But since they boast a high amount of fat and calories as well as proteins, nuts are best used in moderate amounts. Fortunately, even a light sprinkle of nuts will add noticeable flavor and texture to a variety of dishes such as pasta, salad, or ice cream.

A Guide to Nuts

ALMOND The meat found inside the pit of a dry fruit related to peaches, the almond is delicate and fragrant. It has a pointed, oval shape and a smooth texture that lends itself well to elegant presentations.

BRAZIL NUT Enclosed in a dark, hard, roughly textured shell shaped like a small orange segment, Brazil nuts taste somewhat like the meat of a coconut. They are the seeds of 250-foot-high trees that grow only in tropical regions of South America and require great labor to harvest. Best eaten as snacks or used in desserts.

CANDLENUT Looking like large macadamias, and sold packaged in Asian markets, these nuts of a native Malaysian bush are traditionally ground and mixed into the curries and spice pastes of the region to add body and richness. Macadamia or Brazil nuts or cashews may be substituted. The nut's name comes from the fact that Malaysian natives sometimes used the ground nuts as candles.

CASHEW A smooth, kidney-shaped nut from a tree native to Africa and India. They are always sold removed from their hard shell and caustic lining. Most commonly eaten whole as a snack, cashews also make excellent nut butter.

CHESTNUT Known as *marrons* in France, chestnuts are large and wrinkled and have a smooth, shiny, mahogany-colored shell shaped like a turban slightly flattened on one side. Unlike other nuts, they contain a high amount of starch and little oil. Often treated as a vegetable and almost always cooked, such as in a puréed soup or mixed with Brussels sprouts, sweet and rich chestnuts are also popular simply roasted whole and eaten while still hot.

You must cook chestnuts by briefly boiling or roasting them to loosen their tough outer shells and thin, bitter skins. Note that if you let the chestnuts cool after roasting or blanching them, they will again become difficult to peel. If they do cool, simply return them to a hot oven or hot water for 5 minutes to warm them up. For large amounts, roast or blanch and peel the nuts in batches, working steadily and without distractions.

HOW TO *Boil Chestnuts*

1. Using a small, sharp knife, score, or shallowly cut, an X in the flat side of the nut, being careful not to cut through the nutmeat.

2. Put the nuts into a large pot of boiling water and boil for 12 to 15 minutes. (They take 30 to 45 minutes if you're going to eat them plain.)
3. Drain and return the nuts to the still-hot pot (turn off the heat below it). Cover the pot to keep the nuts warm.
4. Take the nuts 1 or 2 at time from the pot, using a kitchen towel or pot holder. Peel back the scored X using your fingers or the knife. Peel off the outer shell and the thin, beige inner skin. Discard both the outer and inner skins.

HOW TO *Roast Chestnuts*

1. Using a small, sharp knife, score, or shallowly cut, an X in the flat side of the nut. Be careful not to cut through the nutmeat.

2. Lay the nuts in a single layer on an ungreased baking sheet and roast in a 350°F oven until the nuts are fragrant and the scored portions begin to separate from the shells, 15 to 20 minutes. (If you're going to eat them plain, increase the heat to 400°F and bake until they give slightly when pressed with oven mitt–protected fingers.)

3. Transfer the nuts to a platter or heatproof surface and cover with a damp kitchen towel to keep them warm.
4. Using a kitchen towel or pot holder, pick up each nut and, using your fingers or the knife, peel back the scored X. Peel off the hard outer shell and the thin, beige, soft inner skin. Discard both outer shell and inner skin. Discard any nuts that, once peeled, look dried out.

5. Eat the chestnuts immediately or use as directed in a recipe.

Quick Tip

Chestnuts have traditionally been roasted in fireplaces. They should be scored with an X first and nestled in the hot ashes of a dying fire. After 15 to 20 minutes, they will be fragrant and easy to shell.

continued

Nut, continued

COCONUT Like the almond, the coconut is the actual seed of a tree, a palm that grows in almost every tropical area. A dark brown, fibrous husk and a very hard shell enclose the rich, white flesh inside. See also COCONUT.

FILBERT See Hazelnut, below.

HAZELNUT Also known as filberts, grape-sized hazelnuts have hard shells that come to a point like an acorn, cream-colored flesh, and a sweet, rich, buttery flavor. Difficult to crack, they usually are sold already shelled.

MACADAMIA NUT Usually sold shelled, this rich nut originated in Australia but is now also grown widely in Hawaii. Smooth, off-white, and round, it resembles a large chickpea. Macadamias add crunch and sweet, buttery flavor to curries, salads, rice, cookies, candies, and ice cream.

PEANUT Actually not a nut but rather a type of legume that grows on underground stems, peanuts are seeds nestled inside waffle-veined pods that become thin and brittle once dried. The peanut has long been a nutritious staple throughout South America, Africa, and Asia, where it often flavors curries and garnishes salads. The peanut is also well known in North America in its puréed state as peanut butter; see also PEANUT BUTTER.

PECAN A native of North America, the pecan has two deeply crinkled lobes of nutmeat, much like its relative, the walnut. Hundreds of varieties exist, but they all have smooth, brown, oval shells that break easily. Their flavor is sweeter and more delicate than closely related walnuts.

PINE NUT The seed of pine trees, nestled in the scales of their cones. Pine nuts are small, rich nuts with an elongated, slightly tapered shape and a resinous, sweet flavor. Important in southern Europe and the Middle East, they appear in salads, stuffings, and sauces (most famously, pesto), as well as in baked goods and desserts.

PISTACHIO Used widely in Mediterranean, Middle Eastern, and Indian cuisines, the pistachio has a thin but hard shell that is creamy tan and rounded. Bright red nuts owe their color to vegetable dye. Pistachios are often used in desserts. As the nut ripens, its shell cracks to reveal a light green kernel inside.

WALNUT The furrowed, double-lobed nutmeat of the walnut has a rich, assertive flavor. The most common variety is the English walnut, also known as Persian walnut, which has a light brown shell that cracks easily. Black walnuts, native to North America, have dark shells that are extremely difficult to break. Almost always sold whole, black walnuts are a challenge to find and have a stronger, slightly astringent flavor desirable for desserts. The mild white walnut, or butternut, has a light tan shell.

Selecting Nuts in the shell remain fresh longer and are preferable if you have the time and inclination to shell them yourself. Look for whole nuts that are free of holes, cracks, and mold. Shake their shells; a rattling sound inside indicates old and dried nutmeats. Look for whole nuts sold in bulk at health-food stores or in specialty markets. Buying nuts in bulk is economical, but be sure that the store has a rapid turnover so you can purchase the nuts as fresh as possible. Nuts in the shell are best from autumn to early winter.

Shelled nuts should be plump and crisp. Avoid kernels that look withered or lack a snap when broken. Shelled nuts come whole, halved, chopped, and sometimes ground. Almonds can also be blanched (skinned), slivered, or sliced, and chestnuts are available dried, vacuum-packed, candied, or puréed. Supermarkets stock shelled nuts in plastic bags or vacuum-sealed jars and cans year-round.

Many nuts are available raw, roasted, or dry-roasted. Commercial roasted nuts tend to have more flavor, since they are actually fried in oil. On the other hand, no additional oil is used in the preparation of dry-roasted nuts. Nuts for snacking may be salted, smoked, or sweetened. Popular flavorings include garlic, jalapeño, and honey.

Occasionally, fresh green almonds or walnuts appear at farmers' markets during the late summer. Their tender, buttery flesh is a treat for snacking or grinding into a flavorful spread.

Storing Since they contain high amounts of oil, nuts will eventually turn rancid. Raw, unshelled nuts keep well for 6 months to 1 year if stored away from light, heat, and moisture. On the other hand, shelled nuts, especially chopped and unsalted ones, are convenient but have a shorter shelf life. Store shelled nuts in an airtight container for 1 to 2 months at room temperature, 3 to 6 months in the refrigerator, or 9 months to 1 year in the freezer in a zippered plastic freezer bag. (Exceptions: pistachios with partially opened shells will keep for only about half as long as other nuts; fresh chestnuts should be kept for no more than 1 week at room temperature, 1 month in the refrigerator, or 6 months in the freezer.) Be sure to check nuts for freshness before adding to recipes; rancid nuts will ruin the flavor of other foods.

Quick Tip

Generally, you will obtain about ½ pound nutmeats, or approximately 2 cups, from 1 pound unshelled nuts.

Although nut butters can remain at room temperature for several weeks, it is best to keep them in the refrigerator, where they will keep for up to 6 months. Since they are highly perishable, keep nut oils in the refrigerator for up to 4 months once they have been opened. Store nut flours in an airtight container or zippered plastic freezer bag in the freezer for 6 to 9 months.

Cracking Nuts Although you can shell some nuts, such as pistachios, with simply a press of your fingertips, others have hard shells that require more effort and additional equipment. Black walnuts and Brazil nuts call for a sturdy nutcracker, and macadamias demand a small hammer. There are two basic types of nutcrackers. The familiar stainless-steel lever with two grooved arms connected by a hinge usually comes with thin picks for removing the nutmeats. This effective and versatile cracker is also handy for opening lobster shells. Wooden screw-type nutcrackers have a small cup that holds a nut while you twist a knob that squeezes and eventually cracks the shell. Special nutcrackers are available for obtaining whole, intact nutmeats from pecans and walnuts.

continued

Nut, continued

For best results, soften the shells by covering them in boiling water and setting them aside to soak for about 15 minutes. Drain and dry well before cracking. Alternatively, bake the whole nuts in a 350°F oven for 15 to 20 minutes to make the shells more brittle. Let cool before cracking. Crack nuts lightly in several different places rather than in one big, crushing squeeze. Walnuts and pecans should be cracked along the seam in order to get an unbroken nut.

Quick Tip

If, after cracking nuts, you find a lot of shell bits mixed in with the kernels, pour the nutmeats into a large bowl of cold water. Slowly stir the nuts and let the pieces of shell float to the surface of the water. After skimming off the shells, drain and dry the nutmeats completely before using.

Skinning Nuts Some nuts have a thin, dark protective skin that can taste rather bitter. Blanching or toasting, depending on the type of nut, will loosen the skin for easy removal.

HOW TO *Skin Nuts by Blanching*
Works for almonds or pistachios.
1. Place the shelled nuts in a large bowl and pour boiling water over them.
2. Let sit for about 1 minute.
3. Drain in a colander and rinse with cold running water to cool.
4. Pinch each nut to slip the skin off.

HOW TO *Skin Nuts by Toasting*
Works for hazelnuts, walnuts, and peanuts.
1. Toast the nuts in a dry skillet over medium heat for 10 to 15 minutes, or until fragrant and golden. Shake the pan or stir occasionally as the nuts toast. Alternatively, toast in the oven; see Toasting Nuts, below.

2. While they are still warm, wrap them completely in a coarse-textured kitchen towel and rub vigorously to remove the skins.
3. An easy (albeit messy) way to sift nuts from the loose skins: Transfer the nuts and skins to a shallow bowl or pan. Toss while you blow or fan them over a sink or outdoors. The papery skins will fly up, leaving behind the nuts.

Chopping Nuts For the best texture, chop nuts by hand with a large, sharp knife. A food processor can crush and extract too much oil from nuts, quickly reducing them to a paste. However, if you are in a hurry or have a lot of nuts to chop, the food processor is the easiest way to do it. Pay attention and do not overwork them. Pulse the machine instead of running it continuously, in order to control the texture better. If you plan to use chopped nuts in a baking recipe, add a little of the flour or sugar from the list of dry ingredients to absorb excess oil as you process the nuts. This will help keep the nuts dry and help them spread evenly throughout the batter or dough.

Grinding Nuts When nuts are ground, they release their natural oils. The cook must be vigilant when grinding nuts, for they can easily end up as nut butter. A  rotary nut mill, a simple contraption with a hamper for holding the nuts and a manually turned arm, assures the baker of perfectly dry ground nuts every time. For less precise grinds, a food processor can be used. For best results, combine the nuts with a little of the flour or sugar called for in the recipe you are preparing and process for no more than 5 to 10 seconds at a time. Be sure to watch the nuts carefully to prevent overprocessing.

Quick Tip

Full-flavored oils pressed from nuts, like hazelnuts and walnuts, add depth to dressings and sauces. Try substituting 1 to 2 tablespoons walnut oil or hazelnut oil for the same amount of butter or vegetable oil in recipes for pancake batters, cakes, or muffins. Nut oil does go rancid, so always check its flavor before adding it to a recipe.

Toasting Nuts Whether you plan to sprinkle almonds over a salad or fold walnuts into a batter, toasting nuts will intensify their flavor and give them a crisp texture and attractive golden color. Large amounts of nuts are best toasted in the oven. Spread them in a single layer on a baking sheet and bake them in a 325°F oven, stirring occasionally to prevent over-browning at the edges of the pan, until the nuts are golden, fragrant, and coated in a thin layer of their own oil. Depending on the type of nut and the size of the pieces, this may take 10 to 20 minutes.

Quick Bite

Some desserts and sauces call for nut flours, or meals. Look in Italian markets for chestnut and almond flour and in Asian markets for peanut flour.

Toasting nuts in a microwave oven is quick and convenient. Although they will not turn golden, they will have much the same flavor as traditionally toasted nuts. Microwave them on a plate for 3 to 4 minutes, stirring them once about halfway through if the oven does not have a turntable. You can also toast small amounts of nuts in a dry skillet on the stove top. Cook the nuts over medium heat, stirring frequently, until they are golden. Keep a close eye on the nuts, especially pine nuts and sliced almonds, for they burn quickly.

Immediately transfer the nuts to a plate or paper towel and let them cool completely before using. Nuts will continue to toast, so cook them just a shade lighter than desired. They will become darker and crispier as they cool. Nuts easily develop acrid flavor if overbrowned, so just the exterior should be toasted, and the interior should remain lighter colored.

If needed, toast nuts in advance and store them in an airtight container at room temperature for up to 1 week.

See also BLANCHING; FAT & OIL; THICKENING.

Quick Tip

Most nuts contain 70 to 97 percent fat calories (except starchy chestnuts, which have only 8 percent). Fortunately, much of the fat is cholesterol-lowering monounsaturated and polyunsaturated fatty acids. Tropical nuts, especially the coconut, contain higher amounts of saturated fat.

N

O

everything from octopus to oyster sauce

OAT See GRAIN.

OCTOPUS Relatively unusual in mainstream American cuisine, octopus is well loved in Japan and in some of the Mediterranean countries. A diet of clams and scallops gives the octopus a rich flavor, but its meat can be quite tough and rubbery if not properly tenderized and cooked.

Like its relative the squid, octopus is best when cooked quickly over high heat or very slowly over low heat. It can be eaten raw, lightly pickled, sautéed, grilled, fried, boiled, or stewed. Its black ink colors and flavors sauces, stews, pastas, and risottos.
Selecting Look for fresh or frozen octopus in Japanese markets or specialty fish markets. If buying a whole octopus, ask the fishmonger to clean it for you, since it is an involved process. Usually, already-peeled and portioned tentacles are sold, and these can be found precooked.
Storing Keep octopus in the refrigerator, using it as soon as possible and keeping it for no more than 2 days. Defrost frozen octopus completely before cooking.
Preparing To tenderize octopus before cooking, pound well with a meat mallet, or plunge it several times into boiling water and then let it simmer for 5 to 6 minutes. Slice the tentacles crosswise or on a bias.

OFFAL See ORGAN MEATS.

OIL See FAT & OIL.

OKRA A slender, grayish green, ridged pod that contains numerous small, edible seeds, okra originated in Africa. Also called ladies' fingers, the tasty pods are now common fare throughout warmer climates, from India to the American South. Its mild flavor, similar to that of green beans, is often enlivened with spicy sauces, while its viscous quality thickens soups and stews such as gumbo. Okra is also delicious deep-fried.
Selecting Choose okra that is bright in color and free of bruises or soft spots. Its skin can be smooth or slightly fuzzy, depending on the variety. Okra pods grow up to 9 inches long, but they become increasingly tough and fibrous. Look for young, tender pods that are less than 4 inches in length. Although okra is available throughout the year in the South, it is most plentiful elsewhere in the country from May to October. Frozen okra (good for simmered dishes) and pickled okra are also marketed.
Storing The pods will keep for up to 3 days in the refrigerator, wrapped in a paper towel inside a perforated plastic bag. You also can blanch them briefly and freeze them for up to 8 months.
Preparing Small pods can be cooked whole, with only their tops sliced off. Larger pods are better if thickly sliced. If you don't like the sliminess typical of okra, however, cut off only the stem and do not cut the pod.

OLALLIEBERRY See BERRY.

OLIVE First cultivated in the Mediterranean basin thousands of years ago, the olive is one of the oldest and most important crops in the world. The fruit of a hardy, long-lived tree, fresh olives are too bitter to eat, even when completely ripe. After harvest, they are either pressed to make olive oil or coaxed by long curing into table olives.

The color of olives depends on when they are picked. Green olives are harvested before they ripen, while black olives have been left on the tree until completely ripe. Both are cured, and methods vary according to country and region, but the process basically involves months of sitting in oil, salt, water, brine, or in the sun. Alternatively, they can be processed in an alkaline solution for only a few days. With the American industrial method, half-ripe olives are bathed in lye and oxidized to develop a black color. These are called California or Mission olives and are the soft, mild ones available in cans.

Olives packed in brine stay plump, smooth, and relatively firm. Salt- or oil-cured olives become dry, wrinkled, and pleasantly bitter in flavor, and the best obtain a silky texture and rich flavor.
Selecting Olives are available pitted or unpitted. They may be packed in brine, dried in salt, marinated in oil with herbs and spices, or even stuffed with pimientos, anchovies, or almonds. Look for them in cans, jars, and plastic containers in the refrigerated section of the supermarket, and in bulk in the deli section. Choose evenly colored olives free of white spots.
Storing Covered completely with water, brine, or oil, olives will keep for 1 year in the refrigerator. Store salt-packed olives in an airtight, nonmetallic container for up to 6 months.

Olive Glossary

GAETA Brownish black and with a nutty flavor, the Gaeta, from Italy, is salt-cured but soft and smooth.
GREEK When "Greek olives" are called for in a recipe, most likely Kalamata olives are meant.
KALAMATA Most popular variety from Greece. Almond shaped, purplish black, rich, and meaty, the Kalamata is brine-cured and then packed in oil or vinegar.
MOROCCAN Can refer to either a large brine-cured, reddish green olive or a salt-cured, wrinkled, black one. Moroccan green olives are soft and salty-tart, while Moroccan black olives boast a glistening, silky texture and a meaty, slightly smoky, and pleasantly bitter flavor.
NIÇOISE A small, brownish black olive from Provence. Brine-cured, then packed in oil with lemon and herbs, the mellow and nutty olives appear in stews and authentic tapenade.
PICHOLINE Medium-sized, green, smooth, and very salty olives from France.
SICILIAN Large, green, tart, and meaty olives sometimes flavored with red pepper or fennel.
SPANISH Large, green, and dense, these olives are commonly pitted and stuffed with pimientos, almonds, or anchovies.

O

Preparing To remove the pits of smaller olives, use a cherry pitter or an olive pitter.

HOW TO *Pit Olives When You Don't Own a Pitter*

1. Spread the olives in a single layer on a cutting board.
2. Crush them gently with a rolling pin, the bottom of a pan, or the flat side of a chef's knife.
3. Most of the pits should roll out of the cracked olives. You can quickly pop out any stubborn pits with your fingers. Or carefully open the olive with a small sharp knife to remove the pit.

See also FAT & OIL.

OMELET An egg dish in which beaten eggs are cooked in a shallow pan, producing a firm exterior and soft interior. The omelet is usually folded over or rolled around a savory filling. Rolled omelets are called French omelets, and they might be filled with a simple scattering of fresh herbs or shredded cheese or more bountiful additions. There are also flat omelets, which resemble frittatas, and soufflé omelets, in which the egg whites are beaten to create a light and fluffy end result. Omelets can be made with whole eggs, egg whites alone, or a mixture of whole eggs and egg whites.

Any skillet may be used, but specialized omelet pans with rounded flared sides, often nonstick, make it easier to turn the omelet out of the pan, folding it in the process.

When beating eggs for omelets, try not to beat too much air into them. Foamy eggs interfere with an omelet's texture.

HOW TO *Make an Omelet*

1. Break the eggs called for in a recipe into a mixing bowl. Using a wire whisk or a fork, beat the eggs and a little water, just until the eggs are blended and only slightly frothy.

2. Heat an omelet pan or a skillet over medium heat. Add the butter and, once it melts and foams, the eggs. As the eggs begin to set along the edges and bottom, use a spatula or fork to push the edges toward the center, tilting the pan to let the liquid egg on top flow to the edges and run underneath.
3. When the eggs are almost set but still slightly moist on top, spoon the prepared filling, if using, over the half opposite from you. Shake the pan to loosen the omelet, then tilt the pan to let the filled half slide halfway up the side of the pan. Use the spatula or fork to fold the far edge over itself or the filling.

4. Gently roll the omelet onto the serving plate, folding it over itself (and any filling).

Onion

Belonging to the same family as garlic and leeks, this multi-layered bulb is a staple in nearly every kitchen. "Cook the onions until soft and golden" is the familiar first step in countless savory dishes, from tomato sauces to beef stews.

Onions are crisp and pungent when raw and become soft and sweet when cooked. Two types of onions are available, fresh or spring onions and dried or storage onions, the latter being the kind most of us think of when we consider the onion. Fresh onions include green onions and such sweet onions as Vidalia or Maui. Dried onions have been cured by drying, a process that causes their skins to tighten and protect against spoilage. The curing also concentrates their flavor, dries their skins, and brings out the colors that help shoppers identify the different types.

Assorted onions.

A Guide to Onions

GREEN ONION Also known as scallion or, sometimes, spring onion. Green onions are the immature shoots of the bulb onion, with a narrow white base that has not yet begun to swell and long, flat green leaves. Recipes often specify whether to use only the white base, the

green tops, or both. Green onions have a mild flavor and can be enjoyed raw in salads, while their chopped or minced green tops are often used as a garnish. They are used extensively in Chinese cooking, especially in stir-fries. Whole green onions can also be grilled—in this form a popular addition to Mexican plates—or braised like leeks, and the white base of green onions may be used as a substitute for harder-to-find shallots.

MAUI, VIDALIA, AND WALLA WALLA ONIONS Fresh onions that are mild, sweet, and juicy and named for their place of origin, since, due to soil and climate, they lose their characteristic sweetness if grown elsewhere. Maui and Vidalia onions, from Hawaii and Georgia, respectively, come into season during spring, and Walla Walla, from Washington, during late summer. Worth hunting down in well-stocked supermarkets and finer produce markets, they are best

continued

O

Onion, continued

eaten raw in sandwiches, in salads, or, enthusiasts insist, out of hand. Usually sold loose.

Vidalia onion.

PEARL AND BOILING ONIONS Pearl onions are small, dried onions no more than 1 inch in diameter. They are traditionally white, although red ones are now available. Boiling onions are also white and slightly larger. Both pearl and boiling onions have a mild flavor similar to that of green onions. They are often served as a garnish for stews, roasted meats, and marinated salads, or used for braised or creamed onions. Also available pickled or frozen.

Pearl onions.

HOW TO *Peel Pearl and Boiling Onions*

Peeling a pile of pearl onions may seem daunting, but blanching them first will help the task pass more quickly and easily.

1. Bring a large pot of water to a full boil.
2. Put the onions in the boiling water. Cook for 1 minute, counting from when the water returns to a boil.
3. Drain the onions in a colander. Rinse them under cold running water, tossing continuously, until they are cool.
4. With a sharp paring knife, trim the root and stem ends of each onion.

5. Pinch the onions to remove their skins.

6. Many cooks score, or shallowly cut, an X in each pearl onion's root end to shorten cooking time, ensure even cooking, and help keep the layers from telescoping.

RED ONION Also called Italian onion and Bermuda onion. Mild and slightly sweet, this purplish red onion is delicious raw in salads, sandwiches, and relishes and briefly cooked in vegetable mixes. Extended cooking will dull the color to gray. Sweet elongated varieties, found in farmers' markets, are called torpedo onions.

Red torpedo onion.

SHALLOT This small member of the onion family looks like a large clove of garlic covered with papery bronze or reddish skin. Shallots have white flesh lightly streaked with purple, a crisp texture, and a flavor that is subtler than that of an onion. They are often used for flavoring sauces and salad dressings that would be overpowered by the stronger taste of onion. The white part of a green onion may be substituted for a shallot.

SPANISH ONION Very large, round yellow onion. Similar to yellow onions and used in the same way.

WHITE ONION More pungent than the red onion, but milder and less sweet than the yellow, the white onion is a favorite of the Mexican cook. Large, slightly flattened, mild white onions are sometimes called white Spanish onions.

YELLOW ONION The yellow globe onion is the common, all-purpose onion sold in super-markets. It can be globular, flattened, or slightly elon-gated and, since it is dried, has a parchmentlike golden brown skin. It usually is too harsh for serving raw but becomes rich and sweet when cooked, making it the ideal onion for caramelizing.

Selecting Choose fresh onions that look perky. For green onions, the shoots should be green with white bulb ends. For Vidalia and Maui, seek out fresh-looking, tubular green stems. For dried onions, choose firm specimens with smooth, dry skins. Avoid any with soft spots, particularly at the stem end; green shoots; moldy areas; or moist, wrinkled skins.

Storing Store green onions in a perfo-rated plastic bag for up to 2 weeks in the refrigerator. Keep other onions in a cool, dark, well-ventilated place. Do not leave them in plastic bags, using instead a basket or crate to allow air circulation. Storing them alongside other vegetables (such as potatoes) that may give off gases or mois-ture will spoil the onions quickly. Discard

onions that begin growing shoots, as they will taste bitter.

Preparing Nearly everyone wants the secret to preventing the tears that spring to your eyes when chopping a strong onion. Ideas range from the folksy (clamp a wooden spoon or kitchen match between your teeth) to the somewhat scientific (freeze the onions briefly to slow enzymes, or light candles to burn off irritating sulfur compounds) to the purely pragmatic (wear swimming goggles) to the foolish (keep your eyes closed). Since most of the tear-inducing sulfuric compounds are concen-trated near the roots, trimming the stem end first, peeling downward, and cutting the root end last may help delay the onset of tears. The easiest preventives are to use your sharpest knife, avoid touching your face with oniony fingers, and work as quickly as you possibly can.

Onions can be chopped in a food pro-cessor, but the pieces will be irregular. More important, the processor's blade also

continued

Onion, continued

crushes the onion, releasing more juice and altering its flavor and texture.

When using green onions, you need only trim away the root end and any wilted or brown portions of the tops; both the green and white parts can be used, and recipes generally specify.

Cut all onions as close to cooking or serving time as possible. Their flavor deteriorates while their aroma intensifies over time.

HOW TO *Slice an Onion or a Shallot*

1. Peel the onion.
2. Slice a small piece from the onion's side to create a flat surface.

3. Place the onion flat side down on a cutting board. Now that the onion is stable, proceed to slice it, keeping fingertips safely clear of the blade.

Note that this technique is useful for slicing nearly all round fruits and vegetables.

HOW TO *Chop an Onion or a Shallot*

1. Cut the onion in half lengthwise from stem to root end, then peel it.
2. Put an onion half flat side down on a cutting board, hold the stem end with your fingertips safely curled under and away from the blade, and, with the knife tip pointed toward the stem end, make a series of parallel vertical cuts through the onion half, at right angles to the cutting board. Do not cut all the way through the stem end.

3. Turn your knife so that it is parallel with the cutting board and perpendicular to the first series of cuts, and make a series of horizontal cuts in the onion half, again not cutting through the stem end. The onion half should stay in one piece, more or less.

4. To chop the onion, simply slice the onion across the first cuts made in step 1.

See also LEEK.

ORANGE The orange was first cultivated in China more than two thousand years ago and is now grown around the world. Long a symbol of abundance and prosperity, orange trees decorate royal palaces, their flowers grace bridal bouquets, and their juicy, sweet-tart fruit appears on tables fresh, juiced, and incorporated into countless savory and sweet dishes.

These international fruits fall into two broad categories: sweet and bitter. Sweet oranges are further divided into three groups: common, navel, and blood. The most popular common orange is the Valencia, considered the best for juicing because of its thin skin and juicy pulp. Navel oranges are sweet, easy to peel, and almost always seedless, making them ideal for eating out of hand. Blood oranges, originally from Sicily, have distinctive red flesh and juice and a flavor reminiscent of berries. As versatile as they are dramatic, blood oranges can be eaten out of hand or used in salads, sauces, desserts, and drinks.

Blood oranges.

Bitter oranges have dry pulp, a thick rind, and an extremely bitter flavor. Hardly candidates for the fruit bowl, bitter oranges and their flavorful peels make excellent marmalades, candies, sauces, syrups, and liqueurs. Seville and Bergamot, oils from the latter being what gives Earl Grey tea its elusive flavor and aroma, are the two best-known varieties.

Selecting Choose oranges that are heavy for their size and have smooth skins. Don't look askance at an orange with brown surface patches. The imperfect peel may be hiding an extra dose of juice and sweetness. Color is not a good indicator of quality, since oranges are sometimes dyed and fully ripened oranges may regreen, particularly Valencias. Do avoid fruits with soft or moldy spots, however.

Oranges are available all year, but they have different peak seasons depending on variety. Valencias are at the height of their season from May through July, navels are best from January through March, and blood oranges peak from mid-December through March.

Storing Oranges can be left at room temperature for 1 week or kept in the refrigerator for up to 3 weeks.

Preparing For best flavor, serve oranges raw or cook them only briefly. Before peeling an orange, squeeze it between your palms or roll it on a countertop, pressing down. This will make the orange a little juicier and easier to peel. Special plastic orange peelers have a small cutting edge and a flat, curved blade that is slipped beneath the peel to separate it quickly and cleanly from the flesh. But, often the best way to serve oranges as a snack is to cut them, peel and all, into thick wedges.

Quick Tip

Don't overlook the pleasures of cooking with oranges. Add a little orange juice to the cooking water for rice to get a tangy pilaf to serve with chicken or lamb. Or toss orange segments with sliced fennel and endive for a refreshing appetizer salad.

O

HOW TO *Section an Orange*

1. Slice off the orange's top and bottom.
2. Stand the orange upright. Following the contour of the fruit, slice off the peel, pith, and membrane in thick strips.

3. Holding the fruit over a bowl, cut along each side of the membrane between the sections, letting each freed section drop into the bowl.

See also JUICING; ZESTING.

OREGANO See HERB.

ORGANIC With consumers ever more concerned about the quality and safety of the foods they eat, the term *organic* continues to rise in the public consciousness and appear on food labels in farmers' markets, health-food stores, and supermarkets alike. While government definitions may vary, the term generally refers to foods—whether plant or animal in origin—produced naturally, without the use of chemical-based pesticides, fungicides, or antibiotics. While the jury remains out on whether organic products are inherently safer or more nutritious, or whether those produced by conventional means are less so, organic products do offer one distinctive advantage: often, they are grown locally, ensuring that the products found in your market will be fresher, more flavorful, and possibly higher in nutrients.

ORGAN MEATS Sometimes also referred to by the term "offal," these types of animal proteins derive from internal organs. In general, when properly prepared and cooked, they combine very soft, tender texture with distinctive flavor. Most common types include liver, which may come from beef, veal, lamb, chicken, goose, or duck; kidneys, of which veal and lamb have the mildest flavor; sweetbreads, the tender and subtly sweet thymus glands of veal, lamb, or pork; and brains from lamb or veal, which are surprisingly delicate in both taste and texture.

OVEN Nowadays, ovens keep time, schedule dinner, clean themselves, and can even turn a roasting chicken for you. Despite all the available bells and whistles, ovens can be divided into three basic kinds. Each uses different types of energy and, more important, has different heating characteristics. Knowing what each one can and cannot do will help ensure that your roast is moist and flavorful, your casseroles creamy, and your cookies perfectly golden brown. Now available is a combination oven that offers all three functions.

Oven Options Three basic oven types are available for home kitchens.

THERMAL OVEN Uses radiant heat from gas flames or electric elements to cook foods with dry heat. Hot spots can occur, so be sure to check the food and turn it as needed for even cooking. Large pans or baking sheets can block heat and create noticeable variances in temperature between racks. Electric ovens tend to cook food more quickly and evenly than gas ovens. Most standard stoves are fitted with thermal ovens.

CONVECTION OVEN Has a fan that blows heated air throughout the oven. No matter how many pans or what their size, food cooks quickly and evenly in the moving air. A convection oven can cut cooking time by one-third, and most recipes will need to be adjusted accordingly. These ovens are excellent for smaller cuts of meat and for cookies, breads, cakes, and pies. Large roasts can dry out, however, and are best cooked more slowly in a conventional thermal oven. A convection oven is generally more expensive than a thermal model of comparable quality.

MICROWAVE OVEN Uses moist heat generated by the food itself, produced when its molecules are agitated by short, high-frequency microwaves. See also MICROWAVE OVEN.

OVEN MITT See COOKING TOOLS.

OYSTER This unassuming bivalve has enjoyed a long and varied history. Early Romans extolled the oyster's aphrodisiac qualities, while American colonists begrudgingly depended on  them to survive long, harsh winters. Few combinations are as simple and elegant as freshly shucked oysters and chilled Champagne. Lemon, lime, saffron, coconut milk, chiles, lemongrass, leeks, miso, and cream all complement oysters. Oysters also star in soups, stews, and fillings.

Selecting Always buy oysters from reputable merchants who can vouch that they come from safe, clean, unpolluted waters. Fresh live oysters in the shell have a mild, sweet smell. Their shells should be closed tightly and feel heavy with water. Do not buy any oysters that remain open when touched. A strong fishy or ammonium odor indicates the oysters are no longer fresh, so pass them by. Any oysters intended for eating raw should be bought fresh and shucked within a few hours of serving. Do not buy shucked oysters for eating raw unless you know that the fishmonger shucked them specially for your order.

When buying containers of shucked oysters, check that the shellfish are plump and their liquor is clear, without a trace of milkiness. Some grocery stores and fish markets sell frozen shucked oysters. Also available are canned smoked oysters.

While oysters are spawning during the summer months, their flesh becomes soft, milky, and less sweet. They are not toxic but simply taste unpleasant. In the United States and Europe, oysters are in season during the months that have the letter r in them—in other words, from September to April. Now, however, with sterile varieties cultivated, oysters are increasingly available all year long. A clear exception to the alphabet rule is the Kumamoto oyster, which spawns during the autumn months.

Storing Spread live oysters in a large container and cover them with a damp cloth. If needed, keep them in the refrigerator for 1 to 2 days, making sure the cloth stays moist. They will die if submerged in tap water, stored on ice, or sealed in an airtight container. Cover shucked oysters in their own liquor and refrigerate them in an airtight container for no more than 2 days. Store cans of smoked oysters in a cool, dry place for up to 2 years. Keep frozen oysters for up to 3 to 4 months.

Preparing Before opening oysters, be sure to scrub them with a stiff brush and rinse well. When opening, reserve their liquor and use it in place of other liquids when making soups and sauces. Add oysters toward the end of cooking, allowing just enough time to heat them through. Overcooking toughens them.

O

*Scrubbing
an oyster.*

WHICH WAY IS UP? The top shells of oysters tend to be flatter than the more bowl-shaped bottom shells. For serving on the half shell, open the oyster with its top shell facing up, and leave the oyster in its bottom shell.

Caution!

Since oysters are susceptible to water contaminants and "red tides" of poisonous plankton, be sure to read posted signs and check with local health or game agencies before collecting your own oysters.

HOW TO *Open Oysters*

Oyster knives have thick handles for easy gripping and turning. Their wide, dull blades are strong enough to lever open the shell. (Although similar, oyster knives are stubbier than clam knives.) Stainless-steel oyster knives will not transfer any metallic flavor to the oyster.

Oyster knife.

1. For protection and a better grip, use a folded cloth or an oven mitt to hold the oyster in one hand. (Right-handers should hold the shell with their left hand, and vice versa.) Position the shell so the rounded edge points out toward the space between your thumb and your fingers and the hinge end points toward you.

2. Holding the oyster knife in your other hand, insert its tip into the dark, rounded spot at the oyster's hinge. (The shell's ridges and dark rays emanate from the hinge.)

3. Twist the knife sharply to break the hinge.
4. Once the shell opens, slip the knife carefully up along the inside surface of the top shell, severing the adductor muscle that grips it. Take care not to cut the oyster itself or to spill its liquor.

5. Lift the top shell away and discard.
6. Carefully cut the muscle under the oyster to loosen it from the bottom shell. Remove any small particles of shell.

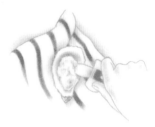

Speed Shucking There are a few ways to open a large number of oysters quickly for use in a recipe. Do not try to use these methods for raw oysters on the half shell,

✥ Oyster Glossary ✥

Since water-filtering oysters readily take on the flavor of their environment, they traditionally are named after the area where they grow. In general, colder waters develop a firmer texture and sharper, saltier flavor, while warmer waters create a milder, softer oyster.

ATLANTIC OYSTER Tends to have a bumpy, elongated shell and a briny flavor with strong mineral notes. Varieties include Blue Point, Cape Cod, Chesapeake, Kent Island, Long Island, Malpeque, and Wellfleet. Atlantic oysters, also called Eastern oysters, account for most of the oysters sold at market.

PACIFIC OYSTER Also known as Japanese oysters, these specimens have more subtle, slightly fruity flavors and more distinctly fluted shells than their Atlantic cousins. Popular varieties are

the Hama Hama, Hog Island, Quilcene, and Tomales Bay. The sweet, popular Kumamoto oyster is actually a separate species, but it is often grouped with the Pacific oysters.

OLYMPIA OYSTER A species indigenous to the American Northwest. Olympia oysters are tiny (about the size of a quarter), slow growing (taking 4 years to mature), and highly prized for their flavor. They are almost always served on the half shell.

FLAT OYSTER Native to European waters but now grown in both the Atlantic and Pacific. Varieties found in the waters off Maine and northern California have especially intense flavors. Small oysters inside large, round shells, they are commonly known by the name Belon, after a French region where they were once abundant.

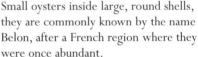

because they will be partially cooked and thus very unpleasant.

The first way is to steam them for about 1 minute. Use very little water, so the liquor that drains from the open oysters will not be overly diluted. Another trick is to spread the oysters in a large, shallow baking dish and heat the oysters in a 375°F oven just until they open, 1 to 2 minutes. Or, you can microwave them on High for about 1 minute.

See also SHELLFISH.

OYSTER SAUCE A thick, dark brown sauce made from oyster extracts and sea-

sonings. With its distinctive smoky-sweet flavor, this all-purpose seasoning is used in Cantonese cuisine to give body, deep color, and rich flavor to the sauces in noodle, meat, vegetable, and seafood dishes. Stir-fried Chinese broccoli simply drizzled with oyster sauce is a popular dish.

Selecting The best brands, made only from dried oysters and salt, have a briny, slightly sweet flavor. Now, however, soy sauce, sugar, and cornstarch may replace some or all of the oysters.

Storing An unopened bottle will keep indefinitely. Once opened, it will keep for up to 2 years in the refrigerator.

everything from paella to purslane

PAELLA Originating in the Valencia region of Spain, paella is a dish of saffron-infused rice cooked with various meats, seafood, and vegetables. It is prepared in a large, round, shallow pan called a *paellera* that usually ranges from 13 to 14 inches in diameter. At its most traditional, *paella valenciana* contains chicken, rabbit, snails, broad green beans, white beans, tomatoes, and saffron; but countless variations exist, from an elaborate all-seafood dish to a hearty recipe using chorizo sausage to a version that consists of only tomatoes and rice. Italian Arborio rice may be substituted for the Spanish medium-grain rice (the Spanish call it short-grain rice; the best comes from Calasparra and is called Bomba) used in paella; unlike risotto, however, paella should never be stirred once the other ingredients have been added.

Paellera.

PAK-CHOI See BOK CHOY.

PALM See HEART OF PALM.

PAN BROILING See BROILING.

PANCAKE Variously known as griddle-cakes, flapjacks, hoecakes, and Indian cakes, these flat, round cakes are made from a thin batter poured onto the surface of a hot griddle or skillet and cooked on both sides. Pancakes are a staple of America's breakfast table. More famous incarnations include yeasted flannel cakes, modest silver dollar cakes, Dutch babies, and Rhode Island's cornmeal johnnycake. Most pancakes are slightly leavened, although some, like crepes and johnnycakes, are not. Commonly topped with butter, fresh fruit, and maple syrup, pancakes are now made in many colors and flavors, including whole wheat with banana and walnuts, lemon ricotta with blueberries, and jalapeño-cornmeal. Although once made with sourdough starter, most pancake recipes are now leavened with baking powder or baking soda.

Pancake Savvy When making pancakes, keep the following in mind:

- Using a whisk, stir the batter only a few times, stopping as soon as it begins to come together and all the ingredients are moistened. The batter should have small lumps. Too much stirring will develop the gluten in the flour and create tough pancakes.
- Use a griddle or heavy pan and heat it thoroughly before spooning or ladling in the batter.
- Turn a pancake only once, when bubbles appear on the surface and the bottom is golden brown.
- Serve pancakes as soon after cooking as possible. Ideally, flip them from the pan directly onto a plate set in front of a hungry eater.

■ If you must hold pancakes before serving, do not stack them more than 2 or 3 high, or they will steam and become soggy.
See also CREPE; WAFFLE.

PANCETTA This flavorful bacon, which derives its name from the Italian word for "belly," has a moist, silky texture. It is made by rubbing a slab of pork belly with a mix of spices that may include cinnamon, cloves, or juniper berries, then rolling the slab into a tight cylinder and curing it for at least 2 months. Since it is not smoked, pancetta is moister than American slab bacon. In Italy, chopped pancetta sautéed in olive oil is used to flavor soups, sauces, meats, and vegetables. 
Selecting Pancetta may be purchased from a good butcher or Italian deli. Ask for it to be sliced thin or thick. When unfurled, the slices look like strips of bacon.
Storing Keep sliced pancetta wrapped in plastic in the refrigerator for up to 2 weeks.
Preparing Pancetta is generally chopped before use in a recipe.
    See also BACON.

PANFRYING See FRYING.

PANKO See BREAD CRUMBS.

PAN ROASTING See ROASTING.

PAN SIZES Cookware and bakeware come in a wide range of sizes. A household's pots and pans, from pressure cookers to skillets to saucepans to roasting pans, are typically selected according to the needs of that household, both in terms of number and size. Some specialty pans, such as a fish poacher, are a fairly standard size,

Volume of Standard Baking Pans	
PAN DIMENSIONS*	**VOLUME**
Square	
8 x 8 x 1½ inches	6 cups
8 x 8 x 2 inches	8 cups
9 x 9 x 2 inches	10 cups
10 x 10 x 2 inches	12 cups
12 x 12 x 2 inches	16 cups
Rectangular	
11 x 7 x 2 inches	8 cups
13 x 9 x 2 inches	12 cups
Jelly roll	
10½ x 15½ x 1 inch	10 cups
12½ x 17½ x 1 inch	12 cups
Loaf	
8 x 4 x 2½ inches	4 cups
8½ x 4½ x 2½ inches	6 cups
9 x 5 x 3 inches	8 cups
Round	
6 x 2 inches	3¾ cups
8 x 1½ inches	4 cups
8 x 2 inches	7 cups
9 x 1½ inches	6 cups
9 x 2 inches	8½ cups
10 x 2 inches	10¾ cups
12 x 2 inches	15½ cups
14 x 2 inches	21 cups
Springform	
9 x 2¾ inches	10 cups
9 x 3 inches	12 cups
10 x 2¾ inches	12 cups
Bundt	
9 x 3 inches	9 cups
10 x 3½ inches	12 cups
Tube	
9 x 3 inches	10 cups
10 x 4 inches	16 cups
8 x 2½-inch heart	8½ cups
9½ x 6½-inch oval	6 cups

Measured on inside of pan.

while others, such as saucepans, come in several capacities. In general, however, if a cook substitutes, for example, a 3-quart

P

saucepan for the $2\frac{1}{2}$-quart pan specified in a recipe, little adjustment is needed to the cooking process.

The sizes of bakeware, in contrast, are more critical. If you use a larger cake or bread pan than that called for in a recipe, for example, you will need to shorten the baking time. The batter or dough will be shallower and have more surface area, thus cooking more quickly. Likewise, the same batter or dough put into a smaller, deeper pan will require more time in the oven to cook them through and perhaps a slightly lower oven temperature to keep from over-browning with the increased cooking time. When purchasing bakeware, remember that the largest pan that will fit in most home ovens is about 17 by 14 inches. Also, when measuring the dimensions of insulated pans or other heavy baking dishes made of glass or ceramic, be sure to measure only the inside space and not include the thickness of the sides themselves.

You can determine a pan's volume by filling it with water, then pouring the water into a large liquid measure or marked pitcher. Use the chart on page 327 to compare the volumes of pan sizes when substituting one pan for another.

See also BAKEWARE; COOKWARE.

PAPAYA With its distinctive earthy aroma and flavor, papaya is the quintessential tropical fruit, although botanically speaking it is actually a berry. Native to Central America, it is now cultivated from Hawaii to South Africa to the Philippines. The papaya looks somewhat like a large pear, with thin, pale green skin that ripens to blotches of yellow and orange. Some people think it resembles a melon and call papayas "tree melons." Such nomenclature may be a result of the fruit's hollow center, which holds a shiny mass of small, slick black seeds, which are edible and have a slightly peppery flavor. Some English speakers call the fruit papaw, a name that also refers, confusingly, to a sweet fruit with a custardlike flesh that is native to North America.

In Southeast Asia and Latin America, crunchy green papaya is treated like a vegetable and appears shredded in salads. Unripe papaya contains papain, a powerful digestive enzyme that rapidly breaks down proteins. Cooks throughout the world rub meat with green papaya or wrap meat in the tree's leaves to marinate and tenderize. Today, papain is the active ingredient in most powdered meat tenderizers.

Selecting Since they bruise easily, most papayas are transported while still hard, with shippers knowing they will ripen in storage. Try to buy a papaya that gives slightly when pressed. Look for skin that is smooth and has already started to turn yellow. Different varieties come in varying sizes, from palm-sized 6-ounce to giant 20-pound fruit, but most of the papayas in markets weigh about 1 pound. Since the tree simultaneously flowers and bears fruit and is cultivated around the world, papayas are available year-round. Look for the nectar in cans at Asian and Latin American markets. Dried papaya spears are available in bulk and packaged in plastic bags at well-stocked supermarkets and health-food stores.

Storing Leave papayas at room temperature to ripen. Once the fruit is ripe, you can peel, cut, and store it in an airtight container in the refrigerator for up to 2 days. The fruit quickly loses its flavor when chilled. Keep unopened cans of papaya nectar for up to 1 year in a cool, dry place; once opened, refrigerate for 2 or 3 days. Store dried papaya in an airtight container in the refrigerator for up to 6 months.

Preparing Small papayas can be halved and eaten with a spoon like custard. A squeeze of lime juice deepens the flavor. For larger fruit, remove the skin with a vegetable peeler, cut the papaya in half, and scoop out its seeds with a large spoon. The seeds can be rinsed and added to salads or other dishes to deliver a peppery bite.

Can't Wait for Your Papaya to Ripen?

Here's a shortcut to reduce the bitterness of a slightly underripe papaya:

1. Cut several shallow score lines through the skin along the length of the fruit. Expose the flesh but avoid cutting into it.
2. Prop the papaya, with its stem down, in a large glass or jar.
3. Leave it at room temperature overnight or, preferably, 1 day. The exposure to air deactivates the bitter papain enzyme. This will make the fruit taste sweeter. (This will not, however, make an already-ripe fruit sweeter.)

PAPRIKA See SPICE.

PARBOILING To cook food partially in boiling water, sometimes as a preparatory step before combining ingredients with different cooking times or finishing with another cooking method. Parboiling is closely related to blanching but usually implies longer cooking. Although parboiling traditionally referred to cooking food until nearly half done, modern cookbooks often use the term for brief cooking times as well, which can confuse longtime cooks.

PARCHMENT PAPER Treated to resist moisture and grease, parchment paper provides a nonstick surface for lining cake pans and baking sheets. Because parchment has undergone a process that strengthens it and makes the surface smooth and impermeable, the paper keeps the food from sticking and makes cleanup easier. Essential in a classic French kitchen, parchment paper folds into tidy packages for cooking food (called *en papillote*), covers floating fruit while it poaches, lines the bottom of cake pans, and folds quickly and neatly into pastry cones for decorating cakes (see also PIPING). Parchment can withstand high heat in the oven, but it must never be used in the broiler or directly on a burner. If touched by a flame or an electric burner, it will ignite. Parchment also maintains its strength when wet. Look for rolls of parchment paper in grocery stores and cookware shops. Large sheets and precut triangles are available at baking-supply stores. Waxed paper cannot replace parchment in cooking or baking; it will burn and smoke when heated.

PARING Another term for peeling; see PEELING.

PARMESAN An aged, firm cheese of medium butterfat content with a pale yellow to medium straw yellow color and a piquant, slightly salty flavor. Made from partially skimmed cow's milk, Parmesan is aged for 1 to 3 years in large wheels to achieve a granular texture and a rich, complex flavor that is at once mild, savory, and fragrant. The trademarked name Parmigiano-Reggiano, stenciled vertically on the rind, refers to true Parmesan, produced in the Emilia-Romagna region of northern Italy under stringent standards that are protected by law. While the cheese is best known as a grated topping for pasta, it is also excellent stirred into risotto, shaved over salads, and presented in shards accompanied by wine.

P

Selecting For fuller flavor, buy Parmesan in wedges, never pregrated. The cheese dries out and begins to diminish in flavor soon after grating and should be kept whole for as long as possible.

Storing Keep wrapped tightly in plastic wrap or aluminum foil in the refrigerator for up to 2 weeks or wrapped airtight in the freezer for several months.

Quick Tip

If Parmesan begins drying out, wrap it first in a damp cloth and then loosely in aluminum foil. Refrigerate for 1 day. Remove the cheese from the cloth and seal it again tightly in plastic wrap or aluminum foil.

Preparing Grate or shave Parmesan only as needed just before using in a recipe or serving. If possible, during meals provide a small hand grater so diners may top their own pasta with cheese.

See also CHEESE.

PARMIGIANO-REGGIANO See PARMESAN.

PARSLEY See HERB.

PARSLEY, CHINESE Another name for cilantro; see HERB.

PARSNIP A relative of the carrot, this ivory-colored root closely resembles its brighter, more familiar cousin. Parsnips have a slightly sweet flavor and a tough, starchy texture that softens with cooking. Excellent roasted, steamed, boiled, or baked, parsnips can be prepared in almost any way that potatoes or carrots are. Because they become mushy more quickly than other root vegetables, add them toward the end of cooking to stews and soups. Very young, tender parsnips may be grated or thinly sliced and added raw to salads.

Selecting Although now available year-round, parsnips are at their peak during the winter months, when the frosty weather converts their starches to sugar. In fact, some devotees of the root find spring-dug parsnips the sweetest of all. (Today, cold storage helps do the same at other times of the year.) Look for small to medium parsnips that are firm and unblemished. Larger ones can be tough and stringy and have a woody core that must be removed.

Storing Wrapped in a perforated plastic bag, parsnips will keep in the refrigerator for up to 1 month.

Preparing Scratch parsnips with your fingernail to check for waxy coating. If the vegetables are waxed, be sure to peel them. Otherwise, they may be scrubbed with a vegetable brush or peeled, as you wish. Cut out and discard the tough, fibrous core found in large parsnips. Because they undergo discoloring when exposed to air, cook cut parsnips immediately or sprinkle them with lemon juice.

See also STEAMING.

PASSION FRUIT Though it is juicy, highly aromatic, and undeniably seductive, this tropical fruit was named not for any aphrodisiac qualities but by Spanish Jesuit missionaries in South America who thought the structure and patterns of its flower recalled the Crucifixion. Passion fruit may be enjoyed simply by slicing open the palm-sized, purplish sphere and spooning it straight from its skin. The yellow-orange pulp, at once sweet and tart, also adds exotic flavor and aroma to fruit salads, sauces, dressings, desserts, and beverages. Even the crunchy, spicy-tasting, glossy black seeds may be eaten, although they are often discarded. Commercially packaged passion fruit juice and nectar are also available.

Selecting The passion fruit is at its best when it looks its worst, the skin uniformly wrinkled and sometimes showing traces of mold. Eat such specimens within a day or so. Otherwise, buy smooth-skinned fruits, which will ripen within 3 to 5 days.

Storing Keep underripe passion fruits at room temperature until wrinkled. Refrigerate fully ripe fruits and use within 2 days. Freeze whole ripe fruits or their pulp for up to 6 months.

Preparing Use a sharp knife to halve a ripe passion fruit. To separate seeds from pulp, rub through a sieve.

PASTA See page 332.

PASTRY Another term for unleavened dough, as opposed to bread dough. Pie and tart dough is often referred to as pastry. See FILO; PIE & TART.

PASTRY BAG See BAKING TOOLS.

PASTRY BLENDER See BAKING TOOLS.

PASTRY BOARD See BAKING TOOLS.

PASTRY BRUSH See BAKING TOOLS.

PASTRY CLOTH See BAKING TOOLS.

PASTRY WEIGHTS Another term for pie weights; see BAKING TOOLS; BLIND BAKING.

PÂTÉ Taken from the French word for paste, a pâté is typically a rich, finely ground meat mixture. It can be made from almost any meat or combination of meats,

the most common being pork, veal, and rabbit, as well as chicken liver and foie gras. It may also be made from fish and shellfish. Some pâtés are blended to a silky smooth texture. Others are chunky and rustic. Still others are studded with ingredients, such as blanched asparagus, hard-boiled eggs, peppercorns, pistachios, diced mushrooms, strips of ham, or whole truffles. Pâtés can be served either hot or cold, with a crust or without. Purists will insist that any meat mixture cooked and served in a terrine dish should also be called a terrine, and that it is only a "pâté" if and when it is unmolded. Today, this distinction is rarely followed, so the two terms are often used interchangeably.

Selecting Look for prepared pâté in the deli section of food markets or specialty grocers. It is available packaged in miniature plastic terrine dishes or as individual slices wrapped in plastic.

Quick Tip

To test the flavor of a homemade pâté (or any meat mixture) before it is cooked, fry up a little patty in a small skillet. Taste and then adjust the seasoning of the mixture. The flavors will mellow as the pâté sits, so season with a bold hand. Also, food served at room temperature needs more seasoning because the lower temperature masks many flavors.

Storing Keep pâté in the refrigerator, sealed in plastic wrap or an airtight container. Serve it within 1 week. The flavor of homemade pâté improves if left to rest for 2 to 3 days in the refrigerator. Freezing pâté is not recommended, for its texture will suffer.

Preparing Before serving pâté, let it sit at room temperature for 30 minutes or so to take the chill off and bring out its flavor. See also TERRINE.

P

Pasta

"Paste," as the Latin root of *pasta* unglamorously translates, doesn't begin to hint at the glorious dishes that result from combining flour and water (and sometimes eggs or flavorings) and forming the mixture into sheets, ribbons, or shapes. Pasta, for all its simplicity, is one of the world's most versatile foods.

Although popular legend has it that Marco Polo discovered noodles on his travels to China in the late 13th century and brought them home to his countrymen, more reputable sources suggest that Italians and Asians learned how to shape and boil pastes of ground wheat independently of each other. Although the term *pasta* used to refer only to wheat noodles found in Italian cooking, pasta long ago transcended Italy's borders to become a dish of universal appeal. Today, nearly every country in the world incorporates pasta into its cuisine, whether it is topped with a sauce, stuffed or layered and baked, added to soups, or dressed with a vinaigrette.

Another common Western-style noodle is the egg noodle. Both fresh and dried, these have a delicate character and silky finish. They are wonderful tossed with a sauce, of course, but also are a fine addition to soups (undercook them, then stir them in for the last few minutes of cooking); serve as a satisfying base for stews; and accompany main dishes, often tossed with butter and grated cheese.

Pick of the Pastas Hundreds of pasta shapes exist, many of them with descriptive or fanciful Italian names. More than 30 of the most commonly available types, both dried and fresh, are listed below. Choose the sizes and shapes of pasta that suit the sauce or other treatment you are using:

thin strands for light sauces; small shapes for broths or soups; broader strands, ribbons, or tubes, or larger shapes for more robust or chunky sauces; and wide ribbons or large, hollow tubes or shapes for layered or filled baked dishes.

ACINI DI PEPE Small "peppercorns." Spherical shapes for adding to soups.

AGNOLOTTI Crescent-shaped filled pasta.

BUCATINI Long, narrow tubes resembling hollow spaghetti; good for chunky, full-flavored sauces.

CANNELLONI Rolled tubes of fresh or dried pasta used for stuffing.

CAPELLINI/CAPELLI D'ANGELO "Little hairs" or "angel hair," resembling fine spaghetti strands. Best for simple, light, smooth sauces.

CONCHIGLIE "Shells" in various sizes. Used for soups or, in the case of larger shells, stuffing and baking.

DITALI Tubes resembling "thimbles," tossed with sauces or used in salads or soups. Ditalini are small ditali, used primarily in soups.

FARFALLE Bite-sized "butterflies." Also called bow ties. Farfalline are the smaller version.

FEDELINI Thin spaghetti strands; good served with medium- to full-bodied sauces.

FETTUCCINE Long, wide "ribbons," often fresh pasta. Good for hearty, rich, and chunky sauces.

FUSILLI "Fuses." Long, twisted strands or short, corkscrew-shaped tubes. Best with chunky, substantial sauces.

GEMELLI "Twins." Two short, intertwined strands, served with sauces or in salads or baked dishes.

LASAGNE Large, flat ribbons of dried pasta or ribbons or squares of fresh pasta, for layering. Sometimes made with ruffled edges.

LINGUINE "Little tongues." Flat, narrow ribbons of the same general length as spaghetti; best when served with light, smooth sauces or medium-bodied sauces.

LUMACHE "Snails." Large shells for stuffing.

MACARONI Small, short tubes curved like elbows; great for casseroles and salads.

MANICOTTI "Muffs." Hollow tubes for stuffing.

MOSTACCIOLI "Moustaches." Narrow tubes served with sauces or in salads or baked dishes.

ORECCHIETTE "Little ears." Small, indented circular shapes, good for chunky sauces.

ORZO "Barley." Slender, seedlike shapes that look not unlike large grains of rice. Good for soups.

PAPPARDELLE Wide ribbons of fresh pasta used with hearty sauces.

PENNE "Quills." Narrow tubes with angled ends resembling pen nibs. Traditionally used for

casseroles and chunky tomato-based sauces. Small penne are pennette.

PERCIATELLI Another name for bucatini.

RADIATORI Bite-sized, ridged shapes resembling "radiators"; served with sauces or in salads or baked dishes.

RAVIOLI Classic stuffed pasta, usually square but often round.

RIGATONI Ridged bite-sized tubes. Hold up well under robust, chunky tomato sauces and in baked dishes.

ROTELLE Many-spoked wheels; served with sauces that catch in the spokes or in salads or baked dishes.

RUOTE More bite-sized wheels; served with sauces or in salads or baked dishes.

SEMI DI MELONE "Melon seeds." Similar to orzo.

SPAGHETTI Long, thin, cylindrical strands. From the word *spago,* "string." Spaghettini is a thinner version of spaghetti.

STELLINE "Little stars." Tiny shapes used typically in soups.

TAGLIARINI Long, flat, narrow ribbons, usually of fresh pasta. Also referred to as tagliolini.

TAGLIATELLE Ribbons similar to but slightly wider than fettuccine, usually of fresh pasta. Good with hearty, sturdy sauces.

TORTELLINI "Little pies." Small, circular stuffed pasta.

TUBETTI Short, stout "tubes" served in soups or with sauces. Tubettini are small tubetti.

VERMICELLI "Little worms." A slender form of spaghetti similar to spaghettini. Good for light, smooth sauces.

ZITI Hollow tubes in short and long forms, for hearty sauces.

continued

P

Pasta, continued

Selecting Pasta is sold in a wide variety of shapes and sizes (see Pick of the Pastas, page 332) and in both dried and fresh forms. Well-stocked food stores and Italian delicatessens offer the best selection of both dried and fresh pastas. The finest dried pasta begins with semolina flour ground from durum wheat, the hardest variety grown, which gives the resulting pasta shapes their desired firmness and elasticity. Fresh pasta is made from either all-purpose or semolina flour combined with eggs. Sometimes another ingredient, such as spinach, tomato, beet, saffron, or squid ink, is added to provide color and a subtle flavor. Despite a recent tendency in this country to consider fresh pasta better than dried, each has its place in a menu. Dried pasta goes best with tomato or oil-based sauces, while more tender fresh pasta is better suited to sauces featuring butter, cream, or cheese.

When buying dried egg noodles, check that eggs are, in fact, one of the ingredients listed; many are imitation egg noodles.

Storing Dried pasta keeps well in the manufacturer's packaging at room temperature for up to 2 months. Transferred to an airtight container away from moisture, heat, and light, it will keep for up to 1 year. Wrap homemade or store-bought fresh pasta in plastic and store in the refrigerator for no more than 3 days, or wrap in freezer-weight plastic and store in the freezer for up to 1 month.

About Cooking Pasta Both fresh and dried pastas should be cooked al dente, tender but still chewy. Use a two-handled pot large enough to let the pasta float freely during cooking, and plan on 5 quarts of water for each 1 pound of fresh pasta or 1 to 1¼ pounds of dried pasta. These amounts usually are sufficient for 8 first-course servings or 4 main-course servings.

Bring the water to a full rolling boil, salt it, and then add the pasta. (Unsalted water may result in bland pasta, and the finished dish may demand heavier seasoning.) As soon as the water returns to the boil, start timing. Cooking time will vary with the pasta's dryness, shape, and size. Fresh pasta usually cooks within 1 to 3 minutes, depending on thickness. Commercial dried pasta generally cooks in 3 to 15 minutes; check the manufacturer's packaging for suggested times. To test for doneness, at the earliest possible suggested time, remove a strand or piece with tongs, a long-handled fork, or a slotted spoon, let cool briefly, then bite into it.

Removing pasta for testing.

If the pasta seems too chewy, cook 1 minute more before testing again. As soon as it is ready, drain the pasta immediately, pouring it through a colander set in the kitchen sink.

The only exception to cooking pasta at a rolling boil is fresh filled pastas such as ravioli, which are more tender and should be simmered so they will not break apart.

HOW TO *Make Homemade Pasta*
1. On a work surface, heap the flour specified in a pasta recipe and make a well in its center. Break the eggs into the well.

2. With a fork, lightly beat the eggs. Then, in a circular motion, gradually incorporate flour from the sides of the well until combined.

3. With the heel of your hand, knead the dough—pushing it down and away and turning it repeatedly, using a dough scraper if it sticks—until it is smooth and elastic, at least 5 minutes. If it sticks or seems a little soft, sprinkle it with flour. Gather the dough into a ball.

ROLLING AND CUTTING BY HAND

4. On a clean work surface dusted with flour, flatten the kneaded dough with your hand. With a flour-dusted rolling pin, roll it out to desired thickness as given in a recipe.

5. Loosely roll up the pasta around the rolling pin and unroll onto a flour-dusted kitchen towel, leaving it until dry to the touch but still flexible, about 10 minutes (less if the air is very dry).

6. On the work surface, roll the pasta into a cylinder. With a small, sharp knife, cut crosswise into ribbons of desired width.

ROLLING AND CUTTING BY MACHINE

Start by following steps 1 to 3 above.

4. Adjust the rollers of a hand-cranked pasta machine to the widest setting. Cut the kneaded dough into manageable portions of 2 to 3 ounces each. Lightly dust a portion of dough and crank it through the rollers.

5. Lightly dust the sheet of dough with flour and fold it into thirds.

6. Reset the rollers one width narrower; roll the dough again. Repeat the process until the dough reaches desired thickness.

7. Secure a cutting attachment to the machine. Cut the pasta sheet into easily manageable lengths and crank each length through the cutter to make pasta strands.

See also FLOUR; NOODLE.

PEA, FRESH The pea is one of the major groups within the vast legume family. Peas can be divided into three general categories: whole pea pods eaten young and fresh, shelled peas eaten fresh, and shelled peas that are dried.

Peas eaten fresh as whole pods include the broad, flat snow peas that star in Chinese stir-fries, as well as plumper, rounder, bright green sugar snap peas.

Sugar snap and snow peas.

The most common variety for shelling is the English, or garden, pea. Baby peas, or *petits pois,* refer to tiny, sweet English peas, while so-called early or June peas are larger and have more starch. The smaller ones need barely any cooking and are wonderful stirred into risotto at the last minute with a little grated Parmesan cheese. Most are harvested for freezing.

The final category of peas, those that are usually dried, include yellow and green split peas, chickpeas, and black-eyed peas. These are better grouped with beans and lentils because of their similar flavors and uses. See BEAN, DRIED.

Black-eyed peas are sometimes available fresh in the summer. If you buy them still in the pod, you'll need to shell them before using them.

Selecting Choose fresh peas with crisp, smooth, glossy, bright green pods. Avoid any that are wilted, dried, puffy, or blemished. Try to purchase them from a farmers' market for the sweetest flavor.

Canned peas bear so little resemblance to fresh peas that it is better to go without if they are the only option. Frozen shelled peas, on the other hand, are decent substitutes, especially if they will be cooked with other ingredients. Look for those labeled "baby" or "petite" for smaller, more delicate peas. Snow peas are available frozen as well, but frozen snow peas turn fairly soft and flavorless once cooked.

Storing Because their natural sugar begins converting to starch immediately after they are picked, peas should be prepared and eaten as soon as possible, preferably the day of purchase. Peas will stay crisp for 3 to 4 days if stored in a plastic bag in the refrigerator, but do not expect them to retain their characteristic sweetness after a day.

Preparing For whole pea pods, snap off the tips of the pods, pulling down the length of the pod to remove any tough strings as well. Although many modern hybrids have no strings or the peas are processed before reaching the store, it doesn't hurt to check. Whether pods or shelled, peas are best if steamed or blanched very briefly to retain their crisp texture and vibrant color.

Quick Tip

If raw snow peas wilt, let them stand in cold water for 10 to 15 minutes to recrisp them.

HOW TO *Shell English Peas*
Shell peas just before cooking to prevent them from drying out.

1. Work over a large bowl. After checking for and removing any strings as described above, squeeze the pod and press your thumb against the seam to split it open.

2. Continuing the same movement, sweep your thumb down along the inside of the pod to pop out the peas.
3. Discard the pod. (If making soup, save a few to sweeten the simmering stock.)
4. If needed, refrigerate the peas for up to 1 day. Cover with damp paper towels or cold water to keep them moist.

See also BEAN, FRESH; BLANCHING; BOILING; STEAMING.

PEACH A sweet and fragrant peach, ripe enough to drip juice down your chin, is one of the joys of summer. Native to China, where legends tell of this fruit's power to confer immortality, peaches now also grow in temperate regions of North America and Europe. Related to cherries, apricots, and plums, peaches are members of the stone fruit family, their flesh concealing a large, wrinkled pit. Peaches are often classified as clingstone or freestone, depending on how difficult or easy it is to separate the pit from the flesh. The flesh ranges from bright yellow to white, the latter being less common and more perishable but also generally sweeter and juicier. In more recent years, the fruit's downy skin has fallen into disfavor among consumers. Popular hybrids reduce the fuzz to a mere softness.

Peaches make excellent jams, pies, and sauces. Use them in salsas or marinades for pork or toss thin slices into a green salad. For dessert, enjoy peach halves prepared simply: poached in spiced white wine or broiled with a touch of butter and lime juice. Or bake peaches in a wide variety of homestyle classics, from peach pie to peach cobbler to peach variations of upside-down cakes.

Selecting Choose peaches that give slightly to gentle pressure, that emanate a flowery fragrance, and that are free of bruises and blemishes. The amount of red in a peach's skin depends on its variety and has little relation to its ripeness. Avoid any with tinges of green, however; they were picked too early and may never ripen properly. Once picked, a peach will eventually become softer and juicier but not significantly sweeter. Unfortunately, most peaches arrive at market stone hard. Handle even unripe peaches with care, for their flesh bruises easily. Peaches come to market from May to October, but most varieties peak in late June to early August.

Peach halves and slices are available canned in sugar syrup, water, or fruit juice. Other forms convenient for cooking include frozen slices and dried chunks.

Storing Keep peaches at room temperature in a smooth bowl until they are ripe. (The ridges of a basket can leave bruised indentations in ripening peaches.) Hasten the ripening process by placing them in a paper bag with an apple or a banana. Once they are soft, store peaches in the refrigerator in a plastic bag for 4 to 5 days.

Keep dried and canned peaches in a cool place away from light and moisture.

Preparing Wash peaches just before cooking or serving. If there's a good deal of fuzz, rub the peach briefly while washing. The fuzz will come right off. Like many fruits, fresh peaches will have a sweeter, fuller flavor if served at room temperature. Since the flesh of peaches discolors when exposed to air, toss cut pieces immediately with citrus juice, wine, or liqueur.

P

Quick Bite

Although the nectarine looks like a peach with smooth skin and is a member of the extended peach family, it is not, as some folks believe, a hybrid. Like the peach, however, it comes either freestone or cling, with yellow or white flesh, and it is sweet and juicy.

HOW TO *Halve a Peach*

1. Using a small, sharp knife, cut the peach in half lengthwise, cutting carefully around the round pit at the center.

2. Rotate the halves in opposite directions to separate them.

3. Scoop out the pit with the tip of a knife and discard.

For peeling peaches, see BLANCHING.

PEANUT First grown in South America, peanuts quickly spread to Asia, Africa, and the American South aboard the ships of early Spanish and Portuguese explorers and slave traders. Known also as groundnuts, goobers (from the African word *nguba*), or goober peas, peanuts belong to the legume family, along with lentils, beans, and peas. The vinelike plant is unique in that its flower stalks, after fertilizing themselves, each grow a stem that bores into the soil. The seedpods then develop and mature underground. The primary types grown commercially are the jumbo Virginia, the oval Valencia, the smaller and rounder Spanish variety covered with a red skin, and the runner peanut with evenly sized kernels, which are ideal for producing peanut butter. The world's leading growers are India and China, where the plants flourish in the hot climates.

Peanuts are one of the most common ingredients in snacks and sweets, adding texture as well as flavor to cookies, candies—who isn't tempted by peanut brittle?—and countless snack mixes. With a high amount of protein and tremendous thickening power, peanuts appear in soups, stews, breads, and sauces around the

Quick Tip

If a recipe calls for 1 pound shelled peanuts, you will need to buy about 1½ pounds peanuts in the shell.

world, from West African chicken and peanut stew to Sichuan noodles tossed with a peanut-sesame-chile sauce to the rich, creamy sauce made from peanuts and coconut milk that accompanies saté, a specialty of Indonesia's many street vendors.

The colorless oil derived from pressed peanuts has a mild flavor and a particularly high smoking point, making it ideal for stir-frying and deep-frying. It is especially typical of Asian cuisines.

Selecting Peanuts are sold in a wide variety of ways. They are available with or without their shells, with or without their papery skins, roasted or unroasted, salted or unsalted, mixed with other nuts or alone. Although usually dried, they occasionally appear fresh at farmers' markets during the late-summer harvest. If buying them whole, shake the peanuts to check that they do not rattle in their shells, a sure sign that the nuts inside are old and dry. Once shelled, they are most commonly roasted and then vacuum-packed in cans or glass jars. Bags of unroasted (raw) skinned peanuts can be found in Asian and Latin American markets.

Storing Because of their oil content, peanuts go rancid fairly quickly if left at room temperature. Wrap unshelled peanuts in a plastic bag and keep them in the refrigerator for up to 6 months. Store unopened jars or cans of peanuts at room temperature for up to 1 year; once you open them, be sure to refrigerate them. They will stay fresh for 3 months in the refrigerator and for 2 years in the freezer. Store peanut oil for no longer than 2 months in an airtight container away from light and heat.

Preparing To shell peanuts, firmly and evenly press your thumb lengthwise along the shell. It will easily split and pull away.

See also FAT & OIL; NUT; PEANUT BUTTER.

PEANUT BUTTER This creamy or slightly crunchy peanut spread, made by grinding shelled dry-roasted peanuts to a paste, has come a long way from its humble beginnings. Commercially developed as an easily digested source of protein, peanut butter is now enjoyed by young and old alike in sandwiches, cookies, candies, and such unforgettable snacks as peanut butter fudge or "ants on a log," the classic combination of celery stalks, peanut butter, and raisins. It is also used in some savory dishes such as a spicy peanut soup.

Selecting Peanut butter is available smooth or chunky, that is, with chopped peanuts stirred in for texture. Many commercial peanut butters include additives to improve spreadability and flavor. Natural peanut butters have a slightly grainy texture and a layer of oil that must be stirred back

in before using. Variations include honey flavored, grape jelly or marshmallow swirled, and reduced fat.

Storing Some brands contain salt, sweeteners, stabilizers, and preservatives. These peanut butters can be kept for up to 1 year in a cool, dark place. The oils of "natural" or "old-fashioned" peanut butter will separate over time. Keep these peanut butters in the refrigerator for up to 6 months.

Preparing Use peanut butter as a convenient replacement for ground roasted peanuts in sauces or soups. The flavor of peanut butter pairs well with chocolate, banana, caramel, and marshmallow.

PEAR A perfectly ripe pear has soft, juicy flesh with delicately floral flavor. Sweet, fragrant pears are available year-round, but their peak season is during the cold months of winter, a time when their freshness is especially welcome. The many different varieties of pear are all generously curved in the fruit's well-known shape, but they range in color, contour, texture, and flavor. The French in particular have long admired and cultivated pears.

Selecting Pears are picked when mature but still hard, rather than when they are ripe. This prevents them from becoming too granular and soft. Look for smooth,

Bartlett and Comice pears.

unblemished fruits with their stems still attached. They should be fragrant and just beginning to soften near the stem. They must be left at room temperature to soften and sweeten and are ready to eat when they

P

P

Pear Glossary

Although thousands of pear varieties have been developed since the fruit was first cultivated 4,000 years ago in Asia, today relatively few choices are available commercially.

ANJOU An almost egg-shaped pear with green skin, often with a yellow tinge even when ripe, although a rarer red variety blushes to reddish green. A ripe Anjou is juicy, yet keeps its shape when sliced for salads, cooked in desserts, or baked whole. In season from October to May.

BARTLETT Known as the Williams pear in Europe, with thin skin that ripens from dark green to light green and then yellow and an aromatic, slightly musky flesh that is very soft when ripe. This good eating and all-purpose cooking pear is available from August to November. The sturdier red Bartlett is not always as juicy.

BOSC A versatile pear with a long, tapered neck, green skin with distinct brown russeting, and sweet, creamy white flesh. Excellent for eating fresh and for baking or poaching. Eat Bosc pears when they yield only slightly to finger pressure. In season from September to May.

COMICE Widely available, Comice is the best pear for eating out of hand, with sweet, meltingly juicy, "buttery" flesh and a hint of spiciness. It is quite round, with hardly noticeable shoulders, and its greenish yellow skin blushes to a soft red. It also bakes well. The Comice is fragile and is not a good traveler. In season from October to January.

SECKEL Among the smallest of pears. Ideal for making preserves, it has smooth, dark green skin with reddish hues and firm, slightly granular flesh. In season from August to January.

WINTER NELLIS A short pear with almost no neck and with a brownish green peel with russeted dots. The slightly spicy flesh is enjoyed raw, holds its shape well when baked or poached, and is good for preserving. In season from November to May.

wrinkle a little at the stem end and are slightly soft at the blossom end. Pears are also available dried and canned in light sugar syrup or in fruit juice.

Storing Handle pears gently, for they bruise easily. Leave them at room temperature for a few days to ripen. Pears are notorious for having an extremely brief period of ripeness between being still too hard to eat and heading toward spoiling. They can be refrigerated in plastic bags for 3 to 5 days, depending on their degree of ripeness, but for the best flavor, be sure to bring them back to room temperature before eating. Because of their delicate texture, pears do not freeze well.

Keep canned pears for up to 2 years in a cool, dry place. Refrigerate dried pears

Quick Bite

The colorless French pear brandy known as *poire Williams* is made from Bartlett pears.

Quick Tip

Pears may be substituted for apples in many apple desserts.

in an airtight container or zippered plastic bag for up to 6 months.

Preparing Pears can be left unpeeled for eating fresh, but be sure to peel pears before cooking. Although the peel is edible, some fruits may have tough skins with a slightly bitter flavor that is accentuated when cooked. When cutting pears for salads or hors d'oeuvres, halve them lengthwise, then scoop out the core with a small spoon or melon baller. Like cut apples, cut pears should be tossed with a little lemon juice to prevent discoloring.

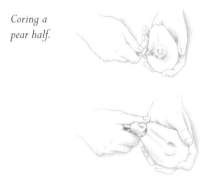

Coring a pear half.

To core a whole pear while leaving the stem end intact, use a small spoon, a grapefruit spoon, or the large end of a melon baller to scoop out the seeds and membrane from the pear's blossom end.

Coring a whole pear.

See also PEAR, ASIAN.

PEAR, ASIAN A relative newcomer in the American produce aisle, the Asian pear somehow manages to be both superbly crisp and extremely juicy. Belonging to a species completely different from regular pears, Asian pears resemble large, pale yellow-green apples. They are also known as Japanese pears, Chinese pears, and apple pears. Asian pears have a flowery fragrance, a mildly sweet flavor, and a slightly granular texture that bursts with juice from the first bite.

Asian pears are best enjoyed fresh as a snack or dessert. You can cut them into translucent, paper-thin slices for salads, cheese trays, and dessert garnishes. They can be cooked in many of the same ways as regular pears, but they require significantly longer cooking and remain relatively firm. The delicate flavor of Asian pears is lost if they are mixed with more strongly flavored fruits or ingredients. Stick to such subtle partners as citrus fruits, ginger, lemongrass, or almonds.

Selecting Varying in skin color from soft green to clear yellow depending on the variety, Asian pears often have a delicate scattering of russeted spots. They are sometimes sold wrapped in protective webbing to prevent bruising. Unlike regular pears, Asian pears are a little firm when ripe.

Storing Once ripened at room temperature, store Asian pears in a plastic bag in the refrigerator. They will keep well for up to 2 weeks, far longer than regular pears.

Preparing Asian pears can be left unpeeled for eating fresh but should be peeled before cooking.

PECAN See NUT.

PECORINO ROMANO See CHEESE.

PECTIN Pectin is a water-soluble carbo-hydrate, a flavorless, gelatinlike substance found naturally in fruits, valued for its ability to "set" or jell jams, jellies, and pre-serves. Concentrated in the seeds and skin of tart and underripe fruits, pectin dimin-ishes as the fruit fully ripens. Pectin works effectively only when the correct balance of sugar and acid is present. The acid, which allows the release of the pectin, is often present in the fruit itself, and then cooking with sugar produces a soft set.

Some fruits naturally contain more pectin than others. For example, apples are naturally high in pectin, while peaches and strawberries contain low amounts. For making preserves from fruit with a low pectin content, you can buy liquid or powdered pectin to add as directed.

Selecting Liquid and powdered pectin are available in major supermarkets. Pectin sugar, which combines powdered pectin and sugar for use in preserving, may be found in specialty-food or baking-supply stores.

Storing Keep liquid and powdered pectin and pectin sugar in airtight containers away from light and moisture.

Preparing Different forms of pectin are not interchangeable and vary in how they are used. Follow instructions on the pack-age and in specific recipes. With low-pectin fruits, additional pectin, a high-pectin fruit, or a greater amount of sugar must be added to set jams, jellies, and candies.

Pectin Content of Various Fruits

HIGH PECTIN

apple; cranberry; currants, red and black; lemon; orange; plum; quince

LOW PECTIN

banana; cherry; grapes; mango; peach; pineapple; strawberry

PEELING Removing the skin from fruits and vegetables is one of the first steps in preparing many dishes. Although peels fre-quently are edible and contain concentrated amounts of nutrients, they may add un-wanted texture, color, or bitterness to a dish. Some fruits, vegetables, and nuts, such as peaches, tomatoes, and almonds, have thin skins that slip off more easily after blanching. Others, such as peppers and eggplant, have skins that will peel away quickly once they are roasted or charred.

A simple vegetable peeler or a sharp paring knife is used for peeling most foods. You can buy special peelers designed for specific foods. Unusual-shaped utensils for peeling asparagus, avocados, oranges, and pineapples are practical if you serve any of them frequently or in large amounts. See also BLANCHING.

PEPPER, BELL See BELL PEPPER.

PEPPER, HOT See CHILE.

PEPPERCORN See SPICE.

PERSIMMON In late autumn, bright orange persimmons hang from leaf-bare trees like small lanterns. Dramatic in color and demanding in temperament, these showy fruits reward the patient cook with a rich, sweet flavor that epitomizes the harvest season. Originally cultivated in China and later carried from Japan to the West by Commodore Perry, the persim-mons most familiar to us today belong to the *kaki* species. Many countries still know the fruit by this name. A species na-tive to the United States is now difficult to find, although the word *persimmon* derives, in fact, from an Algonquian word.

Two basic varieties are available, both derived from the *kaki* persimmon but each with different characteristics. The Hachiya is large, acorn shaped with a pointed end, and deep orange. It must be ripened until meltingly soft to rid it of its mouth-puckering astringency. Once ripe, the flesh

Hachiya and Fuyu persimmons.

is creamy and rich, with a flavor hinting of honey and pumpkin. Puréed, it is wonderful added to muffin and quick-bread batters, custard, pudding, ice cream, or pie. It also makes flavorful jams, jellies, and confections. The Fuyu persimmon has a lighter color and a smaller, rounder shape, like a tomato. Popular for eating out of hand, it is still crisp when ripe and is also completely free of the bitter tannin present in the unripe Hachiya. Halved and broiled briefly, with butter and brown sugar, Fuyus can accompany roast pork or poultry.

Selecting Choose plump fruits heavy for their size and free of blemishes. Their skin should be smooth and shiny, with no hint of yellow. Look for intact stem caps that are green, not gray and brittle. Handle the Hachiya persimmons carefully, for any bruises will encourage rot as they ripen. For this reason, it's a good idea to buy them still a little firm (not rock hard) and let them ripen in peace on your countertop. Persimmons are in peak season from late October to late February.

Storing Arrange Hachiya persimmons stem down on a plate or in a large shallow bowl, and then leave them at room temperature for 1 to 2 weeks until ripe, when they will be very soft, and the flesh, encased in the now-wrinkled skin, will feel almost liquefied. To speed up ripening, place them

inside a paper bag with a banana or an apple. Some claim that freezing persimmons will hasten the ripening, but this only softens them without developing their sweetness. Once ripe, persimmons should be eaten right away or refrigerated in a plastic bag for 2 days. Persimmon purée freezes well for up to 1 year.

Preparing Peel ripe Hachiya persimmons before eating. Fuyus can be eaten unpeeled.

PHYLLO See FILO.

PIE & TART See page 344.

PIE PLATE See BAKEWARE.

PIE WEIGHTS See BAKING TOOLS; BLIND BAKING.

PILAF See RICE.

PIMIENTO Also spelled pimento. From the Spanish for pepper, the pimiento is a sweet, scarlet pepper about 4 inches long. Essential to Hungarian cuisine, ground dried pimientos are better known as paprika. With wide shoulders tapering to a point, the fresh pepper has the shape of a heart. Its thick flesh is more flavorful than that of red bell peppers, and it ranges in heat from mild to hot.

Selecting Fresh pimientos can be found in specialty markets from late summer to early fall. Select firm, smooth peppers with no soft spots. Pimientos are available year-round whole, chopped, or sliced, preserved in brine or vinegar in cans or jars.

Storing Wrapped in a paper towel and then in a plastic bag, a fresh pimiento will keep refrigerated for about 1 week. Store unopened jars and cans for up to 1 year in a cool, dark place. Once opened, jarred pimientos begin to mold rather quickly.

Preparing See BELL PEPPER.

Pie & Tart

"Good apple pies," wrote Jane Austen, "are a considerable part of our domestic happiness." So, too, any lover of the pastry maker's art might add, are pumpkin pies, strawberry tarts, lemon meringue pies, chocolate cream pies, mincemeat tarts, Key lime pies, and other sweet—or occasionally savory— treats that combine a filling with one or two layers of crust.

Pies, which are usually baked in a pie pan with sloping sides, may feature two crusts or just a bottom crust. The crust is usually made from pastry dough that bakes up crisp and flaky. Some pies, however, may feature a more crumbly, tender pastry like those found in tarts. Still other pies use crusts made of crushed cookie or graham cracker crumbs, like those that form the crust for some cheesecakes.

Tarts almost always have only a bottom crust, which tends to be firmer, richer, and more crumbly than pie pastry. Rustic tarts, like a *pizza rustica,* may also be made with more chewy, breadlike, yeast-leavened dough. Tarts are usually baked in tart pans, which have straight or fluted vertical sides and sometimes removable bottoms that let you slip the rim away after baking and cooling. Some tarts, however, are free-form—shaped by hand on a baking sheet. Some of these may also be called *galettes.*

About Crusts "Flaky" and "tender" are the two basic styles of crust. Flaky crust is achieved by keeping the fat in discrete, cold bits within the dough. Once the dough reaches the oven, the bits of fat melt, giving off puffs of steam that lift the pastry into flakes and create air pockets. This airy, flaky texture defines a classic pie crust. A tender crust is flavorful and crumbly, like short-bread, and is created by blending fat and flour more thoroughly. The fat in the dough literally cuts the gluten strands in the flour, making them short and fragile. This is often desirable for tarts.

Such variety alone can lead to the impression that making pies and tarts is difficult work. In truth, however, it is fairly easy to master the basics.

Quick Tip

Crusts with sugar will brown more quickly than those without. A high-sugar crust may scorch if not watched carefully.

Some makers of pies and tarts swear by vegetable shortening for their pastry, while others prefer butter, margarine, lard, or suet. There are even old-fashioned pie crusts made with vegetable oil. Each type of fat contributes its own characteristics to the final results. For any particular recipe, choose a fat—or combination of fats—that gives you the effect you prefer and best complements the filling.

Which Fat Should I Use?

BUTTER Makes a rich-tasting, tender crust.

VEGETABLE SHORTENING Produces the flakiest results, without contributing distinctive flavor of its own.

BUTTER PLUS VEGETABLE SHORTENING
Combines flakiness with tenderness and
rich flavor, a combination that many bakers
swear by. Replace up to half the butter
called for in a recipe with shortening.
LARD Makes an extremely light, flaky, rich
but almost flavorless crust. Some bakers
think it complements a savory filling better
than a sweet one.
MARGARINE Makes a slightly oily dough
with good flavor. Use only solid stick
margarine, never whipped.
SUET Makes a rich-tasting, firm-textured
crust that is best for savory fillings.
Pie and Tart Crust Savvy When
making pie and tart crusts, keep the following tips in mind:

- For a flaky, airy pie crust, keep all ingredients and equipment cold and work
  quickly. For a tender, crumbly crust, use
  ingredients and equipment at room temperature and blend the fat and flour
  well. See CUTTING IN and RUBBING IN
  for more details.
- Measure pastry ingredients precisely.
  Even slightly wrong proportions of
  flour, fat, and liquid can produce less-
  than-ideal crusts.
- Bake pies and tarts using nonreflective
  cookware, so heat will transfer well to
  the crust and cook it properly.
- Bake pies and tarts on the bottom rack
  in the oven for crisper bottom crusts.

Quick Tip

When a fully baked tart shell is to be filled with
fresh fruit, its inside is sometimes sealed to
prevent the fruit's juices—or the pastry cream
base for the fruit—from making the pastry
soggy. The sealant often is little more than a
brushing of melted jam or jelly. Alternatively,
melted chocolate may be used, which hardens
to a thin, crisp coating that also complements
the flavor of the fruit.

HOW TO *Roll Out Pie or Tart Pastry Dough*

Beginning bakers often like to roll out
dough between two sheets of waxed or
parchment paper or plastic wrap. This prevents the dough from sticking to the work
surface and also makes the dough easy to
transfer to the pan. With a little practice,
however, you will become able to roll out
easily any ordinary nonsticky dough.

1. Sprinkle flour lightly over both the work surface and the rolling pin. If using a pastry sleeve
   or pastry cloth, rub flour into it, too.
2. Using your hands, shape the dough into a flat,
   round disk. Place it on the work surface and
   tap it 3 times with the rolling pin, at the top,
   middle, and bottom of the disk, to flatten and
   spread it out a bit. Give the disk a quarter turn
   and tap it again 3 times to spread it out.
3. Starting with the pin in the center of the disk,
   roll the pin away from you toward the far edge.
   Stop rolling and lift the pin at a finger's width
   from the edge of the dough (so that the edge
   does not become too thin). Bring the pin back
   to the center of the disk and roll it toward you,
   again stopping just shy of the edge. Use firm
   and steady pressure as you roll the pin, and
   work quickly so that the fat in the dough does
   not have time to melt too much.
4. Give the dough a quarter turn and repeat
   step 3. Turning the dough after each couple of
   strokes prevents it from sticking to the work
   surface. A second safeguard against sticking:
   add sprinklings of flour beneath the dough and
   on the rolling pin. Repeat turning and rolling
   until the dough is rolled out about $\frac{1}{8}$ inch thick,
   with about 1 inch to spare around the circumference of your pan for pies or $\frac{1}{2}$ inch for tarts,
   or as directed in a recipe.
5. Place your pie or tart pan in the center of the
   dough circle and, with a small knife, trim the
   dough into a neat circle, including the extra
   $\frac{1}{2}$ or 1 inch around the outside of the pan. Save
   any trimmings, if you like, to make decorations
   for a top crust.

continued

P

Pie & Tart, continued

HOW TO *Transfer Dough and Make a Pie or Tart Crust*

1. Roll the round of dough loosely around the rolling pin and unroll it over the pie or tart pan, draping it loosely over the top of the pan.

2. Lift up the edges of the dough circle as you gently ease it into the contours of the pan. Do not stretch the dough.

3. If not already done, use a knife or scissors to trim the overhanging dough to 1 inch for pies, ½ inch for tarts.

4. FOR PIES:
Tuck the overhang under itself to create a rim. This rim may be decoratively fluted or crimped (see page 348); for a double-crust pie, wait until the top crust is laid over the filling before crimping and sealing them (see opposite).

FOR TARTS:
Fold the overhang back into the pan and pat it into the sides of the pan, making the tart's sides a little thicker than the bottom.

Press the dough well into the sides of the pan, raising the dough slightly above the rim of the pan. The crust will likely shrink slightly during baking.

5. Before baking, place the crust in the freezer for 15 minutes to "relax the dough." The process of making dough and rolling it out develops a network of elastic gluten strands in the flour, and this cooling-down period will help avoid a chewy crust.

HOW TO *Make a Double-Crust Pie*

Follow these guidelines for forming a top crust on a pie.

1. After filling the pie and rolling out the top crust as directed in the specific recipe, brush the rim of the bottom crust with water.

Transfer the rolled-out top crust as described above, laying it over the pie.

2. Trim the pastry all around so you have about ½ inch of overhang.
3. Fold the overhang under the bottom crust.

4. With the tines of a fork, crimp, or press firmly, around the rim to seal the crusts together.

5. With a small knife, cut 4 or 5 vents, or slits, in the top crust so steam can escape from the filling during baking.

HOW TO *Make a Lattice Top*

1. With a straight or fluted pastry wheel or a sharp knife, cut the rolled-out dough for the top crust into 12 strips of varying lengths, each about ½ inch wide.
2. Invert the pie pan on top of a sheet of waxed paper and run the tip of a table knife around its rim to make a visible indentation in the paper. Place the paper on top of a rimless baking sheet and spray lightly with nonstick spray.
3. Using the circle as a guide, lift up every other strip and place it on the paper, arranging the strips parallel and 1 inch apart, with the longest in the middle and the shortest at the sides.
4. Fold back every other strip halfway and lay the longest remaining strip perpendicular to the unfolded strips across their centers. Unfold the folded strips over the perpendicular one. Fold back the other strips and place another strip parallel to and 1 inch from the first perpendicular one. Continue to form one side of the lattice, then repeat to form the other side.
5. Glaze the lattice, if desired. Brush the rim of the filled bottom crust with water. Slide one edge of the lattice to the edge of the baking sheet. Line up the edge of the lattice with one side of the crust. While securely holding the waxed paper and baking sheet together, carefully slide them out from under the lattice, draping the lattice on top of the pie.
6. Press down on the edges of the lattice to secure them to the crust. Use kitchen scissors or the tip of a small, sharp knife to trim the edges of the lattice even with the rim.

continued

Other Decorative Effects

Experiment with all sorts of simple techniques to make the tops of your pies look more attractive.

CRIMPING Pressing around the rim of a pie crust or pastry with the tines of a kitchen fork, the blunt side of a knife, or a special crimping tool. See also CRIMPING.

EGG GLAZE For a shiny top crust, beat together 1 egg yolk with 1 teaspoon milk or cream and brush over the crust before baking.

FLUTING Press your thumb at regular intervals all around the rim of a single-crust pie to give it a scalloped edge. Or, use the thumb of one hand and the thumb and forefinger of the other to pinch the pastry around the rim in V shapes. Double-crust pies are better crimped (above) to seal the crusts together. See also FLUTING.

PASTRY CUTOUTS Reserve scraps of pastry dough left over from trimming the crusts for a double-crust pie. Roll them out and cut them into decorative shapes such as leaves or representations of the fruit being used in the pie. Moisten the undersides with water and place them in a pattern on the top crust.

SUGAR SPRINKLES Before baking, lightly brush the top crust with cold water and then sprinkle with granulated sugar or coarser sugar granules. The sugar will bake into sparkling jewel-like crystals.

VENTS Instead of cutting simple steam vents, use small cookie or candy cutters or the tip of a small, sharp knife to cut a pattern of decorative vents. It is easiest to do this before setting the top crust.

Pie and Tart Blues

Got a problem with your pie or tart? Find the simple explanation here.

PASTRY CRACKS DURING ROLLING OUT. If small cracks cannot be repaired by pressing them together with your fingers, dough is too dry. Cover with a damp kitchen towel and refrigerate for 30 minutes. If problem persists, discard the dough and start over.

CRUST SHRINKS FROM SIDES OF PAN DURING BAKING. Dough was stretched too tightly while being put in pan. Always loosely drape and press dough into pan to avoid shrinkage, chill it briefly before baking, and weight it during blind baking.

CRUST EDGES BROWN TOO FAST. Your oven may be too hot or its heat not distributed evenly. Shield the crust edges during the final minutes of baking by covering with strips of aluminum foil, shiny side out.

CRUST ISN'T BROWNING QUICKLY ENOUGH. Oven is too cool, or there's not enough fat in the dough. Turn up the oven slightly, taking care not to overbake the pie. Even if the crust doesn't brown sufficiently, it should still be cooked through and tasty.

FILLING BUBBLES OVER AND DRIPS. Pie may be too full; pie dish may not be deep enough; or filling may be too moist. Next time, use a deeper dish or include a little more starch in the filling to thicken the juices. Meanwhile, place a sheet of aluminum foil on the rack below the pie (or place a foil-lined baking sheet directly underneath the pie) to catch drips.

TOP CRUST SAGS. The pie may not have enough filling, or dish may be too deep. To help support the crust in deep-dish pies, use a pie bird, an old-fashioned ceramic device—sometimes shaped like a bird—placed upright in the center of the filling.

See also BAKEWARE; BAKING TOOLS; BLIND BAKING; CRIMPING; FLUTING; ROLLING OUT; UNMOLDING.

PINCH This measuring term refers to the tiny amount of an ingredient that is picked up by pinching together thumb and forefinger. This informal measuring technique is used especially when adding a hint of strongly flavored ground spices such as cayenne or nutmeg and sometimes when seasoning with salt or pepper. A pinch is generally considered to be $\frac{1}{16}$ teaspoon.

PINEAPPLE Its oval shape and rugged, scalelike texture inspired the Spanish to name the pineapple after a *piña,* or "pinecone." Long cultivated in South America and the West Indies, the pineapple took Europe by storm after the explorers returned with samples of the fruit, odd and unwieldy on the outside but fragrant, sweet, and juicy inside. The pineapple now grows in hot regions from Hawaii to Malaysia and ranks as one of the world's most popular tropical fruits. It is also used as a symbol of hospitality.

Selecting Pineapples at the market usually weigh between 3 and 7 pounds. Look for a pineapple that gives slightly when pressed and sports deep green, fresh, healthy leaves. A center leaf usually pulls out easily from a ripe specimen. A ripe pineapple will smell fragrant, but an overly sweet, strong odor reveals that it has begun to ferment. As a pineapple ripens, it turns yellow from the bottom end up, but color is not an accurate indicator of the fruit's maturity. Avoid any pineapple with dried, wilted, or yellowed leaves. Check that the eyes on the skin are dry, pale, and free of mold. Dark, damp eyes reveal that it has been refrigerated too long. These fruits also tend to have browned flesh. This is more of a problem in winter, when pineapples imported from below the equator have to travel long distances to the market.

Look in the refrigerated section of the produce department for already peeled and cored pineapples; whole or sliced, they come in plastic containers or sealed in Cryovac. Pineapples are also available canned in juice or sugar syrup as slices, chunks, or crushed pulp. The fruit is also frozen, dried, and candied.

Storing Although a pineapple will not become any sweeter once picked, it will soften if left at room temperature for a few days. Once it is ready, use it as soon as possible. Otherwise, peel it, cut the flesh into pieces, and store it in an airtight container in the refrigerator for up to 4 days.

HOW TO *Peel a Pineapple*
1. Cut off the crown of leaves and the bottom end.
2. Set the pineapple straight up on one end and pare off the skin, cutting just below the surface in long, vertical strips and leaving the small brown eyes on the fruit. (If you cut deeper, much of the fruit will then be wasted.)

3. Place the pineapple on its side. Lining up the knife's blade with the diagonal rows of eyes, cut shallow furrows, following a spiral pattern to remove all the eyes.

continued

4. Today's pineapple hybrids have softer, less fibrous cores that do not require trimming. Still, it's always a good idea to take a taste of the core and, if at all woody, remove it with a knife or small cookie cutter.

Pineapple contains an enzyme, bromelin, which readily breaks down protein. Meat marinated in fresh pineapple juice will become mushy quickly, and any gelatin dish containing even a hint of pineapple will not set. But since heat completely destroys the enzyme, you can use cooked or canned pineapple in such cases.

PINE NUT See NUT.

PINK BEAN See BEAN, DRIED.

PINTO BEAN See BEAN, DRIED.

PIPING Frosting, whipped cream, or a similar mixture can be spooned into the wide end of a pastry bag and piped out of the narrow end through a tip to make a variety of decorative effects or to write messages on cakes. The same technique can also be used  to form decorative rosettes or scrollwork of soft mashed potatoes, which may then be browned in the oven or beneath a broiler.

Bound with eggs and flour, the piped potato shapes may be fried as croquettes.

Many different tips can be inserted into the narrow end of a conical pastry bag for different piping styles. The bag is then filled and held with one hand guiding the tip and the other squeezing the mixture from the top of the bag out through the tip.

Disposable pastry bags are available. You also can fashion one from parchment paper, or cut a small corner off a plastic bag. Parchment cones are best for delicate work because their openings usually are very small. Plastic bags work for small, less precise jobs requiring narrow piping lines, such as decorating large cookies or applying stripes of melted chocolate to cupcakes.

HOW TO *Use a Pastry Bag*

To dress up a cake, decorate it with piped greetings, colorful flowers, or scalloped borders. Use frostings that are firm enough to hold their shape, yet soft enough to flow smoothly. Decorating bags with couplers and screw-on tips are most convenient because they allow you to switch tips quickly, but any 12- to 16-inch pastry bag will work fine.

1. Fold the edge of the bag down about 6 inches to create a cuff. If necessary, you can prop the bag upright inside a glass or tall container while you fill it. Fill the pastry bag no more than halfway, as overfilled bags are difficult to hold and tend to leak frosting out the top.

2. Unfold the cuff, press all the frosting down toward the tip, squeeze out as much air as possible, and then twist the bag several times to seal.

3. Grip the bag at the twisted part with your dominant hand; squeeze only with this hand. Lightly support the bottom of the bag, just behind its tip, with your other hand; this hand will guide your movements as you pipe. You may wish to practice on a sheet of waxed paper.

4. Hold the pastry bag at a 45-degree angle and maintain a small gap between the tip and the surface of the cake. Squeeze with steady pressure for an even line. More force will create larger shapes and less force smaller ones. Twist the bag regularly to keep it smooth and taut over the frosting.

Quick Tip

Before starting to pipe, practice on waxed paper. Then, as a guide, lightly trace designs and words in the frosting with a toothpick.

HOW TO *Make a Parchment Paper Cone for Piping*

1. Cut a triangle from parchment paper with two equal sides, each measuring about 15 inches long. The base of the triangle should measure about 17 inches.

2. Curl one of the points of the base of the triangle over and position it at the top point of the triangle.

3. Wrap the third point under the other two points. Pull the paper as you work to make a tightly rolled cone.

4. Fold the stacked points together. Tuck them securely inside the top. Fill the cone.

5. Using scissors, snip off the tip of the cone. Smaller openings produce more delicate lines.

See also BAKING TOOLS; FROSTING, ICING & GLAZE; PARCHMENT PAPER.

PISTACHIO See NUT.

PITA See BREAD.

P

PIZZA Italian visitors to America may sometimes be surprised by the thick, gooey concoctions we often call pizza. On the other hand, when faced with an authentic Italian pizza, thin and minimalist, some American tourists in Italy may dismiss it as a glorified cracker. Even in the States, three schools of pizza making vie for top honors: In the Northeast, tomato-smeared slices tend toward the thin and crispy. Chicago or Sicilian-style pizzas, appropriately nicknamed deep-dish, bake up thick, soft, and cheesy in special pans with high sides. An individual-sized crisp crust topped with ingredients from cuisines the world over and then baked in a wood-fired oven sets the California style.

Pizza and pizza wheel for cutting.

Although take-out, delivery, and frozen pizzas have become the ultimate noncook's convenience, making your own pizza at home is simple. Good-quality frozen and refrigerated pizza dough is available now in most supermarkets. In the time it takes to wait for the delivery of a pizza, you can shape, top, bake, and then eat a hot homemade one.

Quick Tip

Use a pizza wheel, a rotating circular blade, for cutting slices, starting at the center and rolling outward so you won't drag the toppings across the pizza.

HOW TO *Shape a Pizza Crust*

1. After punching down the pizza dough, use your hands to shape the ball into a flattened disk.

2. On a floured work surface, gently press, lift, and stretch the dough into the desired flat shape and thickness. For a soft crust, press it out to a thickness of 1/2 inch; for a crisp crust, press it out to a thickness of about 1/4 inch.

3. Press with your fingertips to form a slightly raised rim.

Topping Ideas An empty pizza shell is like a blank canvas. Some combinations, both classic and contemporary, to inspire the chef and artist in you:

- Chopped tomatoes, anchovies, and fresh or dried oregano
- Thinly sliced tomatoes, slivered garlic, and torn fresh basil leaves
- Roasted onions, zucchini, red bell pepper, and yellow squash
- Pancetta, spinach, and ricotta

- Caramelized onions, anchovies, and black olives
- Sautéed Swiss chard, plumped currants, and pine nuts
- Fontina, Gorgonzola, mozzarella, and goat cheeses
- Sliced mushrooms, onion, and spinach
- Asparagus tips, julienned ham, and shredded Gruyère cheese
- Artichoke hearts, red bell pepper, black olives, and pesto
- Crumbled Italian sausage and julienned red, yellow, and green bell pepper
- Sliced smoked chicken, arugula, and Asiago cheese
- Gorgonzola, caramelized onions, pine nuts, and fresh thyme
- Smoked salmon, dill, and capers
- Tuna, tapenade, and capers

Pizza Savvy Follow these insider's tips to help you achieve perfect pizzas at home:

- Preheat the oven fully. The best pizzas bake quickly in very hot ovens.
- Use a pizza stone or baking stone, or ceramic baker's tiles, placed on the lowest oven rack. These will absorb heat as your oven preheats, approximating the radiant heat of a traditional baker's oven. When the pizza is cooked directly on top, without a pan, the stone or tiles help absorb moisture from the dough, producing a crisp crust.
- Buy a baker's peel, a thin-edged metal or wooden paddle used for transferring pizzas or breads into or removing them from the oven. It slides easily under a pizza crust, making for smooth, mishap-free moving.
- Patch any tears in the crust before topping the pizza. This will keep sauce or toppings from bleeding through during baking, thus preventing the pizza from sticking to the pan, stone, or tiles.
- Don't add too much sauce. Excess sauce makes a pizza soggy.
- Don't add too many toppings. A heavy load of toppings makes pizza harder to cut and eat.

See also BAKING TOOLS; PREHEATING.

PIZZA PAN See BAKEWARE.

PLANTAIN Beloved of Caribbean, Latin American, African, and Indian cooks, this fruit, a close relative of the banana, tastes like a less sweet, blander version of its cousin but has a higher starch content that allows it to be cooked in many more ways. Unlike the banana, the plantain is eaten only when cooked, as all but the very ripest raw plantains are high in mouth-puckering tannin. Also unlike the banana, the sturdy plantain won't fall apart or become mushy when deep-fried, panfried, baked, or stewed, so it may be used like a vegetable in many dishes. Its bland flavor can be paired with a variety of sauces and combined with a large number of other ingredients. A popular way of serving plantains is to make *tostones:* cut plantains into thick slices, smash them to break their fibers, and fry them. Thinner slices are sometimes fried and eaten as a snack, like potato chips. Fried plantains are also wonderful mashed and served with roasted meats.

Selecting Plantains are available year-round. Look for them in major supermarkets or in Latin markets, where they may be labeled *platanos*. Choose fruits that are firm and have peels free of tears or breaks. Fully ripe plantains will have an almost completely black skin and be soft to the touch. Buy plantains at this stage of ripeness for dishes in which they are mashed or quickly cooked; they are much sweeter than in their less-ripe state. For sautéing, deep-frying, and stewing, use firm green plantains, with a yellow-green skin, or semiripe plantains, with black-spotted yellow skins.

P

Storing Leave plantains at room temperature for several days, or until they reach the desired ripeness. Afterward, refrigerate them for up to 1 week. They will not ripen any further once refrigerated, however. Like bananas, plantains freeze well. Simply wrap the peeled fruit tightly in plastic wrap and freeze for 2 to 3 weeks.

Preparing Plantains are harder to peel than bananas, as the peel tends to cling to the fruit. Because the skin contains a substance that can leave dark stains on your hands and fingernails, rub your hands with a very small amount of oil or with a lime half before you begin to peel.

HOW TO *Peel a Plantain*

1. Cut off the top and bottom of the plantain, then cut it in half crosswise.
2. Make a lengthwise cut through the skin down to the flesh on either side of each half and peel back the skin.

PLASTIC WRAP First introduced to consumers in the early 1950s as an improvement on waxed paper, plastic wrap has become an almost indispensable kitchen asset. Most often used for storage, the wrap is also used in microwave cooking to trap steam and aid in heat distribution.

Brands differ widely in quality. Some are easy to use and cling tightly to a variety of surfaces, while others don't trap moisture well and allow food to dry out. Some wraps have a frustrating tendency to cling to themselves, making them impossible to unravel. Experiment until you find a wrap that works well.

In recent years, consumers have voiced concern about the chemical plasticizers found in plastic wrap (and plastic containers used for food), as these substances are thought by some to be potential health hazards. When microwaving, you may wish to prevent the plastic wrap from touching food directly; or look for plastic wrap made from polyethylene.

When wrapping food for freezing, be sure to use freezer-weight plastic wrap or bags. Insufficient wrapping can lead to freezer burn, the drying out and discoloration that occurs when ice crystals from the food's surface evaporate into the drier air of the freezer. Freezer burn degrades the taste and texture of the food.

See also ALUMINUM FOIL; PARCHMENT PAPER; WAXED PAPER.

PLUCKING To pull the feathers from poultry and game birds. Modern processing practices have made plucking all but obsolete for most home cooks. Sometimes, however, a few feathers (usually tiny pinfeathers) remain on poultry, especially specialty game birds from small producers. Use your fingers, tweezers, or needle-nosed pliers to remove these.

PLUM Thanks to crossbreeding, hundreds of varieties of this summer-ripening stone fruit exist. Take a trip to the farmers' market during plum season and you'll find plums in colors that range from yellow and green to many shades of pink, purple, and scarlet. Among the most common are Santa Rosa, Greengage, Red Ace, Damson, and prune plum, also called Italian plum. More unusual varieties include Queen Rosa, Black Amber, and Elephant Heart. Small beach plums, wild plums that grow near beaches or alongside country roads on the East Coast, are excellent for jams and jellies.

Quick Tip

One of the simplest of summer desserts is plums poached in a mixture of water, sugar, and lemon juice. Reduce the cooking liquid and spoon it over the warm plums.

In general, cooking plums are smaller and more acidic than the larger, juicier plum varieties. The latter are best used uncooked in tarts, shortcakes, and other desserts and for eating out of hand.

Selecting The first plums of the season ripen in mid-May, and fruits remain in the market through mid-September. To find a ripe plum, hold one in the palm of your hand. It should feel heavy and there should be some give, particularly at the blossom end. Tasting is the best indication of ripeness, so if you are shopping at a farmers' market, ask for a sample before you buy.

Storing To soften hard plums, put them in a paper bag and let sit at room temperature for a couple of days. Because their sugars must develop on the tree, plums won't sweeten appreciably once they've been picked. Perfectly ripe plums can be refrigerated for 3 to 5 days.

Quick Tip

Always taste plums before cooking. Tart varieties usually demand the addition of sugar, sometimes more than a recipe indicates. Balance the flavor of sweeter varieties with a squeeze of fresh lemon juice.

Preparing If you're using plum slices or halves in a pie or tart, leave the skins intact. They lend a pretty color to the finished dish. But if you're making a plum purée to flavor an ice cream or for jelly or jam, the skins will be unpleasantly acidic and should be removed. When plums are fully ripe, the skin should easily pull away, although it may need to be coaxed with a knife. If the plums are quite firm and the skin clings stubbornly to the fruit, slice a small X in the skin and blanch for 1 to 2 minutes in boiling water. The skins will then slip off easily.

See also PRUNE.

PLUMPING To rehydrate dried fruit, such as raisins, currants, prunes, and dried apricots, by soaking them in a liquid, most often warm water. Some recipes call for soaking the fruit in an unheated spirit, such as rum; the soaking liquid is then used in the recipe as well. Plumping softens dried fruits, making them more pleasant to eat and easier to incorporate into batters and sauces; it also restores flavor to dried fruits that have hardened during storage.

HOW TO *Plump Dried Fruits*
1. Cover the fruits with warm or hot water.
2. Cover and let stand for 10 to 20 minutes.
3. Drain, reserving the soaking liquid if called for in the recipe.

See also DRIED FRUIT; LIQUEUR.

PLUM SAUCE A mixture of plums, apricots, chiles, vinegar, and sugar, this thick, amber-colored, sweet-and-sour sauce is a frequently used condiment in Chinese restaurants. A popular accompaniment to roast duck, it's often called duck sauce and also is served with egg rolls, spareribs, and roast pork.

Selecting Look for jars of plum sauce in Asian markets or the Asian-foods section of supermarkets.

Storing Once opened, the jar of sauce should be placed in the refrigerator, where it will keep for up to 1 year.

PLUNGING After partial or complete cooking, foods are sometimes plunged, or immersed quickly, in cold water to stop the cooking, to brighten and set the color, or both. The French term for this technique translates to "refresh"; another term used is "shock." The water should be ice cold, especially for green vegetables, which need the dramatic temperature change to brighten them after blanching.

p

To plunge, have a large container of cold or ice water ready. Either remove the food from its cooking pan with a skimmer or slotted spoon, or simply pour the food and its cooking water into a sieve or colander set in the sink; then use the skimmer, spoon, sieve, or colander to transfer the food to the container of cold water. Use a large container, so the food won't warm up the water immediately. Remove the food as soon as it has cooled, 2 to 3 minutes, and don't leave it for more than 4 minutes. Soaking in water too long will leach out flavor and ruin texture, particularly in the case of green vegetables.

See also BLANCHING.

POACHING The technique of gently cooking foods in not-quite-simmering water or other seasoned liquid. The water should barely move, although a few small bubbles may break the surface. Although poaching and simmering are often used interchangeably, technically poaching is cooking food at a slightly lower temperature (160° to 180°F) than a simmer (185°F). Many recipes for poaching, however, specify cooking the food, especially larger pieces, at a low simmer.

Poaching is ideal for delicate foods that need careful treatment to avoid breaking apart or overcooking, such as eggs, fish, chicken, asparagus, and pears. It also is used for foods that need long cooking in order to tenderize them, such as beef or pork. (Two examples are classic French pot-au-feu and tough cuts of beef and pork to be shredded for Mexican dishes.) Usually, foods are poached either whole, as for whole chickens and fish, or in large pieces, as for chicken breasts and fish fillets. This helps to keep the food moist.

Either water or a flavored liquid is used to poach foods. In the latter case, the liquid will add flavor to the food being poached, and the liquid may then be used as the basis for a sauce for the cooked food. A common poaching liquid for savory foods is court-bouillon, a light, quickly made stock. Poaching chicken in chicken stock or fish in fish stock is also common. Pears and other fruits may be poached in wine or in simple syrup to which flavorings are added. Eggs and vegetables are usually poached in salted water that has already reached the almost-simmering stage. In the case of eggs, a small amount of vinegar sometimes is added to help the eggs hold their shape.

Poaching eggs.

In poaching, the food to be cooked is partially or completely submerged in liquid, in a pan not much larger than the food, and the pan is usually covered to prevent excessive evaporation. Whole fish are classically cooked in a fish poacher, a long, covered narrow pan just large enough for a good-sized fish; many such pans include a perforated platform with handles for lifting the fish in and out. The fish may also be wrapped in a long length of cheesecloth that extends beyond its ends and sides; when the fish is cooked, the ends of the cloth are used to lift the fish out of the poacher or pot. Some recipes, especially French ones for delicate foods such as fillets of sole, call for the pan to be covered with a circle of buttered waxed paper or parchment paper, rather than a lid. This prevents the excessive heat and steam buildup caused by a tight lid. The dish is then poached in the oven.

Fish poacher.

Quick-cooking foods like eggs or smaller cuts of meat and fish are added to the water once it has reached the almost-simmering stage, while larger foods, like whole chickens, are added to cold water that is brought just to a boil and then reduced to poaching temperature. This prevents overcooking of small foods and allows larger foods to heat gently and remain tender. The cooking time is clocked from the moment the liquid reaches the poaching stage. Smaller pieces of food are removed from the pan as soon as they are ready to avoid overcooking, while larger pieces, such as whole chickens or large pieces of meat, may be left to cool in the liquid.

Caution!

Note that poached eggs are not cooked to 160°F, the temperature needed to kill salmonella bacteria. For more information, see EGG.

See also COOKWARE.

POBLANO See CHILE.

POLENTA One of the glories of Italian cooking, polenta is cornmeal that is cooked in either water or stock until it thickens and the grains of the cornmeal become tender. In Italy, polenta may be either yellow or white, made from either coarsely ground or finely ground cornmeal, but the classic version is made from coarsely and evenly ground yellow corn. Traditionally, it was poured right onto the middle of a wooden table or onto a wooden board as soon as it was ready and then cut with a string for serving after cooling.

Polenta can be spooned up straight from the pot when still soft. Just-cooked polenta is often enriched and softened with butter and Parmesan cheese and served as a base for a thick stew, absorbing savory meat juices and adding its own sweet taste of corn. It is a wonderful hot cereal as well, topped with butter, milk, and sugar or with poached eggs and grated cheese. Polenta in this stage is often referred to as "soft polenta," though true soft polenta, a southern Italian variation of polenta also known as *polentina,* is a thinner, porridgelike mixture that stays softer longer as it cools. The softness of polenta depends on the amount of liquid used. More liquid renders a softer polenta. Polenta that is to be cooled and cooked further is made with less liquid, so it is firmer and easier to cut.

Soft polenta can be poured into a flat pan and cooled until firm, then cut into shapes to be grilled, fried, sautéed, or baked. Thin slices can be layered with tomato sauce, cheese, and vegetables and baked like lasagne. Squares of firm polenta can be browned in butter or oil or brushed with oil and broiled or grilled, and then used in place of toast as the base for appetizers topped with sautéed greens, grilled peppers, or mushrooms.

Traditional Italian cooks make polenta in a special unlined copper polenta pot. They add the cornmeal to boiling water or stock in a slow, steady stream and stir with a wooden spoon, ideally in the same direction throughout cooking, until the polenta thickens to a golden mass and pulls away from the sides of the pan and the polenta grains are tender to the tongue. This usually takes 40 to 45 minutes. A serviceable polenta can be made after about 20 minutes of cooking, as it will have thickened and

P

357

cooked sufficiently by this time, but only the long-cooked kind will have a tender, silken texture. Some food writers are now recommending stirring-free oven-baked polenta.

Adding polenta to boiling liquid.

Stirring polenta.

Selecting Choose an imported Italian polenta cornmeal or, if you prefer, stone-ground domestic cornmeal in a fine grind. Stone-ground cornmeal has more fiber and minerals than the more commonly available degerminated cornmeal, and some cooks find it has a richer corn flavor as well. Polenta is available in instant form, too, although for the best consistency, instant polenta should be cooked for about 15 minutes, which is longer than the instructions on most packages indicate. To purists, the flavor and texture of instant polenta suffer in comparison to regular polenta; it is best reserved for dishes in which polenta is one of several ingredients. Polenta is also available cooked, cooled, and shaped into plastic-wrapped cylinders, a great time-saver for making fried and grilled sliced polenta.

Storing Stone-ground cornmeal must be refrigerated. Degerminated cornmeal has a longer shelf life and can be stored at cool room temperature.

Quick Tip

The kind of pot you use for cooking polenta makes a difference. To keep the polenta from sticking and scorching, make sure the pot is heavy. Unless you have a copper polenta pot, enameled cast iron is the best choice.

See also CORNMEAL; GRAIN.

POMEGRANATE This deep red fruit has a thick, leathery skin, which when split open reveals an abundance of seeds—each surrounded by slightly translucent, ruby-red pulp—sectioned between tough white membranes. The pomegranate is an important food throughout the Middle East, where its fruity, sweet-sour juice is used in stews, sauces, marinades, glazes, salads, and drinks. Pomegranate seeds add sparkle and crunch to salads and make a pretty garnish for soup. Use them, too, in tarts and fruit desserts. Pomegranate juice is used to flavor syrups and drinks and to make sorbet and ice cream.

Quick Bite

Pomegranate molasses, or concentrated pomegranate juice, is an essential ingredient in many eastern Mediterranean cuisines. The thick, deep red, sweet-tart juice is used to flavor salad dressings and in sauces for grilled fish and chicken. Look for it in Middle Eastern groceries and in well-stocked supermarkets and specialty-food stores.

Selecting Pomegranates arrive in the market in the fall and early winter. Look for deeply colored, large fruits, which will have a greater proportion of the clear red, juicy, crisp pulp. Heavy fruits promise more juice. The tough skin should be thin and nearly bursting with seeds. Press the fruits gently; if they release a powdery cloud, return them to the bin; the pulp is dry as dust.

Storing Pomegranates have a much longer shelf life than most fresh fruits. They can be kept at room temperature for 3 to 5 days or refrigerated in a plastic bag for up to 3 weeks. The seeds and the whole fruit can be frozen for about 3 months.

HOW TO *Seed a Pomegranate*

1. Working over a bowl, cut off the peel from the blossom end of the fruit, removing it with some of the white pith, but taking care not to pierce the seeds.

2. Don't cut into the fruit with a knife. You'll break the seeds, releasing their juice and making a mess of your kitchen and clothing. Instead, lightly score, or shallowly cut, the peel into quarters, starting at the blossom end and working down to the stem end. Carefully break the fruit apart with your hands, pull back the skin, and use your fingertips to remove the seeds.

Quick Tip

Work over a bowl and wear an apron when seeding pomegranates. Their bright red juices leave stubborn stains on whatever they touch.

Quick Tip

For a refreshing drink, roll a pomegranate on a hard surface, pressing down firmly, to release the juice from the seeds. Cut a small hole in the peel, insert a straw, and sip.

POPOVER This classic quick bread is characterized by a crisp, brown exterior and moist, almost hollow center. Made from a thin batter of equal parts flour and milk enriched with butter and eggs, popovers have no added leavening. Operating on the same principles as the paste for cream puffs and the batters for Yorkshire pudding and Dutch babies, popover batter rises when the liquid in the batter turns to steam and the proteins in the eggs and flour coagulate to form an elastic shell that traps the steam inside. Although you can use standard muffin pans or individual custard cups, for best results use old-fashioned cast-iron popover pans, which have deep cups, or the newer black-steel popover pans, whose deep cups are attached only by metal strips. Many recipe writers call for the batter to be poured into preheated pans and put immediately into a hot oven, but others insist that popovers made in unheated pans and started in a cold oven will rise just as high. Try both ways yourself and decide.

Popover molds.

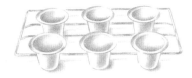

Popover Savvy When making popovers, keep the following in mind:

■ Make sure that the popover batter is cold. It should be refrigerated for at least 1 hour or as long as overnight

359

before baking. If using black-steel popover pans, reduce the oven temperature by 25°F.

- For the highest-rising popovers, use a pan with smaller cups. The batter will have nowhere to go but up. Fill cups of any size no more than two-thirds full.
- Make sure the popover cups are well buttered or sprayed with cooking spray to prevent sticking.
- Place individual popover molds on a baking sheet.
- While popovers are baking, do not open the oven door for the first 30 minutes.
- After 30 minutes, pierce the side of each popover with a small, sharp knife to allow steam to escape and prevent a soggy interior. Continue baking until you reach the specific time.

- After baking, pierce the popovers again, unmold quickly, and serve at once.

POPPY SEED See SPICE.

PORCINO See MUSHROOM.

PORK A marvel of fertility and abundance, the pig, source of pork, has long been one of the most valuable farm animals. Prolific, omnivorous, easy to raise, and possessing an abundance of succulent meat and fat, the pig is the primary source of meat in many cultures. Almost every part of the pig is eaten, from its feet to the bits and pieces left over from hog butchering, which become scrapple and headcheese. The fresh meat is used in stews, roasts, steaks, and chops. When cured, it becomes ham, bacon, and sausages that can be eaten on their own or used as flavoring in other dishes. In fact, the keeping ability of cured pork has always been one of the greatest assets of this versatile meat.

Thanks to its sweet, mild taste, pork pairs well with fruit, particularly dried fruit such as prunes, which may be used in a stuffing for a pork loin roast or made into a sauce to accompany sliced pork or grilled kabobs. Applesauce is a classic pork accompaniment, and quince also seems to go naturally with this meat. Or, try a mango or papaya salsa with grilled pork. Such piquant and spicy ethnic condiments as hoisin sauce also complement this popular meat.

Pork may be divided into two distinct categories: fresh and cured. Chances are you will find a wider variety of cured pork products available in your market than different cuts of fresh pork.

Selecting Fresh pork should have a clean smell, white fat, and dark pink or rosy pink flesh, depending on the cut. The premium cuts, such as loin roasts and chops, are available in any supermarket or specialty butcher shop. Pork shoulder, fresh leg of pork, picnic shoulder, fat back, fresh pigs' feet, and fresh hocks may have to be ordered, but you will probably find them readily available in ethnic markets such as Chinese, German, or Mexican.

Storing Keep fresh pork in the cold bottom rear of the refrigerator for 2 to 3 days. Pork wrapped in butcher paper should be rewrapped in waxed paper or plastic and, to catch any escaping juices, placed on a plate. Carefully wrap pork to be frozen in freezer-weight plastic wrap or zippered plastic freezer bags; freeze large cuts for up to 6 months, smaller cuts and ground pork for up to 3 months.

Store all other cured pork products in the refrigerator. Even though bacon, ham,

❧ Pork Glossary ❧

Pork cuts.

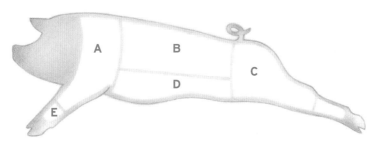

Like any food animal, a butchered pig is divided into primal cuts, the wholesale cuts from which smaller pieces of meat are carved for the market. The two primal cuts of pork most often sold in fresh form are the loin and the pork shoulder. Meat from three other primal cuts, the leg, the side and belly, and the picnic shoulder, is more often cured but occasionally sold fresh.

SHOULDER (A) The shoulder is divided into the upper and lower shoulder section. The upper shoulder, known as pork shoulder, pork butt, or Boston shoulder, is highly valued in many ethnic cuisines. Because it is marbled with fat, this cut is juicy and flavorful. It is ground, cut into kabobs, cut into cubes for stews, cooked as pot roasts, or cut into steaks. In Mexican cuisine, this is the meat used to make *carnitas;* in Chinese cuisine, it is cut into shreds and used in stir-fries or ground and used in spicy fillings; and in regional American cooking, it is used in soups and in stuffings for chicken and turkey and is ground for meat loaf and meatballs. Many of the recipes that today call for tenderloin, such as kabobs and stir-fries, have traditionally used the fattier pork shoulder. It may be boned for ease in cutting.

The foreleg and lower shoulder of the pig, known as the picnic shoulder, is usually smoked for picnic ham, but it is occasionally available fresh. This cut can be used in all the same ways as pork shoulder. The bottom portion of the picnic shoulder is cut off to make pork hocks, which can be added whole to flavor soups and stews and often are found smoked. The picnic shoulder may be boned.

LOIN (B) This upper back section is the most tender part of the pig. The front part of the loin, known as the blade and center loin, has rich, tender meat that is cut into large blade roasts or sliced into bone-in blade chops. Toward the center of the loin, the meat becomes juicier and more tender still.

Center-cut loin chop.

continued

Pork Glossary, continued

The loin may be cut into chops for grilling, broiling, or sautéing. A section with rib bones attached may be shaped and tied into the descriptively named crown roast. The tender back ribs from this section are excellent for barbecuing.

The sirloin, the back section of the loin, is the source of the tenderloin, a narrow cylinder about a foot long and 3 inches in diameter. The most tender of all pork cuts, it may be quickly roasted, grilled, or stir-fried; cut into medaillons; or flattened into scallops. The tenderloin is usually served with a sauce to complement its mild flavor and buttery texture. Loin chops also may be cut from this section for grilling, broiling, or sautéing.

The ribs from a boned pork loin are sold as baby back ribs.

LEG (C) A fresh leg of pork, which is one of the hind legs of the pig, usually becomes a smoked ham, but in the old days it was often roasted and served as a festive farmhouse dinner.

SIDE AND BELLY (D) Below the loin, or upper back, section of the pig are the sides and belly, the source of spareribs and fresh side pork, respectively. Pork spareribs are usually barbecued or grilled but, as with beef ribs, can also be braised. Fresh side pork is sometimes cooked, but usually it is smoked and turned into bacon, or salted and turned into salt pork.

Spareribs.

FEET (E) Also known as trotters. Fresh pigs' feet are usually found only in ethnic meat markets these days. They may be prepared in a variety of ways, including roasting, pickling, smoking, and braising in a flavorful sauce.

and some sausages are cured, they will lose flavor and begin to spoil in the refrigerator. It is best to use them within about 1 week.

Preparing The biggest challenge when cooking pork is to keep it from drying out. Over the years, pigs in the United States have been bred to have a lower fat content, and in some cuts there is little internal fat to insulate and lubricate the meat. Many cooks find that cooking pork gently to an internal temperature of 150° to 160°F ensures the best flavor, tenderness, and juiciness. However, an internal temperature of 160°F is needed to destroy any bacteria in pork (see also Pork Safety, below). Avoid cooking pork to temperatures above 160°F, with the exception of slow-cooked barbecue, which is cooked until the meat falls from the bone.

Even in its new lean incarnation, however, pork is still more succulent and tender than most beef cuts, and the various pork cuts can be cooked by either moist or dry heat. In other words, a cut of pork can be cooked almost any way you want to cook it: broiled, braised, roasted, panfried, poached, stir-fried, or grilled. Some cooks also help keep fresh pork moist nowadays by presoaking it in brine. For more information, see BRINE.

Quick Tip

Keep a piece of boned pork shoulder, well wrapped, in your freezer to use in stir-fries. Simply cut off thin slices of the meat with a chef's knife and stir-fry without defrosting to add to vegetable mixtures.

Pork Safety Though the internal doneness temperatures suggested in Preparing, above, yield what many cooks feel is the optimum taste and texture for pork, they are lower than those suggested by the U.S. Food Safety and Inspection Service guidelines. In order to destroy any lurking bacteria, cook pork to an internal temperature of 160°F. See also DONENESS.

Quick Bite

For many years, trichinosis was a major health concern in the consumption of pork, as this disease of microscopic parasites can be deadly in meat that is not thoroughly cooked. Thanks to advances in the sanitary conditions of pig husbandry, the incidence of trichinosis is rare today in the United States—but raw meats and poultry may harbor other harmful bacteria and should still be fully, diligently cooked.

Never taste pork before it is cooked. If you need to test the seasoning in a mixture containing uncooked pork, cook a small portion of the mixture until no trace of pink remains in the center, then taste it.

Thoroughly wash your hands, cutting board, knives, grinder, and any other utensils that have touched raw pork in hot, soapy water after use.

Don't use a marinade in which pork sat to baste the cooking meat or to serve with the cooked meat unless the marinade has first been brought to a boil and then boiled for about 5 minutes.

See also BACON; CANADIAN BACON; HAM; PANCETTA; PROSCIUTTO; ROASTING; SAUSAGE.

PORTOBELLO See MUSHROOM.

POTATO The Incas of Peru gave us this ancient vegetable. Not only did they cultivate more varieties than we now enjoy, but they also freeze-dried them at high altitudes for long keeping. This vegetable, a member of the nightshade family and once considered exotic by Europeans, is today a symbol of normality and comfort. Easy to grow and to store, the starchy, faintly earthy-tasting potato is compatible with many other foods and endlessly adaptable to various cooking methods.

Red, russet, and white potatoes.

The reliable tuber may be boiled and puréed into mashed potatoes, baked and topped with sour cream, or thinly sliced and layered with cheese and cream to bake in a gratin. It is cut into long, thin sticks and deep-fried for French fries, cut into paper-thin slices and deep-fried for potato chips, or cut into wedges and roasted until crisp. It is simmered in stews and soups, made into a variety of potato salads, or grated and panfried as hash browns or potato pancakes. In addition, potato flour is used as a thickening agent, potato cooking water and puréed potatoes add moisture and flavor to yeast breads, and potatoes are used to make vodka. Even the skins of potatoes are fried or rebaked and eaten.

❧ Potato Glossary ❧

Thousands of potato varieties grow in the world, although we see only a handful in the markets. Increasingly, specialty potatoes are finding their way into produce bins.

RUSSET POTATO Also called baking potato, Idaho, or russet Burbank (named for Luther Burbank, a famed American horticulturalist, who developed the variety in Massachusetts in 1872). Large and oval, with a dry, reddish brown skin. Its starchy flesh is perfect for baking and mashing, and for making French fries and potato gnocchi. Specialty russets include the Lehmi, a large, brown potato with white flesh, similar to classic baking potatoes but more flavorful; and the Butterfinger, with brown russet skin and golden flesh.

RED OR WHITE POTATO Also known simply as the boiling or all-purpose potato. These round potatoes have a thin red or white skin and a waxy flesh that keeps its shape, making them perfect for grating for hash browns and potato pancakes; slicing for cottage fries; cutting into chunks for roasting; or boiling and then cubing or slicing for potato salads. Specialty red potatoes include Red Gold, flavorful tubers with yellow flesh and netted red skin; Red Dale, which are slightly flattened potatoes with white flesh and red skin; All Red, which have both rosy skin and flesh; and Rose Fir, which have pink skin and yellow flesh. Long white potatoes, which were developed in California and are also called white rose potatoes, are a specialty white potato that is oval and has a thin, cream-colored skin and relatively few, very small eyes.

YUKON GOLD Thin-skinned potatoes with a yellowish skin and golden, fine-grained, buttery-tasting flesh. These all-purpose potatoes hold their shape well when boiled, and so may be used in all the same ways as red, white, and new potatoes, but they also make colorful mashed potatoes. Yellow Finn is a similar variety.

NEW POTATO An immature potato, usually of the round red or round white variety, although you may also find new Yellow Finn and Rose Fir potatoes. Most often available in spring and early summer, new potatoes are low in starch and perfect for potato salad, for roasting and grilling, and to use in creamed dishes. Be aware that not all small red and white potatoes are new. A true new potato is freshly harvested, will have a thin skin, and will not keep long.

FINGERLING POTATOES Certain varieties of white potato are called fingerlings because of their narrow, knobby shape. Waxy fingerlings may be used in all the same ways as new potatoes and are good steamed or boiled and served with butter or olive oil.

BLUE OR PURPLE POTATOES With a dark blue or purple skin and flesh, these potatoes will catch your eye in the market. They can be mashed or boiled.

Selecting Most potato varieties are available year-round, although new potatoes may appear only in the spring and early summer and sporadically at other times. Choose firm specimens that are not blemished, wrinkled, tinged with green, or cracked. The buds, commonly called eyes, of the potatoes should not have sprouted.

Quick Tip

If you've oversalted a soup or stew, cut a boiling potato into slices and add it to the pot. Simmer the mixture for 5 to 10 minutes, and then remove the potato slices, which will have absorbed some of the salt.

Different potatoes are used in cooking in different ways. There are three basic types of potato: starchy or mealy, waxy, and all-purpose. Starchy or mealy potato varieties, such as russets, are best for baking and mashing because they cook up dry and fluffy but do not hold their shape well. Waxy potatoes, such as red or white potatoes, are low in starch. Use them for potato salads and other recipes where you want them to hold their shape and are not relying on their starch content to thicken a soup or sauce. All-purpose (that is, medium-starch-content) potatoes, such as Yukon Golds, are good for both uses.
Storing Store potatoes in a cool, dark place with good air circulation for up to 2 weeks; do not refrigerate and do not store in the same bin with onions. These vegetables together produce gases that cause rapid spoilage. New potatoes have a much shorter shelf life than other potatoes. To make the most of their fresh, sweet flavor and texture, use them within 2 or 3 days of purchase.
Preparing Potatoes are used both peeled and unpeeled. If you plan to eat the peels, try to use organic potatoes, as commer-

Quick Tip

If you must peel and cut potatoes ahead, put them in a bowl of cold water to keep them from discoloring, unless the recipe directs you not to do so. Some recipes, such as for latkes, rely on the surface starch of just-cut potatoes to bind the potato mixture during cooking. Other recipes, such as for French fries, will direct you to rinse potatoes in order to remove the starch that might otherwise cause the pieces to stick to one another or to the pan.

cially grown ones are subjected to a wide variety of pesticides that concentrate in the skin. Whether or not you peel the potatoes, scrub them well with a stiff brush under cold running water to remove any dirt. (When washing new potatoes, be aware that their thin skins will come off if scrubbed too hard.) If baking, prick the skins in a few places with a fork. If peeling, use a potato peeler, cutting out the eyes with a paring knife or the tip of the peeler if necessary. If the flesh is tinged with green spots, be sure to pare away all traces of them, for they will taste bitter.

Quick Tip

For the fluffiest, lump-free mashed potatoes, use a ricer or food mill. See RICING.

See also BOILING; MASHING; PURÉEING; STEAMING.

POT HOLDER See COOKING TOOLS.

POUNDING To tenderize or flatten food by pounding it with a heavy object. Thin, relatively tough cuts of meat, such as round steaks, are tenderized by pounding them with a meat mallet. This tool has blunt teeth on two of its sides that break down the connective tissue of the meat. Swiss steak and country-fried or chicken-fried steak are tenderized in the same way.

Some recipes call for pounding or pressing food to ensure faster and more even cooking. Boned chicken and turkey breasts and beef, lamb, veal, or pork fillets may be pounded thin so that they will cook quickly or be thin enough to roll around a filling. To flatten a fillet evenly, place it between two sheets of waxed paper or plastic wrap and strike it with glancing blows, working from the center to the edge with the smooth side of a meat mallet or with a meat pounder (a smooth, heavy disk on a short handle), rolling pin, or the bottom of a heavy skillet. The idea is not to pound down directly on the food but to come at it from an angle as if to spread it out. Slices of veal tenderloin are pounded to make veal scallops (or scallopini), and pork tenderloin is pounded to make pork scallops.

See also SCALLOP.

POWDERED SUGAR See SUGAR.

PRAWN See SHRIMP.

PREBAKING See BLIND BAKING.

PREHEATING The process of bringing an oven, a grill, or a pan to the desired cooking temperature before adding food to be cooked. Without adequate preheating, the actual cooking time will not match the time given in a recipe, and food may cook unevenly, stick tenaciously, or fail to rise, brown, reduce, or otherwise transform itself as the recipe requires.

An oven should be preheated for 15 to 20 minutes before baking. Preheating is particularly important for baked goods, which need to be exposed to the correct temperature at the very beginning of baking in order for the leavening process to take place. When using a baking stone to bake pizzas or breads, the oven should be preheated for at least 45 minutes, to allow the stone to heat through completely. To make sure your oven is preheated to the correct temperature, use an oven thermometer. It is equally important to preheat skillets and sauté pans before pan broiling, sautéing, and stir-frying to prevent foods from sticking.

Quick Bite

Many recipes will tell you to preheat a broiler. This is needed for electric broilers, not gas ones, and electric broilers need only about 5 minutes of preheating.

PRESSURE COOKER This special cooking pot is equipped with an airtight locking lid that forces pressure to build up inside the pot as the liquid within it comes to a boil. The trapped steam causes the internal temperature to rise beyond what it would be capable of doing in a covered pot, decreasing cooking times by two-thirds or more. Dried beans can be cooked in 20 minutes or less, as compared to hours of normal cooking. The increased

Quick Tip

Buy a pressure cooker with a minimum 6-quart capacity. Since safety precautions demand that pressure cookers never be completely filled, anything smaller will be limiting.

pressure also softens the fibers in foods, which makes pressure cookers ideal for cooking tough cuts of meats.

While early models sometimes exploded under pressure and were considered dangerous by some cooks, current designs include safety features that make such problems impossible.

PRICKLY PEAR See NOPAL CACTUS.

PROOFING Yeast, a living organism that can weaken over time, may be tested or proofed to determine whether it is active and capable of leavening bread dough. The yeast is mixed with warm water and allowed to sit for a few minutes until creamy or foamy, which indicates that it is active. Today's commercial active dry yeast is quite reliable, and if used before the expiration date on the package, it should not require proofing. Proofing, however, also gives yeast a head start on multiplying before it is added to the other ingredients, thus giving it a boost in raising the dough. It is also recommended for compressed fresh yeast, which is more perishable than active dry yeast. See YEAST for more detail.

The second rise, or fermentation period, of a yeast dough, after it has been shaped, may also be referred to as proofing.

PROSCIUTTO This Italian ham is a seasoned, salt-cured, air-dried rear leg of pork. Prosciutto is not smoked or cooked, and it is treated with a minimum of salt, but it is cured enough to be eaten without cooking. The result is a meat with a distinctive fragrance and a subtle flavor that make prosciutto one of the world's favorite hams. Aged from 10 months to 2 years,

prosciutto from Parma in the Italian region of Emilia-Romagna is considered the best. The process for curing Parma prosciutto is dictated by law and is overseen by the Parma Ham Consortium.

Prosciutto's intense flavor goes a long way. It is best when served raw or only lightly cooked, since cooking can toughen the meat. Sweet melon wedges, fresh figs, and ripe pears are classic accompaniments that provide a sweet foil to the slightly salty flavor of the ham; together they make a fine first course. Prosciutto is also an excellent addition to an antipasto platter. Just a few paper-thin slices will make a luxurious sandwich on thick bread with butter and arugula. Prosciutto is often used in recipes as a flavoring agent as well. Add a bit of shredded prosciutto to pasta and egg dishes. Drape whole slices or scatter chopped bits on just-baked pizza.

Quick Tip

A blanched prosciutto rind makes a good seasoning for soup, such as minestrone. Ask the butcher to set one aside for you and blanch it before use. If your butcher carries bone-in prosciutto, ask him for the bone to use for making soups.

Selecting Under the rind, a whole prosciutto should be covered with a thick layer of creamy white fat that fades to rose where it touches the meat. The meat itself should be a soft, rosy pink. Before buying any prosciutto, ask for a taste. It should have a sweet, earthy flavor with a slight saltiness in the background. Don't buy any ham that tastes even slightly rancid, an indication that it has not been stored properly.

For prosciutto from Parma, check for the five-pointed Parma crown seared into the side of the intact ham. All consortium-approved hams bear this seal.

In general, prosciutto is sliced paper-thin, for otherwise it may be rather tough. This is best done by the butcher using a mechanical slicer. Once sliced, the delicate flavor of the ham begins to fade, so try to buy it the day you plan to serve it. Thin slices should not be stacked one directly on top of another, but separated by pieces of waxed paper or plastic; otherwise, you'll tear them as you try to pull them apart.

Storing Store sliced prosciutto well wrapped and sealed in the refrigerator. Bring to room temperature about an hour before serving. Never freeze prosciutto, or you'll ruin its creamy texture and diminish its flavor.

See also HAM; PORK.

PROVOLONE See CHEESE.

PRUNE Although this dried plum too seldom gets the respect it deserves, it is an absolutely delicious fruit. For centuries, prunes have been a specialty of the Agen district of Bordeaux in France. Today, most of the prunes eaten in the United States are produced in California, but the most common plum for drying is still the prune d'Agen, introduced to California by French settlers in the mid-1800s. Prune plums are freestone fruits whose pits separate easily from the flesh. They also have a high sugar content that allows them to dry without fermenting.

Many traditional recipes for prunes date back to medieval times and combine the fruits with meat and other savory ingredients. The sweet, rich flavor of the fruit marries well with pork, lamb, or duck. One classic French recipe combines prunes with eel, and another pairs them with tripe. As a special treat, stuff a slit prune with a bit of foie gras. Prunes also lend themselves to desserts. Poach them in wine or Armagnac, alone or with other dried or fresh fruits, to make a compote; or use them in cakes, tarts, and puddings.

Selecting Prunes are graded according to size, from small to jumbo. Bigger is usually better. They should be plumper and moister than other dried fruits, with an even blackish purple color. Some are sold with the pits still in them, others pitted.

Storing Store prunes in a tightly covered container in a cool, dry place for up to a month. You can store them for up to 6 months in the refrigerator. Dried foods readily absorb other flavors, so keep prunes away from strong-flavored foods.

Quick Tip

Because of the concentrated sugar content of prunes, crystals sometimes form on their surface. This does not affect their quality, but you can rid prunes of the crystals by dipping them briefly in boiling water and then drying them.

Preparing If the prunes are very dry, plump them in hot water for 15 to 20 minutes. If they are to be cooked, lengthy soaking is unnecessary, as they will continue to plump as they cook.

See also DRIED FRUIT; PLUM; PLUMPING.

PUDDING The term *pudding* is a source of confusion for some people, and with good reason. In Britain, it seems as if the name is pinned to nearly every dessert. For Americans, however, the definition narrows to a handful of distinct categories. First, and most familiar, are thick, creamy, cornstarch-thickened milk puddings, of which the most popular flavors are chocolate, vanilla, butterscotch, banana, and coconut. Next in popularity are probably rice puddings, which may be thickened custard style with eggs or simply by the starch in the rice itself. The same description applies to tapioca puddings, which feature the pearly granules of the cassava root.

More robust puddings are based on bread or on batters or doughs. Bread puddings start with firm-textured, sometimes stale bread, soaked and bound with milk and egg, sweetened with sugar, and flavored or embellished in a variety of ways. Most bread puddings are baked in the oven. Other starchy puddings may also be baked, such as the cornmeal-and-maple Indian pudding. Another cakelike variety traditional to the English kitchen is the steamed pudding, in which a rich and flavorful batter is cooked for several hours in an enclosed ceramic or metal mold in a large pot of simmering water. The results are incomparably moist and flavorful, the classic example being the Christmas pudding redolent of spices and dried fruit.

Pudding Savvy When making pudding, keep the following in mind:

- For cornstarch puddings, use a heavy-bottomed saucepan to prevent sticking and scorching, and stir and scrape constantly with a wooden spoon.
- For rice puddings, avoid using pre-cooked "converted" rice, which will not thicken sufficiently.
- Avoid overcooking tapioca pudding, simmering only until the granules or pearls are translucent. The pudding will continue to thicken as it cools.
- When making bread puddings, feel free to experiment with a different type of bread than what is called for in the recipe and to substitute milk for cream.

- For a steamed pudding, set the mold atop a trivet in the pot, to keep the bottom of the pudding from overcooking. Be sure to replenish the pot with more boiling water, maintaining the level just over halfway up the mold's side.

PUFF PASTRY The high, flaky layers of a French napoleon or mille-feuille (literally, "thousand leaf"), the crisp, delicate folds of a fruit-filled turnover, and other ethereal baked goods depend for their rich taste and fine texture on this classic pastry dough. Puff pastry is made by rolling out a simple dough of flour, salt, water, and butter; layering it with more butter; folding it envelope fashion; refrigerating it to firm up the butter; and then rolling out the dough again and repeating the whole process. The end result is several hundred ultrathin layers of dough and butter that literally puff up in the oven. Making puff pastry dough from scratch takes more time and patience than skill. Fortunately, commercial puff pastry dough may be found packaged and frozen in well-stocked food stores.

Selecting Shop around for a good-quality brand of puff pastry dough that includes real butter. Check any sell-by or use-by dates on the packaging.

Storing Keep the carefully wrapped dough in the freezer until ready to use.

Preparing Following package instructions, defrost the dough in the refrigerator, keeping it cold until ready to roll it out.

PUMPKIN A popular cold-weather member of the gourd family. Pumpkins are round to oblong with a distinctive ridged shell, and range in color from pale ivory to a deep red-tinged orange. The biggest pumpkins found in the market usually

P

tip the scale at 30 pounds or more, and some, grown by ambitious farmers or gardeners seeking to win agricultural prizes or to outdo their neighbors, can weigh more than 200 pounds. Others weigh just a few ounces and will fit in the palm of your hand. For cooking, seek out small, sweet varieties with a thick flesh and a fairly small seed cavity, such as the Sugar Pie, Baby Bear, or Cheese pumpkin. Field pumpkins have a fibrous flesh that is not good for cooking. Reserve them for jack-o'-lanterns.

When making savory pumpkin dishes, turn to seasonings such as garlic, onions, herbs, or curry to balance the pumpkin's natural sugars. Bakers of pies, custards, muffins, and quick breads can rely on maple syrup, molasses, brown sugar, and warm spices like nutmeg and cinnamon to emphasize pumpkin's sweet side.

There are many excellent brands of canned pumpkin purée, all of which offer considerable convenience to pumpkin-loving cooks. Some are unsweetened and plain, while others, labeled as pie filling, include sugar and spices.

Selecting Choose pumpkins that feel solid and heavy for their size. As they age, they dry out and become lighter. The skin should be hard, with no cracks, blemishes, or soft spots.

Storing Hard shells protect pumpkins from easy spoilage. Most will keep for a month or longer if stored in a cool, dry place. Once cut, pumpkins should be wrapped tightly in plastic, refrigerated, and used within 3 to 4 days.

Preparing The greatest challenge to cooking a pumpkin is cutting it open. Steady the pumpkin on a thick towel, very carefully insert a large, heavy knife near the stem, and cut down through the curved side. Always cut away from you. Turn the pumpkin 180 degrees and repeat on the other side. A more dramatic, messier method is simply to drop the pumpkin onto newspapers spread on a hard floor. It will break into pieces. Once you've cracked into the pumpkin, use a large metal spoon to scrape out the seeds and any fibrous strings in the seed cavity. If you like, save the seeds for roasting (see below).

HOW TO *Make Pumpkin Purée*

1. Place a small whole pumpkin on a baking sheet and roast it in a preheated 350°F oven until it can be easily pierced with a knife, 1 to 1½ hours. For a shorter roasting time, slice the pumpkin in half and roast it cut side down in 1 inch of water in a baking dish for about 45 minutes, or until tender.
2. Let cool, then cut the pumpkin in half crosswise (if not already done) and scoop out and discard the seeds. Scoop out the flesh with a large spoon and purée the flesh in a blender or food processor or with a food mill.

HOW TO *Roast Pumpkin Seeds*

The seeds of the pumpkin can be cleaned off and toasted to serve as a snack or to use in recipes as an ingredient or a garnish. Toasting makes the hulls crisp and edible.

1. Wipe or pick off any pumpkin flesh or strands. Sauté pumpkin seeds in a little canola oil until lightly browned.
2. Transfer them to a baking sheet and sprinkle with salt.
3. Bake in a preheated 350°F oven until crisp, about 10 minutes.
4. Drain on paper towels, cool, and store in a covered container in the refrigerator for up to 1 month.

See also SQUASH; STEAMING.

PUNCHING DOWN Once a yeast dough has gone through its first rise, it is punched down, or pressed, before a second rise. This step redistributes the yeast to give it a fresh food supply as it continues to ferment and raise the dough, and it expels larger carbon dioxide bubbles that have already been created by the fermenting yeast, resulting in a more even crumb to the bread. Punching down also keeps the elastic gluten in the bread from becoming overstretched or broken by the gases trapped within the dough, which would result in a heavy and coarse baked bread.

To punch down, press down on the mass of dough with both hands. Bread dough that is removed from the bowl and shaped before the second rise—or that doesn't call for a second rise—doesn't need to be punched down, as the act of handling the dough achieves the same end.

Punching down.

See also BREAD; RELAXING; RISING; YEAST.

PURÉEING Reducing solid food to a smooth, thick consistency by blending, mashing, or pushing it through some kind of sieving device. Puréed vegetables, such as mashed potatoes, make a comforting side dish. They are also used for soups, dips, and spreads and to add body to sauces. Fruit purées are used as fillings for cookies, cakes, and tarts.

There are many tools to help the cook prepare purées. Food can be mashed into a purée in a mortar using a pestle or pushed through a strainer with a wooden spoon. A chinois is a specialized conical strainer with a wooden pestle for just this purpose. Handheld immersion blenders do a fine job of puréeing without your having to transfer hot food from its pot. Food processors may be used to make coarser purées, while blenders are unsurpassed as a quick way of making very smooth purées. Many cooks prefer using a food mill for making purées, as many food mills have two or more plates with different-sized holes that allow the cook to control the degree of smoothness of the purée, from fine to coarse.

See also BLENDER; FOOD MILL; FOOD PROCESSOR; STRAINER.

PURSLANE Once gathered only in the wild but now also grown for market, this green resembles jumbo clover. The succulent, fleshy leaves have a pleasant tang. In the American Southwest, the green is known by the Spanish term *verdolages*.
Selecting Purslane is in season from late spring to early summer. Choose bright green, relatively small and tender leaves.
Storing Refrigerate, enclosed loosely in a plastic bag. Use within 3 or 4 days.
Preparing Add sprigs of fresh purslane to mixed green salads or chop them up as a garnish for sliced tomatoes. Purslane may also be cooked like spinach; used as an embellishment for pastas, mashed potatoes, and soups; or quickly sautéed on its own.

See also GREENS, DARK; GREENS, SALAD; HERB.

P

Q·R

*everything from quail
to rutabaga*

q·r

QUAIL The American quail is a non-migratory, stay-at-home bird, prized for its light, lean flesh and sweet, nutty flavor. It is not related to European quail, although they resemble each other.

Quail are small and delicate birds, weighing about 6 ounces, with most of the meat in the breast. They are almost always served whole or halved. If a recipe calls for boned or butterflied quail, ask the butcher to do this for you, as it requires a fair amount of precision. (A boned quail is really only partially boned, with the legs and wings left intact.) Quail are generally roasted, fried, or grilled. Boned quail can be stuffed and roasted; butterflied quail is often marinated or rubbed with a spice mixture and then grilled.

Selecting The quail sold today are farm raised. Better butchers offer frozen quail (which are fine) or can special-order fresh. Asian markets are another good source for quail. When buying frozen birds, avoid torn packages or packages with pink-tinged ice (indicating thawing and refreezing). When buying fresh quail, look for plump birds with even color.

Storing Cook quail within 2 days of purchase. Refrigerate them as soon as you get home, in the original packaging. Thaw frozen quail in the refrigerator.

Preparing Allow at least 2 quail per person for a main course. Prepare as for any poultry: remove the innards, wash and pat dry, and pluck any remaining feathers with a sturdy pair of tweezers or needle-nosed pliers. It is often necessary to truss the birds or secure them with small metal skewers to help them maintain their shape during cooking.

QUATRE ÉPICES (KAH-tray-PEACE) Literally "four spices," a mixture of spices sold bottled in nearly every grocery in France. *Quatre épices* commonly appears in ingredient lists in French recipes, signaling Gallic cooks to use their own favorite mixture. *Quatre épices* usually combines white pepper, cinnamon or ginger, nutmeg, and clove, in proportions that vary. The blend seasons soups and stews as well as sausages, pâtés, and marinades for meats.

QUICHE A savory custard usually baked like a pie in a pastry crust and flavored with ingredients such as ham, cheese, mushrooms, and vegetables. The quiche originated in Lorraine in eastern France, where it is traditionally served as an hors d'oeuvre. Many different kinds are made in the area, as well as in neighboring Alsace, but the so-called quiche Lorraine, a common brunch dish in the United States, is the best known. To make this classic tart, bacon bits are layered atop a flaky pastry shell and then a mixture of eggs beaten with cream and seasoned with salt and pepper is poured into the crust. Sometimes Gruyère cheese, onion, or leeks may be included as well.

Quick Bread

There are yeast breads, and there are quick breads. Banana bread, muffins, biscuits, popovers, and corn bread are examples of quick breads. Yeast breads are leavened with yeast, while quick breads rapidly rise thanks to baking powder and/or baking soda, resulting in denser, moister textures.

They rarely require kneading (some doughs for biscuits and scones are kneaded briefly), and do not need to rise before baking, hence their name.

Quick-bread batters frequently contain fats and sweeteners, as well as flour and liquid. They also may be mixed with fresh or dried fruit, nuts, vegetables, cheese, herbs, spices, and other ingredients to create rich and flavorful breads and muffins.

To test a quick bread for doneness, open the oven at the earliest time specified in the recipe and insert a toothpick into the center of the loaf or muffin. It should come out clean or with only a few moist crumbs clinging to it. As they bake, the tops of some quick bread loaves may crack and split.

Quick Bread Savvy When making quick breads, keep the following in mind:

- Careful measuring of both liquid and dry ingredients is needed to achieve the correct texture in quick breads. (This is true of all baking, from breads to cakes to cookies.) See BAKING; MEASURING.
- Replace baking powder or baking soda that has been open in your pantry for more than 6 months, as its leavening power gradually dissipates.
- Coat baking containers thoroughly with fat such as butter, oil, or cooking spray to prevent sticking and promote browning. A light dusting of flour over the fat also helps (or use a baking spray that includes flour).
- Mixing batters with a light hand, just until combined but still slightly lumpy, keeps flour's gluten from overdeveloping and producing a tough texture.
- Bake quick breads as soon as possible after mixing. The leavening effect of the baking powder or baking soda gradually wears off if not exposed to heat. See BAKING POWDER & BAKING SODA for more details about how these chemical leaveners work.
- For convenience, you can mix the dry and wet ingredients separately and hold them apart until you are ready to combine them and bake the bread.
- When the minimum baking time called for in the recipe has elapsed, check for doneness by inserting a long wooden toothpick or thin wooden skewer into the center. (Old cookbooks often called for a clean broom straw.) If it comes out clean, the quick bread is done.
- Let quick-bread loaves or muffins cool in their pans for about 10 minutes, allowing them time to firm up. Then unmold and transfer to a wire rack to complete cooling, so their crusts won't grow damp from moisture trapped in the pan.

See also BISCUIT; CORN BREAD; FLOUR; MUFFIN; POPOVER.

QUINCE A relative of the rose, the quince has a heady aroma that can fill a room. These fruits, which look something like misshapen yellow apples, have hard, dry flesh, with an overwhelmingly astringent flavor; once cooked, however, it becomes a deep rose pink and increases in fragrance. Even cooked, however, quinces remain sour and need the addition of other ingredients to be palatable.

Quinces are old-fashioned fruits, predating their close cousins apples and pears. They were great favorites of the Romans, and the early American colonists eagerly planted quince trees in their orchards. The fruit has fallen from favor in more recent centuries, probably because it requires long cooking and cannot be eaten raw as a quick snack.

An extraordinary amount of pectin is packed into quinces, making them ideal for jellies and jams, especially those containing other fruits lower in pectin, such as pears. Quinces take well to all sorts of cooking methods, too. They can be poached, stewed, baked, or braised. They hold their shape even after long cooking and are traditionally combined with meats and used to flavor stews in the kitchens of Iran, Morocco, and Romania. Quinces are a wonderful addition to fruit compotes and make delicious pies and tarts. Quince paste, made by cooking the pulp with a high proportion of sugar, is served with soft cheese as a favorite European and Latin American dessert.

Selecting Quinces are available from October through December. Look for them in farmers' markets and specialty-food stores. They are harder to find in supermarkets. Large, smooth fruits are easiest to peel and are less wasteful than smaller ones. Blemishes and scars aren't an issue, since quinces are always cooked, but fruits that are too battered tend to spoil more quickly than others. Buy them before they ripen, when they are still quite firm and their skin is just beginning to turn from green to gold.

Storing Store unripe quinces at room temperature for up to 1 week or longer, where they will ripen from green to yellow and fill the room with their fragrance. Once they are ripe, refrigerate them in a plastic bag for up to 2 weeks. Ripe quinces bruise easily, so wherever you store them make sure that they won't be jostled and bumped.

Preparing Although edible, the peel of a quince can be somewhat bitter and is usually removed before cooking. The hard flesh will resist a knife. You may need a hefty cleaver and an extra bit of effort and care to cut the fruit open. Remove the core and the seeds unless you're planning to put the quince through a food mill or otherwise strain it.

QUINOA See GRAIN.

RAAB See BROCCOLI RABE.

RACLETTE See CHEESE.

RADICCHIO See CHICORY; GREENS, SALAD.

RADISH Although radishes come in a tremendous diversity of sizes, shapes, and colors, they all belong to a single subspecies of the mustard family. Aside from the familiar round red radishes, there are thin white ones, known as icicle radishes; Easter egg radishes that range in color from purple and white to lavender and red; and deep red, elongated French breakfast radishes, which fade to white at the root. Central Europeans serve grated black radishes as a first course. Although radishes are sometimes boiled, steamed, or sautéed, their flavor and texture are perhaps best appreciated when raw. They are sliced and used to add color and crunch to salads. Spring radishes, accompanied with sweet butter and bread, are a classic French hors d'oeuvre.

Red radish.

In addition, several different Asian radishes exist, which are cooked, pickled, or eaten raw. The most common is the daikon, a cylindrical vegetable that grows up to 20 inches long and about 2 inches in diameter. It is used extensively in Japanese cooking. Fried dishes are almost always accompanied by fresh daikon, as it is thought to aid the digestion of oily foods. It is grated and eaten in salads or pickled to eat with rice, and it turns up in long, thin threads on platters of sushi. The Chinese also use daikon, but they prefer to cook chunks of it in stews and other dishes.

Daikon.

Selecting Look for smaller, round radishes in spring and elongated ones as summer arrives. Large Asian radishes are in season in autumn, and black radishes are in season in winter. Some more unusual varieties of radish are found in Asian groceries and farmers' markets. All radishes should be firm, with smooth skins and unwilted green leaves.

Storing If you are planning to serve the radishes whole as an hors d'oeuvre, don't remove the leaves; serve the radishes within a day or two of purchase. Otherwise, remove the leaves before storing small radishes in a perforated bag in the refrigerator for up to 1 week. Large radishes such as daikon can be refrigerated for up to 2 weeks. Use the greens in salads or cook them like other greens. See also GREENS, DARK; GREENS, SALAD.

Preparing Scrub the radishes and trim both ends, unless you are serving them as an hors d'oeuvre, in which case you may want to trim the root end but leave 1 inch of the leaves.

Quick Tip

If the radishes you buy are not as crisp as they should be, put them into a bowl of ice water and refrigerate them for a few hours.

RAISIN While you might think that a raisin is a raisin is a raisin, there are actually several different types of this popular dried fruit. All raisins are, of course, simply dried grapes, but the type of grape used determines the characteristics of the raisin. In addition to the common dark, seedless raisins made from sun-dried Thompson grapes that turn up in cereal boxes, dot oatmeal cookies, and are mixed with nuts and seeds in nearly every hiker's supply of trail mix, there are golden raisins, also called sultanas, which are Thompson grapes that have been treated with sulfur dioxide and dried in a dehydrator. During the winter holiday season, fat Muscat raisins are sometimes available. These large, plump raisins have an intense fruity flavor that is favored by many bakers. And tiny dried

q·r

currants are not really currants at all, but actually dried Zante grapes.

Rich in iron, raisins make a great snack for eating out of hand. Add them to cookies, cakes, and yeast breads. Raisins also go well with many savory dishes. Add them to salads or use them to flavor stews.

Selecting Look for plump, moist raisins. They are usually the freshest.

Storing Raisins can be stored in a covered container at room temperature for about a month, or refrigerated for up to 6 months.

Preparing If your raisins are dry and hard, soak them in hot water for about 20 minutes to plump them.

See also DRIED FRUIT.

RAMEKIN A small, round ceramic baking dish, usually 3 to 4 inches in diameter, used for making individual portions of sweet and savory dishes. Custard cups or individual soufflé dishes may be substituted. The term also refers to a small baked pastry filled with a creamy cheese filling.

RAPE See BROCCOLI RABE.

RAPINI See BROCCOLI RABE.

RASPBERRY See BERRY.

REACTIVE A metal that produces a chemical reaction when it comes in contact with an acidic food is said to be reactive. Copper, aluminum, and, to a lesser extent, cast iron are reactive metals. See also ACID; NONREACTIVE.

RECONSTITUTING To bring dehydrated foods back to their original consistency or strength, usually by adding liquid. This term is also used for the process of correcting a sauce that has separated.

See also REHYDRATING.

RED BEAN See BEAN, DRIED.

REDUCING Simmering or boiling a liquid in order to decrease its quantity through evaporation, while concentrating the flavor and thickening the consistency. Reducing is a handy sauce-making technique, typically used when food is being sautéed. Braising liquids, stocks, wine, cream, balsamic vinegar, and other liquids can all be reduced to make flavorful sauces. For a perfectly smooth texture, strain reduced sauces before serving. Meat and poultry stocks are particularly desirable for reduction sauces, since as they reduce their proteins give the sauce a silky, viscous texture unmatched by any starch-thickened sauce. Be careful when using commercial broths for reduction, as they may contain a good deal of salt, which will become concentrated. Opt for reduced-sodium broth when you're planning to make a reduced sauce, and salt to taste at the end.

HOW TO *Make a Simple Reduction Sauce*

For a quick sauce to accompany sautéed poultry or meat, deglaze the pan:
1. Add a small amount of wine, vermouth, or chicken or meat stock to the pan after removing the sautéed food.
2. Stir with a wooden spoon over medium-high heat, scraping up the browned particles from the bottom of the pan, until the liquid has reduced in volume slightly and has thickened.
3. Pour the reduction sauce over the sautéed food, through a strainer if desired, and serve.

Quick Tip

Season reduction sauces after they've reached the desired consistency. If you season them before reducing, you may find them too strong tasting and salty.

Quick Tip

Use a wide, heavy saucepan to speed reducing and to keep the liquid from scorching.

See also DEGLAZING.

REFRESHING See BLANCHING; PLUNGING.

REHYDRATING The process of restoring moisture to dried foods, also called plumping. Although drying is a wonderful way of preserving foods, often giving them a more intense and intriguing flavor than when fresh, it can leave foods with an unpalatable texture. By soaking dried foods in liquid, usually hot water, you can rehydrate them, essentially putting back some of the moisture that was lost during the drying process, making the food tender and pliable again. See also MUSHROOM; PLUMPING; SUN-DRIED TOMATO.

RELAXING Allowing dough to rest after punching down so that the elastic gluten strands in it can relax. For bread, relaxing the dough makes it easier to shape and helps to ensure a well-risen loaf.

Quick Tip

Recipes for bread dough may not specify allowing the dough to relax for a few minutes before shaping it into loaves. But including this step in your bread-making routine will make a better loaf: before shaping the dough for the oven, form it into a tight round, cover it with plastic wrap or a damp cloth, and let it sit for 15 minutes, then shape the dough into the desired form.

The dough for flat breads, such as pizza and focaccia, will often resist being rolled out or pressed into pans, tightening up when you try to do so. When this happens, cover the dough with a kitchen towel and let it relax or rest for about 10 minutes, then finish rolling it out or pressing it into a pan. You will find the relaxed dough much easier to handle.
See also BREAD; RESTING; RISING.

RELISH A sweet or savory condiment, usually made of cooked or pickled fruits or vegetables. Relishes include the green pickle relish used for hot dogs, piccalilli, pickled vegetables, corn relish, spiced pears, and pickled watermelon rind. Pickles and chutneys are types of relishes, although relishes are generally considered more spicy than either.

RENDERING No matter how snowy white it appears, all animal fat in its natural state contains some amount of meat tissue, and the only way to separate the fat from the tissue is to melt it, a process known as rendering. As the fat melts, it separates from the bits of meat tissue, which sink to the bottom of the pan. The pure fat is then strained to remove these crisp bits, which are known as cracklings and are sometimes used, like crumbled bacon, as a garnish or as an ingredient. The fat of poultry, especially ducks and geese, is rendered when the birds are roasted. It is simply a matter of straining the pan drippings to capture the rendered fat. When bacon is cooked, it renders most or all of its fat, producing a favorite cooking medium in many kitchens.
Lard and schmaltz (rendered chicken fat), duck fat, and goose fat can all be purchased from specialty-food purveyors.

RESERVING Saving an ingredient or recipe component for use later in the recipe or for another dish.
See also SETTING ASIDE.

q·r

RESTING To allow food to sit undisturbed for a period of time during the course of preparing a dish. Resting is an important step in bread recipes, as it allows the gluten to relax, making the dough easier to shape and giving the final product a better texture. Pie dough is allowed to rest in the refrigerator, usually for a minimum of 30 minutes, to chill and firm the fat and to allow the moisture to distribute evenly throughout the dough. The cold slows down the development of gluten, which is desirable in bread dough but not in pastry. The batter for crepes should be allowed to rest in the refrigerator before using. The flour particles will then expand in the liquid, and the resulting crepes will be more tender.

Roasted meats should be allowed to rest after cooking and before carving or slicing. During cooking, the meat near the surface dries out due to evaporation and because some of its juices have been forced farther into the interior. Carving the meat right out of the oven results in dry edges and loss of juices from the center of the roast. A resting period allows the juices to redistribute themselves through the meat, making it uniformly juicier. Keep in mind that the internal temperature of meat and poultry will rise 5° to 10°F during resting, so account for this when judging roasting times.

See also RELAXING; ROASTING.

RHUBARB Although technically a vegetable, rhubarb is treated like a fruit in the kitchen. Its long, celery-like stalks range in color from cherry red to pale pink. Rhubarb usually is cooked with a good dose of sugar to balance its tartness. The delicious transformation after sweetening and cooking has earned rhubarb the nickname "pie plant."

Although hothouse-grown rhubarb is available all year in some areas, field-grown rhubarb is a spring crop, with the bulk appearing in April and May. Rhubarb is often paired with strawberries, which appear in the same season and whose sweetness provides a nice contrast. Oranges are another common flavor pairing. A favorite for pies and tarts, rhubarb also makes wonderful jams and preserves. Rhubarb chutneys and relishes are an excellent accompaniment to roast pork or duck.

Caution!

Rhubarb leaves are mildly toxic and should always be discarded.

Selecting Look for crisp, firm stalks without blemishes or cuts and with good color. Avoid rhubarb stalks that are turning from red or pink to green. Field-grown rhubarb has a bright red color and a more pronounced flavor than pale pink hothouse-grown stalks. Any leaves attached to the stalks should be fresh looking, not wilted, although the leaves should not be eaten.

Storing Whole stalks can be refrigerated for up to 3 days. Store them in the crisper in perforated plastic bags.

Quick Tip

To enjoy rhubarb long after its season has passed, cut the stalks into chunks, put into heavy-duty plastic freezer bags, and freeze for up to 8 months.

Preparing Trim away the leaves and stalk ends and peel any brown spots. If stalks are fibrous, remove the strings with a vegetable peeler. Stalks that are more than 1½ inches wide should be halved lengthwise.

Rice

From steaming bowls of plump, clingy rice served alongside Japanese sashimi to aromatic rice accompanying Middle Eastern kabobs to creamy Italian risotto, this seed of a species of grass is the most widely eaten of all the grains.

More than 40,000 distinct varieties of rice have been identified, explaining the diverse characteristics of rice dishes around the world. Nevertheless, far fewer types of rice lend themselves to commercial cultivation, and these may be readily classified into a handful of easily identifiable categories.

Rice Styles One or more of the following terms are likely to be found on the packaging of rice you encounter for sale. Some define a specific variety or type of rice, while others specify characteristics the rice has when cooked.

ARBORIO RICE Northern Italian variety of medium-grain rice with a high surface-starch content that dissolves when the rice is simmered and stirred, forming a creamy sauce that complements the chewy rice as in the classic Italian dish risotto. Two other, similar Italian varieties, Carnaroli and Vialone Nano, may be substituted. So, too, may other medium-grain rice varieties. See also Medium-Grain Rice, page 380.

AROMATIC RICE Varieties that give off pronounced aromas when cooked, such as Della, basmati, jasmine, and pecan rice.

BASMATI RICE Highly aromatic, long-grain variety, grown primarily in India, Iran, and the United States, with a sweet, nut-like taste and perfume. Both white and brown basmati rices are sold. Basmati is the best rice to use in pilafs. American-grown basmati rice is sometimes commercially labeled Texmati after its state of origin.

BLACK RICE Southeast Asian variety of unmilled sticky rice with a black hull that turns dark purple when cooked.

BROWN RICE Refers to any rice that has not been processed by milling or polishing, leaving its brown hull intact. Brown rice takes longer to cook than comparable white rice and has a chewier texture and a nutlike taste. Technically speaking, both black and red rice are brown rice.

CONVERTED RICE Refers to commercially sold white rice that was parboiled before the removal of its bran. This rice cooks quickly and is high in B vitamins.

DELLA RICE A hybrid rice of the American South similar to basmati. It has a taste and aroma that has been likened to popcorn.

GLUTINOUS RICE A short-grain rice that becomes soft, moist, sticky, and translucent when cooked. Also called sticky or sweet rice. Uncooked, it is opaque and almost as round as a pearl. It is also ground into flour. There is no substitute for glutinous rice in sticky rice desserts.

JASMINE RICE A long-grain rice variety from Thailand with a sweet floral scent.

LONG-GRAIN RICE Any rice variety with grains three to five times longer than they are wide. When cooked, the grains are generally fluffy and separate. Long-grain rice is traditionally used in such dishes as pilafs, which are cooked in stock and may include vegetables, poultry, meat, or seafood.

continued

Rice, continued

MEDIUM-GRAIN RICE Rice varieties with grains 2 to 3 times longer than they are wide. Note that the United States is the only country that uses "medium grain" as a category of rice. In other countries, all rice is divided into either "short grain" or "long grain." Therefore, the rice used in Spain for paella and in Italy for risotto is referred to as short grain, although both are more accurately described as medium grain.

PECAN RICE An aromatic long-grain white rice grown in Louisiana and enjoyed for a taste and scent reminiscent of pecans.

RED RICE Long-, medium-, or short-grain rice variety with red-colored bran, sold unmilled and enjoyed for its bright color.

RICE FLOUR See FLOUR.

SHORT-GRAIN RICE Most common in Asian and Caribbean kitchens, these almost-spherical grains yield very sticky, chewy results when cooked. Short-grain rice is used in many desserts. It is also ground into rice flour, to be used as a thickening agent.

SUSHI RICE Medium-grain white rice. What makes sushi rice so distinctive is the method of cooking that involves soaking and rinsing the grains as well as fanning them while they cool.

WHITE RICE Any rice that has been milled to remove its brown hull and bran.

WILD RICE Not actually a type of rice at all, but the seed of an aquatic grass. It is native to Minnesota, where it grows wild. It is also cultivated. The dark brown, unpolished kernels have a rich, nutlike flavor and texture. See also WILD RICE.

Selecting Most food stores today carry several different kinds of rice. For an even wider selection, seek out specific types in natural-food stores, ethnic markets, or specialty-food shops.

Storing Store rice in an airtight container away from moisture, heat, and light. White rice will keep for up to 2 years; brown rice, other unhulled rices, and wild rice will keep for up to 1 year, or longer if refrigerated.

Preparing Many cooks rinse rice before using it to remove excess starch that may create a gummy texture. Place the rice in a large pot and rinse it several times, gently swishing the rice with your fingers, until the water runs clear.

Rice may be boiled in a large quantity of liquid and then drained, like pasta; simmered in a covered pan with a carefully measured amount of liquid, which steams the grains; cooked in a microwave oven with a measured amount of liquid; or prepared in an Asian-style rice cooker, following the manufacturer's instructions. Substituting stock, coconut milk, or another savory or sweet liquid for its cooking water flavors rice as it cooks.

HOW TO *Steam Rice*

For plain rice follow these simple instructions and proportions, adding, if you wish, $\frac{1}{4}$ to $\frac{1}{2}$ teaspoon salt for each 1 cup rice.

1. Combine water (in the proportion listed below, depending on the type of rice) and rice in a small saucepan that has a tight-fitting lid.
2. Bring to a boil over high heat, stir, reduce the heat to low, cover, and cook until tender, according to the times suggested.
3. After cooking, let the rice sit undisturbed for 10 to 20 minutes to "steam" it before serving.

BROWN RICE Simmer, covered, in 2 parts water to 1 part rice until tender, 45 to 60 minutes.

LONG-GRAIN RICE Simmer, covered, in $1\frac{3}{4}$ parts water to 1 part rice for 15 to 20 minutes.

SHORT- OR MEDIUM-GRAIN RICE Simmer, covered, in $1\frac{1}{2}$ parts water to 1 part rice for 15 to 20 minutes.

WILD RICE Simmer, covered, in 3 parts water to 1 part rice until tender but still chewy, about 1 hour; drain off any excess liquid.

See also NOODLE; PAELLA; RICE COOKER; RISOTTO.

q·r

RICE COOKER Also called a rice steamer, this electric appliance takes the guesswork and worry out of cooking rice. The cooker sits on the countertop. It is fitted with an insert for steaming rice. Some models have additional inserts for steaming other foods such as vegetables. Rice cookers typically cook from 2 to 24 cups of rice, depending on the size.

RICE PAPER Thin, dried translucent paper made from rice flour, water, and salt is known as rice paper, rice sheets, or spring roll wrappers. Indispensable to the Vietnamese kitchen, rice papers are distinguished by the cross-hatching that results from being dried on bamboo mats under a tropical sun.

Selecting Rice papers may be round or triangular, and they come in a range of sizes from small to large. Vietnamese spring rolls are usually made from 8-inch round rice papers, which come in 1-pound packages of about 50 papers.

Storing Rice papers will keep indefinitely in a tightly closed plastic bag stored on a cupboard shelf.

Preparing Brush or spray each paper with water on both sides, or simply dip it quickly in a bowl of cold water and shake to remove the excess water. Set the moistened rice paper on paper towels for 1 to 2 minutes to soften. Fill and roll. Spring rolls made with rice paper may be served without further cooking or deep-fried.

RICE VERMICELLI See NOODLE.

RICE VINEGAR See VINEGAR.

RICE WINE There are several variations of this sweet wine, which is made from glutinous rice. (See RICE.) Sake, the traditional Japanese beverage, is often served warm to pour into tiny cups or wooden boxes, though some sake is meant to be sipped chilled. Rice wine is also used in cooking, most often in sauces and marinades. Mirin, or sweet sake, a sweetened rice wine, is used exclusively for cooking and is an important ingredient in Japanese cuisine. Dry sherry may be substituted.

The best-known Chinese rice wine is Shaoxing. Like sake, it is often served warm. It is considered an essential ingredient in Chinese cooking, from stir-fries to braises. This is the spirit that is used in large quantities in "drunken" Chinese dishes, such as drunken shrimp. A dry sherry is the only substitute.

Selecting Look for rice wine in the ethnic-foods section of the supermarket or in Asian groceries.

Storing Rice wine will keep indefinitely in a cool, dark place.

Quick Bite

Although sake is called rice *wine*, it is actually made in a process that is more akin to that used to make beer.

RICING Ricing is a method of making a fluffy mash or purée. It is most commonly used for making extremely fine mashed potatoes. A ricer looks like a small pot with holes in the bottom and a plunger attached to the rim. Cooked potatoes are put in the "pot," which is positioned over a warmed bowl. The potatoes are then forced through the perforations with the plunger, which turns them into soft ricelike kernels. Finally, hot milk or cream and butter is gently stirred into the riced potatoes. The resulting texture is very refined and smooth.

r·t

You can also rice other sturdy vegetables, such as carrots, parsnips, or celery root.

Ricing potatoes.

Quick Tip

If you use organic potatoes, you can cook and rice them without having to peel them. Scrub the potatoes well before cooking to remove dirt. After they are cooked, cut them into chunks if necessary and put them through the ricer, stopping periodically to scrape off the peels from the plunger.

See also COOKING TOOLS; POTATO.

RICOTTA See CHEESE.

RIND The tough, and usually thick, exterior coat of some foods, such as melons, citrus fruits, slab bacon, and ham. Citrus rinds consist of both the colored zest and the white pith. (See also ZESTING.) Like melon rinds, citrus rinds are generally inedible. But they may be cooked or packed in salt for an extended time to soften them, as for preserved lemons. Citrus rinds can also be candied. Melon rinds, or peels, particularly those of watermelons, are preserved by pickling. Ham and bacon rinds are often removed before cooking, but are sometimes reserved to use as a flavoring and thickening agent in soups and stews.

Many aged cheeses have a rind, which varies in texture, thickness, and color, depending on the cheese. See also CHEESE.

RIPENING Fruits are best eaten at the point of ripeness, that is, when they have reached their peak of flavor and texture. Fruits play a key role in a plant's reproduction process: fruits are carried away and eaten by animals, dispersing their seeds far and wide. So it is to a plant's advantage that its fruit be as appealing to the animal senses as possible at the moment when its seeds become viable. There are four main sensory indicators of ripeness: a change in color, usually from green to a bright shade; a burst of scent; a softening of texture; and a decrease in acid content, highlighting the fruit's sugar content and sweet taste.

It's not always easy to come across fruits at their point of ripeness. Pears, for example, often are hard when you buy them and should sit at room temperature for a few days before eating out of hand. Some fruits are picked unripe for distribution to markets and so need to ripen after purchase. Bananas, plantains, peaches, and tomatoes are picked before they reach their peak and will benefit from sitting at room temperature. Avocados, in fact, do not ripen fully until *after* they have been picked.

To hasten the ripening process and to prevent fruit from spoiling before it ripens completely, put the fruit in a paper bag to trap the ethylene gas the fruit emits. Be sure to punch several holes in the bag to let the fruit breathe.

RISING The increase in volume of a mixed batter or dough is referred to as rising. A leavener causes these mixtures to increase in volume. Heat and steam alone are enough to induce some batters or light doughs to rise. Three other kinds of leaveners are eggs and butter (both aerating leaveners—beaten to incorporate air, which expands to raise the batter), yeast, and chemical leaveners such as baking soda and baking powder.

See also BAKING POWDER & BAKING SODA; EGG; LEAVENING; YEAST.

RISOTTO Like pasta and polenta, risotto is an example of the Italian talent of turning the simplest ingredients into a sublime dish. It is made from certain varieties of medium-grain rice that possess an outer layer of soft starch. During cooking, the rice is constantly stirred while hot liquid is gradually added, causing the starch to dissolve and form a creamy sauce that complements the chewy rice.

The varieties of Italian rice most commonly used are Arborio, Carnaroli, and Vialone Nano; Arborio is by far the best known and most widely available in the United States.

There are two styles of risotto made in Italy: the cohesive and slightly sticky dish from Lombardy and Emilia-Romagna is what we usually think of as risotto in the United States. The best-known example is probably *risotto alla milanese,* made with saffron and a sprinkling of Parmesan cheese. The second style, from the Veneto, is thinner and more like a porridge; the best-known example is the *risi e bisi* of Venice, which is rice with peas.

Risotto can be plain, with only Parmesan cheese added, or it can incorporate one or more of a wide variety of flavoring ingredients. Any risotto usually starts with finely chopped onion cooked in butter or, less frequently, olive oil. The rice is added and stirred just long enough to coat the grains. Next, about ½ cup of liquid is added at a time, and the rice is stirred constantly until almost all the liquid is absorbed. Often dry white wine is the first liquid addition, followed by a hot stock, typically chicken. This step is repeated, along with constant stirring, until the rice is creamy on the outside and al dente at the center: tender but firm to the bite. This process takes 20 to 30 minutes of closely monitored cooking and stirring.

Risotto may be served as a first course, side dish, or main course. It may also be molded before serving. In one classic dish, it is made from the stock of a poached chicken, and the bird is served in the center of a ring of the risotto. Risotto is the basis for *arancini* and *supplì,* deep-fried cheese-stuffed croquettes. It may also be formed into cakes, sautéed, and served as a side dish or as a bed for other foods.

Risotto Savvy When making risotto, keep the following in mind:
- The right pan is the secret to a good risotto. The pan must be large, of about 1-quart capacity for each serving made, and heavy enough to keep the rice from scorching or cooking too fast during the lengthy process of becoming risotto. An enameled cast-iron saucepan is ideal.
- Taste-test the rice after about 20 minutes, but plan for 25 to 35 minutes of total cooking time.
- If you run out of liquid before the rice is al dente, use hot water to finish the cooking process.
- Often the final step in making risotto is to stir in 1 or 2 tablespoons of butter or a good amount of grated Parmesan cheese, or both, depending on the other

ingredients. This process takes from 1 to 2 minutes and makes the final dish even creamier. Use a light hand: if you stir too vigorously, the rice will become gummy.

■ Although it will not be quite as creamy, you can partially cook the risotto ahead of time and finish it just before serving. To do so, cook the risotto until half of the hot liquid has been added, remove it from the pan, and spread it out on a rimmed baking sheet to arrest the cooking process. Return the rice to the heat and complete the risotto's preparation right before serving, adding a little more cheese or butter, or both, than called for in the recipe.

See also RICE.

ROASTING This dry-heat method of oven-cooking foods in an uncovered pan should be reserved for tender meats with plenty of marbling or interior fat. Though marinating, coating with oil or butter, and basting will also help keep the surface of roasted meat moist, nothing will keep a roast's center moist if you overcook it. Paying attention to the internal temperature is the only final assurance of juicy, succulent meat. Leaner meats also can be roasted, but they should be well barded to supplement their moisture (see BARDING).

Cooks have developed various techniques for keeping the interior of roasted meats moist while developing a rich, brown exterior. Larger roasts are best cooked at a lower roasting temperature of 325° to 350°F, to help prevent the outer section of the roast from overcooking before the center is done. If the roast isn't as brown as it should be by the end, the temperature can be raised to 400°F for the last minutes of cooking. Smaller roasts, including beef tenderloins, do better roasting quickly at higher temperatures. They need the higher heat to brown since they are not in the oven as long.

Equipment A roasting pan has low sides in order to allow the oven heat to reach as much of the surface of the food as possible, while catching any juices from the roasting food. For roasts and poultry, choose a heavy roasting pan to keep the bottom of the food and the pan juices from burning. Although a pan with a nonstick surface makes cleanup easy, a regular surface allows more brown bits to stick to the pan during roasting, which means better gravy.

Roasting pan with rack.

A metal rack keeps the bottom of the food from stewing in the pan drippings and sticking to the pan. It also produces clearer pan drippings, which means better-tasting gravy. You can use a wire cake rack in a pinch, but a V-shaped nonstick roasting rack is preferable, as it elevates the food

Roasting Times for Various Foods

Food	Oven Temperature	Approximate Time	Internal Temperature
Beef			
Prime rib	550°F to preheat, 350°F to roast	18 to 20 minutes per pound	Medium-rare: 130° to 140°F*
Rolled roast	550°F to preheat, 350°F to roast	25 to 30 minutes per pound	Medium-rare: 130°F to 140°F*
Tenderloin (whole)	500°F to preheat, 400°F to roast	10 minutes per pound	Rare: 120° to 130°F;* Medium-rare: 130° to 140°F*
Lamb			
Boneless leg	450°F to preheat, 325°F to roast	20 to 25 minutes per pound	Medium-rare: 130°F*
Rack	400°F	25 minutes total	Medium-rare: 130°F*
Pork			
Boneless loin or shoulder	450°F to preheat, 325°F to roast	30 to 35 minutes per pound	Medium: 150° to 160°F*
Tenderloin	500°F	18 to 20 minutes total	Medium: 150° to 160°F*
Veal, leg, shoulder, or loin (barded)	425°F to preheat, 325°F to roast	15 to 20 minutes per pound (turn once)	Medium: 145° to 155°F*
Chicken (whole)	450°F to preheat, 350°F to roast	20 to 25 minutes per pound	150° to 160°F* in breast; 165° to 175°F in thigh
Turkey (whole)	450°F to preheat, 325°F to roast	15 to 20 minutes per pound (10- to 15-pound birds); 13 to 15 minutes per pound (birds over 16 pounds)	170°F in breast; 185°F in thigh
Fish	500°F	8 to 9 minutes per inch of thickness	135° to 137°F
Vegetables			
Asparagus	500°F	8 to 10 minutes total	
Beets (whole)	300°F	45 to 75 minutes total	
Winter squash (whole)	375°F	45 to 90 minutes total	

*Although the internal temperatures for meats and poultry in this chart yield what many cooks feel are the optimum taste and texture for these foods, they are lower than those suggested by the U.S. Food Safety and Inspection Service guidelines; see DONENESS.

q·r

more and allows more of its surface to brown. You can also place the meat or poultry on a bed of aromatic vegetables, such as chopped carrots, onions, and celery. The vegetables serve the same function as a rack, with the added benefit that they may be puréed and combined with the degreased pan juices and the deglazing liquid to make a sauce for the roasted food.

About Vegetables Vegetables such as whole potatoes and sweet potatoes in their skin, sliced and oiled root vegetables, and softer vegetables such as tomatoes take well to roasting, as it concentrates their natural sugars and heightens their flavor. Beets roasted in their skins are a revelation, becoming almost as sweet as candy, and asparagus comes out crisp-tender and deep green. Except for baked potatoes, vegetables should be given a coating of olive oil before roasting: place them in a baking dish or roasting pan, sprinkle or spray with olive oil, and toss them to coat. Toss again with salt, pepper, and other seasonings.

Roasting Times Note in the chart on page 385 that the doneness temperatures are different for different meats and birds, and that cooking times are approximate. Keep in mind that the internal temperature of roasts and birds will continue to rise after they are out of the oven. In many cases, the oven is preheated to a high temperature, and the temperature is then reduced when the food is put in the oven to roast. The chart is based on unstuffed, room-temperature meats and poultry. For stuffed meats and smaller stuffed poultry, add a few minutes more per pound; the same rule also applies to stuffed turkeys over 12 pounds.

Pan Roasting Like pan broiling, this term refers (usually) to cooking in a dry skillet on the stove top. Pan roasting differs from pan broiling in that the heat is lower and the food is cooked more gently. In Mexican cooking, fresh chiles, tomatoes, onions, tomatillos, and garlic are all pan roasted on a *comal,* a flat carbon-steel griddle, until browned and tender. This concentrates the flavor in the vegetables as they cook by evaporating some of their moisture and giving them a slightly charred taste. You can use a griddle or a cast-iron skillet over medium heat for pan roasting these types of vegetables. You may want to line the griddle or pan with aluminum foil for easier cleanup. (They can also be cooked under a broiler.)

Another version of pan roasting is used for boneless chicken breasts and salmon, tuna, or swordfish fillets: the food is seared on one side—in a little oil heated over medium-high heat in a cast-iron or other heavy, ovenproof skillet—for a few minutes. The food is not turned, and the skillet is placed in a preheated 450°F oven for about 10 minutes, resulting in chicken or fish with a very crisp exterior and a tender, juicy interior.

See also BARDING; DEGLAZING; DONENESS; LARDING; MARINATING; RESTING; TEMPERATURE; individual types of poultry and meat.

ROCK CORNISH GAME HEN See CORNISH GAME HEN.

ROCKET See ARUGULA.

ROLLING OUT To flatten dough using a rolling pin. Pie dough and cookie dough are rolled out on a work surface, such as a countertop or pastry board, which is usually floured first to prevent sticking. Pastry sleeves (for the pins) and pastry cloths (for the surfaces) may be used to prevent sticking, too. A recipe usually specifies the final size and/or thickness of the dough and the shape. Bread doughs can be rolled out for pizza and various flat breads.

HOW TO *Roll Out Dough*

1. Sprinkle flour lightly over both the work surface and the rolling pin.
2. Using your hands, shape the dough into a flat, round disk. Place it on the work surface and tap it 3 times with the rolling pin, at the top, middle, and bottom of the disk, to flatten and spread it out a bit. Give the disk a quarter turn and tap it again 3 times to spread it out.
3. Starting with the pin in the center of the disk, firmly and steadily roll the pin away from you to within a finger's width of the far edge.
4. Give the dough a quarter turn and repeat the rolling. Continue in this manner, giving the dough a quarter turn and rolling away from you until the dough is the thickness indicated in the recipe. If the dough begins to stick, lift it and sprinkle flour beneath it.

Rolling Out Savvy for Pie, Tart, and Cookie Doughs

■ Some sticky doughs need to be placed between two sheets of waxed or parchment paper before rolling. Beginners may like to roll out all doughs this way, since it prevents any sticking to the work surface and makes the transfer to the pan easy. With practice, you will be able to roll out dough without paper.

Rolling out between waxed paper sheets.

When you are ready to transfer the dough, remove the top layer of paper and gently flip the dough round over.

■ Although many recipes recommend chilling the dough disk before rolling it out, in order to relax it, this step can make the dough difficult to roll. Sometimes, it's better to chill dough just after you have cut the fat into the flour but before you have added water (if you find the fat is starting to melt) or after the dough has been rolled out and shaped.

■ Any time the dough begins to stick to the work surface or the rolling pin, lift up the dough and lightly flour the surface, the pin, and the top of the dough. You can also turn the dough over periodically, lightly flouring all the surfaces.

■ Periodically shape the dough into a circle with your cupped hands. If the edges begin to crack, press them together with your fingertips.

■ Make sure you roll the dough evenly, to avoid thin spots and holes. Patch any holes with a piece of dough brushed with a little water.

■ Do not push too hard on the dough with the rolling pin. Instead, flatten it with firm, quick, steady strokes.

■ Pie pastry is usually rolled out ⅛ inch thick. If the dough is too thick, it can be tough after baking; if too thin, it can fall apart or tear as you put it in the pie pan.

See also BAKEWARE; COOKIE; PIE & TART; RESTING.

ROLLING PIN See BAKING TOOLS.

ROMAN BEAN See BEAN, DRIED.

ROMANO BEAN See BEAN, FRESH.

ROSEMARY See HERB.

ROUNDED A "rounded" measure is one in which the ingredient forms a lightly rounded dome above the rim of the measuring spoon or measuring cup. See also MEASURING.

ROUX See SAUCE; THICKENING.

RUB Mixtures of spices and herbs, often in the form of powders and pastes, rubs are pressed or massaged onto the surface of meat or poultry. Many recipes call for allowing the foods to sit for several hours to absorb the flavors. The salt and spices draw the juices of the meat or poultry to the surface, so that eventually the food literally marinates in its own flavored juices. Rubs can also be applied directly before cooking. Either way, these concentrated dry mixtures are cousins to marinades, which are acid-based liquid concoctions that bathe the food, flavoring and tenderizing.

To help it adhere, a rub may contain a small amount of alcohol or juice to bind the dry ingredients, or the food may be lightly coated with oil.

Rub Savvy When using rubs, keep the following in mind:

- For better flavor, toast spices before combining in a rub.
- Before using a rub, let it stand overnight to meld and develop its flavors.

See also MARINATING.

RUBBING IN To break and flatten fat into small pea-sized pieces by rubbing it into flour with your fingertips. Used in the making of pie or biscuit dough, this technique is designed to create layers of fat and flour to ensure flaky or tender pastry. Many cooks prefer using fingers rather than cutting in the fat with two knives or a pastry cutter, as they believe the result is more thorough. When making flaky pastry, rubbing in must be done quickly and carefully to avoid melting the butter with the heat of your fingertips. The butter should remain in discrete pieces. For a crumbly, tender crust, the fat is worked into the flour more thoroughly, so this is not a concern. See also BISCUIT; CUTTING IN; PIE & TART.

RUM See SPIRITS.

RUTABAGA This member of the cabbage family looks something like an overgrown turnip, to which it is closely related. Sometimes known as swedes, Swedish turnips, and yellow turnips, rutabagas come in a variety of colors, from brown to yellow to white. Their firm, yellow flesh has a strong mustardlike taste that mellows and becomes sweeter when cooked. They can be substituted for turnips in most recipes, and cooking time will depend on age, with smaller young ones taking as little as 10 minutes and older, larger, and tougher roots taking up to an hour.

Rutabagas make wonderful purées, especially when enriched with butter or cream, or when combined with milder vegetables such as potatoes that offset their sometimes strong flavor. Braise them in chicken stock or use them in gratins. Cut into slices or chunks and brushed with oil, rutabagas are excellent roasted and stewed, either alone or mixed with other root vegetables.

Selecting Rutabagas are best during the cool-weather months of the late fall and early winter. Small ones are generally sweeter. Rutabagas should be firm and heavy for their size. Avoid those that look faded, have a strong smell, or feel at all soft. Some look shiny, which indicates they are coated with clear paraffin to hold in moisture. This is harmless and comes off with the peel.

Storing Keep rutabagas in a cool, dark place for up to 10 days, or store in a plastic bag in the refrigerator for up to 1 month.

Preparing Trim the ends and peel with a paring knife. Sprinkle cut pieces with lemon juice to prevent discoloring.

RYE See GRAIN.

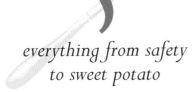

*everything from safety
to sweet potato*

SAFETY A few simple precautions and smart habits will help ensure safety in the kitchen. See also FOOD SAFETY.

Guarding against Accidents

- Keep knives sharpened and fingers clear of the blade during use. See also KNIFE.
- Always dry your hands thoroughly before handling any electrical appliances or their plugs or cords.
- Keep pan handles away from the edge of the stove and from adjacent hot burners or pilot lights.
- Do not leave metal spoons or other utensils inside pots during cooking, since they will heat up.
- To avoid splattering or scalding, never mix hot fats with water.
- Do not drop food into hot fat or boiling water; gently slip it in, using a slotted spoon or long-handled tongs. You may want to wear oven mitts to protect your hands.
- Always be especially cautious at every stage of frying and deep-frying, from heating fats or oils to adding food, regulating temperatures, and removing food and leaving oil to cool.
- When pouring hot liquids, pour away from yourself to avoid spills.

Guarding against Fire

- Keep your hands, sleeves, hair, pot holders, kitchen towels, cookbooks, and other flammable objects well clear of your stove's burners and pilot lights.
- Keep a fully charged, up-to-date fire extinguisher in your kitchen. Know where it is and how to use it.
- Whenever a fire breaks out, call for help immediately.
- For a fire contained in a small pan on the stove, turn off the heat and cover the pan with a tight-fitting lid to smother the flames; or, from a safe distance, toss handfuls of baking soda at the base of the flames to extinguish them. Do not try to move the pan. If the pan contains oil or fat, do not throw water on it. Water will spread a grease fire.
- Use the fire extinguisher to put out any small fires away from the stove. Do not attempt to fight large or quickly moving fires. Instead, yell "Fire!" and get everyone out of the house. Phone the fire department from a neighbor's house.

SAFFRON See SPICE.

SAGE See HERB.

SALAD Salads can consist of one ingredient or many; can be cooked or raw, hot or cold; and can be served as an appetizer, main course, or dessert. The one constant seems to be that they are usually dressed in a sauce that contains a tart element, such as vinegar or lemon juice. Most salads have at least one raw ingredient, and at least one that is either a vegetable or a fruit.

A salad should celebrate the freshness of its seasonal ingredients. Make sure that your vegetables, fruits, and salad greens are at their height of flavor and look their best.

See also DRESSING; GREENS, SALAD; VINAIGRETTE.

SALAD SAVOY See GREENS, SALAD.

SALMON A king among culinary fish, salmon has a beautiful, flavorful flesh rich in heart-beneficial omega-3 oils. Salmon is often included on lists of the most healthful foods, as it is also high in protein and A and B-complex vitamins, but it is favored by cooks and diners above all for its taste, appearance, and texture.

As a firm, meaty, oily fish, salmon is a good choice for poaching, baking, pan roasting, panfrying, steaming, broiling, and grilling. It is used fresh or canned as an in-gredient in chowders and other stews, and in casseroles, gratins, and creamed dishes and to make salmon cakes. Fresh salmon's deep color and sweet, full flavor are com-plemented by assertive and colorful sauces and salsas such as tapenade, aioli, and pesto. Smoked salmon is always a delicacy, no matter what smoking method is used.

Salmon is native to both North Amer-ican coasts. Atlantic Coast salmon stocks have declined greatly due to pollution in the United States, although Canada still provides Atlantic salmon. The majority of salmon comes from the Pacific Coast in Alaska. Salmon is now farmed in Norway, Chile, and the United States, but the farmed product has a blander flavor and softer texture.

Of the different species of salmon, the large Chinook, or king, salmon is the most prized for cooking. The silver, or coho, salmon is smaller, looks a lot like a trout, and has slightly leaner flesh. The sockeye, or red, salmon and the pink, or humpback, salmon are often used for canning. The chum, or dog, salmon is a lean fish with a pale color.

Selecting Farm-raised salmon are sold year-round. Wild Atlantic salmon is in season from summer to early winter, and wild Pacific salmon is available from spring through fall. The smallest Chinook salmon is around 6 pounds, and it is available whole or cut into chunks, steaks, or fillets. Like all fish, fresh salmon should smell sweet and clean and have clear eyes and firm flesh.

Storing Plan to cook fresh salmon the day it is purchased, or within 24 hours at the most. Wrap large fish in plastic wrap and place smaller fish in a zippered plastic bag, then refrigerate. Place the fish on a bed of ice cubes or crushed ice in the refrigerator if storing for more than a few hours.

Preparing Whole and chunk salmon are easily skinned and boned after cooking. Salmon fillets, however, must be checked carefully before cooking for pinbones, which are often buried vertically in the thickest part of the flesh. To find the bones, press the flesh gently with your fingers, then remove the bones using sturdy tweez-ers or needle-nosed pliers.

See also FISH.

SALT Since the dawn of civilization, salt has been a valuable commodity whose availability helped to found some cultures, while other cultures often created ex-tensive trade routes to reach it. Salt is the most basic of seasonings. It is the one essential flavoring ingredient in almost all savory dishes, and a tiny amount helps to bring out the flavors in many sweet dishes. Salt substitutes such as ground seaweed and lemon juice will also heighten flavor, but they add a flavor of their own that can distract from food in a way that the proper amount of salt does not.

Aside from flavoring foods, salt per-forms a range of chemical actions that are important in cooking and preserving. It draws moisture away from bacteria and mold cells in food, for example, slowing their growth. In early history, when adequate food storage was crucial, salt was valued for its ability to preserve food as much as for its flavor. Many foods, such as bacon, ham, cured sausage, and pickles, originated because food had to be salted to keep it from spoiling.

Of the various kinds of salt available, the most common is table salt, which usually contains added iodine (a practice started in the 1920s as a public-health measure to help prevent hypothyroidism, or the formation of goiters) along with additives that prevent it from caking and keep it pouring easily. Table salt is granular and is made by evaporation in vacuum pans.

Sea salt, by contrast, has no additives, but it has more minerals than table salt. Naturally evaporated, sea salt is available in coarse or fine grains that are shaped like hollow, flaky pyramids. As a result, it adheres better to foods and dissolves more quickly than table salt. It also has more flavor than table salt, and sometimes a smaller amount is sufficient to season the same amount of food. Sea salt is also preferred for bread making, as its mineral content helps in the development of gluten. Most sea salt comes from France, England, or the United States. Salts from different areas carry a subtle difference in flavor. One of the most prized sea salts is the grayish-ivory Fleur du Sel from Brittany.

Kosher salt is another favorite of cooks because its large flakes are easy to handle. This coarse-grained salt, made by compressing granular salt, has no additives. It is used in the preparation of kosher meats, as its large surface and jagged shape help to draw more blood from meat, one of the aims of koshering. Since it is not as salty as table salt, it can be used more liberally. Besides, kosher salt has a superior flavor.

Rock salt is mined from salt deposits rather than being processed by evaporation. It has less taste than other salts and is pri-

marily used in making ice cream in hand-cranked ice cream makers (because salt lowers the freezing point of water, making the melting ice cold enough to freeze the ice cream) and as a bed for roasting oysters on the half shell and other foods (the bed of salt keeps the foods level).

Pickling salt is finely ground and has no additives. It is used in pickling and canning because it dissolves quickly and won't cloud liquids.

Salt Savvy When using salt, keep the following in mind:

- Add a spoonful of salt to the boiling water when you cook soft-boiled or hard-boiled eggs. It will help the egg white coagulate quickly to close any cracks in the eggs.
- Add salt to emulsions based on egg yolks to help thicken the yolks.
- Because salt absorbs moisture, drawing it out of foods, many recipes specify salting eggplant, cucumber, and zucchini to make them less watery.
- Add salt to boiling water for cooking vegetables and pasta to replace the salt leached from the food by boiling. Add salt to water after it comes to a boil, not before (Italians believe that adding salt to water before it boils makes the water taste bitter).
- A pinch of salt at the beginning of the cooking process will help to develop the flavor in almost any food (the exception is corn on the cob; salt toughens it), but wait until the end of cooking to season to taste with salt, or the dish may become too salty during cooking. This is especially true for any dish that cooks a long time, any reduced sauces or other liquids, and dishes containing such salty foods as cheese, ham, or anchovies.
- Although many cookbooks advise against salting dried beans until the very end of cooking, based on a belief that an excess

of salt will toughen the beans, tests have shown that a pinch of salt will not interfere with their cooking. Salt beans very lightly, however, as the liquid will reduce during the long cooking process, concentrating the saltiness.

- To remove salt from an oversalted dish, add more unsalted liquid, vegetables, or starches such as potatoes, pasta, or rice. You can alleviate the saltiness of some sauces by diluting the sauce with unsalted liquid (you may then need to add thickener) or a tiny bit of brown sugar and/or vinegar.
- Some people feel that salt draws off too much moisture when roasting or grilling meats, but the actual effect of salt on meat cooked by dry heat is minimal.
- If you live in a coastal area, you probably ingest more than enough iodine from your drinking water (which absorbs iodine from the soil near seawater) and from eating seafood, so that you do not need iodized salt. If you live in the Midwest, particularly in one of the North Central states, you should use iodized salt to protect against hypothyroidism.

SAUCE The French brought the technique of saucing foods to its height, but every cuisine in the world has developed sauces that are as distinctive and varied as the cultures from which they come. Any liquid used to dress a food is technically a sauce, although the narrower definition of sauce usually refers to a liquid of some thickness. Thinner sauces are usually called dressings, vinaigrettes, or condiments. The basic French sauces may be classified by the method used to thicken them. Because each kind is the basis for a variety of other sauces, the French call these mother sauces. WHITE SAUCES White sauces are thickened with a roux, which is a mixture of butter and flour. The roux is cooked for 2 to 3 minutes to eliminate the raw taste of the flour, but it is not allowed to color. The two main white sauces are béchamel, which has milk added to the roux, and velouté, which uses a white stock as the liquid. Classic cream sauces are made by adding cream to either a béchamel or a velouté sauce. Béchamel is the sauce used to make creamed dishes of vegetables, chicken, eggs, and pastas, and it is also the basis for most savory soufflés. A velouté sauce is usually the basis for many dishes made with poultry, fish, or meat, as well as many creamed soups.

Quick Bite

Modern-day cream sauces are often made without a roux and gain thickness by simply reducing heavy cream with savory elements such as pan drippings or seasonings. See REDUCING for more details.

BROWN SAUCES Brown sauces are the most prestigious sauces in the entire system of classic French sauce making. Traditionally, brown sauces were based on rich, meaty beef and veal stock that was slowly reduced over a matter of days to concentrate its flavor. The resulting sauce is referred to as demi-glace and is used as the base of a legion of brown sauces. Demi-glace is deep and complex, with a thick, glossy texture derived from the gelatin naturally present in the stock. For economy's sake, many chefs now shortcut the process by using brown roux (cooked until the flour turns a nut brown) to thicken their reduced stock. Brown sauce is often flavored with wine, tomatoes, or herbs, and traditionally served with beef, lamb, duck, and other meats. BUTTER SAUCES Butter sauces are divided into two groups: those thickened with butter and egg yolks, and those thickened with butter only. The first group contains the celebrated hollandaise and béarnaise sauces. Like all butter sauces, they are delicate and will separate if overheated. The egg yolks must be whisked constantly over the correct level of heat as they thicken, and the melted or clarified butter must be beaten very gradually into the yolks. Finally, the sauce must be kept warm, if necessary, over tepid water. If these sauces separate they can often be saved. Hollandaise is best known as a topping for poached eggs, while béarnaise is served with steak and grilled fish.

Beurre blanc represents the second group. It is made by gradually beating small cubes of cold butter into a reduced mixture of shallots, vinegar, and white wine. It should be served as soon as it is made, but it may be kept a short time over tepid water. If this sauce separates, you can save it by beating 1 tablespoon of the sauce in a cold bowl, then gradually beating in the rest of the sauce by teaspoonfuls. Beurre blanc is traditionally served with fish.

MAYONNAISE Mayonnaise, thickened by gradually beating oil into beaten egg yolks, is the well-known sandwich spread and binder for dishes such as egg salad, chicken salad, and tuna salad. It is also used as a dressing for composed salads. You can vary mayonnaise by adding green herbs or flavored oils. Aioli, the famed garlic mayonnaise of Provence, may be served with meat, fish, chicken, or vegetables. Tartar sauce is another flavored mayonnaise, made by adding mustard, capers, chopped dill pickle, and herbs. If any of these mayonnaise-based sauces separates, beat a fresh egg yolk in a dry, warm bowl, then beat in the rest of the sauce by teaspoonfuls.

VINAIGRETTE Vinaigrettes are French sauces that are usually considered salad dressings in the United States, although many chefs also use them to top meats, fish, and chicken. See also VINAIGRETTE.

TOMATO SAUCE Tomato sauce is thickened by cooking tomatoes until they dissolve and their pulp reduces. Usually flavored with onion, garlic, and herbs, it is used in a myriad of dishes, including pizzas and a wide variety of pastas.

OTHER SAVORY SAUCES Other sauces include gravy and simple pan sauces made by using stock and/or wine to deglaze a pan used to sauté meat, chicken, or fish. Among many other sauces around the world are Philippine *adobos,* Mexican moles, fresh and cooked salsas, Spanish *romesco* sauce, Indian *raita,* chile sauce, barbecue sauce, and teriyaki sauce, as well as those often considered as condiments and flavorings, such as Worcestershire sauce and soy sauce.

SWEET SAUCES Sweet sauces, part of the realm of desserts, constitute another large category and are as varied as the ingredients they feature. Those based largely on sugar include caramel and butter-and-cream-enriched butterscotch sauces. Chocolate sauces range from fluid cream-enriched versions to thick hot fudge. Cream- and egg-based sauces have thick, velvety texture and rich flavor. They range from simple lightly whipped cream to the airy beaten egg sauce known as a sabayon to thick custard sauces such as the classic French crème anglaise. Puréed fruits give vibrant color and taste to other sweet sauces, such as light but flavorful raspberry *coulis* and thick, old-fashioned applesauce.

See also BARBECUE SAUCE; CURDLING; DEGLAZING; DRESSING; GRAVY; MAYONNAISE; REDUCING; STOCK; THICKENING.

SAUCEPAN See COOKWARE.

SAUERKRAUT A dish of salted, fermented green cabbage. Although known as a German specialty, sauerkraut likely originated in Asia or ancient Rome, where

S

fermentation was widely used to preserve vegetables. Traditional recipes for sauerkraut call for layering shredded cabbage with pickling salt and sometimes other seasonings such as juniper berries or caraway seeds, and then allowing it to ferment. The strong, pungent flavor of raw sauerkraut mellows with long, slow cooking. There are many devotees who won't consider eating a hot dog without a generous topping of sauerkraut. It goes well, too, with other sausages and alongside roast pork. *Choucroute garnie,* braised sauerkraut served as a bed for bacon, ham, and sausages, is a classic Alsatian dish.

Selecting Purchase sauerkraut in bulk or in a clear plastic bag so that you can see what you're getting. It should be moist but not soupy.

Storing Like other fermented foods, sauerkraut has a long shelf life. Refrigerated in its own juices in a nonmetal container, it will last for 1 month or longer.

Preparing Sauerkraut can be served raw or braised with stock, hot or at room temperature. Rinse raw sauerkraut before serving. Always taste sauerkraut before cooking. If it is very salty, you may want to soak it in cold water for 15 minutes and then drain it before using.

SAUSAGE Most sausages are made from ground meat and fat mixed with salt and other seasonings and packed into casings, although country sausage is made by simply forming bulk sausage meat into patties or into rolls to be sliced and cooked. Originally concocted to use up every last scrap of meat after hog butchering, including the intestines, which serve as casings, sausages are often made of pork, although almost any meat, fish, poultry, shellfish, or game may be used. While sausages are traditionally high in fat, many lower-fat versions are now available, as are vegetarian sausages

made from vegetables and/or bean curd. The three basic sausage categories are fresh, cooked, and semidry or dry.

Fresh Sausages Made with raw meat, fresh sausages must be cooked, whether or not they have been lightly smoked. The best-known fresh sausages include bockwurst, made of veal sometimes mixed with pork; chorizo, made with pork and available in the spicy Mexican version and the milder, usually smoked, Spanish version; and Italian sausage, which is also made with pork and may be either spicy or mild. In recent years, some sausage makers have introduced new varieties of fresh sausages, often made with chicken, turkey, or seafood mixed with ingredients such as apples, herbs, and sun-dried tomatoes. Like other fresh sausages, these varieties contain no preservatives.

Fresh sausages are excellent grilled or sautéed. They may be eaten whole, or sliced and sautéed further, then added to casseroles or sautés. Try sliced sautéed Italian sausages in tomato sauce over polenta or pasta, or sauté sliced chicken sausages in a skillet dish with vegetables.

HOW TO *Sauté Fresh Sausages*

1. Puncture the casing of each sausage twice on each of its four sides with the tines of a fork.
2. In a skillet, bring water to a depth of about $1/4$ inch to a simmer and add the sausages. Cook until the water evaporates.
3. Continue to cook, turning the sausages as necessary in the fat they have released, until they are browned on all sides, 5 to 10 minutes, adding a little olive oil if necessary for very lean sausages.
4. Cut open the sausages to make sure the sausages are cooked through if serving whole. If serving sliced, transfer the sausages to a cutting board and cut them into 1-inch-wide diagonal slices. Return the slices to the pan and sauté them until browned on both sides.

HOW TO _Grill Fresh Sausages_

1. Puncture the sausages as above.
2. Cook over medium-hot coals until browned on all sides.
3. Cover the grill and cook for several more minutes, turning the sausages once or twice. The total cooking time will be 10 to 12 minutes.

Mexican chorizos and Italian sausages are often removed from their casings and cooked as a recipe ingredient.

Cooked Sausages These sausages may also be smoked or unsmoked. They are fully cooked at purchase but most are usually reheated to serve. Some of the most common are andouille, a smoked sausage made of tripe and often used in Cajun cooking or sliced and eaten cold; bratwurst, a pork or pork-and-veal sausage, which is also available fresh; and knockwurst, which is made from one of several meats and is usually eaten whole. Bologna and frankfurters are thoroughly Americanized sausages; the first is served sliced and eaten cold on sandwiches, while frankfurters are the beloved grilled or boiled hot dog. Mortadella is a popular Italian cooked sausage and is eaten as a cold cut.

_Andouille
sausage._

Bratwurst.

_Mortadella
sausage._

Semidry and Dry Sausages Both semidry and dry sausages may be eaten without cooking, as they have been cured, or preserved, by extensive smoking and/or drying. They may be eaten cold, reheated, or used in cooking. Semidry sausages, sometimes called summer sausages, are smoked to remove some of their moisture and preserve them during the heat of summer. Dry sausages are dried for 1 to 6 months and may or may not be smoked. They include kielbasa, a smoked garlic sausage of Polish origin usually made of pork. Most often cooked in casseroles, soups, and stews, or poached and served with sauerkraut or potatoes, it may also be eaten cold. Linguiça, a pork sausage native to Portugal, is flavored with garlic and red pepper. It is used, like chorizo, as an ingredient in other dishes, and it may also be grilled. Pepperoni and salami are dried sausages of Italian origin. Pepperoni, spicy with red and black pepper, is a favorite antipasto ingredient and pizza topping. Salami comes in many different styles and sizes and is usually sliced and eaten on sandwiches or as an hors d'oeuvre.

Storing Store uncooked fresh sausages in the refrigerator for up to 2 or 3 days or in the freezer for up to 2 months. Spanish chorizo and other smoked fresh sausages will keep, refrigerated, for 1 week. Store cooked sausage in the refrigerator for up to 1 week or freeze for up to 2 months. You can keep semidry sausages at room temperature for up to 3 days or refrigerate them for up to 3 weeks. Unsliced dry sausage may be kept at room temperature for up to 6 weeks. Once it has been sliced, refrigerate it for up to 2 weeks.

SAUTÉING One of the basic French cooking methods, sautéing takes its name from the verb *sauter,* meaning "to jump." In its classic form, this action is a skillful one that some home cooks envy: the pan is moved briskly back and forth, lifting slightly on the backward motion to make the contents jump. But the food can just as easily be stirred as tossed. Sautéed foods are cooked quickly, usually over medium or medium-high heat, in a small amount of fat. The food is tossed or stirred in the pan to cook its outside evenly without overcooking the inside.

Foods to be sautéed should be cut into small pieces or fairly thin slices, so they can cook quickly. Chicken, tender cuts of meat, tender vegetables, and tougher, starchy vegetables that have been blanched are all good choices for sautéing. Be sure to dry all foods to be sautéed on paper towels before adding them to the pan, to keep moisture from steaming the foods and, if you wish, to allow the foods to brown slightly. For the same reason, don't crowd the pan. Too much food can lower the temperature in the pan as well as trap moisture that will cause the food to steam instead of brown.

Use either a sauté pan (a wide pan with straight sides) or a skillet (a wide pan with slightly sloping sides). If you want the flavor of butter in your dish, use half butter and half oil, as butter alone will burn quickly over medium to high heat. Another alternative is to use clarified butter, which will not burn as quickly. (See BUTTER.) Pure olive oil, canola oil, and other vegetable oils may be used alone or with butter for sautéing.

HOW TO *Sauté*
1. Preheat the pan briefly over medium to medium-high heat and then add the oil and/or butter and heat for a few seconds until the oil is fragrant, the surface of the oil wavers, and small bubbles appear, or until the butter has foamed and begins to subside.
2. Add the food, in batches if necessary, and stir, toss, or turn it as it cooks, watching carefully to make sure it does not burn and adjusting the heat as necessary.
3. Sauté the food according to the recipe instructions. Foods may or may not be browned or cooked through, and some foods, such as onions, may be sautéed briefly just to bring out their flavor.

See also BUTTER; FAT & OIL; FRYING.

SAUTÉ PAN See COOKWARE.

SAVORY See HERB.

SCALDING Heating a liquid, usually milk, to almost simmering. Because milk scorches and boils over easily, recipes that require hot milk specify scalding as a safeguard against overcooking.

HOW TO *Scald Milk*
1. To keep milk from spilling over the pan edges as it simmers, select a saucepan large enough to allow for a few inches of rising.
2. Fill the pan with a little cold water, swirl, and then pour it out. The thin layer of water prevents milk from sticking to the pan.
3. Pour the milk into the pan and place it over medium heat. Stir occasionally to prevent scorching at the bottom and to dissolve the thin film that will form on the surface.
4. Heat just until small bubbles appear around the edge of the pan. Watch the milk carefully, for it can boil over quickly.

See also MILK.

SCALE See BAKING TOOLS.

SCALLION Also known as green onion; see ONION.

SCALLOP (MEAT) A slice of boneless meat or fish. Pork, veal, beef loin, turkey breasts, and other tender cuts may all be sliced into boneless cutlets, which are then pounded to an even thinness to tenderize them and so that they can be cooked quickly. (See also POUNDING.) Scallops may be breaded and are usually sautéed. Veal scallopini, Wiener schnitzel, and French *escalopes* are all meat scallop dishes.

SCALLOP (SHELLFISH) A popular mollusk, plump and flavorful. In the United States, the bivalves are shucked almost immediately after they are caught, while in Europe they are often sold in their pretty shells. The edible portion is actually the adductor muscle used to open and close the shell. Scallop roe and milt (eggs and male reproductive glands) are delicious but quite perishable and, with rare exceptions, are discarded when scallops are shucked. Scallops are often served creamed in scallop shells as coquilles Saint-Jacques. They may also be seared quickly and served with a sauce.

Scallops in their shells.

Selecting Choose sea scallops that are creamy white or slightly pink, rather than bright white, an indication that they have been soaked (see below). Bay scallops should be pale pink or light orange.

Although shucked scallops will always have some odor, choose those with the mildest scent. If you are lucky enough to find scallops still in their shells, snap them up. They cost more than shucked scallops, but their fresh taste is well worth the expense. The shells usually gape open a bit. They should close slightly when pinched and smell fresh. Don't turn up your nose if offered quick-frozen scallops. Because they are frozen as soon as they are shucked, these scallops often have a better flavor than those that have languished in a ship's hold for several days before they were delivered to the market.

Some wholesalers soak sea scallops in a tripolyphosphate solution to help preserve them. Although soaking may make the scallops last longer, the meat absorbs much of the water, which increases the weight (and thus the price) of the scallops and dilutes their flavor. Wholesalers are required to label their scallops "soaked" or "dry" (unsoaked), but retailers do not always pass this information on to their customers. Two indicators will help you to identify treated scallops. Unsoaked ones range in color from pale ivory to pale coral. If the scallops offered to you are shiny and bright white, you can be almost certain that they've been soaked. Another clue is that soaked scallops tend to clump together, while unsoaked ones remain separate.

Dried scallops are considered a delicacy by the Chinese. Called *conpoy* and sold by weight (large ones fetch exorbitant prices), they are used in steamed dishes and soups.

Storing Buy scallops the day you plan to serve them and keep them refrigerated until ready to cook. If still in the shell, put the scallops in a bowl and cover the bowl with a damp kitchen towel. Shuck them just before cooking.

Preparing Scallops in the shell are easier to shuck than oysters or clams.

Scallops take well to a wide range of recipes and cooking methods. The only caveat is to watch your cooking time carefully. Scallops need just a few minutes of heat to cook. If left for too long, they quickly turn rubbery and dry. If you like raw fish, you should know that scallops are one of the safest shellfish to eat raw. Like all shellfish, they filter large amounts of seawater for the nutrients they need to stay alive and accumulate some toxins in the process. But the scallop's filtration mechanism is discarded during shucking and what is eaten is likely to contain few toxins.

✦ Scallop Glossary ✦

BAY SCALLOP The most highly regarded of all scallops, these little morsels—about $\frac{1}{2}$ inch in diameter—have a sweet, delicate flavor. Bay scallops are harvested from a small region of the Atlantic Ocean and are rarely found outside of East Coast fish markets during their short season, which begins in October and runs through March. Unscrupulous markets sometimes try to pass off less-expensive calico scallops or cut and trimmed sea scallops as bay scallops.

Bay scallops and sea scallops.

CALICO SCALLOP Tinier than bay scallops, calicos are found off the east coast of Florida and in the Gulf of Mexico. They are quite good and are often offered at a very reasonable price. The important thing to remember when preparing them is not to overcook them. Because shucking the small shells is too expensive for most processors, the shells are steamed open and the scallops arrive in the market already partially cooked, so they must be exposed to heat for no more than a few minutes during cooking.

SEA SCALLOP These are the most common scallops. At about $1\frac{1}{2}$ inches in diameter, they are larger than bay scallops but not quite as tender. Because scallop boats fishing for sea scallops stay out on the ocean for weeks at a time, freshness is always an issue with sea scallops.

SINGING PINK SCALLOP Also known as swimming scallops, these are named for their translucent pink shell, about 3 inches in diameter, which propels them through the water by opening and closing. They are found in the Puget Sound of the Pacific Northwest.

HOW TO *Shuck Scallops*

1. Slide a knife sideways into the crack between the shells. Rotate the knife to open the shell.

2. Run the knife around the scallop meat to free it and then remove it, along with any roe.
3. Peel the tough white tissue off the side of the scallop and discard it, along with the dark-colored innards.

SCALLOPING To cook vegetables or seafood in milk or cream, usually topped with bread crumbs and sometimes cheese. Typical dishes include scalloped potatoes and scalloped oysters.

SCANT This term is used to describe measurements, such as "1 scant tablespoon," that are slightly less than full. See also MEASURING.

SCHMALTZ See FAT & OIL.

SCISSORS See COOKING TOOLS.

SCORING Making shallow cuts in food. Scoring is done for several reasons: It can help flatten a piece of meat, such as flank steak. It allows marinades or seasonings to flavor the interior of the meat. It can aid in the tenderizing of a piece of meat by cutting through some of the tough meat fibers. Whole fish are often scored in the thickest part to allow heat to penetrate to help the flesh cook evenly. Scoring the fat layer of whole hams encourages the fat to drain and creates a decorative appearance.

Breads are often scored, or slashed, before baking, both for decoration and to help them rise. Breads that are not scored can burst from the pressure that builds up inside the baking loaf or fail to rise at all if the crust sets before the bread has a chance to expand. Scoring the dough before it bakes provides an escape route for the gases. Similarly, pastry crusts are vented and pricked to allow steam to escape during baking. See also SLASHING.

SCRAPER A dough, or bench, scraper; see BAKING TOOLS.

SCRUBBING Many foods, such as potatoes and clams, carry dirt from the fields or impurities from the sea and should be scrubbed clean before eating. In fact, any vegetable that is cooked or eaten unpeeled, including citrus fruit that is to be zested, should be scrubbed. Special vegetable brushes made for this purpose are sold in supermarkets and cooking-supply shops, although you can use any brush with firm bristles. Scrub foods under cold running water, brushing or rubbing vigorously to remove all traces of dirt. If the brush scrubs off a vegetable's skin with the dirt, for example, if you are cleaning mushrooms, try a softer brush, or simply use your thumb to rub away the dirt.

SEAFOOD Although the dictionary definition of seafood is "edible *marine* fish and shellfish," the word is often used to mean all edible fish and shellfish, freshwater as well as seawater. See also FISH; SHELLFISH.

SEARING To brown a food—usually meat, poultry, or seafood—quickly over high heat, usually to prepare it for a second, moist cooking method such as braising or stewing. For years, cooks believed that searing sealed in juices and kept the meat from drying out, but food scientists have proven that it does just the opposite, drawing juices to the surface and releasing them into the pan or fire. But cooking meat over high heat with a small amount of fat sets off a series of reactions between the sugars and the proteins, essentially caramelizing the surface, which results in a more complex and richer flavor. The crisp, browned surface of a seared piece of meat is also more appetizing than the dull, gray look of meat that hasn't been properly browned before moist cooking.

Searing Savvy When getting ready to sear, keep the following in mind:

- Be sure to pat meat dry with paper towels before searing, or the moisture will hinder proper browning.

- Use a large, heavy pan such as a cast-iron frying pan or a dutch oven.
- Oil the food to be seared rather than the pan, for an oiled pan will soon start to smoke at the high temperatures needed for searing.
- Allow space between pieces of meat or one piece of meat and the sides of the

Seasoning Chart

KIND OF FOOD	SEASONING
Beans or peas, dried	Bay leaf, parsley, thyme
Beans, green	Basil, marjoram, savory, thyme
Beef	Allspice, bay leaf, black pepper, celery seed, chili powder, cumin, garlic, ginger, nutmeg, thyme
Beets	Basil, dill, ginger, mint, parsley
Carrots	Cinnamon, cloves, dill, lemon juice, mint, nutmeg, parsley, savory, tarragon, thyme
Cauliflower	Chives, curry powder, lemon juice, nutmeg, parsley
Chicken	Bay leaf, chives, cinnamon, cloves, cumin, curry powder, garlic, ginger, lemon, marjoram, mustard, rosemary, sage, tarragon, thyme
Corn	Basil, chives, chili powder, dill, lime juice, parsley
Duck	Orange, parsley, sage, thyme
Eggplant	Basil, cumin, garlic, parsley, thyme
Fish	Bay leaf, chervil, chives, cumin, curry, dill, marjoram, mint, mustard, oregano, paprika, parsley, saffron, savory, tarragon, thyme
Goose	Allspice, caraway, marjoram, thyme
Lamb	Cumin, curry powder, garlic, mint, oregano, rosemary
Peas	Basil, marjoram, mint, parsley, savory, tarragon
Pork	Allspice, bay leaf, cumin, fennel, garlic, ginger, marjoram, mustard, rosemary, sage, thyme
Potatoes	Chives, dill, garlic, parsley
Spinach	Curry powder, garlic, nutmeg
Squash, summer	Basil, chives, garlic, marjoram, oregano, parsley, savory
Squash, winter	Allspice, cinnamon, cloves, ginger, lemon, mace, nutmeg
Sweet potatoes	Cayenne, cinnamon, cloves, lime juice, mace, nutmeg
Tomatoes	Basil, chives, garlic, marjoram, oregano, parsley, savory, tarragon, thyme
Turkey	Bay leaf, rosemary, sage, savory
Veal	Basil, bay leaf, lemon, parsley, savory, tarragon, thyme

pan. Too much food crowding the pan will lower the temperature, trap moisture, and create steam, preventing the meat from browning properly.

■ Turn the meat frequently to brown it evenly on all sides.

■ Make the most of the pan drippings created by searing by deglazing the pan before continuing with the recipe.

See also BRAISING; BROWNING.

SEASONING The use of aromatic herbs and spices to enhance the flavors of ingredients in a dish is called seasoning. Some seasonings naturally seem to go well with some foods—rosemary with lamb, nutmeg with spinach—but seasoning is also a matter of taste. Much of the satisfaction of cooking comes from learning which flavors you like to bring together. Keep an assortment of spices and dried herbs, as well as fresh herbs, if you can, and experiment by replacing the seasonings called for in different dishes or changing the amounts. Start out with a small amount of seasoning, and learn as you go. To bring out the fullest flavors, season each component of a recipe and taste as you go along. (But take care not to taste meat, poultry, or seafood before it is done.) Never serve a dish without one last tasting to see if it needs a final seasoning.

See the chart at left for some tried-and-true combinations of ingredients and herbs and spices to use as a starting point when mixing and matching flavors.

The term *seasoning* also refers to the treating of cast-iron cookware to prevent it from rusting and foods from sticking. Pans are heated and coated with oil before the first use and whenever the coating starts to wear away and rust starts to appear.

HOW TO *Season a Cast-Iron Pan*

1. Heat the pan over high heat until a drop of water sizzles and evaporates immediately.

2. Coat the inside of the pan with vegetable oil, using paper towels to spread the oil and rub it well into the metal. Blot up any excess. If seasoning a new pan, repeat several times until the pan blackens.

See also ADJUSTING THE SEASONING; TASTING.

SEAWEED The ocean yields this foodstuff, rich in nutrients and tasting of the sea, which is widely used in Asian cooking. The Japanese use more kinds of seaweed than any other culture, beginning with the nori used in making sushi. Dried nori, like many other seaweeds, is available in Japanese markets, most natural-food stores, and some supermarkets. It comes in dark green, dark brown, or black thin sheets that are either toasted or untoasted. Dark brown to grayish black, kombu is kelp that is dried, cut, and folded. It is often mixed with dried bonito flakes as an ingredient in dashi, the typical Japanese stock. Wakame is a deep green or brown seaweed shaped like long strings and eaten in soups and salads. Agar-agar is sold in long strands or sticks. It may be soaked and eaten in soups like noodles, but its primary use throughout East Asia is as a gelatin-like thickener. In the West, agar-agar is prized by vegetarians as a replacement for animal-based gelatin.

HOW TO *Use Agar-Agar as a Gelatin*

1. To jell 4 cups of liquid, measure out about $2/3$ ounce strips or sticks, break into pieces, and soak in water to cover for about 20 minutes.

2. Wring the pieces dry. Put them in a saucepan with cold water to cover.

3. Bring to a boil over medium heat. Reduce the heat to a simmer and cook, stirring occasionally, until dissolved.

4. Add the ingredients to be jelled and bring just to a boil. Mold and chill them as required.

SEEDING For details on various techniques for removing seeds, see entries for individual foods.

SEIZING When melted chocolate comes into contact with any amount of moisture, the fine, dry particles of cocoa solids suspended in the cocoa butter can clump together, hardening the chocolate in a phenomenon known as seizing, or stiffening.

Paradoxically, a larger amount of liquid (at least 25 percent of the weight of the chocolate) will prevent seizing. This explains why some recipes can successfully instruct you to add liquid to chocolate as it melts. As long as you have at least 1 tablespoon of liquid for each 2 ounces of chocolate, the chocolate will not seize.

You can salvage seized chocolate by taking it off the heat and working in a bit of water, a tablespoon at a time. This restored chocolate will be smooth and shiny and fine for use in icings and fillings, but it will not work in recipes where the chocolate must set up, such as for candies. In these instances, you will need to discard the chocolate and start over.

When melting chocolate in a double boiler, always do so over barely simmering water, as briskly simmering or boiling water creates steam. Steam is moist and will cause chocolate to seize if the two come in contact. Melting chocolate in a microwave will also prevent seizing. Cool the chocolate uncovered to prevent contact with steam.

See also CHOCOLATE; TEMPERING.

SEMOLINA See GRAIN.

SEPARATING To separate the white of an egg from the egg yolk. This is more easily done when an egg is cold, and several different techniques may be used. For details, see EGG.

The word *separate* is also used to describe the curdling action of sauces; for more information, see CURDLING.

SERRANO See CHILE.

SESAME PASTE See TAHINI.

SESAME SEED Sesame seeds are widely used in Indian, Asian, African, Middle Eastern, and Latin American cuisines. In fact, these tiny, flat seeds have been used in cooking for at least 5,000 years. Brown, red, and black sesame seeds are available, but the most commonly available ones are a pale tan. They add a nutty flavor to any food and are often sprinkled over savory dishes as a garnish. Many breads and cookies are strewn with sesame seeds before baking. Ground sesame seeds are used to make halvah, a Middle Eastern candy, and tahini, a paste used in many Middle Eastern dishes. The seeds are crushed to make two kinds of highly polyunsaturated oil, one pale in color and often used in salad dressings and for deep-frying, and the other made with toasted sesame seeds and commonly called Asian sesame oil. This dark brown oil is highly flavorful and is used to season savory Asian dishes, but is seldom used for cooking.
Storing Because of their high oil content, sesame seeds can go rancid quickly and should be stored in the refrigerator.

See also FAT & OIL.

SETTING To firm up a food by letting it sit at room temperature or by chilling it. Some foods that need to set before serving are baked custards, lasagne, gelatin dishes, candies, chocolate decorations, and frostings and icings. The recipe method should either tell you how much time a dish will need in order to set or indicate this in some way other than time.

Some recipe components, such as custards incorporating eggs or mixtures including gelatin, need to thicken before they are added to other ingredients. This is done by refrigerating the mixture until thickened, usually for about 2 hours, or by placing a bowl containing the mixture in a larger bowl filled with ice cubes and stirring constantly until the mixture thickens.

SETTING ASIDE To put a component of a dish to one side while preparing other parts of the dish. When a recipe instructs you to set aside part of a dish and to keep it warm, you should cover it with a lid, a plate, or aluminum foil and keep it in a warm place, perhaps on the stove top. In some cases, a recipe will specify keeping a component or a finished dish warm in a low (180° to 200°F) oven, in a hot water bath, or over tepid or hot water. Other solutions, depending on the food, are candle warmers, electric heating trays, and the warming ovens found in some stoves.

Quick Tip

Some sauces, such as hollandaise, will separate if kept over water that is hotter than tepid. A solution to keeping such delicate sauces warm is to pour them into a thermos.

The term *reserve* is used when preparing an ingredient that yields two components, such as pears and their poaching liquid, or diced mushrooms and their soaking liquid. One component is used in the recipe sooner than the other, which is reserved for a later stage. Or, the second component may be reserved for use in another recipe altogether.

SHALLOT See ONION.

SHEARS See COOKING TOOLS.

SHELLFISH From raw oysters on the half shell to chilled cooked jumbo shrimp peeled and ready to dip in cocktail sauce to garlicky steamed mussels, shellfish offer a wide array of gastronomic delights.

For all their variety, shellfish may be easily grouped into two broad categories: crustaceans and mollusks. Crustaceans are the more animated group, scurrying or swimming about with legs or fins, their bodies protected by a tough external skeleton. These include crabs, lobsters, crayfish, and shrimp. Mollusks include bivalves, shellfish that live within two hinged shell halves, such as oysters, clams, and mussels; cephalopods, whose shells are actually penlike bones within their bodies, such as squid and octopus; and finally univalves, or gastropods, which have one shell that protects their soft bodies, such as abalone, snails, and conch.

See also individual shellfish.

SHELLING Removing the hard outer covering of a food such as nuts or shellfish. Eggs and vegetables such as green peas and fava beans are also shelled.

See individual foods; SHUCKING.

SHERBET See SORBET.

SHIITAKE See MUSHROOM.

SHIRRING A way of baking eggs. Although eggs are essential to many baked goods, such as cakes and quick breads, they may also be baked themselves, in a ramekin or custard cup. When a bit of cream or butter is added before baking, the baked eggs become shirred eggs.

403

SHOCKING See BLANCHING; PLUNG-
ING.

SHORTENING Any solid fat can be
referred to as shortening, particularly in
baking and frying recipes, although this
is not the current usage of the word. When
modern recipes call for shortening, they
mean vegetable shortening. See FAT & OIL;
VEGETABLE SHORTENING.

SHREDDING To cut food into thin,
narrow strips. Medium-soft cheeses, such
as Cheddar and Monterey jack, and vegetables, such as carrots, usually are shredded
on the largest holes of a box grater. Grating, on the other hand, means to reduce
foods (such as Parmesan cheese) into tiny
particles using the fine rasps of a grater.
Cabbage and other stiff leaf vegetables are
shredded by cutting them with a large knife
into long pieces about ¼ inch wide. To
shred soft leaves such as spinach and basil,
roll individual leaves or stacks of leaves
into a tight roll and cut crosswise into thin
shreds with a large knife. (Very thin shreds
are called chiffonade.) Mandolines and
food processors fitted with a shredding disk
may also be used to shred.
　See also FOOD PROCESSOR; GRATING;
MANDOLINE.

SHRIMP There are thousands of shrimp
varieties in the world. The main ones eaten
in the United States are Gulf shrimp from
the Gulf of Mexico; tiger shrimp from
Asian waters,
easily identi-
fied by their
black stripes;
and Monterey
prawns, also
known as spot
prawns. Available in many different
colors, from pink to brown and white,

shrimp also vary in size, from "colossal" to
"miniature." The most common sizes are
jumbo (10 to 15 shrimp per pound); large
(16 to 20 shrimp per pound); medium
(25 to 30 shrimp per pound); and miniature (about 100 shrimp per pound). Jumbo
and large shrimp are also labeled U-15 or
U-12 to indicate there are fewer than 15 or
12 per pound. Miniature shrimp are also
known as bay shrimp and are almost always
purchased already cooked.

Quick Bite

Giant and jumbo shrimp are often called
prawns in the United States, although true
prawns are actually either a type of freshwater
shrimp or certain miniature members of the
lobster family.

　Shrimp are a favorite food for appetizers, often served with cocktail sauce, and
for grilling, sautéing, and stir-frying. Boiled
with flavorings, they are eaten straight
from the shell, or they may be shelled and
cooked in soups such as shrimp bisque, or
in flavorful stews such as the Greek dish
of shrimp with feta and tomatoes or Cajun
shrimp jambalaya and gumbo.
　Dried shrimp are used to make shrimp
paste, a pungent fermented flavoring used
widely in Asia. It comes in two forms, as
a thick, moist paste and as a dried paste.
The former is usually labeled shrimp sauce
or shrimp paste and is easily found in
Chinese and Southeast Asian markets. The
latter is variously labeled *kapi* (Thailand),
trasi (Indonesia), and *blacan* (Malaysia).
Commonly found in Southeast Asian markets, it is sold in small bricks. Once opened,
the fresh paste must be refrigerated, while
the dried paste will keep for months in a
cool, dry cupboard. Either way, store the
pungent-smelling shrimp paste sealed in
an airtight jar or zippered plastic bag.

Bay shrimp.

> ## Quick Tip
>
> Raw shrimp should be cooked quickly, usually for only about 2 minutes, depending on their size. As soon as the shrimp turn evenly pink, they are done.

Selecting Choose firm, sweet-smelling fresh shrimp still in the shell when possible. All but the freshest shrimp will have had their heads already removed. Most shrimp sold has been previously frozen and thawed. You may do better buying still-frozen shrimp, since its quality is the same or better than thawed, and you'll be able to decide more freely when to use it. Previously frozen shrimp should not be refrozen. Bay shrimp are usually available only shelled and cooked.

Pass over shrimp with yellowing or black-spotted shells, an "off" odor, or a gritty feel. In general, avoid preshelled and deveined shrimp. Their texture and flavor will likely have suffered more during the freezing process than shrimp in the shell. Shrimp cooked without their shells are also less flavorful than those cooked in their shells.

> ## Quick Tip
>
> Although a shrimp may be deveined with nothing more than your hands and a small knife, a shrimp cleaner, a tool resembling a knife tapered sharply like a bird's beak, removes a shrimp's shell and vein in one motion.

Most Gulf shrimp, tiger shrimp, and Chinese white shrimp are available year-round, while Monterey prawns are in markets from spring through fall.

Storing Fresh raw shrimp should be used the day of purchase or within 24 hours at the longest. Keep them in a zippered plastic bag in the refrigerator on a bed of ice before using. Cooked shrimp may be refrigerated for up to 3 days. Frozen shrimp may be kept for up to 3 months. Once defrosted, shrimp should not be refrozen, or their texture will deteriorate.

Preparing Shrimp are often shelled and deveined before they are cooked. See instructions below.

To freshen frozen shrimp before cooking, soak in salted water for 10 to 15 minutes, then rinse well. Shrimp are very sensitive to heat and must be cooked quickly, or they will turn tough and chewy. When possible, cook shrimp in their shells; unshelled grilled shrimp are always juicier. The Chinese customarily stir-fry large shrimp in their shells for the same reason.

Rinse and drain canned shrimp before using them. Thaw frozen shrimp in the refrigerator.

HOW TO *Shell Shrimp*
1. If the shrimp still has its head, pull it off or lop it off with a knife.
2. Carefully pull off the legs on the inside curve of the shrimp.
3. Peel off the shell, beginning at the head end of the shrimp, pulling off the tail as well unless the recipe calls for it to be left attached.

HOW TO *Devein Shrimp*

Shrimp may be deveined before or after cooking.

1. Shell the shrimp. See How to Shell Shrimp, page 405.
2. With a small knife, cut a shallow groove along the back of the shrimp.

3. With the tip of the knife, gently lift and scrape away the dark vein, then rinse the shrimp under cold running water (if raw). Drain the shrimp on paper towels and proceed with the recipe.

See also BUTTERFLYING.

SHUCKING To remove a bivalve, such as an oyster, a mussel, a scallop, or a clam, from its shell. Peas and beans are sometimes said to be shucked, rather than shelled, while to shuck corn means to remove its husk and silk. When shucking bivalves such as clams and oysters, make sure you have the right equipment. The correct knives make all the difference in safety and ease of shucking.

See also CLAM; CORN; MUSSEL; OYSTER; SCALLOP.

SIEVE See STRAINER.

SIFTING Passing an ingredient through a sifter or strainer to aerate it, give it a uniform consistency, and eliminate any large particles. Although most all-purpose flour is sold presifted, some baking recipes still specify sifted all-purpose flour. Because sifting significantly increases volume, you should not sift before measuring unless a recipe specifies this. (A good baking recipe is written so that you know by the order of the words if the flour is to be measured before sifting: "1 cup sifted flour" means that you are measuring sifted flour—in other words, you should sift before measuring— while "1 cup flour, sifted" means to measure the flour first, then sift it.) In recipes that do not specify sifted flour, the flour should be stirred or whisked to aerate it before measuring and sifted afterward if desired.

Flour sifters are metal or plastic canisters that force flour through a layer (or two or three) of wire mesh. A simple fine-mesh strainer may be used instead, its rim tapped to pass the flour through.

Sifter.

Sifting flour with other dry ingredients such as salt and baking soda is the best way to combine and aerate these ingredients so that they distribute evenly and readily into a batter, although you can also stir or whisk these ingredients together instead.

Soft pastry and cake flours clump easily and should always be sifted to remove any lumps. Trying to remove lumps later in the mixing process can result in overmixing and may toughen a dough.

Confectioners' sugar and cocoa powder regularly clump and often should be sifted before using. Use the back of a spoon to push these ingredients through a fine-mesh strainer, rather than sifting them in a flour sifter; they will be sifted more efficiently this way, and you won't have to clean the flour sifter before using it for flour.

See also STRAINER.

SIMMERING When liquid is maintained at a temperature just below a boil, about 185°F, it is called a simmer. Tiny bubbles barely breaking on the surface signal that a liquid has reached a gentle, or low, simmer. If the bubbles are larger and move a little more rapidly, the liquid is at a full simmer, or is "simmering rapidly" or "briskly." The temperature in this case will be closer to 200°F. Once the bubbles are quite large and numerous, filling much of the liquid and breaking when they reach the surface, the liquid is at a boil. Simmering is the ideal temperature for many soups and sauces, but only a gentle simmer or a slightly lower temperature should be used for braising or poaching meat and fish. See also BOILING; BRAISING; POACHING.

SIMPLE SYRUP See SUGAR.

SKEWERS See COOKING TOOLS.

SKILLET Also known as a frying pan; see COOKWARE.

SKIMMING To remove the top layer from the surface of a liquid. Many soups and stocks produce a white scum, or foam, during the cooking process that should be skimmed off and discarded. Use a large spoon or a skimmer to skim solids from liquids. A skimmer has a long handle and a slightly concave head

made of fine wire mesh or perforated metal. The fat that rises to the top of soups and stocks is often skimmed in a process called degreasing. Cream that rises to the surface of whole milk is also skimmed off to make heavy cream or to be churned into butter.

See also DEGREASING.

SKINNING Removing the thin outer membrane of a food. Poultry is often skinned to quicken the cooking process, to allow seasoning to penetrate the flesh more easily, or to lower the fat content of the final dish. Vegetables such as tomatoes and fava beans and foods such as hazelnuts and almonds also are often skinned, or peeled, for reasons of appearance, texture, or taste.

SLASHING Making shallow cuts with a sharp blade in the surface of a food, such as bread dough or whole fish, before cooking. See also SCORING.

Slashing bread dough.

SLICING To cut a food into relatively flat pieces of varying possible thicknesses, as with bread or meat, or into wedges, as with cake or pie. Food is often sold by the slice in delicatessens. See also CHOPPING.

SLIVERING Cutting a small piece of food, such as a garlic clove or an almond, into thin pieces. Garlic is often slivered and inserted into pieces of meat to add flavor, and almonds are sold already slivered for use in desserts and other dishes. Thin wedges of pie or cake also may be referred to as slivers.

SLOW COOKER See CROCKPOT.

SMASHING Crushing a food, usually in order to release its flavor. See also BRUIS-ING; CRUSHING.

SMOKE POINT The temperature at which a fat begins to break down and emit smoke. Some fats have a higher smoke point than others, and so are preferred for cooking techniques that employ a high heat, such as deep-frying. Also, keeping oil hot for any extended period of time will lower the smoke point. Each time you use a batch of oil for deep-frying, its smoke point is lowered.

Butter has one of the lowest smoke points of all fats, as the milk solids suspended in the butterfat begin to burn after only a few seconds over medium heat. Combining vegetable oil with butter will raise the smoke point, allowing you to add the taste of butter to sautéed food without burning the butter. Clarified butter, which has been separated from its milk solids, has a higher smoke point while retaining the flavor of butter. The smoke point of different types of oils varies, with safflower, peanut, canola, and corn oil having high smoke points and extra-virgin olive oil having a relatively low one.

Oil that has reached the smoke point gives off a noxious smell and may be chemically altered into saturated fat.

See FAT & OIL; FRYING.

SMOKING To preserve and flavor a food by either hot smoking or cold smoking. In most cases, particularly with cold smoking,

foods are partially cured in brine beforehand. Cold smoking, a slow-curing method, happens at low temperatures of 70° to 90°F, can take several weeks, and is done in traditional or makeshift smokehouses. Cold-smoked foods retain more moisture than hot-smoked foods and will have a more tender texture. Salmon is a frequent candidate for cold smoking. Hot smoking takes place at higher temperatures of 100° to 190°F for as long as it takes to cook the food partially or completely. It may be done in a commercial charcoal-water smoker, a tall, cylindrical device that concentrates the smoke from charcoal and smoking woods. These smokers are constructed in layers, with a fuel grate and water pan in the bottom, topped by one or more cooking racks; adjustable vents control the amount of smoke. Outdoor grills can be modified to smoke foods as well, by adding smoking woods to a charcoal fire and covering the grill during cooking. Stove-top smokers are also available.

See also GRILLING.

SNAIL As any gardener knows, the snail loves the tender leaves of salad greens and other vegetables. Snails also love grape leaves; when the ancient Romans brought grapevines to France, they also brought one of their favorite foods, the snail. Today, the large, black Burgundy, or vineyard, snail is considered to be the premium food snail, and an entire ritual has developed around their consumption in the French wine country of the same name, and wherever snails are available. The petit-gris snail, as its name indicates, is smaller and gray; it is found in the southern part of France.

Specially designed serving pieces known as snail plates, tongs, and forks make eating snails easier. A snail plate includes small indentations that hold snail shells securely in place. Snail tongs let the diner handily grip each usually butter-drenched snail shell while extracting its meat with a narrow two-pronged snail fork.

Snail serving plate.

Quick Bite

Gardeners in France harvest the snails in their gardens and also collect them in the fields and along roadsides after a rain.

Selecting Fresh farm-raised snails are available in some specialty markets; these have already been cleansed. You are much more likely to find canned snails, however, the best ones being imported from Burgundy. Snails are also available frozen.
Storing If you should find fresh snails, eat them on the day they are bought.
Preparing Fresh snails must be washed, soaked for 2 hours in a mixture of salt, vinegar, and a pinch of flour, then washed again and blanched. Then they are removed from their shells, and the black end of the tail is removed and discarded. Next, the snails are braised in a mixture of white wine and stock for 3 to 4 hours before they

are allowed to cool. If using the shells for serving, they must be boiled for 30 minutes in water with a pinch of baking soda, then drained, rinsed, and dried. Canned snails have already gone through all these steps; the shells are purchased separately to use and reuse for serving.

SNAP BEAN See BEAN, FRESH.

SOAKING To immerse a food in liquid. Some foods must be soaked to make them more tender or to remove salt or brine. Salt-packed anchovies and capers, and salt-dried fish such as cod, benefit from a cold-water soak to rinse away some of their salt. Without soaking, these foods would remain unpalatably salty and hard. See also BEAN, DRIED.

SORBET The name for this family of frozen desserts has a ring of elegance, and like many elegant things, much of its style derives from simplicity. Sorbets are made with merely fresh fruit (or sometimes chocolate, coffee, wine, or herbal infusions), sugar, usually water, and lemon juice, without the addition of milk, cream, or eggs. Sorbets were the rage in the late 19th and early 20th centuries, when they were often served as palate-cleansers between rich, heavy courses of formal meals. A *sorbetto,* the more intense Italian version, generally has more fruit and less water, resulting in a softer, less icy texture. Fruit ices, also known by the Italian name *granita* or the French *granité,* resemble sorbets but have more grainy textures, the result of being frozen in a simple freezer tray and repeatedly scraped and refrozen to form icy particles. A sherbet, similar to a sorbet, usually includes some milk or cream or, sometimes, egg whites, resulting in a flavor and consistency midway between those of sorbet and ice cream.

Sorbet Savvy When making sorbets and other related desserts, keep the following in mind:

- Use only fresh fruit for fruit-flavored sorbets. Those made with cooked or canned fruit will taste like cold jam.
- When making syrup for sorbets, use a hydrometer to measure its density and a candy thermometer to measure its temperature, following any specifications given in recipes. For sorbet to freeze properly, the syrup must have the correct density.
- For making granitas and other ices, use a stainless-steel pan, which will help the mixture freeze faster. As a layer of crystals forms, scrape it up occasionally with a metal spoon, until the desired consistency is reached.
- Alternatively, freeze mixtures for granitas in ice-cube trays until almost but not completely solid, then chop to the desired consistency in a food processor.
- If you enjoy serving sorbets, consider investing in a countertop electric machine that will stir and freeze the mixture.

See also ICE CREAM.

SORREL See GREENS, DARK; HERB.

SOUFFLÉ The soufflé is an airy concoction of beaten egg whites stabilized by a thicker base, often a béchamel sauce. Its name is based on the verb *souffler,* meaning "to blow" or "to puff up." The classic soufflé may be either savory, as in a cheese or vegetable soufflé, or sweet, as in a chocolate, lemon, or berry soufflé. In either case, it emerges hot and trembling from the oven and is eaten at once. But cold dessert soufflés, stabilized usually by gelatin and often by freezing, also exist, although they more properly should be called mousses. Soufflés may be cooked in one large soufflé dish or in individual ones; layered with other foods, such as poached eggs or fish fillets; baked in a shallow casserole or gratin dish; or baked in a water bath and served unmolded. Some soufflés are served with sauces, such as the whipped cream or berry coulis accompanying chocolate soufflés.

The French porcelain soufflé dish, with its high, straight sides, allows the soufflé to rise to its most dramatic heights. If you don't have a soufflé dish, use a charlotte mold, or fit a round casserole dish with a collar. The batter should come to within 1 inch of the rim. For savory recipes, the sides of the dish are buttered and sprinkled with bread crumbs or grated cheese to help the soufflé mixture climb upward as the beaten egg whites expand in the oven. In dessert soufflés, the buttered dish is sprinkled with sugar. Some recipes for savory soufflés forgo the bread crumbs or grated cheese and instead chill the buttered dish. The cold butter gives the soufflé mixture some traction on the dish's sides.

Soufflé dishes.

The French prefer their soufflés undercooked by American standards, that is, creamy in the center. This is a matter of taste, however, and you may prefer a drier, more fully cooked soufflé, especially if you are concerned about the possibility of salmonella from undercooked eggs. If so, bake your soufflé until a skewer inserted from the side into the center of the soufflé crown comes out clean. Some especially dense soufflés, such as those made of chocolate, will always remain a bit moist in the center.

HOW TO *Make a Soufflé Collar*

1. Measure the circumference of the mold and cut a strip of aluminum foil or heavy brown paper 1 or 2 inches longer than the circumference and 6 to 8 inches wide.
2. Fold the foil or paper in half lengthwise and tie it around the dish with kitchen string. It should rise no more than 2 to 3 inches above the rim.
3. Butter and sprinkle the exposed interior of the foil or paper when you prepare the interior of the dish.

SOUP Served for any course, including dessert, soup can be hot or cold, and it can be made from almost any ingredient. Among the various kinds are clear soups, which range from a simple stock to a clarified consommé and may have other ingredients, such as dumplings, added; cream soups, which have milk or cream added to a base of stock and are usually thickened with either puréed ingredients or a roux; and soups that blur the line between soups and stews, like chili, gumbo, and bouillabaisse. (In general, a stew has larger pieces of food cooked in a relatively smaller quantity of thicker, saucelike liquid.)

Storing Store soup, tightly covered, in the refrigerator for 2 to 3 days, depending on the soup. Some soups are better the day after they are made, as the flavors have had a chance to meld and deepen. Degrease meat soups after chilling, and reheat slowly over low heat. Most frozen soups will keep for 3 to 6 months. Do not freeze soups with potatoes, however, as they will turn into mush.

Soup Savvy When making soup, keep the following in mind:
- When a soup recipe calls for stock or broth, start with the best quality. If you don't make and store your own, look for good frozen, vacuum-packed, or canned broth, choosing a brand that has a flavor you like and that is not too salty.
- Many soups can be made vegetarian simply by substituting vegetable stock or broth for meat, chicken, or seafood stock or broth.
- Conversely, vegetarian soups can gain more robust appeal for meat eaters by the use of meat or poultry stock or the addition of smoked ham or bacon.
- In summer, consider serving a cold soup such as Spanish gazpacho, cream of avocado or cucumber, or iced melon soup.
- To give puréed soups sufficient body, include starchy or full-bodied ingredients such as potatoes, carrots, tomatoes, bread crumbs, or cooked grains.
- Because soups reduce in volume during cooking, concentrating their flavors, season them only at the end of cooking.
- Don't forget to garnish your soups, adding flavor and texture while enhancing their appearance. Easy garnishes include puréed bell pepper, pesto, herbs, shredded cheese, or croutons.

See also STEW; STOCK.

SOUR CREAM Sour cream is cream that has been deliberately soured. By adding a bacterial culture to the cream, producers can control the souring process as the lactose in the cream converts to lactic acid. Sour cream comes in low-fat and nonfat versions. When sour cream is used in baking, its lactic acid makes for a more tender crumb, and the sour cream lends cakes and muffins a pleasingly tart taste. Sour cream is sometimes used in salad dressings, such as for carrot-and-raisin salad or coleslaw, and for topping baked potatoes. Many sauces are enriched with sour cream as well, although the cream should be added at the very end of cooking, as it will curdle if exposed to high heat.

Storing Check sour cream containers for sell-by dates before purchasing, then store in the refrigerator for up to 1 week.

SOYBEAN See BEAN, DRIED; SOY FOODS.

SOY FOODS The humble soybean is mother to an entire family of soy foods that are high in protein and vitamins.
BEAN CURD Called *tofu* in Japanese and *dou-fu* in Chinese, bean curd comes in silken, soft, medium, firm, and extra-firm ivory-colored blocks and has a mild flavor. It comes packed in water and should be drained, rinsed, and then drained again before use. If you are deep-frying bean curd or using it in some other preparation that would suffer from too much liquid, place it on a plate, top with a second plate and a weight, such as a 1-pound can, and let stand for about 1 hour, to release more moisture. Bean curd is also sold pressed, pickled, and dried in sheets and sticks.
TEMPEH Indonesian tempeh, a firm, slab form of fermented bean curd with a yeasty flavor, is a favorite meat substitute for vegetarians, as it is as high in protein as beef or chicken while containing no cholesterol. Often made with a mix of fermented grains to add flavor and texture, tempeh can be baked, broiled, grilled, stir-fried, or deep-fried and used like cooked meat in salads, sandwiches, soups, and casseroles.
SOY SAUCE The ubiquitous seasoning of Asia, soy sauce is made from fermented soybean meal and wheat. Look for soy sauce labeled as naturally brewed. Synthetic versions made with sweeteners and coloring agents are inferior. Tamari sauce, soy sauce made without wheat, is thicker and more intense. Japanese soy sauce *(shoyu)* is a fairly light soy sauce that is less salty than Chinese soy. The two main types of Chinese soy sauce are dark and light (or thin). Dark soy sauce has had molasses added, and because it is rich and flavorful, it is often used with red meats and other robust foods.
MISO A staple food in Japan, this fermented soybean paste is made by crushing boiled soybeans; adding wheat, barley, or rice; inoculating the mix with a yeastlike culture; and then aging it. White miso, also called light or yellow miso, is aged from 2 to 6 months. It has a mild, sweet flavor and is used in soups, sauces, and salad dressings. Red, or dark, miso is aged from 3 months to 3 years. It has a strong, salty taste and is used in robust dishes.
SOY MILK Made by puréeing soybeans with water, and then straining, cooking, and filtering the purée, soy milk is sold plain or sweetened and flavored and is also used as the basis for soy-based cheeses.

Soybeans are also the basis for a number of other condiments and pastes, such as salted black beans, bean paste, hot bean sauce, hoisin sauce, and sweet bean sauce. All of these intense-tasting sauces may be added to stir-fries and other dishes to deepen the flavor. Look for soybean sprouts in Asian markets, or look for fresh soybeans in their pods in natural-food stores and some Asian markets for sprouting at home. The young, tender green soybeans in the pod are also a wonderful and nutritious snack. About 2 inches long, and called by their Japanese name, *edamame,* they are simply boiled in their shells in heavily salted water for 5 to 10 minutes, drained, cooled to room temperature, and popped from their pods and eaten.

SPATULA See BAKING TOOLS; COOKING TOOLS.

Spice

The average person's love for spices comes second only to his or her love for salt and sugar. These highly scented seeds, barks, roots, and fruits have been commodities since prehistory. They have been used since ancient times in sacred rituals, to anoint royalty, to mask the taste of spoiling foods, and to add aroma and flavor to prepared dishes.

For centuries, spices had to be brought overland by camel from Asia and India, and the spice trade was monopolized by the Arabs. By medieval times, spices were almost as valuable as gold, and Venice controlled their commerce, becoming a great power in the process. Christopher Columbus was only one of many European explorers who hoped to break the Venetian hold on the spice trade by finding a sea route westward to the spice lands. North America just happened to be in the way.

Coriander, star anise, and cumin.

Spices are still valuable today, for only a small amount is needed to add a haunting or heady fragrance and taste to food. The cuisines of India and Indonesia, the two countries where most spices are still grown, use a wide range of them. Spain, Mexico, Ethiopia, and North Africa also depend on blends of spices to perfume their foods, reflecting their ancient connections with Arabic cuisine. Northern European countries continue to demonstrate their love of spices in a wide range of foods both sweet and savory, including gingerbread, sauerbraten, honey cake, mulled wine, and cardamom-scented butter cookies.

The Spice Pantry

ALLSPICE The berry of an evergreen tree, allspice tastes like a combination of cinnamon, nutmeg, and cloves. It is used ground or whole in many sweet and savory dishes, including some cakes, cookies, breads, braised meat dishes, tomato sauces, marinades, pickled foods, and stewed fruits.

ANISEED The seed of the anise plant, belonging to the parsley family, aniseed is used whole and ground and has a licorice taste. It is a popular addition to European baked goods, especially Italian breads and cookies. Aniseed is one of the flavorings used in the liqueurs pastis and anisette.

ANNATTO SEED Also called achiote, annatto seeds are the small, hard seeds of the annatto tree. The dark red seeds are ground and used in spice pastes or as part of a

continued

Spice, continued

dry-rub mixture for grilled and roasted meats, giving the food a musky, earthy taste and a reddish color. Annatto seeds are used in Indian, Spanish, and Mexican cooking, especially in seasoning pastes for meat and stews and to color rice.

CARAWAY SEED Caraway seed is a member of the parsley family. It has a strong, pungent taste that is closely identified with rye bread. Caraway seed is used in many other breads throughout northern and central Europe and is added to rich meat and poultry dishes and casseroles. It is almost always used whole.

CARDAMOM This intense spice is the dried fruit of a plant in the ginger family. Cardamom has an exotic, highly aromatic flavor and is used ground in curries, fruit dishes, and baked goods.

It may also be added whole to mulled wine, the spicy tea known as chai, and braised dishes. Cardamom is sold in small round pods or as whole or ground black seeds. The seeds are best removed from the pod and ground, although the whole pod also may be ground.

CAYENNE A very hot ground red pepper made from dried cayenne and other chiles, cayenne is used sparingly in a wide variety of preparations—hummus, salsas, chili, curries, chutneys—to add heat or to heighten flavor. Because different blends vary in heat, and because only a little is needed, always begin with a very small amount and add more to taste in small increments.

CELERY SEED This tiny dried seed of the wild celery plant has a strong celery flavor and is used whole in potato salad, coleslaw, and pickling mixtures. Use it sparingly.

CINNAMON While in American cooking cinnamon appears most often in sweets, such as apple pie and cinnamon rolls, the Greeks, Indians, and Moroccans use it in both sweet and savory dishes. The dried bark of a tree, cinnamon comes from two sources: the commonly available cassia cinnamon, which is a dark red-brown and has a strong, sweet taste; and pale tan, delicate-tasting Ceylon cinnamon, which is grown only in Sri Lanka and is considered by many to be true cinnamon. Buy cinnamon in stick form or already ground. To grind your own, first break or crush the stick into pieces.

CLOVE Shaped like a small nail with a round head, the almost-black clove is the dried bud of a tropical evergreen tree. It has a strong, sweet flavor with a peppery quality. Ground cloves are added to desserts such as spice cakes and to meat dishes such as sauerbraten, while whole cloves are used to stud hams and to flavor pickling mixtures.

Quick Bite

The word *clove* derives from the French word *clou,* which means "nail."

CORIANDER SEED The dried ripe fruit of fresh coriander, or cilantro. Coriander is a relative of parsley. Its tiny, round ridged "seeds" have an aroma said to be like a combination of lemon, sage, and caraway. The ground seeds add an exotic flavor to both savory and sweet foods, including stews and baked goods. Coriander is used in Indian, Scandinavian, and Middle Eastern cuisines, among others.

CUMIN The seed of another parsley family member, cumin has a sharp, strong flavor and is much used in Latin American, Indian, and Moroccan cooking. Mixed with ground chile, it is one of the ingredients in chili powder and is used in assertively flavored dishes like Mexican black beans and Texas chili. Cumin is available ground and whole. For superior flavor, buy whole seeds and toast them before grinding.

FENNEL SEED The seed of the common fennel has a licorice-like flavor and is used in savory dishes such as bouillabaisse, sausage, and pork stews and roasts. It is also used in some breads and desserts and to flavor liqueurs. Fennel seed may be used ground or whole.

FENUGREEK The characteristic bittersweet aroma of curry powder is due in part to the tiny yellow-brown seeds of the fenugreek plant. Highly aromatic, fenugreek seeds are actually legumes and are eaten as such in Ethiopia. They are also used to flavor Indian chutneys and Moroccan breads. The seeds are best purchased whole, as they quickly lose flavor after grinding. Fenugreek seeds should be toasted and soaked in water until soft before grinding.

GINGER Indispensable in Asian cooking, the warm, perfumy taste and spice of ginger is also a favorite flavoring of American and British cooks. See also GINGER.

JUNIPER BERRY This pea-sized berry from the evergreen juniper bush is blue-black and pungent. Juniper berries are used to flavor gin; in marinades for assertive-tasting meats such as lamb, venison, and boar; and as an important ingredient in sauerbraten and Alsatian sauerkraut. Use the berries whole; toast them lightly first and then crush them before adding to marinades or sauces.

MACE When the bright red, lacy membrane that covers the nutmeg seed is removed and dried, it turns orange-yellow and is sold as mace, usually in ground form. When sold whole, it is called blade mace. The flavor is a deeper and more pungent version of nutmeg. The spice is used in Indian, Moroccan, and Indonesian dishes and is also added to baked goods such as pound cake and to fruit dishes. Ground mace loses its flavor quickly, so buy it in small amounts and refrigerate it.

MUSTARD The seeds of the mustard plant come in three colors: white (also called yellow), brown, and black. Mustard seeds, which have a pungent, hot taste, are used whole as a primary ingredient in pickling mixtures and for flavoring marinades. Dry, or powdered, English mustard is used in sauces and dressings, and it may also be used to make prepared mustard at home. See also MUSTARD, PREPARED.

Quick Tip

Water triggers the chemical reaction in mustard seed that produces its distinctive hot flavor. If a recipe calls for dry mustard, mix it with a little tap water, let it stand for 10 minutes for the flavors to develop, and then add the paste to the other ingredients. One teaspoon of dry mustard is roughly equivalent to 1 tablespoon of prepared mustard.

NUTMEG The oval brown seed of a soft fruit, a nutmeg is about ¾ inch long, with a warm, sweet, spicy flavor. It has a hard shell that is in turn covered by the membrane that becomes mace. A beloved spice, nutmeg is used to dust

continued

Spice, continued

custards and eggnog and is one of the spices used to flavor sweet potato and winter squash dishes, pumpkin pie, spice cakes, breads, and cookies. The whole nutmeg keeps its flavor much longer than ground nutmeg. Specialized nutmeg graters, usually with small compartments for storing a nutmeg or two, are available for this purpose.

Quick Tip

If you do not have a nutmeg grater or other fine grater, very carefully shave a whole nutmeg seed crosswise with a sharp knife. The shavings will break apart into coarse powder. Mince them more finely with a knife, if needed.

See also NUTMEG.

PAPRIKA Made from ground dried red peppers and ranging from orange-red to red, paprika is used both as a garnish and as a flavoring. A dusting of paprika gives color to foods such as potato salad, macaroni salad, deviled eggs, fish, and creamed dishes. It is also used to give color and flavor to sausages and is an ingredient in spice mixes and rubs. Hungary and Spain make the finest paprika. Three basic types are available: sweet, half-sweet, and hot. Sweet paprika is often specified in recipes.

PEPPER Although small in size, peppercorns pack a wallop of piquancy that is essential to many dishes and is the natural flavor partner of salt. Both black and white peppercorns, which are the same spice picked at different stages of ripeness and processed differently, are used whole or ground to varying degrees of fineness.

*Black
peppercorns.*

White peppercorns, which are actually tan, are slightly milder than their black kin and are used for aesthetic reasons in light-colored preparations such as cream sauce. Green peppercorns are harvested when still green and unripe, then packed in water or brine or dehydrated. They are less pungent than black and white peppercorns. So-called pink peppercorns are not true peppercorns but rather the brightly hued berries of a type of rose plant. All pepper is much more aromatic when freshly ground.

POPPY SEED Tiny in size and ranging from beige to blue-black in color, poppy seeds add crunch and a slight nutty flavor to foods. Black poppy seeds are used in central European cooking as a filling ingredient and as a garnish for baked goods such as strudel, cake, and cookies as well as for yeast breads and noodle dishes. Beige and brown poppy seeds are used in Indian and Middle Eastern cuisines. Because they are high in oil, poppy seeds should be stored in the refrigerator. Toasting the seeds brings out their flavor.

SAFFRON In flavor, saffron, the stigmas of a type of crocus, is pungent and earthy, with a slight bitterness. When soaked in liquid, it turns the liquid a dark yellow. Because it must be hand-picked, and because each crocus has only three stigmas, saffron is the world's most expensive spice. Only a tiny bit, however, is needed to tint and flavor rice (paella, risotto), chicken, breads, and many other dishes. It is available as "threads" (stigmas) or powdered. Thread saffron, although more expensive, is preferable, as powdered saffron is sometimes adulterated with other ingredients to extend it, and it loses flavor more rapidly.

Saffron is usually soaked in a small amount of hot water or other liquid before it is added to any dish. When possible, add saffron toward the end of the cooking process to preserve its highly aromatic flavor.

STAR ANISE Although it has an aniselike flavor, star anise is a seed-bearing pod from a Chinese evergreen tree related to the magnolia. The brown pods are indeed star shaped; each contains eight seeds. Slightly more bitter in flavor than aniseed, star anise is used in Asian cuisine to flavor teas and savory dishes. In the West, it is used in baked goods. Star anise is often used whole or snapped into points, and is also ground as one of the spices in Chinese five-spice powder.

TURMERIC Like saffron, turmeric is valued for both its taste and its bright color. The root of a plant belonging to the ginger family, turmeric is used fresh and dried. Fresh turmeric resembles fresh ginger in shape but is smaller and has orange-tinted skin. It is primarily used in Southeast Asian and South Asian cooking, in stews and curries. Dried and ground, the bright-orange flesh becomes yellow-orange. Ground turmeric is one of the primary ingredients in Indian curry powder and is also used to impart color to some prepared mustards.

VANILLA The favorite sweet flavoring of many Americans, vanilla is indigenous to the New World. In whole form, vanilla beans are the dried fruit of a tropical orchid; they are also used to make vanilla extract. See also VANILLA.

Selecting Ideally, spices should be bought whole and ground just before use. But in the interest of convenience, cooks stock many spices in two forms, whole and ground. Buy your spices, especially ground ones, in the smallest amounts you can, as they lose flavor over time. It's better to go to a natural-food store or a specialty-food shop that sells spices in bulk and buy only a little of each than to buy jars or cans of

spices that will grow stale and have to be thrown out. Be sure your merchant stores spices in a cool, dark place.

Storing Keep spices in tightly closed containers in a cool, dark place such as a pantry, rather than beside the stove or elsewhere in a bright kitchen. Some cooks keep their spices in alphabetical order for ease of selection. If you buy your spices in bulk, purchase some empty glass spice jars for storing them. Whole spices kept this way will last for about 1 year; ground spices should be replaced after 6 months.

Preparing For grinding small quantities of spices, use a mortar and pestle or a pepper mill reserved for spices. Or buy a small electric coffee grinder and use it only for grinding spices. Grind just the amount you need. To add whole spices to stews and mulled wine, tie them in a cheesecloth square or place them in a tea ball for easy removal. If using an orange or onion and whole cloves, stud the orange or onion with the cloves. Whole peppercorns should be bruised or cracked before using.

Putting spices in a tea ball.

To intensify their flavor, toast spices in a dry skillet. It is best to toast whole spices before grinding, but ground spices may be toasted if you keep a close eye on them. Some recipes call for frying spices in oil. Take great care not to burn them.

HOW TO *Toast Spices*

1. Put the spices in a small, heavy skillet (cast iron is ideal) over medium heat.
2. Toast, stirring constantly, until fragrant. Immediately empty the spices into a bowl and stir them to stop the cooking.

Spirits

Alcoholic spirits can be distilled from almost any food that contains sugar and can be fermented. The list ranges from apples, corn, and potatoes to barley, watermelons, milk, cactus, grape skins, and wine itself.

The Arabs originated the art of distilling, in which a fermented solution is boiled in a pot still, a large, closed kettle with a long, very narrow spout. Alcohol, which has a lower boiling point than water, evaporates first, and the resulting steam condenses and is channeled off.

Spirits such as whiskey, rum, gin, and vodka are labeled with their proof, a number that indicates the alcohol content of the beverage and is always twice the actual percentage. For example, 80 proof bourbon is 40 percent alcohol. Distilled spirits, such as whiskey, are barreled at well over 100 proof and then diluted with water when bottled to reach the desired proof.

Quick Bite

The term *proof* derives from an old custom of testing the quality of liquor by mixing it into a little gunpowder and holding it over a flame. If it ignited, the spirit was said to be "proved," indicating that it contained at least 50 percent alcohol (100 proof). If it only fizzled, the spirit didn't prove and was labeled inferior.

The Liquor Cabinet Spirits are used as appetizers, as digestives, and in cooking. Some of the most common spirits follow.

AQUAVIT Distilled from grain or potatoes, this Scandinavian liquor is flavored with caraway. It is kept in the freezer and served as single shots before or after dinner.

BOURBON See Whiskey, below.

BRANDY Brandy, which has an ancient heritage, is distilled from wine or fermented fruit juice. Cognac is brandy that comes from six regions clustered around the town of Cognac in western France. Known as the best of all brandies, Cognac is distilled from wine made from Charente grapes and is aged in Limousin oak in a highly controlled process. It is usually sipped after dinner, but it is also used in desserts, sauces, and consommés. Cognac is added to French onion soup and used to flambé a variety of both sweet and savory foods. Armagnac is brandy made from wine in the Gascony area of France. It is aged in black oak and has a pungent aroma and a more robust flavor than Cognac. It is also taken after dinner and is occasionally used in cooking.

Fruit brandies, also known as eaux-de-vie, or "waters of life," are strong, colorless spirits distilled from fermented fruit juice. Most of these are made in eastern France, Germany, and Switzerland. They are drunk before or after dinner and are widely used in desserts, especially those made with fruit. Fruit brandies are made from pears (poire Williams), raspberries (framboise), cherries (kirsch), and other fruits, including prunes and apricots. Calvados, an apple brandy, comes from northern France, where apples are plentiful but grapes are not grown. A dry brandy aged in oak, Calvados is taken after dinner and, in

Normandy, even as a digestive between two courses of a long meal. It is also an important ingredient in the dishes of Norman cuisine.

Calvados.

GIN This grain-based liquor gets its distinctive flavor from juniper berries and is often enjoyed as an ingredient in before-dinner mixed drinks. The most popular of these beverages is the dry martini, but dozens of gin mixed drinks exist, from gin and tonic to the Negroni (Campari, sweet vermouth, and gin) to the gimlet (lime juice and gin) to the salty dog (grapefruit juice, gin, and salt).

RUM Distilled from sugarcane juice or molasses, this Caribbean liquor comes in different colors, each stronger in flavor, from milk white or silver to golden, amber, dark, and Demerara, the darkest one. With its slightly sweet taste, rum is enjoyed straight, particularly in the Caribbean; in a Cuba libre and other highballs; and in a variety of cocktails, from a classic daiquiri to a martini in which the rum stands in for the gin. It is also widely used in Caribbean cooking, especially in fruit desserts, in ice cream, and in baked goods.

SCOTCH See Whiskey, below.

TEQUILA Made from fermented agave juice and named after its place of origin, Tequila, Mexico, this heady spirit ranges in color from white to golden and is the basis of the popular margarita. It is also drunk neat, with salt and a squeeze of lime, or sipped alternately with *sangrita,* a spicy mixture of tomato and lime juices.

VODKA Originally made from potatoes, today vodka is usually made from grain. Unaged and clear, vodka has little taste and so may be blended with a variety of other liquids. It is kept in the freezer to drink neat and also is sold in flavored form. A flavored, or infused, vodka is treated with one of a wide variety of ingredients, from lemon zest to chile. Vodka is occasionally used in cooking, as in a vodka-flavored cream sauce for pasta. It is also used as a base for homemade liqueurs.

WHISKEY Including bourbon, Canadian, Irish, rye, and Scotch, whiskeys are all made from grain. Scotch whisky, correctly spelled without an *e,* is also called simply Scotch. It is made throughout Scotland, and five kinds are produced: grain whisky, which is used in blended Scotch; and four distinctive malts, all made from malted barley in different areas of the country. Most Scottish malt whiskies are blended, except for the "single," or unblended, whiskies of the Highlands and other areas, which are considered the finest. Scotch is drunk on the rocks before dinner and is used in some mixed drinks. Bourbon takes its name from a county in Kentucky and is made from fermented grain, primarily corn. Indeed, so-called straight bourbon must be at least 51 percent corn. This slightly sweet whiskey is served before dinner over ice or in drinks such as eggnog. In cooking it may be added to barbecue sauce or baked beans, or used in bourbon balls or fruitcakes.

Quick Tip

Two common small bar tools that simplify measuring are the jigger (1½ ounces) and the pony (1 ounce), both small cups with flared sides. Sometimes they are available as a single double-ended measure. Most drinks call for 1½ ounces of alcohol; some call for 1 or 2 ounces.

See also LIQUEUR; WINE.

SPINACH See GREENS, DARK; GREENS, SALAD.

SPIRITS See page 418.

SPLIT PEA See BEAN, DRIED.

SPOON Stirring and spooning up food are simple tasks, but having a selection of different kinds of spoons to choose from makes them even easier. Wooden spoons are indispensable in the kitchen, as they are sturdy, do not scratch bowls or pans, or add a metallic taste to foods, and their handles do not get hot. Their only drawback is that they need to be washed by hand, not in a dishwasher, and if allowed to soak in water for extended periods, they will eventually warp, crack, and split. Metal spoons are nice for stirring large quantities of thick foods, such as stews, although their primary use is transferring food from one container to another. The slotted spoon is not used for stirring, but it is an essential tool for removing solid foods from liquid. The ladle is a necessary utensil for serving soups and sauces in the kitchen and at table. Scoops are used to remove dry foods from their containers. Ice-cream scoops come in several different sizes, and devoted cookie makers value them for scooping uniform balls of dough nearly as much as for scooping ice cream.

Wooden and metal spoons and ladle.

Measuring spoons help keep even the most intuitive cook on track. Choose metal ones that are linked, so you won't lose any. Precise measurements are critical in many recipes, especially those for baked goods.

See also BAKING TOOLS; COOKING TOOLS; MEASURING.

SPRINGFORM PAN See BAKEWARE; CAKE.

SPROUT Beans and seeds, germinated until they form a tender stalk and often their first leaves, are valued for their fresh, crisp taste and high nutritional content. Sprouts are rich in enzymes, which aid digestion, and are much higher in vitamins than are unsprouted seeds and beans.

Caution!

Raw sprouts have emerged as a possible source of food-borne illness. They may carry the pathogenic salmonella and *E. coli* bacteria. Alfalfa and clover sprouts have been involved in outbreaks most often, but all raw sprouts may pose a risk. If you are pregnant or older, are cooking for young children or older people, have a compromised immune system, or want to limit your exposure to bacterial risk as much as possible, you should cook all sprouts before eating them.

Any live seed can be sprouted, but the most commonly available sprouts are mung bean, alfalfa, radish, sunflower, and red clover sprouts. Mung bean sprouts, often called simply bean sprouts, are used in stir-fries and salads. Radish sprouts, sunflower sprouts, and red clover sprouts are also good salad ingredients, and alfalfa sprouts are often used in sandwiches and in stuffed pita breads. Broccoli sprouts have recently become popular, as they have been shown to be higher in nutrition than full-grown broccoli. Lentil and wheat berry sprouts are also available in many natural-food stores. Soybean sprouts are available in both natural-food stores and Asian markets.

Alfalfa and soybean sprouts.

Selecting Sprouts should be as fresh as possible. Try to buy them in bulk, rather than packaged, so you can make sure they are not dry, wilted, discolored, or slimy. Recent studies have shown that sprouts that are past their prime may actually be detrimental to one's health. To be absolutely sure of freshness, try growing your own.

Storing Place sturdy sprouts, such as mung bean, sunflower, and radish sprouts, in an airtight plastic container and store in the refrigerator for up to 3 days. Store delicate sprouts, such as alfalfa, in a perforated plastic bag in the crisper of the refrigerator for no more than 2 days.

Preparing Rinse the sprouts lightly with cool water and shake dry. Pull them apart and, if you don't like the looks of the little tails on mung and soy sprouts, pull them off and discard them. They are, however, edible. Soy sprouts, which are a little larger and thicker than other sprouts, should always be cooked instead of eaten raw.

Toss sprouts into a stir-fry or into boiling water for only about a minute, so they will stay crunchy. Scatter raw sprouts over salads or use in sandwiches.

SQUAB A young farm-raised pigeon with a rich, succulent meat. Because the birds never fly (exercise that builds muscles and toughens meat), their flesh is also exceedingly tender. Usually weighing under 1 pound, they may be substituted for poussins and Cornish hens. Like duck, the meat of a squab is all somewhat dark and rich.

Selecting When shopping for squab, look for ones that are plump and firm. Fresh squab is available in some markets during the summer months. It may also be ordered from specialty-meat markets and from Asian meat markets. The rest of the year, rely on frozen birds.

Storing Store squab in the coldest part of the refrigerator, usually the rear bottom shelf or in a meat drawer. If not prepared within 48 hours, freeze until ready to use. Defrost frozen squab in their packaging in the refrigerator.

Preparing Like other birds, squab takes well to a wide range of cooking methods. It can be roasted, grilled, broiled, sautéed, or smoked but should never be cooked above medium-rare. The birds are done when the juices are still slightly pink. If overcooked, the meat takes on a gamy, liverlike flavor.

See also DONENESS.

SQUASH The large, sprawling squash clan, all members of the gourd family and native to the Americas, may be neatly divided into two branches: winter squash and summer squash. Winter squashes are allowed to mature until their flesh is thick and their shells are hard, and they have a long shelf life. They come in many shapes, colors (white to red to green to near-black), and sizes. Summer squashes are generally eaten while small and tender, and are best eaten young and fresh. The blossoms of winter and summer squashes are eaten as well.

Squash Blossoms Squash blossoms, particularly those of pumpkins and zucchini, can be sautéed and used in quesadillas, pastas, or soups. They can also be filled with a seasoned white cheese, then battered and deep-fried.

Zucchini with blossoms.

Summer Squash All summer squashes are similar in flavor. They may be shredded or cut into thin slices and eaten raw or cooked by sautéing, stir-frying, boiling, steaming, or broiling. Zucchini and crookneck yellow squash can be cut into lengthwise slices, coated with olive oil, and grilled, while pattypans or scallopini may be sliced crosswise and cooked the same way. Sliced summer squashes can be battered and panfried or deep-fried. All summer squashes can be halved, hollowed out, filled, and baked; or they may be made into soups and stews, perhaps most notably ratatouille. Enormously versatile, they can be steamed whole, or sliced and sautéed as a side dish or as a topping for pasta.

CROOKNECK SQUASH
This bright yellow squash is about the same size as zucchini, but with a curved neck.

PATTYPAN SQUASH
Also known as scallop squash, this pale green, yellow, or white squash is about 4 inches in diameter, with scalloped edges.

SCALLOPINI Shaped like the pattypan, the scallopini is larger, thicker, and speckled green, like zucchini.

ZUCCHINI These narrow green squashes, some of which grow to an enormous size and capture ribbons at county fairs, are best eaten when small and young, before their tender flesh begins to toughen. Zucchini come in bright gold as well as the better-known green. A pale green round zucchini, known as Ronde de Nice, is sometimes available in farmers' markets and better produce stores. It is especially nice for panfrying.

See also ZUCCHINI.

Selecting Summer Squash Look for small summer squash early in summer. Throughout the season, select firm, unblemished specimens.

Storing Summer Squash Put summer squashes in a perforated plastic bag and keep them in the crisper section of the refrigerator for up to 3 days. Use squash blossoms within 24 hours; place them in one layer on a baking sheet lined with paper towels and refrigerate them until using.

Preparing Summer Squash Trim the ends of summer squashes, then hollow them with a tablespoon if you plan to stuff them, or slice, chop, or shred them as called for in a recipe.

Acorn and pattypan squashes.

Winter Squash Compared to summer squashes, winter squashes have a strong taste and dense texture (with the exception of the long strands of the spaghetti squash). They may be baked whole or in halves, slices, or cubes; or they may be cubed or sliced, then steamed or simmered and puréed if you like. Small winter squashes such as acorns and golden nuggets are the perfect size for halving, stuffing, and baking. Large squashes such as butternuts may be sliced and baked, or cut into pieces, then cooked and puréed. Sliced or cubed squash is also good in soups and stews or glazed and baked.

ACORN SQUASH About 6 inches in diameter, this squash has a dark green, ribbed shell and orange flesh.

BANANA SQUASH A squash with peach-colored skin and orange flesh, shaped like its namesake, although it can grow several feet long. It is often sold cut into pieces.

BUTTERNUT SQUASH Large, usually a foot long or more, with a beige skin and orange-yellow flesh, the butternut is identifiable by the round bulb at one end. It has a flavorful, dense flesh and is especially good for baking and puréeing.

DELICATA SQUASH A squash with green-striped yellow skin and yellow flesh that tastes a bit like a sweet potato. It is about 3 inches in diameter and 6 to 8 inches long.

GOLDEN NUGGET SQUASH Resembles a small pumpkin about 4 inches in diameter.

HUBBARD SQUASH Weighing 10 pounds or more, the Hubbard has yellow flesh and gray-green, blue, or dark green skin with small bumps. It makes an excellent purée that is a good substitute for pumpkin in pies.

KABOCHA SQUASH This squash, with its bright green skin marked with paler green stripes, has pale orange flesh. It usually weighs 2 to 3 pounds and may be substituted for acorn squash in recipes.

PUMPKIN Divided into field and cooking varieties; see PUMPKIN.

SPAGHETTI SQUASH Roughly the shape and size of a football, with bright yellow skin. Baked whole, the cooked flesh of the spaghetti squash forms long, thin strands when pulled from the shell with a fork, thus its name.

Spaghetti squashes should be baked whole, then halved and their strands pulled out; serve them like pasta.

SWEET DUMPLING SQUASH Actually an Asian gourd about 4 inches in diameter, the sweet dumpling has a very flavorful flesh and can be cooked and eaten like a winter squash. It is best when fully mature, its skin yellow with dark-orange stripes.

TABLE QUEEN Resembling an acorn squash in size and shape, this variety, also sometimes known as a golden acorn, has a bright orange shell and sweet, mild-tasting flesh.

TURBAN SQUASH This exotic-looking specimen has a top-knot and a multihued skin in oranges, yellows, and greens. It comes in varied sizes and shapes.

Selecting Winter Squash Some winter squash varieties are available year-round, but the widest selection is found during fall and winter. Squashes should be firm and unblemished and feel heavy for their size. To stuff and bake winter squash, choose a small squash, such as an acorn, that will yield two servings. For puréeing and cubing, choose a larger squash with more meat, such as the butternut.

Storing Winter Squash Cut winter squashes may be kept in the refrigerator for up to 1 week; whole winter squashes may be kept for months in a cool, dark place.

Preparing Winter Squash Using a chef's knife, cut winter squashes into halves or wedges. Using a large metal spoon, spoon out the seeds and strings, then peel the squash.

Scooping out the seeds.

HOW TO *Roast (or Bake) a Winter Squash*

1. Using a large, sharp knife, carefully cut the squash in half lengthwise through its stem and flower ends. If the skin is very hard, use a kitchen mallet to tap the knife carefully once it is securely wedged in the squash.

2. Place the squash halves cut side down in a baking dish and add water to a depth of 1 inch to the dish. Bake at 350°F until the squash is tender when pierced with a fork, 30 minutes to 1¼ hours, depending on variety. Add more water to the dish if it evaporates.

3. Once the squash is cooked and tender, scooping out the seeds and fibers is easy.

See also STEAMING.

SQUID One of the best values in the fish market, squid, sometimes called by its Italian name, calamari, is also one of the most delicious items you'll find there. This member of the cephalopod family (see SHELLFISH) has a sweet, mild flavor that takes well to a wide range of preparations. Many shops sell it already cleaned, cutting down dramatically on the cook's labor.

Whatever recipe or cooking method you choose, cook squid quickly, for 1 or 2 minutes, or slowly, for at least 1 hour. Otherwise, your squid will have the taste and texture of rubber bands.

Cuttlefish, which is similar in appearance to squid but much larger, is popular in Japan and some Mediterranean countries. Because its body walls are thicker than those of squid, it must be tenderized (see POUNDING) before cooking.

Selecting Fresh squid is shiny and firm, with a delicate ocean smell. The membrane that covers the squid should be gray. A purple or pink cast indicates that the squid may not be fresh.

Storing Squid is highly perishable and should be refrigerated on a bed of ice for no more than 2 days before cooking and serving. If you purchase frozen squid, don't defrost it more than a day before you plan to use it.

HOW TO *Clean Squid*

1. Pull the head and tentacles away from the body, or pouchlike part, of the squid. The innards, including the ink sac, should come away with the head.

2. Reach into the pouch and remove the long, plasticlike quill and discard it.

3. Cut off the tentacles from the rest of the head just below the eyes and discard the head and innards. Squeeze the cut end of the tentacles to remove the hard, round "beak" at the base and discard it.

4. Rinse the squid body, inside and out, and the tentacles under cold running water and pull off the gray membrane that covers the pouch. You may want to use a paring knife to help scrape it off. If the 2 small fins on either side of the pouch come off, reserve them to cook with the squid. Once cleaned, the pouch, fins, and tentacles can be sliced or left whole.

STAR ANISE See SPICE.

STARFRUIT Also known as the star apple or carambola, this bright yellow, 4- to 6-inch-long subtropical fruit, a native of China and India, gets its name because of its deeply ribbed exterior, which forms a star when the fruit is cut crosswise. The juicy flesh has a taste reminiscent of pineapple, plum, and lemon. It may be enjoyed raw or cooked in sweet and savory dishes.

Selecting Choose shiny-skinned, firm specimens. It's okay if they have a touch of green to them, as they will ripen well in your kitchen.

Storing Keep at room temperature until uniformly golden, a sign of ripeness; then refrigerate and eat within several days.

Preparing The fruit may be eaten peel and all. Cut crosswise for the most attractive presentation.

STARTER See YEAST.

STEAMER BASKET See COOKING TOOLS.

STEAMING To cook food over boiling water in a covered pan. Also, to cook some foods, such as mussels and clams, in a small amount of simmering liquid in a covered pan. Steaming is an especially good cooking method for delicate foods such as fish and vegetables, as it cooks by a more gentle process than boiling, simmering, or even poaching, thereby retaining the food's shape, color, flavor, and texture. In addition, steamed foods will not take on excess water, which could dilute their inherent flavor. Steaming is the technique of choice for cauliflower and broccoli, as it keeps them from becoming waterlogged. Steaming is also the most healthful of all cooking techniques, because it uses no fat, and it allows more nutrients to remain intact.

Caution!

Take care when uncovering a steaming pot. Be sure to avert your face and lift the lid away from you as you uncover the pot, and wear oven mitts to protect your hands and arms from the hot steam. It can scald you just as boiling water can.

Steamers are large pots fitted with a perforated basket and a lid. Often pasta pots will include a steamer basket that can be used in place of the perforated pasta basket. Collapsible steamer baskets can turn almost any saucepan or stockpot into a steamer. They have feet that keep the basket above the level of the water, and a ring for lifting the basket out of the pan. In lieu of a steamer basket, a metal colander or strainer can be set inside a large saucepan or a stockpot. Chinese bamboo steamer baskets are designed to fit snugly against the sides of a wok above the water. They can be stacked three high, so you can steam a meal of meat, fish, and vegetables, all in separate baskets but in the same pot.

Steaming Times for Various Foods

Artichoke, medium	40 minutes
Asparagus	
Thin spears	3 to 4 minutes
Thick spears	5 to 6 minutes
Beets	30 to 35 minutes
Broccoli	
Florets	4 to 5 minutes
Spears	5 to 6 minutes
Brussels sprouts	7 to 11 minutes
Cabbage, cut into wedges	6 minutes
Carrots, 1/4-inch-thick, 2-inch-long pieces	6 to 8 minutes
Cauliflower	
Head	12 to 15 minutes
Florets	4 to 6 minutes
Corn on the cob	5 minutes
Fennel	
Whole, trimmed	20 to 35 minutes
Quartered	7 to 10 minutes
Green beans	4 to 5 minutes
Kale	4 to 5 minutes
Parsnips, 1 1/2-inch pieces	8 to 10 minutes
Peas	2 minutes
Potatoes	
New	12 minutes
2-inch chunks	15 minutes
Pumpkin & winter squashes	
Peeled 2-inch chunks	15 to 20 minutes
Spinach, 1 pound	4 to 5 minutes
Sweet potatoes	
Whole	40 to 50 minutes
1-inch chunks	12 to 15 minutes
Swiss chard	
Leaves	4 to 6 minutes
Ribs, in 2-inch pieces	10 to 12 minutes
Zucchini, 1/4-inch slices	5 to 7 minutes

Foods may also be steamed in the microwave or by tightly sealing them in parchment paper or aluminum foil and cooking them in the oven.

Steaming Savvy When steaming foods, keep the following in mind:

- Fill the pot with several inches of water if using a steamer, or about ½ inch of water if using a collapsible steamer basket. Make sure the water will not touch the bottom of the basket or other container used to hold the food.
- Bring the water to a boil, then fill the steamer basket with food and add the basket to the pot. Cover and cook for the time specified in the recipe. Remove the basket as soon as the food is cooked.
- If the food must steam for a long time, and especially if you are using a small amount of water with a collapsible basket, check periodically to make sure the water has not boiled dry. Add more boiling water as needed.
- When steaming vegetables, especially strong-flavored ones like broccoli and cauliflower, try cooking by smell: when the vegetable begins to give off its fragrance, it is crisp-tender.

Vegetables are hands down the most popular food category to cook by steaming. Use the times suggested in the chart at left as guidelines only, relying more on taste and tenderness to help you determine when a vegetable is done to your liking.

STEEPING Extracting flavor from an ingredient by soaking it in a hot liquid. The point is to transfer the flavor from the solid ingredient to the liquid, which is then consumed or used as a flavoring. Steeping tea leaves in hot water makes tea. Ice creams are often flavored by steeping a flavoring such as coffee beans in the cream base and then straining out the beans after the base has taken on their flavor.

STEMMING To remove the stem from a fruit or vegetable. Many fruits and vegetables arrive in the market with their inedible stems still attached. Some stems, such as those on cherries, can simply be plucked off. Others foods, like artichokes, have thick stems that must be cut away with a knife. Greens and herbs such as spinach, watercress, basil, and parsley are usually stemmed before using, as the stems tend to be fibrous and somewhat bitter. See individual foods.

Stemming spinach.

STEW A stew is made by simmering pieces of meat, fish, and/or vegetables slowly in liquid. Usually thicker and more substantial than a soup, a stew is commonly served as a main course. It is similar to a braise, although stews generally use more liquid and the food for them is cut into smaller pieces.

Stews are among the basic dishes found in almost every cuisine, from the meat or seafood stews of France to the clay pots of Asia. A few famous French stews are the daube (which can also be a whole piece of braised beef), the ragout, and *boeuf bourguignonne*. The meat for stews is often browned to add flavor to the liquid, which gradually thickens as the meat cooks, although some dishes, such as fish stews and *blanquette de veau* (white veal stew) are made without browning.

Stews are economical, as they are usually made with foods that require long cooking for tenderness, such as root vegetables and tougher cuts of meat. They also have the advantage of usually tasting better the day after they are made. Refrigerating a stew overnight allows the flavors of the different ingredients to deepen.

Stew Savvy When making stew, keep the following in mind:

- When browning meat or vegetables for stews, follow the rules for searing: dry the food first on paper towels, add it to hot oil without crowding, and don't stir too often, to allow the meat to brown and to create browned bits on the bottom of the pan, which will flavor the sauce.

- An enameled cast-iron dutch oven or covered casserole is a perfect vessel for stewing, as it allows you to brown, cook, store, reheat, and serve the stew in the same container.

- The liquid in a stew should cover or almost cover the pieces of food.

- Stews and braises may be cooked on top of the stove, but medium-low oven heat allows for more even cooking and for a lower temperature, thus ensuring more tender results.

- Add quicker-cooking foods, such as potatoes and peas, when the meat is tender, and then cook them until tender, usually only 10 to 20 minutes. If you are making the stew a day ahead, add these foods the next day when reheating it.

- To make a stew 1 day ahead, let it cool to room temperature, then refrigerate. The next day, lift off any congealed fat from the surface, then slowly reheat the stew.

See also SOUP.

STIR-FRYING An Asian cooking technique of rapidly frying small pieces of foods in oil over high heat. The wok is the perfect implement for stir-frying, as it exposes the food to the maximum cooking surface

while keeping it from flying out of the pan as you stir. A large, deep cast-iron skillet or heavy sauté pan is a good substitute, however. Almost any vegetable or meat can be stir-fried, as long it is cut into small pieces. Although Asian-flavored dishes are the most obvious choices for stir-fries, you can also fashion simple Italian-style stir-fries, using such ingredients as sun-dried tomatoes, basil, and fresh vegetables, to top pasta or to serve as side dishes.

HOW TO *Stir-fry*

For approximately 1 pound of vegetables and ½ pound meat or tofu.

1. All food to be stir-fried should be cut into bite-sized pieces about 1½ inches long or into ½-inch dice. Cut red meat into strips against the grain, cut chicken or fish into thin slices or strips or into dice, and cut tofu into dice. Shrimp should be left whole and may be shelled or not. Vegetables such as carrots and zucchini should be cut into matchsticks or very thin slices, while long, thin vegetables such as green beans and asparagus should be cut on the diagonal to help them cook more quickly.

Cutting chicken into strips.

Cutting vegetables into small pieces.

2. Marinate meat, chicken, fish, shellfish, or tofu for about 15 minutes in a little soy sauce and vegetable oil, flavored with garlic, grated fresh ginger, and dry sherry or Shaoxing rice wine.

3. Preheat the wok over high heat until hot, then pour about 1½ tablespoons canola or peanut oil into the wok. Carefully tilt and rotate the pan in a circle so that the oil is distributed 6 inches up the sides of the pan. The oil should spread out in fragrant waves.

4. Add the meat or other foods; stir the food rapidly and push it up the sides of the wok until the meat, fish, chicken, or tofu is just beginning to brown, 2 to 3 minutes; shrimp should just have turned pink. Using a slotted spoon, transfer the meat to a bowl and set aside.

5. Add another tablespoon of oil to the pan, heat, and stir-fry the vegetables until their color turns bright, about 1 minute.

6. Add 2 to 3 tablespoons stock or water and cover the pan.

Reduce the heat to medium-high and cook for a few minutes, or just until the vegetables are crisp-tender. Vegetables such as broccoli, carrots, and cauliflower will take 3 to 4 minutes; bell peppers and zucchini will take 1 to 2 minutes; tender vegetables such as bean sprouts and snow peas need only 30 seconds or less.

7. Return the meat, chicken, fish, shellfish, or tofu to the pan along with the marinade and any other flavoring ingredients, such as black beans, soy sauce, chile oil, or Asian sesame oil. If you would like a thickened sauce, dissolve 2 teaspoons cornstarch in about ⅓ cup cold stock or water, add to the pan at the very end of cooking, and stir until the liquid is thickened. Serve at once.

See also COOKWARE.

STOCK The word *stock* is often used interchangeably with *broth* to describe the liquid made by cooking a food such as chicken, beef, fish, or vegetables in water for a few hours. More specifically, a stock is a homemade broth, a well-flavored liquid made by cooking meat and/or bones, fish parts and/or bones, the shells of shellfish, or vegetables with aromatic ingredients such as spices, herbs, onions, garlic, and other vegetables. Stock is used as the basis for countless soups, stews, and sauces and is used as a source of flavor and moisture in many other savory dishes.

Stock Savvy When making stock, keep the following in mind:

■ The more meat you use, the more flavorful your stock will be.

■ Ask your butcher for meaty soup bones or chicken parts for making stock (ask him or her to saw and/or chop them into 2- to 3-inch pieces for you). Or you can make your own stockpile by freezing leftover bones, meat scraps, chicken carcasses, bony chicken parts (backs, necks, and wings), and giblets (without the livers), both cooked and uncooked.

- Some strong-flavored vegetables, such as turnips and members of the cabbage family, will overpower the flavor of the stock, while starchy vegetables, like potatoes, will cloud and thicken the stock, and other vegetables, like beets, will color it.
- Don't let a stock being made with meat, fish, or chicken come to a boil, or it will become cloudy. Always cook the stock at a low simmer.
- Don't cover the pot completely while it is cooking, or the stock can sour. Cook with the lid askew so steam can escape, and let the stock cool uncovered.
- See SKIMMING and DEGREASING for tips on those processes.
- If you do not have homemade stock on hand, use a good-quality, low-salt commercial broth.

See also BROTH.

STOCKPOT See COOKWARE.

STRAINER A strainer, also called a sieve, is used to separate lumps or larger particles of food from smaller ones. It also is used to drain pieces of food of their liquid, and to purée soft foods, which are pushed through the strainer with the back of a large spoon.

Strainer and skimmer.

Wire-mesh strainers come in a variety of sizes, from very small to large, with either fine or coarse mesh. Some strainers have a long handle, plus a metal hook that allows them to fit onto a bowl; others are freestanding. Strainers are used in blanching, to move food quickly from boiling water into an ice bath. Use fine-mesh strainers to strain delicate foods such as consommés and custard sauces; to make the strainer even more effective, line it with a double thickness of cheesecloth.

The chinois is a conical French-style strainer, named after its resemblance to a Chinese hat of the same shape. A fine-mesh chinois is used to clarify stocks, while others with coarser mesh are used in making jelly. A chinois of perforated metal instead of mesh is used to make very smooth purées. It employs a long, pointed wooden pestle that is used to force the food through the perforations. Lacking the pestle, you can use the back of a large spoon or the bottom of a ladle.

Chinois.

The colander is a freestanding strainer, with two handles and perforated holes; it is used to rinse foods and to drain foods such as pasta and vegetables.

Colander.

See also BLANCHING; COOKING TOOLS; PURÉEING.

STRAINING To pass a liquid or dry ingredient through a strainer in order to separate out unwanted particles. Straining is different from draining, in which food is rid of its liquid. The word *strain* also means to purée food by pressing it through a strainer or sieve with the back of a large spoon or another implement. See also PURÉEING; STRAINER.

STRAWBERRY See BERRY.

STRING BEAN See BEAN, FRESH.

STUDDING To decorate and/or flavor food by inserting seasonings such as garlic, spices, or nuts into the surface of the food. Whole cloves are commonly used to stud hams, while lamb and pork roasts are sometimes studded with garlic slivers or anchovy fillets. Breads containing raisins or other dried fruit are said to be studded with the fruit.

STUFFING Any mixture of food used to stuff another food and then cooked is called stuffing. Another word for stuffing is "dressing," a usage more common in the South and East. (In other parts of the country, dressing is cooked alongside the bird rather than stuffed into it.) Stuffed Thanksgiving turkey is the classic example, but any food with a natural or hollowed-out cavity, such as other kinds of poultry, squashes, vegetables, and fruits, may be filled with a stuffing. Other foods, such as meats, may be butterflied, stuffed, and tied closed or may have pockets cut into them for stuffing.

Although it was long believed that stuffing helped to flavor a bird, the stuffing is actually the main flavor beneficiary: the stuffing in a bird is always moister and more delicious than stuffing baked separately. Because a stuffed turkey takes longer to cook, however, and may become drier than a turkey without stuffing, many cooks prefer to bake the stuffing separately. If you do choose to stuff poultry, make sure that you stuff the bird loosely, giving the stuffing room to expand, and be sure to observe the safety rules given below.

One of the simplest stuffings for poultry and meats is a bread stuffing made from torn pieces, cubes, or crumbs of bread mixed with herbs, eggs, butter, chopped celery and onions, and stock. Torn pieces of bread seasoned with lemon, butter, and parsley is another, rather rustic stuffing. Foods such as nuts, vegetables, and oysters, may be added to bread stuffing. Other favorite poultry and meat stuffings have a base of corn bread, rice, or wild rice. Pork is often stuffed with a mixture of dried fruits; fresh fruits may be stuffed with sweet or savory mixtures.

Stuffing Safety

- Prepare stuffing just before roasting. This way, warm stuffing can be put into the bird and directly into the oven. A made-ahead and refrigerated stuffing will take longer to cook. If you do make it ahead, warm it before filling the bird.
- Never put stuffing into a bird the day before (or even several hours before) roasting. The warm stuffing can breed bacteria from the bird.
- Cook stuffing to 165°F on an instant-read thermometer. If it is not done and the bird is, transfer the stuffing to a baking dish and bake until it tests done.
- If adding meat to a stuffing, cook it thoroughly first. Stuffings made with raw meats may not cook through properly.

Quick Tip

Figure on ½ cup of stuffing for each pound of meat when stuffing poultry.

- To serve, spoon all the stuffing out of the bird at once. Do not let it sit more than 2 hours in the turkey or chicken.
- Store leftover stuffing separately from the bird in the refrigerator for no longer than 2 days.

SUBSTITUTIONS & EQUIVALENTS The following chart lists the equivalent weight or amount for specific measurements of certain foods, as well as acceptable substitutes for certain foods, when available.

Substitutions and Equivalents

FOOD	AMOUNT	EQUIVALENT/WEIGHT	SUBSTITUTE
Almonds, whole	1 cup	$^3/_4$ cup ground	
Anchovy			Fresh sardines or anchovy paste
Apples	3 whole	$2^1/_2$ cups sliced	
Apricots, dried	1 cup	6 oz	
Arrowroot			Same amount of cornstarch; twice as much flour
Bacon	1 lb 1 slice, cooked	30 thin slices or 15 thick slices 1 tbsp, crumbled	
Baking powder	1 tsp		$^1/_4$ tsp baking soda plus $^5/_8$ tsp cream of tartar or $^1/_2$ cup buttermilk or yogurt
Bananas	3 to 4 (1 lb)	$1^1/_2$ cups mashed, 2 cups sliced	
Barley	1 cup	$3^1/_2$ cups cooked	
Beans, dried	1 cup (7 oz)	2 to $2^1/_2$ cups cooked	
Beans, green	1 lb	3 cups	
Beans, shelling	1 lb	1 cup shelled	
Bean sprouts	1 cup	4 oz	
Beets	1 lb, trimmed	2 cups cooked and sliced	
Bread crumbs, dried	$^1/_4$ cup	1 slice bread	
Bread crumbs, fresh	$^1/_2$ cup	1 slice bread	
Bread cubes, fresh	1 cup	1 slice bread	
Bulgur wheat	1 cup	$3^1/_2$ cups cooked	
Butter	$^1/_2$ stick 1 stick 2 sticks 4 sticks 4 tbsp	4 tbsp, $^1/_4$ cup, 2 oz 8 tbsp, $^1/_2$ cup, 4 oz 1 cup, 8 oz 2 cups, 16 oz (1 lb)	 $^7/_8$ cup vegetable oil or 1 cup lard 3 tbsp clarified butter

Substitutions and Equivalents, continued

Food	Amount	Equivalent/Weight	Substitute
Buttermilk	1 cup	8 oz	1 cup milk plus 1 tbsp fresh lemon juice, or 1 cup plain yogurt
Cabbage	1 head (1 lb)	4½ cups shredded or sliced	
Carrots	6 to 7 (1 lb)	3 cups shredded or sliced	
Cauliflower	2 lb	3 cups cut and cooked	
Celery	1 large rib	½ cup sliced or chopped	
Celery root	1 lb	3 cups grated or julienned	
Cheese	1 cup grated 1 cup crumbled feta 1 cup ricotta	4 oz 5 oz 8 oz	
Cherries	1 lb	2 to 2½ cups pitted	
Chestnuts	1½ lb	2½ cups peeled	
Chicken	1 whole (3½ lb)	3 cups cooked meat	
Chickpeas, dried	1 cup	2½ cups cooked	
Chocolate	1 square (1 oz)	4 tbsp grated	
Chocolate chips	6-oz pkg	1 cup morsels or bits	
Coconut, shredded	1 cup	4 oz	
Corn	2 ears	1 cup kernels	
Corn bread	8-in round or 9-in square	4 cups crumbs for stuffing	
Cornmeal	1 cup	4 cups cooked	
Cornstarch	1 tbsp		2 tbsp flour or 1 tbsp arrowroot
Couscous	1 cup	2½ cups cooked	
Crab	1 lb live	1 cup cooked meat	
Cracker and cookie crumbs	1 cup		28 soda crackers, 7 graham crackers, or 22 vanilla wafers
Cranberries	12-oz bag	3 cups	
Cream, heavy	1 cup	2 cups whipped	
Cream cheese	3-oz pkg	6 tbsp	
Cucumber	2 medium	3 cups sliced	

Substitutions and Equivalents, continued

FOOD	AMOUNT	EQUIVALENT/WEIGHT	SUBSTITUTE
Currants, dried	1 cup	5 oz	
Dates	8 oz whole	1¼ cups chopped	
Eggs	1 large		¼ cup liquid egg substitute
	1 whole, large		2 yolks plus 1 tbsp water (for baking)
	1 white, large	2 tbsp	
	1 yolk, large	1 tbsp	
	5 whole, 7 whites, or 14 yolks, large	1 cup	
	3 large		2 jumbo, 3 extra-large, 3 medium, or 4 small
	4 large		3 jumbo, 4 extra-large, 5 medium, or 5 small
	6 large		5 jumbo, 5 extra-large, 7 medium, or 8 small
Figs, dried	1 lb	3 cups chopped	
Filo leaves	1-lb pkg	about 25 leaves	
Flour, all-purpose and whole wheat	1 lb 1 cup 1 cup	3½ cups unsifted	 1 cup plus 2 tbsp cake flour 1 cup self-rising flour; omit any salt and baking powder listed in the recipe
Flour, cake	1 lb 1 cup	4½ cups sifted	 1 cup less 2 tbsp all-purpose flour (with 2 tbsp cornstarch added if possible)
Flour, self-rising, unsifted	1 cup	5 oz	1 cup all-purpose flour plus 1½ tsp baking powder and ½ tsp salt
Garlic	2 medium cloves	1 tsp minced	
Gelatin	1 envelope	1 tbsp	4 sheets gelatin
Ginger, fresh	2-inch piece	2 tbsp grated or chopped	
Green onions, white part only	1 bunch (about 7)	½ cup chopped	
Hazelnuts, shelled	1 cup	5 oz	
Herbs	1 tbsp (3 tsp) fresh	1 tsp dried herbs	

	Substitutions and Equivalents, continued	
FOOD	**AMOUNT**	**EQUIVALENT/WEIGHT SUBSTITUTE**
Horseradish, fresh	1 tbsp grated	2 tbsp prepared horseradish
Kasha (buckwheat groats)	1 cup	2½ to 3 cups cooked
Leeks	2 lb trimmed	4 cups sliced or chopped
Lemons	1 medium	1 to 3 tbsp juice, 1½ tsp zest
Lentils, dried	1 cup	2½ cups cooked
Lettuce, butter	1 head	4 cups torn leaves
Lettuce, leaf and romaine	1 head (1 lb)	8 cups torn leaves
Limes	1 medium	1½ to 2 tbsp juice
Lobster	2 lb live	⅔ to 1 cup cooked meat
Mangoes	1 lb	1½ cups chopped
Milk, whole	1 cup	• ½ cup evaporated milk and ½ cup water; reduce the sugar in the recipe slightly • 1 cup skim milk plus 1 tbsp cream or melted butter
Mushrooms, fresh	4 oz	1 cup sliced, 1½ cups chopped
Mustard, dry	1 tsp	1 tbsp prepared mustard
Nectarines	3 to 4 (1 lb)	2 cups sliced
Nuts, whole	4 oz	¾ to 1 cup chopped, 1 cup ground
Oats	1 cup	2 cups cooked
Onions	1 medium	½ to ⅔ cup chopped
Oranges	1 medium	⅓ cup juice, 2 to 3 tbsp zest
Pasta	8 oz	3½ cups cooked
Peaches	4 medium (1 lb)	2 cups peeled and sliced
Pears	3 medium (1 lb)	2 cups peeled and sliced
Peas	1 lb in shell 10-oz pkg	1 cup shelled 2 cups
Pecans	1 cup	4 oz
Peppers, bell	1 large	1 cup chopped
Pineapple	1 medium	3 cups cubes
Pistachios	1 lb in shell	2 cups shelled
Plums	6 medium (1 lb)	2½ cups halved and pitted

Substitutions and Equivalents, continued

Food	Amount	Equivalent/Weight	Substitute
Potatoes, white and sweet	1 lb	3 cups sliced, 2 cups mashed	
Prunes	1 lb	2½ cups pitted	
Pumpkin	3 to 4 lb	3½ cups puréed	
Purée	½ cup	About 1 cup berries, fruit, or cooked vegetables	
Raisins	1 cup	5 oz	
Rhubarb	1 lb	2 cups cooked	
Rice, brown	1 cup	3 to 4 cups cooked	
Rice, white and wild	1 cup	3 cups cooked	
Shallots	1 large	1 tbsp minced	
Shortening	1 lb	2 cups	2 cups butter (baking)
Shrimp	1 lb jumbo 1 lb large 1 lb medium	10 to 15 16 to 20 25 to 30	
Sour cream	1 cup	8 oz	1 cup plain yogurt
Spinach	1 lb bunched, or 10-oz bag	¾ cup chopped and cooked	
Split peas	2 cups	2½ cups cooked	
Squash, summer	1 lb	3½ cups sliced	
Squash, winter	3 lb	3 cups puréed	
Sugar, brown	1 lb 1 cup	2¼ cups packed	1 cup granulated sugar combined with 2 tbsp light or dark molasses
Sugar, confectioners'	1 lb	3½ to 4 cups	
Sugar, granulated	1 cup	8 oz	⅞ cup honey
Tapioca, instant	1 tbsp		1 tbsp flour
Tapioca flour	½ tbsp		1 tbsp flour
Tomatillos	5 to 6 whole		13-oz can, drained
Tomatoes	3 medium (1 lb)	1½ cups chopped	
Tomato sauce	2 cups		¾ cup tomato paste plus 1 cup water

Substitutions and Equivalents, continued

FOOD	AMOUNT	EQUIVALENT/WEIGHT	SUBSTITUTE
Vanilla	1 tsp extract		1-inch piece vanilla bean, halved and scraped
Yeast, active dry	1 pkg	2¼ tsp	1 cake (0.06 oz) compressed yeast
Yogurt, plain	1 cup	8 oz	

SUET See FAT & OIL.

SUGAR The Arabs introduced sugar to Europe and cultivated sugarcane in Sicily and Spain. Later it was shipped there from the sugarcane fields cultivated in the New World colonies. It was an expensive luxury until 1747, when a German physicist discovered that sugar could also be extracted from a type of beet. Only then did it become widely available in Europe. Today, it is sold in many different forms and has become an essential ingredient in cooking. Sugar sweetens, helps foods to caramelize and to stay fresh longer, encourages yeast to grow in bread dough, gives stability to egg whites, and preserves foods.

Granulated Sugar The most common sugar is granulated white sugar, which has been extracted from sugarcane or beets and refined by boiling, centrifuging, chemical treatment, and straining. For baking recipes, buy only sugar that is specifically labeled cane sugar; beet sugar will have an unpredictable effect on many recipes. SUPERFINE When finely ground, granulated sugar becomes superfine sugar,

known as castor or caster sugar in England. Because it dissolves rapidly, it is preferred for cold recipes such as mixed drinks (it is also sold as bar sugar) and delicate mixtures such as beaten egg whites.

Confectioners' Sugar Crushed to a powder and mixed with a little cornstarch to prevent lumping, granulated sugar becomes confectioners' (or powdered) sugar, known as icing sugar in England. It is used for dusting foods and decorating plates and in icings and candies. Even though confectioners' sugar has been treated, it still forms little lumps in the package and should be sifted before using in most recipes.

Dusting a cake with confectioners' sugar.

Brown Sugar Brown sugar is simply granulated sugar colored with molasses. It has a rich flavor and a soft, moist texture and is available as mild-flavored light brown sugar or the more strongly flavored dark brown sugar. Granulated brown sugar, also called Brownulated sugar, is good for

Quick Tip

To make your own superfine sugar, simply whirl granulated sugar in a blender or in a food processor fitted with the metal blade.

sprinkling because it is dry and doesn't clump. It should not be used as a substitute for brown sugar in baking, however.

BROWN SUGAR SAVVY When using brown sugar, keep the following in mind:

- To soften hardened brown sugar, place a cut piece of apple in a container or plastic bag of brown sugar and close it tightly for a day or so. It can also be softened by sprinkling it with a little water and placing it in a 200°F oven for a few minutes.
- To sprinkle brown sugar evenly over dishes such as crème brûlée, push it through a small sieve with the back of a spoon.
- To keep brown sugar soft, refrigerate it in a tightly closed container.

Other Sugars

COARSE SUGAR Coarse sugar, also called sugar crystals or sanding sugar, comes in large granules and is used to decorate cookies, cakes, sweet breads, and candies. It is available in some cookware stores and in specialty-food stores.

COLORED SUGAR Colored sugar comes in different hues and in both coarse and fine grains. It is used for decorating cakes and cookies and is available in most well-stocked supermarkets.

DATE SUGAR Date sugar is made from ground dried dates. It does not dissolve well, but it may be used in cooking and some baking.

JAGGERY SUGAR Also called palm sugar, jaggery is made from palm tree sap or sugarcane. This unrefined sugar has dark, coarse grains and is used in Indian and Southeast Asian cooking. It is available as a soft spread and as a solid cake. Look for it in Indian markets. Dark brown sugar may be substituted for piloncillo and jaggery.

MAPLE SUGAR Maple sugar is made by boiling maple sap almost dry. It is twice as sweet as granulated white sugar and is often made into molded candies attractively packaged for gift giving.

PILONCILLO SUGAR Piloncillo is an unrefined Mexican sugar that is formed into blocks or dark brown tapered cones. It is available in Latin markets.

RAW SUGAR The sugars marketed as "raw" in the United States are actually partially refined. Turbinado, which has light brown coarse crystals, has been washed with steam. Demerara sugar and Barbados sugar are also raw sugars that have been purified. A sugar that retains much of the nutritive value of unrefined sugar is Sucanat, which is a dark brown granulated sugar made by dehydrating the juice of organically grown sugarcane. It has a nutty, molasses-like flavor. Organic sugar is also made from evaporated sugarcane juice, clarified to make a light tan granulated sugar that pours easily and has a warm, clean flavor.

ROCK SUGAR Amber-colored rock sugar, used in some Chinese dishes, comes in large crystals and is made by cooking sugar until it begins to caramelize. It is not as sweet as granulated white sugar.

HOW TO *Make Simple Syrup*

Make a jar of this syrup and keep it on hand in your refrigerator to use in making cocktails, ice cream and sorbet mixtures, frostings and candies, and for poaching fruit. For a heavy syrup, use equal parts sugar and water; for a medium syrup, use 2 parts water and 1 part sugar; and for a thin syrup, use 3 parts water and 1 part sugar. Plan on the following yield: 1 cup sugar will make about 1 cup heavy syrup, 2 cups medium syrup, or 3 cups thin syrup.

1. Combine equal parts granulated sugar and water in a heavy saucepan. Place over low heat and stir until the sugar has dissolved.
2. Bring to a boil and cook without stirring for 1 minute. Pour into a glass jar. Cover and refrigerate indefinitely.

See also CANDY MAKING; CORN SYRUP; HONEY; MAPLE SYRUP; MOLASSES.

SUGAR SYRUP See CANDY MAKING; SUGAR.

SUNCHOKE See JERUSALEM ARTICHOKE.

SUN-DRIED TOMATO Fresh tomatoes dried in the sun (or in special dehydrators or in a very low oven) take on a deep, intense tomato flavor and chewy, dense texture. Sun-dried tomatoes make a simple topping for a pizza or can 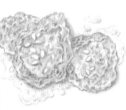 be tucked inside a sandwich. Use them in salads or to season braises and stews.

Selecting Sun-dried tomatoes are sold dry, often loose in plastic bags or in bulk, or packed in jars of olive oil. Those packed in oil tend to be sweeter and have more flavor than the dry-packed ones.

Storing Once opened, jars of oil-packed sun-dried tomatoes should be stored in the refrigerator. Dry-packed tomatoes should be stored airtight in a cool, dry place. They will last indefinitely.

Preparing Oil-packed sun-dried tomatoes can be used straight from the jar, after being drained. Dry-packed ones must be rehydrated before using.

HOW TO *Rehydrate Dry-Packed Sun-Dried Tomatoes*

1. In a bowl, cover the tomatoes with hot water and let stand for about 30 minutes.
2. Drain the tomatoes, reserving the soaking liquid. It can lend a good tomato flavor to soups, braises, and stews.

Quick Tip

A second, more flavorful, way to rehydrate dry-packed sun-dried tomatoes is to cover them with extra-virgin olive oil and let stand for 24 hours. Refrigerate the tomatoes in the oil and keep them for several months. Use the oil for salad dressing, drizzle it over toasted bread, or toss it with hot pasta.

The oil in which sun-dried tomatoes are packed has a rich tomato flavor and is often too good to be discarded. Taste it and use it for making salad dressings or brush it over pizzas still warm from the oven.

SWEATING A French technique of cooking food, usually vegetables, over low heat in a little fat in a covered pan. Sweating causes the food to release its juices and to cook without browning, thereby concentrating the flavor of the food. A variation of this technique is the preliminary step in many recipes that calls for sautéing onions, shallots, and/or garlic until translucent or just tender.

SWEETBREADS The thymus glands of calves or lambs. Each gland has two lobes, one elongated and the other round, both with the same subtle, rich flavor and delicate texture. Veal sweetbreads are widely considered better, while those of lamb are less common. Sweetbreads are blanched, then often breaded and fried and sauced.

Selecting Look for sweetbreads that are plump, compact, and surrounded by a shiny membrane. There should be no dark spots.

Storing Sweetbreads are highly perishable. Refrigerate them as soon as you get home, and serve the day of purchase.

Preparing Sweetbreads must be peeled and firmed before cooking. Long cooking will destroy their delicate texture; cook

s

them quickly to preserve their tenderness. Sweetbreads can be poached whole or sliced and sautéed.

HOW TO *Peel and Firm Sweetbreads*

1. Cover the sweetbreads with water, bring to a gentle boil, reduce the heat to low, and simmer for about 5 minutes.
2. Drain and transfer to a bowl of cold water. Pull off the membrane that covers each sweetbread and remove any fat and tubes, working with the sweetbreads in the water.
3. Drain and put the sweetbreads on a tray and cover with plastic wrap. Top with a plate and weight it evenly with heavy cans or other items. Refrigerate until firm, about 3 hours.

SWEETENED CONDENSED MILK
See MILK.

SWEET PEPPER See BELL PEPPER.

SWEET POTATO Another of the New World's contributions to the world larder, the sweet potato has either yellow-brown skin and yellow flesh, or dark reddish or purplish skin and dark orange flesh. The latter is commonly known in the United States as a yam, although it is a different species from the true yam.

Sweet potato (below) vs. "yam" (above).

Both types of sweet potato may be cooked in a wide variety of ways. Baked whole, they are served with or without a sweet or savory topping. Cubed or sliced, they are baked with a sweet glaze. They also can be cooked and puréed and served alongside meat or poultry—often pork, ham, or turkey—or used to make a pie filling similar to pumpkin pie. A staple of Southern and tropical cooking, sweet potatoes are puréed and topped with marshmallows, then baked as a Thanksgiving side dish; added in chunks to stews and soups; and candied as a holiday treat in Mexico.

Selecting Sweet potatoes are available year-round, but their true seasons are fall and winter. Choose firm, unblemished sweet potatoes without any breaks in their thin skin.

Storing Sweet potatoes do not keep well. Store them in a cool, dark place, but plan to use them within a week or so.

Preparing To bake whole sweet potatoes, scrub them well first and prick their skins in a few places with a fork. Place them on a baking sheet to catch their juices, and bake in a preheated 400°F oven until they are tender when pierced with a knife, about 45 minutes. They may then be peeled and sliced or cut into chunks for glazing, or puréed. You can also peel uncooked sweet potatoes and cook them in salted boiling water until tender before glazing or puréeing.

See also STEAMING; YAM.

SWISS CHARD See GREENS, DARK; STEAMING.

T

*everything from tahini
to turnip*

TAHINI This paste, made from ground sesame seeds, has a rich, creamy flavor and a concentrated sesame taste. Tahini, also called sesame paste, is used in the popular chickpea spread known as hummus and in baba ghanoush, a Middle Eastern eggplant purée. It is also combined with lemon juice and seasonings to make *taratoor,* a thin Middle Eastern sauce used as a dip for vegetables and pita bread, as a dressing for salads, and as a sauce for fish, vegetables, and falafel. The oil often separates from the paste and should be stirred in before using.
Storing After opening, tahini can be refrigerated for up to 2 months.

Quick Tip

Turn a jar of tahini upside down occasionally and let it stand for a few days so that the oil redistributes itself throughout the paste.

TAMARIND Also known as Indian date, tamarind is the fruit of a tropical tree. The long, dark pods are filled with small seeds and a distinct sweet-and-sour pulp that is dried and used in Indian, Southeast Asian, and Middle Eastern kitchens in much the same way that cooks in the West use lemon

juice. Tamarind is available in several forms. In addition to whole pods, you may find blocks of tamarind paste and frozen pouches of pulp. There is also frozen nectar, sweetened tamarind syrup, and tamarind concentrate.

Tamarind pulp.

Tamarind pairs beautifully with aromatic seasonings such as ginger, garlic, chiles, and coconut milk, and Indian cooks have long used it in chutneys, relishes, curries, and preserves. In Mexico, tamarind is used to flavor one version of the refreshing fruit drinks known as *aguas frescas.* Western cooks have begun to experiment with the fruit, using it in sorbets and salad dressings. Tamarind's natural acidity helps to tenderize tougher cuts of meats, making it a popular ingredient for marinades in both Asian and Latin American kitchens.
Selecting Locating tamarind in pod form may take a bit of searching. It is increasingly available in large supermarkets, but you may need to search your local specialty-food stores and Asian, Latin, or Middle Eastern markets to find it. Fresh whole pods should bend easily in your hands. As an alternative, look for packaged blocks of paste or frozen pouches of pulp.
Storing Pods and unopened packages of tamarind paste will keep indefinitely when stored in a cool, dry place. Once opened, packages of paste can be refrigerated for about 3 months.
Preparing To use the whole dried pods: For 1 cup of tamarind pulp you will need about 4½ ounces dried pods. Open the pods and remove the seeds. Combine the

t

pods with 1 cup of warm water and let soak for about 20 minutes. Pour through a fine-mesh sieve, pressing the pulp through the sieve with the back of a large wooden spoon. Stir to combine, then refrigerate in a tightly sealed glass jar for up to 1 week.

HOW TO *Use Packaged Tamarind Paste*

1. Use a knife to cut off about 2 ounces of the pulp. In a bowl, combine the pulp with about ½ cup warm water.
2. Soak for about 20 minutes before straining. Makes about ¾ cup.

TAMARI SAUCE See SOY FOODS.

TANGERINE See MANDARIN ORANGE.

TAPAS (TOP-uhs) Small, flavorful appetizers that appear in bars and restaurants all over Spain. Tapas may be hot or cold, as simple as a bowl of olives or a more involved dish such as Spanish tortilla, which is related to an omelet; fried squid; or grilled pork with romesco sauce.

TAPENADE Capers, anchovies, and garlic are some of the other ingredients that go into this classic Provençal olive spread. The ingredients are mashed into a paste, preferably with a mortar and pestle, and the paste is used as a spread for grilled bread, smeared on pizzas, or used as a dip for vegetables and crudités. It may also be used as an ingredient in sauces, such as for pasta, and marinades, especially for grilled foods. A little tapenade goes a long way, as its flavor is highly concentrated and salty. The ingredients (other than olives) and their proportions often vary, although the word *tapenade* comes from the Provençal word *tapeno,* meaning capers, and these tiny buds are usually considered an essential part of the dish. Some tapenades contain lemon juice or other seasonings and/or tuna fish. By contrast, *olivada* is an Italian spread made only of black olives, olive oil, and black pepper.

Both green and black tapenades, made from either green or black olives, are usually available in jars in specialty-food stores and many supermarkets in the United States. In their home in the south of France, a dazzling variety of tapenades, freshly made from a wide range of olives, are sold at weekly street markets.

Storing Once opened, tapenade should be kept in the refrigerator for up to 6 months.

See also ANCHOVY; CAPER; OLIVE.

TAPIOCA A starchy substance derived from the root of the cassava plant, tapioca can be used to thicken sauces and fruit fillings for pies, as well to make a dessert enjoyed by children everywhere. Tapioca comes in three basic forms, pearl (small dried balls of tapioca starch), granulated (coarsely broken-up pearl tapioca), or instant (very finely granulated pearl tapioca). Asian markets and some supermarkets carry tapioca flour, also called tapioca starch, which is used much like cornstarch.

Selecting For tapioca pudding, choose either pearl, granulated, or instant tapioca. To thicken sauces and fruit fillings, choose either instant tapioca or tapioca flour.

Storing All forms of tapioca will keep indefinitely in a cool, dark place.

Preparing Pearl tapioca should be soaked in cold water for an hour before using. Granulated and instant tapioca do not need soaking. As a thickener, 1 tablespoon instant tapioca or 1½ teaspoons tapioca flour can be substituted for 1 tablespoon flour.

TARRAGON See HERB.

TART See PIE & TART.

TARTAR SAUCE See SAUCE.

TART PAN See BAKEWARE.

TASTING The tasting of a dish during and after preparation is one of the keys to good cooking because the level of the seasoning needed can be affected by many factors. For example, some fruits need more or less sugar, depending on their natural sugars and degree of ripeness, while some vegetables and other foods not at their peak of flavor may need more seasoning. Temperature also affects the taste of foods. Flavors are strongest when heated, so chilled and frozen foods need relatively more seasoning. Ice cream, for example, must be made from a base that tastes very sweet at room temperature, as freezing will dull the sweetness. The good cook tastes a dish throughout the making of it. If a dish doesn't taste right at any stage of preparation, it won't taste right when it's done.

Recipes often specify salt and other ingredients "to taste" or give a range of amounts, as some people need to limit their salt intake and others prefer their dishes more or less spicy or piquant. When using salt or such assertive flavors as cayenne or rosemary, always use the smallest amount specified. You can always add more later to suit your taste—but you can't take it away.

"To taste" is not always meant literally, however. In foods that can't be tasted with pleasure, such as salted raw eggplant, or that could endanger your health, such as raw poultry or meat mixtures, this phrase means to use the seasoning lightly or moderately, as you prefer. (Some people are careful not to taste batters made with raw egg, because of concern for salmonella. A small portion of a raw meat mixture can be cooked until it has lost all pinkness throughout and then tasted for seasoning.)

Whether or not a recipe method says to "taste and adjust the seasoning," always taste a completed dish before you plan to serve it, and add more of any of the seasonings it seems to need. This is particularly true for highly or complexly seasoned dishes that depend for their success on the proper balance of seasonings.

See also ADJUSTING THE SEASONING.

TEA A cup of tea manages to be both calming and stimulating at the same time. Perhaps that's why tea always has gone hand in hand with meditation and reflection. The amount of theophylline, a close relative of caffeine, in black tea is just enough to keep you awake and aware, while the act of drinking the hot, fragrant brew seems to offer comfort and solace. Native to China, tea began to be cultivated there around 2000 B.C. Exported to Europe in the 17th century, it created a sensation, especially in England, where it is still favored over coffee, that other stimulating beverage.

There are three common types of tea leaves: black, green, and oolong. (A fourth kind, white tea, is very rare.) These three all come from the same species of plant, which produces different-tasting teas depending on where the plant was grown and how it was processed. The best teas grow at the highest altitudes and consist of the smallest new-growth leaves and the unopened leaf buds, picked by hand. Black tea leaves are fermented, then heated and dried. Green tea leaves, by contrast, are steamed and dried without fermenting, and oolong tea is made from leaves that are partially fermented. Black tea leaves produce a dark, full-flavored brew, while green tea is a pale greenish yellow with a flowery flavor and astringent taste. Oolong tea is lighter than black tea and darker than green. The best known is Formosa oolong, which is appreciated for its bright and fruity flavor.

The names of black teas can be confusing. Many black tea blends, for example, were long ago given an arbitrary name, such as Earl Grey, English breakfast, or Prince of Wales, designed to intrigue the British consumer. Other teas—such as Assam and Ceylon—are instead named for their place of origin. Still other black teas are named for the size of their leaves, such as pekoe (medium leaves) and orange pekoe (small leaves), while the *souchong* in Lapsang Souchong signifies large leaves.

Green teas have a grassy, slightly bitter taste that seems to go perfectly with Asian food. Like black tea, green tea is high in vitamin C, while containing less theophylline, tea's natural stimulant. In addition, both black and green teas are beneficial to healthy teeth and gums.

A number of flavored teas exist, from Earl Grey (which is flavored with bergamot oil) and teas scented with flowers to newer teas flavored with fruits such as mango and peach. Herbal teas, known also as tisanes, are not technically teas but rather infusions of herbs and other flavorings. They are valued for their reputed health benefits, which vary from herb to herb.

In the United States, tea is often served cold, sweetened and iced, usually with lemon. Bottled iced teas are also popular. Instant iced tea and decaffeinated black tea may be found in supermarkets.

Tea is also used as a cooking ingredient, the best-known examples being tea-smoked duck and tea eggs. The latter are flavored and colored by steeping them in tea. Green tea is used to make a refreshing ice cream.

Selecting The world of tea is wide and varied. As with wine, there are so many different styles and flavors that you could spend years learning about this drink. Common commercial brands are made from blends of inferior bits of leaves. Look instead for high-quality teas sold in coffeehouses, tea shops, or specialty-food stores. Herbal teas are available in natural-food stores.

Storing Teas are available in loose form or in tea bags in foil- or plastic-lined packages. Store tea in its packaging in an airtight container in a cool, dark place for up to 1 year.

Preparing Although the tea bag is a marvel of convenience, it does not make the best tea, as the leaves are unable to circulate in the hot water and fully release their essence. The best solution is to spoon loose tea into the bottom of a pot. If you prefer not to deal with a few tea leaves in the bottom of your cup, use a strainer or a pot that comes with its own infuser, or buy the largest metal-mesh tea ball you can.

Tea ball.

HOW TO *Make a Pot of Tea*

1. Choose a ceramic teapot that is just the size of the amount of tea you are making. Bring a teapotful of water to a boil in a kettle.
2. Pour the boiling water into the teapot, cover the pot with its lid, and set it aside to warm. Fill the kettle with 1 cup fresh cold spring water or filtered water per cup of tea you are brewing and bring it just to a boil.
3. Turn off the kettle and let it sit for a minute. (Like coffee, tea is best when made with water that is slightly below boiling temperature.) Empty the teapot. Add 1 level teaspoon loose tea per cup to the teapot, to the teapot's infuser, or to a large metal-mesh tea ball. Add the infuser or tea ball, if using, to the pot and pour in the hot water. Cover the pot.
4. Let the tea steep for 1 to 3 minutes for green tea and 3 to 6 minutes for black tea. Oolong teas take from 6 to 8 minutes, while herbal teas need 8 to 12 minutes.
5. Stir the tea in the pot or in the infuser or swirl the tea ball around in the tea to extract more flavor from the leaves, then remove the infuser or ball from the pot. If necessary, pour the tea through a strainer into each cup.
6. If you have made more than 2 cups, use a tea cozy or wrap the teapot in a thick kitchen towel to help keep the tea hot.

HOW TO *Make Sun-Brewed Iced Tea*

1. Fill a clear glass or plastic container with cold water, keeping track of the amount of water as you fill the container.
2. Measure 3 tablespoons of leaves per quart of water. Place in a tea ball (you may need more than one).
3. Placing the container in direct sunlight, steep the tea in the water for 2 to 3 hours, or until it is strong enough for your taste.

TECHNIQUES Those folks fortunate enough to have grown up in a household with a good cook who shared his or her knowledge will find the ability to execute cooking techniques an almost natural occurrence when they are finally in their own kitchen. After years of watching while standing beside someone who is comfortable in the kitchen, these students will instinctively know how to seed a tomato, measure a cup of flour, or truss a chicken. When a recipe calls for reducing a sauce, blanching a green vegetable, clarifying a stock, barding a lean bird, or deglazing a pan, they will act almost without thinking.

Not everyone is so fortunate. But anyone can learn to become a good cook by trial and error, persistence, and openness to gleaning insights from any source he or she can find.

The complete mastery of cooking techniques begins with understanding how to perform the most basic kitchen tasks, such as chopping an onion, dredging a chicken breast, beating egg whites until stiff, or frosting a cake. Depending on the specific interests of a particular cook, it can extend to such exotic techniques as opening a sea urchin, assembling a *pâté en croûte,* hanging a game bird to age and season, or fashioning a marzipan blossom. Technique reaches all the way to presentation, whether the recipe calls for piping an attractive filling for stuffed eggs, hollowing out a pineapple to hold a fruit salad, or floating paper-thin vegetable slices atop a clear soup.

For complete information on basic cooking techniques, see individual technique listings throughout this book.

TEMPEH See SOY FOODS.

TEMPERATURE The definitions of some key temperatures vary, as you will see if you compare temperature charts among several different cookbooks. The chart on page 446 shows commonly accepted temperatures for different stages of cooking, oven heats, and other conditions.

Key Temperatures Chart

Freezer	0°F
Refrigerator	8° to 40°F
Cool room temperature	65°F
Warm room temperature	70° to 75°F
Lukewarm (tepid) liquid	95°F
Warm liquid	105° to 115°F
Hot liquid	120°F
Boiling water	212°F
Warm temperature for rising bread	80°F
Low/slow oven	180° to 200°F
Warm oven	300° to 325°F
Moderate oven	350° to 375°F
Hot oven	400° to 450°F
Very hot oven	475° to 500°F

See also DONENESS; HIGH-ALTITUDE COOKING; MEASURING; ROASTING; SAFETY.

TEMPERING Tempering means to melt and cool chocolate to very specific temperatures in order to create a shiny, smooth patina once it rehardens. Tempering also means to heat beaten eggs slightly before adding them to hot liquid, in order to keep them from curdling.

Tempered chocolate is preferred for candy coatings, molded candies, and decorations because it is silkier and more malleable and flavorful than untempered chocolate, and it breaks with a "snap" when bitten. Tempering chocolate also prevents "bloom," the white coating caused by excessive heat or humidity.

To temper bittersweet or semisweet chocolate, the melted chocolate is heated to 115° to 118°F, which breaks down the microscopic structure of the cocoa butter crystals. The chocolate is then cooled to 89° to 91°F, which causes the crystals to align perfectly. (The temperatures for tempering milk chocolate and white chocolate are slightly lower.)

HOW TO *Temper Bittersweet or Semisweet Chocolate*

This is one of the simplest ways to temper chocolate. It is sometimes known as the quick tempering method.

1. Chop the chocolate with a large chef's knife. Melt two-thirds of the chocolate in a double boiler over not-quite-simmering water until it reaches a temperature of 115° to 118°F on a candy thermometer. Make sure the bottom of the chocolate pan does not touch the water, and stir the chocolate occasionally as it melts.

2. Remove the upper portion of the double boiler from the bottom portion. Stir in the remaining one-third chopped chocolate until the mixture cools to 89° to 91°F, or until a little of the chocolate dabbed on your upper lip or inside wrist feels cool.

3. Place the pan in a larger pan of tepid water or on a heating pad to keep the chocolate at a constant 89° to 91°F while you work with it. If the temperature falls so much that the chocolate becomes hard to work with, you may reheat it to a maximum of 91°F. If you exceed this temperature, however, the chocolate will lose temper and you will have to repeat the entire process again.

Quick Tip

To test whether chocolate is in temper, spoon a little on a saucer and refrigerate it until hardened and set, 2 to 3 minutes. If it looks glossy, the chocolate is in temper.

To temper eggs, beat a little hot milk or cream into the beaten eggs, then gradually whisk the egg mixture into the hot liquid.

TEMPURA In its simplest description, Japanese tempura is batter-coated, deep-fried fish and vegetables. The basic method was introduced to the island nation by Portuguese missionaries in the 16th century (the word *tempura* reputedly comes from the Portuguese *tempora,* a day of abstinence from meat), but the Japanese developed it into an art, producing lacy, nongreasy, crisp morsels. The requisite dipping sauce is made from fish stock, soy sauce, and mirin (sweet cooking wine).

TENDERIZING See POUNDING.

TEQUILA See SPIRITS.

TERIYAKI A favorite Japanese dish among Americans, although its definition differs depending on whether you are in Japan or the United States. In the former, teriyaki is a sauce brushed onto chicken, fish, or meat during the final stages of grilling or panfrying, while in the latter the term refers to chicken, fish, or meat that has been marinated in the sauce before grilling, or sometimes simply coated with the sauce just before grilling. The bottled sweet sauce is widely available in supermarkets and can be used as a glaze on nearly any grilled food. You can make a simple home version by mixing equal parts sake, mirin (sweet cooking wine), or sherry and dark soy sauce with sugar to taste.

TERRINE A rectangular or oval heat-proof cooking and serving dish. Pâté mixtures are classically cooked in terrines. When served from the dish, the food is also called a terrine, or *pâté en ter-*  *rine,* although it may also simply be called a pâté. The dishes are usually made of heavy earthenware or enameled iron, but porcelain or Pyrex are also used.

See also PÂTÉ.

THAWING The process of restoring frozen food to room temperature is called thawing, or defrosting. Frozen poultry, meat, and fish should be thawed in the refrigerator to keep bacteria from multiplying. Large pieces of meat (over 4 pounds) will take 4 to 7 hours per pound to defrost this way; steaks and chops will take 8 to 14 hours or overnight. A whole chicken will take 12 to 16 hours, while a frozen turkey, depending on size, can take 2 to 5 days to thaw fully; figure on 3 to 4 hours per pound of poultry.

Thin pieces of meat, fish, or chicken may be thawed at room temperature in less than 2 hours. Or, put the food in a zippered plastic bag and immerse it in a large container or sink of cold water. This will generally cut the thawing time by about one-third. Food defrosted this way, however, will lose more of its juices and be drier when cooked.

Caution!

Thawing food in warm water is not safe. This encourages the growth of bacteria.

Meat, fish, or chicken may also be thawed in a microwave, although it will also lose some of its moisture and must be watched carefully. Wrap the food in waxed paper and microwave on Low in 5-minute increments; let the food stand for 5 minutes; and then check to see if it has thawed. Repeat as necessary until the food is barely thawed. Food thawed this way should be cooked immediately.

Vegetables may be safely thawed at room temperature or by cooking them in a small amount of boiling water.

See also FOOD SAFETY; FREEZING.

THERMOMETER See BAKING; COOK-ING TOOLS; SAFETY; TEMPERATURE.

THICKENING Sauces depend on numerous ingredients and techniques for the alchemy that turns a thin liquid into a velvety substance to dress or accompany food. Other dishes, from soups to desserts, also use thickeners to give them body. Following is a list of thickening agents and methods used in various cuisines and dishes.

Agar-agar A seaweed-based gelatin used in Asia and preferred by vegetarians to animal-derived gelatin. See SEAWEED.

Arrowroot Often used in place of cornstarch or flour in puddings and sauces, as it doesn't have the chalky taste of undercooked cornstarch and it is more easily digested than wheat. Use half as much arrowroot as flour and the same amount as cornstarch, and stir it into liquid before adding it to a dish. Arrowroot will give a sauce a lovely sheen. The thickening effect will not hold up to reheating.

Butter A little butter (1 tablespoon per $\frac{1}{4}$ cup of sauce) stirred into sauce at the end of cooking will "finish" or "mount" the sauce, adding gloss and flavor and thickening it very slightly. Serve immediately.

Cornstarch Used in Asian cooking to thicken stir-fry sauces and in American cooking to thicken some pie fillings and puddings, cornstarch will give a sauce a glossy sheen. It should be dissolved in cold liquid before being added to other ingredients: stir 1 tablespoon cornstarch into 2 tablespoons water in a small cup until dissolved. This amount will thicken about 1 cup liquid. To substitute for flour, use half as much cornstarch as flour. Cornstarch can have a chalky taste if it is undercooked, so when adding it to sauces, be sure to stir for several minutes over heat. Boiling can cause a cornstarch-thickened sauce to separate. See also CORNSTARCH.

Cream Heavy cream added to a hot sauce or soup will thicken it slightly. Add 2 tablespoons per $\frac{1}{4}$ cup of sauce. Beaten heavy cream is used to thicken mousses and some puddings and other desserts.

Egg Yolks When olive oil or melted butter is beaten into egg yolks, the yolks gradually absorb the liquid and emulsify, thickening to make mayonnaise and butter sauce, respectively. Egg yolks beaten with wine and sugar over heat thicken to make zabaglione, also called sabayon or sabayon sauce, and when whisked over heat with warm milk and sugar they thicken to become crème anglaise, or custard sauce. Heat gently to avoid curdling.

Flour Flour is a common thickener, but it must be used correctly. When you add flour directly into a liquid, it may clump. It will also add the raw taste of flour to a mixture unless the mixture is cooked for at least several minutes after the flour is added. Flour can be gradually whisked into a small amount of milk, water, or stock until all lumps disappear. The mixture, known as a slurry, is then added to another liquid and cooked to thicken it. Or, flour may be mixed with fat, as when making a roux (see below), and cooked for a few minutes to remove the raw flour taste before it is incorporated into a liquid.

Quick Tip

The consistency of a gravy or sauce depends on the amount of flour used: for thin, use 1 tablespoon flour for 1 cup of liquid; for medium-thick, use 2 tablespoons flour for 1 cup of liquid; and for thick, use 3 tablespoons of flour for 1 cup of liquid.

BEURRE MANIÉ A French technique for thickening and enriching sauces and stews at the end of cooking is to blend equal parts flour and soft butter to make a paste, *beurre manié.* The sauce is removed from the heat, the paste is whisked in, and the sauce is stirred over heat until thickened.

Roux Another mixture of flour and fat, roux is the basis of a béchamel sauce and is also used to thicken soups and other foods. It is made by heating fat and whisking in flour. After cooking out the raw taste of the flour, liquid is whisked in. A white roux is cooked for 2 to 3 minutes over medium heat. It is usually made with butter, although a mixture of butter and olive oil or all olive oil can be used. For some dishes, the roux is cooked to a pale tan. This blond roux has a toasted taste. Brown roux, cooked until dark and nutty in taste, is made with butter, drippings, or lard, and is one of the foundations of Cajun and Creole cuisine. The darker a roux, however, the less thickening power it has.

For a thin sauce or for soup, make a roux of 1 tablespoon butter mixed with 1 tablespoon flour per 1 cup liquid. For a thicker sauce, use 2 tablespoons butter and 2 tablespoons flour per 1 cup liquid.

Gelatin This animal protein–based substance is dissolved in liquid to add to mixtures that are then allowed to set and thicken. See GELATIN.

Reduction Boiling or simmering a liquid to reduce it in volume both thickens it and concentrates its flavor. See REDUCING.

Starch Pasta cooking water contains starch, so a bit of this water may be reserved and added to a pasta sauce. Potato cooking water is also a good source of starch for thickening sauces.

Tapioca Either tapioca flour or instant tapioca may be used to thicken fruit pie fillings (as long as they are not baked in a lattice-top pie), puddings, or sauces. Don't boil a mixture after tapioca flour has been added, or its consistency can turn gluey. To substitute for flour, use an equivalent amount. See TAPIOCA.

Tomato Paste Use tomato paste to thicken and intensify the taste of a tomato-based sauce. See also TOMATO.

Vegetable Purée Some cooks use puréed vegetables to thicken soups and sauces in place of butter, cream, flour, or egg yolks, both for the sake of lowering calories and fat content and for the clean, interesting tastes that vegetable purées provide. Many soups, such as corn, bean, and potato, are made by puréeing some of the contents for thickness and leaving the rest whole for texture.

THYME See HERB.

TIN FOIL See ALUMINUM FOIL.

TOASTING To heat foods until they are fragrant or lightly browned in order to bring out their flavor and/or to crisp them. Bread is toasted in a toaster, under a broiler, or on a grill to make such toasts as croutons and *crostini,* which are used plain or as a base for butter or other spreads or foods. Nuts, spices, and dried chiles may all be toasted to intensify their flavor before using them in recipes. The quickest way to toast these foods is in a dry pan over medium heat. The food should be stirred frequently and watched carefully to prevent it from burning. The minute it becomes fragrant and/or lightly browned, empty it onto a baking sheet or into a bowl. Even if taken off the heat, the food will continue to cook in the pan, and it might burn. Some cooks prefer to toast nuts in the oven; but watch them very carefully or they may burn. See CHILE; NUT; SPICE.

TOFU The Japanese word for bean curd, or soybean curd. See SOY FOODS.

TOMATILLO Although they look like small green tomatoes and are called *tomates*

t

verdes in Mexico, tomatillos are relatives of the Cape gooseberry, not the tomato. Strip away the papery husk that encloses them to get at one of the essential ingredients for *salsa verde,* the popular Mexican table sauce. Tomatillos have a lemony, herbal flavor that's sharply tart when raw and somewhat tempered by cooking. Some recipes, such as those for raw green salsas, use raw tomatillos, while most others specify poaching them until tender or roasting them on a griddle or in a skillet. Tomatillos are also used in pork stews and in green moles. Canned tomatillos, available in many Latino food stores, lack the spark of fresh but are an acceptable substitute.

Selecting Tomatillos are available off and on throughout the year; they are at their best from August through November. They are most commonly found in Latino markets but are increasingly available in supermarkets and specialty-produce stores. Choose firm, unblemished tomatillos with tightly clinging husks.

Storing Keep tomatillos in a perforated plastic bag in the refrigerator crisper for up to 2 weeks.

Preparing Tomatillos must be husked before use. Use your fingers to peel the brown papery husk under warm running water, and the husk and the sticky, resinous substance that lightly coats the fruit will rinse right off.

Once husked, fresh tomatillos may be added to sauces raw and chopped, to simmer with other ingredients. Some recipes call for them to be briefly boiled in water until their skins split, about 15 minutes. Still other recipes require that they be roasted, either on a dry griddle, in a dry cast-iron frying pan, or on the end of a long-handled fork over a low flame, turning the tomatillo until its surface is evenly golden brown and its flesh is slightly soft, 5 to 10 minutes. No further peeling is required.

TOMATO Once feared as poison, then considered a possible aphrodisiac, the "love apple" now adds its vivid color and delicious flesh to innumerable dishes. Like the potato, this fruit (which is generally treated as a vegetable) is a member of the nightshade family and is native to South America.

After finally gaining acceptance as food in Europe and the United States, tomatoes became an inextricable part of many cuisines, especially those of the Mediterranean. In Italy, they are used to make sauce for pasta, pizza, and many other dishes and are served sliced in salads. Slices of tomato, for example, are served with sliced fresh mozzarella and fresh basil leaves, and the trio is sprinkled with olive oil. Other dishes that depend on tomatoes for their character include minestrone, gazpacho, ratatouille, Greek salad, and tomato soup. And, of course, tomatoes are a staple of New World cuisine, from the American South's fried green tomatoes to Texas's chili con carne, from Latin America's *salsa cruda* to bacon, lettuce, and tomato sandwiches.

Today's health-conscious cooks know that, far from being poisonous, the tomato is high in vitamin C and cancer-fighting antioxidants. The tomato comes in a wide range of sizes, from tiny currant tomatoes no bigger than blueberries to fat beefsteaks up to 5 inches in diameter. The colors are varied, too, from white to purple-black to reddish black, with green-striped zebra tomatoes somewhere in between. Dedicated gardeners have traced and reintroduced a number of heirloom tomatoes, that is, old-fashioned varieties that don't work as well for modern commercial processing. (They may not keep as long, have thinner skins that won't stand up to jostling, or may just have a taste that, delicious though it may be, is less of a crowd-pleaser.) Look for heirloom tomatoes in a wide variety of colors and patterns, with evocative names like Elephant Heart, Lemon Boy, and Golden Jubilee. At the other end of the spectrum, hybridists have introduced many new varieties for the sake of variation in color, size, and other attributes, including thriving in a range of growing conditions.

Sun-dried tomatoes and tomato sauce, purée, and paste are commonly used to flavor a wide variety of dishes. Tomato sauce can be used straight from the can in sauces and casseroles. Tomato purée is a more concentrated version of the sauce, while tomato paste is the thickest and most intense mixture of all. Tomato purée and tomato paste are often used as flavoring agents in soups and sauces.

Selecting Although tomatoes are available year-round, they are at the top of the list of produce that is best when eaten at the height of its natural season. You can find hothouse or imported Mexican tomatoes during the off-season, but in general it is a good idea to wait until local vines are producing, usually June through September, to serve them sliced. If you must choose fresh tomatoes out of season, plum tomatoes and cherry tomatoes are the best bet, as they have more flavor and a better texture than hothouse slicing tomatoes. Otherwise, use canned (or packaged) imported plum tomatoes, usually called Italian tomatoes. They will have a much better flavor than will poor-quality fresh tomatoes.

For the best summer tomatoes, visit farm stands, farmers' markets, and natural-food stores for vine-ripened tomatoes, or grow your own. Most supermarket tomatoes are picked unripe and then ripened with ethylene gas, so they never develop a full flavor. Choose organic tomatoes, if possible, as they are likely to be more flavorful.

Storing Store ripe tomatoes at room temperature for up to 3 days. If they are slightly unripe, put them in a sunny place for several days and they will ripen further. Although whole fresh tomatoes should not be refrigerated, cut tomatoes should be wrapped in plastic or waxed paper and refrigerated. Put leftover canned tomatoes, sauce, purée, and paste in glass jars, cover, and refrigerate for several days.

Preparing Wash and dry tomatoes to be sliced. Cut out the stem end and leave the tomatoes whole or cut them into crosswise or lengthwise slices or into wedges, or chop, according to the recipe. Pull off the stems of cherry tomatoes.

*Chopping
a tomato.*

Some recipes call for peeled and/or seeded tomatoes, usually when the tomatoes are to be chopped for a sauce. For peeling tomatoes, see BLANCHING.

Tomato Glossary

BEEFSTEAK Large, meaty, and delicious variety, bright red to orange.

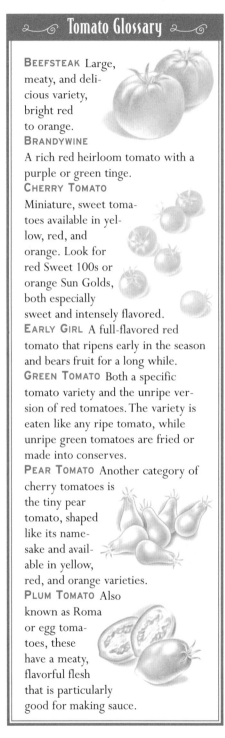

BRANDYWINE A rich red heirloom tomato with a purple or green tinge.

CHERRY TOMATO Miniature, sweet tomatoes available in yellow, red, and orange. Look for red Sweet 100s or orange Sun Golds, both especially sweet and intensely flavored.

EARLY GIRL A full-flavored red tomato that ripens early in the season and bears fruit for a long while.

GREEN TOMATO Both a specific tomato variety and the unripe version of red tomatoes. The variety is eaten like any ripe tomato, while unripe green tomatoes are fried or made into conserves.

PEAR TOMATO Another category of cherry tomatoes is the tiny pear tomato, shaped like its namesake and available in yellow, red, and orange varieties.

PLUM TOMATO Also known as Roma or egg tomatoes, these have a meaty, flavorful flesh that is particularly good for making sauce.

HOW TO *Seed Tomatoes*

1. Cut the tomatoes in half crosswise.
2. Holding each half in turn over a sink or bowl, lightly squeeze and shake it to dislodge the seeds. Use a finger if needed to help ease the seeds out of each half.

A Clever Way to Purée Tomatoes

1. Cut a tomato in half and seed it.
2. Using the small rasps, grate the cut side of the tomato half on a handheld grater.
3. Spread your fingers and press the tomato skin flat as its edges curl up, so that you grate only its pulp. You should end up with a flattened piece of tomato skin.
4. Discard the skin.

See also SUN-DRIED TOMATO.

TOMATO PASTE See TOMATO.

TOMATO PURÉE See TOMATO.

TONGS See COOKING TOOLS.

TOOLS Although only a few basic cooking tools are essential, the right tool can make a difference in the quality of the finished dish and can make cooking more enjoyable. For guidance in developing your own selection of culinary tools, see BAKING TOOLS; COOKING TOOLS.

TORTILLA When the Spanish conquistadores came to Mexico, they found the Indians preparing thin cakes of ground corn, as they had done for centuries. The

Spanish dubbed them *tortillas,* meaning "little round cakes." (In Spain, the word *tortilla* describes a round omelet. The best-known Spanish tortilla is the potato tortilla, popular as a tapa and as a lunch dish. See also FRITTATA; UNMOLDING.)

Corn tortillas were originally made completely by hand from fresh *masa,* a paste made from dried corn that has been softened in a solution of water and the mineral lime. Some are still made that way, but most tortillas today are factory produced. Some cooks use fresh *masa* but form the tortillas in a tortilla press rather than pat them out by hand. When fresh *masa* is unavailable, *masa harina,* a flour made from dried *masa,* is used. After wheat was introduced to Mexico, flour tortillas were developed in the northern part of the country.

Selecting Fresh hand-patted corn tortillas are sometimes available from restaurants or Latino markets. They are thicker and more uneven than tortillas made in a tortilla press, and they are especially good for serving as a bread alongside Mexican food. Look for the freshest corn tortillas you can find. Those purchased directly from a restaurant, market, or tortilla factory will be more pliable and tender than those that have sat in plastic in a supermarket for days. To make your own tortillas, try to get fresh *masa* from one of the same places, as it is easier to work with than dough made from *masa harina.*

Quick Tip

To heat corn or flour tortillas, wrap them in aluminum foil or put them in a clay tortilla warmer and heat in a low oven for about 20 minutes. To heat in a microwave, wrap the tortillas in plastic wrap and heat for 1 minute on one side and 30 seconds on the other.

Quick Tip

Don't throw away stale tortillas. Cut them into triangles and fry or bake them for tortilla chips, or cut them into shreds and fry or bake them for a salad or soup garnish. Mexicans cut stale tortillas into shreds or bits and use them in tortilla soup or bake them with chiles and cheese as casseroles called *chilaquiles.*

Storing Keep tortillas in an airtight plastic bag in the refrigerator. They will keep for several days but are best used sooner rather than later.

See also CORN.

TOSSING To mix ingredients lightly, or to coat them with a sauce or dressing by turning them over several times with two large spoons or your two hands. A somewhat riskier method is to pick up the container and jerk it so that the ingredients fly up in the air a few inches. Salads are customarily tossed to coat them with dressing. Other ingredients such as cooked vegetables that might be crushed or smashed by stirring are also tossed. Professional chefs often toss foods while sautéing or frying them in order to cook them quickly over high heat without burning. See also SALAD; SAUTÉING; STIR-FRYING.

TREE OR WOOD EAR MUSHROOM See MUSHROOM.

TRITICALE See GRAIN.

TRUFFLE No other food has developed quite the same mystique as this knobby, aromatic underground fungus. Until now it has been impossible to cultivate, so finding it has traditionally been a matter of having a good truffle dog or pig who could smell a truffle buried in the earth under oak trees

t
—

453

in Europe. The two most valuable kinds of truffle are the black truffle (sometimes called "black gold") of France, particularly from the Périgord and Quercy areas, and from Umbria in Italy, and the white truffle of the Piedmont in Italy. Truffles have a strong, earthy aroma and are used to flavor a variety of foods. The white truffle is even more powerfully scented than the black, although its flavor is somewhat milder. Black truffles may be cut into very thin slices or matchsticks and added to pâtés and terrines, and they are often used to flavor foie gras. Minced or shaved black truffles are used as a counterpoint to mild foods such as eggs and are added to sauces for meats and poultry for rich flavor. White truffles are used raw, grated or shaved, over cooked pasta, polenta, or risotto.

Black truffles.

White truffle.

Selecting Truffle season begins in late autumn and lasts through the winter. Look for fresh truffles in specialty-food stores. A single truffle is usually packed on a bed of rice in a glass jar. The rice absorbs moisture and keeps the truffle from spoiling. (Be sure to cook the rice, which will have taken on the flavor of the truffle.) Whole, minced, or sliced truffles are available in jars or cans year-round, as is truffle paste in tubes and truffle oil in bottles. Truffle oil is an espe-

cially good way to add the truffle's haunting fragrance to pasta dishes, salads, and main courses. Sprinkle it on hot foods just before serving to preserve the truffle flavor.

Quick Tip

To scent eggs with a truffle, remove it from its jar and bury it in a bowl of eggs in their shells. Cover and refrigerate for 2 to 3 days.

Storing Keep a fresh truffle, in its jar of rice, in the refrigerator, but use within a few days of purchase, or the truffle will dry out and lose fragrance. Canned and jarred truffles, truffle paste, and truffle oil will keep indefinitely in a cool, dark place. Refrigerate them after opening.

Preparing For fresh truffles, brush the truffle clean with a soft mushroom brush or damp kitchen towel. Peel black truffles, saving the peel to flavor other dishes or to infuse olive oil, but use white truffles unpeeled. Grate truffles on a grater, or cut them into paper-thin slices, or shavings, with a vegetable peeler, a mandoline, or a tool called a truffle slicer. Slices of black truffles may be used whole or minced with a chef's knife.

Quick Bite

Chocolate truffles are so-called because their irregular spherical forms and cocoa dusting mimic the appearance of a black truffle with its coating of earth.

TRUSSING To tie a food, usually poultry or boned roasts, into a rounded, compact shape before cooking. Trussing gives a roast a plump, tidy form that holds even when the trussing string is removed. This technique should be reserved for birds that are presented whole at table, as poultry actually cooks more evenly untrussed.

HOW TO *Truss Poultry*

1. Have ready the bird, kitchen scissors, and kitchen string.

Tuck the first joint of each wing under the second joint.

2. Cut a long piece of kitchen string (4 to 5 times the length of the bird) and lay it across the board. Place the bird on its back on top of the string, so that the string is just under the tail. Cross the string over the legs, pulling them together and crossing the ends of the drumsticks; then loop the string under the end of the crossed drumsticks.

3. Fold the tail up into the cavity and pull on the string until it is tight. Pull each end of the string up toward the breast.

4. Turn the bird breast side down, bringing each string end over each wing and tucking the neck skin under the string. Cross the string ends and pull them tight. Tie securely in a knot and clip

the string ends. To remove string after the bird is cooked and has rested, cut it at the knot and pull it free.

TUBE PAN See BAKEWARE; CAKE.

TUNA A prized food fish, the tuna comes from a family of large fish with rich, oily, firm flesh. Tuna is the most popular fish for canning and is widely available in cans in several different forms. The albacore, a small tuna (10 to 60 pounds) with the palest flesh of all the tunas, is mild in flavor and almost white in color when cooked. The bluefin is a very large fish—it can grow to more than 1,000 pounds—whose mature flesh is dark red and strongly flavored. Bonitos are small fish (up to 25 pounds) and have the most pronounced flavor among all the tunas. Skipjack tunas are usually quite small (6 to 8 pounds), with meat similar to that of the yellowfin. Yellowfin tuna, which can reach a weight of 300 pounds, is called ahi in Hawaiian. It has slightly more flavor than albacore.

Because its meat is oily and firm, tuna takes well to pan roasting or grilling. It is typically cooked until seared on the outside and rare on the inside. Fresh tuna is also used for Japanese sashimi and sushi. Canned tuna is served as part of an antipasto plate and is used to make salads, sandwiches, and casseroles.

Selecting Fresh albacore is usually available from spring through fall, while yellowfin is available year-round but is most plentiful in summer. The different kinds of

t

fresh tuna are interchangeable for cooked dishes, although yellowfin steaks are often preferred for grilling and pan roasting. For sushi and sashimi, look for the freshest-possible fish, usually labeled "sushi-grade," "sashimi grade," "tuna loin," or "tuna belly."

When choosing canned tuna, imported Italian tuna packed in olive oil is considered the premium kind for antipasto, salads, and sandwiches, although you may prefer a lower-calorie tuna packed in spring water. Domestic tuna is also packed in vegetable oil. Solid albacore tuna is the most expensive domestic canned tuna, followed by chunk light tuna, and then flaked light tuna. Solid albacore can be somewhat dry, however, and some cooks prefer chunk light tuna. "Dolphin-safe" or "line-caught" tuna has been caught by methods that do not endanger dolphins.

Storing Pat fresh tuna dry with paper towels and put it in a heavy-duty zippered plastic bag. Place the bag on top of a bowl of ice cubes or cracked ice and refrigerate. Cook the fish the day you buy it. If you must wait, it should be kept no longer than 24 hours. Freezing degrades the texture and flavor of fish somewhat, but if you must freeze tuna, place it in a freezer-weight plastic bag and freeze for up to 1 month. Defrost in the refrigerator. Unopened canned tuna may be kept indefinitely.

Preparing Fresh tuna may be grilled, broiled, panfried, pan roasted, or poached. Canned tuna is usually drained before using in a recipe.

TURKEY Benjamin Franklin wanted to make the turkey the national bird of the United States, and it unofficially becomes just that every year at Thanksgiving, when Americans consume this bird in incredible numbers. Turkey is nearly as popular at Christmas and is also eaten throughout the year, often as a low-fat substitute for red meat. Ground turkey is made into turkey burgers and meat loaves, and sliced cooked turkey breast is a favorite meat for sandwiches. Turkey breast halves are roasted whole, sliced raw and sautéed, or boned, stuffed, rolled, and roasted.

Sooner or later, though, every cook is faced with roasting a whole turkey, and an entire culture of techniques, advice, and lore has grown up around this process. Turkeys are cooked in covered roasters or paper or plastic bags; roasted under a tent of aluminum foil; packed in a thick layer of salt and baked; grilled; roasted breast down; boned, rolled, and roasted; or soaked in brine, then roasted. Whole turkeys are even deep-fried. All of these methods have one aim in mind: to produce a bird with juicy meat throughout. And for most people, the juicy meat must be combined with crisp, well-browned skin. The great problem in cooking a turkey, of course, is that by the time the skin is crisp and the dark meat is done, the white meat is usually overcooked and dried out.

A simple way to combat this is to roast the turkey at a moderate temperature of 325°F and to cover the breast of the turkey with aluminum foil to keep it moist, and then remove the foil toward the end of roasting so the breast will brown.

Selecting For the best taste, pick a turkey over 10 pounds; if you want a small bird, a capon or a turkey breast half is a better choice. Figure on ¼ pound per person for serving, although you will probably want twice that (or more) for leftovers. If at all possible, choose a fresh bird (frozen turkeys have drier meat) that was raised free range and fed organic grain. Although they are more expensive, these turkeys have more flavor than those raised on factory farms. Order them from specialty butchers or natural-food stores.

Storing Store turkey in its original wrapping in the cold bottom back shelf of the refrigerator. Cook fresh or thawed turkey within 2 days. Pick up your whole turkey the day before it is to be roasted, unless it is frozen, in which case it will most likely take longer than a day to thaw (see THAWING). Fresh turkey may be frozen for up to 6 months, but previously frozen turkey should not be refrozen.

Preparing Two hours before roasting, remove the whole bird from the refrigerator, remove the packaging, and remove the package of giblets from the body and/or neck cavity. Remove the giblets from their packaging and rinse them. Use them now (with the exclusion of the liver) to make a stock to use in the turkey gravy, or place them in a bowl, cover it with plastic wrap, and refrigerate until ready to use. Rinse the turkey inside and out (both neck and body cavities) under cold water. Remove and discard any bloody bits. Pat the bird dry inside and out with paper towels. Pluck any leftover feathers, using tweezers or needle-nose pliers if necessary. Fold the wings under the bird. Let the bird sit at room temperature on a baking sheet until roasting.

If stuffing the bird, do so just before putting it into the oven, packing the stuffing loosely into the neck and body cavities to allow it room to expand. If not stuffing the bird, sprinkle the cavities with salt and pepper and put an onion half and a coarsely chopped carrot and celery rib inside the body cavity.

See also CARVING; DONENESS; GIBLETS; GRAVY; ROASTING; STUFFING; TRUSSING.

TURMERIC See SPICE.

TURNING OUT Removing a food, such as a baked pastry or a molded dessert, from its container; see UNMOLDING.

TURNIP Like so many other root vegetables, the turnip, which grows well in poor soil, has long been a staple of northern European cooking. It typically has crisp white flesh and a white skin with a purple cap, although some varieties have yellow flesh, and the cap might be green, red, white, or even black. Very young turnips are tender and have a mild, sweet flavor. The flavor grows stronger and the flesh woodier with age. Young turnips are delicious raw, eaten like radishes, or they may be cooked whole, along with their greens. Turnips are delightful in soups and stews, braised in butter, puréed with potatoes, glazed, roasted along with other root vegetables, or served in braises with duck and pork.

Selecting Although available year-round, turnips are at their best in winter. Baby turnips, with their greens attached, are 1 to 2 inches in diameter. Older turnips are usually 3 to 4 inches in diameter and are sold with their greens removed. Choose unblemished, firm, sweet-smelling turnips.

Storing Keep baby turnips, with their greens attached, in a perforated plastic bag in the refrigerator crisper for 1 to 2 weeks. Older turnips will keep for several weeks in a cool, dark place.

Preparing Peel and trim baby turnips, but leave them whole. Peel older turnips and slice them or cut them into chunks. If older turnips have a strong smell, blanch them for 3 to 5 minutes to remove some of the harshness.

t

U·V

*everything from unmolding
to vinegar*

U·V

UNMOLDING To remove a food from the container in which it cooked or set, a step that can sometimes be the trickiest part of making the dish. Preparing the mold beforehand and cooking the dish properly are the keys to successful unmolding. Nonstick bakeware and cookware have been a boon to unmolding foods easily. A coating of cooking spray is added insurance against food's sticking to the pan and falling apart as it leaves the mold. Cast-iron skillets and other similar pans must be properly seasoned; many cooks wash them only in hot water (without soap) in order to preserve the seasoning.

To unmold such foods as frittatas and Spanish tortillas in order to cook them on the second side, make sure to use enough butter and/or oil at the beginning and to heat it well before adding the food to the pan. Make sure the mixture is browned on the bottom, and shake the pan to loosen it, or dislodge it with a thin spatula if necessary. You may invert a plate over the pan and then quickly invert both plate and pan if the pan is small and light enough; or you can slide the food out of the pan onto a plate, cooked side down, then top it with the upside-down pan and invert the two.

Jelled foods are easier to unmold if the mold has been oiled or sprayed with cooking spray before filling. To unmold, dip the base of the mold into a pan of very hot water for no more than 4 or 5 seconds. Remove the mold from the water and rock it slightly to see whether the food has loosened inside the mold. If not, dip it again in hot water. Rinse the serving plate with cold water, then place it upside down over the mold. Holding the mold and plate together tightly, invert the two quickly and place on the countertop. Tap the bottom of the mold to make sure the food drops onto the plate. If all else fails, loosen the edges of the food by slipping a thin knife along the inside edge of the mold, and then leave the mold upside down on the serving plate until the food falls out.

*Lowering mold
into hot water.*

*Setting plate
upside down
on mold.*

*Inverting mold
and plate
together.*

Most cakes, muffins, and loaf breads are cooked until they begin to pull away from the sides of the pan. Usually, they are allowed to cool for a few minutes in their pan on a wire rack, during which time they shrink slightly, making them easier to unmold. Run a thin knife around the inside edges of the pan before unmolding.

For ease in unmolding cakes, make sure to follow the recipe instructions for preparing the pans. Some cakes require a circle of parchment paper in the bottom and/or a coating of butter, and some need a sprinkle of flour or sugar over the butter. Many cakes are baked in springform pans in order to unmold them easily, while most tarts and tart shells are baked in a tart pan with a removable bottom. When using this type of pan, place it on a baking sheet for baking, and slide the tart pan onto a wire rack to cool. To unmold, push up on the false bottom of the pan so that the pan ring falls away. Cut and serve a filled tart while it is sitting on the pan's false bottom.

See also BAKING; MOLDING; PIE & TART; SEASONING.

VANILLA Lending perfume, depth, and nuance to a wide variety of dishes, including some savory ones, vanilla is one of the West's prime flavors for ice creams, cookies, cakes, custards, pastry cream, and puddings. It may be used either in its whole-bean form or as vanilla extract, a commercial product made by chopping the beans, soaking them in a mixture of alcohol and water, and then aging the solution. Because the beans are hand-pollinated and hand-picked, they are expensive, but they may be reused several times.

Vanilla beans.

Selecting Whole beans, which are sold in bulk or packaged singly in plastic cylinders, are available in natural-food stores, specialty-food stores, and some supermarkets. They should be moist and pliable. The best-quality beans will develop a natural coating of vanillin, a white powder. Of the three most common kinds—Tahitian, Mexican, and Bourbon-Madagascar—the Mexican and Bourbon-Madagascar beans are more strongly scented, while Tahitian are more delicate. Mexican beans are in short supply, however, while Bourbon-Madagascar beans make up about three-fourths of the total supply.

The best vanilla extracts identify the type of bean used. Buy only pure vanilla extract, not imitation vanilla, which is made of artificial flavorings and has an inferior taste. Vanilla powder, the ground vanilla bean, is available by mail order and from some specialty-food stores. Some cooks prefer it because its flavor does not dissipate when it is heated.

Storing Vanilla beans sold in a plastic cylinder should be kept in the cylinder, and loose beans should be placed in an airtight jar. Keep in a cool, dark place for up to 6 months. The tightly capped extract keeps indefinitely stored in a cool, dark place.

Preparing Use the whole bean, or cut the bean in half lengthwise, scrape out the seeds, and add them, with the pod, to the liquid in the dish you are preparing. Some recipes will instruct you to steep the vanilla bean first. After use, rinse and dry whole beans, store as above, and reuse.

Scraping a vanilla bean.

U·V

When adding vanilla extract to hot food, first let the food cool for a few minutes. When the extract is added to hot food, the alcohol evaporates, taking with it some of the vanilla flavor.

HOW TO *Make Vanilla Sugar*
Use vanilla sugar as a replacement for regular granulated sugar to add flavor in desserts, sauces, and drinks. One tablespoon vanilla sugar equals ¼ teaspoon vanilla extract in flavoring power.
1. Bury a vanilla bean—whole or halved—in 1 cup granulated or confectioners' sugar.
2. Cover tightly and let sit for at least 24 hours. Replace sugar as it is used and replace the bean after 1 year.

HOW TO *Make Homemade Vanilla Extract*
1. Cut a vanilla bean in half lengthwise and crosswise. Place the pieces in a clean glass jar.
2. Add ¾ cup vodka. Cover tightly and let steep for 6 months before using.

VEAL The meat of a calf up to the age of 3 months, or sometimes slightly older but still less than 6 months (when it becomes "baby beef"). The most tender and white veal is from a milk-fed calf that is no more than 3 months old. "Formula-fed" veal is raised on a diet of milk solids, milk fats, and other various nutrients and may be up to 4 months old. This kind of veal, sometimes referred to as "Dutch method" veal, is tender and pale but inferior in flavor to that of true milk-fed veal. The tenderness of the meat is also a result of restricting the calf's movement, which in recent years has raised concerns and protest. Most producers have responded by improving conditions; a good-quality butcher should be able to tell you about the practices of his or her suppliers.

When a calf is weaned from milk and fed on grass and grain, its flesh becomes redder due to the iron in the food, and some cooks prefer this "free-range" veal, as it has a meatier flavor.

Veal is a traditional European meat. The relative lack of pastureland in Europe has always made it practical to slaughter cattle at a younger age. Thus, France has developed such dishes as *blanquette de veau,* Germany has its traditional Wiener schnitzel, and Italy has its veal scallopini, among a host of other veal dishes.

Selecting For traditional dishes calling for veal scallopini or chops, look for milk-fed veal, distinguished by its creamy pink color and fine-grained texture. The redder meat of free-range veal is especially good in more hearty dishes such as stews.

Storing Ground veal may be refrigerated for up to 2 days, steaks or chops for 3 days, and roasts for 4 days. Freeze ground veal for up to 3 months; steaks, chops, and roasts may be frozen for up to 9 months.

Preparing Unlike beef, veal is low in fat and has little or no marbling. Thus all veal cuts, except the ones from the loin, leg, and rib, should be cooked by methods that involve moisture, such as stewing or braising, or else barded (see BARDING) to give them extra insulation during cooking.

Unlike beef and lamb, roasted veal should be cooked no less than medium (145° to 155°F). Braised and stewed cuts are cooked until tender.

VEGETABLE See individual vegetables; BLANCHING; BOILING; BRAISING; ROASTING; STEAMING.

VEGETABLE OIL See COOKING SPRAY; FAT & OIL.

VEGETABLE PEAR See CHAYOTE.

VEGETABLE PEELER See COOKING TOOLS.

U·V

Veal Glossary

Veal cuts.

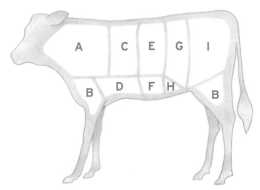

rom the primal, or wholesale, cuts of veal come the smaller roasts, chops, and other cuts available from the butcher.

SHOULDER (A) Source of roasts for braising, stewing, or roasting. The shoulder may also be cut into steaks, which likewise should be braised. Ground veal is often shoulder meat.

SHANK (B) The shank is cut into slices and sold as veal shanks or osso buco. Many cooks feel hind shanks make better osso buco. This gelatinous meat is rich in flavor, and long braising turns the meat and its marrow meltingly tender. The same cut is a fine choice for making stock.

Veal shanks.

RIB (C) Veal rib, or rack of veal, may be roasted as a rack or a crown roast, or boned and roasted. Usually, however, it is cut into rib chops.

BREAST (D) The breast is a source of less expensive cuts that are traditionally stuffed and braised. The breast may be used for ground veal.

LOIN (E) The loin, the section beneath the ribs and above the leg, is the source of whole loin roast, either bone in or boned and stuffed, for roasting or braising. The loin is also cut into chops, which may be sautéed or grilled.

Veal loin chops.

FLANK (F) Combined with trimmings from other cuts to make ground veal.

SIRLOIN (G) Cut into chops, which may be sautéed or grilled. The sirloin is also cut into roasts for grilling or broiling.

TIP (H) Sliced into cutlets, which are often pounded to become veal scallops.

Veal scallops.

ROUND (I) Source of rump and round roasts for roasting, as well as round steaks for braising.

U·V

VEGETABLE SHORTENING A solid white fat made by hydrogenating a vegetable oil, such as cottonseed or soybean. (The hydrogenation process consists of pumping hydrogen atoms into the oil.)

Because about 10 percent of its volume is air, shortening requires less creaming than butter does. And shortening contains millions of tiny bubbles, which trap the air that's beaten in during the creaming process, making tender, light-textured cakes. Shortening remains solid even at warm room temperature, so there's no risk of its melting and absorbing flour the way that butter can. This ability to remain solid over a wide temperature range means that cookies made with shortening hold their shape and don't spread the way ones made with butter do. And unlike butter, which contains a small percentage of water, shortening is 100 percent fat. This lack of water means that shortening makes flakier pie crusts and crisper cookies than butter does. Shortening also is used for deep-frying because it has a high smoke point.

Recently, the use of vegetable shortening has caused health concerns because the hydrogenation of vegetable oil converts the oil into saturated fat and creates trans fatty acids. Some researchers believe that these saturated fats are more harmful to the body than regular saturated fats.

Because it's virtually flavorless, shortening is often combined with butter in baked goods, in order to get both the delicious flavor of butter and the flakiness created by using shortening.

Quick Tip

Butter may be substituted for shortening in most baking recipes.

Storing Once opened, store shortening in the refrigerator for up to 1 year.

VELOUTÉ See SAUCE.

VENISON See GAME.

VERMOUTH See WINE.

VINAIGRETTE The most basic of salad dressings, *sauce vinaigrette* is a simple mixture of oil and vinegar, plus seasonings. The proportions usually run 3 or 4 parts oil to 1 part vinegar. Vinaigrettes as simple as oil and vinegar plus seasonings shaken together in a glass jar offer a multitude of possibilities. By first whisking the vinegar with a spoonful of mustard and then drizzling in the oil as you whisk, you can create a creamier, better emulsified vinaigrette that will coat evenly. Experiment with different oils, vinegars, herbs, and spices.

Quick Tip

Before recycling a just-emptied mustard jar, add oil, vinegar, salt, and pepper and shake to make a mustard-flavored vinaigrette.

Vinaigrettes may also be used as marinades or as a sauce for meat, chicken, seafood, vegetables, and grains. See also EMULSION; SAUCE.

VINEGAR The first vinegar was probably a wine gone bad: *vin aigre,* French for "sour wine." A multiplicity of uses was soon found for this fortuitous discovery. Not only did it provide just the right tartness for dressing salad greens when mixed with oil, but it also preserved foods, cleaned surfaces, brightened hair, and was used as a medicine and a poultice. Before refrigeration, the keeping quality of vinegar was of major importance. It was used to pickle meats, fruits, and vegetables, preventing spoilage while altering taste and texture in ways resembling cooking. Several traditional dishes, such as

U·V

pickled herring, dill pickles, piccalilli, sauer-braten, and adobo, remind us of this function. Today, vinegar is made from a variety of red or white wines, and you will even find varietal wine vinegars in some specialty-food stores. Sherry vinegar, which originated in Spain, has a nutty taste and is especially good on vegetables and in dressings.

In addition to wine vinegars, there are a number of vinegars based on fruit and grain, including cider vinegar and rice vinegar. Cider vinegar, a fruity vinegar made from apples and used in many traditional American recipes, was once more common in this country than wine vinegar. Distilled white vinegar, made from grain alcohol, is used in pickling and in other recipes where its clean taste is desired. Malt vinegar, a mild vinegar made from malted barley, is popular in England as a dressing for fish and chips. Rice vinegar, made from fermented rice, is widely used in Asian cuisines. It is used to add a slight acidity in cooked dishes and to make dressings for delicate greens. It is available either plain or sweetened; the latter is marketed as seasoned rice vinegar. The Chinese make white, red, and black rice vinegars, with the deeply flavored black type used in cooking and as a condiment and the milder red type used in much the same way. Many vinegars, whatever their source, are further seasoned by the addition of fresh herbs, fruit, garlic, or other ingredients.

Herb-flavored vinegar.

Balsamic Vinegar A specialty of the Italian region of Emilia-Romagna, primarily in the town of Modena, balsamic is an aged vinegar made from the pure wine must—unfermented grape juice, which may contain stems, skins, and seed—of white Trebbiano grapes. Authentic balsamic vinegar is designated by the word *tradizionale* or an Italian consortium seal on the label and is aged for as little as 1 year and on up to 25 years, 50 years, 75 years, and sometimes far longer, slowly evaporating and growing sweeter and mellower with time. It is aged in airy attics in a series of wooden casks of decreasing sizes, each a different wood that contributes to its flavor. Long-aged balsamic is an intense, expensive, syrupy vinegar that should be used sparingly; only a few drops are necessary. True balsamic that is aged for a shorter time is also available. Younger balsamic makes a superb salad dressing and is used, often reduced, in sauces for other foods, or is sprinkled over fruit.

What is often sold as balsamic vinegar is a relatively inexpensive duplication of the true product, made from grape must mixed with high-quality vinegar, but it makes a decent salad dressing.

Quick Tip

When making a vinaigrette with balsamic vinegar, use 3 parts olive oil or less to 1 part balsamic. Its flavor is less sharp than that of some other vinegars.

Storing All vinegar should be stored in glass bottles in cool, dark cupboards. It keeps indefinitely. Although vinegar may cloud with time, it is still usable and may simply need to be filtered through a heavy paper towel or coffee filter.

VODKA See SPIRITS.

U·V

everything from waffle to wine

WAFFLE Cunningly devised to combine the maximum amount of crisp-tender crust while trapping the maximum amount of syrup or sauce, a waffle can be sweet or savory. Waffles are usually leavened by baking powder and/or baking soda, but they may also be made from a yeast dough. Like pancakes, they may be lightened with foamy beaten egg whites or made more tender by incorporating buttermilk, sour cream, or yogurt. Standard waffles have a grid of small depressions, while Belgian waffles are thicker and have larger and deeper depressions, a crisp exterior, and an airy interior.

Waffle iron.

Waffles are a traditional breakfast or brunch dish, topped with maple syrup, yogurt, or a fruit sauce, but savory waffles may also be served as a quick, light lunch or supper, topped with creamed chicken, tuna, or vegetables.

Waffle irons come in a variety of shapes, including squares, circles, and hearts. They may be heated on the top of the stove, like European cookie irons, but are more commonly electric. Most of today's waffle irons are nonstick, but if you prefer one with a regular surface, make sure to season it according to the manufacturer's instructions. Seasoned or nonstick waffle irons do not need greasing. Make sure that the light on an electric iron indicates that the iron is ready to use, and wait until the top of the iron lifts easily away from the waffle to remove it from the iron. Do not immerse an electric waffle iron in water, and do not wash the grids after use. If crumbs have stuck to the surface, simply brush them out.

See also CREPE; PANCAKE.

WALNUT See NUT.

WATER BATH A water bath, sometimes called a bain-marie, is created by setting a baking dish or pan holding food inside a larger pan and then pouring either hot or nearly boiling water into the larger pan. The water, which should reach about halfway up the sides of the dish containing the food, insulates the food from the direct heat of the oven or stove, promoting gentle, moist, even cooking. Water baths provide a moist environment for baking delicate foods such as custards, mousses, cheesecakes, and puddings, or they can keep sauces, soups, or coffee warm on the stove top, acting as a sort of double boiler.

Water bath.

Although specialty water baths, or bain-marie pans, are available, it is easy to fashion a water bath from pans you already have on hand. The safest way to assemble a water bath intended for the oven is to line a large pan such as a roasting pan with a folded kitchen towel, and place the towel-lined pan on a pulled-out oven rack.

Quick Bite

Lining the water bath's outer pan with a folded towel keeps custard cups from rattling and shaking as they cook and also insulates them from the hot pan bottom.

Place the baking dish holding the food inside the larger pan, then pour the hot water into the larger pan. If using a springform pan, wrap it in aluminum foil before setting it in the water to prevent any leakage. Be sure the outer pan is large enough to hold a substantial amount of water, or the water will evaporate too quickly. Finally, slide the rack carefully into the oven. It's advisable to check the water level at regular intervals during cooking, pouring in more hot water as necessary.

Quick Bite

Bain-marie means "Marie's bath" in French, and some historians believe that the name for this mild cooking method alludes to the gentle nature of the Virgin Mary.

WATER CHESTNUT Cultivated in streams, ponds, and rivers throughout China and Southeast Asia, water chestnuts are the underwater stem tips of a type of water grass found in many parts of the world. In the past, the seeds of the water chestnut were sometimes used for making rosaries, inspiring a second name: Jesuit's nut. When it is fresh, the popular Asian vegetable looks something like a more spherical cousin of the tree-borne chestnut. It has a wonderfully crisp texture, welcome in stir-fries and salads, and a sweet, refreshing flavor all its own. Canned water chestnuts, whether whole or sliced, lack the sweetness of fresh ones and offer little more than a mild flavor and crunchy texture.

Selecting Look for fresh water chestnuts in Asian markets. Choose those that are rock hard with a slight sheen. Soft spots and a dull color are signs of mushy, soured fruit. Test various brands of canned water chestnuts until you find a good one.

Quick Tip

If using canned water chestnuts, cook them in boiling water for about 10 minutes, drain, and rinse with cold water. This will help rid them of any metallic flavors they may have absorbed from the can.

Storing Refrigerate fresh water chestnuts in a plastic bag for up to a week. Canned water chestnuts should be transferred to a plastic or glass container, covered with water, and refrigerated for up to 10 days.

Preparing If using fresh water chestnuts, rinse off any dirt. Cut off the flat top and bottom and peel the skin with a small knife or vegetable peeler. Cut out any yellow or brown bits of flesh. Keep peeled water chestnuts immersed in cold water until ready to use to prevent discoloration.

WATERCRESS Characterized by a refreshingly peppery flavor, watercress grows wild along streams and is cultivated in water. Like other members of the mustard family, it has an agreeably assertive taste that makes it a classic filling for tea sandwiches; a dull green, lively tasting soup; a refreshing salad, either on its own or combined with other greens or with fruit; and an attractive garnish.

Selecting Watercress is available year-round, but it is at its peak in late spring and early summer. Look for brightly colored leaves. Pass over those that droop or are tinged with yellow.

Storing Place in a perforated plastic bag in the refrigerator for up to 2 days.

Preparing Wash and pick over the sprigs, discarding all but the freshest ones. Remove and discard the thick stems, then dry the watercress in a salad spinner. Or, line a baking sheet with paper towels and top with a layer of rinsed watercress sprigs. Repeat until all the watercress is washed, top with a final layer of paper towels, and gently roll up to dry.

See also GREENS, SALAD.

WATERMELON See MELON.

WAX BEAN See BEAN, FRESH.

WAXED PAPER Waxed paper is tissue-thin paper that has been coated on both sides with wax. This moisture-resistant, grease-resistant paper has largely been replaced in today's kitchens by aluminum foil, plastic bags and plastic wrap, and parchment paper, but it still has a place in the kitchen, especially since it is more ecologically friendly than plastic or foil. It does have some limitations, however. Waxed paper tears easily, and moisture or grease will eventually begin to soak through. Also, unlike parchment paper or foil, it cannot be directly exposed to heat in the oven, as its coating will melt. Nonetheless, it is often used to line cake pans to prevent sticking, as the batter protects the paper

from direct heat. Chocolate decorations and some candies such as divinity may also be spooned or piped onto waxed paper to set. Waxed-paper sandwich bags may be used for microwaving leftovers. Waxed paper is also useful for wrapping frozen food to be thawed in a microwave oven.

Quick Tip

Roll out pie dough and other sticky pastry between sheets of waxed paper. The dough won't adhere to its slick surface, allowing you to remove the paper easily.

WEIGHTS AND MEASURES See MEASURING.

WELL DONE When a food is cooked through completely, it is referred to as well done. In the case of meat, no trace of pink should remain. See also DONENESS; individual meats.

WET INGREDIENTS This term refers to the liquid ingredients in a baking recipe. Wet ingredients are usually water and/or milk, eggs, and liquid flavorings such as lemon juice, brandy, wine, or vanilla extract. Flour, sugar, salt, and other ingredients such as baking powder or baking soda are called dry ingredients. The wet ingredients are generally mixed together until blended, and dry ingredients are sifted or stirred together until blended. The wet and dry ingredients are then mixed together until blended or just combined. See also BAKING; DRY INGREDIENTS; MEASURING.

WHEAT See GRAIN.

WHIPPING Beating a food such as heavy cream or egg whites to increase its volume by incorporating air into it. Whipped ingredients are sometimes used to lighten the texture of heavier mixtures, such as adding whipped cream to custard to make it less dense, or folding whipped egg whites into a cake batter to facilitate rising.

Whipping can be accomplished using a wire whisk, an electric mixer, or a rotary beater. A balloon whisk will add the maximum amount of air to whipped cream or beaten egg whites.

Surprisingly, both egg whites and heavy cream are more quickly whipped by hand than with an electric mixer. Hand-beaten whites mound higher and are more stable than those beaten with an electric beater, while hand-beaten whipped cream is smoother and lighter.

Quick Tip

To whip egg whites or heavy cream, use a large bowl. The larger the bowl, the easier it is to incorporate air. A deep bowl also prevents the cream from splattering.

See also CREAM; EGG; WHISKING.

WHISKEY See SPIRITS.

WHISKING To beat, or whip, rapidly with a whisk, an implement with a head of thin looped metal wires and a metal or wooden handle.

Wire whisks.

Also known as whips, whisks are made in various sizes and shapes and with differ-

ent thicknesses, flexibilities, and quantities of wire, depending on the kind of food for which they will be used. Sauce whisks are the basic model, used to mix ingredients thoroughly without adding excess air. Balloon whisks, which are more rounded, are used to incorporate air into egg whites and cream. Flat whisks are used for stirring gravies and sauces as they thicken, while also pressing out and smoothing lumps. Tiny whisks are made for whisking mixtures in cups or small pans.

See also BAKING TOOLS; COOKING TOOLS.

WHITE BEAN See BEAN, DRIED.

WHITE MUSTARD CABBAGE See BOK CHOY.

WILD RICE A different species of grain from true rice, this seed of a marsh grass is native to the northern Great Lakes of the United States, where it has long been harvested in boats by Native Americans. It now is also farmed elsewhere in the Midwest, in Canada, and in California. Wild rice is dark brown, almost black in color, and the long, narrow grains are pointed on both ends. With a pronounced nutty flavor, wild rice is pleasantly chewy and is a perfect accompaniment to game or wild mushrooms. It is especially good as an autumn pilaf or stuffing, mixed with nuts and raisins or currants. Wild rice may be substituted for white or brown rice in most recipes. Keep in mind, however, that its texture is firmer and it takes longer to cook. Combine it with white or brown rice to make a milder-tasting dish.

See also RICE.

WINE See page 468.

WOK See COOKWARE.

Wine

Certain connoisseurs have presented the convincing argument that wine is not so much a beverage as a food, citing its complex flavor, aroma, and body and the many ways in which those characteristics can interact with other elements of a meal.

Wine has indeed been an integral part of good dining for millennia, since humankind first discovered the happy results of fermentation in grape juice caused by airborne yeasts, followed by the subtle, yet profound, changes that can occur as wine ages in a cask or bottle. A thoughtfully chosen wine can greatly enhance the pleasure derived from the food it accompanies.

The Wine Cellar A significant factor in wine's compatibility with food lies in the fact that it can be made from many different grape varieties, each of which has unique characteristics of flavor, body, and color that are imparted to the finished wine. When a wine is made entirely or predominately from one grape variety, it is said to be a varietal wine. Today, most wines made in the Americas, Australia, and New Zealand are made and labeled as varietals. Most European wines, by contrast, are traditionally named after the regions in which they are produced. But each such region, as a rule, makes its wines from a predominant type of grape, and its wines will demonstrate that grape's signature varietal qualities as well as those of the land and climate in which the grapes were grown.

CABERNET SAUVIGNON (cab-er-NAY SO-vi-nyon) A robust red wine often described as fruity, spicy, or herbaceous, made from the same grape as the wines of Médoc and Graves in the Bordeaux region of France. Good with hearty red meat dishes, whether roasted, grilled, stewed, or braised.

CHAMPAGNE AND OTHER SPARKLING WINES Most often based on Chardonnay grapes, Champagne or sparkling wine describes a process rather than a grape. These wines delight with their fine bubbles of carbon dioxide, produced in the most authentic, highest-quality form by a secondary fermentation within the bottle. Dry Champagne or sparkling wine, which may be labeled "brut" or "extra sec," is appropriate nearly any time you would serve light white wine. It's excellent with foods such as caviar, fresh oysters, shrimp, salty cheeses, nuts, eggs, and smoked salmon.

Quick Bite

Though the term is used loosely in this country, *Champagne* specifically refers to sparkling wine made in the Champagne region of France, where the manufacturing process (called the *méthode champenoise*) and labeling are strictly controlled.

CHARDONNAY A rich and fruity white wine, which can range in taste from big and oaky to buttery and spicy to bracingly dry and flinty. The same grape yields the great white Burgundies of France—Chablis, Côte de Beaune, Mâcon, Meursault, and

Montrachet. Serve big, buttery Chardonnays with roast chicken, seafood, or creamy pastas, or even grilled veal or red meat; spicy Chardonnays with appetizers, light grilled meat or poultry, or pasta with tomato sauces; and flinty Chardonnays with raw or cooked shellfish or broiled whitefish.

GEWÜRZTRAMINER (guh-VURTZ-tra-meen-er) Popular in Germany, northeastern France, northern Italy, the United States, Australia, and New Zealand, this fruity, highly aromatic, spicy white wine is especially good with assertively spiced Asian dishes and with smoked fish and meats.

MERLOT (mer-LOW) Soft, rich, fruity, and full-bodied, this red wine comes from a grape also featured in the wines of Saint-Émilion and Pomerol in the Bordeaux region of France. Excellent with grilled or braised red meat, roast duck, or even grilled seafood.

PINOT NOIR (PEE-noh NWAHR) Many people consider this wine, with its silken body and a complex flavor and bouquet abounding in fruity, spicy, and floral characteristics, to be the greatest of the red wines. The same grape produces the renowned red wines of France's Burgundy region. Pinot noir may be served with a wide range of rich or complex-tasting dishes, from chicken braised in red wine to spicy Asian dishes.

RIESLING (REESE-ling) A crisp, floral white wine native to Germany, with a flavor that may variously bring to mind summer tree fruits, flint, or even a hint of smoke. Serve drier Rieslings on their own as a refreshing aperitif or with light appetizers or seafood; sweeter versions go well with blue cheeses or spicy food.

ROSÉ AND BLUSH WINES Made from red wine grapes of numerous varietals, these pink-tinged wines result from briefly leaving the skins in contact with the juice. Fresh and fruity, they go well with a wide range of casual foods, particularly well-seasoned Mediterranean dishes such as French seafood stews or Spanish paella.

SAUVIGNON BLANC (SO-vi-nyon BLAHNK) Crisp and acidic with herbaceous or grassy overtones, this white wine—made with a grape featured in France's great white Bordeaux—goes well with seafood of any kind or with dishes featuring (similarly acidic) tomato sauces. It is also known as Fumé Blanc.

ZINFANDEL Based on a popular California grape, Zinfandel is most often produced today as a hearty red wine with a flavor that brings to mind berries, cherries, and spices. It goes especially well with roasted or grilled red meats, robust stews, and game. Zinfandel is also produced in a lighter style similar to the Beaujolais Nouveau of France, ideal for drinking with casual meals of tomato-based pasta dishes or grilled poultry. So-called white Zinfandel is made by leaving the crushed grapes only briefly in contact with their skins, then straining the skins away. The result is a popular "blush" wine with a deep pink tint and a light, fruity flavor.

Selecting Wine Many food stores today carry a good range of reasonably priced wines. For the best selection, however, seek out a reputable wine store. A first-rate

Quick Bite

When applied to wine, the term *dry* refers to the amount of residual sugar in the wine. The less sugar, the drier the wine. Sweeter wines may be referred to as dessert wines or late-harvest wines.

continued

Wine, continued

merchant will be able to guide you to good bottles within your budget that will complement the foods you plan to serve. See The Wine Cellar, page 468, for a few pointers; for extra guidance on particular wine makers and on the best-quality vintages— that is, specific years in which wines are bottled—consult one of the many books or periodicals on the subject.

Storing Wine Bottles you plan to drink within a few days or weeks may be stored in your pantry, away from heat or light. For long-term storage of high-quality wines, keep the bottles undisturbed in an environment with a controlled constant temperature of 50° to 55°F, to slow their aging. They should rest on their sides in a wine rack to keep their corks moist and swollen, thus preventing outside air from coming into contact with the wine.

Serving Wine Red wines are best appreciated at cool room temperature, within the range of 55° to 65°F. More robust reds may be served at the warmer end of that range, and the lightest reds should be poured slightly cooler. The ideal serving temperature for white wines ranges from 40° to 50°F, with sparkling wines at the colder end of that range and big, full-bodied white wines at the warmer. Wines may be chilled in the refrigerator for up to 2 hours before serving time, or for about 20 minutes in an ice bucket filled with equal parts cold water and ice cubes. When using an ice bucket, fold a clean kitchen towel or napkin around the neck of the bottle to help catch drips when the bottle is removed for pouring.

Several styles of corkscrews are available; for details, see CORKSCREW. To open Champagne or sparkling wine, place a folded towel or napkin over the cork. With one hand, hold the bottle steady and pointing away from you and other people while you use your other hand to untwist and remove the wire cage that holds the cork in place. Then, grip the cork and gently twist the bottle to loosen the cork, letting the pressure within the bottle slowly force it out while you keep the cork in your grasp. Never cavalierly shoot the cork out of the bottle, which can lead to possible injury as well as loss of wine.

Loosening the cage.

Twisting the bottle.

When pouring wine, fill glasses to only about two-thirds of their capacity, allowing

Quick Bite

Opening a bottle of wine ahead of time to allow it to "breathe" is not generally necessary. While exposure to air does change and bring out the flavors of wine, wine is well aerated as it is poured into a glass. A very young or tannic wine may be decanted and allowed to breathe and mellow for up to several hours before serving. This step is not recommended for older wines, as their bouquet fades rather quickly after pouring.

room at the top of the bowl for the wine's bouquet to develop upon exposure to air and for its aroma to be fully appreciated by those who drink it.

WINEGLASSES You will find wineglasses within a wide price range and in many different colors, patterns, sizes, and shapes. To best appreciate good wine, look for clear, unadorned glasses that do not interfere with the view of the wine's color and clarity. The rim of a wineglass should be narrower than the widest point of the bowl, to capture and hold the wine's bouquet. Generally, the bowls of glasses for red wine are more spherical, allowing more room for their bigger bouquets to develop. The bowls of white wineglasses, while still rounded, tend to be taller and narrower. All-purpose glasses for everyday use are also available. Champagne and sparkling wine are best appreciated in tall, slender glasses called flutes, which help to conserve their signature effervescence.

White and red wineglasses.

Champagne flute.

Wine connoisseurs always hold their wineglasses by the stem, not by the bowl, for two reasons. One is that touching the bowl with your fingers will subtly heat the wine, altering its flavor. While this might be a fine point for most wine drinkers, we can all appreciate the second concern: touching the bowl of the wineglass will leave unsightly fingerprints.

Matching Wine with Food "Red with meat, white with poultry and seafood"; so goes the old saw about matching wine and food. There is some wisdom in that advice, based on the logical assumption that a hearty red wine will better complement a hearty roast beef, while a more delicate white is a more sensible choice for, say, a delicate fish fillet. But pairing wine and food can become, depending on how you choose to look at it, far more complicated or even simpler.

Complexity is a factor when you consider the effects of sauces and seasonings not only on a given dish but also on the taste of the particular wine you pair with it. For instance, grilled fish with an aromatic rub of Indian spices might go very well with a light, fruity red Pinot Noir. Or the wine itself might dictate a departure from the rule, as when a particular white Chardonnay is big, buttery, and oaky enough to stand up to a chop.

While such examples illustrate how many fine considerations are possible in food and wine pairing, with a slight shift of perspective the same examples may also be seen as making a far more reassuring point. That is, if you enjoy drinking any particular type of wine, there is no good reason why you shouldn't feel free to try it as a companion to any food that you think it might complement.

Cooking with Wine While you would not want to pour a rare, expensive vintage wine into your stockpot, you should cook

continued

Wine, continued

with a wine that you'd actually want to drink. Avoid any products labeled "cooking wine," which tend to be needlessly seasoned, inferior products. Wines can add flavor to soups, such as a classic sherry-laced consommé; sauces, such as beurre blanc or a quick pan sauce made by deglazing with white wine; braises and stews, including such traditional French dishes as beef bourguignonne and coq au vin; and even desserts, such as pears poached in red wine.

Quick Bite

When cooking with wine, for the best pairing of wine and food at table, pour a wine made with the same grape variety to accompany the dish. Or, cook with the same wine you're serving.

Fortified Wines Some special types of wine are preserved through fortification, by the addition of brandy or a neutral spirit to raise the wine's total level of alcohol from the usual 7 to 14 percent to a range of 17 to 21 percent. Three of the most popular forms of fortified wine are Madeira, Port, and sherry.

MADEIRA From the Portuguese island of the same name, Madeira ranges in flavor from nutty and dry aperitifs to sweet after-dinner varieties.

PORT A classic, rich-tasting, and sweet fortified wine of Portugal, Port is excellent after dinner with nuts and cheeses. It comes in several styles, ranging from sweet, red ruby Port to drier tawny Port to complex, red vintage Port.

Port glass.

SHERRY A specialty of the Jerez region of Spain, sherry is now also made elsewhere. In its driest form, it may be served as an aperitif or with well-seasoned appetizers, while sweet sherries go well with mild to sharp cheeses after dinner. Fino sherries are characteristically very dry and tangy and drunk younger than oloroso sherries, which are aged to create a lovely brown color and rich, nutty bouquet.

Sherry glass.

VERMOUTH This fortified white wine is flavored with various spices, herbs, and fruits. Dry vermouth, which contains just 2 to 4 percent sugar, can be served as an aperitif and is an essential ingredient in many cocktails, starting with the martini. Sweet vermouth, sometimes called Italian or red vermouth, has a minimum of 14 percent sugar, and is used for sweet cocktails such as Manhattans or is enjoyed alone over ice.

Quick Tip

Keep a bottle of dry vermouth on hand to use in recipes that call for white wine. Because it is fortified, once opened, it will last indefinitely stored in a cool cupboard. Use a little vermouth and stock to deglaze a pan that was used to sauté chicken or meat, thereby making a simple sauce.

See also ALCOHOL; CORKSCREW; DECANTING; DEGLAZING; LIQUEUR; REDUCING; SPIRITS.

y·z

everything from yam to zucchini

YAM In the United States, orange-fleshed sweet potatoes are often referred to as yams. The true yam is a different species of plant, however, and is not widely available in this country.

Throughout Latin America, much of Asia, India, West Africa, the South Pacific, and the Caribbean, yams are one of the most important crops, with an annual production topping 25 million tons. There are over 600 varieties, which range in size from a few ounces to several hundred pounds. They may be brown, black, or tan, with white, pink, or yellow flesh. Shapes vary, too. Some yams resemble a giant animal foot or a misshapen hand, while others look like large potatoes. They have a slightly nutty flavor, with a texture that ranges from firm and chewy to moist and tender. Yams—boiled, stewed, fried, or baked— are often served as a foil to spicy sauces and to rich foods such as pork and ham. Grated and steamed yams are sometimes used to flavor breads and cakes.

Selecting Yams are available year-round in some Latin, Japanese, or African markets. Look for ones that are rock hard with no cracks or soft spots. Before you buy a yam, scrape it with your fingernail. It should be slippery and juicy inside. If it's dry, leave it at the market. Yams and sweet potatoes are interchangeable in most recipes.

Storing Yams can be stored at room temperature for up to 1 week.

Preparing Yams can cause skin irritation, so it is a good idea to wear rubber gloves when handling them. Scrub yams well and use a paring knife to cut away the skin and underlayer. Cut the yams into chunks or slices as needed for specific recipes. Rinse and keep in a bowl of acidulated water (to prevent oxidation) until ready for use.

See also SWEET POTATO.

YEAST Yeast has been called the soul of bread, for it is the living substance that animates dough, eating its sugars and giving off carbon dioxide and ethyl alcohol to expand the gluten in the flour and raise the bread. Although many different strains of yeast exist, there are two main categories: brewer's yeast, also called nutritional yeast, and baker's yeast. Both are living single-cell organisms, but only baker's yeast is a leavener. Brewer's yeast is grown on hops and is used to make beer. Because it is high in B vitamins, it is also sold in natural-food stores as a nutritional supplement.

Baker's Yeast Baker's yeast is available as active dry and as compressed fresh yeast.

ACTIVE DRY YEAST Active dry yeast may be purchased in 4-ounce jars, in bulk in natural-food stores, or in small ($\frac{1}{4}$-ounce) foil-lined envelopes. One envelope of dry yeast equals about $2\frac{1}{4}$ teaspoons. Check the expiration date on the package, then proof it if desired (see page 474). Store yeast in the freezer to prolong its shelf life.

Active dry yeast may be either regular or quick-rise, also known as rapid-rise yeast. This accelerated yeast will cut the rising time of a bread in half, but most bakers find that a shorter rising time makes for less flavor in the finished loaf. Quick-rise yeast does not need to be dissolved separately. It may be combined with the other dry ingredients, to which a warm liquid is added, thus activating the yeast.

A third kind of active dry yeast, instant dried yeast, is three times more powerful than regular dry yeast. Also called European yeast, it is a stronger, more stable yeast developed for commercial bakers. Some bakers feel that it has an objectionable taste, and it should not be used in sweet bread doughs or those that require long, slow risings.

COMPRESSED FRESH YEAST Compressed fresh yeast comes in small (0.60-ounce) foil-wrapped packages and is found in the refrigerated section of some markets. Since it has largely been replaced by active dry yeast, compressed yeast can be difficult to locate. It can be ordered in larger blocks from commercial bakers if you plan to do a lot of baking. Compressed yeast is much more perishable than dry yeast, however, and will keep under refrigeration for only about 10 days. Use it by the expiration date on the package. It may be frozen for up to 2 months and should be defrosted at room temperature and used at once. Proofing is recommended for fresh yeast; see A Word on Proofing, below. One cake of compressed yeast is equivalent to one package of active dry yeast.

A Word on Proofing Proofing yeast means to test the yeast to make sure it is still active, or alive. It is not really necessary for today's active dry yeast, but many bakers feel it doesn't hurt to check. It's a good idea to proof fresh yeast, as it is more perishable. Since all yeasts except quick-rise and instant dried are first dissolved in water before being mixed with dry ingredients, the dissolving process is essentially the same as proofing. Simply check to make sure that the mixture is bubbly or creamy after it sits for 5 to 10 minutes.

HOW TO *Proof Yeast*

1. Dissolve active dry yeast in a small bowl of warm (105° to 115°F) water (or another liquid, if called for in the recipe). Fresh yeast cake should be crumbled into lukewarm (90° to 100°F) liquid. If the water is too hot, it will kill the yeast; if the water is too cold, the yeast will not be activated.

2. If desired, add a pinch of sugar or another sweetener, such as honey, for the yeast to feed on (this is not necessary). Flour works well, too. Do not add salt; it inhibits the yeast.

3. Let the mixture stand for 5 to 10 minutes. If it becomes creamy, active dry yeast is indeed active and can be used for baking. Fresh yeast should bubble and foam. If it does, continue immediately with the recipe. If not, discard the yeast and purchase new yeast.

Yeast starters and sourdough starters are also used to leaven bread; they may be made at home or purchased. Yeast starter is a mixture of flour, water, sugar, and yeast that has been allowed to ferment. A portion of the starter is used as the leavener for yeast bread, and the remaining starter is kept alive indefinitely by replenishing it with equal parts flour and water. Sourdough starters are made without any (or with a very small amount of) baker's yeast. Instead, a mixture of flour and water, and sometimes a crushed vegetable or fruit, is allowed to sit at room temperature, where it will capture the wild yeasts always present in the atmosphere. Flour also contains some wild yeasts. A kitchen where yeast bread has been made from baker's yeast in the past is more likely to have an abundance of wild yeasts present in the air.

See also BAKING; BREAD.

YEAST BREAD See BREAD.

YOGURT Made from milk fermented with friendly bacterial cultures, yogurt is

Y·Z

thick and tart with a custardlike texture. Like the milk it is made from, yogurt can be full fat, low fat, or nonfat. Available plain or sweetened and flavored, yogurt is made from cow's, goat's, or sheep's milk. Enjoy yogurt straight from the container, use it as a salad dressing or a topping for both savory and sweet dishes, or let it lend both body and flavor to sauces and soups.

The bacterial cultures in yogurt (*Lactobacillus bulgaricus* and *Streptococcus thermophilus;* a third kind, *Lactobacillus acidophilus,* is also sometimes added) are prized as an aid in digestion. They also give yogurt tenderizing properties that make it useful as a marinade for meats. Bakers like yogurt for the tender crumb it produces in quick breads and cakes. Frozen yogurt is refreshing, although freezing makes the friendly bacteria inactive. Likewise, heating yogurt over 120°F will kill the bacteria.

Yogurt may be drained in cheesecloth for several hours or overnight to make a thick substance known as yogurt cheese, which is used to make dips, desserts, and spreads for canapés and sandwiches. When making yogurt cheese and homemade yogurt, be sure to use a natural yogurt, made without gelatin or other stabilizers.

Selecting Check the sell-by date and make sure the yogurt you buy is fresh.

Storing Store in the refrigerator. Yogurt grows tarter with age, so enjoy it soon after purchase.

Yogurt Savvy When cooking with yogurt, keep the following in mind:

- Bring yogurt to room temperature before heating. When adding yogurt to hot food, make sure to do so toward the end of the cooking process, or it can curdle. For longer cooking, the yogurt should be stabilized (see below).
- To substitute yogurt for milk, cream, sour cream, or buttermilk in baking, add $\frac{1}{2}$ teaspoon baking soda per cup of yogurt.

- For a lower-fat soft whipped cream, use half the amount of heavy cream. Beat it until stiff peaks form, then blend in an equal amount of plain nonfat yogurt.

HOW TO *Stabilize Yogurt for Cooking*

1. Stir 1 tablespoon all-purpose flour into 1 cup plain yogurt until blended. Use to replace cream in soups, casseroles, and sauces.

HOW TO *Make Yogurt at Home*

1. In a large, heavy saucepan, bring 1 quart whole, low-fat, or nonfat milk just to a boil, stirring to prevent a skin from forming. If a skin does form, skim it off with a spoon.

2. Remove from the heat and let cool to 112° to 115°F, or until a few drops sprinkled on your inner wrist are almost body temperature.

3. If using low-fat or nonfat milk, or for a high-protein yogurt made with whole milk, put $\frac{1}{3}$ cup instant nonfat dried milk in a clean ceramic or glass bowl. Gradually whisk in about $\frac{1}{2}$ cup of the warm milk until the mixture is smooth. Whisk in 2 tablespoons plain yogurt (made without gelatin or stabilizers) until well blended. Slowly whisk in the remaining warm milk until blended.

4. Cover tightly with plastic wrap. Set in a warm place (90° to 115°F) and let stand, without moving or otherwise disturbing the bowl, until thickened, 6 to 8 hours or overnight. (An oven with a gas pilot light is a good choice; if you have an electric oven, preheat it to 120°F, then turn it off. Or wrap the bowl in a heavy bath towel and place it on top of the refrigerator.) The longer the yogurt stands, the tarter and thicker the end product will be.

5. Use the yogurt at once, or refrigerate it. For the best flavor, use within 4 days.

ZESTING Citrus zest, the colored portion of the peel, is rich in flavorful oils that can perk up all sorts of foods. When used to flavor baked goods or salads, zest is

y·z

usually grated or minced. Large strips of zest should be removed from braises, stews, and sauces before serving.

When zesting fruit, be sure to scrub the fruit well to remove any wax or chemicals. Even better, buy organic citrus fruit if you need the peel. Use only the thin, colored layer of the rind, taking care not to include the bitter white pith. Zest may be removed with a tool known as a zester, which is designed to be pulled across the fruit's rind, removing the zest in thin strips. This is the best method for making attractive zest strips to use as a garnish or decoration.

Zesting with a zester.

A vegetable peeler or a paring knife is a useful tool for removing zest in long strips, but these pieces may be larger and more irregular than needed, needing to be trimmed with a chef's knife. Zest strips may be chopped or minced, or zest may be removed with the fine rasps of a handheld grater, a technique that produces tiny bits of zest and eliminates any need for chopping it.

Zesting with a peeler.

Slicing zest strips.

ZUCCHINI Nearly every backyard vegetable gardener has experienced a bumper crop of zucchini. Fortunately, this best-known member of the summer squash family is highly versatile. It can be cut into sticks and eaten raw; sliced and sautéed or fried; shredded or cooked and puréed in soups; cut into lengthwise slices, oiled, and grilled; and hollowed out, stuffed, and baked. It is a classic ingredient in ratatouille and other Provençal vegetable dishes, as well as in Middle Eastern stews. Shredded zucchini is also an ingredient in delicious quick breads and muffins.

Immature zucchini measuring no more than 3 to 5 inches long sometimes turn up at the market with their brilliant yellow flowers still attached. Marketed as baby zucchini, these tender, tiny squashes are favored for their delicate flavor and the fine texture of their flesh. The flowers are also edible and can be stuffed, battered, and fried or used as a filling for omelets.

Selecting Zucchini are available year-round, thanks to imports from Mexico. Local zucchini are at their best and most abundant in summer. Look for small zucchini for the most tender bite. The best have thin skins with a bright, even color and no blemishes or scars.

Storing Zucchini are at their best just after harvest. Serve them soon after you buy them, or store them for up to 3 days in a perforated plastic bag in the crisper of your refrigerator.

Preparing There's no need to peel zucchini; simply wash, trim the ends, and then slice, chop, or shred as desired. Some recipes call for salting zucchini to remove excess moisture.

See also SQUASH.

For Further Reading

GENERAL FOOD REFERENCE

Chalmers, Irena. *The Great Food Almanac: A Feast of Facts from A to Z.* San Francisco: Collins Publishers, 1994.

Clingerman, Polly. *The Kitchen Companion.* Gaithersburg, Md.: The American Cooking Guild, 1994.

Davidson, Alan. *The Oxford Companion to Food.* New York: Oxford University Press, 1999.

Fortin, François, ed. *The Visual Food Encyclopedia.* New York: Macmillan, 1996.

Herbst, Sharon Tyler. *The Food Lover's Tiptionary.* New York: Hearst Books, 1994.

——. *The New Food Lover's Companion.* 2nd ed. Hauppauge, N.Y.: Barron's Educational Series, 1995.

Herbst, Sharon Tyler, and Ron Herbst. *Wine Lover's Companion.* Hauppauge, N.Y.: Barron's Educational Series, 1995.

Horn, Jane, ed. *Cooking A to Z: The Complete Culinary Reference Source.* New and rev. ed. Santa Rosa, Ca.: Cole Group, 1997.

Kamman, Madeleine. *The New Making of a Cook: The Art, Techniques, and Science of Good Cooking.* New York: William Morrow & Co., 1997.

Lang, Jenifer Harvey, ed. *Larousse Gastronomique: The New American Edition of the World's Greatest Culinary Encyclopedia.* New York: Crown Publishers, 1988.

Mariani, John F. *The Dictionary of American Food and Drink.* New York: Hearst Books, 1994.

Willan, Anne. *La Varenne Pratique: The Complete Illustrated Cooking Course.* New York: Crown Publishers, 1989.

FOOD HISTORY

Root, Waverly. *Food: An Authoritative and Visual History and Dictionary of the Foods of the World.* New York: Smithmark, 1980.

Sokolov, Raymond. *Why We Eat What We Eat: How the Encounter Between the New World and the Old Changed the Way Everyone on the Planet Eats.* New York: Summit Books, 1991.

Trager, James. *The Food Chronology: A Food Lover's Compendium of Events and Anecdotes, from Prehistory to the Present.* New York: Henry Holt & Co., 1995.

FOOD SAFETY

Bailey, Janet. *Keeping Food Fresh.* New York: Harper & Row, 1985.

Kilham, Christopher S. *The Bread & Circus Whole Food Bible: How to Select and Prepare Safe Healthful Foods without Pesticides or Chemical Additives.* Reading, Ma.: Addison-Wesley Publishing Co., 1991.

Mendelson, Cheryl. *Home Comforts: The Art and Science of Keeping House.* New York: Scribner, 1999.

FOOD SCIENCE

Corriher, Shirley O. *Cookwise: The Hows and Whys of Successful Cooking.* New York: William Morrow & Co., 1997.

Hillman, Howard. *Kitchen Science: A Guide to Knowing the Hows and Whys for Fun and Success in the Kitchen.* Rev. ed. Boston: Houghton Mifflin Co., 1989.

continued

McGee, Harold. *On Food and Cooking: The Science and Lore of the Kitchen.* New York: Scribner, 1984. Reprint, New York: Fireside, 1997.

COOKWARE AND TOOLS

Ettlinger, Steve. *The Kitchenware Book.* New York: Macmillan, 1992.

SPECIALTY

Alford, Jeffrey, and Naomi Duguid. *Seductions of Rice: A Cookbook.* New York: Artisan, 1998.

Bremness, Lesley, and Jill Norman. *The Complete Book of Herbs & Spices: The Ultimate Sourcebook to Herbs, Spices & Aromatic Seeds.* New York: Viking Studio Books, 1995.

Choate, Judith. *The Bean Cookbook.* New York: Simon & Schuster, 1992.

Clarke, Oz. *The Essential Wine Book: An Indispensable Guide to the World of Wines.* New York: Fireside, 1997.

Cost, Bruce. *Bruce Cost's Asian Ingredients: Buying and Cooking the Staple Foods of China, Japan, and Southeast Asia.* New York: William Morrow & Co., 1988.

Davidson, Alan. *Fruit: A Connoisseur's Guide and Cookbook.* New York: Simon & Schuster, 1991.

DeWitt, Dave, and Nancy Gerlach. *The Whole Chile Pepper Book.* Boston: Little, Brown & Co., 1990.

Ellis, Merle. *Cutting-up in the Kitchen: The Butcher's Guide to Saving Money on Meat & Poultry.* San Francisco: Chronicle Books, 1975.

Jenkins, Steven. *Cheese Primer.* New York: Workman Publishing Co., 1996.

Perry, Sara, et al. *The Complete Coffee Book: A Gourmet Guide to Buying, Brewing, and Cooking.* San Francisco: Chronicle Books, 1991.

Peterson, James. *Fish and Shellfish.* New York: William Morrow & Co., 1996.

Pratt, James Norwood. *The Tea Lover's Treasury.* San Francisco: 101 Productions, 1982.

Rosengarten, Frederic, Jr. *The Book of Spices.* Wynnewood, Pa.: Livingston Publishing Co., 1969.

Schneider, Elizabeth. *Uncommon Fruits & Vegetables: A Commonsense Guide.* New York: Harper & Row, 1986.

Wood, Rebecca. *The Splendid Grain.* New York: William Morrow & Co., 1997.

About the Contributors

ABOUT THE AUTHORS

SARAH PUTMAN CLEGG is an editor and writer specializing in cookbooks. She lives in the San Francisco Bay Area.

MARY GOODBODY is a nationally known food writer and cookbook editor based in Connecticut. She has written or contributed to more than 45 books, including *The Basque Table; Sunday Dinner;* and *Spring Evenings, Summer Afternoons.* More recently, she collaborated on *Alfred Portale's 12 Seasons Cookbook, Prime Time: The Lobels' Guide to Great Grilled Meats,* and *No Need to Knead,* which was nominated for a 1999 James Beard Cookbook Award. Ms. Goodbody is also a senior contributing editor for *Chocolatier* and *Pastry Art & Design* magazines and is the editor for the *IACP (International Association of Culinary Professionals) Food Forum Quarterly.*

CAROLYN MILLER is a writer and book editor living in San Francisco. She is the author of *Savoring San Francisco: Recipes from the City's Neighborhood Restaurants* and *The Christmas Table: A Holiday Menu Cookbook.* Her writing has also been featured in many cookbooks, including *Chocolate: A Sweet Indulgence* and *Espresso: Culture and Cuisine.* In addition, she has edited innumerable other cookbooks for publishers nationwide.

THY TRAN is a San Francisco–based food and travel writer who specializes in the history and culture of cooking. A graduate of the California Culinary Academy, she has honed her craft working at numerous restaurants, catering, and testing recipes and writing for national food magazines. Ms. Tran is the owner of Wandering Spoon, a cooking school in San Francisco, where she teaches classes on traditional Asian ingredients and techniques.

ABOUT THE ILLUSTRATOR

ALICE HARTH, a San Francisco–based artist and graphic designer whose clients have included magazines, book publishers, and food producers, illustrated the multi-volume Williams-Sonoma *Kitchen Library* and *Lifestyles* series. Ms. Harth studied fine art and design at the University of California at Los Angeles. In addition to good food, travel, drawing, and painting are her passions.

weldon**owen**

415 Jackson Street, Suite 200, San Francisco, CA 94111
www.weldonowen.com

COOK'S WISDOM

Conceived and produced by Weldon Owen Inc.
Copyright © 2000 Weldon Owen Inc.
and Williams-Sonoma, Inc.

This book has been previously published as
Williams-Sonoma Kitchen Companion

Printed in China

This edition first printed in 2012
10 9 8 7 6 5 4 3 2 1

Library of Congress Cataloging-in-Publication
Data is available.

Weldon Owen is a divsion of
BONNIER

ACKNOWLEDGMENTS

Weldon Owen wishes to thank the following
people for their generous support in producing
this book: Pam Anderson, Mu' frida Bell, Desne
Border, Linda Bouchard, Carrie Bradley, Ken
DellaPenta, Susan Derecskey, Judith Dunham,
Ellen Klages, Norman Kolpas, Jan Marti, Joan
Olson, Sharon Silva, Molly Stevens, TonBo Designs

ISBN-13: 978-1-61628-456-5
ISBN-10: 1-61628-456-0